MW01010021

PRAISE FOR
SUPERABUNDANCE

"With great writing and a mountain of good evidence, Tupy and Pooley remind us that we are immeasurably better off than our ancestors. In this day of pestilence, war, and climate change, we need that reminder, and we can hope that the doom-mongers will be wrong about the future, just as they have always been wrong about the past."

—Angus Deaton, Nobel Prize–winning economist and
Dwight D. Eisenhower Professor of Economics and
International Affairs Emeritus, Princeton University

"As the number of humans grew from millions to billions, the much-feared crisis of resource scarcity turned out to be a mirage. Fifty years ago, the Club of Rome said that civilization would collapse because of a scarcity of fossil fuel. Now, any thinking person has to recognize that the real, and very dangerous, problem is that there is too damn much. We live with the benefits (and occasional costs) of the superabundance exhaustively documented by the authors, yet for far too many people, the mirage of the scarcity crisis has hardened into delusion. Because they deny the many real benefits from superabundance, they cannot grasp the simple fact that when harmful side-effects are present, it is abundance that threatens us, not scarcity. As a result, they fail to see that all it takes to address the few cases of harmful abundance is to redirect the dynamic of discovery behind superabundance. After scientists learned that CFCs were destroying the ozone layer, governments adopted policies that halted the production of CFCs and encouraged an abundance of safe alternatives. If the facts documented here can free people from the apathy of delusion and help them see the optimistic possibilities revealed by pervasive superabundance, the way forward will be obvious."

—Paul Romer, Nobel Prize–winning economist and
former chief economist, World Bank

"People don't depend on stuff; they depend on *ideas*—formulas, algorithms, knowledge—which allow stuff, useless by itself, to satisfy our wants. In this lucid and illuminating book, Tupy and Pooley lucidly use this insight to explain a fact that, surprisingly, surprises people: over the centuries, our increasing knowledge has made more stuff available to us."

—Steven Pinker, author of *Enlightenment Now:*
The Case for Reason, Science, Humanism, and Progress

"We are living in signal times. The rate at which everything is changing is unparalleled, as is the increase in that rate itself. Two starkly divergent paths therefore present themselves before us, more clearly than ever before: movement toward an era of superabundance, where everyone could have everything they needed and perhaps even most of what they wanted, or degeneration into a state of apocalypse-inspired, faux-compassionate, authoritarian hell, perhaps worse than anything we saw in the most extreme excesses of the 20th century. Could we choose the former path? Tupy and Pooley, anything but naive optimists, say yes and explain why. Read this book. It's a valid antidote to demoralization, cynicism and hopelessness."

—Jordan Peterson, author of *12 Rules for Life: An Antidote to Chaos*

"*Superabundance* pulls off the remarkable feat of being both exhaustive and entertaining at the same time. It adds a critical piece to the growing canon of books documenting the rapid improvements in the quality of human life: an explanation that is grounded in rapid population growth. Anyone who cares about the future of humanity should read this book."

—Jason Furman, professor of the practice of economic policy, Harvard University, and former chair of the Council of Economic Advisers

"There are those who wish for scarcities, and who work to inhibit economic growth, so that government can claim an excuse to ration this and that.

Happily, they have met their match in Tupy and Pooley, who demonstrate that population growth is not a problem, it is the solution—the most important resource."

—George Will, *Washington Post*

"My father, Julian Simon, would have treasured Tupy and Pooley's *Superabundance*. Its breathtaking scope, encyclopedic data, and deep and precise analysis of both economics and history powerfully confirm that people are indeed the ultimate resource—and that a growing population, particularly with greater freedom, has and will overcome every challenge and will, in virtually every measurable way, continue to enjoy greater prosperity."

—David M. Simon, senior fellow, Unleash Prosperity

"The decline of poverty and famine and disease and violence over the past few decades has been spectacular, as Tupy and Pooley demonstrate. There is every reason to think it can continue and our grandchildren will look back on today's world with horror and pity. This book is a comprehensive, detailed, and devastating riposte to the perpetual pessimists who dominate modern discourse."

—Matt Ridley, author of *The Rational Optimist:
How Prosperity Evolves* and *How Innovation Works:
And Why It Flourishes in Freedom*

"Our future is a battle between positive-sum technology and zero-sum mentalities. Tupy and Pooley show that we have the numbers on our side and that the long-term trend in resource abundance is promising."

—Balaji Srinavasan, former chief technology officer,
Coinbase

"Pessimism sells, which is strange. But the scientific evidence shows that optimism is a lot more sensible. Stop weeping. Read the book and smile."

—Deirdre McCloskey, author of *Why Liberalism Works: How True Liberal Values Produce a Freer, More Equal, Prosperous World for All* and distinguished professor emerita of economics and history, University of Illinois at Chicago

"It's true that we live on a delicate planet that is composed of a finite number of atoms. But as this fascinating and heartening book shows, it's also true that we humans can increase both our population and prosperity as much as we want without endangering the earth. The key, as Tupy and Pooley show, is innovation. Read *Superabundance* to have your assumptions challenged and your sense of hope restored."

—Andrew McAfee, author of *More from Less: The Surprising Story of How We Learned to Prosper Using Fewer Resources—and What Happens Next*

"Every generation has a new Malthusian panic about world population growth, but every generation also produces a voice of reason to counter the panic. Tupy and Pooley's brilliant book is deeply convincing that natural resources are actually becoming *less* scarce with growing population, pointing the way to continued economic progress."

—William Easterly, author of *The Tyranny of Experts: Economists, Dictators, and the Forgotten Rights of the Poor*

"In their essential and provocative new book, Tupy and Pooley show that the ultimate resource remains human ingenuity. *Superabundance* is a must-read for anyone who cares about the fate of humankind and our bountiful, beautiful planet."

—Michael Shellenberger, author of *Apocalypse Never: Why Environmental Alarmism Hurts Us All*

"In a tsunami of bad news about Russian revanchism, nuclear saber rattling, global warming, inflation, supply chain shortages, and a pandemic emerges *Superabundance*, a data-fueled corrective to the doom and gloom the media daily heaps upon us. Tupy and Pooley have done the world a service with this fact-filled reminder of how good our lives are compared to ages past, and how much more human flourishing is in store if we unleash human innovation."

—Michael Shermer, author of *The Moral Arc: How Science and Reason Lead Humanity toward Truth, Justice, and Freedom*

"More people produce more ideas and innovations. They also produce more nonsense. It is not resources but hope and common sense that are scarce. Human ingenuity can come up with a solution for every scarcity, though, and now we have an antidote to nonsense as well: this magnificent, groundbreaking book by Tupy and Pooley."

—Johan Norberg, author of *Open: The Story of Human Progress*

"Tupy and Pooley document beyond the faintest doubt that we ordinary men and women in modern market economies today enjoy a material standard of living that is indescribably superior not only to that of our pre-industrial ancestors, but to that of our grandparents and even—in many ways—to that of our parents. The expertly assembled evidence in this book should finally silence the many professors and pundits who peddle the false tale that, over the past half-century, only the rich have gotten richer. Tupy and Pooley bust the myth of middle-class stagnation to smithereens."

—Donald J. Boudreaux, professor of economics, George Mason University

"A compelling account of humanity's cooperative victory over the Hobbesian state of nature and Malthusian constraints to growth. Tupy and Pooley provide a much-needed and convincing manifesto for optimism that celebrates people as the ultimate resource for progress."

—Charles Kenny, author of *Getting Better: Why Global Development Is Succeeding—and How We Can Improve the World Even More*

"*Superabundance* is the best antidote I've read in 30 years to counter the never-ending doom-and-gloom predictions of the extreme environmentalists and anti-growth proponents. Using their breakthrough "time price" series, Tupy and Pooley forcefully demonstrate that we need to stop selling capitalism short. In *Superabundance*, they show that through ingenuity and the proper incentives, there is no limit to economic growth and our rising standard of living, and we can do so without destroying the planet and the environment. *Superabundance* is in the grand tradition of the optimist Julian Simon and deserves to be read by a wide audience."

—Mark Skousen, presidential fellow, Chapman University, and founder of FreedomFest

"We flourish through freedom. For good after good after good, Tupy and Pooley show that the time we must work to buy the good is less than it was before, whether "before" is 40 years ago or 170. Higher population is a boon, not a peril, because more free people means more innovations. At a time when we are stressed by censors and violence, *Superabundance* reminds us of what is possible if we preserve hope and stand up for freedom."

—Arthur Diamond, professor of economics, University of Nebraska Omaha

SUPERABUNDANCE

SUPERABUNDANCE

The Story of Population Growth,
Innovation, and Human Flourishing on
an Infinitely Bountiful Planet

Marian L. Tupy and Gale L. Pooley

To find data files, explanatory videos, a resource calculator, and other valuable resources, scan with your QR reader or visit www.superabundance.com.

Print ISBN: 978-1-952223-39-6
eBook ISBN: 978-1-952223-40-2

Cover design: Lindy Kasler, Faceout Studio,
   Luis Ahumada Abrigo, and Guillermina Sutter Schneider
Text design: Paul Nielsen, Faceout Studio
Imagery: Shutterstock

Library of Congress Cataloging-in-Publication Data

Tupy, Marian L., author. | Pooley, Gale Lyle, author.
   Superabundance : the story of population growth, innovation, and human
   flourishing on an infinitely bountiful planet / Marian L. Tupy and
   Gale L. Pooley.
      pages   cm
   Washington, D.C. : Cato Institute, 2022.
   Includes bibliographical references and index.
   ISBN 9781952223396 (hardcover) | ISBN 9781952223402 (ebook)
   1. LCSH: Population—Economic aspects. 2. Economic development
   3. Natural resources.
   HB849.41 .T75 2021
   DDC 304.6—dc23   2022016156

Printed in Canada.

CATO INSTITUTE
1000 Massachusetts Ave. NW
Washington, DC 20001
www.cato.org

Marian L. Tupy:

To Arthur and Kim,
for their friendship and support.

Gale L. Pooley:

To Helen and DeAnna,
creators of life.

The outward feature that immediately differentiates the present world from mankind before 1800 is the recent astonishing increase in the numbers of people. . . . This is obviously the result of material progress, but the number of people is itself as much cause as consequence of this progress.

Fernand Braudel, *The Structures of Everyday Life*

CONTENTS

PART ONE

Thanos's deadly idea: from antiquity to the present and beyond

PART TWO

Measuring abundance: new methodology, empirical evidence, and in-depth analysis

PART THREE

Human flourishing and its enemies

FOREWORD

With economic models and equations constrained by limits, central to all economic thought is the issue of abundance and scarcity. In 1932, renowned British economist Lionel Robbins defined economics as the science of scarcity. He wrote, "Economics . . . studies human behavior as a relationship between ends and scarce means which have alternative uses."

For centuries, the ivory towers of academia have echoed this sentiment of multitudinous ends and limited means. In this supremely contrarian book, Marian L. Tupy and Gale L. Pooley overturn the tables in the temple of conventional thinking. They deploy rigorous and original data and analysis to proclaim a gospel of abundance. Economics—and ultimately, politics—will be enduringly transformed.

Overthrown in the process is Reverend Thomas Malthus's historic concept of a fatal conflict between the geometrical expansion of populations and the linear growth of food to sustain them. In 1798, Malthus launched the still-current fashion of declaring population growth as ultimately "unsustainable" in the face of the finite resources of a limited planetary environment.

After World War II, the British philosopher Bertrand Russell revived the issue of overpopulation as a global crisis. He observed that even war had proven "disappointing" as a remedy to population growth. He suggested dourly that in the future "perhaps bacteriological war may prove more effective."

Tupy and Pooley prove this idea itself unsustainable. They consummate the argument of their inspirer, the late economist Julian Simon, showing that the only ultimate scarcity is human lives. Tupy and Pooley reshape economics from a "dismal science of scarcity" into a redemptive science of abundance and creativity. The test and testament of economic abundance is an almost eightfold rise in world population since 1800, with people living on average 45 years longer than their forebears and consuming exponentially more commodities of all kinds.

People sustain themselves by working for one another and trading with each other. In the process, they both create new resources and provide and prove their capability of enabling even far greater populations. In *Superabundance*, Tupy and Pooley provide a mountain of data that makes "sustainability" a picayune distraction of people without vision. At the same time, they offer a new model of economic measurement based on a theory of information.

The ultimate test and measuring stick of wealth is time. What remains scarce when all else becomes abundant is our minutes, hours, days, and years. Time is the only resource that cannot be recycled, stored, duplicated, or recovered. Money is most fundamentally tokenized time. When we run out of money, we are really running out of the time to earn more. Measured by this only universal gauge of value—time—we are in a crowning golden age of capitalism.

The single greatest breakthrough in 21st-century economics is the comprehensive and creative translation of prices into time—*time prices*. Time prices calculate the hours and minutes needed to earn the money to buy goods and services. Unlike money prices, time prices are unequivocal and universal; they are the true prices. All other prices are circular, measuring value by measured values, commodities by commodities, market caps by money markets. Tupy and Pooley take this fundamental economic concept and make it the pivot of a providential new theory of economic measurement.

Going back to 1850, the data collected by Tupy and Pooley show that for more than a century and a half, measured by time prices, resource abundance has been rising at a rate of 4 percent a year. That means that every 50 years, the real-world economy has grown some sevenfold. Between 1980 and 2020, while population grew 75 percent, time prices of the 50 key commodities that sustain life dropped 75 percent. That means that for every increment of population growth, global resources have grown by a factor of 8. Tupy and Pooley confirm Simon's revolutionary insight: people are not a burden on resources but the source of them.

In the face of all the claims of inflation and devaluation of money and runaway debts and subzero interest rates, Tupy and Pooley show that this rate of real growth has even increased. The spearhead may have shifted from California to Texas, from the United States to China, India, Israel, and even Africa. But everywhere entrepreneurs are free to create and market their inventions, time prices fall. Time prices show that for the first 20 years of the century, China's economy grew an average of over 10 percent a year.

Every person, whether he is rich or poor, has only 24 hours in a day. But as time prices decline, it is often poor people who benefit vastly and differentially. Instead of a Sisyphean struggle for subsistence, they now have more free time to invent and innovate. Thus, instead of having to spend every waking hour hunting and gathering food to live, typical humans today earn their food in a matter of minutes.

As *Superabundance* shows, the time price to acquire rice as food for a day in India has dropped from about seven hours in 1960 to under an hour today, while the time price of a comparable supply of wheat in Indiana has dropped from an hour to 7.5 minutes. In a striking reduction in inequality, the Indian peasant has gained six hours and two minutes to do other things while the Indiana wheat purchaser gained only some 52 minutes.

The Tupy-Pooley time price revolution stems from and enriches the development of the information theory of economics. This theory translates into economics the central findings behind the information economy. As established by the mathematician Claude Shannon, who applied an information calculus to telecommunication networks and first defined the bits and bytes of computer science, information is unexpected bits. It is measured by *surprisal.*

Shannon called it "entropy," following the physicist Ludwig Boltzmann's information theory of the thermodynamics of *disorder.* Thus, Shannon confused generations of geniuses still devout in their faith in information as *order* and discomfited economists galore in their mathematics of equilibrium. In standard economics, equilibrium is death. Information economics, in contrast, is about disruption and disorder.

The information theory behind *Superabundance* provides the foundation for economics driven not by equilibrium or order but by falsifiable entrepreneurial surprises. Order is predictable and thus low information and low entropy. As Shannon showed, however, it takes a low-entropy carrier, without surprises, to bear high-entropy messages or enterprises.

The most reliable low-entropy carrier is the electromagnetic spectrum, which is governed everywhere by the speed of light. But the U.S. Constitution and English common law have sufficed as structures to sustain enterprise. Economies prosper to the extent that knowledge, intrinsically dispersed through the system in the minds of individuals, is complemented by a similar dispersal of power. Free markets and uncontrolled prices typically achieve this goal. Combinations of government and business frustrate it.

Money is the device or token that enables the scarcity of time to be translated into transactions and valuations. It is *tokenized time*. As Tupy and Pooley demonstrate, defining everything in economics is finally the hours and minutes and seconds of time prices.

Almost all sciences find that their ultimate measuring sticks are measured in time—frequencies and spectra rooted in the speed of light. The *systeme internationale* of measuring sticks enshrined in Pavillon de Breteuil in Saint Cloud, France, encompasses mass, distance, time, temperature, electrical current, brightness, and moles of individual chemical elements. Except for the mole, all the other metrics—from the meter and kilogram to degrees Kelvin and amperes of electricity to the candela of luminosity—ultimately are rooted in *time*. The constant is the velocity of light per second. Defining the second is the transitional radioactive frequency of the ground state of cesium, itself specified in cycles per second. Tupy and Pooley, pioneering money as time, bring economic science into the *systeme internationale*.

Refined and documented by Tupy and Pooley, the time price method of gauging value and economic progress is a huge breakthrough. It can transform nearly all economic calculations and assumptions, from the rate of economic growth to the weight of debt to the degree of inequality to the impact of atmospheric carbon dioxide to the level of true interest rates.

When I wrote *Knowledge and Power* (2013), I talked about time prices in a chapter titled "The Light Dawns." It told the story of the economist William Nordhaus, a Yale University Nobel laureate, who demonstrated by studying the ever-declining cost of lighting that prevailing accounts of economic history may underestimate real economic advance by a factor of nearly a hundred thousand.

This is an exponential "oops!" moment in which an existing paradigm resoundingly gives way. As I wrote, economists erred because "they concentrated on money prices rather than real labor costs—how many hours workers had to labor to buy light." After many experiments with the historical technologies of illumination, Nordhaus ended up calculating the number of hours a worker had to toil to buy lighting.

Introducing time prices for the modern era, Nordhaus's approach was an elaborate analysis of "service characteristics" of output, in this case lighting a room at night. Because he was intrigued with the impact of the industrial revolution on lighting costs, he examined in scrupulous detail the comparative efficiency of all the different ways people have produced light over the millennia, from cave fires to Babylonian wick lamps to candles to incandescent bulbs to fluorescent lights.

In his 1994 essay "Do Real Income and Real Wage Measures Capture Reality? The History of Lighting Suggests Not," for the National Bureau of Economic Research, Nordhaus concluded, "One modern 100-watt incandescent bulb burning for three hours each night would produce 1.5 million lumen hours of light per year. At the beginning of 'last century' [1800] obtaining this amount of light would have required burning 17,000 candles, and the average worker would have had to toil almost 1,000 hours to earn the dollars to buy the candles. In the modern era, with a compact fluorescent bulb, the 1.5 million lumen hours would need 22 kilowatt hours, which can be bought for about 10 minutes work by the average worker [in 1990]," or six thousand times less.

However, the Nordhaus approach is not scalable. No one can evaluate the "true" effects of all the endless improvements and changes in all the multifarious and interrelated goods and services in a modern economy. Tupy and Pooley transcend Nordhaus by making his insights scalable. They show that time prices obviate endless ad-hoc calculations by combining in one number the two key effects of innovation: the rise in wages and the decline in costs.

Prices are subjective. Workers decide what to buy with their hours of toil. Gauging the value of something, therefore, consists simply of the number of hours and minutes a typical person is willing to spend to earn the money to buy it. Forget all the "hedonic" adjustments and estimates of the utility or worth of goods and services. All you need to do is divide number of hours of work into gross domestic product (GDP), however it is calculated. The result is the correct estimate in the rise in the standard of living.

As Tupy and Pooley show, globally between 1980 and 2018, despite all the monetary noise and the cultural "headwinds," workers have been able to buy some 252 percent more goods and services with their hours and minutes. During this same period, the world's population increased 71.2 percent, yielding a 503 percent increase in global resource abundance. Despite claims of "extreme weather," agricultural and marine commodities—including tea and coffee and shrimp and salmon—have become radically cheaper. There's no need to figure out the physical efficiencies and yields of every item in the basket. Just compute the hours and minutes of work and divide them into any monetary measure of the relevant part of the economy. That's a breakthrough, but it's still only the beginning of wisdom.

Time prices show that economic progress continues far faster than economists estimate. Far from plunging into negative realms, as if time could move backward, real interest rates remain at between 3 and 4 percent. And China has been growing faster than even the Communist Party claims. This means that China, with its radically lower government spending than the United States as a share of GDP, may so far have provided a freer environment for business.

The leading threat to capitalism today comes not in red but green. The extreme environmentalists say that capitalism is using up the natural resources that the materialists mistake for wealth, that capitalism is destroying the very climate on which life depends, and that capitalism is killing the planet. Today's green socialism enjoys greater popular acceptance than the red variety ever achieved. Amid unprecedented plenty and human well-being, the cries of doom are deafening.

Capitalism cannot defend itself from socialism because, whatever their differences in policy, their metaphysics are identical. Capitalist theory, at least from Adam Smith on, has rested on the same materialist superstition that sustains socialism; the one inevitably leads to the other.

The materialist superstition is this: that wealth consists of things rather than thoughts, of accumulated capital rather than accumulated knowledge—that people are chiefly consumers rather than creators, mouths rather than minds.

The materialist error has been eloquently identified. More than 40 years ago, the economist Thomas Sowell, expounding the argument that wealth is essentially knowledge, not material resources, wrote, "The cavemen had the same natural resources at their disposal as we have today, and the difference between their standard of living and ours is a difference between the knowledge they could bring to bear on those resources and the knowledge used today."

What we lack to go with our information economy is an information economics. Capitalist theory remains bound in a language that cannot escape materialist premises. Those premises fundamentally distort not merely the content but the very purpose of economic thought.

As Smith's heirs, including John Stuart Mill and Alfred Marshall, fleshed out the theory, self-interest appeared quantifiable as "demand" and "supply" mediated by the common denominator of "utility" by which the two could achieve "equilibrium." The clockworks were in place.

In imitating Isaac Newton, however, Smith made a disastrous mistake. To explain recurrent physical phenomena, one wants a determinist system, governed by constant laws. All apples must fall from the tree. If, however, wealth is knowledge, growth is learning, and innovation explains the gap between the Stone Age and the information age, then the choice of a deterministic model is fatal to economic theory.

If the fundaments of wealth are unpredictable, if innovation always comes as a surprise, no deterministic theory can explain wealth. As long as economics is justified by its ability to predict outcomes in detail—as long as it remains mechanical and deterministic—it will be intellectually unpersuasive and morally indefensible. Profit will remain a mystery and a scandal.

For this new battle we need a new economics. Above all we need an economics that can not only explain economic growth but vindicate it. We need an economics of mind, an economics of information grounded in the truth that the growth of recent centuries has been achieved not by ravishing "natural" resources but by regenerating them, not by accumulating matter but by replacing it with mind, not by wasting energy but by using it more ingeniously. Information theory shows that we accumulate wealth not by stealing from the earth but by adding to our store of knowledge.

We need an economics of information. *Superabundance* is the pioneering text on this new frontier of economic truth.

George Gilder

INTRODUCTION

Generations of people throughout the world have been taught to believe that there is an inverse relationship between population growth and the availability of resources, which is to say that as the population grows, resources become more scarce. In 2021, for example, we were told that "the world's rapidly growing population is consuming the planet's natural resources at an alarming rate. . . . [It is estimated] that the world currently needs 1.6 Earths to satisfy the demand for natural resources . . . [a figure that] could rise to 2 planets by 2030."[1]

Is that really true?

Start with a brain teaser. It is 1980, and you are getting married. Your parents invite 100 guests to the wedding reception. The reception costs them $100 per person, or $10,000 in total. Fast-forward to 2018. Now it is your turn to throw a wedding reception for your child. The guest list has increased by 72 percent. Some of the old folks are no longer around, but the cousins have grown in number. That means that you are now catering for 172 people. If the price per guest had remained the same, your bill would amount to $17,200. Instead, the bill comes to $4,816, which is less than half of what your parents paid for you. You ask the caterer: How is this possible? The caterer responds that for every 1 percent increase in attendance, the bill fell by 1 percent. While the number of guests rose by 72 percent, then, your bill has declined by 72 percent. Surely, things like that don't happen in real life.

Or do they?

In fact, this is exactly what has happened to the abundance of 50 basic commodities between 1980 and 2018. Over that period, the world's population rose by 71.2 percent,[2] yet the average working time required to earn enough money to buy 50 kinds of energy, food, raw materials, and metals fell by 71.6 percent. Put differently, the amount of effort required to buy 1 basket of the 50 commodities in 1980 bought 3.5 baskets in 2018.[3] As we will explain, abundance occurs when the nominal hourly income increases faster than the nominal price of a resource. Furthermore, when the abundance of resources grows at a faster rate than population increases, we call that relationship "superabundance." This relationship between population growth and the abundance of resources is deeply counterintuitive, yet it is no less true.[4]

So what's going on? In the animal world, a sudden increase in the availability of resources such as grass after an unusually rainy season leads to an explosion in the animal population. The population explosion then leads to an exhaustion of resources. Finally, the exhaustion of resources leads to population collapse.

Likewise, human beings were much more exposed to the vicissitudes of fortune in the past. Over time, however, people have developed sophisticated forms of cooperation that increase their wealth and chances of survival. Consider, for example, trade and exchange. In his 1776 magnum opus, *The Wealth of Nations*, the Scottish economist Adam Smith (1723–1790) wrote about humanity's "propensity to truck, barter, and exchange one thing for another."[5] Smith noted that trade is one of the characteristics that distinguishes humanity from nonhuman animals:

> It [trade] is common to all men, and to be found in no other race of animals, which seem to know neither this nor any other species of contracts. . . . Nobody ever saw a dog make a fair and deliberate exchange of one bone for another with another dog. Nobody ever saw one animal by its gestures and natural cries signify to another, "This is mine, that yours; I am willing to give this for that."[6]

More recently, the British writer Matt Ridley noted, "There is strikingly little use of barter in any other animal species. There is sharing within families, and there is food-for-sex exchange in many animals including insects and apes, but there are no cases in which one animal gives an unrelated animal one thing in exchange for a different thing."[7] Trade is particularly valuable during famines. A country struck by drought, for example, can purchase food from abroad. That's not an option available to other animals.

The most important difference between people and nonhuman animals, though, is our superior intelligence and the use of that intelligence to invent and to innovate. "In a way, everything is technology," noted the French economic historian Fernand Braudel (1902–1985): our "patient and monotonous efforts to make a mark on the external world; the rapid changes and the slow improvements in processes and tools; and those innumerable actions which may have no immediate innovative significance but which are the fruit of accumulated knowledge."[8]

And so, over many millennia of trial and error, we have accumulated a store of knowledge that has allowed us to reach escape velocity from scarcity to abundance somewhere toward the end of the 18th century. The Four Horsemen of the Apocalypse (war, famine, pestilence, and death) have not completely disappeared—that would be a miracle, not progress—but the world today is incomparably richer and more productive than it was just two centuries ago. If you don't believe this, ponder, if only for a moment, the 768 types of breakfast cereal that you can buy at Walmart by putting forth just a few minutes of labor at minimum wage.[9]

Trivial, you say? All right. Consider, then, the proper nutrition, high rates of literacy, widespread availability of antibiotics, and countless other conveniences now so commonly available in modern life.

We measure abundance in time prices.[10] A time price denotes the length of time that a person has to work to earn enough money to buy something. It is the money price divided by hourly income. Money prices are expressed in dollars and cents, while time prices are expressed in hours and minutes. If a barrel of oil, for example, costs $75 and you earn $15 an hour, the time price will come to five hours. If the price of oil increases to $80 a barrel and your income increases to $20 an hour, the time price will decrease to four hours.

Time prices make much more sense than money prices for at least three reasons. Time prices avoid the contention and subjectivity of commonly used inflation adjustments.[11] Since innovation shows up in both lower prices and higher incomes (more productive people are better-paid people), time prices more fully capture the effects of innovation. And time prices are independent of currency fluctuations. Instead of gauging the standards of living in India and the United States by comparing the adjusted "purchasing power parity" prices of a gallon of milk in Indian rupees and American dollars, time prices provide a universal and standardized way (hours and minutes) to measure changes in well-being.

That brings us to the most important contribution of time prices to economic discourse. The American economic commentator George Gilder argues that wealth is knowledge, growth is learning, and money is time. From these three propositions, we have derived a theorem, which states that the growth in knowledge—which is to say innovation, productivity, and standards of living—can and ought to be measured with time. *Superabundance* operationalizes this theorem within a new analytical framework. When we applied this framework to a wide variety of goods and services spanning two centuries, we were astonished by the near-ubiquitous and apparently accelerating growth in abundance. The purpose of this book is to share with you, the reader, what we found.

Our research into time prices and the abundance of resources began when we looked at updating the famous wager between the University of Maryland economist Julian Simon (1932–1998) and three scholars: Stanford University biologist Paul Ehrlich; University of California, Berkeley ecologist John Harte; and University of California, Berkeley scientist and the future director of President Barack Obama's White House Office of Science and Technology John P. Holdren.[12] The wager was based on the inflation-adjusted prices of five metals: chromium, copper, nickel, tin, and tungsten, and it lasted from 1980 to 1990. Ehrlich et al. predicted that because of population growth, metals would become scarcer and hence more expensive. Simon argued that because of population growth, metals would become cheaper.

Ehrlich thought like a biologist who did not seem particularly interested in economics. In 1971, for example, Ehrlich and Holdren wrote that as "a population of organisms grows in a finite environment, sooner or later it will encounter a resource limit. This phenomenon, described by ecologists as reaching the 'carrying capacity' of the environment, applies to bacteria on a culture dish, to fruit flies in a jar of agar, and to buffalo on a prairie. It must also apply to man on this finite planet."[13] In 1997, Ehrlich still believed this:

> Since natural resources are finite, increasing consumption obviously must "inevitably lead to depletion and scarcity." Currently, there are very large supplies of many mineral resources including iron and coal, but when they become "depleted" or "scarce" will depend not simply on how much is in the ground but also on the

rate at which they can be produced and the amount societies can afford to pay, in standard economic or environmental terms, for their extraction and use. For most resources, economic and environmental constraints will limit consumption while substantial quantities remain. . . . For others, however, global "depletion"—that is, decline to a point where worldwide demand can no longer be met economically—is already on the horizon. Petroleum is a textbook example of such a resource.[14]

Simon thought like an economist who understood the powers of incentives and the price mechanism to overcome resource shortages. Instead of the quantity of resources, he looked at the prices of resources and at the human creativity that higher prices awaken. He saw resource scarcity as a temporary challenge that can be resolved through greater efficiency, increased supply, development of substitutes, and so on. The relationship between prices and innovation, he insisted, is dynamic. Relative scarcity leads to higher prices, higher prices create incentives for innovations, and innovations lead to abundance. Scarcity gets converted to abundance through the price system. The price system functions as long as the economy is based on property rights, the rule of law, and freedom of exchange. In relatively free economies, therefore, resources do not get depleted in the way that Ehrlich feared they would. In fact, resources tend to become more abundant.

Simon won his bet with Ehrlich et al. when the real (which is to say inflation-adjusted) price of the bundle of five metals fell by 36 percent. Simon's victory would have been even more impressive had he used time prices. Between 1980 and 1990, those fell by 40 percent.[15] Unfortunately, it will take much more than a single bet between two scholars or, for that matter, a book like this one, to rid the world of the outdated idea that population growth and resource depletion inevitably go hand in hand,[16] but we have to start somewhere, and the customary place to start is with Chapter 1.

PART ONE

Thanos's deadly idea:
from antiquity to the present
and beyond

CHAPTER 1

Are we in the midst of progress, or are we facing the apocalypse?

Little one, it's a simple calculus. This universe is finite, its resources finite. If life is left unchecked, life will cease to exist. It needs correction.

Thanos, *Avengers: Infinity War* [1]

Chapter summary

This is a book about facts. Paradoxically, it starts with fiction. Thanos, the villain from the blockbuster movie *Avengers: Infinity War*, is an intergalactic warlord in search of superpowers that will allow him to destroy half the life in the universe. This, he feels, is necessary and even, in a way, good. The resources in the universe are finite, he believes, and the needs of living creatures are infinite. By reducing all life by half, he reasons, there will be plenty of resources left for the rest. He succeeds, and disaster ensues.

Thanos may be fictional (in fact, he first appeared in a comic book in 1973, a time when Paul Ehrlich and like-minded thinkers dominated the public debate in the United States), but the human appetite for apocalyptic movies is very real. In fact, the number of disaster flicks has been increasing since the 1950s in spite of the world becoming richer, healthier, better fed, more educated, freer, safer, and in some ways, environmentally friendlier over the intervening seven decades. The world, in other words, has experienced tremendous progress.

What is progress? The American writer P. J. O'Rourke (1947–2022) wrote that "if you think that in the past, there was some golden age of pleasure and plenty to which you would, if you were able, transport yourself, let me say one single word: dentistry."[2] Since antiquity, in fact, people have thought of humanity as regressing from a good state to a bad state rather than progressing from a bad state to a good state. That started to change during the Renaissance. By the 18th century, the upward trends in human knowledge and (in some places) wealth became undeniable, and leading intellectuals of the day started to theorize about the causes and effects of human progress.[3]

Of course, as soon as they started to think about human progress, they started to critique it. Progress, some argued, would corrupt the human soul and destroy our species.[4] As we shall explain, humans have evolved to focus on the negative. That makes looking at the brighter side of life difficult, if not altogether foreign to us. In fact, some people find the notion of a coming apocalypse strangely reassuring. Thus, while traditional sources of apocalyptic thinking may be in abeyance, new ones have come to the fore.[5]

The movie that everyone was talking about

Avengers: Infinity War, the penultimate movie in the Avengers film series, was a blockbuster in the United States and beyond. While it has since been surpassed by *Avengers: Endgame, Infinity War* smashed through the previous opening weekend records, earning over $640 million worldwide. That means that despite being the fourth most expensive film ever produced—it cost $312 million to make—*Infinity War* brought home more than double its production costs in the opening weekend alone. From its April 23, 2018, premiere in Los Angeles and subsequent release in 59 countries to its theatrical close on September 13, 2018, the film earned a total of $2.048 billion, thus becoming the fifth highest-grossing movie of all time. Domestically, the film made $678.8 million at the box office.[6] If we divide that figure by $9.11, the average U.S ticket price in 2018, we end up with a staggering 74.5 million tickets sold.[7] That means that if every ticket holder saw *Infinity War* only once, about one out of every five Americans viewed the film.

If you missed seeing the film in the theater, here's a brief summary. Most of the movie consists of Thanos, a giant purple alien warlord, searching the universe for six magic crystals called infinity stones that he is trying to steal. Each stone is left over from the creation of the universe, and collectively, they encompass all of its supposed aspects: reality, time, space, power, mind, and soul. As he collects these gems, Thanos attaches them to his magic gauntlet, becoming more powerful with each stone. His end goal? To use the infinity stones to eliminate half of all life in the universe. The Avengers and their allies try to stop him at every turn, but they are unsuccessful, mostly because they refuse to sacrifice each other's lives in the process. In the opening scene, Loki gives up the space stone in an attempt to save Thor, his brother. In another, Gamora reveals the location of the soul stone after Thanos tortures her sister, Nebula. Finally, Wanda refuses to destroy the mind stone embedded in her lover's forehead, despite it being the easiest way to stop Thanos from acquiring it.

Thanos, on the other hand, has no qualms about sacrificing his loved ones. In a pivotal moment, he weeps before throwing his beloved daughter Gamora off a cliff in order to collect the soul stone. You see, Thanos's mission isn't destruction for its own sake. In order to preserve the future of life, Thanos plans to destroy half of it. After the final battle with the Avengers, Thanos snaps his jeweled fingers, and the audience gasps as half of their favorite characters dissolve on screen. The tragic irony of the film is that Thanos defeats the Avengers by exploiting their value for life, the very thing that makes them heroes. Because they refuse to "trade lives," Thanos is able to destroy half of them.

This book is not a retort to Thanos.[8] It is instead intended as an antidote to a pernicious idea with roots in deep antiquity. According to this idea, population growth leads to the exhaustion of resources, shortages, hunger, and, eventually, death. Counterintuitively, we will use empirical evidence and theoretical analysis to show that humans can overcome shortages through innovation. Contrary to what many people have been expecting, the growth of the human population from roughly 1 billion in 1800 to 7.8 billion in 2020 has not been accompanied by a lowering of living standards but by an explosion in material abundance. If you approach this volume with an open mind, you will be astounded by the progress that humanity has made, especially over the last 200 years or so. The book will affirm the moral and practical value of every additional human being, leave you appreciative of the abundance that you are enjoying today, and even hopeful about the future fate of humanity.

A (very) brief history of apocalyptic thought

According to Washington State University scholars Mary K. Bloodsworth-Lugo and Carmen R. Lugo-Lugo, the number of apocalyptic movies released between 1980 and 1999 was 59. Between 2000 and 2013, the number of such releases rose to 90.[9] "The author's [sic] survey of apocalyptic films produced over the last 100 years found that only a handful of end-of-the-world motion pictures were produced in the period before 1950, and with each passing decade after 1950 until the 1980s, the number of films released to audiences steadily increased. During the 1980s and 1990s, the number of apocalyptic films released remained steady before an explosion of apocalyptic films in the

21st century."[10] Most have dealt with such apocalyptic subjects as runaway climate change, asteroid impacts, nuclear holocausts, resource depletion, disease pandemics, the end of days, zombie apocalypse, cybernetic revolts, dysgenics, and alien invasions.

In recent years, popular movies with a Thanos-like character or an emphasis on overpopulation as a key global problem included *Kingsman: The Secret Service* (2014) and *Inferno* (2016). In the former movie, a billionaire businessman named Richmond Valentine offers everyone in the world SIM cards guaranteeing free cellular and internet connectivity. In fact, Valentine plans to use his satellite network to send a neurological signal to people's cell phones, thereby making humanity rageful and murderous. The culling of most of the world's population in an orgy of violence, Valentine believes, will avert global warming and extinction.[11] In the latter movie, a hero named Robert Langdon has to track down a hidden bioweapon called Inferno, which has the potential to kill half of humanity. The weapon was created by another mad billionaire, Bertrand Zobrist, who believes that the world's population is growing at an exponential pace. In order to save half of humanity, the other half has to perish. Thankfully, the world is saved by Langdon and heroic agents from the World Health Organization.[12]

If you are wondering why so many movies about the future of humanity are filled with doom and gloom, you are not alone. On his popular HBO show on June 14, 2019, the host of *Real Time with Bill Maher* observed, "Not every movie set in the future has to be a super clean utopia or a smoldering post-apocalypse." Maher asked, "Isn't there something in between? It's always either the earth is a giant Apple store or Burning Man got way out of control."[13] Maher was onto something. Movies about humanity's future are almost exclusively pessimistic. Even when humanity does manage to survive, it is only after a great deal of hardship and close calls with oblivion.

Was there a golden age?

Pessimism about the future of humanity is of ancient vintage. Most civilizations have conjured up some theory of decline from a perfect original state that underpinned their prevalent belief systems. The garden of Eden and the fall of man appear in all Abrahamic religions and are well known, but similar stories can be found in Buddhism, Taoism, and Hinduism.[14] Buddhism, for example, divides the period after Buddha's death into three ages: the age of the "true law" during which the Buddha's teachings were upheld; the age of the "copied law" when Buddhist doctrines only resembled the Buddha's teachings; and the age of the "latter law," in which Buddhist doctrines "degenerated."[15] In China, Zhuang Zhou (369–286 BCE), one of the founders of Taoism, observed that

> the men of old dwelt in the midst of crudity and chaos; side by side with the rest of the world, they attained simplicity and silence there. At that time the yin and yang were harmonious and still, ghosts and spirits worked no mischief, the four seasons kept to their proper order, the ten thousand things knew no injury, and living creatures were free from premature death. Although men had knowledge, they did not use it. This was called the Perfect Unity. At this time, no one made a move to do anything, and there was unvarying spontaneity.[16]

Similarly, James Madison University religion professor Alan Levinovitz noted the following in his 2020 book, *Natural: How Faith in Nature's Goodness Leads to Harmful Fads, Unjust Laws, and Flawed Science*:

> During the mythic Hindu epoch known as the Satya Yuga, there was no need for agriculture, no one fell ill, and the weather was always nice. . . . Even the preagricultural peoples who star in modern golden age myths had their own versions of the same. A myth from the South American Bororo people describes "days when diseases were still unknown and human beings were unacquainted with suffering."[17]

In ancient Greece, the poet Hesiod (750–650 BCE) outlined human history as a series of degenerating stages beginning with a golden age when people "lived like gods without sorrow of heart, remote and free from toil and grief: miserable age rested not on them."[18] The ages of man decayed from gold to silver, from silver to bronze, and from bronze (via a heroic age) to iron. Hesiod, incidentally, believed that he was living in the Iron Age, which he characterized as a wretched era of misery and strife. He wrote that "for now truly is a race of iron, and men never rest from labor and sorrow by day and from perishing by night, and the gods shall lay sore trouble upon them."[19]

To be sure, there are intimations of human progress in the plays of the Greek tragedians. They include *Prometheus Bound* by Aeschylus (525/524–456/455 BCE), *Antigone* by Sophocles (497/496–406/405 BCE), and *The Suppliant Women* by Euripides (480–406 BCE).[20] But as the Anglo-Irish historian John Bagnell Bury (1861–1927) argued in his 1920 book, *The Idea of Progress: An Inquiry into Its Origin and Growth*, "these recognitions of a progress were not incompatible with the widely-spread belief in an *initial* degeneration of the human race, nor did it usually appear as a rival doctrine [emphasis added]."[21]

By and large, the Romans shared the Greek view of human development. For example, the Roman historian Sallust (86–35 BCE) wrote that in the past, "men's lives were still free from covetousness; each was quite content with his own possessions."[22] Likewise, the Roman historian Tacitus (56–120 CE) thought that "primeval man, untouched as yet by criminal passion, lived his life without reproach or guilt and consequently without penalty or coercion."[23] A similar sentiment can be observed in *Poem 64* by the Latin poet Catullus (84–54 BCE).[24] Finally, Livy (59 BCE–17 CE) noted the following in the preface to his *History of Rome*:

> The subjects to which I would ask each of my readers to devote his earnest attention are these—the life and morals of the community; the men and the qualities by which through domestic policy and foreign war dominion was won and extended. Then as the standard of morality gradually lowers, let him follow the decay of the national character, observing how at first it slowly sinks, then slips downward more and more rapidly, and finally begins to plunge into headlong ruin, until he reaches these days in which we can bear neither our diseases nor their remedies.[25]

Once again, there were partial exceptions to the rule. The Roman Stoic philosopher Seneca (4 BCE–65 CE) expected future growth in human knowledge when he wrote that "the day will come when posterity will marvel at our ignorance of things that will then appear to be so evident."[26] Seneca did not, nonetheless, expect that new knowledge would result in human betterment and remained wedded to the theory of degeneration.[27]

The Epicureans rejected the notion of a golden age. "For them," wrote Bury, "the earliest condition of men resembled that of the beasts, and from this primitive and miserable condition, they laboriously reached the existing state of civilization, not by external guidance or as a consequence of some initial design, but simply by the exercise of human intelligence." To quote the Epicurean philosopher Lucretius (99–55 BCE):

> Thus time draws forward each and everything
> Little by little into the midst of men,
> And reason uplifts it to the shores of light.
> For one thing after other did men see
> Grow clear by intellect, till with their arts
> They've now achieved the supreme pinnacle.[28]

Even Lucretius and the Epicureans, though, did not expect continuous improvements in human well-being and thought that the world would end in ruins. What happened between their time and the advent of universal ruin did not interest them. As with the Stoics, theirs was "a philosophy of resignation."[29]

Or is history a cycle of destruction and renewal?

The theory of world cycles flourished throughout antiquity. In Hinduism, we encounter an infinite number of universes that both preceded and will follow our own.[30] The cycle of universal creation and destruction is controlled by a deity named Kāla, or Time. In Buddhism, by contrast, the cycle of destruction and renewal happens without the intervention of a deity.[31] In both religions, universal destruction is generally preceded by social degradation, while universal renewal is marked by the return of virtue and peace.

This theory of cycles in human society was also popular in both ancient Greece and Rome. Two centuries after Hesiod and Homer, the Greek philosopher Plato (428/427–348/347 BCE) argued that Hesiod's ages corresponded to the rotation of Earth, first in one direction, then another. In the first rotation, the gods oversaw human affairs and tended to human needs. According to Plato, the golden age occurred in that period. When Earth's rotation changed, the gods left humans to manage their own affairs with predictably disastrous results.[32]

Some Pythagoreans also embraced the notion of infinite universes but believed that each new universe would be exactly the same as the one that preceded it (i.e., the abduction of Helen would be repeated ad infinitum). The same was true of the Stoics. In the words of the Roman Emperor Marcus Aurelius (121 CE–180 CE), the rational soul

> goes over the whole Universe and the surrounding void and surveys its shape, reaches out into the boundless extent of time, embraces and ponders the periodic rebirth of the Whole and understands that those who come after us will behold nothing new, nor did those who came before us behold anything greater.[33]

Polybius (200–118 BCE), a Greek historian who spent much of his life in Rome, used some of Plato's and Aristotle's ideas concerning the ideal form of government to develop a cyclical theory of politics known as anacyclosis (from the Greek term ἀνακύκλωσις).[34] Polybius distinguished between three "benign" forms of government (i.e., monarchy, aristocracy, and democracy), which he thought were weak and unstable, and three "malignant" forms of government (i.e., tyranny, oligarchy, and ochlocracy), which he thought were oppressive and thus undesirable. According to a modern interpretation of Polybius's model,

> political communities are first ruled by kings. Kingship is eventually corrupted into tyranny. The last tyrant is deposed or forced to share power with an aristocracy. Aristocracy degenerates into an oppressive oligarchy. Occasionally, an independent middle economic stratum—a middle class—emerges, hoi mesoi in Aristotelian terms. If this middle class is entrenched, democracy emerges. In time, however, a plutocracy emerges, stratifying society between

opulent and dependent. The hopes of the dependent masses fuel an intensifying competition among their political patrons, transforming democracy into mob-rule, perhaps better described as rule by demagogues. This tournament of demagogues rages among a narrowing field of popular leaders until a single champion arises victorious, dragging political society back to some form of monarchy, thus completing the cycle.[35]

So amid the general chaos and decline, the ancients grasped at a ray of hope, an emergence of a hero so virtuous that he (and it was always a male) could, so to speak, turn back time and return humanity to the happy days of yore. In Roman imperial propaganda, that hero was Caesar Augustus (63 BCE–14 CE). In celebration of his reign, Virgil (70–19 BCE) penned the *Fourth Eclogue*, in which he wrote, "A great new cycle of centuries begins . . . The Golden Age returns, and its first-born comes down from heaven."[36] As each virtuous hero inevitably dies, however, the world slides back into iniquity. It is, perhaps, not coincidental that according to one mythological tradition, chaos is the child of Chronos (i.e., time).

Or are we even heading toward a Judgment Day?

The Zoroastrians developed the idea of the final judgment: a day of reckoning when the wicked are punished (and later forgiven), evil is defeated, and humans gain immortality and enjoy harmonious coexistence with the creator of the universe, Ahura Mazda, and the virgin-born messiah, Saoshyant.[37] And so in Zoroastrianism, we encounter the concept of a final denouement that is quite distinct from the continuous process of degeneration or, for that matter, a continuous cycle of death and renewal.

The Day of Judgment or Yawm ad-Din reappears in Judaism and is presaged, according to one tradition, by the coming of the Messiah. A different tradition avers that everyone will be judged immediately after death. On Judgment Day, "some Jews believe that everyone will be resurrected so that they can be judged, while others believe that only those who are morally good will be resurrected."[38] Most Muslims believe that after death, the soul enters Barzakh, a limbo where the former waits until Yawm al-Din, or Judgment Day. On that day, Allah will decide who goes to heaven and who goes to hell. Thereafter, the world will be destroyed.[39]

As we shall see later in this chapter, the idea of a gradual and continuous process of human improvement emerged in 18th-century Western Europe. It is therefore appropriate to consider in greater detail Christian eschatology (from the Greek ἔσχατος meaning "last" and the English ending -ology meaning "the study of") and its impact on the thoughts and actions of Western Europeans from the rise of Christianity in the fourth century (Emperor Constantine the Great Christianized the Roman Empire in the first three decades of the fourth century, and Emperor Theodosius I made Nicene Christianity the state religion of the Roman Empire on February, 27, 380 CE) to the Enlightenment.

The Christian view that was developed by the Church Fathers, especially Saint Augustine (345–430 CE), and that dominated Christian thought and life throughout the Middle Ages was in some ways incompatible with the idea of human progress. In the Gospel of Matthew, Jesus is quoted as saying,

> When the Son of man shall come in his glory, and all the holy angels with him, then shall he sit upon the throne of his glory, and before him shall be gathered all nations, and he shall separate them one from another, as a shepherd divideth his sheep from the goats. And he shall set the sheep on his right hand. . . . Then shall the King say unto them on his right hand, "Come ye, blessed of my father, inherit the kingdom prepared for you from the foundation of the world" (Matt. 25:31).

By implication, the whole of human history has been preordained since the dawn of time, and the Christian era "would endure only so long as to enable the Deity to gather in the predestined number of saved people."[40] The early Christians assumed that the Second Coming and, concomitantly, eternal life in heaven were imminent. From that perspective, the current state of humanity, let alone any improvements in human well-being, was immaterial.

Moreover, Saint Augustine's formulation of original sin seemed to negate the notion of free will, thus making moral progress impossible. There were two aspects of Christian thought, however, that proved quite propitious to human progress in the long run.

First, Christians borrowed from the Jews a view of history that had a clear meaning in the form of a desirable future goal (i.e., salvation). When the belief in the active role of a deity in the guidance of human affairs (i.e., divine providence) later subsided, the Western world did not revert to the cyclical theory of the ancient Greeks. In the future, humans would understand themselves to be responsible for their own improvement.

Second, the Christians borrowed from the Greeks and the Romans an ecumenical view of the world. With the conquests of Alexander the Great (356–323 BCE), the ancient distinction between the Greek and barbarian worlds started to break down. Also, the Romans justified their conquests "by the establishment of a common order [and] the unification of mankind in a single, world-embracing political organism."[41] Rome was to be all-encompassing (*orbis terrarum*) and peaceful (*Pax Romana*), with Augustus as its savior (*salvator*).

After the fall of Rome, the universal empire of the Caesars gave way to the Christian idea of the "universal church," the ultimate goal of ambitious rulers from the Frankish king Charlemagne (748–814) through the Holy Roman Emperor Charles V (1500–1558) and French King Louis XIV (1638–1715). While they may not have succeeded, "the conception of the intercohesion of peoples as contributors to a common pool of civilization" endured. "When the idea of progress at last made its appearance in the world, [human intercohesion] was to be one of the elements in its growth."[42]

Some people find apocalyptic thinking strangely reassuring

Considering the centrality of apocalyptic thinking to most of the world's dominant belief systems that continue to guide the moral sentiments of the vast majority of human beings even today, it is worth pausing to consider what (if any) utility people derive from entertaining apocalyptic thoughts and expectations.

In their 2016 paper, "Death and End Times: The Effects of Religious Fundamentalism and Mortality Salience on Apocalyptic Beliefs," psychologists Clay Routledge, Andrew A. Abeyta, and Christina Roylance place the roots of apocalyptic thinking in the human search for transcendence and meaning. Religion, they note, is one of the defining features of humanity. It has existed for thousands—maybe even hundreds of thousands—of years.[43]

Religion's astounding endurance is partly due to one universal aspect of the human psyche: the fear of death. By affirming the immortality of the soul, many religions promise life after death, whether in the form of a blissful afterlife or some form of reincarnation. Religion is also attractive to humans because it can give meaning to life. It interprets natural and random phenomena as though they have been created for a purpose. From a religious perspective, accidental events can be perceived as being a part of a larger design. Rather than face an infinite and impersonal cosmos, religion allows humans to sleep soundly "knowing" that a strong hand is guiding the universe. Finally, religion provides people with a moral code that in turn helps give structure to everyday life and connects individuals to broader moral communities.

Interestingly, prophecies predicting widespread death and destruction can be a source of comfort to certain individuals. According to Routledge and his coauthors, religious fundamentalists are more likely to believe that a natural disaster, for example, is a sign of a coming apocalypse. Furthermore, when asked to consider their own deaths, fundamentalists become even more likely to report apocalyptic beliefs. The fundamentalists are motivated to interpret natural disasters as apocalyptic because the ensuing destruction reinforces their worldview, and that gives them comfort in death and meaning in life.

The apocalypse is also attractive to some secularists. As Daniel Wojcik from the University of Oregon notes in his 1997 book, *The End of the World as We Know It: Faith, Fatalism, and Apocalypse in America*, popular apocalyptic narratives usually include a small group of survivors destined to rebuild civilization as a utopia. This fantasy leads people to believe that if they survive, they may have a more meaningful life after the corrupt world of yore has been destroyed. Wojcik also argues there is an inherent romance to the apocalypse, which gives the disillusioned something to look forward to, even if they do expect to die.[44]

There is nonetheless no shortage of positive trends in the world today

Unfortunately for the apocalypticists and fortunately for the rest of us, the state of the world continues to improve along many different dimensions. Astonishingly, those improvements have become most pronounced over the same period that saw the number of apocalyptic movies explode.

Let's start with income, for richer societies can afford more food, better health care, higher levels of education, and so on. Between 1950 and 2020, the average income per person in the United States rose from $15,183 to $62,941, or 315 percent. In the United Kingdom, it rose from $11,772 to $43,906, or 278 percent. The population-weighted average global income per person rose from $4,158 to $16,904, or 307 percent (all figures are in 2018 U.S. dollars).[45]

Increased prosperity was not confined to developed nations. Some of the world's poorest countries benefited handsomely from income growth between 1950 and 2020. The growth in Chinese incomes (from $688 to $14,009) amounts to a staggering 1,936 percent. India saw its average income rise from $842 to $6,649, or 690 percent. Even sub-Saharan Africa, the world's poorest region, saw its per capita income rise from $2,214 to $4,025, or 82 percent (all figures are in 2018 U.S. dollars).[46]

Except for a handful of war-torn African countries such as the Democratic Republic of the Congo and failing socialist countries such as Venezuela, real incomes rose throughout the world over the last half century, often substantially.

Now, consider the population-weighted average global life expectancy, which rose from 52.6 years in 1960 to 72.4 years in 2017, or 37.6 percent. In the United States, it rose from 69.8 years to 78.5 years, or 13 percent. In the United Kingdom, it rose from 71.1 years to 81.2 years, or 14 percent.

Once again, the world's poorest nations experienced some of the greatest life expectancy gains between 1960 and 2017: China, from 43.7 years to 76.4 years, or 75 percent; India from 41.2 years to 68.8 years, or 67 percent; and sub-Saharan Africa from 40.4 years to 60.9 years, or 51 percent.[47] There is not a single country in the world where life expectancy was lower in 2017 than it was in 1960.

The reasons for increasing life spans include the dramatic decline in infant mortality and improved nutrition. Between 1960 and 2018, the infant mortality rate per 1,000 live births fell from 25.9 to 5.6 in the United States, from 22.9 to 3.6 in the United Kingdom, and from 161 to 30 in India. That's a reduction of 78 percent, 84 percent, and 81 percent, respectively.

Between 1990 and 2018, the population-weighted average global infant mortality rate fell from 64.7 to 28.9, or 55 percent. In sub-Saharan Africa, it fell from 107 to 53, or 51 percent. In China, it fell from 83.7 in 1969 to 7.4 in 2018, or 91 percent.[48]

The population-weighted average global food supply per person per day rose from 2,115 calories in 1961 to 2,917 calories in 2017, or 38 percent. Over the same period, it rose from 2,880 calories to 3,766 calories, or 31 percent, in the United States; from 3,231 calories to 3,428 calories, or 6 percent, in the United Kingdom; from 1,415 calories to 3,197 calories, or 126 percent, in China; and from 2,010 calories to 2,517 calories, or 25 percent, in India.[49]

To put these figures in perspective, the U.S. Department of Agriculture recommends that moderately active adult men consume between 2,400 and 2,600 calories a day and that moderately active adult women consume 2,000 calories a day.[50]

In sub-Saharan Africa, a region that once seemed destined for hunger (many of us remember the horrifying photos of malnourished babies from the Horn of Africa in the early 1980s), food supply rose from 2,004 calories in 1961 to 2,447 calories in 2017. That's a 22 percent increase. Put differently, the world's poorest region now enjoys access to food that is roughly equivalent to that of the Portuguese in the early 1960s.[51]

In fact, scientists from the African Population and Health Research Center in Kenya estimated that in 4 out of 24 African countries surveyed in 2017, obesity prevalence among urban women exceeded 20 percent. It ranged between 10 and 19 percent in the other 20 countries.[52] Today, obesity tends to be a bigger problem than starvation in many parts of the world, and famines have disappeared outside of active war zones (e.g., Yemen in 2020).

Speaking of violence, the global homicide rate, according to the Institute of Health Metrics and Evaluation in Seattle, has dropped from 6.4 per 100,000 in 1990 to 5.3 per 100,000 in 2016. That's a reduction of 17 percent over a remarkably short period of 26 years.[53]

Similarly, researchers at the Peace Research Institute in Oslo have documented a steep decline in the rate at which soldiers and civilians were killed in combat in the post–World War II era. The rate of battle deaths per 100,000 people reached a peak of 23 in 1953.[54] By 2016, it had fallen to just over 1. That's a decline of about 95 percent.[55]

Genocides, noted the Harvard University psychologist Steven Pinker in his 2018 book, *Enlightenment Now: The Case for Reason, Science, Humanism, and Progress*, tend to go hand in hand with wars. In the late 1930s, for example, the global genocide death rate among civilians hovered around 100 per 100,000 per year. During World War II, it reached a peak of 350. It then gradually declined. Since 2005, it has stood at statistical zero.[56]

Also, more people go to school and are able to read. The population-weighted gross primary school enrollment rate in the world stood at 89 percent in 1970. By 2018, it stood at over 100 percent (because some students will be over-aged, under-aged, or grade repeaters, the gross rate can exceed 100 percent).[57] The population-weighted gross secondary school enrollment rate rose from 40 percent to 76 percent over the same period.[58] Finally, the population-weighted gross tertiary school enrollment rate rose from 9.7 percent to 38 percent.[59]

The population-weighted global literacy rate among men aged 15 and older came to 74 percent in 1975. That number rose to 90 percent in 2018.[60] The literacy rate among women aged 15 and older rose from 56 percent in 1976 to 83 percent in 2018.[61] In 2018, 90 percent of women between the ages of 15 and 24 were literate.[62] That number was almost 93 percent among men of the same age.[63] The age-old literacy gap between the sexes has all but disappeared.

The rates of extreme poverty have plummeted, with the share of people living on less than $1.90 per day declining from 42 percent in 1981 to less than 10 percent in 2015. In China, it fell from 66 percent in 1990 to an astonishingly low 0.5 percent in 2016. In India, it fell from 62 percent in 1977 to 21 percent in 2011.[64]

Today, extreme poverty is no longer a global problem but is still an African problem, yet even the world's poorest region saw extreme poverty decline from 55 percent in 1990 to 42 percent in 2015.[65] That reduction may seem underwhelming until we realize that the population of sub-Saharan Africa doubled from 512 million to 1.006 billion over the same period.

Speaking of Africa, Mauritania became the last country in the world to outlaw chattel slavery (in 1981) and to criminalize the practice of enslavement (in 2007).[66] A scourge of humanity for thousands of years, chattel slavery is legal no more.

Consider political freedom as well. The Center for Systemic Peace in Virginia evaluates the characteristics of a political regime in each country on a 20-point scale from −10, which denotes a tyranny like North Korea, to 10, which denotes a politically free society like Norway. "As of the end of 2017, 96 out of 167 countries with populations of at least 500,000 (57 percent) were democracies of some kind, and only 21 (13 percent) were autocracies. . . . [Some] 28 [percent of countries] exhibited elements of both democracy and autocracy. Broadly speaking, the share of democracies among the world's governments has been on an upward trend since the mid-1970s and now sits just shy of its post-World War II record (58 percent in 2016)."[67]

Other positive trends that one of us discussed in a recent book, *Ten Global Trends Every Smart Person Should Know: And Many Others You Will Find Interesting,* include the rise in global happiness, declining global income inequality, the falling share of the world's population living in slums, the political and economic empowerment of women, the uneven but pronounced rise in IQ scores, the decriminalization of same-sex relationships, the continued rise in vaccinations against contagious diseases, the decline of contagious diseases (such as HIV/AIDS, malaria, and tuberculosis), falling cancer death rates, declines in the use of capital punishment, falling rates of military spending and conscription, the shrinkage of nuclear arsenals, declines in working hours that leave more time for leisure, falling rates of child labor and work-place accidents, increasing access to electricity, improving access to sanitation and clean drinking water, and internet-driven access to information.[68]

In fact, it is much easier to compile a list of global trends that are worsening than a list of global trends that are improving, for the former is much shorter than the latter.

The most obvious worry to a diverse group of people, ranging from the apocalypticists at the one end to merely concerned citizens at the other end, is the state of the planet's environment. While other potential threats such as the rise of artificial intelligence and autonomous machines, nuclear conflict, the spread of viruses and superbugs, and even future asteroid impacts on Earth are widely discussed, we will show in Chapter 3 that it is the possibility of an environmental apocalypse that has been dominating the headlines and exercises a powerful hold on the imagination of millions of people.

This book is not about the present state of environmental science, the causes and the extent of global warming, and the precise nature and potential consequences of climatic changes. That said, it is worth noting that even within the environmental sphere, there is plenty of positive news. Between 1982 and 2016, for example, the global tree canopy cover increased by an area larger than Alaska and Montana combined.[69] As *Reason* magazine science correspondent Ronald Bailey put it, "Expanding woodlands suggests that humanity has begun the process of withdrawing from the natural world, which in turn will provide greater scope for other species to rebound and thrive."[70]

According to the same author, "The chance of a person dying in a natural catastrophe—earthquake, flood, drought, storm, wildfire, landslide or epidemic—has declined by nearly 99 percent since the 1920s and 1930s. . . . Buildings are better constructed to survive earthquakes; weather satellites and sophisticated computer models provide early storm warnings that give folks time to prepare and evacuate; and broad disease surveillance enables swift medical interventions to halt developing epidemics."[71]

The Rockefeller University environmentalist Jesse H. Ausubel estimated in 2014 that due to the continued improvements in the efficiency of farming practices, including rising crop yields, the world will see "a net reduction in use of arable land (i.e., land used for farming) in about 50 years totaling 10 times the area of Iowa, and shrinking global cropland to the level of 1960."[72]

In 2017, the World Database on Protected Areas reported that 15 percent of the planet's land surface was covered by protected areas. That's an area almost double the size of the United States. Marine protected areas covered nearly 7 percent of the world's oceans. That's an area more than twice the size of South America.[73]

Part of the reason for rising marine conservancy is fish farming, which enables humans to consume increasing quantities of fish without decimating aquatic wildlife. "In 1950," noted Bailey, "aquaculture produced less than a million metric tons of fish. In 2016, aquaculturists raised more than 80 million metric tons of fish—51 million tons on inland fish farms and 29 million tons at sea."[74]

We are also getting better at producing goods and services in ways that are less harmful to the environment. For example, the global sulphur dioxide emissions (SO_2 is a toxic gas that is a byproduct of copper extraction and the burning of fossil fuels) declined from a peak of 152 million metric tons in 1980 to 97 million metric tons in 2010—a reduction of 36 percent over a comparatively short period of 30 years.[75] The volume of SO_2 emissions in the United States decreased from about 31 million metric tons in 1970 to about 2 million metric tons in 2019, a reduction of 94 percent.[76]

Speaking of burning fossil fuels, the average global CO_2 emissions per dollar of output declined by 41 percent between 1960 and 2014 from 0.84 kilograms to 0.5 kilograms.[77] Those are the latest figures that we had access to. We suspect that the recent switch from burning coal to burning natural gas in many countries (natural gas emits between 50 and 60 percent less CO_2 when combusted in a new, efficient natural gas power plant compared with emissions from a typical new coal plant)[78] will help reduce CO_2 emissions per dollar of output even further, and that's not accounting for the rise in non–fossil fuel sources of power such as wind and solar.

The long-term relationship between the intensity of CO_2 emissions and economic development is furthermore quite notable. "On average," wrote Hannah Ritchie and Max Roser from Our World in Data, a non-profit organization based in the United Kingdom, "we see low carbon intensities at low incomes; carbon intensity rises as countries transition from low-to-middle incomes, especially in rapidly growing industrial economies; and as countries move towards higher incomes, carbon intensity falls again."[79]

That's precisely what we are seeing in the data. To be sure, global CO_2 emissions are still rising—they reached 36.44 billion metric tons in 2019— but looking at individual countries provides a more positive picture. For example, in the United States, CO_2 emissions declined from a high of 6.13 billion metric tons in 2007 to 5.28 billion metric tons in 2019, a 14 percent reduction in 12 years. In the European Union, they fell from a peak of 4.1 billion metric tons in 1979 to 2.92 billion metric tons in 2019.[80]

We are also getting better at saving freshwater, which is used widely in agriculture as well as in industrial production. The World Bank estimates that the United States increased its water productivity, or inflation-adjusted dollars of GDP per cubic meter of freshwater withdrawn, from $13 in 1980 to $36 in 2010; China from $0.8 in 1980 to $15 in 2015; Japan from $34 in 1980 to $67 in 2009; Germany from $58 in 1991 to $104 in 2010; and the United Kingdom from $91 in 1980 to $314 in 2012.[81]

Finally, consider the revolutionary findings of Massachusetts Institute of Technology scientist Andrew McAfee in his 2019 book, *More from Less: The Surprising Story of How We Learned to Prosper Using Fewer Resources—and What Happens Next*. For a long time, economists knew that the profit motive compels companies to decrease the use of natural resources per dollar of output. When aluminum cans were introduced in 1959, for example, they weighed 85 grams. By 2011, they weighed 13 grams.[82] Why pay more for inputs if you don't have to?

But as McAfee discovered by looking at the U.S. consumption of 72 resources from aluminum to zinc, the absolute annual use of 66 resources peaked prior to 2019. Likewise, energy use decreased between 2008 and 2017, even though the U.S. economy expanded by 15 percent over the same period. The U.S. economy, in other words, has reached such a level of efficiency and sophistication that it is possible for it to produce an ever-increasing amount of goods and services while at the same time using ever-fewer resources.[83] There is every reason to expect that as other economies become similarly advanced, they too will reduce their absolute consumption of resources.

The aforementioned data will not come as a total surprise to readers interested in the welfare of our species. Over the past decade or so, a number of highly regarded authors have turned their considerable intellects toward exploring the state of humanity. They included British writer Matt Ridley in his 2010 book, *The Rational Optimist*; Swedish scholar Johan Norberg in his 2017 book, *Progress: Ten Reasons to Look Forward to the Future*; Hans Rosling and Anna Rosling Rönnlund in their 2018 book, *Factfulness: Ten Reasons We're Wrong About the World—and Why Things Are Better Than You Think*; Nobel Prize–winning economist Angus Deaton in his 2013 book, *The Great Escape: Health, Wealth, and the Origins of Inequality*; American writer Gregg Easterbrook in his 2018 book, *It's Better Than It Looks: Reasons for Optimism in an Age of Fear*; Ronald Bailey in his 2015 book, *The End of Doom: Environmental Renewal in the Twenty-First Century*; Bailey and Tupy in their 2020 book, *Ten Global Trends Every Smart Person Should Know: And Many Others You Will Find Interesting*; and last but not least Harvard University psychologist Steven Pinker in his 2011 book, *The Better Angels of Our Nature: Why Violence Has Declined*, and his 2018 book, *Enlightenment Now: The Case for Reason, Science, Humanism, and Progress*. All of them found considerable evidence for human progress.[84]

What is progress? Where did it come from? And why is it controversial?

In previous sections, we looked at the persistence and, if Hollywood movies are any indication, the flourishing of apocalyptic thinking. We have also looked at the steady stream of good news about the state of human affairs that ought to give people pause when entertaining a variety of end-of-times fantasies. The numbers that we have provided came from globally recognized, credible, reliable external sources that include independent scholars, accredited academic institutions, and international organizations. In this section, we will look at the very idea of human progress. What does it mean? And where did it come from?

As we already saw, the ancient conceptions of time tended to see the physical world through the prism of decline and destruction. The Dark Ages that followed the fall of Rome seemed to confirm that negative view of human development. During the Renaissance (the 15th and 16th centuries), a time when the Europeans rediscovered the works of the ancients and reengaged with the latter, scholars still assumed that the best humanity could hope for was to match the intellectual and social sophistication of the Greco-Roman world. As Bury argued, however, things were slowly changing.

The French jurist and political philosopher Jean Bodin (1530–1596), for example, rejected the theory of human degeneration outright, arguing that there was no a priori reason why conditions conducive to human flourishing in the past (i.e., antiquity) could not reappear in the future.[85] Both Bodin and French classicist Louis LeRoy de Coutances (1510–1577) went as far as to argue that some 16th-century European knowledge was superior to that of the ancients. Similarly, the Italian polymath Gerolamo Cardano

(1501–1576) noted that the "whole of antiquity has nothing equal" to the maritime compass, the printing press, and gunpowder, which the Europeans started using in the Middle Ages.[86]

It was at this time that Europe saw two essential intellectual advancements, if not revolutions. In England, Lord Verulam, the 1st Viscount St. Alban (1561–1626), better known as Francis Bacon, popularized the notion that experimentation was key to unlocking the secrets of nature. In the future, knowledge would be discovered through the scientific method, not derived from the pronouncements of those in authority (including those of the ancients). In France, René Descartes (1596–1650) insisted on "the supremacy of reason and the invariability of the laws of nature."[87] No longer would the fate of humanity be subjected to active interventions of a deity (divine providence). That, Bury noted, "was equivalent to a declaration of the Independence of Man."[88]

It was only during the Enlightenment (17th to 19th centuries), though, that the first true exponent of the idea of progress emerged. Bernard Le Bovier de Fontenelle (1657–1757) was a French author who recognized that human knowledge was cumulative and therefore limitless. Prior to Fontenelle, scholars eschewed frontal attacks on the wisdom of the ancients such as Plato and the Greek philosopher Aristotle (384–322 BCE). Fontenelle acknowledged that the ancients had much wisdom to offer, but he averred that many of the ancient insights could be (and indeed were being) superseded by modern scholars who increasingly relied on the experimental method, something that the ancients (with the exception of Archimedes) did not do, preferring deductive reasoning instead.[89]

The growth of knowledge, as we shall argue in the chapters to follow, depends on human cooperation. The same is true of material enrichment.[90] That's one of the reasons why many "enlightened" scholars favored free trade between nations (the other reason being the establishment of international peace).[91] And so, while the 17th-century English philosopher Thomas Hobbes (1588–1679) still talked of human instincts leading to "war of all against all," the 18th-century Scottish scholar Francis Hutcheson (1694–1746) was arguing that humans were basically cooperative.

Hutcheson, who mentored both Adam Smith and the Scottish philosopher David Hume (1711–1776), thought that humans longed to be with one another and argued that progress resulted from "natural bonds of beneficence and humanity in all [people]."[92] The idea of universal human bonds was embraced by the thinkers of the Enlightenment, who developed, in Arthur Herman's words, the "first secular theory" of human progress or "civilization."[93]

Arguably, the first intimations of a secular theory of progress can be found in the writings of Anne-Robert-Jacques Turgot, Baron de l'Aulne (1727–1781). Turgot was a noted economist and philosopher as well as the first minister of state to French king Louis XVI (1754–1793). In his 1750 book, *Philosophical Review of the Successive Advances of the Human Mind*, Turgot outlined progress in the arts and sciences, culture, manners, mores, institutions, legal codes, and the economy. He divided human history into four successive stages (hunter-gatherer, pastoral, agricultural, and commercial) and averred that the speed of progress was accelerating.

The thinkers of the Scottish Enlightenment—Adam Smith in his *Lectures on Justice, Police, Revenue, and Arms* (1763); Adam Ferguson (1723–1816) in his *Essay on the History of Civil Society* (1767); John Millar (1735–1801) in his *Observations Concerning the Distinction of Ranks in Society* (1771); and Henry Home, Lord Kames (1696–1782) in his *Sketches of the History of Man* (1774)—embraced Turgot's ideas, further developing and popularizing the latter.

In a way, Turgot and the Scottish philosophers turned Hesiod's thesis on its head. According to the ancient scholar, the ages of man decayed from gold to silver, from silver to bronze, and from bronze to iron. The moderns, by contrast, argued that humanity was ascending from rude beginnings to ever higher states of knowledge, wealth, and sophistication.

The 18th-century praise of commerce and the birth of the bourgeoisie . . .

In the first stage, the Scots argued, humans survived by hunting and gathering. In the second stage, they embraced pasturage. In the third stage, they turned to agriculture. In the fourth stage, people gathered in towns and cities and began to live through industry and commerce. With each stage, humans become more productive, more connected, and more civil. Increasingly, people specialized in distinct tasks and lived through exchange. People who might have been rivals become trading partners and friends. As human relationships become more complex, people become socialized, polite, and refined. All of that stimulating conversation eventually led to advances in art and science.

While all "enlightened" scholars (before Rousseau) believed that the human capacity to reason was the main driver of human progress, many also emphasized the beneficial role played by commerce. In the words of Scottish historian William Robertson (1721–1793), commerce "softens and polishes the manners of men. It unites them, by one of the strongest of all ties, the desire of supplying their mutual wants."[94] Charles-Louis de Secondat, Baron de La Brède et de Montesquieu (1689–1755) agreed, writing that "commerce cures destructive prejudices. . . . Wherever lifestyles are gentle, there is commerce; and wherever there is commerce, lifestyles are gentle."[95] In a similar vein, the English writer Samuel Johnson (1709–1784) observed that "there are few ways in which a man can be more innocently employed than in getting money."[96]

People who might have otherwise hated each other, in other words, were brought together in the pursuit of profit. By the 18th century, the extent of human cooperation within the context of the market economy reached levels that the French philosopher François-Marie Arouet (1694–1778)—also known as Voltaire—could write,

> Go into the London Stock Exchange—a more respectable place than many a court—and you will see representatives from all nations gathered together for the utility of men. Here, Jew, Mohammedan and Christian deal with each other as though they were all of the same faith and only apply the word infidel to people who go bankrupt. Here the Presbyterian trusts the Anabaptist and the Anglican accepts a promise from the Quaker. On leaving these peaceful and free assemblies, some go to the Synagogue and others for a drink, this one goes to be baptized in a great bath in the name of Father, Son and Holy Ghost, that one has his son's foreskin cut and has some Hebrew words he doesn't understand mumbled over the child, others go to their church and await the inspiration of God with their hats on, and everybody is happy.[97]

Besides creating wealth and friends, commerce created the middle class or "bourgeoisie." Like the upper class, the middle class was educated. Unlike the nobility, which lived off land rents and was exempt from taxation, the bourgeoisie had to work and pay taxes. As the wealth of the middle class grew, so did its confidence and resentment of the nobility. Soon the former started to question the political dominance of the latter. Given that the middle class became wealthy and influential without the need for the land of the nobility, the bourgeoisie started to question the need to obey the laws imposed by the nobility.[98]

To enlightened thinkers like Adam Smith and French historian François Guizot (1787–1874), dependency and tyranny were remnants of humanity's barbarian past, while liberty and self-governance marked the final phase of the civilizing process. The French mathematician and philosopher Nicolas de Caritat, Marquis de Condorcet (1743–1794), went as far as to predict the global triumph of liberty. He wrote:

> Then will arrive the moment in which the sun will observe in its course free nations only, acknowledging no other master than their reason; in which tyrants and slaves, priests and their stupid or hypocritical instruments, will no longer exist but in history and upon the stage; in which our only concern will be to lament their past victims and dupes, and, by the recollection of their horrid enormities, to exercise a vigilant circumspection, that we may be able instantly to recognise and effectually to stifle by the force of reason, the seeds of superstition and tyranny, should they ever presume again to make their appearance upon the earth.[99]

As Herman points out, however, "there was also a keen awareness that this improvement could be a transformative as well as a cumulative process, in which each stage of civilization's advance required the destruction of what came before."[100] The English historian Edward Gibbon (1737–1794) brought that perspective to his monumental study, *The Decline and Fall of the Roman Empire* (1776). He argued that the rise of modern Europe depended on the fall of the "corrupt" and "degenerate" empire and warned that Rome's "prosperity ripened the principle of decay."[101]

In the words of another English historian, James Anthony Froude (1818–1894), Rome's "virtue and truth produced strength, strength [produced] dominion, dominion [produced] riches, riches [produced] luxury, and luxury [led to] weakness and collapse."[102] The specter of a Roman Empire destroyed by its own excesses haunted the European consciousness. Would history, some members of the European intelligentsia wondered, repeat itself?

. . . gives way to the doubts of the 19th century

The English cleric and economist Thomas Malthus (1766–1834), who will feature prominently in the chapters that follow, adopted that pessimistic view and questioned whether Europe's newfound wealth was sustainable. He predicted that with more resources, the population would grow faster than the human ability to produce food. He argued, therefore, that if population growth was not controlled, humanity was destined for poverty and famine. We shall return to Malthus in Chapter 2.

The French philosopher Jean-Jacques Rousseau (1712–1778) took a different angle. He agreed that reason was the foundation of civilization, but he thought that civilization did not constitute progress, for it came at the expense of morality. According to Rousseau, civilization generates learning, wealth, and sophistication, but learning, wealth, and sophistication lead to moral degradation. Before reason was awakened, Rousseau conjectured, people lived in an ideal state of simplicity, equality, and solitude. Their limited needs were easily met through hunting and gathering.[103]

Then civilization "destroyed natural liberty, [and] established for all time the law of property and inequality . . . and for the benefit of a few ambitious men, subjected the human race henceforth to labor, servitude, and misery."[104] As Duke University political scientist Geneviève Rousselière observed, Rousseau consistently declared that "commercial society prevents us from being free because it makes us dependent on others and on endless desires in ways we cannot control."[105]

Rousseau's critique of the Enlightenment inspired an entirely new political philosophy, Romanticism, and by the end of the 18th century, theories of progress had divided. To be sure, everyone agreed that civilization made humanity richer, but that's where the agreement ended. The thinkers of the

Enlightenment believed that civilization made us friendly, thoughtful, and free. Romantics, in contrast, argued that civilization made us jealous, weak, and enslaved. The great intellectual endeavor of the 19th century was to try to bridge the gap between the two views of progress.

The German philosopher Georg Friedrich Hegel (1770–1831) believed that the Enlightenment and Romantic visions could be reconciled in a "holistic" understanding of progress. According to Hegel, individual freedom could be preserved and the degeneracy of modern society arrested through what he saw as the final type of political entity: the nation-state. In this new ethical and social realm, people would be able to express their "true" freedom, while an army of professional bureaucrats would work to counteract the negative side effects of progress.[106]

The German philosopher Karl Marx (1818–1883) was greatly inspired by Hegel's ideas. Marx agreed with Hegel that history was the struggle for human freedom, but he disagreed on the endpoint. Instead of Hegel's commercial nation-state, Marx advocated stateless socialism, which would usher in the final stage of human liberation. He predicted that capitalist "exploitation and decadence" would eventually cause a global revolution and usher in the global "dictatorship of the proletariat."[107] With time, he thought, the nation-state would dissolve into a perfect, classless society that was finally free from all coercion.

Other thinkers took their cues from the intellectual revolution unleashed by the English naturalist Charles Darwin (1809–1882) and his revolutionary works, including *On the Origin of Species by Means of Natural Selection, or the Preservation of Favoured Races in the Struggle for Life* (1859) and *The Descent of Man, and Selection in Relation to Sex* (1871). Darwin's cousin, the English polymath Francis Galton (1822–1911), for example, ignored the former's objections and launched a new discipline of eugenics. Eugenics sought to improve human well-being by improving the quality of the human species via selective breeding.

By the end of the 19th century, then, Western Europe, which was at the cutting edge of technological and scientific advancement, political and economic institutional development, and social and artistic sophistication, became synonymous with civilization itself. While European leaders and intellectuals thought that they understood how Europe had advanced so far, they had trouble explaining why the rest of the world had not. They began to turn their attention to such notions as religion, culture, and race to explain "the systematic failure of the rest of the world to be like them."[108]

Wrong turns: spreading "progress" at the point of a bayonet

By this point in our narrative of progress, a careful reader will have spotted dark clouds gathering over the horizon. First of these dark clouds was imperialism or, as the French economist Pierre Paul Leroy-Beaulieu (1843–1916) termed it, *la haute mission civilisatrice de la colonisation*.[109] The European *mission civilisatrice* brought many benefits to the undeveloped world, including modern science, life-saving medicine, and sophisticated technology. Unfortunately, these benefits were often accompanied by discrimination, humiliation, prejudice, and even genocide.

The second of these clouds was socialism and its much bloodier cousin, communism. Marx, as is well known, wanted to replace "exploitative" capitalism (i.e., commercial society so beloved by many "enlightened" thinkers) with classless, stateless, and moneyless communal living. Communist revolutionaries from the Soviet Union and China to Cambodia and North Korea consequently set out to create a Marxist utopia by eliminating capitalism. Communism brought about the destruction of the last vestiges of feudalism in the former Russian empire, parts of China, and some other places, but it came at the steep price of some 100 million lives.[110]

The third of these clouds was fascism and its more horrific cousin, national socialism. The Italian *duce* Benito Mussolini (1883–1945) and the German *Führer* Adolf Hitler (1889–1945) fetishized the Hegelian nation-state as the apex of human achievement, although their distaste for capitalism owed much to Marx.[111] Mussolini's motto "All within the state, nothing outside the state, nothing against the state" was clearly reminiscent of Hegel's injunction that "we must . . . worship the State as the manifestation of the Divine on Earth."[112] Hitler's statement "I have learned a great deal from Marxism, as I do not hesitate to admit [that] . . . the whole of National Socialism is based on it" speaks for itself.[113]

The 20th century, then, endured imperialism, communism, and nationalism. It saw the Boer War, the Great War, the Armenian genocide, the Russian revolution, the Soviet Gulag and the Holodomor, the Second World War and the Holocaust, the deployment of atomic weapons, the wars in Korea and Vietnam, the greatly misnamed Great Leap Forward, the killing fields of Kampuchea, the bloody genocide in Rwanda, the Yugoslav Civil War, and more. After all that slaughter and suffering, humanity still entered the present century living longer and healthier lives and being better fed, better educated, more equal, and more free. Given all that, how should we think about progress?

How should we think about progress, anyway?

The *Oxford English Dictionary* defines progress as "advancement to a further or higher stage or to further or higher stages successively; growth; development, usually to a better state or condition; improvement . . . applied especially to manifestations of social and economic change or reform."[114] But what do "higher stage" and "better state" mean? Are those terms purely subjective, or can we devise an objective understanding of human progress? In his book *Enlightenment Now*, Steven Pinker proposed one possible answer. He wrote,

> Most people agree that life is better than death. Health is better than sickness. Sustenance is better than hunger. Wealth is better than poverty. Peace is better than war. Safety is better than danger. Freedom is better than tyranny. Equal rights are better than bigotry and discrimination. Literacy is better than illiteracy. Knowledge is better than ignorance. Intelligence is better than dull-wittedness. Happiness is better than misery. Opportunities to enjoy family, friends, culture, and nature are better than drudgery and monotony. All these things can be measured. If they have increased over time, that is progress.[115]

Some people will no doubt object, asserting that there is more to life than the above indicators of human well-being. The search for the meaning of life, religious fulfillment, heroic accomplishments, and personal self-discovery have been important drivers of human thought and action for millennia, and that won't change. Pinker's definition of progress nonetheless seems like a reasonable start.

As the American psychologist Abraham Maslow (1908–1970) showed in his 1943 paper, "A Theory of Human Motivation," humans have a hierarchy of needs. At the bottom of the Maslow pyramid are basic needs such as food, water, warmth, and safety. Then come psychological needs such as friendships, relationships, prestige, and feelings of accomplishment. At the top of the pyramid rest self-fulfillment needs, including self-actualization and creative pursuits.

Bearing the Maslow pyramid in mind, it is much easier to search for the meaning of life and self-actualization on a full rather than an empty stomach. To quote *Enlightenment Now* again,

> It's easy to extol transcendent values in the abstract, but most people prioritize life, health, safety, literacy, sustenance, and stimulation for the obvious reason that these goods are a prerequisite to everything else. If you're reading this, you are not dead, starving, destitute, moribund, terrified, enslaved, or illiterate, which means that you're in no position to turn your nose up at these values— nor to deny that other people should share your good fortune.[116]

Keep in mind, also, that progress denotes incremental improvements upon the past. It does not denote perfection or utopia. "Utopia" combines two Greek words: οὐ (ou, "not") and τόπος (tópos, "place, region"). As such, it literally means "no place." Using English language tenses as an analogy, utopians compare the present with the future perfect, not the past imperfect. It is nonetheless the past imperfect that is the proper lens through which living conditions today should be evaluated, or as Bury explained a century ago,

> Theories of Progress ... [can be differentiated] into two distinct types, corresponding to two radically opposed political theories

and appealing to two antagonistic temperaments. The one type [is] that of constructive idealists or socialists, who can name all the streets and towers of "the city of gold," which they imagine as situated just around a promontory. The development of man is a closed system; its term is known and is within reach. The other type is that of those who, surveying the gradual ascent of man, believe that by the same interplay of forces which have conducted him so far and by a further development of liberty which he has fought to win, he will move slowly towards conditions of increasing harmony and happiness. Here the development is indefinite; its term is unknown and lies in the remote future. Individual liberty is the motive force, and the corresponding political theory is liberalism.[117]

Note also that the "line" of progress is jagged, not smooth. Western Europe, for example, experienced tremendous economic, political, technological, scientific, and medical advances during the century that separated the end of the Napoleonic Wars (1803–1815) and 1914, only to descend into the barbarism of the First and Second World Wars. Yet Europe rebounded, just as it did after the fall of Rome and the subsequent Dark Ages.

There are, in other words, rational grounds for cautious optimism, but optimism should not be confused with inevitability. We could yet destroy our civilization through human action such as nuclear war, or watch helplessly as an asteroid hurtles through the sky and wipes out most of life on Earth.

Finally, progress does not mean that we'll ever reach a paradisiacal end state where everything will be optimal for everyone everywhere. New problems will arise, and they will have to be solved, however imperfectly, by future generations. As such, the world will never be a perfect place. After all, the beings who inhabit it are themselves imperfect. As the German philosopher and advocate of gradual human progress Immanuel Kant (1724–1804) observed in 1784, "From such crooked timber as humankind is made of, nothing entirely straight can be made."[118] The best we can hope for is to make tomorrow's world better than it is today.

In spite of many improvements, we have evolved to focus on the negative

Previously, we looked at the proliferation of apocalyptic movies and a possible explanation for their continued attractiveness. We have also noted the mismatch between the increasing supply of apocalyptic offerings and the increasing stream of good news about the state of humanity.

However, it needs to be recognized that the human obsession with decline and the "end of times" is only part of a much larger, well-documented array of negative biases that have accumulated in our brains over the span of human evolution, a period of hundreds of thousands of years during which time the world that *Homo sapiens* navigated was much less hospitable to human survival than our own. "Our modern skulls house a Stone-Age mind," noted Leda Cosmides and John Tooby from the University of California, Santa Barbara, and that mind is often better at dealing with problems encountered by our foraging ancestors than the problems that we face today.[119]

Think of it this way. If the latest archeological discoveries are correct, the *Homo sapiens* species is roughly 300,000 years old.[120] For most of that time, we were foragers, subsisting in a way that's observable among the Hadza in Tanzania and the Ache of Paraguay. Humanity began to embrace agriculture some 12,000 years ago, but change remained painfully slow. An ordinary person born some 6,000 years ago in Sumer, the world's oldest civilization, would find much about daily life in England at the time of the Norman Conquest (1066 CE) or in the Aztec Empire at the time of Columbus quite familiar.

In the last two hundred years or so, though, the standard of living among many people has skyrocketed. We shall explore that miraculous if highly contingent improvement in the human condition in subsequent chapters. For now, it is useful to recognize that from a historical perspective, material abundance is incredibly recent, amounting to no more than 0.08 percent of our time on Earth. Blink and you will miss it.

Let's take a closer look at the mysteries of the human mind. "Organisms that treat threats as more urgent than opportunities," wrote eminent Princeton University psychologist Daniel Kahneman in his 2013 book, *Thinking, Fast and Slow*, "have a better chance to survive and reproduce."[121] Put differently, humans have evolved to prioritize bad news. That's true of our hardware or the physical structure of the brain and software or the evolved programs with which we react to the world around us.

Human beings, explain Peter H. Diamandis and Steven Kotler in their 2012 bestselling book, *Abundance: The Future Is Better Than You Think*, are constantly bombarded with information. Because our brains have limited computing power, they have to separate what is paramount (such as a lion running toward us) from what is mundane (such as a bed of flowers). Because survival is more important than all other considerations, most information is first sifted through the amygdala, a part of the brain that is "responsible for primal emotions like rage, hate, and fear." Information relating to those primal emotions gets our attention first "because the amygdala is always looking for something to fear."[122]

That is a very powerful impulse that can deceive even the most dispassionate and rational observers. As Mark Trussler and Stuart Soroka from McGill University found in their 2014 paper, "Consumer Demand for Cynical and Negative News," even when people expressly say that they are interested in more good news, eye-tracking experiments show that they are in fact much more interested in bad news. "Regardless of what participants say," the authors of the study conclude, people "exhibit a preference for negative news content."[123]

As Pinker noted, the nature of cognition and nature of news interact in ways that make us think that the world is worse than it really is. News, after all, is about things that happen. Things that did not happen go unreported. As he points out, we "never see a reporter saying to the camera, 'Here we are, live from a country where a war has not broken out.'" Newspapers and other media, in other words, tend to focus on the negative. As the old journalistic adage goes, "If it bleeds, it leads."[124]

Furthermore, the media seldom provide comparative analysis or put terrible events in their proper, long-term, context. Pinker points to research conducted by Kalev Leetaru from Georgetown University, who has analyzed the emotional tone of articles in the *New York Times* between 1945 and 2005 and articles and broadcasts from 130 countries between 1979 and 2010. Leetaru found that, in spite of all the improvements we have noted in the previous section, both articles and broadcasts have become increasingly gloomy over time.[125]

The reasons for pessimism change, but the stream of apocalyptic warnings continues to gush forth. As the 64-year-old British author Matt Ridley wrote in his bestselling book, *The Rational Optimist,* in 2010,

> In my own adult lifetime, I have listened to the implacable predictions of growing poverty, coming famines, expanding deserts, imminent plagues, impending water wars, inevitable oil exhaustion, mineral shortages, falling sperm counts, thinning ozone, acidifying rain, nuclear winters, mad-cow epidemics, Y2K computer bugs, killer bees, sex-change fish, global warming, ocean acidification and even asteroid impacts that would presently bring this happy interlude to a terrible end. I cannot recall a time when one or other of these scares was not solemnly espoused by sober, distinguished and serious elites and hysterically echoed by the media.[126]

To make matters worse, the arrival of social media makes bad news immediate and more intimate. Until relatively recently, most people knew very little about the countless wars, plagues, famines, and natural catastrophes happening in distant parts of the world. In 1759, the Scottish philosopher Adam Smith wrote in his *Theory of Moral Sentiments,*

> The most frivolous disaster which could befall [a man] himself would occasion a more real disturbance. If he was to lose his little finger tomorrow, he would not sleep tonight; but, provided he never saw them, he will snore with the most profound security over the ruin of a hundred millions of his brethren, and the destruction of that immense multitude seems plainly an object less interesting to him, than this paltry misfortune of his own.[127]

Contrast the ignorance of Smith's 18th-century man with the widespread shock and empathy that the 2011 Japanese tsunami elicited from people throughout the world who watched the disaster unfold in real time on their smartphones.

The human brain also tends to overestimate danger due to what psychologists call "the availability heuristic"—that is, the process of estimating the probability of an event based on the ease with which relevant instances come to mind. Unfortunately, human memory recalls events for reasons other than their rate of recurrence. When an event turns up because it is traumatic, the human brain will overestimate how likely it is to reoccur.

Consider our fear of terrorism. According to John Mueller from the Ohio State University, "In the years since 9/11, Islamist terrorists have managed to kill about seven people a year within the United States. All those deaths are tragic of course, but some comparisons are warranted: lightning kills about 46 people a year, accident-causing deer another 150, and drownings in bathtubs around 300."[128] We nonetheless continue to fear terrorism much more than drowning in a bathtub.

Moreover, as psychologists Roy Baumeister from the University of Queensland and Ellen Bratslavsky from Cuyahoga Community College found, "bad is stronger than good." Consider how much happier you can imagine yourself feeling. Then consider how much more dejected you can imagine yourself to feel. The answer to the latter question is "infinitely." Research shows that people fear losses more than they delight in gains; harp on setbacks more than relishing successes; resent criticism more than being encouraged by praise.[129] Or, as Adam Smith put it, between our normal state

> and the highest pitch of human prosperity, the interval is but a trifle. Between it and the lowest depth of misery, the distance is immense and prodigious. Adversity, on this account, necessarily depresses the mind of the sufferer much more below its natural state than prosperity can elevate him above it.[130]

Good and bad things also tend to happen on different timelines. Johan Galtung and Mari Holmboe Ruge from the Peace Research Institute Oslo observed in their 1965 article, "The Structure of Foreign News," that "there is a basic asymmetry in life between the positive, which is difficult and takes time, and the negative, which is much easier and takes less time—compare the amount of time needed to bring up and socialize an adult person and the amount of time needed to kill him in an accident: the amount of time needed to build a house and to destroy it in a fire, to make an airplane and to crash it, and so on."[131]

Consider, moreover, a 2018 finding by Harvard psychologists David Levari and Daniel Gilbert that's known as "prevalence-induced concept change in human judgment." In an experiment, the two scholars found that the more rarely they made blue dots on a computer screen, the more likely people were to call purple dots "blue." The more rarely they made threatening faces, the more likely people were to describe a face as threatening. "From low-level perception of color to higher-level judgments of ethics," they wrote, "there is a robust tendency for perceptual and judgmental standards to 'creep' when they ought not to."[132]

"Our studies show that people judge each new instance of a concept in the context of the previous instances," Gilbert noted in an interview. "So as we reduce the prevalence of a problem, such as discrimination, for example, we judge each new behavior in the improved context that we have created. Another way to say this is that solving problems causes us to expand our definitions of them. . . . When problems become rare, we count more things as problems. Our studies suggest that when the world gets better, we become harsher critics of it, and this can cause us to mistakenly conclude that it hasn't actually gotten better at all. Progress, it seems, tends to mask itself."[133]

Other psychological effects apply as well. As we grow older, we start recalling more and more stories from our childhood. This phenomenon is known as the "reminiscence bump." As such, people tend to develop rosy nostalgia for the days of their youth—when they were young, virile, and full of potential. By feeling good about the past, dissatisfied with the present, and gloomy about the future, people fail to reflect on the real improvements in the world around them. Instead, they superimpose their physical and mental decline on their surroundings.

Pessimism moreover reduces expectations, thereby narrowing the gap between possible and actual outcomes. "Expecting things to be bad," explained former *Wall Street Journal* financial columnist Morgan Housel, "is the best way to be pleasantly surprised when they're not."[134] Consider Cambridge University theoretical physicist Stephen Hawking, who was diagnosed with a motor-neuron disease that left him paralyzed and unable to talk in 1963. Hawking was only 21 years old. In an interview with the *New York Times* in 2004, Hawking used his famous computer to express his excitement at selling books to a popular audience. "Are you always this cheerful?" the interviewer asked. "My expectations were reduced to zero when I was 21. Everything since then has been a bonus," Hawking replied.[135] Nobel Prize–winning Chapman University economist Vernon Smith put it this way: "It's always better to be pleasantly surprised than disappointed."[136]

Finally, humans suffer from a psychological quirk known by such names as pessimism extrapolation, or the end of history illusion. As Housel observed, even people who are aware of the progress that humanity has made in the past "underestimate our ability to change in the future." "If you underestimate our ability to adapt to unsustainable situations," he noted, "you'll find all kinds of things that currently look bad and can be extrapolated into disastrous. Extrapolate college tuition increases and it'll be prohibitively expensive in 10 years. Extrapolate government deficits and we'll be bankrupt in 30 years. Extrapolate a recession and we'll be broke before long. All of these could be reasons for pessimism if you assume no future change or adaptation, which is crazy, given our long history of changing and adapting."[137]

This is a book about innovation and adaptation. Contrary to many commentators, we do not believe that humanity is bound to destroy itself. Using data spanning close to two centuries, reason, and analysis, we will show you that humans, unlike other members of the animal kingdom, are intelligent beings who are uniquely capable of innovating their way out of pressing problems. We will show you that unlike other species, we have developed sophisticated forms of cooperation that increase our chances not only to survive but to prosper. We will, in other words, show you that there are rational grounds for optimism about your future. And while it is true that, as the financial brokers like to say, past performance is no guide to future performance, note the words of the British historian and statesman Thomas Babington Macaulay (1800–1859), who wrote this in 1830:

> In every age everybody knows that up to his own time, progressive improvement has been taking place; nobody seems to reckon on any improvement in the next generation. We cannot absolutely prove that those are in error who say society has reached a turning point—that we have seen our best days. But so said all who came before us and with just as much apparent reason. . . . On what

principle is it that with nothing but improvement behind us, we are to expect nothing but deterioration before us?[138]

As you read this book—indeed, as you go through life—remember all the different ways in which your mind is playing tricks on you. Recognize that you are a member of a species that's always on the lookout for danger and that your predisposition toward the negative provides a market for purveyors of bad news, be they doomsayers who claim that overpopulation will cause mass starvation or scaremongers who claim that we are running out of natural resources. The negativity bias is deeply ingrained in our brains. It cannot be wished away. The best that we can do is to realize that we are suffering from it.

CHAPTER 2

Thanos's intellectual and practical progenitors

The power of population is so superior to the power of the earth to produce subsistence for man that premature death must in some shape or other visit the human race.

Thomas Robert Malthus, *An Essay on the Principle of Population, as It Affects the Future Improvement of Society, with Remarks on the Speculations of Mr. Godwin, M. Condorcet, and Other Writers*[1]

Chapter summary

Thanos may be a fictional character, but the ideas that drove him toward genocide are real enough. Since antiquity, scholars have been at best ambivalent toward population growth. More often than not, they saw the increase in human numbers as a problem to be addressed. Midway through the 18th century, a new, more optimistic perspective on human affairs emerged in the form of the Enlightenment. Confident in technological and scientific progress and imbued with the idea of humanism, the scholars of the Enlightenment argued that population growth could go hand in hand with growing prosperity.

That was a novel and a controversial idea that quickly drew the ire of an English pastor who had an immense influence on the quarter of a millennium that followed. Thomas Malthus believed that in the absence of countermeasures, the population would grow at a much faster pace than the world's ability to feed the swelling ranks of humanity. Disaster would surely follow. From Malthus's time through 2020, the world's population has risen from about 1 billion to 7.8 billion,[2] yet few people would be willing to argue that the world is worse off today than it was when King George III sat upon the British throne.

That spectacular forecast failure has not stopped Malthus's disciples over the past 200 years from periodically revisiting the pastor's thesis, only to be met with further disappointment. In this chapter, we will look at the main tenets of Malthusianism. We will also look at the proponents and opponents of the pastor's ideas. Finally, we will look at the application of Malthus's ideas in practice. Malthusianism, it should be remembered, is much more than an interesting academic debate. It is, above all, a set of policy prescriptions that had catastrophic consequences for those unfortunates who have lived and died under governments that took Malthusian ideas seriously.

Should we see Thanos as a mass murderer or a tragic hero?

In *Poetics*, which he wrote in the 4th century BCE, Aristotle noted that a tragic hero must be neither a bad man nor a good man, but a "character between these two extremes . . . whose misfortune is brought about not by vice or depravity, but by some error or frailty." That ambiguity, Aristotle claims, will "excite pity and fear . . . [which is] the distinctive mark of tragic imitation."[3]

If Thanos were to destroy half the life in the universe out of sheer vice or depravity, he would not be a particularly compelling character. Generally speaking, people tend not to empathize or connect with characters who kill for the sake of killing, such as the Terminator, the Predator, and the Alien. Thanos's destructiveness, by contrast, is fueled by a higher purpose. He sees his mission of destruction as one of mercy. That's because he believes that life cannot go on expanding indefinitely. Resources upon which life depends, he believes, are finite. At some point, they will surely run out. To ensure that at least some might live, others must die. Thanos, in other words, is driven by an idea, however erroneous.

In his monumental work, *The Gulag Archipelago*, the Russian writer Aleksandr Solzhenitsyn (1918–2008) teased out the distinction between the two types of evildoing beautifully. It is worth quoting him at length:

> It is permissible to portray evildoers in a story for children, so as to keep the picture simple. But when the great world literature of the past—Shakespeare, Schiller, Dickens—inflates and inflates images of evildoers of the blackest shades, it seems somewhat farcical and clumsy to our contemporary perception. The trouble lies in the way these classic evildoers are pictured. They recognize themselves as evildoers, and they know their souls are black. And they reason: "I cannot live unless I do evil." . . . But no; that's not the way it is! To do evil a human being must first of all believe that what he's doing is good. . . . The imagination and the spiritual strength of Shakespeare's evildoers stopped short at a dozen corpses. Because they had no ideology. Ideology—that is what gives evildoing its long-sought justification and gives the evildoer the necessary steadfastness and determination. . . . That was how the agents of the Inquisition fortified their wills: by invoking Christianity; the conquerors of foreign lands, by extolling the grandeur of their Motherland; the colonizers, by civilization; the Nazis, by race; and the Jacobins (early and late), by equality, brotherhood, and the

happiness of future generations. Thanks to ideology, the twentieth century was fated to experience evildoing on a scale calculated in the millions.[4]

Recall the scene that follows Thanos's finger snap. Having destroyed half the life in the universe, the exhausted and apparently saddened Thanos is transported to an ethereal realm where he meets what appears to be the young version of his daughter, Gamora. A brief conversation between the two ensues:

GAMORA: Did you do it?
THANOS: Yes.
GAMORA: What did it cost?
THANOS: Everything.[5]

What are we to make of that scene? Rather than being exultant, Thanos is mournful. Instead of rejoicing in the accomplishment of his dream, he reflects on the personal loss, including filicide. The viewers may abhor his methods, while at the same time they understand and perhaps even appreciate the dilemma that Thanos faced. *Tout comprendre c'est tout pardonner.*[6] In the end, Thanos achieves the seemingly impossible: he excites a modicum of pity in the audience. Aristotle would have approved.

Where did Thanos get his ideas?

Scholars have been debating the costs and benefits of population growth since antiquity. In ancient China, Confucius (551–479 BCE) and many of his followers saw population growth in a favorable light, but they also believed that population growth needed to be controlled. They theorized that there was an ideal ratio of land to population. When the population grew beyond that ratio, they reasoned, labor productivity and quality of life would diminish, leading to social discord. Therefore, they argued, it was the duty of the government to maintain that ratio by forcing people to migrate to less populated areas. They also recognized certain checks on population growth such as starvation at the time of food shortages and noted that early marriages lead to higher infant mortality rates.[7]

The Greeks analyzed population growth from the perspective of the city-state and were mostly concerned with the implications of human fecundity for governance and state security. They thought that a population should be large enough to be economically self-sufficient but not so large as to make democratic governance impossible. Plato had a specific ideal population in mind, arguing that 5,040 citizens per city-state would maximize the well-being of the polity. He advocated reproductive incentives and immigration if the population was too low, and birth control and colonization (i.e., emigration) if the population was too high. Similarly, Aristotle worried that since cultivated land could not be increased as quickly as the population could grow, it was necessary to abort or expose (i.e., leave to die) some children.[8]

The Romans analyzed population growth from the imperial (i.e., expansionist) perspective and welcomed the contribution of a growing population to Rome's military strength. Under Caesar Augustus, married and child-rearing couples were given legal privileges, while unmarried people faced discrimination. Celibacy was discouraged.[9]

The Indian philosopher Chanakya (371–283 BCE) expressed a similar view, arguing that a large population leads to greater economic and military power. He also acknowledged checks on rapid population growth such as war, famine, and plague.[10]

Hebrew texts emphasized procreation, and childlessness was regarded as a misfortune.[11] Early and medieval Christians saw population growth from a distinctly ethical perspective. They condemned population control through abortion, infanticide, and abandonment but praised virginity and sexual restraint. They also discouraged second marriages. Some Christians attributed poverty to overpopulation and believed that war, famine, and plague were God's way of culling humanity. High mortality rates, however, "predisposed most writers towards the maintenance of a high birth rate."[12]

In the 14th century, the Arab scholar Ibn Khaldun (1332–1406) developed a fairly comprehensive theory on population. He argued that dense populations were key to raising standards of living, as they allowed for greater division of labor, and he thought that economic expansion and population growth went hand in hand. Ibn Khaldun also maintained, though, that history moved in a cycle of expansion and decline. He wrote that "in the wake of . . . periods of economic progress came luxury, rising taxes and other changes, which in several generations produced political decline, economic depression and depopulation."[13]

In 16th-century Europe, mercantilism began to take root. Influenced by the ideas of the Italian diplomat and philosopher Niccolò Machiavelli (1469–1527) and those of Jean Bodin, mercantilists believed that the goal of national policy ought to be the maximization of the wealth and, consequently, the power of the state. They welcomed population growth, believing that it would swell the government's coffers while depressing wages and the cost of labor. Implicit in the mercantilist thinking was the notion that population growth, while strengthening the state, also led to the immiseration of the populace.[14]

The physiocratic school—an economic theory developed by a group of French economists in the 18th century—arose in opposition to the mercantilists. The physiocrats rejected the mercantilist idea that population growth should be welcomed even if overall living standards fell. The physiocrats believed that agricultural production was key to the overall health of the economy. They accepted the advantages of population growth as long as it went hand in hand with increasing agricultural yields and consequently higher standards of living. Implicit in the physiocratic thinking was the notion that, given the right economic policies, agricultural production could potentially keep pace with population growth.[15]

The 18th century, as we have already shown and will reemphasize throughout this book, marked a fundamental change in human affairs and ushered in the modern age that is marked by innovation and abundance. It is, therefore, appropriate to pause and take stock of what we have learned so far. With a few exceptions, most scholars from antiquity onward were either hostile to population growth or deeply ambivalent about its potential effects on human welfare. Of course, more people meant larger armies and more taxpayers, which is what mattered to the feudal lords of yesteryear, but population growth also meant greater pressure on available resources and other calamities.

That was not an irrational prism through which to view population growth. For thousands of years, the world was, in fact, stuck in what came to be known as a Malthusian trap. The world's population fluctuated, growing during the times of good harvests and collapsing when food got scarce or war and pestilence reigned. According to the U.S. Census Bureau, the world's population at the time of Caesar Augustus was somewhere between 170 and 400 million. Fourteen centuries later, it was somewhere between 350 and 374 million.[16] In 2020, in contrast, the world's population stood at 7.8 billion.

In the 18th century, some scholars started to look at population growth with greater optimism. They began to see human life as intrinsically valuable and problems concomitant with population growth as eminently solvable. The French economist Nicolas Baudeau (1730–1792) argued that the "productiveness of nature and the industriousness of man are without known limits" because production "can increase indefinitely." As such, "population numbers and well-being can go on advancing together."[17] English journalist and political philosopher William Godwin (1756–1836) argued that scientific progress would increase food production, thus increasing leisure time. Moreover, he thought that human reason would keep the world's population from outrunning the food supply.[18] Condorcet "professed the same faith [as Godwin] in the power of science . . . [which] would be able to prolong life span without any worsening of the human condition through a production of food . . . and also because reason would come in to play to prevent irrational population growth."[19] You can see now why the Enlightenment is also commonly referred to as the Age of Reason!

Other leading intellectuals of the day went as far as to argue that good government is one that leads to the maximization of the human population and its well-being. David Hume, for example, noted that "wherever there are most happiness and virtue and the wisest institutions, there will also be most people."[20] Even Rousseau held that "the Government under which . . . the citizens increase and multiply the most is infallibly the best."[21] These were, to put it mildly, revolutionary ideas, and the almost inevitable backlash against them soon arrived.

Reverend Thomas Robert Malthus (1766–1834) was born in Westcott, England. He studied English, classics, and mathematics at Cambridge University. In 1789, he took holy orders in the Church of England and later became a professor of history and political economy at Haileybury College near London. Over time, Malthus became fascinated with geometric and arithmetic growth rates. A geometrically growing value increases in proportion to its current value, such as always doubling (for instance, 1, 2, 4,

8, 16, 32, 64, 128, 256, 512, 1024). An arithmetic growth rate, in contrast, increases at a constant rate (1, 2, 3, 4 or 1, 3, 5, 7).[22]

In 1798, Malthus published *An Essay on the Principle of Population as It Affects the Future Improvement of Society, with Remarks on the Speculations of Mr. Godwin, M. Condorcet, and Other Writers.* He argued that "population, when unchecked, increases in a geometrical ratio. Subsistence [by contrast] increases only in an arithmetical ratio. A slight acquaintance with numbers will show the immensity of the first power in comparison to the second."[23] He then warned that if

> the proportion of births to deaths for a few years indicate an increase of numbers much beyond the proportional increased or acquired produce [i.e., food] of the country, we may be perfectly certain that unless an emigration takes place, the deaths will shortly exceed the births.... Were there no other depopulating causes, every country would, without doubt, be subject to periodical pestilences or famine.[24]

Malthus acknowledged natural constraints on population growth or "positive checks," as he called them, including the classic trio of miseries: war, famine, and plague. He declared, however, that these checks would cause "misery" and were therefore undesirable. To avoid running into positive checks, Malthus favored "preventative checks" on population growth. Those included "the sort of intercourse which renders some of the women of large towns unprolific; a general corruption of morals with regard to the sex, which has a similar effect; unnatural passions and improper arts to prevent the consequences of irregular connections."[25] Scholars generally interpret that statement as a veiled reference to prostitution, venereal disease, homosexuality, abortion, and birth control.

Malthus believed that history validated his theory, which it did. He also insisted that what was true in the past would also be true for all eternity, and that was not to be. Malthus in fact lost his main argument even before his first book went to print. Between 1700 and 1798, the population of England increased from 5.2 million to 7.754 million, or 49.1 percent.[26] Over the same period, nominal GDP per person per year increased from £12.37 to £23.97 or 93.8 percent.[27] Finally, the nominal price of flour increased from 1.67p per kilogram to 2.25p per kilogram, or 34.9 percent.[28] That means that the ratio or the "quantitative relation between two amounts showing the number of times one value contains or is contained within the other" between the nominal price of flour and the nominal GDP per person per year declined from 0.135 in 1700 to 0.094 in 1798 or 30.4 percent.[29] That translates to a 43.6 percent increase in the abundance of flour that, when converted to bread, supplied most of the peasantry with daily sustenance.[30] Put differently, as the population of England increased by 49.1 percent, flour became 43.6 percent more abundant.

It is too bad that Malthus didn't check his theory against the facts. During his own lifetime, the abundance of the main food staple among the poorest stratum of English society was growing at almost the same rate as the population. As our analyses in Chapters 5 and 6 demonstrate, food abundance grew faster than population in subsequent years. Contrary to Malthus, in other words, there is no logical reason why the human population should grow geometrically, while food production can only grow arithmetically. In fact, empirical evidence suggests that the abundance of food can grow geometrically while population grows arithmetically.

Despite his failure to acknowledge the improvements that were happening around him, Malthus's ideas spread across the globe like wildfire. Part of his success rests, as we have explained before, in human bias toward the negative. Part of it rests in Malthus's skill as a mathematician and a writer. He covered his arguments with a patina of mathematical respectability and used a rhetorical technique of implying that anyone unfamiliar with mathematics would be unable to comprehend the obviousness of his assertions. Both are common in the writings of his disciples to this day.

In fact, Malthus is a good example of the oft-seen failure to subject a theory that's stated in mathematical terms to historical or empirical testing. As the economic historian at the University of California, Davis, Gregory Clark noted in his 2008 book, *A Farewell to Alms: A Brief Economic History of the World*, Malthus's family line died out because his children failed to procreate.[31] So much, then, for the geometric growth of Malthus's own family.

While Malthus was proven spectacularly wrong, his theory remains influential. In the 20th century, a number of scholars whom we shall encounter in the next section adapted Malthus's theory to the modern world. To those scholars, we can also add Thanos. It is due to the remarkable staying power of Malthus's ideas that we shall refer to overpopulation concerns as "Malthusianism" throughout the remainder of this book.

The core arguments of Thomas Malthus and his disciples

In their 2018 book, *Population Bombed: Exploding the Link between Overpopulation and Climate Change*, Pierre Desrochers and Joanna Szurmak from the University of Toronto identified five distinct justifications for the supposed "need to curb ever-growing human demands on the life-support capacities of natural systems." First, "continued growth in a finite system is unsustainable." Second, "everything else being equal, a reduced population will enjoy a higher standard of living." Third, "decreasing returns to investment in natural resources result in lower standards of living." Fourth, "technological innovation and synthetic products cannot be substituted for the natural" endowment of the planet. Fifth, "past successes in overcoming natural limits are irrelevant to present conditions."[32]

The first justification for population controls and consumption limits deals with the basic question of supply and demand. If the planet can supply only a limited quantity of resources and human demand for those resources continues to expand, at some point those resources will deplete, and a catastrophe will ensue. This view has been adhered to by such scholars as Malthus, Machiavelli, American biologist Paul Ehrlich, Danish cleric Otto Diederich Lütken (1719–1790), English-American economist Kenneth Boulding (1910–1993), and John P. Holdren.[33] It was this concern with the "depletion" of resources that drove Thanos to exterminate half the life in the universe.

The second justification for population controls ties to the first. If demand for resources matches the supply of resources, people will enjoy a sustainable existence. If the population declines, but everything else remains the same, the demand for resources will decrease, and those people who remain will enjoy access to more resources. Put differently, their standard of living will increase. That was the view shared by Malthus, Ehrlich, American ecologist and ornithologist William Vogt (1902–1968), the British politician Edward Henry Stanley (1826–1893), the chairman of President Richard Nixon's Commission on Population Growth and the American Future John D. Rockefeller III (1906–1978), American climatologist Reid Bryson (1920–2008), British filmmaker David Attenborough, and American primatologist Jane Goodall. This is, to borrow a term that American Nobel Prize–winning economist Milton Friedman (1912–2006) first used: the "fixed pie fallacy."[34] Since the size of the resource pie is supposedly fixed, the fewer people there are, the larger portion of the pie they will enjoy.

The third justification for population controls deals with diminishing returns on investment. According to this view, the planet contains finite amounts of high-quality land and easily accessible resources. Once those are accessed, it will become more difficult to cultivate more land and mine more resources. The low-quality land will then produce less food, and deeper mines will produce more expensive resources. Both will result in a lower standard of living for an expanding population. The people who embraced this viewpoint included Ehrlich, Holdren, English philosopher John Stuart Mill (1806–1873), American geneticist and demographer Robert Carter Cook (1898–1991), Dutch demographer John Bongaarts, English economist William Stanley Jevons (1835–1882), and American economist and historian Robert Heilbroner (1919–2005).

Throughout this book, we shall argue that the quantity of resources on Earth is not fixed. We will show you that human ingenuity allows our species to expand the stock of planetary resources ad infinitum. Our view directly contradicts the fourth justification for population controls and consumption limits, which states that "technological innovation and synthetic products cannot be substituted" for existing resources.[35] According to that view, technological solutions to the coming environmental catastrophe can never be as perfect as the natural earth processes. Synthetic fertilizer, for example, may work to grow plants, but it is generally less effective than regular soil nutrients. This "techo-pessimist" view has been shared by such scholars as Vogt,

Heilbroner, Ehrlich, Holdren, and American paleontologist and geologist Henry Fairfield Osborn (1857–1935).

The fifth justification for population controls states that past successes in overcoming natural limits are irrelevant to present conditions. Put differently, past successes in overcoming population growth and consumption increases are immaterial to the modern world because the scale of the problems that humanity faces are much greater than they used to be. The scholars subscribing to this point of view include Cook, Jevons, Vogt, British economist Alfred Marshall (1842–1924), American geochemist Harrison Brown (1917–1986), and American geneticist Edward Murray East (1879–1938). In Chapter 1, we called this approach the pessimism extrapolation, or the end of history illusion.

The validity of Malthusian ideas has always been challenged

Needless to say, we are not the first writers to raise objections to overpopulation concerns. Throughout the centuries, there were many distinguished scholars who refused to countenance pessimistic analysis and gloomy predictions concerning the future of humanity. They expressed "confidence in the ability of humans and their technologies to overcome any problems— including environmental problems" and to "shape the natural world for [humanity's] own benefit."[36] Desrochers and Szurmak identify four main arguments against population controls. First, "a larger population that engages in trade and the division of labor will deliver greater material abundance per capita." Second, "human creativity can deliver increasing returns." Third, "standards of living are not constrained by local resources." Fourth, "past achievements are grounds for cautious optimism."[37]

The first objection to population controls holds that population growth enables humanity to produce more goods and services, cultivate more land, and access hitherto unused resources. Population growth, in other words, enables greater division of labor, which makes production cheaper and more abundant. The overpopulation alarmists tend to focus only on growing demand while ignoring the expansion of supply. When demand increases, so does supply. When demand decreases, so does supply. That's why locales with dense populations tend to be richer on a per person basis than locales with sparse populations. The scholars holding this view have included British economist and historian Edwin Cannan (1861–1935), French economist Jean-Baptiste Say (1767–1832), American political economist and journalist Henry George (1839–1897), Hungarian economist Peter Bauer (1915–2002), British writer Matt Ridley, and American journalist and urban scholar Jane Jacobs (1916–2006).

The second objection to population controls holds that population growth results in increasing returns on investment. Human beings are the only animal capable of sustained innovation. The greater the population, the more likely it is that a creative mind will emerge to invent a solution to a pressing problem (i.e., increase supply to meet growing demand). Moreover, human beings are the only animals capable of building on past inventions. Therefore, as the population grows, information accumulates and innovation accelerates.[38] The people who held some combination of these views include Ridley, Jacobs, George, British political economist William Petty (1623–1687), German philosopher Friedrich Engels (1820–1895), American economists Harold Barnett (1917–1987) and Chandler Morse (1906–1988), British social theorist Herbert Spencer (1820–1903), American entrepreneur Edward Atkinson (1827–1905), Scottish agriculturalist James Anderson (1738–1809), German economist Karl Brandt (1899–1975), Austrian economist Fritz Machlup (1902–1983), American investor and economist George Gilder, American popular science writer Steven Johnson, and the American Nobel Prize–winning economist Paul Romer.

The third objection to population controls holds that "human standards of living are not constrained by local resources" because human ingenuity enables people to transcend resource limitations.[39] Humans can and do, for example, increase their food supply by plowing more fields or increasing yields from existing fields. By contrast, nonhuman animals have to rely on what mother nature does or does not provide. As American economist Jacqueline Kasun (1924–2009) put it, "in the same territories where earlier (and less populated) men struggled and starved, much larger populations today support themselves in comfort. The difference, of course, lies in the knowledge that human beings bring to the task of discovering and managing resources."[40] Scholars subscribing to this view included George, Jacobs, Russian revolutionary and scientist Pyotr Kropotkin (1842–1921), German economist Erich Zimmermann (1888–1961), British economist Colin Clark (1905–1989), English geographer Peter Taylor, American futurist Herman Kahn (1922–1983), and last but not least, American economist Julian Simon (1932–1998).

The fourth objection to population controls states that "past achievements are grounds for cautious optimism."[41] Of course, we cannot predict the future. Consequently, there is no guarantee that the prosperity that humanity currently enjoys will continue indefinitely. That said, the past provides a window into the future. As Bauer noted, "It is only the past that gives us any insight into the laws of motion of human society and hence enables us to predict the future."[42] Looking at the long-term interaction between population growth and resource availability as we shall do in the following chapters should fill the readers with cautious optimism. In doing so, we shall follow in the footsteps of such scholars as Cannan, Bauer, Simon, Ridley, and German economist Hans Landsberg (1913–2001).

Putting Malthusianism into practice: the tragic cases of China and India

Unfortunately, Malthusian "remedies" for population growth have not been limited to intellectual theorizing. In the mid-1970s, India, for example, pursued policies that limited population growth that carried out enforced sterilization of both men and women and social ostracism of people with large families. Nowhere in the world, however, did Malthusianism gain as much purchase as in China between 1980 and 2015. It is in that communist dictatorship that the most horrific abuses of the populace took place. The scale of human suffering that was caused by government-enforced sterilizations, prenatal and postnatal abortions, and wanton cruelty is difficult to comprehend. Let's begin with China.

China's one-child policy (1980–2015)

In 1970, Chinese Premier Zhou Enlai announced a five-year plan to limit the country's population growth. The Chinese Communist Party believed that a rapidly growing population would hinder China's economic development. Zhou Enlai's plan later evolved into a two-child policy that would last for much of the 1970s. Although China's fertility rate had plummeted as a result of the two-child policy, the government felt that population growth was still too high. In 1980, the Chinese leadership organized a meeting in Chengdu, Szechuan Province, to discuss further fertility restrictions. One participant of the meeting, Song Jian, had recently returned from a trip to Europe where he had read two influential books concerning the supposed dangers of population growth.

The first was the Club of Rome's 1972 report, *The Limits to Growth*.[43] The report looked at the interplay between industrial development, population growth, malnutrition, the availability of nonrenewable resources, and the quality of the environment. It concluded that

> if present growth trends in world population, industrialization, pollution, food production, and resource depletion continue unchanged, the limits to growth on this planet will be reached sometime within the next one hundred years.... The most probable result will be a rather sudden and uncontrollable decline in both population and industrial capacity.... Given present resource consumption rates and the projected increase in these rates, the great majority of currently nonrenewable resources will be extremely expensive 100 years from now.[44]

The second book was *A Blueprint for Survival*. Originally published as an article in the January 1972 edition of the *Ecologist*, it was republished in book form later that year.[45] Signed by over 30 of the leading scientists of the day, *Blueprint* noted that "continued exponential growth of consumption of materials and energy is impossible. Present reserves of all but a few metals will be exhausted within 50 years if consumption rates continue to grow as they are. Obviously, there will be new discoveries and advances in mining technology, but these are likely to provide us with only a limited stay of execution."[46] It called for a radical overhaul of human institutions in order to prevent "the breakdown of society and the irreversible disruption of the life-support systems on this planet." It used a "tribal model" to argue in favor of small, decentralized, and mostly deindustrialized communities. People in such communities, the authors averred, would lead more moral, ecologically sound, and fulfilling lives. According to the authors,

> an examination of the relevant information available has impressed upon us the extreme gravity of the global situation today. For, if current trends are allowed to persist, the breakdown of society and the irreversible disruption of the life-support systems on this planet, possibly by the end of the century, certainly within the life-times of our children, are inevitable. Governments, and ours is no exception, are either refusing to face the relevant facts or are briefing their scientists in such a way that their seriousness is played down. Whatever the reasons, *no corrective measures of any consequence are being undertaken* [emphasis added].[47]

Song became convinced that a one-child policy was necessary in order to curb China's population growth. He calculated that the ideal size of the Chinese population fell between 650 and 700 million (i.e., roughly two-thirds of the Chinese population in 1980). Song presented his findings to members of the Chinese Academy of Sciences. With their help, he managed to convince China's leadership of the veracity of his claims, and the one-child policy was adopted by the Fifth National People's Congress in September 1980.

In a recent paper, Chelsea Follett from the libertarian Cato Institute in Washington, DC, outlined some of the measures that the Chinese government implemented to achieve its policy goals, as well as the suffering that the one-child policy caused.[48] She noted how the government incentivized local officials with bonuses to abort pregnancies and sterilize adults and punished local officials with wage cuts and dismissal for not meeting a quota of one child per couple. To achieve the quota, officials could destroy property, jail people, and even threaten to confiscate children. Legal restrictions went beyond the one-child limit. The government outlawed single-parent families and required married couples to obtain a permit to have a child. Women were sometimes punished for intimacy out of wedlock or without contraception. Some were forced to take a pregnancy test every two weeks by urinating into cups in public.

In the 1980s, intrauterine devices (IUDs) became state-mandated for women who had already given birth. Unlike typical IUDs, which only last a decade, the government-approved IUDs were modified to last until menopause and designed to be extremely difficult to remove. The government regularly had x-rays performed on women with the government-approved IUDs to make sure that the contraceptive was still functional. After having two children, women were surgically sterilized. Between 1980 and 2014, the government's official statistics estimate, 324 million Chinese women were fitted with modified IUDs, and 107 million underwent tubal ligation surgery (i.e., they got their "tubes tied"). That averages to 9.5 million modified IUDs and over 3 million tubal ligation surgeries annually.

Punishment for noncompliance could be ruthless. One official that Follett mentions recalled his part in the enforcement of the one-child policy, describing how he and his team tore down a family's house after the mother tried to avoid a state-mandated tubal ligation. Fees for breaking the one-child policy were exorbitant, usually around 5 to 10 times a person's annual disposable income. The Chinese government raked in $2.7 billion from these "social compensation fees" in 2013. While wealthy families who wanted multiple children could afford the fees, the poor were often bankrupted, spending years of their lives paying the fees off. If the families could not pay, state officials would send teams of enforcers to raid the parents' homes for valuables.

Children conceived illegally were born without *hukou*, the legal registration necessary to study, work, marry, or have children of their own. Around 13 million people in China still do not have *hukou* and are forced to either pay huge fines, acquire a false identity, or survive without access to mainstream society. Occasionally, the state allows unregistered individuals to gain *hukou* through amnesty and registration programs, but the process can be very difficult. One man that Follett mentions spent $7,000 over three years in a failed attempt to get his adopted daughter registered so she could go to school.

Some Chinese families tried to get around the one-child policy by giving their illegal children to friends, family members, and neighbors. In response to these attempts to circumvent the one-child policy, the Chinese government outlawed adoption of healthy children except by older, childless couples. Children who were adopted illegally were seized by the Chinese government and put up for adoption internationally. International adoptions steadily increased throughout the one-child-policy period, eventually peaking at 14,000 per year in 2005. In total, over 120,000 children were adopted internationally during the years of the one-child policy.

Unfortunately, many children were simply aborted, killed, or abandoned by their families. Given the Chinese cultural preference for sons, females were killed at higher rates than males, causing a skewed gender ratio that peaked at 121 boys for every 100 girls in 2008. Without enough women to marry, Chinese men have had a lot of trouble finding life partners. Not surprisingly, the shortage of women has resulted in increased instability. One study found that for every 1 percent increase in the gender disparity, there was a 5 to 6 percent increase in crime.[49]

The state also often forced women to abort their children. Often, these abortions happened after six months of pregnancy. Although late abortions are officially illegal in China, a family planning official who performed 1,500 abortions estimated that around one-third were late term.[50] One study concluded that one-fourth of rural women married in the 1970s had an abortion in the next two decades. Half of those abortions were late term.[51]

Follett notes the example of Wang Liping, who was 23 years old and seven months pregnant when she was beaten, abducted, tied to a bed, and induced into labor by family planning officials. The baby was born conscious but lived for mere minutes. Afterwards, Wang Liping was asked to pay the hospital for the operation.

Sometimes, the baby would live longer. In such cases, Chinese officials would kill the babies themselves. Mao Hengfeng, for example, gave birth to a living baby after being forced into premature labor. It emerged alive, only to be drowned in a bucket by family planning officials.[52]

While these forced abortions and infanticides were sometimes criticized in China, the criticism was never directed at the one-child policy itself. In 2012, for example, photos of a mother and the corpse of her would-be child, taken shortly after the woman had been restrained and injected with an abortive agent in her third trimester, went viral on Weibo, a Chinese social media platform. The Weibo chief editor denounced the forced abortion but maintained his support for the one-child policy, stating that "the world's resources cannot afford to feed a China with billions of people."[53] An editorial in *Global Times*, an English-language newspaper controlled by the Chinese government, argued that forced late-term abortions should be abolished. But the editorial endorsed the one-child policy, claiming that it "freed China from the burden of an extra 400 million people."[54]

■ Box 2.1. How much more prosperous would the world be without China's one-child policy?

In 1968, Stanford University biologist Paul Ehrlich published his immensely popular and influential book, *The Population Bomb*. In it, Ehrlich claimed that population growth would result in mass starvation. More recently, he argued that "You can't go on growing forever on a finite planet. The biggest problem we face is the continued expansion of the human enterprise."[a]

Ehrlich's early work launched a frenzy of studies, books, and articles concerning the supposedly negative relationship between population growth and resource scarcity. Two of them, the Club of Rome's *The Limits to Growth* (1972) and the special edition of the journal *The Ecologist*, *A Blueprint for Survival* (1972), were taken seriously by the Chinese Communist Party.

In 1980, the Chinese communists implemented the so-called "one-child policy." The American journalist Charles C. Mann reported that the birth limit "led to huge numbers—possibly 100 million—of coerced abortions, often in poor conditions contributing to infection, sterility, and even death. Millions of forced sterilizations occurred [as well]."[b]

The National Population and Family Planning Commission, which was tasked with implementing the one-child policy, grew into a gigantic bureaucracy with half a million full-time employees and 85 million part-time employees.[c] According to the Chinese government itself, the policy prevented 400 million births.[d]

The primary victims of Ehrlich's policy recommendations were females. Mothers suffered, and the Chinese cultural preference for sons meant that girls were aborted more often than boys. It is estimated that there were 34 million more men than women in China in 2018.[e] Under normal circumstances, there should be a rough parity between sexes. China relaxed its one-child policy in 2015, and Ehrlich was incensed. He tweeted (in all caps), "GIBBERING INSANITY—THE GROWTH-FOREVER GANG."[f]

Contrary to Ehrlich, we believe that China's one-child policy was a mistake. The policy caused mass suffering and death. Moreover, analysis suggests that without China's birth limit, global resources would be almost twice as abundant today.

Our method for estimating the abundance of global resources is simple. It is based on economics instead of physics and prices instead of quantities. We start by calculating the changes in personal resource abundance, a calculation of whether the average inhabitant of the earth can afford to buy more or less. We then multiply that value by the size of the population. Finally, we compare the size of the global resource pie at two different points in time to see if resource abundance rose or fell.

Personal resource abundance is measured with time prices. We buy things with money, but we pay for them with time. A time price is the hours and minutes of work it takes to earn the money to buy an item. It is the ratio of the (nominal) money price divided by the (nominal) hourly income.

To determine whether resource abundance is rising or falling, we analyzed the time prices of 50 basic commodities between 1980 and 2020 including energy, food, materials, minerals, and metals. Our data came from three reputable organizations: the World Bank, the International Monetary Fund, and the Conference Board.

We found that the average time price of the 50 basic commodities fell by 75.2 percent. That means that the time required to earn the money to buy one unit in our basket of 50 basic commodities in 1980 would get you 4.03 units in 2020. So, the average inhabitant of the planet saw a 303 percent increase in personal resource abundance.

Between 1980 and 2020, the world's population rose from 4.434 billion to 7.795 billion, or 75.8 percent. Put differently, every 1 percent increase in the world's population corresponded to a 1 percent decrease in time prices (-75.2 percent $\div$ 75.8 percent $= -0.992$).

Given that personal resource abundance increased by 303 percent and the world's population increased by 75.8 percent, we can say that global resource abundance (i.e., the increase in personal resource abundance multiplied by the increase in the world's population) rose by 609 percent.[g]

What would have happened to our findings if the world's population rose by an additional 400 million people? Instead of a global population of 7.8 billion, the planet would now be inhabited by 8.2 billion people, an increase of 84.8 percent between 1980 and 2020 instead of 75.8 percent.

Recall that our findings suggest that for every 1 percent increase in the world's population, time prices decrease by 1 percent. If that relationship held in a world populated by 400 million more people, time prices would have fallen by 84.8 percent instead of 75.8 percent.

For the same length of time required to earn enough money to buy 1 unit in our basket of 50 basic commodities in 1980, you would get 6.59 units (rather than 4.03 units) in 2020. That represents a 559 percent increase in personal resource abundance (rather than 303 percent). That also means global resource abundance would have increased by 1,118 percent (rather than 609 percent).[h]

Such is the miracle of compounding! Thomas Malthus, the English pastor who was Ehrlich's intellectual precursor, recognized exponential growth but mistakenly thought that the population would grow faster than resources. Two hundred years of empirical evidence suggests that the opposite is true.

China has experienced a great economic boom since the start of its economic reforms in the late 1970s. At the same time, the Chinese people suffered from the one-child policy that reduced the potential Chinese population by 400 million people. Just imagine how much more prosperous China could be today if its economy employed 400 million more young (and somewhat more free) people!

In the late 1970s, the Chinese Communist Party assumed that unless they implemented strict population controls, China would never escape poverty. Of course, we know today that economic policy (namely, greater economic freedom), not population control, was responsible for China's success.

As we showed, though, the rest of the world also suffered. If the global population were 9 percent higher, the average time price of the 50 basic commodities would be 9 percent lower. Instead of a 303 percent increase in personal resource abundance, the average inhabitant of the world would be 559 percent better off. Instead of a 609 percent increase in global resource abundance, the world's resources would be 1,118 percent more abundant. ∎

The Indian Emergency (1975–1977)

In 1975, Indian Prime Minister Indira Gandhi declared a state of emergency. To justify her actions, she noted supposedly imminent "internal and external threats" to the country.[55] During "the Emergency," Gandhi ruled by decree, voting rights and freedom of the press were suspended, and Gandhi's political opponents were thrown in jail. To make matters worse, Gandhi empowered her son, Sanjay, to implement a set of far-reaching programs. They included the Each One Teach One program intended to achieve complete literacy, the Plant Trees program intended to achieve ecological balance, the Abolish Dowry program intended to abolish "a social evil," the Eradicate Casteism program intended to destroy social prejudice, and the Family Planning program intended to achieve "a prosperous future for the country."[56]

Implicit in Sanjay Gandhi's thinking and justification for the Family Planning program was the supposed connection between fewer people on the one hand and prosperity on the other hand. By the time that Sanjay Gandhi was able to implement the Family Planning program, India was full of Malthusian ideas. Follett found that

> from the United States, both the Johnson and the Ford administrations encouraged India's Prime Minister Gandhi to pursue population control more aggressively. . . . Western population professionals thronged to India's capital in the 1960s, backing surveys, doling out research grants, proselytizing neo-Malthusianism, and training many of India's demographers, doctors, and public health professionals. In conjunction with India's elite, Western organizations helped design and bankroll policies such as sterilization targets aimed at curbing the fertility of the country's poor. . . . By the 1960s, the U.S. government, UNFPA [the United Nations Population Fund], Ford Foundation, and World Bank accounted for most of the $1.5 billion in annual aid that India received. In 1974, the UNFPA issued its largest grant ever to India, and in 1976 the Swedish Development Authority loaned India $60 million for "family planning," some of which ultimately funded coerced procedures. Between 1972 and 1980 the World Bank loaned India

$66 million for "population control." Upon returning from a visit to India in 1976 during the Emergency, then–World Bank president Robert McNamara declared, "At long last, India is moving to effectively address its population problem," noting without alarm coercive policies including, in his words, "compulsory abortion" and "sterilization laws."[57]

The majority of Sanjay Gandhi's 11 million victims were vasectomized men. An additional 1 million women were fitted with IUDs, often without regard for the appropriate health and safety standards.[58] Government officials pursued Sanjay Gandhi's quotas so vigorously and carelessly that some 2,000 people died while undergoing sterilization procedures. One government official compared the program to a war and the deaths to "misfiring out of enthusiasm."[59]

All government agencies were expected to participate in the sterilization drive. Government officials withheld water and salaries from those who refused sterilization. Sometimes, the former seized the latter's property. Hospitals refused service to the unsterilized and performed sterilizations without consent on patients who showed up for other kinds of operations. Sanjay Gandhi's program incentivized sterilizations, not reductions in the birth rate. Age and fertility were of no importance to family planning officials, so the young, the childless, and the already infertile elderly were sterilized alike. Some were even sterilized twice.[60]

In the schools, members of the faculty were threatened with salary cuts unless they got sterilized. They were expected to encourage their students' parents to do so as well. One student reported that his school administration and teachers threatened to fail students with unsterilized parents.[61] Sometimes, the police would simply capture random groups of people off the street and bring them to sterilization camps. People were terrified, hiding in the woods and sugar fields to avoid the roundups. To enlist the help of the private sector, the government would withhold licenses unless business owners assisted in the sterilization drive.

The sterilization program intersected with other government initiatives. When the government destroyed slums in its numerous "beautification drives," the 700,000 displaced people were given new land only if they agreed to be sterilized or convinced others to be sterilized in their place. Those who circumvented the government bureaucrats and obtained a plot without being sterilized could be evicted. "In an area in Delhi known as Turkmen's Gate, local resistance to the sterilization drive and demolitions resulted in authorities killing at least 12 resisters, with some sources estimating a much higher death toll."[62]

CHAPTER 3

Julian Simon and the bet that made him famous

Our supplies of natural resources are not finite in any economic sense. Nor does past experience give reason to expect natural resources to become more scarce. Rather, if history is any guide, natural resources will progressively become less costly, hence less scarce, and will constitute a smaller proportion of our expenses in future years.

Julian Simon, *The Ultimate Resource 2*[1]

Chapter summary

While many scholars expressed optimism about the effects of population growth on prosperity, Julian Simon is arguably the best known of the cornucopians, a label that former *New York Times* columnist John Tierney gave to individuals who argue that the environmental problems faced by humanity can be solved by technology and free enterprise.[2] Malthusian scholar Paul Ehrlich was Simon's greatest intellectual opponent. He saw population growth in terms of the carrying capacity of natural systems, arguing that people, like rabbits, procreate until destroying the supporting environment that surrounds them, leading to both environmental and population collapse.

It was the intellectual battle between Simon the cornucopian and Ehrlich the Malthusian that revived the debate over the precise nature of the relationship between population growth and prosperity for the modern era. As we shall see, Simon won the debate by virtue of a much-publicized bet on the future price of a selected number of resources, yet Malthusianism did not go away. In recent years, it made a remarkable comeback in the guise of "running out of nature" theory and mathematical models that purport to calculate how much consumption is compatible with "sustainable" economic development. Finally, we will conclude with a brief look at the role that the media has played in increasing ecological anxiety by uncritically repeating the most outrageous claims of the doomsayers.

Julian Simon: the life and thought of the ultimate Avenger

Simon was born on February 12, 1932, in Newark, New Jersey. His parents gave him the middle name Lincoln because he was born on Abraham Lincoln's birthday. His parents were lower-middle-class children of Jewish immigrants who arrived in the United States from Central and Eastern Europe in the late 19th century. Simon grew up in Newark and then Millburn, New Jersey. He attended Harvard College on a Navy scholarship and served for three years as a naval officer. He tried his hand at business and then studied business economics at the University of Chicago, where he earned a master's degree in business administration in 1959 and a doctorate in business economics in 1961. Simon then started and operated a successful mail-order business. In 1963, he joined the faculty of the University of Illinois as a professor of advertising. In 1969, he became a professor of economics and business administration. In 1983, he moved to the University of Maryland, where he worked until his death on February 8, 1998.[3]

Simon was a polymath, but his main interest concerned the economic effects of changes in population. His books, including *The Ultimate Resource* (1981), *The Ultimate Resource 2* (1996), and *Population Matters: People, Resources, Environment, and Immigration* (1990), discussed long-term trends concerning the availability of resources, quality of the environment and population growth, as well as the interactions among the three. These books, which were intended for noneconomists, developed ideas that Simon introduced in his first technical book concerning population, *The Economics of Population Growth* (1977), as well as later technical books such as *The Resourceful Earth* (edited with Herman Kahn in 1984), *Theory of Population and Economic Growth* (1986), *Population and Development in Poor Countries* (1992), and *The State of Humanity* (1996).

In his books, Simon acknowledged that population growth causes short-term problems such as temporary increases in the prices of resources, but he insisted that people are also the means to solve those problems. He wrote,

> Greater consumption due to increase in population and growth of income heightens scarcity and induces price run-ups. A higher price represents an opportunity that leads inventors and business people to seek new ways to satisfy the shortages. Some fail at [a] cost to themselves. A few succeed, and the final result is that we end up better off than if the original shortage problems had never arisen. That is, we need our problems, though this does not imply that we should purposely create additional problems for ourselves.[4]

People, Simon observed, are the ultimate resource. By applying their intelligence and ingenuity, people—individuals—make all the other resources more abundant. He observed,

> It is your mind that matters economically, as much or more than your mouth or hands. In the long run, the most important economic effect of population size and growth is the contribution of additional people to our stock of useful knowledge. And this contribution is large enough in the long run to overcome all the costs of population growth.[5]

Simon concluded that there is no a priori reason why material life on Earth should not continue to improve indefinitely. He emphasized that facts, not preexisting beliefs, led him to his conclusions. As he wrote in the preface to *The Ultimate Resource 2,*

> When (starting about 1969) ... I began to work on population studies, I assumed that the accepted view was sound. I aimed to help the world contain its "exploding" population, which I believed to be one of the two main threats to humankind (war being the other). But my reading and research led me into confusion. Though the then-standard economic theory of population (which had hardly changed since Malthus) asserted that a higher population growth implies a lower standard of living, the available empirical data did not support that theory.[6]

Simon tried to reconcile the conflict between the theory and empirical evidence. In the end, he had to admit that "population growth does not hinder economic development or reduce the standard of living."[7] Instead, empirical evidence led him to believe that "population growth has positive economic effects in the long run."[8]

Simon's work challenged widely accepted and strongly held positions by most of the scientific establishment, governmental institutions, and popular media. The strength of his iconoclastic work made him the target of decades of the most intense personal criticism. He was, for example, accused by Ehrlich and other influential critics of stupidity, scientific ignorance, dishonesty, and deceptive manipulation of statistics. His critics also attempted to prevent the publication of his books and articles. Some sought to have him fired. Simon did not respond in kind to the ad hominem attacks leveled against him. Instead, he focused on science.

One anecdote can illustrate the appalling way in which Simon was treated. University of Wisconsin sociologist William Freudenburg (1951–2010), who witnessed lengthy and venomous attacks on Simon during a question-and-answer session that followed the latter's speech at that institution in 1989, wrote to Simon, sarcastically noting "the 'hospitality' that all of us, collectively, offered to you and to your ideas." Freudenburg expressed his admiration "for the equanimity with which you responded to behaviors that I found to be downright childish." Freudenburg found "it quite ironic that the people who think of themselves as 'real' scientists were the ones coming up with excuses for not dealing with data, resorting to ad hominem attacks, and generally showing a disdain for scientific methods that I formerly thought would be found only among book-burners."[9]

The intensity of the criticism reinforced Simon's adherence to the highest scientific standards and unparalleled precision in his work, thus driving his opponents to ever more exotic criticisms. As he noted in the epilogue to *The Ultimate Resource 2*, Ehrlich "and his colleagues based their criticism of my 1980 *Science* article [which we will discuss at length later in this chapter] . . . on what turned out to be a typographical error in a source. If I had been in their shoes, I would have been chagrined and embarrassed when this was discovered."[10] He also maintained a sense of humor and humility. Asked about Ehrlich's win of the MacArthur Foundation's Genius Award, Simon quipped: "I can't even get a McDonald's!"[11] When the December 1993 issue of *Washingtonian* magazine listed Simon as being among the 25 "smartest people" in Washington, DC, he commented that he would have preferred to be one of the 25 "sexiest Washingtonians."[12]

In 1981, at the height of the attacks against him, Simon received an unexpected lifeline of support: letters from, in Simon's words, "as great an economist as has lived in the 20th century, Nobel Prize winner Friedrich Hayek."[13] The first letter from Hayek began thusly: "I have never before written a fan letter to a professional colleague, but to discover that you have in your *Economics of Population Growth* provided the empirical evidence for what with me is the result of a life-time of theoretical speculation, is too exciting an experience not to share it with you." Another letter included the following:

> I have now at last had time to read [*The Ultimate Resource*] with enthusiastic agreement. . . . Your new book I welcome chiefly for the practical effects I am hoping from it. Though you will be at first much abused, I believe the more intelligent will soon recognize the sound-ness of your case. And the malicious pleasure of being able to tell most of their fellows what fools they are, should get you the support of the more lively minds about the media. If your publishers want to quote me, they are welcome to say that I described it as a first class book of great importance which ought to have great influence on policy.[14]

As part of his work on the economics of population growth, Simon also studied the economics of immigration. In his 1989 book, *The Economic Consequences of Immigration*, Simon provided theory and data showing that, on balance, immigrants to the United States make Americans richer rather than poorer. It may sound strange to the modern ear, but many environmentalists of the day were very much opposed to immigration to the United States. The Sierra Club, a wealthy and politically influential northern California group founded in 1892, went as far as to call "for the 'stabilization of the population of the United States as part of a broader policy on global population growth,' and in 1978, it urged the U.S. Congress to 'study the effects of immigration on domestic population growth and environmental quality.'"[15]

Simon wrote on a variety of other subjects, including statistics, research methods, the economics of advertising, and managerial economics. Some of his other books include *How to Start and Operate a Mail-Order Business* (1981), *Basic Research Methods in Social Science* (1969), *Issues in the Economics of Advertising* (1970), *The Management of Advertising* (1971), *Applied Managerial Economics* (1975), *Patterns of Use of Books in Large Research Libraries* (coauthored with the American librarian Herman Fussler in 1961), *Effort, Opportunity, and Wealth* (1987), *The Great Breakthrough and Its Cause* (published posthumously with Turkish American economist Timur Kuran in 2001), *Developing Decision-Making Skills for Business* (published posthumously in 2000), *Hoodwinking the Nation* (published posthumously in 1999), *The Art of Empirical Investigation* (published posthumously in 2003), and *Good Mood: The New Psychology for Overcoming Depression* (published posthumously in 1999).

Simon authored more than 200 professional studies in technical journals and wrote dozens of articles in such outlets as the *Atlantic Monthly, Reader's Digest*, the *New York Times*, and the *Wall Street Journal*. He took great pride in inventing a mechanism for improving air travel that most readers will be familiar with and for which he is the first economist profiled in the American economist Robert E. Litan's 2014 book, *Trillion Dollar Economists*. Before 1978, "airlines arbitrarily bumped passengers when flights were overbooked, creating ill will among travelers left behind. As a result, airlines kept overbooking to a minimum, meaning that flights ran far short of capacity when no-shows exceeded expectations. Simon proposed seeking volunteers instead, offering rewards such as free airfare for a future trip if passengers agreed to wait for a later flight."[16] American economist James Heins noted that this "seemingly subtle switch has provided a $100 billion jolt to the U.S. economy over the last three decades—allowing airlines to run fuller, more profitable flights, [which] in turn has trimmed air fares and increased tax revenue."[17]

Simon takes on Paul Ehrlich, the Thanos of his day

Paul Ralph Ehrlich, like Simon, was born in 1932 to a family of Jewish émigrés from Central and Eastern Europe. His family was based in Philadelphia when he was born and later moved to New Jersey. That, alas, is where the similarities between the two scholars ended. Ehrlich earned a bachelor's degree in zoology from the University of Pennsylvania in 1953 and a master's degree and doctorate from the University of Kansas in 1955 and 1957, respectively. In 1959, he joined the faculty at Stanford University, becoming a professor of biology in 1966.

Ehrlich's background in biology is relevant. In the nonhuman animal world, a sudden increase in the availability of resources leads to a population explosion, which leads to the exhaustion of resources and population collapse. American environmentalist Lester R. Brown from the Worldwatch Institute in Washington, DC, noted in 1998 that "most biologists and ecologists look at population growth in terms of the carrying capacity of natural systems." Economists, in contrast, tend to "see population growth in a much more optimistic light."[18]

In his widely popular 1968 book, *The Population Bomb*, Ehrlich wrote that he was convinced of the threat of unchecked population growth before his 1966 trip to Delhi, India, yet it was during that visit that he saw "overpopulation" first hand. As he later recalled,

> The streets seemed alive with people. People eating, people washing, people sleeping. People visiting, arguing, and screaming. People thrust their hands through the taxi window, begging. People defecating and urinating. People clinging to buses. People herding animals. People, people, people, people. . . . [S]ince that night, I've known the feel of overpopulation.[19]

By 1990, a year the significance of which will soon become clear, *The Population Bomb* had sold 3 million copies and was translated into many languages. It brought Malthusian concerns into the mainstream, both through its dramatic language and Ehrlich's considerable skill at promoting his ideas. The book opened with this oft-quoted prediction: "The battle to feed all of humanity is over. In the 1970s, hundreds of millions of people will starve to death in spite of any crash programs embarked upon now."[20] In 1970, Ehrlich appeared on *The Tonight Show*, an American late-night talk show that has been hosted on NBC since 1954 by six comedians: Steve Allen, Jack Paar, Johnny Carson, Jay Leno, Conan O'Brien, and Jimmy Fallon.

John Tierney notes that Ehrlich "became perhaps the only author ever interviewed for an hour on 'The Tonight Show.'"[21] It was that show that made Ehrlich famous. Phyllis Diller was the first guest and told jokes about her honeymoon night.[22] According to Tierney, the next guest was "a starlet whose one-word answers made things so awkward that Ehrlich was rushed on early to rescue Johnny Carson."

"I went on and did basically a monologue," Ehrlich recalled. "I'd talk until the commercial, and during the break I'd feed Johnny a question, and then

I'd answer it until the next commercial. I got the highest compliment after the show, when I was walking behind Johnny and Ed McMahon [Carson's announcer] up the stairs, and I heard Johnny say, 'Boy, Paul really saved the show.'"[23] The show, wrote Tierney, "got more than 5,000 letters about Ehrlich's appearance, the first of many on the program. Ehrlich has been deluged ever since with requests for lectures, interviews, and opinions."[24]

Back home in Illinois, Simon watched Ehrlich's many appearances on *The Tonight Show* (there were over 20 in total) in a state of frustration. He remembered that Carson, "the most unimpressible of people, had this look of stupefied admiration. He'd throw out a question about population growth and Ehrlich would start out by saying, 'Well, it's really very simple, Johnny.' Now the one thing I knew in those days about population was that nothing about it is simple. But what could I do? Go talk to five people? Here was a guy reaching a vast audience, leading this juggernaut of environmentalist hysteria, and I felt utterly helpless."[25]

Simon and Ehrlich never debated directly. Tierney notes that "Ehrlich has always refused, saying that Simon is a 'fringe character'—but they lambasted each other in scholarly journal articles." In 1980, for example, Simon wrote an article in *Science* magazine, which was then the most widely read scientific publication in the United States. In it, he criticized Malthusian voices such as the National Wildlife Federation, the secretary general of the United Nations, and Ehrlich. Ehrlich couldn't believe that a leading science journal would publish a criticism of his work. He quickly shot back with a scathing counter-article asking, "Could the editors have found someone to review Simon's manuscript who had to take off his shoes to count to 20?" He declared that Simon was part of a "space-age cargo cult" and complained about economists' inability, or unwillingness, to understand the Earth's "carrying capacity." He wrote that "to explain to one of them the inevitability of no growth in the material sector or . . . that commodities must become expensive would be like trying to explain odd-day-even-day gas distribution to a cranberry."[26]

It was around this time that Simon challenged his critics to a bet. "Offering to wager is the last recourse of the frustrated," he wrote. "When you are convinced that you have hold of an important idea, and you can't get the other side to listen, offering to bet is all that is left. If the other side refuses to bet, they implicitly acknowledge that they are less sure than they claim to be."[27] Ehrlich, who predicted in 1970 that "if I were a gambler, I would take even money that England will not exist in the year 2000," seemed to have been foremost on Simon's mind.[28] In fact, Ehrlich, Holdren, and Harte decided to "accept Simon's astonishing offer before other greedy people jump[ed] in."[29] Ehrlich even quipped that "the lure of easy money can be irresistible,"[30] and so the Ehrlich group bet $1,000 on $200 quantities of five metals: chrome, copper, nickel, tin, and tungsten. Then they signed a futures contract that stipulated that Simon would sell these same quantities of metal to Ehrlich's group for the same price in 10 years' time. Since price is a reflection of scarcity, Simon would pay if population increases made these metals scarcer, but if they became more abundant and therefore cheaper, Ehrlich would pay. The bet would last from September 29, 1980 to September 29, 1990.

Over the next 10 years, the two men regularly feuded with each other through articles such as Ehrlich's "An Economist in Wonderland" and Simon's article "Paul Ehrlich Saying It Is So Doesn't Make It So." Aside from these not-so-subtle jabs, Ehrlich continued his personal attacks on Simon, comparing the economist to a flat-earther and stating that "the views of . . . Simon are taken seriously by a segment of the public, even though to a scientist, they are in the same class as the idea that Jack Frost is responsible for ice-crystal patterns on a cold window."[31] During the 1980s, in fact, Simon started to turn some academics to his side. He noted that population and prosperity can go hand in hand and took a public stance against coercive government measures to limit population growth such as China's one-child policy. On Earth Day 1990, while Simon spoke to an audience of 16 specialists, Ehrlich gave a rousing speech about future food riots to a crowd of 200,000. At another event, Ehrlich referenced Simon's book when he declared "the ultimate resource—the one thing we'll never run out of is imbeciles."[32]

That autumn, the wager's timeline finally ran out. All five metals became cheaper, with the prices of three of them falling at a faster pace than inflation. The prices of tin and tungsten fell by more than half. Ehrlich mailed Simon a spreadsheet of metal prices and a check for $576.07, representing a 36 percent decrease in inflation-adjusted prices. Ehrlich's wife, Anne, signed it.

There was no letter accompanying it. Simon sent Ehrlich a thank-you note and an offer to raise the stakes to $20,000 in a future wager, but Ehrlich refused. Simon's triumph was more than a gambling victory. As he had predicted, human ingenuity had made these resources more abundant despite a population increase of over 800 million. New nickel mines had been discovered and exploited, ending a Canadian monopoly on the commodity. Glass cables had replaced copper wires, driving down demand for the metal. Aluminum replaced tin in cans, eventually leading to the collapse of the price-setting international tin cartel. Across the board, technological improvement and entrepreneurship made mining and refining so much more efficient and therefore cheaper that new supply outpaced the rising demand of a growing population. Ehrlich, who is still alive as of this writing, regards his loss as an anomaly. As he noted,

> The bet doesn't mean anything. Julian Simon is like the guy who jumps off the Empire State Building and says how great things are going so far as he passes the 10th floor. I still think the price of those metals will go up eventually, but that's a minor point. The resource that worries me the most is the declining capacity of our planet to buffer itself against human impacts. Look at the new problems that have come up: the ozone hole, acid rain, global warming. It's true that we've kept up food production—I underestimated how badly we'd keep on depleting our topsoil and groundwater—but I have no doubt that sometime in the next century food will be scarce enough that prices are really going to be high even in the United States. If we get climate change and let the ecological systems keep running downhill, we could have a gigantic population crash.[33]

In 2013, Ehrlich and his wife revisited *The Population Bomb* in an article titled "Can a Collapse of Global Civilization Be Avoided?" The pair warned that human civilization "is threatened with collapse by an array of environmental problems. They observed that "the human predicament is driven by overpopulation, overconsumption of natural resources, and the use of unnecessarily environmentally damaging technologies and socioeconomic-political arrangements to service *Homo sapiens'* aggregate consumption."[34] In 2017, Ehrlich was invited to address a Vatican workshop on biological extinction. "You can't go on growing forever on a finite planet. The biggest problem we face is the continued expansion of human enterprise," he said. "Perpetual growth is the creed of a cancer cell. . . . It's the aggregate consumption that ruins the environment," Ehrlich continued.[35]

As Simon would say before his untimely death in 1998, "Paul Ehrlich has never been able to learn from past experience."[36] He also produced his "long-run forecast" for the future:

> The material conditions of life will continue to get better for most people in most countries most of the time, indefinitely. Within a century or two, all nations and most of humanity will be at or above today's Western living standards. I also speculate, however, that many people will continue to think and say that the conditions of life are getting worse.[37]

Subsequent events confirmed Simon's forecast. Material conditions of life have continued to improve for people in rich and poor countries alike (see Chapter 1). The gloomy predictions of the fate of our species, as we will show in later chapters, haven't stopped, though.

Running out of nature: a somewhat different, but equally flawed, take on Malthus

As we conclude this chapter, we should acknowledge that Malthusian concern over population growth is not the only intellectual current within the environmentalist movement. As early as 1970, Kenneth Boulding said that he "would not be a bit surprised if we [i.e., humanity] ran out of pollutable reservoirs before our mines and ores are exhausted. There are signs of this happening in the atmosphere, in the rivers, and in the oceans."[38] Even Ehrlich, who usually put a heavy emphasis on "overpopulation," sometimes hedged his bets. In 1981, for example, he wrote:

> There is no danger whatever of humanity "running out" of non-fuel mineral resources, and I have not said there is. Those resources

remain on the surface of the earth after mining and use. Humanity is not destroying them—it is dispersing them. What will run out, however, is the capacity of the environment to absorb the punishment associated with mining ever-lower grades of ore or reconcentrating what is already dispersed. Secondarily, the ability to do the job at an attractive cost will also "run out."[39]

The focus on environmental damage as a byproduct of population growth, economic growth, and growth in consumption gathered steam in the 1980s and the 1990s. In 1982, for example, a group of "ecological economists" met in Stockholm and published a manifesto warning of natural limits on human activity. "Ecological economists distinguished themselves from neo-Malthusian catastrophists by switching the emphasis from resources to systems," wrote one historian of this period. Their "concern was no longer centered on running out of food, minerals, or energy. Instead, ecological economists drew attention to what they identified as ecological thresholds. The problem lay in overloading systems and causing them to collapse."[40]

The American climate change activist Bill McKibben is a good example of the intellectual pilgrimage from worrying about running out of resources to worrying about running out of nature. As late as 1989, "McKibben argued [in his book The End of Nature] that humankind's impact on the planet would require the same Malthusian program developed by Ehrlich and [Barry] Commoner in the 1970s. Economic growth would have to end. Rich nations must return to farming and transfer wealth to poor nations so they could improve their lives modestly but not industrialize. And the human population would have to shrink to between 100 million and 2 billion."[41]

By 1998, McKibben explained, "It's not that we're running out of stuff. What we're running out of is what the scientists call 'sinks'—places to put the by-products of our large appetites. Not garbage dumps (we could go on using Pampers till the end of time and still have empty space left to toss them away) but the atmospheric equivalent of garbage dumps."[42] Overconsumption, in other words, will not exhaust planetary resources. Instead, the environmental catastrophe will be brought about by the destruction of humanity's broader environmental support systems such as high-quality soil, ground-water deposits, biodiversity, and so on.

Many prominent scientists and policy makers share McKibben's pessimism. The American climatologist Michael E. Mann, for example, argued that "climate change is simply one axis in a multi-dimensional problem that is environmental sustainability. They all stem from the same problem—too many people using too many natural resources."[43] The former head of the Intergovernmental Panel on Climate Change, Robert Watson, worries that the "more people we have on the Earth and the richer they are, the more they can demand resources."[44] Rajendra K. Pachauri, Watson's successor, wrote that people have "been so drunk with this desire to produce and consume more and more whatever the cost to the environment that we're on a totally unsustainable path."[45] The German atmospheric physicist Hans Joachim Schellnhuber, who advised Pope Francis when the latter wrote his 2015 encyclical *Laudato Si*, estimates Earth's carrying capacity at "below 1 billion people."[46]

"The notion that current levels of population and affluence are already exceeding natural limits," wrote Desrochers and Szurmak, "has been expressed and elaborated in a number of influential [mathematical] frameworks, which . . . equate smaller population numbers and greater material poverty with lesser environmental impact."[47] The most influential of these models is the IPAT, a brainchild of Ehrlich and Holdren. The IPAT is a formula that calculates the human impact (I) on the environment using population size (P), income or affluence (A), and technology or amount of pollution per dollar of output (T). It has been heavily criticized by a variety of scholars and scientists.[48] That said, let us make four points that should put this particular take on Malthus in a proper perspective.

First, as Ted Nordhaus from the Breakthrough Institute in California observed in 2019, the frameworks assume that humans will continue to reproduce with abandon. In reality, data show that as an economy becomes more developed, birth rates begin to fall. The massive population growth in recent decades is due to rising life expectancy, not rising fertility.[49] The birth rates of the United States, Europe, Japan, China, and large parts of Latin America have actually fallen below the replacement level of 2.1 children per woman for some time. That means that their populations are actually starting to shrink. It's likely that the rest of the world will follow that trend. What does that mean?

According to Bailey, the "world population will likely peak at 9.8 billion people at around 2080 and fall to 9.5 billion by 2100 in the medium fertility scenario calculated by demographer Wolfgang Lutz and his colleagues at the International Institute of Applied Systems Analysis. Alternatively, assuming rapid economic growth, technological advancement, and rising levels of educational attainment for both sexes—all factors that tend to lower fertility—Lutz projects that world population will more likely peak at around 8.9 billion by 2060 and decline to 7.8 billion by the end of the twenty-first century."[50]

Considering that there were 7.8 billion humans on the planet in 2020, it is possible that the world's population will be roughly the same size 80 years later. If Lutz's latter estimates are correct, then the world may actually end up facing an underpopulation rather than an overpopulation problem. That's because, in the absence of artificial intelligence, human beings remain the sole producers of ideas, inventions, and innovations that drive technological, scientific, and medical progress. We will discuss the interplay between human beings and innovation in Chapter 9.

Second, modern doomsayers, who recognize that the human population may actually shrink in the future, worry that free enterprise will continue to drive human consumption of resources to higher and higher levels.[51] Again, the data do not agree. We have already noted McAfee's 2019 book, *More from Less: The Surprising Story of How We Learned to Prosper Using Fewer Resources—and What Happens Next*. Sophisticated economies, he found, are currently producing ever more goods and services, while at the same time using ever fewer resources. That is a result of a sustained transition in advanced countries from industry to less resource-intensive economic activities that deal with services and information.

To that process, we may also add dematerialization, which refers to declining consumption of material and energy per unit of gross domestic product (GDP). According to Jesse Ausubel from Rockefeller University and Paul E. Waggoner from the Connecticut Agricultural Experiment Station, "If consumers dematerialize their intensity of use of goods and technicians produce the goods with a lower intensity of impact, people can grow in numbers and affluence without a proportionally greater environmental impact."[52]

Why would people do that? Dematerialization makes economic sense to producers, since spending less on inputs can swell profit margins and make outputs cheaper and therefore more competitive.[53] It makes sense to consumers as well. Consider, for example, the growing use of smartphones. The product combines functions that previously required a myriad of separate devices, including a telephone, camera, radio, television set, alarm clock, newspaper, photo album, voice recorder, maps, compass, and more.

Replacement of many devices with one produces substantial efficiency gains. How substantial? In 2018, a team of 21 researchers led by Professor Arnulf Grubler from the International Institute for Applied Systems Analysis in Austria estimated the "savings from device convergence on smartphones . . . for materials use (device weight) and for its associated embodied energy use." They found that smartphones can reduce material use by a factor of 300. They can reduce power use by a factor of 100 and standby energy use by a factor of 30.[54]

To summarize, many doomsayers worry that future growth will mirror that during the Industrial Revolution: bigger and deeper mines, bigger and more polluting steel mills, and so forth. But economic growth does not have to come from bigness. On the contrary, it can and does come from miniaturization, such as that observable in the computing industry, which saw replacement of massive mainframe computers with smaller and much more efficient personal computers. The economic historian from Northwestern University Joel Mokyr has this to say:

> The main logical issue here is that economic growth can be resource saving as much as resource-using, and that the very negative effects that congestion and pollution engender will set into motion searches for techniques that will abate them. Such responses may be more effective in democratic than in autocratic regimes because concerned public opinion can map better into public policy, but in the end the need for humans to breathe clean air is about as universal a value as one can find. Investment in soil reclamation, desalination, recycling, and renewable energy count just as much as economic growth as economic activities that use up resources. Whether or not wise policies will help steer technological progress in that direction, the basic notion that per capita income growth has to stop because the planet is finite is palpable nonsense.[55]

Third, doomsayers assume that humanity will sit idly by and allow environmental problems to overwhelm our planet. That is highly improbable given our species' track record of tackling past challenges. According to Nordhaus, it took six times as much land to feed a single person in the Neolithic Age as it does now. If we were still harvesting einkorn with sticks and stones, we would certainly be above our carrying capacity. Instead, we've improved our agricultural efficiency so much that less than 2 percent of the U.S. population actually has to farm at all.[56]

As Ausubel and his colleagues noted in their 2013 article, "Peak Farmland and the Prospect for Land Sparing," if the productivity of the world's farmers increases to U.S. levels, humanity will be able to restore at least 146 million hectares of cropland land to nature. This is an area two and a half times that of France or the size of 10 Iowas.[57] As Bailey observed, "The UN Food and Agriculture Organization reports that land devoted to agriculture (including pastures) peaked in 2000 at 4.915 billion hectares (12.15 billion acres) and had fallen to 4.828 billion hectares (11.93 billion acres) by 2017. This human withdrawal from the landscape is the likely prelude to a vast ecological restoration over the course of this [21st] century."[58]

In fact, as we write, many of the problems identified by the frameworks are being addressed or are on the cusp of being addressed. Forest coverage is growing in rich countries, species are being protected at record levels throughout the world, freshwater reserves are being replenished through desalinization in the Middle East, soil erosion is being reduced through precision agriculture in Israel, and CO_2 emissions have fallen in nuclear energy–friendly France and Sweden. In the future, genetically modified crops could lead to a decline in the use of nitrogen and phosphorus, and wild fish stocks could bounce back through greater use of aquaculture, which is rapidly expanding in China.

What's needed to address current and future problems is freedom and brainpower, and that leads us to the fourth problem with neo-Malthusian thinking. Limiting population growth not only limits brain power; it also means social engineering and violence. Such policies could include reproductive controls, like one-child policies, forced sterilization, or even genocide. Instead of enacting violent policies out of irrational fear, Nordhaus noted, we should evaluate the merits of the frameworks on thousands of years of human history and rational optimism. People have addressed pressing environmental problems in the past and can do so in the future.

Michael Moore's mission to prove that Malthus is alive and well

That being said, you don't have to scratch deep below the surface of the environmental movement in general and theory of limits in particular to notice that Malthusian ideas are alive and well. Given its notoriety, one remarkable example should suffice to prove the above point. In April 2020, a new Michael Moore movie called *Planet of the Humans* was released on YouTube. Moore is a well-known environmentalist and anti-capitalist, recognized for such widely acclaimed movies as *Bowling for Columbine* (2002) and *Fahrenheit 9/11* (2004). He has been vocal in his support of the environmentalist movement, and in 2007, he endorsed the former U.S. Vice President Al Gore for president.

So it came as a massive shock to the environmental movement when in his latest offering, Moore aimed his fire at the environmentalists themselves.[59] The plot of *Planet of the Humans* consists of two parts. The first part of the plot is correct in pointing out that renewable energy (chiefly through wind turbines and solar panels) is not really renewable. Their manufacture relies on extensive mining, processing, and transport (and, therefore, CO_2 emissions), their intermittent operation requires extensive fossil fuel backups (and, therefore, CO_2 emissions), and their eventual deconstruction and disposal require a lot of energy (and, therefore, CO_2 emissions).

Making matters worse are pollutants that are released during the production of renewable energy. Wind turbine magnets, for example, require a great deal of rare earth minerals such as neodymium and dysprosium. "Estimates of the exact amount of rare earth minerals in wind turbines vary, but in any case, the numbers are staggering. According to the Bulletin of Atomic Sciences, a 2 megawatt wind turbine contains about 800 pounds of neodymium and 130 pounds of dysprosium. [Another source] estimates that a 2 megawatt wind turbine contains about 752 pounds of rare earth minerals. To quantify this in terms of environmental damages, consider that mining one ton of rare earth minerals produces about one ton of radioactive waste."[60]

The second part of the plot is pure Malthus. Since green energy cannot, as the movie puts it, prevent a global environmental catastrophe in the future, we have to limit our consumption of energy, and the best way to limit our consumption of energy is to have fewer people using energy in the first place. So the solution to environmental problems is, once again, population control. Sure, the means by which humans supposedly destroy the earth has changed from the depletion of natural resources to planetary limits, but the solution to the supposed environmental apocalypse remains the same: fewer people.

Getting it wrong time and again: a half century of media scaremongering

Ecological doomsayers from Ehrlich to Moore would not have been half as successful in spreading their ideas had it not been for the cooperation of the media. The media plays a vital role in the day-to-day functioning of a democratic society. We rely on the media to expose government corruption and corporate malfeasance. We count on the media to inform us of major political and economic events, as well as ground-breaking scientific and technological discoveries. Above all, we expect them to do all that in a dispassionate and objective way. In return, we provide the media with our trustful readership and viewership.

Today, it is *de rigueur* to complain about the breakdown of trust between the media and their audience. That breakdown, however, has been in the works for a very long time.[61] Consider some of the extraordinary reports that have found their way into the press over the last 50 years or so, thus scarring and scaring two generations of people throughout the world in general and in advanced countries in particular.[62] They represent a tip of the iceberg of the constant diet of gloom that ordinary citizens have been fed for decades.

First there was reporting about future famines . . .

On November 17, 1967, the *Salt Lake Tribune* ran an article titled "Dire Famine Forecast by '75." The article warned that increasing population growth would result in global famine that was destined to peak in 1975. Referencing Ehrlich, the article argued in favor of involuntary birth control and the spread of sterilization agents through such pathways as food and water. Along with these measures, the author of the article argued, the Roman Catholic Church should be "pressured into going along with routine measures of population control."[63]

On August 10, 1969, the *New York Times* ran an article titled "Foe of Pollution Sees Lack of Time, Asserts Environmental Ills Outrun Public Concern." The article warned that by the time society becomes convinced of the seriousness of major environmental problems, it is usually already too late. It quoted Ehrlich as saying, "We must realize that unless we are extremely lucky, everybody will disappear in a cloud of blue steam in 20 years."[64] That is to say, in 1989!

. . . then came reporting about the coming Ice Age . . .

On April 16, 1970, the *Boston Globe* ran an article titled "Scientist Predicts New Ice Age by 21st Century." The article warned that growing electricity use and the concomitant increase in air pollution will lead to an ice age "in the first third of the next century" that would dry up all the rivers and streams in the United States. To avoid these climatological conditions, the article noted a number of world-saving recommendations by James P. Lodge, a scientist at the National Center for Atmospheric Research, including population control.[65]

On July 9, 1971, the *Washington Post* ran an article titled "U.S. Scientist Sees New Ice Age Coming." The article warned that the world was between 50 and 60 years away from the next ice age. Referencing scientists from the U.S. National Aeronautics and Space Administration (NASA), the *Washington Post* asserted that dust from the burning of fossil fuels could lower the world's temperature by six degrees.[66]

On January 29, 1974, *The Guardian*, a British daily newspaper, ran an article titled "Space Satellites Show New Ice Age Coming Fast." The article noted the growing amount of ice coverage worldwide and suggested a link between ice coverage and "adverse changes in our climate."[67]

On June 24, 1974, *Time* magazine ran an article titled "Another Ice Age?" The article warned that atmospheric temperatures would continue to decrease, thus leading to the next ice age. It claimed that the "unexpected persistence and thickness of pack ice in the waters around Iceland" and the "southward migration of a warmth-loving creature like the armadillo from the Midwest" are the telltale signs for the impending ice age.[68]

On January 5, 1978, the *New York Times* ran an article titled "International Team of Specialists Finds No End in Sight to 30-Year Cooling Trend in Northern Hemisphere," which discussed a report from a team of American, German, and Japanese scientists who found that there is "no end in sight" to the cooling trend in the northern Pacific and Atlantic oceans.[69]

. . . which gave way to global warming and climate change

On June 24, 1988, the *Miami News* ran an article titled "More Droughts Likely, Expert Tells Senators." The article detailed the testimony by James Hansen, director of NASA's Goddard Institute for Space Studies, to the U.S. Senate Energy and Natural Resources Committee. In his testimony, Hansen stated that "our climate model simulations for the late 1980s and the 1990s indicate a tendency for an increase of heatwave drought situations in the Southeast and Midwest United States."[70]

On December 12, 1988, the *Lansing State Journal* ran an article titled "Prepare for Long, Hot Summers," which discussed Hansen's prediction that in the next 50 to 60 years, Washington, DC, would see an increase in days with temperatures over 90 degrees from 35 to 85 days a year. According to Hansen, the ocean would rise from anywhere between one and six feet.[71]

On September 26, 1988, the *Canberra Times*, an Australian newspaper, ran an article titled "Threat to Islands." According to the article, the Maldives would be completely underwater in 30 years. The article argued that the end of the islands could come much sooner, since the Maldivian drinking water supply was expected to dry up as early as 1992.[72]

On June 30, 1989, the Associated Press ran a story titled "Rising Seas Could Obliterate Nations: U.N. Officials." The article discussed the claim by Noel Brown, the director of the New York office of the UN Environment Program, who predicted that "entire nations could be wiped off the face of the Earth by rising sea levels if the global warming trend is not reversed by 2020." Brown also claimed that the world had only a 10-year opportunity window to reverse the rising sea level trend.[73]

On March 20, 2000, the *Independent*, a British daily newspaper, ran an article titled "Snowfalls Are Now Just a Thing of the Past," which argued that snow was beginning to disappear. The article quoted University of East Anglia scientist David Viner, who said that snowfall would become "a very rare and exciting event" within a few years. Viner also claimed that "children just aren't going to know what snow is."[74]

On October 23, 2001, *Salon* ran an article titled "Stormy Weather: Floods, Droughts, Hurricanes and Disease Outbreaks—An Expert Explains Why Climate Changes Give Us Yet Another Reason to Find Terror in the Skies." The article detailed a conversation with Hansen, who told the author that in 20 to 30 years' time, "the West Side Highway [which runs along the Hudson River] will be under water" and "you'll have signs in restaurants saying 'Water by request only.'"[75]

On December 23, 2002, *The Guardian* ran an article titled "Why Vegans Were Right All Along." The article argued that "famine can only be avoided if the rich give up meat, fish and dairy." According to the author, population growth and dwindling resources would force the rich to adopt the diet of most of the world (i.e., mostly vegan) and only eat meat on special occasions.[76]

On February 21, 2004, *The Guardian* ran an article titled "Now the Pentagon Tells Bush: Climate Change Will Destroy Us." The article noted that a secret Pentagon report warned that Britain would be "Siberian" by 2020. The report apparently also warned that "nuclear conflict, megadroughts, famine, and widespread rioting will erupt across the world."[77]

On June 24, 2008, the *Argus-Press* ran an article titled "NASA Scientist: We're Toast." The article quoted Hansen as saying that "in 5 to 10 years, the Arctic will be free of sea ice in the summer."[78]

On July 9, 2009, the *Independent* ran an article titled "Just 96 Months to Save the World, Says Prince Charles." According to Charles, "Capitalism and consumerism have brought the world to the brink of economic and environmental collapse" and that "he had calculated that we have just 96 months left to save the world."[79]

On October 20, 2009, the *Independent* ran an article titled "Gordon Brown: We Have Fewer Than Fifty Days to Save Our Planet from Catastrophe." The article summarized a speech given by the British prime minister, who claimed that the United Kingdom had 50 days to "set the course of the next 50 years and more."[80]

On December 14, 2009, *USA Today* ran an article titled "Gore: Polar Ice Cap May Disappear by Summer 2014," which described the claims made by the former U.S. vice president Al Gore at the UN climate summit in Copenhagen. Gore stated that "some of the models suggest that there is a 75 percent chance that the entire north polar ice cap during some of the summer months will be completely ice-free within the next five to seven years."[81]

On July 24, 2013, *The Guardian* ran an article titled "Ice-Free Arctic in Two Years Heralds Methane Catastrophe—Scientist," which described a recent paper by University of Cambridge scientist Peter Wadhams, who claimed that summer sea ice would be gone by 2015.[82]

On December 9, 2013, *The Guardian* ran an article titled "U.S. Navy Predicts Summer Ice Free Arctic by 2016," which detailed a U.S. Department of Energy finding that the Arctic would lose its summer ice as early as 2016. This would come, the agency asserted, about "84 years ahead of conventional model projections."[83]

On May 14, 2014, the *Washington Examiner* ran an article titled "French Foreign Minister: '500 Days to Avoid Climate Chaos,'" which quoted the French foreign minister Laurent Fabius as saying, "we have 500 days to avoid climate chaos."[84]

On October 7, 2018, the *New York Times* ran an article titled "Major Climate Report Describes a Strong Risk of Crisis as Early as 2040." It warned of worsening food shortages, wildfires, and destruction of coral reefs "well within the lifetime of much of the global population."[85]

That same day, the *Washington Post* ran an article titled "The World Has Just Over a Decade to Get Climate Change under Control, U.N. Scientists Say." According to the article, "The world stands on the brink of failure when it comes to holding global warming to moderate levels, and nations will need to take 'unprecedented' actions to cut their carbon emissions over the next decade."[86]

Part One: Summary

In the first part of this book, we contrasted the human propensity toward the negative with the generally improving state of the world. We noted that instead of an apocalypse that humanity has been expecting since the dawn of time, the world has seen great progress. We then outlined one of the persistent sources of concern about the present state of the world and the future of humanity: population growth that may, some people fear, lead to the exhaustion of resources, thus ending in a calamity for the planet and the species that inhabit it. As we explained, there are many reasons why that need not be the case. In the second part of this book, we will subject the concern over population growth and resource abundance to an empirical test. Using publicly available data, we will estimate growth in resource abundance at individual and population levels. As we'll show, resources have been getting more abundant relative to human labor for generations.

PART TWO

Measuring abundance: new methodology, empirical evidence, and in-depth analysis

CHAPTER 4

Introduction to the Simon Abundance Framework

Not understanding the process of a spontaneously ordered economy goes hand in hand with not understanding the creation of resources and wealth, and when a person does not understand the creation of resources and wealth, the only intellectual alternative is to believe that increasing wealth must be at the cost of someone else. This belief that our good fortune must be an exploitation of others may be the taproot of false prophecy about doom that our evil ways must bring upon us.

Julian Simon, *The Ultimate Resource 2* [1]

Chapter summary

In Part Two of this book, we will use empirical evidence to test Malthusian concerns about population growth. As we will demonstrate with data that span almost 170 years, resources and a plethora of goods and services have been growing progressively cheaper and more abundant rather than more expensive and therefore more scarce. Instead of the catastrophic shortages that Malthus and his disciples predicted, humanity is experiencing a period of unprecedented prosperity. That, we maintain, happened not in spite of population growth but in large part because of it.

Before doing so, however, we need to define what we mean by scarcity and abundance, as well as note the many different ways in which historical data will be examined. We call this process of data analysis the "ladder of information hierarchy." As we will explain, measuring the quantities of an item is an inferior approach compared with looking at the nominal or real prices of that item. That in turn is an inferior approach compared with looking at the time prices of various items.

Time price, we will argue, is the most useful figure, for it denotes the length of time that a person needs to work to earn enough money to be able to buy a particular thing. We will then explain the personal resource abundance multiplier, which denotes the increased quantity of items that an individual can buy for the same amount of labor at different points in time. The compound annual growth rate of personal resource abundance will show us the speed at which items—be they commodities, goods, or services—are becoming cheaper for individual buyers. That will then allow us to calculate the personal resource abundance doubling period, which is the amount of time required for a specific item to become twice as affordable for individual buyers.

We realize that this chapter breaks the narrative flow of the book somewhat. The readers who are not interested in the discussion in Chapter 4 may wish to skip it and refer to it retrospectively as needed.

Two levels of analysis: personal resource abundance and population resource abundance

The Simon Abundance Framework (SAF) measures and analyzes the relationship between the abundance of resources and population growth over time. The framework captures all the benefits of innovation. It transcends currency fluctuations, inflation measurement uncertainties, and purchasing parity adjustments. It enables us to see the true prices of all goods and services as expressed in the universal constant of time. The framework consists of two levels of analysis: personal resource abundance analysis and population resource abundance analysis.

In Chapter 4, we will introduce the personal resource abundance analysis methodology. In Chapter 5, we will use that methodology to estimate the growth in abundance of resources across a wide range of periods, resources, and countries and territories. It is vital to keep in mind that the two chapters will look at the abundance of resources from the perspective of an individual human being. The question that Chapters 4 and 5 answer is how much more abundant resources have become for an average inhabitant of the planet or a typical U.S. worker between two distinct points in time.

In Chapter 6, we will introduce the population resource abundance analysis, which estimates the rise in "total abundance" in the world in general and in the United States in particular. It is this population resource abundance analysis that allows us to quantify the relationship between the abundance of resources and population growth, a question that is central to the disagreement between Simon and Ehrlich and consequently at the heart of this book.

If the above explanations are still unclear, you can think about the SAF using the analogy of a pizza. Personal resource abundance measures the size of a slice of pizza per person. Population resource abundance measures the size of the entire pizza pie. (For a complete list of our concepts, abbreviations, and equations, see Appendix 1.)

Why should we measure abundance rather than scarcity?

British economist Lionel Robbins (1898–1984) once defined economics as a science that "studies human behaviour as a relationship between ends and scarce means which have alternative uses."[2] Scarcity is generally recognized by economists as a fundamental reality in the world. What is it? Simply put, people always want more than what is readily available. They want more money, more goods and services, more leisure time, and so on. Some needs, such as safety, food, warmth, and shelter, are basic to survival. Others are extraneous.

A rich person's definition of scarcity is different from a poor person's definition of scarcity. In other words, the former's definition (exemplified by not having a car for every adult in the family, for instance) is more expansive than the latter's definition of scarcity (not having one motorbike in the family). Moreover, every person's definition of scarcity is elastic. Burundian immigrants in Belgium, for example, will expand their understanding of scarcity in accordance with the expanded options that Belgium offers (a nice apartment and a university education for their children, for instance) and Burundi does not. Human wants, in other words, are infinite, which is why scarcity can never be fully eliminated.

Instead of focusing on scarcity, therefore, we propose to measure the changes in the standards of living by quantifying abundance.[3] Abundance reflects how much we have rather than how much we want to have. In our definition, abundance occurs when the nominal hourly income increases faster than the nominal price of a resource. This kind of analysis can be done at any two points in time, as long as both the nominal hourly wages and the nominal prices are known. The quantification of abundance, like the quantification of human progress in general, is essentially backward-looking then. It compares today with yesterday. If people today experience greater abundance than they experienced yesterday, humanity can be said to be better off. In the chapters to follow, we will show that abundance has risen, sometimes dramatically, across 18 resource data sets, dozens of nations, and almost 170 years of human history.

Focus on absolute rather than relative improvements in resource abundance

Before proceeding, we have to address a significant objection to the measurement of absolute increases in abundance. The theory of social comparison, which is also known as status anxiety and relative deprivation, asserts that what matters to many people is not an absolute improvement in their well-being (i.e., how much better off they are relative to their parents) but instead an improvement in their well-being relative to the people around them (i.e., how much better off they are relative to their peers). Human nature provides some evidence for this theory, but our genetic predisposition for thinking in relative terms should be kept in proper perspective.

To start with, not all human impulses are laudable. To think otherwise would be to commit the naturalistic fallacy—that is, to argue that if something is natural it must be good.[4] Also, the evidence from nature is far more subtle than is commonly understood. What matters to a person—let's call him "X"—is not whether he is outperformed in any random domain but whether he is outperformed in a domain that is important to him.

There are, in fact, two competing forces at play. X wants to be part of a successful group. Belonging to such a group during the time of evolutionary adaptation would have allowed for more successful hunts as well as greater protection from predators and enemies. In other words, X wants his peers to succeed, but there is a countervailing evolutionary pressure relating to one's relative position within a group. It is brought about by sexual selection. Group members who obtain a disproportionate share of healthy mates and resources have a better chance of passing their genes on to future generations.

X will consequently feel good if he can outperform his peers in a domain that's important to him. That will increase his chances of finding a mate. Conversely, he will feel bad if he is outperformed by his peers in a domain that's important to him. That will decrease his chances of finding a mate and perpetuating his line. In brief, the inclinations of modern-day people are a product of two distinct pressures—their ancestors' competition against strangers for survival, and compatititon against their peers for sex.

The most common resolution to the two competing forces is for X to admire his peers when they do well in the domains that are not very important to him and envy them when they outperform him in a domain that is important to him. If X's peers outperform him by a sufficient margin in all domains, X will lose much of his mating potential and status within the group and become envious and unhappy.[5]

The theory of social comparison, then, points to a real psychological phenomenon: income inequality will matter most to people whose status in a group is most closely tied to their income. That's surely true of some people but not of everyone. In fact, measuring the effect of income inequality on people's subjective well-being suggests that income inequality is not as much of a problem as it is sometimes assumed.[6]

In 2016, Mariah D. R. Evans and Jonathan Kelley from the University of Nevada, Reno, analyzed the effects of income inequality and on subjective well-being in 68 societies and over 200,000 individuals between 1981 and 2008. They found that "in developing nations, inequality is certainly not harmful but probably beneficial, increasing well-being by about 8 points out of 100." That's because "in the earliest stages of development some are able to move out of the (poorly paying) subsistence economy into the (better paying) modern economy; their higher pay increases their well-being while simultaneously increasing inequality. In advanced nations, income inequality on average neither helps nor harms." Only in ex-communist countries did an increase in income inequality reduce the subjective well-being of the older generation that grew up under communism, while increasing (or having no effect on) the subjective well-being of the succeeding generations.[7]

Let us now move beyond the theory of social comparison and look at some of the ways in which a focus on relative income inequality might be counterproductive in the real world. First, preoccupation with income inequality risks normalizing envy, a happiness-destroying emotion condemned by all the main religions and moral codes. There is nothing wrong with income inequality, provided that it was fairly arrived at. Most people understand, for example, that the wealth of Apple cofounder Steve Jobs was the result of the entrepreneur's vision and hard work. Jobs, in other words, did not steal his money. He earned it by creating value for others. The proper lesson to derive from his achievement ought to be inspiration, not envy.

Second, income inequality is in many ways the midwife of progress. People who break from the pack by developing an innovative, useful product such as an iPhone can become very rich, but by adopting the new product, the society profits as a whole and moves forward. The same is true of new modes of social cooperation, production processes, and the like. Put differently, progress would be impossible if society prevented people from trying out and benefiting from new things. Just consider what the world or the future of humanity would have looked like had the Luddites stopped the Industrial Revolution or the innovation of new drugs and sources of energy had been throttled by the precautionary principle (i.e., risk avoidance).

Let's make our consideration of Jobs's wealth and the social benefits resulting from his innovations more concrete. The Nobel Prize–winning economist William D. Nordhaus has concluded that "only a minuscule fraction of the social returns from technological advances over the 1948–2001 period was captured by producers, indicating that most of the benefits of technological change are passed on to consumers rather than captured by producers." Based on "data from the U.S. nonfarm business section," Nordhaus estimates that "innovators are able to capture about 2.2 percent of the total social surplus from innovation."[8]

When Jobs died, his net worth was $7 billion.[9] If Jobs's $7 billion represented 2.2 percent of the social value he created, then the other 97.8 percent of the social value that Jobs created and passed on to Apple consumers amounted to $311 billion.[10] Similarly, the total market value of Apple stood at $2.26 trillion at the beginning of 2021, implying a social benefit of over $100 trillion that was passed onto consumers of Apple products.[11] We can also look at the social value created by Apple from the sales and profits perspectives. In 2019, Apple's sales amounted to $260 billion, implying a social value of $11.5 trillion. That year, Apple's profits amounted to $55 billion, implying a social value of $2.45 trillion.[12]

Finally, focusing on income inequality rather than absolute improvements in the standards of living can be psychologically destructive, for there will always be people who have more money, more things, better health, higher intelligence, better looks, greater height and strength, and more charisma, among other things. "One secret of happiness," notes the economist Richard Layard in his book *Happiness: Lessons from a New Science*, "is to ignore comparisons with people who are more successful than you are: always compare downwards, not upwards."[13]

Layard's observation works not only in the present but also intertemporally.[14] Pretty much everyone who lived in the past had a quality of life that was inferior to the quality of life enjoyed by the vast majority of people in advanced societies today. In 1924, for example, the son of a U.S. president died of a bacterial infection in a blister on the third toe of his right foot. The blister had developed when Calvin Coolidge, Jr., was playing tennis one day on the White House lawn with his brother. "Many of the best doctors of the day were consulted, multiple diagnostic tests were run, and he was admitted to one of the top hospitals in the country," as Chelsea Follett has written, yet "he died within a week of infection. . . . Deaths from sepsis following the infection of a minor cut or blister were extremely common at the time, and no amount of wealth or power could save a patient."[15] Coolidge's son died just four years before Alexander Fleming discovered penicillin.

What this suggests is that people without historical perspective are at a massive disadvantage. Instead of being grateful for all the good things in their lives, they are resentful because of the things that they lack but others have. Acquisition of a historical perspective is not only prudent from a logical standpoint as the best way to measure progress; it is also conducive to happiness. People with a historical perspective can ponder ways in which they could have been worse off (such as having been born a peasant in 17th-century France) rather than ways in which they could be better off (sipping champagne with the glitterati during Paris Fashion Week). In subsequent chapters, we shall provide you with that historical perspective. You will be amazed by the progress that humanity has made in a relatively short time.

Not all types of measurement are the same: introducing the resource abundance information hierarchy

A key to knowledge is measurement, and measurement requires information. Information, however, can range from worthless to priceless. Consider your weekly trip to the grocery store. Scanning the shelves, you'll notice a massive quantity of loaves of bread. That's an example of close to worthless information, for what really matters to you as a shopper is not the quantity of bread but the price of bread. If the price of the cheapest loaf of bread is $1,000 and you are an ordinary American (or Briton or Motswana), you'll leave the shop empty-handed, so prices provide us more useful information than quantities do. Let's take this example a step further. Let's say that you are Bill Gates, whose net worth was in the neighborhood of $130 billion in 2022, and you find yourself really hungry for a sandwich. If the ridiculously high price of bread is paltry relative to your ridiculously high income, you'll leave the store with a loaf of bread after all. Prices relative to income, which we call time prices, provide more useful information, then, than nominal or even inflation-adjusted prices alone do. Scientific analysis can draw misleading conclusions if it is conducted with the wrong level of information. This section explains different levels of information hierarchy from the measurement of quantities at one end to the measurement of personal resource abundance at the other end.

Measuring quantity of resources is almost useless

The first level of measurement is to count things. Humans began to count using notches on sticks and bones, which later became hieroglyphs and symbols. Today's decimal system is the product of thousands of years of thinking and experimenting by Mesopotamians, Babylonians, Egyptians, Greeks, Romans, Indians, and Arabs. Quantity is the most basic or elementary level of measurement, and quantitative thinking is done with arithmetic and other forms of math. Much of engineering and natural science such as physics and chemistry can be conducted at this level of information. Quantity can generally be considered an objective fact that can provide sufficient knowledge to answer many but not all questions.

Although quantities are interesting and valuable, they can be problematic for a variety of reasons. First, in many cases, quantities are not directly observable. Consider commodities such as oil and gas. We really have no idea how much oil and gas we have because we do not have the know-how to measure the total supply of any given commodity on the planet in a cost-effective way.

Second, there is a large range of quality, grades, and concentration levels of commodities. There are, for example, three basic grades of crude oil. That makes the costs of discovery, extraction, and refinement of commodities highly subjective.

Third, because it is so expensive to perform surveys of commodity reserves, those surveys usually end up having little or no value. To give an example, after more than a century of the intensive use of fossil fuels, we have more known deposits today of oil and gas than ever before. To make matters more complicated, we have only surveyed a tiny portion of the planet, so consequently, the sample size of commodity surveys is minuscule.

Fourth, we often don't know where to look. Although survey technology is improving, the location of new deposits—the Tamar gas field off the coast of Israel discovered in 2009 comes to mind—can come as a welcome surprise.

Fifth, quantities do not account for substitutes and recycling. History suggests that many substitutes for current commodities and ways to recycle those commodities are yet to be discovered. The replacement of guano (seabird and bat manure) with synthetic fertilizer in the early 20th century is a good example.[16]

Sixth, we can't predict future discoveries of new deposits of commodities and improved extractive technologies that may increase the supply of commodities. Horizontal drilling and fracking are two newer technologies that have vastly increased oil and gas production, for example. Likewise, improvements in desalinization technologies have dramatically reduced the cost of obtaining freshwater in dry places like the Middle East.

Seventh, surveyors of commodities face asymmetrical costs. If they overestimate commodity reserves, companies lose money in a very visible way. If surveyors underestimate commodity reserves, exploration does not take place, and the cost to companies is invisible. If there is little or no personal cost to the surveyors associated with being wrong, then, the accuracy of their surveys may be biased.

Finally, the surveyors may also want to underestimate commodity reserves in order to increase their budgets and, consequently, their status. To conclude: although measuring quantities has some value, quantities only provide the most basic level of information. Fortunately, there are several other methods to measure the increase or decrease in the abundance of commodities.

Nominal and real prices provide more information about abundance of resources . . .

As previously noted, people generally do not consider how much of an item is in stock or inventory. It is the price of a loaf of bread that's important, not how many loaves of bread there are on the shelf of a grocery store. Like geology, natural science measures the quantity of commodities, but economic science measures the value of commodities as well as other things such as goods and services. Here we must leave the physical domain of quantities and enter the metaphysical domain of values. How do we measure the value of something? We do so by looking at the prices, which contain a denser level of information than quantities do. Before going further, we must pause and define wealth and capital.

Wealth is anything that people value. Wealth can be health, love, beauty, happiness, and many other things. Money can also be wealth because money allows us to store wealth and buy many of the things that we value such as better health or a trip to Hawaii. Capital is anything that can be used to create wealth. There are different types of capital: physical capital (roads and bridges), human capital (creativity and conscientiousness), intellectual capital (knowledge and skills), financial capital (retail and investment banking), cultural capital (social mobility), and social capital (trust and cooperation). Capital is continuously created and depleted. Prices guide the wealth creation process by valuing all sorts of capital.

Let's look at a concrete example. When oil goes up in price, we can deduce from that increase that the demand for oil has risen relative to the supply of oil. We can further deduce that additional profit can be made through finding an additional supply of oil. Attracted by the potential to make a profit, capital of all kinds (financial, physical, human, intellectual) flows toward new exploration and oil production. New wealth in the form of additional oil is then created, so oil, all other things being equal, declines in price. Capital then moves on in search of other potentially profitable ventures. Prices, in other words, distinguish between a thing and the value that the thing has for those who hold it. Quantities tell us what there is, but prices tell us what to do about what there is, such as create more of it (or not).

Prices are expressed in some type of currency, be it dollars and cents or pounds and pennies. Prices can be converted to different currencies using rates of exchange. Furthermore, prices can be nominal or real. Nominal prices are what the customers see in the grocery store or at the gas station. The value of fiat money (paper money made legal tender by a government decree) tends to decline every year due to inflation, so it is possible for a commodity to "seem" more expensive even though its "real" price has declined or remained the same. If the price of bread, for example, increases by 2 percent but the overall inflation rate (including that of wages) is 3 percent, bread in real terms will be cheaper in spite of its higher nominal price. Real prices, therefore, are nominal prices that have been adjusted for inflation using a deflator such as the gross domestic product (GDP) deflator or the Consumer Price Index (CPI). But where do prices come from?

In a free economy, nobody sets prices. They emerge spontaneously through the revealed preferences of individual buyers and sellers. Every time you buy a cup of coffee on the way to work, for example, you incrementally increase the price of coffee beans. Every time you fail to buy your usual morning cup of coffee, you decrease the price of coffee beans by a tiny amount. If everyone stopped buying coffee, the price of coffee beans would collapse. The movement of prices informs both producers and owners of capital about the goods and services that ought to be produced (cars and smartphones) and goods and services that ought to be discontinued (horse-drawn carriages and the telegraph).

So the market is a mechanism (or, really, a process) for the gathering and exchange of information. Individual decisions made by billions of buyers and sellers generate useful knowledge that ensures the relatively smooth functioning of an economy (no permanent shortages of desired goods or permanent stockpiles of undesired goods) and the continued generation of wealth. The situation is quite different in a planned economy, where prices are set by bureaucrats and bureaucracies. Without the market, bureaucrats have to guess future supply and demand for goods and services. More often than not, they guess wrong. Instead of generating wealth in a sustained fashion, they often destroy it or at least prevent it from being created. That's why market economies are, without exception, richer than planned ones over the long run.

The market is much more than a reflection of the current state of supply and demand. It is also a real-time betting mechanism on the future abundance of goods and services. By betting on the American entrepreneur Jeff Bezos and investing in Amazon, for example, people are expressing their opinions about the future of online sales. Others bet on the future of national currencies and even the price of commodities. A decline in price, therefore, also indicates goods and services that people expect to become more plentiful. Conversely, an increase in price can also indicate what goods and services people expect to become more scarce in the future.

In every transaction there is one price, but two values. Buyers value the things they buy more than the price they pay. Sellers value the things they sell less than the price they receive. Buyers have a value range and will pay no more than the maximum value they ascribe to the purchase. Sellers have a value range as well. They will accept no less than the minimum value they ascribe to the things they sell. When the value ranges of buyers and sellers overlap, a price can be discovered and exchange can take place. If the ranges do not overlap, the transaction does not occur.

Competition ensures that prices reflect the best judgment (or knowledge) of all traders at that point in time. If the price is too low, sellers seek other buyers. If the price is too high, buyers seek other sellers. Note that values are usually not explicit. Traders' preferences are revealed, but precise values are usually not revealed. All that we can conclude after a transaction takes place is that value has been created, at least as far as the perception of both parties goes. In an unfree economy, bureaucrats mandate prices of goods and services. If those prices fall outside the common value range of buyers and sellers, transactions don't take place (unless forced), and wealth creation is harmed.

. . . but time prices are superior to both nominal and real prices

Time is essential because it is the scarcest commodity of all. Everyone, rich and poor alike, dies in the end. The more time we spend at work, the less time we have for other pursuits such as leisure or time spent with our loved ones. Adam Smith understood that well. As the founder of economics put in his 1776 work *An Inquiry into the Nature and Causes of the Wealth of Nations*, "The real price of everything is the toil and trouble of acquiring it. . . . What is bought with money . . . is purchased by labour."[17] Moreover, time is constant. Unlike fiat money or consumer goods, it does not depreciate in value. As George Gilder wrote,

> The International System of Units (SI) . . . has established seven key metrics, each founded on a constant of physics: the second of time, the meter of length, the kilogram of weight, the degree Kelvin of thermodynamic temperature, the ampere of electrical current, the mole of molecular mass, and the candela of luminosity. . . . The SI regime confirms that fundamental to all immutable standards of measure is time. All seven key units rely on physical constants, frequencies, and wavelengths that are bounded in one way or another by the passage of time. As the only irreversible element in the universe, with directionality imparted by thermodynamic entropy, time is the ultimate frame of reference for all measured values.[18]

Wealth and changes in wealth, then, should be measured in time, not money.[19] Time price (TP) denotes the amount of time that a buyer needs to work in order to earn enough money to be able to buy something. That is the relevant price from the individual's vantage point. While money prices are the same for everybody, TP can differ considerably across persons. The $3 gallon of gasoline, for example, is five times more expensive for someone making $10 an hour than someone making $50 an hour.

TP can decline in several ways. First, money prices can go down. Nominal price can decrease if a company reduces the price of a product from one day to the next in order, for example, to boost the sluggish sales of a product. Real price can decline when nominal price increases at a slower pace than inflation. So if the nominal price of bread increases by 2 percent from one year to the next but overall inflation (including that of wages) runs at 3 percent over the same period, bread actually becomes cheaper. Second, people's incomes can increase. Thankfully, incomes tend to rise at a faster rate than inflation because humanity tends to become more productive over time. That's true of our species as a whole (we are more productive than our Stone-Age ancestors), and it's true for individuals in their prime working age (up to a certain point, people tend to become more productive with age).

Unlike money prices, which are measured in dollars and cents, TPs are measured in hours and minutes. The easiest way to calculate TP is to divide the nominal price by the nominal hourly income. If an item costs you $1 and you earn $10 per hour, then that item will cost you 6 minutes of work. If the price of the same item increases to $1.10 and your hourly income increases to $12, then that item will only cost you 5 minutes and 24 seconds of work. The most important thing to remember is that as long as hourly income is increasing faster than the money price, the TP will decrease.[20] The relevant equation here is as follows:

$$TP = Nominal\ Money\ Price \div Nominal\ Hourly\ Income$$

There are a number of advantages to using TPs when evaluating scarcity and abundance. First, innovation (or productivity gains) shows up in many places including lower prices and higher incomes. To capture the full impact of innovation, therefore, we must look at changes in both money prices and incomes. To look at just money prices only tells half the story. TPs make it easier to see the whole picture. Second, TPs transcend all of the complications associated with subjective and disputed inflation adjustments such as the CPI.[21] TPs use the nominal price and nominal income at each point in time. No inflation adjustments are necessary. Third, analysts can use a variety of hourly income rates (hourly wages, hourly compensation that includes nonwage benefits, and others) to calculate the TP. Fourth, TPs can be calculated using any currency and any point in time. Fifth, income and prices are converted to time, which is objective and universal.

Once you know the time price, you can then calculate the percentage change in time price (PCTP) between two points in time

The percentage change in time price (PCTP) over time provides more valuable information than individual TPs can provide. The TP is like a picture. It provides a snapshot of people's standard of living at any given point in time.

The PCTP is like a movie. It allows us to observe long-term patterns in the availability of goods and services.

To calculate the PCTP, we start by selecting a time period to analyze. We then calculate TPs for the start-year of the analyzed period and the end-year of the analyzed period. The time price divisor (TPD) denotes the TP at the end of the analyzed period divided by the TP at the beginning of the analyzed period. The relevant equation here is as follows:

$$\text{TPD} = \text{TP}_{\text{end-year}} \div \text{TP}_{\text{start-year}}$$

Consider, for example, the price of bananas. In 1995, the average nominal U.S. price of bananas was $0.45 per pound.[22] The average nominal compensation rate of the U.S. blue-collar worker was $16.66 per hour.[23] The TP of a pound of bananas in 1995, then, was 0.027 hours, or 1 minute 37 seconds of work. In 2018, bananas cost $0.58 a pound and such workers earned $32.06 per hour, making the 2018 TP of a pound of bananas 0.018 hours, or 1 minute and 5 seconds. The time price divisor would thus amount to 0.018 divided by 0.027, or 0.667.

But what does that mean for practical purposes? That's where the percentage change in time price (PCTP) comes in. PCTP can be calculated as

$$\text{PCTP} = \left(\text{TP}_{\text{end-year}} - \text{TP}_{\text{start-year}}\right) \div \text{TP}_{\text{start-year}}$$

That can be simplified to

$$\text{PCTP} = \left(\text{TP}_{\text{end-year}} \div \text{TP}_{\text{start-year}}\right) - 1$$

That can be simplified even further to

$$\text{PCTP} = \text{TPD} - 1$$

In terms of our banana example, the PCTP would equal $0.667 - 1$, or -0.333. As such, we can say that the TP of bananas fell by 33.3 percent between 1995 and 2018. Note that the decline in the TP over time is not the same as an increase in abundance over time. To see how a decline in TPs translates into the growth in abundance, we have to turn to the personal resource abundance multiplier.

Personal resource abundance multiplier (pRAM) tells you how much more of a resource you can get for the same amount of labor between two points in time

The personal resource abundance multiplier (pRAM) is a vital step on our ladder of resource abundance information hierarchy. The pRAM is the ratio of the time it took to work to earn enough money to buy something at the start of the analyzed period divided by the time it took to work to earn enough money to buy something at the end of the analyzed period. The pRAM tells us how much more or less of an item we can buy with the same amount of labor. The relevant calculation here is as follows:

$$pRAM = TP_{\text{start-year}} \div TP_{\text{end-year}},$$

Let's return to bananas. Given that the TP of a pound of bananas fell from 0.027 hours of work in 1995 to 0.018 hours of work in 2018, the pRAM will equal 1.5. That means that our blue-collar worker was able to buy 50 percent more bananas in 2018 than he or she was able to buy for the same amount of labor in 1995. Keep in mind that as long as the pRAM is greater than 1, the abundance of bananas is increasing. Now, consider the opposite scenario. If the TP of a pound of bananas rose from 0.018 hours of work to 0.027 hours of work, then the pRAM would equal 0.667. Being less than 1, the abundance of bananas would decrease. Our blue-collar worker would be able to buy only three-fifths of the bananas in 2018 that he or she was able to buy for the same amount of labor in 1995.

It is crucial to note that the relationship between the percentage change in TPs and the pRAM is geometric, not linear. If the TP of bananas increases by 99 percent, one hour of work will only get you 50.3 percent as many bananas as before. If the price of bananas falls by 99 percent, one hour of work will get you 9,900 percent (or 100 times) as many bananas as before. It can

Table 4.1. Changes in TP, pRAM, and pRA

Percentage change in time price (%)	Personal resource abundance multiplier	Percentage change in personal resource abundance (%)
0	1.00	0
−5	1.05	5
−10	1.11	11
−15	1.18	18
−20	1.25	25
−25	1.33	33
−30	1.43	43
−35	1.54	54
−40	1.67	67
−45	1.82	82
−50	2.00	100
−55	2.22	122
−60	2.50	150
−65	2.86	186
−70	3.33	233
−75	4.00	300
−80	5.00	400
−85	6.67	567
−90	10.00	900
−95	20.00	1,900
−99	100.00	9,900
−99.9	1,000.00	99,900

Source: Authors' calculations.

Note: TP = time price; pRAM = personal resource abundance multiplier; pRA = personal resource abundance.

be difficult to grasp what a negative percentage change in the TP means, so please take a look at Table 4.1 and Figures 4.1 and 4.2. As you'll be able to see, a 50 percent decline in the TP allows you to purchase two items for the former price of one. A 75 percent decline allows you to purchase four items,

Figure 4.1. Percentage decreases in Time Price (TP, from 0 to –75 percent) and percentage changes in Personal Resource Abundance Multiplier (pRAM)

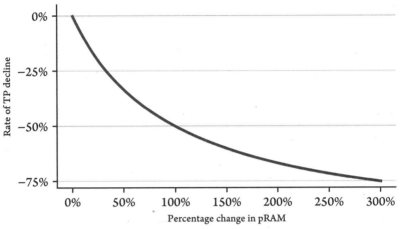

Source: Authors' calculations.

a 90 percent decline will get you 10 items, and a 95 percent decline will get you 20 items. A 5 percentage point decrease from 90 percent to 95 percent, in other words, enhances your gains by 100 percent.

Percentage change in personal resource abundance (pRA) tells you how much better off you have become between two points in time

Once we have the pRAM, we can then proceed to calculate the percentage change in personal resource abundance (pRA) over time. The pRAM functions like an index. Indexes, by definition, have a start, or base, year and a start, or base, value. In the case of the pRAM, our start or base value is always 1. The percentage change in pRA over time can thus be calculated as the pRAM minus 1. The relevant calculation here is as follows:

$$\text{Percentage change in pRA} = \text{pRAM} - 1$$

Let's go back to bananas. If the TP of a pound of bananas in 1995 came to 0.027 hours and the TP of a pound of bananas in 2018 came to 0.018 hours, then the pRAM will equal 1.5. The percentage change in pRA over time can thus be calculated as 1.5 – 1, which equals 0.50 or 50 percent. As such, we

Figure 4.2. Percentage decreases in Time Price (TP, from 0 to −99 percent) and percentage changes in Personal Resource Abundance Multiplier (pRAM)

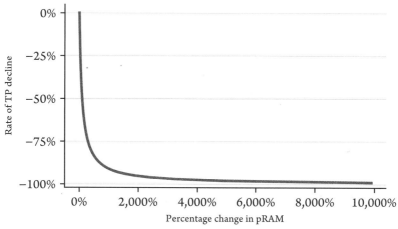

Source: Authors' calculations.

can say that bananas got 50 percent more abundant. Conversely, if the time required to buy a pound of bananas rose from 0.018 hours to 0.027 hours between 1995 and 2018, then the percentage change in pRA over time will equal 0.667 − 1. As such, we can say that bananas became 33 percent less abundant.

Compound annual growth rate of personal resource abundance (CAGR-pRA) tells you the rate of improvement between two points in time

Once we have obtained the pRAM values, we can then calculate the compound annual growth rate of personal resource abundance (CAGR-pRA). The CAGR-pRA represents another step on our ladder of resource abundance information hierarchy because it allows us to calculate the speed at which pRA is changing. The higher the CAGR-pRA is, the quicker an item increases in affordability. The lower the CAGR-pRA is, the slower an item increases in affordability. The relevant equation here is as follows:

$$CAGR - pRA = pRAM^{1/years} - 1$$

Let's return to our banana example. The pRAM for bananas between 1995 and 2018 came to 1.5. That means that the CAGR-pRA equals 0.0107, or 1.07 percent. In other words, the pRA of bananas increased at a rate of 1.07 percent per year. If the CAGR-pRA equaled 3 percent, the pRA of bananas would increase at 3 percent per year. If the CAGR-pRA equaled zero, the pRA of bananas would not change.

Years to double personal resource abundance (YD-pRA) tells you the length of time required for a resource to become twice as abundant

The next step on our ladder of resource abundance information hierarchy is the doubling period. As the name suggests, the doubling period refers to the number of years required for an item to become twice as abundant. To calculate the doubling period, we use the NPER (or "number of periods") function in Excel. This function is based on the equation $(\text{Log}(2) - \text{Log}(1)) \div \text{Log}(1 + \text{CAGR})$. This equation is approximately equal to $70 \div \text{CAGR}$ (commonly known as the rule of 70s). In our banana example, the CAGR-pRA for bananas between 1980 and 2018 came to 1.07 percent. The NPER function indicates that at a CAGR rate of 1.07 percent, bananas will take 65.4 years to double in pRA. If CAGR-pRA were to double to 2.14, the doubling period would fall to 32.7 years. If CAGR-pRA were to fall by half to 0.535, then the doubling period would increase to 131 years.

You need hourly incomes to calculate time prices

In the previous section, we climbed up the ladder of resource abundance information hierarchy from the measurement of quantities at one end to the doubling period at the other end. It is our contention that the value of information increases the further up the ladder of resource abundance information hierarchy we go. Quantities, as we have seen, don't tell us much about abundance. Even money prices, while more informative than quantities, are actually relatively useless unless incomes are taken into account. That is why we believe that abundance should be measured in terms of the TP, the pRAM, pRA, the CAGR-pRA, and the doubling periods. In order to calculate the

TP, the pRAM, pRA, the CAGR-pRA, and years to double, we need to know how much people make per hour of labor. It is that hourly income that allows us to convert money prices from dollars and cents into TPs measured in hours and minutes of labor, or, as the TP equation goes,

$$TP = \text{Nominal Money Price} \div \text{Nominal Hourly Income}$$

The hourly income data come in many varieties. They differ between countries (a typical American makes much more than does a typical Albanian, for instance) and within countries (a typical skilled worker in the United States makes much more than does a typical unskilled worker in the United States). Let us then look at the income measures that we will be using in the next chapter in order to ascertain the level of abundance. As you'll see, most income measures are imperfect, and you should be aware of the pros and cons of each one of them. That said, note the most salient thing: as a general rule, people's hourly incomes have been going up because people are gradually becoming more productive. That's true of people over time and across nations. *Homo erectus* and the Neanderthal were poor because they were relatively unproductive. Instead of using stone axes, today's humans use computers. That makes *Homo sapiens* more productive and our labor more valuable. Of course, productivity differs across the globe. A typical Burundian, for example, has less education and less access to modern technology than a typical Belgian. That's partly why hourly income in Belgium is much higher than what it is in Burundi.

Calculating the average global nominal GDP per hour worked

Our first task in Chapter 5 will be to ascertain abundance at a global level. To do that, we have to come up with an acceptable measure of average nominal hourly income. Unfortunately, the global hourly wage or compensation, which would be ideal for our purposes, is impossible to calculate. Different economies are composed of different mixes of unskilled (and usually low-income) workers and skilled (and usually better paid) workers. In some countries and territories, such as those in sub-Saharan Africa, most people work for themselves and do not report their earnings to anyone. In other regions of the world like Western Europe and North America, our sense of how much people earn is much better. Still, cross-country comparisons in advanced economies are complicated by the differing extent of nonwage compensation, which can include relocation assistance, medical and prescription coverage, vision and dental coverage, health and dependent care flexible spending accounts, retirement benefit plans, group-term life and long-term care insurance plans, legal and adoption assistance plans, child care and transportation benefits, vacation and sick paid time off, and employee discount programs from a variety of vendors, and so on.

As such, it is the accepted practice among economists to use the GDP as the best approximation of global income. This measure has its advantages because it includes income from such sources as wages, benefits, rents, dividends, and profits. Conversely, it has its disadvantages, for it excludes underground economic activity such as black market commerce, household production, volunteerism, and childcare. Moreover, contrary to a long-held view, it would appear that labor's share of the GDP (national income that goes toward worker compensation) is not as constant as was previously thought and may have declined somewhat in recent decades. That said, the GDP figures are the best global figures that we have.

To calculate the average global nominal GDP per hour worked, our methodology requires a measure of the nominal GDP, which is supplied by the World Bank for the period from 1960 to 2019, and a measure of hours worked, which is supplied by the Conference Board, an American nonprofit business membership and research group, for the period from 1950 to 2019.[24]

The work hour adjustment of nominal GDP is necessary because the average number of hours worked per worker is not constant. In general, work hours increase when a country or territory moves from being a preindustrial economy to peak industrialization. Attracted by rising wages, workers put in more hours. Once a certain level of economic development and resulting personal income is reached, people start prioritizing other things including leisure and time with family. The average number of hours worked per worker in South Korea, for example, rose from 2,109 in 1950 to a peak of 2,791 in 1982 before dropping to 2,088 in 2017.[25] South Korea's GDP per

Figure 4.3. The average global nominal GDP per hour worked in 28 countries (1960–2018)

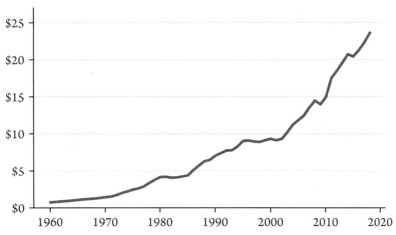

Source: Authors' calculations based on "World Bank, GDP (Current US$)," World Bank (online data set), accessed February 27, 2021; "Total Hours Worked," Conference Board (online data set), accessed February 27, 2021.

person stood at $1,269 in 1950, $6,771 in 1982, and $39,964 in 2017 (figures are in 2018 U.S. dollars).[26]

To get our average global nominal GDP per hour worked, then, we added up nominal GDPs of all countries and territories for which hours worked data were also available. We then divided that nominal GDP total by the total number of hours worked in those same countries and territories. This gave us the average global nominal GDP per hour worked.

In Chapter 5, we will look at global abundance over two periods, 1960–2018 and 1980–2018. Why two periods? Because of data limitations. For the period between 1960 and 2018, we were able to obtain the nominal GDP and hours worked data for 28 countries and territories. Together, these 28 countries and territories accounted for 75 percent of global output. According to our calculations, the average global nominal GDP per hour worked in the above-mentioned 28 countries and territories rose from $0.77 in 1960 to $23.65 in 2018 (Figure 4.3).[27] For more, see Appendix 2.

For the period between 1980 and 2018, we were able to obtain nominal GDP and hours worked data for 42 countries and territories. Together, these 42 countries and territories accounted for 85 percent of global output. According to our calculations, the nominal GDP per hour worked in the

Figure 4.4. The average global nominal GDP per hour worked in 42 countries (1980–2018)

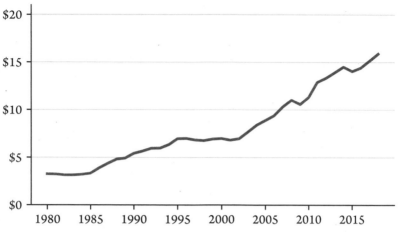

Source: Authors' calculations based on "World Bank, GDP (Current US$)," World Bank (online data set), accessed February 27, 2021; "Total Hours Worked," Conference Board (online data set), accessed February 27, 2021.

abovementioned 42 countries and territories rose from $3.24 in 1980 to $15.88 in 2018 (Figure 4.4).[28] For more, see Appendix 3.

Where does the average nominal U.S. hourly income come from?

After we have estimated abundance at a global level, we will then look at abundance in the United States. We will focus on the United States primarily because of our familiarity with the relevant data, but also because including additional countries in our country and territory analysis would increase the length of this book considerably. Other scholars are encouraged to use our methodology to estimate abundance in their respective countries. University of Illinois at Chicago economist Lawrence H. Officer and Miami University economist Samuel H. Williamson have produced a database of nominal wages in the United States between 1774 and 2018.[29] The database, which is located at https://www.measuringworth.com, is widely recognized and respected as one of the most comprehensive and authoritative sources for historical wage data. The Officer-Williamson data are estimated in nominal rather than inflation-adjusted dollars. As such, we can use the Officer-Williamson data directly without having to "reflate" them using imperfect deflators.

Figure 4.5. The average nominal U.S. hourly wage of unskilled workers and compensation rate of blue-collar workers (1900–2020)

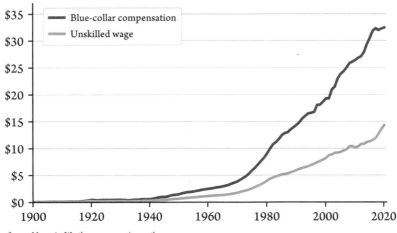

Source: MeasuringWorth, www.measuringworth.com.

In particular, we will be using nominal hourly wages of unskilled workers and nominal hourly compensation rates of production or blue-collar workers between 1850 and 2018.[30] As will become apparent in Chapter 5, we were able to obtain prices of 40 commodities going back to 1900 and 26 commodities going back to 1850. Combining those resource prices with the Officer-Williamson wage data will give us a good sense of rising abundance in the United States over the past 168 years.

We note that nominal blue-collar compensation rates have increased at a faster rate than did the nominal wages of unskilled workers. That's due to a number of factors. Blue-collar workers, for example, have enjoyed a greater increase in nonwage benefits such as medical insurance and retirement programs. Moreover, better education and access to more sophisticated technology have made blue-collar workers more productive and therefore more valuable. Some readers might object that blue-collar compensation rates are not the same as blue-collar take home pay. That criticism, we believe, is unwarranted. Nonwage compensation of blue-collar workers costs the employer real money and provides real benefits to workers. Most employees also prefer nonwage benefits because they are excluded from taxation or otherwise advantaged by the tax code (Figure 4.5).[31]

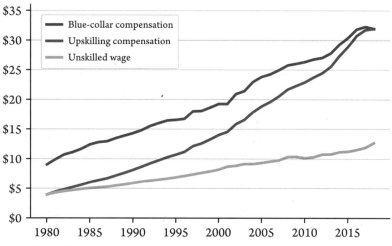

Figure 4.6. The average nominal U.S. hourly income rates (1980–2018)

Sources: MeasuringWorth, www.measuringworth.com; authors' calculations.

Finally, we will use the nominal wages of unskilled workers and nominal compensation rates of blue-collar workers to produce a third kind of nominal hourly income. That will be the nominal hourly compensation rate of upskilling workers. Upskilling workers are workers who started their working lives as unskilled workers but moved up to the blue-collar category through the acquisition of additional skills. A substantial proportion of workers make that jump over the course of their working lives, but given that working life is limited in duration, we will only employ this third kind of nominal hourly income when estimating abundance in the United States between 1980 and 2018 (Figure 4.6).[32] For more, see Appendix 4.

The difference between the mean and the median incomes is irrelevant to our analysis

When calculating pRA in Chapter 5, we will use mean or average incomes as our denominators. We are, of course, aware that average incomes and median incomes differ from each other. An average income is obtained by dividing the total aggregate income of a group such as a nation by the number of units in that group. Median income, by contrast, is the amount that divides

Figure 4.7. Rate of change in the U.S. average and median incomes, indexed to 100 in 1973 (1973–2018)

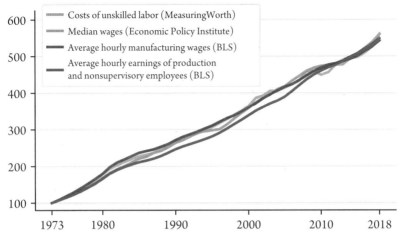

Sources: Jeremy Horpedahl; MeasuringWorth, www.measuringworth.com; Economic Policy Institute; and Bureau of Labor Statistics.
Note: BLS = Bureau of Labor Statistics.

the income distribution in a group into two equal halves with one half earning an income above the median and one half earning an income below the median. Moreover, we recognize that median income is more "telling," or precise, as far as income distribution in a group is concerned. Average income estimates are generally much more common, though, because they are easier to calculate.

Note that the difference between the two measurements is largely irrelevant to our findings as long as the rate of change in average and median incomes is similar.[33] That, fortunately, appears to be the case. University of Central Arkansas economist Jeremy Horpedahl compared U.S. median wages as published by the Economic Policy Institute in Washington, DC, U.S. unskilled labor wage rate as published by MeasuringWorth (https://www.measuringworth.com), average hourly U.S. manufacturing wages, and average hourly earnings of U.S. production and nonsupervisory employees as published by the U.S. Bureau of Labor Statistics (BLS).[34] Horpedahl indexed these four rates to 100, with a base year of 1973. As can be seen in Figure 4.7, the rate of change is almost identical.

Note that the similarity in the rate of change between the four income rates does not imply equality of incomes. Obviously, a 50 percent appreciation in an unskilled wage rate of $5 per hour will be less than a 50 percent appreciation in a $10 compensation rate of a blue-collar worker.

Do we account for global income inequality?

Speaking of equality, note that we do not adjust our average global nominal GDP per hour by measures of global income inequality, nor do we adjust our average nominal U.S. hourly income by measures of U.S. income inequality. That said, it is worth remembering that our estimates of abundance will deal with basic commodities (chicken, corn, oranges, lumber), not yachts or Lamborghinis. The poor benefit most when basic commodities, including food, fall in price. As Gregory Clark noted in *A Farewell to Alms*, "the biggest beneficiary of the Industrial Revolution has so far been the unskilled. There have been benefits aplenty for the typically wealthy owners of land or capital and for the educated. But industrialized economies saved their best gifts for the poorest."[35] Other eminent historians concur.[36]

In fact, it is very likely that our findings underestimate the growth in abundance, especially over recent decades. Why? The most commonly used measure of inequality is the Gini coefficient. Italian statistician and sociologist Corrado Gini (1884–1965) developed a method to measure income inequality at the start of the 20th century. It is based on the work of the American economist Max Lorenz (1876–1959), who developed what came to be known as the Lorenz curve. The Lorenz curve can be plotted using the cumulative share of people on the horizontal axis and the cumulative share of income on the vertical axis. A 45-degree line across the chart would indicate perfect equality (a state of affairs where everyone has the same income). The Lorenz curve illustrates the income distribution as it tends to exist in the real world. The area above the Lorenz curve but below the 45-degree line is denoted as area A. The area below the Lorenz curve but above the horizontal axis is denoted as area B. The Gini coefficient, then, represents the ratio of A area to the A plus B area (Figure 4.8).

A former lead economist in the World Bank's research department and recognized authority on measures of income inequality, Branko Milanovic, found that income inequality has declined substantially since 1980. He compared Gini coefficients between countries on a population-weighted basis

Figure 4.8. The Lorenz curve and the Gini coefficient

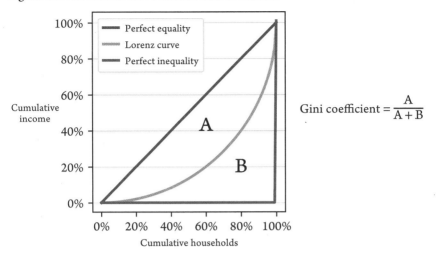

$$\text{Gini coefficient} = \frac{A}{A+B}$$

and calculated that the global Gini coefficient had declined by 26.2 percent from 0.61 in 1980 to 0.45 in 2017 (Figure 4.9).[37] This decline in global income inequality occurred while the global abundance increased (see Chapter 5). Logically, therefore, our estimates of abundance must underestimate the benefits that accrued to the poorest people on the planet, at least for the period between 1980 and 2018.

Instead of income inequality, consider time inequality

Perhaps a better way to think about inequality is by looking at time. While everyone has 24 hours in a day, what you do with your time can be dramatically different. According to our calculations, the global abundance of rice and wheat increased by a factor of 7.32 and 8.06, respectively, between 1960 and 2018. What does that mean for inequality?

Consider Raj in India and Ray in Indiana. In 1960, Raj spent seven hours a day earning the money he needed to buy rice for his meals. By 2018, TP of rice had fallen 86.2 percent. Now Raj's grandson works only 58 minutes to buy his rice. Raj's grandson has six hours and two minutes to do something

Figure 4.9. Global inter-country inequality/Global Gini coefficient, population-weighted GDPs per capita (1952–2017)

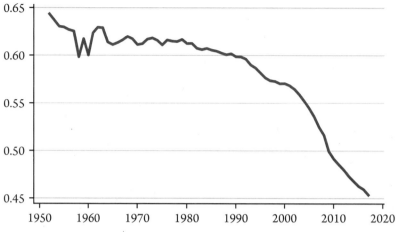

Source: Branko Milanovic, personal communication with coauthor (Marian L. Tupy), July 12, 2019.

else. In 1960, Ray spent one hour a day earning enough money to buy wheat for his meals. By 2018, TP of wheat had fallen 87.5 percent. Now Ray's grandson works only seven and a half minutes to buy his wheat. Ray's grandson has 52.5 minutes now to do something else such as working to buy other goods, going to school, or just relaxing.

Both Raj and Ray are better off, but has inequality increased? That depends on your perspective. In 1960, Raj worked 7 times as long as Ray to buy his food. By 2018, Raj's grandson worked 7.73 times as long as Ray's grandson. From that perspective, it looks as though inequality has increased, but let's look at Raj's and Ray's situations from a different perspective. Between 1960 and 2018, Ray's grandson gained 52.5 minutes of time, but Raj's grandson gained 362 minutes of time. Put differently, Raj's grandson gained 6.9 times more time than Ray's grandson. Time inequality between the two has declined dramatically (Table 4.2).

When basic things get more abundant, it's the poor who benefit the most. This fact is not captured in Gini coefficients. As such, comparing the impact of changes in TPs over time on different groups of people may be much more informative than using Gini coefficients.

Table 4.2. Raj's and Ray's time inequality (1960–2018)

	Minutes to earn daily food			
	1960	2018	Percentage change	Time savings
Raj's rice	420.0	58.0	−86.2	362.0
Ray's wheat	60.0	7.5	−87.5	52.5
Ratio	7.00	7.73	10.5	6.9

Source: Authors' calculations.

Finally, a few words about our commodity price data sources

To calculate abundance in Chapter 5, we will also need nominal commodity prices. When looking at global abundance, we will use two data sets. The first data set, which is called the Basic 50, contains nominal price data for 50 commodities between 1980 and 2018. Nominal price data for 43 commodities in the Basic 50 data set come from the World Bank and 7 come from the International Monetary Fund's Primary Commodity Prices database.[38] The second data set, which is called the World Bank 37, comes solely from the World Bank and covers the period between 1960 and 2018. Ideally, we would have had nominal prices of all 50 commodities going back to 1960. Unfortunately, not all nominal prices were available for that long a period, hence the two data sets.[39] For more, see Appendix 5.

When looking at abundance in the United States, we will use data from economist David S. Jacks at Simon Fraser University in British Columbia.[40] Jacks collected prices of 40 commodities from a variety of sources going back to 1900 and prices of 26 commodities going back to 1850. To suit his research purposes, Jacks adjusted his prices for inflation using the CPI provided by Lawrence H. Officer from MeasuringWorth (https://www.measuringworth.com). We converted Jacks's inflation-adjusted prices back to nominal prices using Officer's CPI. We did that because our methodology requires nominal rather than real prices. We did not make any other adjustments to Jacks's price data.[41]

Finally, a note on the veracity of commodity prices. Earlier in this chapter, we explained that within the context of a free economy, that is, when buyers and sellers are free to conduct trades, prices of goods and services will reflect supply and demand for those goods and services. It has to be remembered that a free economy is an ideal that's seldom adhered to nationally or internationally. Government policies impact prices in a myriad of ways such as through currency inflation, bailouts, tariffs, subsidies, regulations, and corporate taxes.

Consider gold and silver. In addition to their commercial uses—serving as conductors of electricity in switches and cell phones—gold and silver are also stores of value or assets that can be saved, retrieved, and exchanged at a later time. Historically, people in all income groups used gold and silver to hide their wealth from rapacious government officials and in times of war. More recently, both metals rose in price during the inflationary 1970s when many of the world's most widely used currencies, including the U.S. dollar, were rapidly losing their value because of monetary mismanagement. They spiked again after the outbreak of the Great Recession and the subsequent uncertainty about the soundness of the financial system.[42]

Or consider oil. For many decades, the oil market was partly shielded from competitive forces by the Organization of Petroleum Exporting Countries (OPEC), a cartel of oil-producing countries. OPEC nations frequently colluded to restrict the production of oil in order to keep its price artificially high. The extent to which OPEC was able to achieve its goal in the past is subject to much debate, but many experts have come to believe that OPEC's ability to affect the future price of oil is in decline.[43]

Similar observations could be made about the prices of other commodities, including sugar and corn, which are often artificially inflated by tariffs and subsidies. Global commodity prices, then, reflect all kinds of distortions, both at a national level (tariffs and subsidies) and at a global level (conflicts and embargoes). That being said, global commodity price data that are contained in our data sets are the best data that we have.

CHAPTER 5

Personal resource abundance: empirical evidence and analysis

There are many numbers and diagrams in the text. Bear with me, please, the arguments depend on them. If my conclusions were not backed with hard data as proof, some would be laughed away because they violate common sense, and others would be rejected instantly because they starkly contradict the main body of popular writings about population and resources.

Julian Simon, *The Ultimate Resource 2*[1]

Chapter summary

In this chapter, we will use our methodology to estimate the growth in personal resource abundance for a wide variety of basic commodities, food items, finished goods, cosmetic procedures, and a host of individual products. Some of our data go back to 1850. We will begin by analyzing basic commodities, using three comprehensive commodity data sets.

First, we will look at 50 basic commodities—including energy, food, materials, minerals, and metals—that were tracked by the World Bank and the International Monetary Fund (IMF) between 1980 and 2018. The denominator in this analysis will be the average global nominal GDP per hour worked based on data from 42 countries and territories accounting for 85 percent of the global economic output.

After we analyze the personal resource abundance of individual commodities (e.g., how much more abundant beef has become from the perspective of an average inhabitant of the planet), we will then analyze personal resource abundance in individual countries and territories (e.g., how much more abundant beef has become from the perspective of an average Mexican).

Second, we will look at 37 basic commodities that were tracked by the World Bank between 1960 and 2018. The denominator in this analysis will be the average global nominal GDP per hour worked based on data from 28 countries accounting for 75 percent of the global economic output. (As we go further back in time, our data sources become thinner.) As in the previous data set, we will analyze individual commodities first and individual countries second.

Third, we will look at 40 commodities going back to 1900 and 26 commodities going back to 1850. Although we were unable to estimate the average global nominal GDP per hour worked prior to 1960, we were able to obtain excellent data on the hourly wage rates of unskilled workers and hourly compensation rates of blue-collar workers in the United States going back to the early 1800s. Those data will serve as our denominator when estimating the abundance of commodities before 1960.[2]

Fourth, we will consider the growing abundance of food in the United States over a period of 100 years. The nominal prices of 42 food items were collected by the U.S. Bureau of Labor Statistics in 1919. We will compare those historical prices to nominal prices of the same products as found at https://www.walmart.com in 2019. The personal resource abundance of 42 food products will be calculated relative to the hourly wages of unskilled workers and hourly compensation rate of blue-collar workers in the United States.

Fifth, we will go beyond commodities and food and look at the personal resource abundance of 35 finished goods between 1979 and 2019. The 1979 nominal prices come from the 1979 Sears Christmas catalog. The 2019 prices for the same (or similar) products come from https://www.walmart .com. The personal resource abundance of 35 finished goods will be calculated relative to the hourly wages of unskilled workers and hourly compensation rates of blue-collar workers and upskilling workers in the United States.[3]

Sixth, we will look at the abundance of services. Here we readily admit that the personal resource abundance of services is difficult to measure. A trip to a doctor or a dentist in 1920, for example, differs fundamentally (because of new products and better technology) from a trip to a doctor or a dentist in 2020. Making matters more difficult, the delivery of health care is heavily regulated, subsidized, and influenced by third-party insurance policies and payments. As such, the normal functioning of the law of supply and demand is heavily compromised. The same can be said of market competition and its effect on the prices.

Consequently, our very limited findings should be treated as "suggestive" and cause for further research. A quick look at the provision of cosmetic procedures in the United States suggests that when such medical procedures are subjected to greater market competition, they become more abundant. In the same vein, we will also analyze a variety of additional products and services, such as airfares and air conditioning, which have become more abundant over time.

Finally, we will revisit the Simon-Ehrlich wager. Since the original bet between Simon and Ehrlich concluded in 1990, some critics have attempted to minimize the revolutionary nature of Simon's insights by noting the limited extent of the bet (the price of a five-metal basket over 10 years). By looking at the time prices of the five metals between 1900 and the present, we will reaffirm the soundness of Simon's reasoning.[4]

Personal resource abundance: a quick reminder of the methodology

For those who have skipped Chapter 4, here is a short reminder of our methodology. The time price (TP) denotes the amount of time that a person needs to work in order to earn enough money to be able to buy something. The personal resource abundance multiplier (pRAM) denotes the increased quantity of items that the buyer can buy for the same amount of labor at different points in time. The personal resource abundance (pRA) measures the rate of change in pRAM at different points in time. The compound annual growth rate of personal resource abundance (CAGR-pRA) shows us the speed at which items, be they commodities, goods, or services, are becoming cheaper. The CAGR-pRA then allows us to calculate the doubling period (YD-pRA), which is the number of years required for a specific item to become twice as abundant.

Commodities

Julian Simon's bet with Paul Ehrlich included five metals that Ehrlich selected (namely chromium, copper, nickel, tin, and tungsten) and lasted 10 years (1980–1990). To see if Simon's insight that resources grow more abundant over time not in spite of but (in large part) because of population growth holds more generally, we have to extend the scope of our inquiry to many more commodities and longer periods of time.

The Basic 50 (1980–2018)

In this section, we will start by looking at the pRA of 50 individual commodities between 1980 and 2018: aluminum, bananas, barley, beef, chicken, coal, cocoa, coconut oil, coffee, copper, corn, cotton, crude oil, fertilizer, fish meal, gold, groundnuts and groundnut oil, hides, iron ore, lamb, lead, liquefied natural gas (Japan), logs, natural gas (Europe), natural gas (United States), nickel, oranges, palm oil, platinum, plywood, pork, pulpwood, rapeseed, rice, rubber, salmon, sawnwood, shrimp, silver, sorghum, soybeans (including meal and oil), sugar, sunflower oil, tea, tin, tobacco, uranium, wheat, wool, and zinc.[5] We will then look at the overall pRA of 50 commodities in 42 individual countries and territories between 1980 and 2018. The countries and territories are Argentina, Australia, Austria, Bangladesh, Belgium, Brazil, Canada, Chile, China, Colombia, Denmark, Finland, France, Germany, Greece, Hong Kong, Iceland, India, Indonesia, Ireland, Italy, Japan, Luxembourg, Malaysia, Mexico, the Netherlands, New Zealand, Norway, Pakistan, Peru, the Philippines, Portugal, Singapore, South Korea, Spain, Sri Lanka, Sweden, Switzerland, Thailand, Turkey, the United Kingdom, and the United States.

The Basic 50: commodity perspective (1980–2018)

Between 1980 and 2018, the average global nominal GDP per hour worked rose from \$3.24 to \$15.88. Using the nominal prices of the Basic 50 commodities as numerators (the top number of a fraction) and the average nominal GDPs per hour worked as denominators (the bottom number of a fraction), we can calculate time prices.

We find that the average TP of the Basic 50 commodities fell by 71.6 percent. The TP of uranium that is used, among other things, in electricity production, fell the most (−87 percent). The TP of zinc, which is, among other things, a nutrient (or an "essential mineral") that helps the human immune system fight off invading bacteria and viruses, fell the least (−22 percent).

The average pRA increased by 252 percent. The pRA of uranium increased the most (669 percent), and the pRA of zinc increased the least (28 percent). For more, see Figure 5.1. The average pRA of the Basic 50 commodities never fell below its value in 1980 (see Figure 5.2). That means that at no point between 1980 and 2018 did the average of the Basic 50 commodities become less abundant relative to 1980.

The pRAs of 32 individual commodities fell below their 1980 values at least once between 1980 and 2018. That is to say that 32 individual commodities became less abundant relative to 1980 for at least one year during the 38 years analyzed. That said, all 50 commodities were more abundant in 2018 than they were in 1980.

Between 1980 and 2018, the average pRAM rose to 3.52. The pRAM of uranium rose the most (7.69) and zinc the least (1.28). The average CAGP-pRA came to 3.37 percent (5.51 percent for uranium and 0.65 percent for

Figure 5.1. The Basic 50: commodity perspective (1980–2018)

	Change in resource time price	Personal resource abundance multiplier	Change in personal resource abundance	Compound annual growth rate in personal resource abundance	Years to double personal resource abundance
Uranium	−87.0%	7.69	669%	5.51%	12.91
Sugar	−85.9%	7.11	611%	5.30%	13.43
Coffee	−85.4%	6.86	586%	5.20%	13.68
Silver	−84.6%	6.50	550%	5.05%	14.07
Pork	−84.6%	6.50	550%	5.05%	14.08
Cocoa	−82.1%	5.57	457%	4.62%	15.33
Salmon	−80.8%	5.21	421%	4.44%	15.96
Cotton	−80.1%	5.03	403%	4.34%	16.30
Rice	−79.1%	4.79	379%	4.21%	16.81
Palm oil	−77.7%	4.49	349%	4.03%	17.55
Rubber	−77.5%	4.44	344%	4.00%	17.67
Wheat	−76.0%	4.16	316%	3.82%	18.48
Aluminum	−75.8%	4.13	313%	3.80%	18.56
Tin	−75.5%	4.09	309%	3.77%	18.71
Shrimp	−75.4%	4.07	307%	3.76%	18.78
Hides	−74.3%	3.89	289%	3.64%	19.40
Platinum	−73.6%	3.79	279%	3.57%	19.77
Sorghum	−73.3%	3.75	275%	3.54%	19.92
Corn	−73.3%	3.74	274%	3.53%	19.97
Groundnuts etc.	−73.1%	3.72	272%	3.52%	20.06
Soybeans etc.	−72.0%	3.57	257%	3.41%	20.69
AVERAGE	−71.6%	3.52	252%	3.37%	20.94
Rapeseed	−70.5%	3.39	239%	3.26%	21.59
Coconut oil	−69.9%	3.32	232%	3.21%	21.96
Beef	−69.0%	3.23	223%	3.13%	22.49
Logs	−68.9%	3.21	221%	3.12%	22.57
Barley	−67.2%	3.05	205%	2.98%	23.62
Sunflower oil	−67.0%	3.03	203%	2.96%	23.76
Pulpwood	−66.8%	3.01	201%	2.94%	23.90
Bananas	−65.8%	2.92	192%	2.86%	24.55
Fertilizer	−65.1%	2.86	186%	2.81%	25.04
Tea	−65.0%	2.86	186%	2.80%	25.06
Sawnwood	−64.8%	2.84	184%	2.79%	25.21
Plywood	−63.2%	2.72	172%	2.66%	26.36
Natural gas, Eur.	−62.9%	2.70	170%	2.65%	26.55
Crude oil	−62.2%	2.65	165%	2.60%	27.05
LNG, Japan	−61.9%	2.63	163%	2.57%	27.28
Oranges	−59.8%	2.49	149%	2.42%	28.93
Natural gas, U.S.	−59.5%	2.47	147%	2.41%	29.13
Nickel	−59.0%	2.44	144%	2.38%	29.53
Lamb	−58.5%	2.41	141%	2.34%	29.97
Gold	−57.5%	2.35	135%	2.27%	30.81
Tobacco	−56.5%	2.30	130%	2.21%	31.67
Lead	−49.6%	1.98	98%	1.82%	38.43
Iron ore	−49.4%	1.98	98%	1.81%	38.65
Wool	−48.4%	1.94	94%	1.76%	39.77
Coal	−45.7%	1.84	84%	1.62%	43.16
Chicken	−40.0%	1.67	67%	1.35%	51.64
Copper	−39.0%	1.64	64%	1.31%	53.22
Fish meal	−38.4%	1.62	62%	1.28%	54.35
Zinc	−21.8%	1.28	28%	0.65%	107.17

Source: Authors' calculations.
Note: Eur. = Europe; LNG = liquefied natural gas.

Figure 5.2. The Basic 50: change in personal resource abundance of individual commodities, percent (1980–2018)

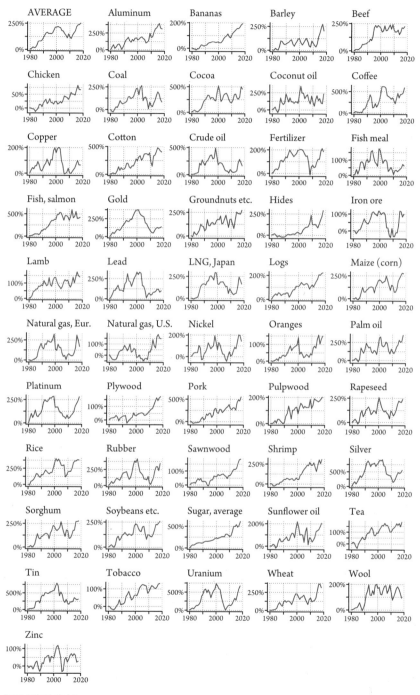

Source: Authors' calculations.
Note: Eur. = Europe; LNG = liquefied natural gas.

zinc). That implies a doubling of the average pRA every 21 years (13 years for uranium and 107 years for zinc). For more, see Appendix 6.

The Basic 50: country and territory perspective (1980–2018)

Now that we have seen how much more abundant the 50 individual commodities became between 1980 and 2018, let us look at the average abundance at a country and territory level. Note that our average global nominal GDP per hour worked, which we used to analyze the 50 individual commodities, consists of data for 42 countries and territories, amounting to 85 percent of the world's economic output. By disaggregating the average global nominal GDP per hour worked into its 42 components, we can estimate the average abundance for individual countries and territories.

Between 1980 and 2018, the average nominal GDP per hour worked rose the most in China (from $0.19 to $9.18, or 5,523 percent) and the least in Mexico (from $4.36 to $10.27 or 135 percent). For more, see Appendix 7.

As Figure 5.3 shows, the average TP of the Basic 50 commodities declined the most in China (−97.5 percent) and the least in Mexico (−41 percent). The average pRA increased the most in China (3,930 percent) and the least in Mexico (69 percent).

In 17 countries and territories, the average pRA of the Basic 50 commodities fell below their 1980 values at least once.[6] That is to say that the Basic 50 commodities became more scarce on average for at least one year in 17 countries and territories (see Figure 5.4). That said, the average pRA of the Basic 50 commodities was higher in all 42 countries in 2018 relative to 1980.

In China, the average pRAM of the Basic 50 commodities skyrocketed to 40.3. In Mexico, it rose only to 1.69. The average CAGR-pRA in China rose by 10.22 percent a year. In Mexico, it rose by 1.39 percent a year. The average pRA doubled every 7.1 years in China and every 50.3 years in Mexico.

The Basic 50: summary (1980–2018)

The average TP of the Basic 50 commodities fell by 72 percent, and the average pRA rose by 252 percent. The average pRAM rose to 3.52, and the average CAGR-pRA increased at 3.37 percent per year, implying a doubling

Figure 5.3. The Basic 50: country and territory perspective (1980–2018)

	Change in resource time price	Personal resource abundance multiplier	Change in personal resource abundance	Compound annual growth rate in personal resource abundance	Years to double personal resource abundance
China	−97.5%	40.30	3,930%	10.22%	7.1
South Korea	−92.1%	12.67	1,167%	6.91%	10.4
Sri Lanka	−88.4%	8.61	761%	5.83%	12.2
Ireland	−88.1%	8.42	742%	5.77%	12.4
Thailand	−87.5%	8.02	702%	5.63%	12.7
Singapore	−84.2%	6.34	534%	4.98%	14.3
Hong Kong	−83.2%	5.95	495%	4.81%	14.8
India	−82.0%	5.55	455%	4.61%	15.4
Portugal	−78.1%	4.58	358%	4.08%	17.3
Bangladesh	−77.3%	4.41	341%	3.98%	17.8
Indonesia	−77.0%	4.35	335%	3.94%	17.9
Turkey	−75.7%	4.12	312%	3.80%	18.6
New Zealand	−75.1%	4.01	301%	3.72%	19.0
Australia	−73.8%	3.82	282%	3.59%	19.7
Finland	−73.7%	3.80	280%	3.58%	19.7
Norway	−73.2%	3.73	273%	3.53%	20.0
Pakistan	−72.9%	3.69	269%	3.50%	20.2
Iceland	−72.7%	3.67	267%	3.48%	20.3
Austria	−72.3%	3.60	260%	3.43%	20.5
AVERAGE	−71.6%	3.52	252%	3.37%	20.9
Malaysia	−70.9%	3.43	243%	3.30%	21.4
United States	−70.6%	3.40	240%	3.28%	21.5
Denmark	−70.5%	3.39	239%	3.27%	21.6
Germany	−70.5%	3.39	239%	3.27%	21.6
Japan	−70.2%	3.35	235%	3.23%	21.8
Chile	−69.5%	3.28	228%	3.18%	22.2
Luxembourg	−68.7%	3.20	220%	3.11%	22.7
Spain	−68.7%	3.20	220%	3.10%	22.7
Switzerland	−68.4%	3.16	216%	3.08%	22.9
Peru	−68.3%	3.16	216%	3.07%	22.9
Brazil	−68.0%	3.13	213%	3.05%	23.1
United Kingdom	−66.5%	2.98	198%	2.92%	24.1
Philippines	−65.8%	2.92	192%	2.86%	24.6
Argentina	−65.7%	2.92	192%	2.86%	24.6
Italy	−64.8%	2.84	184%	2.79%	25.2
Canada	−64.6%	2.83	183%	2.77%	25.3
Colombia	−63.6%	2.75	175%	2.70%	26.0
France	−62.7%	2.68	168%	2.63%	26.7
Belgium	−61.8%	2.62	162%	2.56%	27.4
Greece	−59.3%	2.46	146%	2.39%	29.3
Netherlands	−58.5%	2.41	141%	2.34%	29.9
Sweden	−55.3%	2.23	123%	2.14%	32.8
Mexico	−40.8%	1.69	69%	1.39%	50.3

Source: Authors' calculations.
Note: Hong Kong = Hong Kong SAR, China.

Figure 5.4. The Basic 50: change in personal resource abundance of commodities in individual countries and territories, percent (1980–2018)

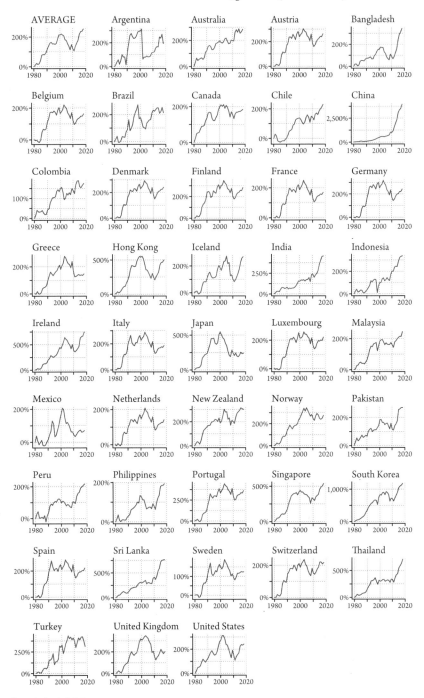

Source: Authors' calculations.
Note: Hong Kong = Hong Kong SAR, China.

of the average pRA every 20.9 years. The average TP fell the most in China (−97.5 percent) and the least in Mexico (−41 percent). The average pRA of the Basic 50 commodities in the two countries rose by 3,930 percent and 69 percent, respectively (abundance growth was 57 times faster in China than in Mexico). The average pRAM in China and Mexico rose to 40.3 and 1.69 The average CAGR-pRA in the two countries increased by 10.22 percent and 1.39 percent, respectively, implying a doubling of the average pRA every 7.1 years in China and every 50.3 years in Mexico.

The World Bank 37 (1960–2018)

In this section, we will start by looking at personal resource abundance (pRA) of 37 individual commodities between 1960 and 2018: aluminum, bananas, barley, beef, chicken, cocoa, coconut oil, coffee, copper, corn, cotton, crude oil, fertilizer, gold, groundnuts and groundnut oil, iron ore, lead, logs, natural gas (Europe), natural gas (United States), nickel, oranges, palm oil, platinum, rice, rubber, sawnwood, shrimp, silver, sorghum, soybeans (including meal and oil), sugar, tea, tin, tobacco, wheat, and zinc. We will then look at the overall pRA of these 37 commodities in 28 individual countries and territories between 1960 and 2018: Australia, Austria, Belgium, Brazil, Canada, Chile, China, Colombia, Denmark, Finland, France, Greece, Hong Kong, Ireland, Italy, Japan, Mexico, the Netherlands, Norway, Peru, Portugal, Singapore, South Korea, Spain, Sweden, Switzerland, the United Kingdom, and the United States.

The World Bank 37: commodity perspective (1960–2018)

Between 1960 and 2018, the average global nominal GDP per hour worked rose from $0.77 to $23.65. Using the nominal prices of the World Bank 37 commodities as numerators and the average nominal GDPs per hour worked as denominators, we can calculate time prices.

We find that the average TP of the World Bank 37 commodities fell by 83 percent. The TP of rubber that is used in, for example, transportation fell the most (−93.4 percent). The TP of crude oil that is an essential source of energy actually increased by 37 percent.

The average pRA increased by 489 percent. The pRA of rubber increased the most (1,425 percent). Crude oil and gold, however, became less abundant, with the pRA of crude oil declining by 27 percent. For more, see Figure 5.5. The average pRA of the 37 commodities never fell below its value in 1960. That means that at no point between 1960 and 2018 did the average of the 37 commodities become less abundant relative to 1960 (see Figure 5.6).

The pRA of 27 individual commodities fell below their 1960 values at least once between 1960 and 2018. That is to say that 27 individual commodities became less abundant relative to 1960 for at least one year over the 58-year period analyzed. That said, 35 out of 37 commodities were more abundant in 2018 than they were in 1960.

Between 1960 and 2018, the average pRAM rose to 5.89. The pRAM of rubber rose the most (15.25). The pRAM of crude oil fell to 0.73. The average CAGR-pRA came to 3.1 percent. The CAGR-pRA was highest with rubber (4.8 percent) and lowest with crude oil (−0.5 percent). The average pRA doubled every 22.7 years. It doubled every 14.76 years for rubber. For more, see Appendix 8.

The World Bank 37: country and territory perspective (1960–2018)

Now that we've seen how much more abundant the 37 individual commodities became between 1960 and 2018, let us look at the average abundance at a country and territory level. Note that our average global nominal GDP per hour worked, which we used to analyze the 37 individual commodities, consists of data for 28 countries and territories accounting for 75 percent of the world's economic output. By disaggregating the average global nominal GDP per hour worked into its 28 components, we can estimate the average abundance for individual countries and territories.

The average nominal GDP per hour worked rose the most in Ireland (from $0.76 to $99.51 or 12,960 percent) and the least in Mexico (from $0.60 to $10.27 or 1,623 percent). For more, see Appendix 9.

As Figure 5.7 shows, the average TP of the 37 commodities declined the most in Ireland (−96 percent) and the least in Mexico (−69.8 percent). The average pRA increased the most in Ireland (2,414 percent) and the least in Mexico (232 percent).

Figure 5.5. The World Bank 37: commodity perspective (1960–2018)

	Change in resource time price	Personal resource abundance multiplier	Change in personal resource abundance	Compound annual growth rate in personal resource abundance	Years to double personal resource abundance
Rubber	−93.4%	15.25	1,425%	4.8%	14.76
Tea	−91.0%	11.06	1,006%	4.2%	16.73
Tobacco	−90.8%	10.93	993%	4.2%	16.81
Palm oil	−90.7%	10.75	975%	4.2%	16.93
Coffee	−90.3%	10.33	933%	4.1%	17.21
Cotton	−89.9%	9.94	894%	4.0%	17.50
Coconut oil	−89.6%	9.59	859%	4.0%	17.79
Wheat	−88.2%	8.45	745%	3.7%	18.83
Corn	−87.9%	8.28	728%	3.7%	19.02
Sugar	−87.3%	7.88	688%	3.6%	19.47
Cocoa	−87.3%	7.86	686%	3.6%	19.50
Rice, Thai	−87.2%	7.81	681%	3.6%	19.56
Soybeans etc.	−86.9%	7.64	664%	3.6%	19.77
Aluminum	−86.5%	7.42	642%	3.5%	20.06
Groundnut oil	−85.5%	6.92	592%	3.4%	20.79
Sorghum	−84.9%	6.64	564%	3.3%	21.24
Sawnwood	−84.1%	6.27	527%	3.2%	21.90
AVERAGE	−83.0%	5.89	489%	3.1%	22.67
Beef	−81.4%	5.37	437%	2.9%	23.91
Oranges	−80.1%	5.04	404%	2.8%	24.87
Iron ore	−80.0%	5.01	401%	2.8%	24.95
Barley	−79.6%	4.90	390%	2.8%	25.30
Chicken	−75.6%	4.09	309%	2.5%	28.52
Fertilizer	−75.3%	4.05	305%	2.4%	28.77
Shrimp	−75.1%	4.01	301%	2.4%	28.92
Bananas	−74.8%	3.97	297%	2.4%	29.14
Nickel	−73.7%	3.81	281%	2.3%	30.08
Logs	−72.4%	3.62	262%	2.2%	31.23
Tin	−70.0%	3.34	234%	2.1%	33.37
Copper	−68.6%	3.18	218%	2.0%	34.75
Platinum	−65.6%	2.90	190%	1.9%	37.70
Lead	−63.2%	2.72	172%	1.7%	40.24
Zinc	−61.2%	2.58	158%	1.6%	42.46
Silver	−43.8%	1.78	78%	1.0%	69.78
Natural gas, Eur.	−38.0%	1.61	61%	0.8%	84.17
Natural gas, U.S.	−26.3%	1.36	36%	0.5%	131.48
Gold	+17.6%	0.85	−15%	−0.3%	N/A
Crude oil	+37.0%	0.73	−27%	−0.5%	N/A

Source: Authors' calculations.
Note: Eur. = Europe; N/A = Doubling period cannot be calculated for commodities that have become less rather than more abundant between two points in time.

Figure 5.6. The World Bank 37: change in personal resource abundance of individual commodities, percent (1960–2018)

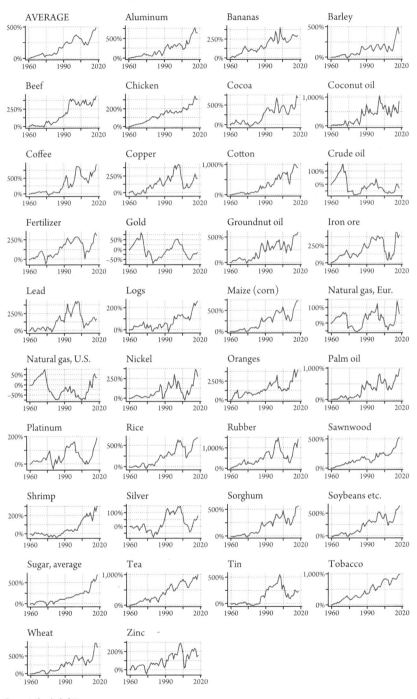

Source: Authors' calculations.
Note: Eur. = Europe.

Figure 5.7. The World Bank 37: country and territory perspective (1960–2018)

	Change in resource time price	Personal resource abundance multiplier	Change in personal resource abundance	Compound annual growth rate in personal resource abundance	Years to double personal resource abundance
Ireland	−96.0%	25.14	2,414%	5.72%	12.5
South Korea	−95.8%	23.85	2,285%	5.62%	12.7
China	−95.2%	20.98	1,998%	5.39%	13.2
Japan	−94.7%	19.01	1,801%	5.21%	13.7
Hong Kong	−94.6%	18.49	1,749%	5.16%	13.8
Spain	−94.4%	17.89	1,689%	5.10%	13.9
Singapore	−92.6%	13.44	1,244%	4.58%	15.5
Austria	−92.3%	12.97	1,197%	4.52%	15.7
Norway	−92.0%	12.58	1,158%	4.46%	15.9
Portugal	−91.5%	11.75	1,075%	4.34%	16.3
Finland	−90.8%	10.91	991%	4.21%	16.8
Denmark	−90.5%	10.53	953%	4.14%	17.1
Italy	−90.3%	10.31	931%	4.10%	17.2
Switzerland	−89.8%	9.79	879%	4.01%	17.6
Netherlands	−89.4%	9.43	843%	3.94%	17.9
Greece	−88.9%	8.98	798%	3.86%	18.3
France	−88.3%	8.52	752%	3.76%	18.8
Belgium	−88.0%	8.36	736%	3.73%	18.9
Brazil	−86.3%	7.30	630%	3.49%	20.2
United Kingdom	−85.9%	7.10	610%	3.44%	20.5
Sweden	−83.3%	5.98	498%	3.13%	22.5
AVERAGE	−79.6%	5.89	489%	3.10%	22.7
Australia	−82.1%	5.60	460%	3.01%	23.3
Chile	−79.2%	4.80	380%	2.74%	25.6
Peru	−73.5%	3.77	277%	2.31%	30.3
United States	−71.5%	3.51	251%	2.19%	32.1
Canada	−71.4%	3.50	250%	2.18%	32.1
Colombia	−71.0%	3.44	244%	2.15%	32.5
Mexico	−69.8%	3.32	232%	2.09%	33.5

Source: Authors' calculations.
Note: Hong Kong = Hong Kong SAR, China.

In five countries, the average pRA of the 37 commodities fell below their 1960 values at least once.[7] That is to say that the average of the 37 commodities became less abundant for at least one year between 1960 and 2018. That said, the average of the 37 commodities was more abundant in all countries and territories in 2018 relative to 1960 (see Figure 5.8).

In Ireland, the average pRAM skyrocketed to 25.14. In Mexico, it rose only to 3.32. The average CAGR-pRA in Ireland rose by 5.72 percent a year. In Mexico, it rose by 2.09 percent a year. The average pRA doubled every 12.5 years in Ireland and every 33.5 years in Mexico.

Figure 5.8. The World Bank 37: change in personal resource abundance of commodities in individual countries and territories, percent (1960–2018)

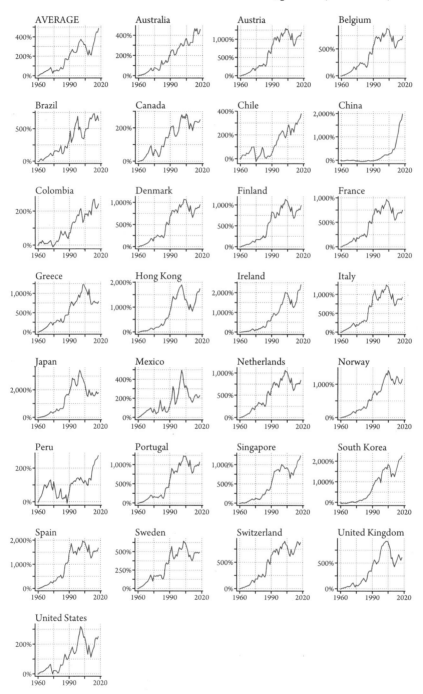

Source: Authors' calculations.
Note: Hong Kong = Hong Kong SAR, China.

The World Bank 37: summary (1980–2018)

The average TP of the World Bank 37 commodities fell by 83 percent, and the average pRA rose by 489 percent. The average pRAM rose to 5.89, the average CAGR-pRA increased at 3.1 percent per year, implying a doubling of the average pRA every 22.7 years. The average TP of the 37 commodities fell the most in Ireland (−96 percent) and the least in Mexico (−69.8 percent). The average pRA of the 37 commodities in the two countries rose by 2,414 percent and 232 percent, respectively (abundance growth was 10.4 times faster in Ireland than in Mexico). The average pRAM in Ireland and Mexico rose to 25.14 and 3.32, respectively. The average CAGR-pRA in the two countries increased at 5.72 percent and 2.09 percent, respectively. That implied a doubling of the average pRA every 12.5 years in Ireland and every 33.5 years in Mexico.

Jacks's 40 commodities (1900–2018)

In the two sections that follow, we will measure the abundance of 40 commodities between 1900 and 2018. The nominal prices of these commodities were collected and published by Simon Fraser University economist David S. Jacks. The 40 commodities that Jacks analyzed are aluminum, barley, bauxite, beef, chromium, coal, cocoa, coffee, copper, corn, cotton, cottonseed, gold, hides, iron ore, lamb, lead, manganese, natural gas, nickel, palm oil, peanuts, petroleum, phosphate, platinum, pork, potash, rice, rubber, rye, silver, steel, sugar, sulfur, tea, tin, tobacco, wheat, wool, and zinc. As noted in Chapter 4, we do not have reliable data on average global nominal GDP per hour worked prior to 1960. We do, though, have excellent data pertaining to the hourly wages of unskilled workers and hourly compensation rates of blue-collar workers in the United States going back to the early 1800s. Those series will serve as our denominators for the Jacks's 40 data set.

Jacks's 40 commodities: the U.S. blue-collar worker perspective (1900–2018)

Between 1900 and 2018, the average nominal hourly compensation rate of blue-collar workers in the United States rose from $0.14 to $32.06. Using the nominal prices of Jacks's 40 commodities as numerators and the average nominal hourly compensation rates of blue-collar workers in the United States as denominators, we find that the average TP of Jacks's 40 commodities fell by 96.1 percent between 1900 and 2018. Rubber fell the most (−99.4 percent) and petroleum fell the least (−48.9 percent).

The average pRA increased by 2,437 percent. The pRA of rubber rose by 17,227 percent, and the pRA of petroleum rose by 96 percent (see Figure 5.9). The average pRA of Jacks's 40 commodities fell below its 1900 value at least once between 1900 and 2018. That means that the average of the 40 commodities became less abundant relative to 1900 for at least one year over the 118 years analyzed (see Figure 5.10).

The pRA of 27 individual commodities fell below their 1900 values at least once between 1900 and 2018. That means that 27 individual commodities became less abundant relative to 1900 for at least one year over 118 years analyzed. That said, all 40 commodities were more abundant in 2018 than they were in 1900.

The average pRAM rose to 25.37. The pRAM ranged from 1.96 for petroleum to 173.27 for rubber. The average CAGR-pRA came to 2.75 percent. The CAGR-pRA ranged from 4.43 percent for rubber to 0.57 percent for petroleum. The average CAGR-pRA figure implies a doubling of the average pRA every 25.51 years, with the pRA of rubber doubling every 16 years and the pRA of petroleum doubling every 122.71 years. For more, see Appendix 10.

Jacks's 40 commodities: the U.S. unskilled worker perspective (1900–2018)

Between 1900 and 2018, the average nominal hourly wage rate of unskilled workers in the United States rose from $0.09 to $12.78. As such, the average TP of Jacks's 40 commodities fell by 94 percent between 1900 and 2018. Rubber fell the most (−99.1 percent), and petroleum fell the least (−17.7 percent).

The average pRA increased by 1,473 percent. The pRA of rubber rose by 10,644 percent, and the pRA of petroleum rose by 21 percent (see Figure 5.11). The average pRA of 40 commodities fell below its 1900 value at least once between 1900 and 2018. That means that the average of 40 commodities became less abundant relative to 1900 for at least one year over the 118 years analyzed (see Figure 5.12).

Figure 5.9. Jacks's 40 commodities: U.S. blue-collar worker perspective (1900–2018)

	Change in resource time price	Personal resource abundance multiplier	Change in personal resource abundance	Compound annual growth rate in personal resource abundance	Years to double personal resource abundance
Rubber	−99.4%	173.27	17,227%	4.43%	16.00
Aluminum	−98.9%	90.83	8,983%	3.86%	18.29
Pork	−98.4%	62.62	6,162%	3.54%	19.94
Potash	−98.2%	54.22	5,322%	3.41%	20.66
Sugar	−98.0%	49.58	4,858%	3.33%	21.13
Rice	−97.6%	41.12	4,012%	3.17%	22.19
Cocoa	−97.1%	34.78	3,378%	3.03%	23.24
Palm oil	−96.9%	32.30	3,130%	2.96%	23.74
Sulfur	−96.9%	31.81	3,081%	2.95%	23.84
Hides	−96.8%	31.60	3,060%	2.94%	23.89
Wheat	−96.7%	30.49	2,949%	2.91%	24.14
Bauxite	−96.7%	30.00	2,900%	2.90%	24.25
Peanuts	−96.2%	26.50	2,550%	2.79%	25.17
Tea	−96.1%	25.68	2,468%	2.77%	25.41
Corn	−96.1%	25.58	2,458%	2.76%	25.44
AVERAGE	−96.1%	25.37	2,437%	2.75%	25.51
Cottonseed	−95.9%	24.36	2,336%	2.72%	25.83
Rye	−95.9%	24.15	2,315%	2.71%	25.90
Cotton	−95.8%	23.57	2,257%	2.69%	26.10
Nickel	−95.0%	20.10	1,910%	2.55%	27.49
Wool	−95.0%	20.02	1,902%	2.55%	27.52
Phosphate	−94.5%	18.12	1,712%	2.46%	28.47
Barley	−94.4%	17.76	1,676%	2.45%	28.67
Coffee	−93.8%	16.18	1,518%	2.37%	29.63
Copper	−91.7%	12.12	1,112%	2.12%	33.06
Iron ore	−91.0%	11.16	1,016%	2.05%	34.20
Lead	−89.5%	9.53	853%	1.91%	36.59
Silver	−89.4%	9.45	845%	1.90%	36.73
Tobacco	−89.4%	9.41	841%	1.90%	36.79
Steel	−86.7%	7.52	652%	1.71%	40.89
Zinc	−85.7%	7.00	600%	1.65%	42.39
Tin	−85.2%	6.74	574%	1.62%	43.23
Manganese	−81.8%	5.48	448%	1.44%	48.49
Natural gas	−80.7%	5.18	418%	1.39%	50.14
Platinum	−79.5%	4.87	387%	1.34%	52.10
Lamb	−78.6%	4.68	368%	1.31%	53.45
Beef	−75.5%	4.08	308%	1.19%	58.66
Chromium	−75.0%	3.99	299%	1.17%	59.58
Gold	−73.2%	3.73	273%	1.11%	62.64
Coal	−67.5%	3.08	208%	0.95%	73.38
Petroleum	−48.9%	1.96	96%	0.57%	122.71

Source: Authors' calculations.

Figure 5.10. Jacks's 40 commodities: change in personal resource abundance of individual commodities, U.S. blue-collar worker perspective, percent (1900–2018)

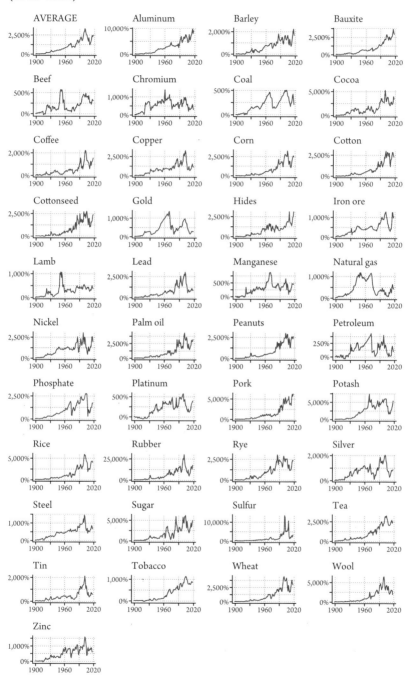

Figure 5.11. Jacks's 40 commodities: U.S. unskilled worker perspective (1900–2018)

	Change in resource time price	Personal resource abundance multiplier	Change in personal resource abundance	Compound annual growth rate in personal resource abundance	Years to double personal resource abundance
Rubber	−99.1%	107.44	10,644%	4.04%	17.49
Aluminum	−98.2%	56.32	5,532%	3.48%	20.29
Pork	−97.4%	38.83	3,783%	3.15%	22.35
Potash	−97.0%	33.62	3,262%	3.02%	23.27
Sugar	−96.7%	30.74	2,974%	2.95%	23.88
Rice	−96.1%	25.50	2,450%	2.78%	25.26
Cocoa	−95.4%	21.57	2,057%	2.64%	26.63
Palm oil	−95.0%	20.03	1,903%	2.57%	27.29
Sulfur	−94.9%	19.73	1,873%	2.56%	27.43
Hides	−94.9%	19.60	1,860%	2.55%	27.49
Wheat	−94.7%	18.90	1,790%	2.52%	27.83
Bauxite	−94.6%	18.60	1,760%	2.51%	27.98
Peanuts	−93.9%	16.43	1,543%	2.40%	29.22
Tea	−93.7%	15.93	1,493%	2.37%	29.55
Corn	−93.7%	15.86	1,486%	2.37%	29.59
AVERAGE	−93.6%	15.73	1,473%	2.36%	29.68
Cottonseed	−93.4%	15.11	1,411%	2.33%	30.12
Rye	−93.3%	14.98	1,398%	2.32%	30.22
Cotton	−93.2%	14.62	1,362%	2.30%	30.49
Nickel	−92.0%	12.46	1,146%	2.16%	32.42
Wool	−91.9%	12.41	1,141%	2.16%	32.47
Phosphate	−91.1%	11.24	1,024%	2.07%	33.81
Barley	−90.9%	11.01	1,001%	2.05%	34.09
Coffee	−90.0%	10.03	903%	1.97%	35.48
Copper	−86.7%	7.51	651%	1.72%	40.55
Iron ore	−85.5%	6.92	592%	1.65%	42.29
Lead	−83.1%	5.91	491%	1.52%	46.04
Silver	−82.9%	5.86	486%	1.51%	46.27
Tobacco	−82.9%	5.84	484%	1.51%	46.36
Steel	−78.5%	4.66	366%	1.31%	53.14
Zinc	−77.0%	4.34	334%	1.25%	55.72
Tin	−76.1%	4.18	318%	1.22%	57.19
Manganese	−70.6%	3.40	240%	1.04%	66.87
Natural gas	−68.9%	3.21	221%	0.99%	70.07
Platinum	−66.9%	3.02	202%	0.94%	74.00
Lamb	−65.5%	2.90	190%	0.91%	76.78
Beef	−60.5%	2.53	153%	0.79%	88.11
Chromium	−59.6%	2.48	148%	0.77%	90.23
Gold	−56.8%	2.31	131%	0.71%	97.50
Coal	−47.6%	1.91	91%	0.55%	126.56
Petroleum	−17.7%	1.21	21%	0.16%	420.99

Source: Authors' calculations.

Figure 5.12. Jacks's 40 commodities: change in personal resource abundance of individual commodities, U.S. unskilled worker perspective, percent (1900–2018)

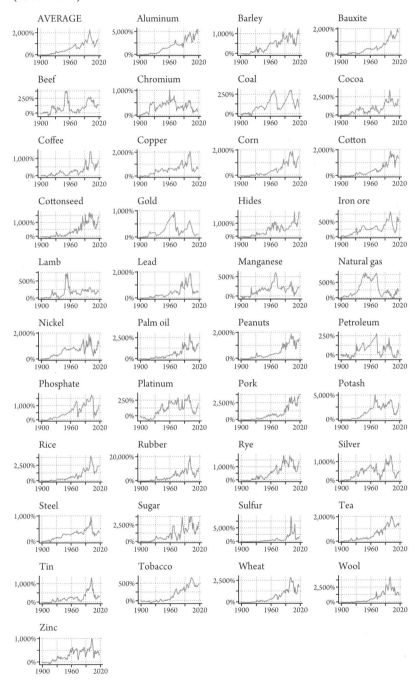

Source: Authors' calculations.

The pRA of 35 individual commodities fell below their 1900 values at least once between 1900 and 2018. That means that 35 individual commodities became less abundant relative to 1900 for at least one year. That said, all 40 commodities were more abundant in 2018 than they were in 1900.

The average pRAM rose to 15.73. The pRAM ranged from 107.44 for rubber to 1.21 for petroleum. The average CAGR-pRA came to 2.36 percent. The CAGR-pRA ranged from 4.04 percent for rubber to 0.16 percent for petroleum. The CAGR-pRA figure implies a doubling of the average pRA every 29.68 years, with the pRA of rubber doubling every 17.49 years and the pRA of petroleum doubling every 420.99 years. For more, see Appendix 11.

Jacks's 40 commodities: summary (1900–2018)

Between 1900 and 2018, the average TP of 40 commodities fell by 96.1 percent for blue-collar workers and by 93.6 percent for unskilled workers. The average pRA of the former rose by 2,437 percent, and the average of the latter by 1,473 percent (see Figure 5.13). The average pRAM for blue-collar workers rose to 25.37, and the average for unskilled workers rose to 15.73. The average CAGR-pRA for the former rose by 2.75 percent a year and for the latter at 2.36 percent a year. Those numbers imply a doubling of the average pRA among blue-collar workers every 25.51 years and among unskilled workers every 29.68 years (see Table 5.1).

Figure 5.13. Jacks's 40 commodities: average change in personal resource abundance, U.S. blue-collar and unskilled worker perspectives, percent (1900–2018)

Source: Authors' calculations.

Table 5.1. Jacks's 40 commodities: summary of the U.S. blue-collar worker perspective and the U.S. unskilled worker perspective (1900–2018)

Jacks's 40 1900–2018	Percentage change in resource time price	Personal resource abundance multiplier	Percentage change in personal resource abundance	Compound annual percentage growth rate in personal resource abundance	Years to double personal resource abundance
Blue-collar	−96.1	25.37	2,437	2.75	25.51
Unskilled	−93.6	15.73	1,473	2.36	29.68

Source: Authors' calculations.

Jacks's 26 commodities (1850–2018)

In the following two sections, we will measure the pRA of 26 commodities between 1850 and 2018. To do so, we will once again rely on commodity data collected and published by Simon Fraser University economist David S. Jacks, who tracked prices of 26 commodities going back to 1850. The commodities are barley, beef, coal, cocoa, coffee, copper, corn, cotton, gold, hides, lamb, lead, nickel, palm oil, pork, rice, rye, silver, steel, sugar, tea, tin, tobacco, wheat, wool, and zinc. Once more, we will examine Jacks's data using hourly wages of unskilled workers and hourly compensation rates of blue-collar workers in the United States.

Jacks's 26 commodities: the U.S. blue-collar worker perspective (1850–2018)

Between 1850 and 2018, the average nominal hourly compensation rate of blue-collar workers in the United States rose from $0.06 to $32.06. Using the nominal prices of Jacks's 26 commodities as numerators and the average nominal hourly compensation rates of blue-collar workers in the United States as denominators, we find that the average TP of Jacks's 26 commodities fell by 98.3 percent between 1850 and 2018. Sugar fell the most (−99.6 percent) and coal the least (−84.2 percent).

The average pRA increased by 5,762 percent. The pRA of sugar rose by 22,583 percent, and the pRA of coal rose by 534 percent (see Figure 5.14).

Figure 5.14. Jacks's 26 commodities: U.S. blue-collar worker perspective (1850–2018)

	Change in resource time price	Personal resource abundance multiplier	Change in personal resource abundance	Compound annual growth rate in personal resource abundance	Years to double personal resource abundance
Sugar	−99.6%	226.83	22,583%	3.28%	21.47
Nickel	−99.4%	181.46	18,046%	3.14%	22.39
Rice	−99.1%	111.49	11,049%	2.85%	24.70
Tea	−99.1%	106.52	10,552%	2.82%	24.94
Rye	−99.0%	99.40	9,840%	2.78%	25.32
Palm oil	−98.8%	82.22	8,122%	2.66%	26.41
Pork	−98.7%	74.91	7,391%	2.60%	26.98
Cotton	−98.5%	68.96	6,796%	2.55%	27.51
Wheat	−98.5%	64.86	6,386%	2.51%	27.91
Cocoa	−98.3%	60.32	5,932%	2.47%	28.40
AVERAGE	−98.3%	58.62	5,762%	2.45%	28.60
Corn	−98.2%	54.85	5,385%	2.41%	29.08
Wool	−98.1%	52.65	5,165%	2.39%	29.38
Coffee	−98.0%	48.79	4,779%	2.34%	29.96
Barley	−97.8%	45.04	4,404%	2.29%	30.58
Hides	−97.7%	44.24	4,324%	2.28%	30.73
Silver	−97.7%	43.94	4,294%	2.28%	30.78
Tobacco	−97.3%	37.03	3,603%	2.17%	32.24
Copper	−96.7%	30.45	2,945%	2.05%	34.09
Lead	−96.5%	28.68	2,768%	2.02%	34.70
Zinc	−92.4%	13.11	1,211%	1.54%	45.26
Steel	−89.5%	9.51	851%	1.35%	51.70
Tin	−88.9%	9.03	803%	1.32%	52.91
Gold	−88.5%	8.71	771%	1.30%	53.81
Lamb	−87.4%	7.96	696%	1.24%	56.14
Beef	−85.3%	6.80	580%	1.15%	60.74
Coal	−84.2%	6.34	534%	1.11%	63.04

Source: Authors' calculations.

The average pRA figures for 26 commodities fell below their 1850 value at least once between 1850 and 2018. That means that the average of 26 commodities became less abundant relative to 1850 for at least one year over the 168 years analyzed (see Figure 5.15).

The pRA of 24 individual commodities fell below their 1850 values at least once between 1850 and 2018. That means that 24 individual commodities became less abundant relative to 1850 for at least one year over the 168 years analyzed. That said, all 26 commodities were more abundant in 2018 than they were in 1900.

The average pRAM rose to 58.62. The pRAM ranged from 226.83 for sugar to 6.34 for coal. The average CAGR-pRA came to 2.45 percent. The

Figure 5.15. Jacks's 26 commodities: change in personal resource abundance of individual commodities, U.S. blue-collar worker perspective, percent (1850–2018)

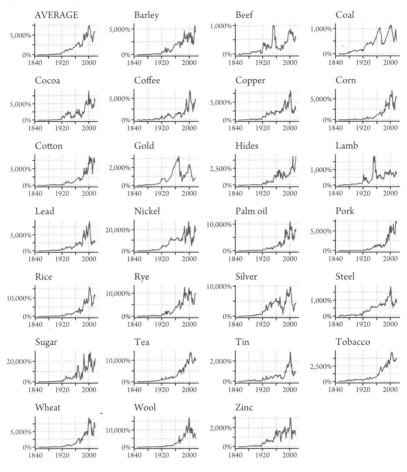

Source: Authors' calculations.

CAGR-pRA ranged from 3.28 percent for sugar to 1.11 percent for coal. The average CAGR-pRA figure implies a doubling of the average pRA every 28.6 years, with the pRA of sugar doubling every 21.47 years and the pRA of coal doubling every 63.04 years. For more, see Appendix 12.

Jacks's 26 commodities: the U.S. unskilled worker perspective (1850–2018)

Between 1850 and 2018, the average nominal hourly wage rate of unskilled workers in the United States rose from $0.05 to $12.78. As such, the average

Figure 5.16. Jacks's 26 commodities: U.S. unskilled worker perspective (1850–2018)

	Change in resource time price	Personal resource abundance multiplier	Change in personal resource abundance	Compound annual growth rate in personal resource abundance	Years to double personal resource abundance
Sugar	−99.1%	107.67	10,667%	2.82%	24.89
Nickel	−98.8%	86.13	8,513%	2.69%	26.13
Rice	−98.1%	52.92	5,192%	2.39%	29.34
Tea	−98.0%	50.56	4,956%	2.36%	29.68
Rye	−97.9%	47.18	4,618%	2.32%	30.21
Palm oil	−97.4%	39.03	3,803%	2.21%	31.78
Pork	−97.2%	35.56	3,456%	2.15%	32.61
Cotton	−96.9%	32.74	3,174%	2.10%	33.38
Wheat	−96.8%	30.79	2,979%	2.06%	33.98
Cocoa	−96.5%	28.63	2,763%	2.02%	34.71
AVERAGE	−96.4%	27.82	2,682%	2.00%	35.01
Corn	−96.2%	26.04	2,504%	1.96%	35.73
Wool	−96.0%	24.99	2,399%	1.93%	36.18
Coffee	−95.7%	23.16	2,216%	1.89%	37.06
Barley	−95.3%	21.38	2,038%	1.84%	38.03
Hides	−95.2%	21.00	2,000%	1.83%	38.25
Silver	−95.2%	20.86	1,986%	1.82%	38.33
Tobacco	−94.3%	17.58	1,658%	1.72%	40.62
Copper	−93.1%	14.46	1,346%	1.60%	43.60
Lead	−92.7%	13.61	1,261%	1.57%	44.60
Zinc	−83.9%	6.22	522%	1.09%	63.71
Steel	−77.8%	4.51	351%	0.90%	77.26
Tin	−76.7%	4.29	329%	0.87%	80.00
Gold	−75.8%	4.13	313%	0.85%	82.07
Lamb	−73.5%	3.78	278%	0.79%	87.62
Beef	−69.0%	3.23	223%	0.70%	99.37
Coal	−66.8%	3.01	201%	0.66%	105.66

Source: Authors' calculations.

TP of Jacks's 26 commodities fell by 96.4 percent between 1850 and 2018. Sugar fell the most (−99.1 percent) and coal the least (−66.8 percent).

The average pRA increased by 2,682 percent. The pRA of sugar rose by 10,667 percent, and the pRA of coal rose by 201 percent (see Figure 5.16). The average pRA figures for 26 commodities fell below their 1850 value at least once between 1850 and 2018. That means that the average of 26 commodities became less abundant relative to 1850 for at least one year over the 168 years analyzed (see Figure 5.17).

The pRA figures for all individual commodities fell below their 1850 values at least once between 1850 and 2018. That means that all individual commodities became less abundant relative to 1850 for at least one year out

Figure 5.17. Jacks's 26 commodities: change in personal resource abundance of individual commodities, U.S. unskilled worker perspective, percent (1850–2018)

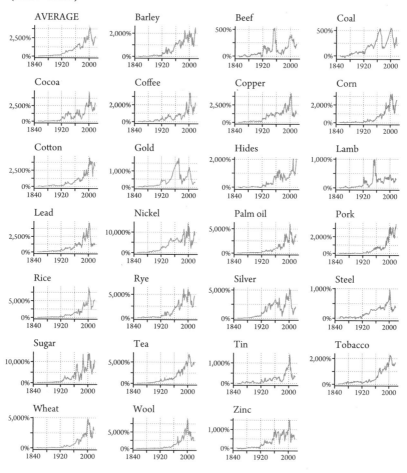

Source: Authors' calculations.

of the 168 years analyzed. That said, all 26 commodities were more abundant in 2018 than they were in 1850.

The average pRAM rose to 27.82. The pRAM ranged from 107.67 for sugar to 3.01 for coal. The average CAGR-pRA came to 2 percent. The CAGR-pRA ranged from 2.82 percent for sugar to 0.66 percent for coal. The average CAGR-pRA figure implies a doubling of the average pRA every 35.01 years, with the pRA of sugar doubling every 24.89 years and the pRA of coal doubling every 105.66 years. For more, see Appendix 13.

Figure 5.18. Jacks's 26 commodities: average change in personal resource abundance, U.S. blue-collar and unskilled worker perspectives, percent (1850–2018)

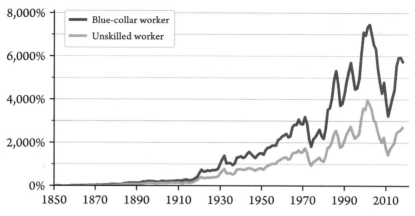

Source: Authors' calculations.

Jacks's 26 commodities: summary (1850–2018)

Between 1850 and 2018, the average TP of 26 commodities fell by 98.3 percent for blue-collar workers and 96.4 percent for unskilled workers. The average pRA of the former rose by 5,762 percent and the average of the latter by 2,682 percent (see Figure 5.18). The average pRAM for blue-collar workers rose to 58.62 and the average for unskilled workers to 27.82. The average CAGR-pRA for the former rose by 2.45 percent a year and the average for the latter at 2 percent a year. These numbers imply a doubling of the average pRA among blue-collar workers every 28.6 years and among unskilled workers every 35 years (see Table 5.2).

Food, finished goods, and beauty

The discussion of commodities may seem esoteric at times, but commodities are the building blocks of most foodstuffs and other finished products. A Big Mac, for example, contains beef, oil, sugar, and wheat. A bicycle contains steel or aluminum and rubber. Coal, gas, and uranium fuel our power plants, and petroleum powers our delivery trucks. Energy-related commodities, therefore, are essential to our factory production processes and our transport systems that use cars, planes, and trains. The cheaper that commodities

Table 5.2. Jacks's 26 commodities: summary of the U.S. blue-collar worker perspective and the U.S. unskilled worker perspective (1850–2018)

Jacks's 26 1850–2018	Percentage change in resource time price	Personal resource abundance multiplier	Percentage change in personal resource abundance	Compound annual percentage growth rate in personal resource abundance	Years to double personal resource abundance
Blue-collar	−98.3	58.62	5,762	2.45	28.6
Unskilled	−96.4	27.82	2,682	2.00	35.0

Source: Authors' calculations.

(inputs) get, the cheaper that products (output) can become. That is exactly what we find when we look at food prices and finished products. Even services can benefit from a greater pRA of commodities. While most of the service-associated costs come from the employment of human labor, people still have to rely on sophisticated machinery and energy that powers it. As such, we will use our methodology to look at the pRA of food (1919–2019), finished goods (1979–2019), and cosmetic procedures (1998–2018) in the United States.

U.S. food prices (1919–2019)

The U.S. Bureau of Labor Statistics (BLS) is a government agency responsible for tracking and reporting the Consumer Price Index (CPI). In 1921, the BLS published *Retail Prices, 1913 to December 1919*, Bulletin of the United States Bureau of Labor Statistics, no. 270. The bulletin contained current (or nominal) prices for 42 common food items: bacon, bananas, beans (baked), beans (navy), bread, butter, cabbage, cheese, chuck roast, coffee, corn, cornflakes, cornmeal, Cream of Wheat, Crisco, eggs, flour, ham, hens, lamb, lard, macaroni, milk (evaporated), milk (fresh), nut margarine,[8] onions, oranges, peas, beef plate,[9] pork chops, potatoes, prunes, raisins, rib roast, rice, rolled oats, round steak, salmon, sirloin steak, sugar, tea, and tomatoes.[10] In 2019, we visited https://www.walmart.com and looked for the same 42 items (including the same quantities of those items) and noted their current (or nominal) prices. We then subjected the two data sets to our analysis.

■ Box 5.1. Life has gotten sweeter, literally (1850–2021)

"Innovism," a term that U.S. economic historian Deirdre McCloskey prefers to the somewhat misleading and pejorative "capitalism," denotes a process of material enrichment based on innovation and trade, or "trade-tested betterment" (another term she coined). Trade benefits humanity in a myriad of ways. It allows us to discover the true value of goods and services. It promotes cooperation by building trust between contracting parties. And, most obviously, it enables us to buy goods and services that we would not be able to produce ourselves.

But trade alone did not bring about the "order of magnitude" enrichment that saw global GDP per person rise from less than $3 in 1800 to more than $40 in 2016 (in 2011 dollars). To explain our unprecedentedly high standards of living, we need to turn to another aspect of innovism: innovation.

To give just one example, agricultural production can increase when more farmers with more plows farm more land. But after the introduction of tractors, GMO crops, and synthetic fertilizers, agricultural productivity skyrocketed. Humanity can now produce more food using fewer workers and less land. By increasing productivity per worker, innovism can make something that was previously unattainable or prohibitively expensive common and affordable.

Consider sugar. People have been sucking on sugarcane for eight millennia. Refined or granulated sugar, which the Indians learned to make between the 1st and the 4th centuries CE, reached Western Europe via the Crusades in the Holy Land in the 11th century. In 1319, sugar sold for two shillings a pound in medieval London.[a] That's equivalent to 10 days of a skilled tradesman's labor.[b]

Assuming an 8-hour workday, the tradesman had to work 80 hours to afford a pound of the sweet stuff.[c] In 2021, the British supermarket chain Tesco sold a pound of granulated sugar for 30p, or 1.89 minutes of labor on Britain's "living wage" of £9.50 ($0.30 \div 9.50 = 0.0315$ hours, or 1.89 minutes).[d]

The "new spice" or the "fine spice," as the Europeans called refined sugar, was akin to pepper, which was more expensive than gold.[e] Sugar remained prohibitively expensive even after the Europeans learned how to extract it from the sugarcane (Venice became the main refining and distribution center on the continent) and began to import granulated sugar from the colonies. (Christopher Columbus introduced sugarcane to the New World in 1492, and

Europeans started to import African slaves to grow sugarcane in the Americas in the 16th century.)

Most Europeans, then, continued to sweeten their food and drink with honey. As late as the 16th century, William Shakespeare implied that "spices" were so precious as to keep them under lock and key in his play *Romeo and Juliet*.

> LADY CAPULET: Hold, take these keys, and fetch more spices, nurse.
> NURSE: They call for dates and quinces in the pastry.
> CAPULET: Come, stir, stir, stir! The second cock hath crow'd. The
> curfew bell hath rung, 'tis three o'clock: Look to the baked
> meats, good Angelica: Spare not for cost.[f]

The real breakthrough in the affordability of sugar came in 1747, when German chemist Andreas Sigismund Marggraf (1709–1782) used alcohol to extract juices from a number of different plants. One of those plants was *Beta vulgaris*, which originated in Silesia (now part of Poland). Today, that plant is popularly known as the sugar beet. Using a microscope, Marggraf noticed that crystallized sugar beet juice was identical to cane sugar. Marggraf's discovery was not fully appreciated until after he died, with the first beet-sugar refinery opening in 1802.

Production of sugar from the sugar beet got a massive boost during the Napoleonic Wars, when the Royal Navy blockaded the European continent—most of it under French control—and cut the French off from their sugarcane-growing colonies in the Caribbean. "To replace the lost source of sweetness," noted one source, "Napoleon directed the creation of a domestic beet sugar industry.... By the tail end of the Napoleonic Wars, 300 French factories were producing nearly eight million pounds of beet sugar."[g] Besides allowing the French to get around the British blockade, beet sugar was produced without slave labor, a fact that appealed to 19th-century abolitionists like the Quakers.

By 1850, productivity gains allowed for sugar to come within the reach of more people, selling for $0.17 a pound in the United States.[h] Given that a factory worker earned $0.06 an hour, he (and it was mostly "he" in that era) had to work 2 hours and 50 minutes to earn enough money to buy one pound of the sweet substance. In 2021, up to 60 percent of the U.S. sugar supply came from the sugar beet (the rest comes from sugarcane) and sold for about $0.32 a pound.[i] (The U.S. government's tariffs and subsidies, which protect domestic sugar producers from global competition, keep the U.S. sugar prices well above the world price of $0.17 a pound).[j]

The hourly compensation rate of a U.S. factory worker, in the meantime, rose to $32.54. A pound of sugar consequently cost 35 seconds of work in 2021. Put differently, the 2 hours and 50 minutes of work required to buy one pound of sugar in 1850 got a factory worker 288 pounds of sugar in 2021. Since 1850, life has gotten 28,700 percent sweeter. Next time you enjoy a cup of coffee and a doughnut, thank human innovation for our astonishing abundance! ∎

U.S. food prices: the U.S. blue-collar worker perspective (1919–2019)

Between 1919 and 2019, the average nominal hourly compensation rate of blue-collar workers in the United States rose from $0.43 to $32.36. Using nominal U.S. food prices as numerators and the average nominal hourly compensation rates of blue-collar workers in the United States as denominators, we find that the average TP of the 42 food items fell by 91.2 percent between 1919 and 2019. Eggs fell the most (−97.2 percent) and tea fell the least (−53.5 percent).

The average pRA increased by 1,032 percent. The pRA of eggs rose by 3,504 percent, and the pRA of tea rose by 115 percent (see Figure 5.19). The average pRAM rose to 11.32. The pRAM ranged from 36.04 for eggs to 2.15 for tea. The average CAGR-pRA came to 2.46 percent. The CAGR-pRA ranged from 3.65 percent for eggs to 0.77 percent for tea. The average CAGR-pRA figure implies a doubling of the average pRA every 28.57 years, with the pRA of eggs doubling every 19.34 years and the pRA of tea doubling every 90.44 years. For more, see Appendix 14.

U.S. food prices: the U.S. unskilled worker perspective (1919–2019)

Between 1919 and 2019, the average nominal hourly wage rate of unskilled workers in the United States rose from $0.25 to $13.66. As such, the average

Figure 5.19. U.S. food prices: U.S. blue-collar worker perspective (1919–2019)

	Change in resource time price	Personal resource abundance multiplier	Change in personal resource abundance	Compound annual growth rate in personal resource abundance	Years to double personal resource abundance
Eggs	−97.2%	36.04	3,504%	3.65%	19.34
Sugar	−96.2%	26.57	2,557%	3.33%	21.13
Corn flakes	−96.2%	26.34	2,534%	3.33%	21.19
Hens	−96.2%	26.27	2,527%	3.32%	21.21
Rice	−96.2%	26.00	2,500%	3.31%	21.28
Corn	−96.0%	24.71	2,371%	3.26%	21.61
Peas	−95.7%	23.20	2,220%	3.19%	22.04
Macaroni	−94.4%	17.87	1,687%	2.93%	24.04
Butter	−94.0%	16.64	1,564%	2.85%	24.65
Tomatoes	−93.7%	15.99	1,499%	2.81%	25.00
Lard	−93.7%	15.95	1,495%	2.81%	25.03
Ham	−93.0%	14.22	1,322%	2.69%	26.11
Milk, evp.	−92.4%	13.13	1,213%	2.61%	26.92
Pork chops	−92.2%	12.76	1,176%	2.58%	27.22
Milk, fresh	−91.7%	12.07	1,107%	2.52%	27.83
AVERAGE	−91.2%	11.32	1,032%	2.46%	28.57
Bananas	−91.0%	11.08	1,008%	2.43%	28.82
Cornmeal	−90.8%	10.89	989%	2.42%	29.03
Bacon	−90.7%	10.78	978%	2.41%	29.16
Cheese	−89.8%	9.83	883%	2.31%	30.33
Crisco	−89.4%	9.41	841%	2.27%	30.92
Beans, baked	−88.7%	8.87	787%	2.21%	31.76
Coffee	−87.7%	8.11	711%	2.12%	33.12
Flour	−87.4%	7.95	695%	2.09%	33.43
Salmon	−86.4%	7.37	637%	2.02%	34.70
Beans, navy	−83.9%	6.20	520%	1.84%	37.99
Rolled oats	−83.9%	6.19	519%	1.84%	38.01
Bread	−83.3%	6.00	500%	1.81%	38.70
Onions	−82.6%	5.76	476%	1.77%	39.59
Raisins	−82.3%	5.65	465%	1.75%	40.02
Prunes	−82.0%	5.56	456%	1.73%	40.41
Cream of Wheat	−81.6%	5.43	443%	1.71%	40.98
Nut margarine	−80.3%	5.08	408%	1.64%	42.67
Plate beef	−79.2%	4.81	381%	1.58%	44.16
Potatoes	−77.2%	4.39	339%	1.49%	46.86
Sirloin steak	−76.9%	4.34	334%	1.48%	47.25
Chuck roast	−76.3%	4.23	323%	1.45%	48.10
Lamb	−75.1%	4.01	301%	1.40%	49.89
Oranges	−73.5%	3.77	277%	1.34%	52.23
Cabbage	−73.0%	3.70	270%	1.32%	52.95
Round steak	−70.6%	3.40	240%	1.23%	56.60
Rib roast	−61.6%	2.60	160%	0.96%	72.52
Tea	−53.5%	2.15	115%	0.77%	90.44

Source: Authors' calculations.
Note: evp. = evaporated.

TP of the 42 food items fell by 87.8 percent between 1919 and 2019. Eggs fell the most (−96.2 percent) and tea the least (−36.1 percent).

The average pRA increased by 722 percent. The pRA of eggs rose by 2,519 percent, and the pRA of tea rose by 56 percent (see Figure 5.20). The average pRAM rose to 8.22. The pRAM ranged from 26.19 for eggs to 1.56 for tea. The average CAGR-pRA came to 2.13 percent. The CAGR-pRA ranged from 3.32 percent for eggs to 0.45 percent for tea. The average CAGR-pRA figure implies a doubling of the average pRA every 32.9 years, with the pRA of eggs doubling every 21.23 years and the pRA of tea doubling every 155.03 years. For more, see Appendix 15.

U.S. food prices: summary (1919–2019)

Between 1919 and 2019, the average TP of the 42 food items fell by 91.2 percent for blue-collar workers and 87.8 percent for unskilled workers. The average food pRA of the former rose by 1,032 percent and the average of the latter by 722 percent. The average pRAM for blue-collar workers rose to 11.32 and the average for unskilled workers to 8.22. The average CAGR-pRA for the former rose by 2.46 percent a year and the average for the latter at 2.13 percent a year. Those numbers imply a doubling of the average pRA among blue-collar workers every 28.57 years and among unskilled workers every 32.9 years (see Table 5.3).

U.S. finished goods (1979–2019)

So far, we have seen that basic commodities and foodstuffs have grown in pRA. What about consumer goods? To answer this question, we went back to the 1979 Sears Christmas catalog and looked at the nominal prices of 35 everyday items. Those items consisted of appliances, men's wear, children's wear, women's wear, and other miscellaneous items.

The items were as follows: slow cookers, covered dutch ovens, stainless steel open skillets, coffeemakers, toasters, blenders, electric can openers, food processors, upright vacuums, dishwashers, washers, dryers, wristwatches, electric men's rotary shavers, leather wallets, three-piece suits, dress pants, button-up cardigans, children's crib sets, boys' bib pants, fleece footed pajamas, girls' panties, women's knit camisoles, two-button blazers, belts with

Figure 5.20. U.S. food prices: U.S. unskilled worker perspective (1919–2019)

	Change in resource time price	Personal resource abundance multiplier	Change in personal resource abundance	Compound annual growth rate in personal resource abundance	Years to double personal resource abundance
Eggs	−96.2%	26.19	2,519%	3.32%	21.23
Sugar	−94.8%	19.31	1,831%	3.00%	23.41
Corn flakes	−94.8%	19.14	1,814%	3.00%	23.48
Hens	−94.8%	19.09	1,809%	2.99%	23.50
Rice	−94.7%	18.89	1,789%	2.98%	23.59
Corn	−94.4%	17.95	1,695%	2.93%	24.00
Peas	−94.1%	16.86	1,586%	2.87%	24.54
Macaroni	−92.3%	12.99	1,199%	2.60%	27.03
Butter	−91.7%	12.09	1,109%	2.52%	27.81
Tomatoes	−91.4%	11.62	1,062%	2.48%	28.26
Lard	−91.4%	11.59	1,059%	2.48%	28.29
Ham	−90.3%	10.34	934%	2.36%	29.68
Milk, evp.	−89.5%	9.54	854%	2.28%	30.73
Pork chops	−89.2%	9.27	827%	2.25%	31.13
Milk, fresh	−88.6%	8.77	777%	2.20%	31.92
AVERAGE	−87.8%	8.22	722%	2.13%	32.90
Bananas	−87.6%	8.05	705%	2.11%	33.23
Cornmeal	−87.4%	7.91	691%	2.09%	33.51
Bacon	−87.2%	7.83	683%	2.08%	33.68
Cheese	−86.0%	7.14	614%	1.99%	35.25
Crisco	−85.4%	6.84	584%	1.94%	36.06
Beans, baked	−84.5%	6.44	544%	1.88%	37.20
Coffee	−83.0%	5.89	489%	1.79%	39.08
Flour	−82.7%	5.78	478%	1.77%	39.52
Salmon	−81.3%	5.35	435%	1.69%	41.31
Beans, navy	−77.8%	4.51	351%	1.52%	46.05
Rolled oats	−77.8%	4.50	350%	1.52%	46.08
Bread	−77.1%	4.36	336%	1.48%	47.09
Onions	−76.1%	4.18	318%	1.44%	48.42
Raisins	−75.7%	4.11	311%	1.42%	49.07
Prunes	−75.2%	4.04	304%	1.41%	49.65
Cream of Wheat	−74.6%	3.94	294%	1.38%	50.51
Nut margarine	−72.9%	3.69	269%	1.31%	53.11
Plate beef	−71.4%	3.49	249%	1.26%	55.44
Potatoes	−68.7%	3.19	219%	1.17%	59.76
Sirloin steak	−68.3%	3.15	215%	1.15%	60.39
Chuck roast	−67.4%	3.07	207%	1.13%	61.79
Lamb	−65.7%	2.92	192%	1.08%	64.78
Oranges	−63.5%	2.74	174%	1.01%	68.78
Cabbage	−62.8%	2.69	169%	0.99%	70.03
Round steak	−59.6%	2.47	147%	0.91%	76.56
Rib roast	−47.1%	1.89	89%	0.64%	108.90
Tea	−36.1%	1.56	56%	0.45%	155.03

Source: Authors' calculations.
Note: evp. = evaporated.

Table 5.3. U.S. food prices: summary of the U.S. blue-collar worker perspective and the U.S. unskilled worker perspective (1919–2019)

U.S. food prices 1919–2019	Percentage change in resource time price	Personal resource abundance multiplier	Percentage change in personal resource abundance	Compound annual percentage growth rate in personal resource abundance	Years to double personal resource abundance
Blue-collar	−91.2	11.32	1,032	2.46	28.57
Unskilled	−87.8	8.22	722	2.13	32.9

Source: Authors' calculations.

fabric backing, dress pants, V-neck pullovers, gold necklaces, blow dryers, Isotoner gloves, sheer hose, butcher block carts, bicycles, stainless steel utensil sets, and jogging shoes.

In 2019, we visited https://www.walmart.com and gathered nominal prices of 35 identical or almost identical items. To convert those nominal prices into TPs, we used three distinct denominators: the U.S. unskilled workers' hourly wage, the U.S. blue-collar workers' hourly compensation rates, and the U.S. upskilling workers' hourly compensation rates.

Unlike in the previous sections where we analyzed commodities and food items as we found them, we picked the data to be analyzed ourselves in the case of U.S. finished goods. With thousands of possibilities to choose from, we tried our best to select items that reflect the familiar needs of everyday people. Our choices were, for once, subjective. Others are urged to analyze other finished goods using our methodology.

■ Box 5.2. Pickup prosperity (1970–2019)

Can you compare a pickup truck built today with one built in 1970? They're almost as different as the famously unreliable and poorly designed Yugo made in communist Yugoslavia and a luxurious, mechanically reliable Lexus made by Japan's Toyota Motor Corporation. In 1970, Ford made the F-100. The F-150 was introduced in 1975 as a way of avoiding certain U.S. emissions control restrictions.

Instead of trying to compare a 1970 F-100 to a 2019 F-150, we found a pickup that is manufactured today and is roughly equivalent to the 1970 Ford pickup. India's Mahindra Bolero Maxi and China's Foton, JAC, and Hilux all make cars that are similar to the 1970 F-100. They sell for about $10,000.[k]

In 1970, a basic Ford F-100 sold for $2,599.[l] Back then, the U.S. blue-collar hourly compensation rate was $3.93. That means that the time price (TP) of the F-100 amounted to 661.3 hours in 1970. The China-India equivalents of the 1970 F-100 sold for $10,000 in 2019. That year, the U.S. blue-collar compensation rate was $32.36 an hour, indicating that the TP of the China-India equivalent of the 1970 F-100 amounted to 309 hours.

That means that pickups have become 53.3 percent cheaper. For the length of working time required to buy one pickup in 1970, the U.S. blue-collar worker could get 2.14 pickups in 2019. Between 1970 and 2019, pickup trucks grew 1.56 percent more abundant each year, suggesting a doubling of the abundance of pickup trucks every 45 years.

In 1970, the U.S. unskilled worker hourly wage rate came to $1.85. That means that the TP of the F-100 amounted to 1,404 hours of work in 1970. The China-India equivalents of the 1970 F-100 sold for $10,000 in 2019. That year, the U.S. unskilled worker hourly wage rate was $13.66 an hour, indicating that the TPs of the Chinese and Indian equivalents of the 1970 F-100 amounted to 732 hours of work.

That means that pickups for unskilled workers have become 48 percent cheaper. For the length of working time required to buy one pickup in 1970, the U.S. unskilled worker could get 1.92 pickups in 2019. Between 1970 and 2019, pickup trucks grew 1.34 percent more abundant each year, suggesting a doubling of the abundance of pickup trucks every 52 years.

Let's turn to upskilling workers. Imagine a U.S. worker who entered the job market in 1970 as an unskilled laborer and retired as a blue-collar worker in 2019. For the same length of working time it took that worker to earn enough money to buy one pickup in 1970, he or she could buy 4.55 pickups in 2019 (see Table B5.2.1).

Table B5.2.1. Personal resource abundance analysis of pickups in the United States: summary of the U.S. blue-collar worker perspective, the U.S. unskilled worker perspective, and the U.S. upskilling worker perspective (1970–2019)

Pickup trucks 1970–2019	Percentage change in resource time price	Personal resource abundance multiplier	Percentage change in personal resource abundance	Compound annual percentage growth rate in personal resource abundance	Years to double personal resource abundance
Blue-collar	−53.3	2.14	114.0	1.56	44.6
Unskilled	−47.9	1.92	91.9	1.34	52.1
Upskilling	−78.0	4.55	354.6	3.14	22.4

Source: Authors' calculations. ∎

U.S. finished goods: the U.S. blue-collar worker perspective (1979–2019)

Between 1979 and 2019, the average U.S. blue-collar worker hourly compensation rate rose from $8.34 to $32.36. Using nominal U.S. finished goods prices as numerators and average U.S. blue-collar worker hourly compensation rates as denominators, we find that the average TP of 35 finished goods fell by 72.3 percent. As such, the average pRA rose by 261 percent, the average pRAM rose to 3.61, and the average CAGR-pRA increased at 3.26 percent per year, indicating a doubling of the average pRA every 21.6 years (see Figure 5.21). For more, see Appendix 16.

U.S. finished goods: the U.S. unskilled worker perspective (1979–2019)

Between 1979 and 2019, the average U.S. unskilled worker hourly wage rate rose from $3.69 to $13.66. As such, the average TP of the 35 finished goods fell by 71 percent. Additionally, the average pRA rose by 244 percent, the average pRAM rose to 3.44, and the average CAGR-pRA increased at 3.14 percent

Figure 5.21. U.S. finished goods: U.S. blue-collar worker perspective (1979–2019)

	Change in resource time price	Personal resource abundance multiplier	Change in personal resource abundance	Compound annual growth rate in personal resource abundance	Years to double personal resource abundance
APPLIANCES	−74.8%	3.97	297%	3.51%	20.10
Food processor	−86.1%	7.21	621%	5.06%	14.04
Vacuum	−83.1%	5.91	491%	4.54%	15.61
Can opener	−80.9%	5.24	424%	4.23%	16.74
Blender	−79.2%	4.80	380%	4.00%	17.67
Toaster	−76.6%	4.28	328%	3.70%	19.08
Skillet	−74.2%	3.88	288%	3.45%	20.45
Coffeemaker	−65.2%	2.87	187%	2.67%	26.29
Washer	−64.6%	2.83	183%	2.63%	26.69
Dutch oven	−63.2%	2.72	172%	2.53%	27.75
Slow cooker	−63.2%	2.72	172%	2.53%	27.75
Dryer	−61.9%	2.62	162%	2.44%	28.77
Dishwasher	−61.5%	2.60	160%	2.42%	29.02
MEN'S	−72.0%	3.57	257%	3.23%	21.78
Cardigan	−81.4%	5.37	437%	4.29%	16.49
Wallet	−78.5%	4.66	366%	3.92%	18.01
Shaver	−73.6%	3.79	279%	3.38%	20.82
Suit	−70.5%	3.40	240%	3.10%	22.68
Pants	−59.7%	2.48	148%	2.30%	30.50
Watch	−42.0%	1.73	73%	1.37%	50.82
CHILDREN'S	−69.8%	3.31	231%	3.04%	23.16
Panties	−78.5%	4.65	365%	3.92%	18.04
Crib	−77.2%	4.38	338%	3.76%	18.77
Pants	−63.7%	2.76	176%	2.57%	27.33
Pajamas	−31.2%	1.45	45%	0.94%	74.07
WOMEN'S	−69.8%	3.31	231%	3.04%	23.15
Camisole	−88.5%	8.73	773%	5.57%	12.80
Gloves	−73.2%	3.73	273%	3.34%	21.08
Sheer hose	−70.3%	3.37	237%	3.08%	22.84
Blazer	−69.1%	3.23	223%	2.98%	23.62
Blow dryer	−67.4%	3.06	206%	2.84%	24.77
Belt	−65.6%	2.91	191%	2.71%	25.96
Sweater	−49.8%	1.99	99%	1.74%	40.20
Pants	−44.8%	1.81	81%	1.50%	46.67
Gold necklace	+3.1%	0.97	−3%	−0.08%	N/A
MISCELLANEOUS	−72.4%	3.62	262%	3.27%	21.55
Butcher block	−82.0%	5.54	454%	4.37%	16.19
Bicycle	−74.2%	3.88	288%	3.45%	20.45
Jogging shoes	−66.7%	3.01	201%	2.79%	25.19
Utensil set	−51.4%	2.06	106%	1.82%	38.43
AVERAGE	−72.3%	3.61	261%	3.26%	21.60

Source: Authors' calculations.
Note: N/A = Doubling period cannot be calculated for commodities that have become less rather than more abundant between two points in time.

per year, indicating a doubling of the average pRA every 22.42 years (see Figure 5.22). For more, see Appendix 17.

U.S. finished goods: the U.S. upskilling worker perspective (1979–2019)

Between 1979 and 2019, the average U.S. upskilling worker hourly compensation rate rose from $3.69 to $32.36. As such, the average TP of 35 finished goods fell by 87.7 percent. Additionally, the average pRA rose by 716 percent and the average pRAM rose to 8.16. The average CAGR-pRA increased at 5.39 percent per year, indicating a doubling of the average pRA every 13.21 years (see Figure 5.23). For more, see Appendix 18.

U.S. finished goods: summary (1979–2019)

Between 1979 and 2019, the average TP of 35 finished goods fell by 72.3 percent for blue-collar workers, 71 percent for unskilled workers, and 87.7 percent for upskilling workers. The average finished goods pRA for blue-collar workers rose by 261 percent, for unskilled workers by 244 percent, and for upskilling workers by 716 percent. The average pRAM for blue-collar workers rose to 3.61, for unskilled workers to 3.44, and for upskilling workers to 8.16. The average CAGR-pRA for blue-collar workers rose by 3.26 percent a year, for unskilled workers by 3.14 percent a year, and for upskilling workers by 5.39 percent a year. Those numbers imply a doubling of the average pRA among blue-collar workers every 21.6 years, among unskilled workers every 22.42 years, and among upskilling workers every 13.21 years (see Table 5.4).

U.S. cosmetic procedures (1998–2018)

University of Michigan-Flint economist Mark J. Perry conducts an annual cost analysis of the 19 most popular cosmetic procedures in the United States. According to Perry, the average nominal price of those 19 procedures increased by 22 percent between 1998 and 2018. The prices ranged from a 47.3 percent decrease for laser hair removal to a 93.3 percent increase for chin augmentation. Over the same period, the CPI increased by 54 percent (in other words, the prices of cosmetic procedures rose slower than inflation, on average). By contrast, the average cost of medical services increased by 109.8 percent, and the average cost of hospital services rose by 201.6 percent

Figure 5.22. U.S. finished goods: U.S. unskilled worker perspective (1979–2019)

	Change in resource time price	Personal resource abundance multiplier	Change in personal resource abundance	Compound annual growth rate in personal resource abundance	Years to double personal resource abundance
APPLIANCES	−73.6%	3.79	279%	3.39%	20.81
Food processor	−85.5%	6.88	588%	4.94%	14.38
Vacuum	−82.3%	5.64	464%	4.42%	16.03
Can opener	−80.0%	5.00	400%	4.10%	17.23
Blender	−78.2%	4.58	358%	3.88%	18.22
Toaster	−75.5%	4.08	308%	3.58%	19.71
Skillet	−73.0%	3.70	270%	3.33%	21.18
Coffeemaker	−63.5%	2.74	174%	2.55%	27.52
Washer	−62.9%	2.70	170%	2.51%	27.96
Dutch oven	−61.4%	2.59	159%	2.41%	29.12
Slow cooker	−61.4%	2.59	159%	2.41%	29.12
Dryer	−60.0%	2.50	150%	2.32%	30.25
Dishwasher	−59.7%	2.48	148%	2.30%	30.52
MEN'S	−70.6%	3.41	241%	3.11%	22.62
Cardigan	−80.5%	5.13	413%	4.17%	16.96
Wallet	−77.5%	4.45	345%	3.80%	18.58
Shaver	−72.3%	3.61	261%	3.26%	21.58
Suit	−69.1%	3.24	224%	2.98%	23.59
Pants	−57.8%	2.37	137%	2.18%	32.17
Watch	−39.3%	1.65	65%	1.25%	55.62
CHILDREN'S	−68.3%	3.16	216%	2.92%	24.11
Panties	−77.5%	4.43	343%	3.79%	18.61
Crib	−76.1%	4.18	318%	3.64%	19.38
Pants	−62.0%	2.63	163%	2.45%	28.65
Pajamas	−27.9%	1.39	39%	0.82%	84.71
WOMEN'S	−68.4%	3.16	216%	2.92%	24.10
Camisole	−88.0%	8.33	733%	5.44%	13.08
Gloves	−71.9%	3.56	256%	3.22%	21.86
Sheer hose	−68.9%	3.21	221%	2.96%	23.76
Blazer	−67.6%	3.09	209%	2.86%	24.60
Blow dryer	−65.8%	2.92	192%	2.72%	25.86
Belt	−64.0%	2.78	178%	2.59%	27.15
Sweater	−47.4%	1.90	90%	1.62%	43.14
Pants	−42.1%	1.73	73%	1.38%	50.68
Gold necklace	+8.0%	0.93	−7%	−0.19%	N/A
MISCELLANEOUS	−71.1%	3.45	245%	3.15%	22.36
Butcher block	−81.1%	5.29	429%	4.25%	16.65
Bicycle	−73.0%	3.70	270%	3.33%	21.18
Jogging shoes	−65.1%	2.87	187%	2.67%	26.31
Utensil set	−49.1%	1.96	96%	1.70%	41.11
AVERAGE	−71.0%	3.44	244%	3.14%	22.42

Source: Authors' calculations.
Note: N/A = Doubling period cannot be calculated for commodities that have become less rather than more abundant between two points in time.

Figure 5.23. U.S. finished goods: U.S. upskilling worker perspective (1979–2019)

	Change in resource time price	Personal resource abundance multiplier	Change in personal resource abundance	Compound annual growth rate in personal resource abundance	Years to double personal resource abundance
APPLIANCES	−88.9%	8.98	798%	5.64%	12.63
Food processor	−93.9%	16.29	1,529%	7.23%	9.94
Vacuum	−92.5%	13.35	1,235%	6.69%	10.70
Can opener	−91.6%	11.84	1,084%	6.37%	11.22
Blender	−90.8%	10.85	985%	6.14%	11.63
Toaster	−89.7%	9.67	867%	5.84%	12.22
Skillet	−88.6%	8.77	777%	5.58%	12.77
Coffeemaker	−84.6%	6.49	549%	4.79%	14.83
Washer	−84.3%	6.39	539%	4.74%	14.95
Dutch oven	−83.7%	6.14	514%	4.64%	15.28
Slow cooker	−83.7%	6.14	514%	4.64%	15.28
Dryer	−83.1%	5.92	492%	4.55%	15.58
Dishwasher	−83.0%	5.88	488%	4.53%	15.66
MEN'S	−87.6%	8.07	707%	5.36%	13.28
Cardigan	−91.8%	12.15	1,115%	6.44%	11.10
Wallet	−90.5%	10.53	953%	6.06%	11.78
Shaver	−88.3%	8.56	756%	5.51%	12.91
Suit	−87.0%	7.67	667%	5.23%	13.61
Pants	−82.2%	5.61	461%	4.41%	16.08
Watch	−74.4%	3.90	290%	3.46%	20.37
CHILDREN'S	−86.6%	7.48	648%	5.16%	13.78
Panties	−90.5%	10.51	951%	6.06%	11.79
Crib	−89.9%	9.90	890%	5.90%	12.09
Pants	−84.0%	6.23	523%	4.68%	15.15
Pajamas	−69.6%	3.29	229%	3.02%	23.30
WOMEN'S	−86.6%	7.48	648%	5.16%	13.77
Camisole	−94.9%	19.73	1,873%	7.74%	9.30
Gloves	−88.1%	8.42	742%	5.47%	13.01
Sheer hose	−86.9%	7.61	661%	5.20%	13.66
Blazer	−86.3%	7.31	631%	5.10%	13.94
Blow dryer	−85.6%	6.92	592%	4.96%	14.33
Belt	−84.8%	6.58	558%	4.82%	14.72
Sweater	−77.8%	4.51	351%	3.83%	18.42
Pants	−75.6%	4.09	309%	3.59%	19.67
Gold necklace	−54.4%	2.19	119%	1.98%	35.31
MISCELLANEOUS	−87.8%	8.18	718%	5.40%	13.19
Butcher block	−92.0%	12.52	1,152%	6.52%	10.97
Bicycle	−88.6%	8.77	777%	5.58%	12.77
Jogging shoes	−85.3%	6.80	580%	4.91%	14.47
Utensil set	−78.5%	4.65	365%	3.92%	18.04
AVERAGE	−87.7%	8.16	716%	5.39%	13.21

Source: Authors' calculations.

Table 5.4. U.S. finished goods: summary of the U.S. blue-collar worker perspective, the U.S. unskilled worker perspective, and the U.S. upskilling worker perspective (1979–2019)

U.S. goods prices 1979–2019	Percentage change in resource time price	Personal resource abundance multiplier	Percentage change in personal resource abundance	Compound annual percentage growth rate in personal resource abundance	Years to double personal resource abundance
Blue-collar	−72.3	3.61	261	3.26	21.60
Unskilled	−71.0	3.44	244	3.14	22.42
Upskilling	−87.7	8.16	716	5.39	13.21

Source: Authors' calculations.

(that is, both medical and hospital costs rose faster than inflation, on average). In this section, we subject Perry's 19 cosmetic procedures to our methodology. Once again, our denominators will include the U.S. blue-collar worker hourly compensation rate, the U.S. unskilled worker hourly wage, and the U.S. upskilling worker hourly compensation rate.

U.S. cosmetic procedures: the U.S. blue-collar worker perspective (1998–2018)

Between 1998 and 2018, the average hourly compensation rate of U.S. blue-collar workers rose from $18.18 to $32.06. Using the nominal prices of U.S. cosmetic procedures as numerators and the average hourly compensation rates of U.S. blue-collar workers as denominators, we find that U.S. blue-collar workers saw the average TP of 19 cosmetic procedures fall by 30.8 percent. The TP of laser hair removal fell the most (−70.1 percent), while the TP of chin augmentation actually increased by 9.6 percent.

The average pRA rose by 45 percent. The pRA of laser hair removal increased 235 percent, while chin augmentation became 9 percent less abundant. The average pRAM rose to 1.45. It rose to 3.35 for laser hair removal and fell to 0.91 for chin augmentation.[11] The average CAGR-pRA increased at 1.86 percent a year. It rose at 6.23 percent a year for laser hair removal and decreased 0.46 percent for chin augmentation. Those numbers imply a doubling of the average pRA every 37.65 years and a doubling for laser hair removal every 11.47 years (see Figure 5.24). For more, see Appendix 19.

■ Box 5.3. Cool innovation (1952–2019)

Air conditioning was invented in 1902 by Willis Carrier in Brooklyn, New York. Carrier invented an air conditioning unit for a local publishing business, which was having problems caused by the hot and humid conditions in its factory. Sweltering Brooklyn summers meant that the printing paper in the publisher's factory would often soak up the moisture from the air. That, in turn, caused the paper to expand and change shape. Finally, paper expansion ruined the alignment of colors on the printed page, causing financial losses.

Although air conditioning was originally used for industrial purposes, it surged in popularity during the post–World War II economic boom in the United States, and its use expanded to offices, hotels, stores, movie theaters, and private homes. One of the most impressive aspects of the history of air conditioning is how quickly it went from being a luxury reserved for large businesses and the richest members of society to being affordable for the masses of ordinary people.

Consider the following data. In 1952, the average U.S. blue-collar hourly compensation rate was $1.72.[m] As Southern Methodist University economists W. Michael Cox and Richard Alm found in their 1997 report *Time Well Spent: The Declining Real Cost of Living in America,* the average cost of a 5,500 BTU air conditioning unit in 1952 came to $350.[n] That meant that a U.S. blue-collar worker had to work 203.49 hours to earn enough money to buy an air conditioning unit in 1952 (see Table B5.3.1).

In 2019, Walmart sold a far more energy-efficient and aesthetically pleasing 6,000 BTU air-conditioning unit (with a remote control) for only $178.[o] With the hourly compensation rate of a U.S. blue-collar worker standing at $32.36, it took just 5.5 hours of work to buy such an air-conditioning unit. That means that the time price (TP) (the number of working hours needed to earn enough money to buy a product) of air conditioning fell by 97.3 percent between 1952 and 2019.

Put differently, for the same length of labor that it took to earn enough money to buy one air-conditioning unit in 1952, a U.S. blue-collar worker could buy about 37 units in 2019. Over the intervening 67 years, in other words, air conditioners became almost 3,600 percent more abundant. Air-conditioner abundance increased at a compound annual rate of about 5.54 percent, implying a doubling of abundance every 12.86 years.

Table B5.3.1. Personal resource abundance analysis of air conditioning: the U.S. blue-collar worker perspective (1952–2019)

Blue-collar worker analysis	1952	2019	Percentage change	Change in personal resource abundance	Percentage change in personal resource abundance	Compound annual percentage growth rate in personal resource abundance	Years to double personal resource abundance
5,500/6,000 BTU AC unit nominal price	$350.00	$178.00	−49.1				
Blue-collar hourly rate	$1.72	$32.36	1,781.4				
Time price in hours	203.49	5.50	−97.3	36.99	3,599	5.54	12.86
Electricity kWh rate	$0.018	$0.139	672.2				
Cost for 1,000 kWhs	$18.00	$139.00					
Hours to earn 1,000 kWhs	10.47	4.30	−59.0	2.44	144	1.34	52.15
Total work hours for AC and power	213.95	9.80	−95.4	21.84	2,084	4.71	15.06

Source: Authors' calculations.

Note: AC = air conditioning.

Unskilled workers in the United States earned $0.83 per hour in 1952, requiring 421.7 hours of work to buy one of the air-conditioning units mentioned by Alm and Cox. By 2019, the hourly wage rate of U.S. unskilled workers increased to $13.66. The TP of an air-conditioning unit at Walmart fell to slightly over 13 hours in 2019. That amounts to a TP decline of almost 97 percent, suggesting a personal resource abundance multiplier of 32.36 and implying a doubling of personal resource abundance every 13.4 years (see Table B5.3.2).

What about the cost of electricity over the same period? The nominal price of electricity has increased from 1.8 cents per kilowatt-hour (kWh) in 1952 to 13.9 cents in 2019, or 672 percent.[P] Recall, though, that the U.S. blue-collar hourly compensation rate increased by 1,781 percent. So, the TP of electricity fell by 59 percent. Similarly, the unskilled wage rate in the United States rose by 1,546 percent. So, the TP of electricity relative to the wages of U.S. unskilled workers fell by 53.1 percent.

The time it took for a U.S. blue-collar worker to earn enough money to buy an air conditioner and 1,000 kWhs of electricity came to 214 hours in 1952. By 2019, it fell to 9.8 hours (a 95.4 percent drop in the TP). Relative to the hourly compensation rate of the U.S. blue-collar worker, air conditioning units and power became almost 22 times more abundant between 1952 and 2019. The time it took a U.S. unskilled worker to earn enough money to buy an air conditioner and 1,000 kWhs of electricity came to 443 hours in 1952. By 2019, it fell to 23.2 hours, amounting to a 95 percent drop in the TP. Relative to the hourly wage rate of the U.S. unskilled worker, air-conditioning units and power became almost 19.11 times more abundant between 1952 and 2019.

Had the entire population of the United States in 1952—158 million people—consisted of blue-collar workers who bought an air-conditioning unit and 1,000 kWhs of electricity, such purchases would have required 33.805 billion hours of work. By 2019, the population of the United States increased to 330 million, a 109 percent increase, yet, it would have taken only 3.233 billion hours of work for every single American to be able to afford an air-conditioning unit and 1000 kWhs of electricity. That means that even as the U.S. population more than doubled, the total cost to provide air conditioning for the whole country fell by more than 90 percent.

Had the entire population of the United States in 1952 consisted of unskilled workers who bought an air-conditioning unit and 1,000 kWhs of electricity,

Table B5.3.2. Personal resource abundance analysis of air conditioning: the U.S. unskilled worker perspective (1952–2019)

Unskilled worker analysis	1952	2019	Percentage change	Change in personal resource abundance	Percentage change in personal resource abundance	Compound annual percentage growth rate in personal resource abundance	Years to double personal resource abundance
5,500/6,000 BTU AC unit nominal price	$350.00	$178.00	−49.1				
Unskilled hourly rate	$0.83	$13.66	1,545.8				
Time price in hours	421.69	13.03	−96.9	32.36	3,136	5.33	13.36
Electricity kWh rate	$0.018	$0.139	672.2				
Cost for 1,000 kWhs	$18.00	$139.00					
Hours to earn 1,000 kWhs	21.69	10.18	−53.1	2.13	113	1.14	61.37
Total work hours for AC and power	443.37	23.21	−94.8	19.11	1,811	4.50	15.74

Source: Authors' calculations.
Note: AC = air conditioning.

such purchases would have required 70 billion hours of work. By 2019, it would have taken only 7.6 billion hours of work for every single American to be able to afford an air-conditioning unit and 1000 kWhs of electricity. That means that the total cost to provide air conditioning for the whole country fell by 89 percent. ∎

U.S. cosmetic procedures: the U.S. unskilled worker perspective (1998–2018)

It may seem a little strange to include a section on the abundance of U.S. cosmetic procedures relative to the wages of U.S. unskilled workers. People at the bottom of the income ladder, we recognize, face more pressing challenges than hair removal and chin augmentations. In the end, we decided to discuss cosmetic procedures from the perspective of unskilled workers for one simple reason. The budgets of the unskilled workers are disproportionately squeezed by fast-growing medical and hospital bills in the United States. We contend that those price increases would be lower if health care in the United States were subjected to some of the competitive forces that operate in the market for cosmetic procedures. By outlining the effect of market competition on the abundance of cosmetic procedures, we hope to show that a somewhat more affordable health care is possible, even for poorer Americans.

Between 1998 and 2018, the average hourly wage rate of U.S. unskilled workers rose from $7.75 to $12.78. As such, U.S. unskilled workers saw the average TP of 19 cosmetic procedures fall by an average of 26 percent. The TP of laser hair removal fell the most (−68.1 percent), while the TP of chin augmentation actually increased by 17.2 percent. The average pRA rose by 35 percent. The pRA of laser hair removal increased 213 percent, while chin augmentation became 15 percent less abundant.

The average pRAM rose to 1.35. It rose to 3.13 for laser hair removal and fell to 0.85 for chin augmentation.[12] The average CAGR-pRA increased at 1.52 percent a year. It rose at 5.87 percent a year for laser hair removal and decreased 0.79 percent for chin augmentation. Those numbers imply a doubling of the average pRA every 46.04 years and a doubling

Figure 5.24. U.S. cosmetic procedures: U.S. blue-collar worker perspective (1998–2018)

	Change in resource time price	Personal resource abundance multiplier	Change in personal resource abundance	Compound annual growth rate in personal resource abundance	Years to double personal resource abundance
Laser hair removal	−70.1%	3.35	235%	6.23%	11.47
Botox injection	−58.4%	2.40	140%	4.48%	15.80
Chemical peel	−52.1%	2.09	109%	3.75%	18.82
Laser skin resurfacing	−35.2%	1.54	54%	2.19%	31.96
Breast reduction	−32.6%	1.48	48%	1.99%	35.10
AVERAGE	−30.8%	1.45	45%	1.86%	37.65
Breast augmentation	−29.4%	1.42	42%	1.76%	39.78
Liposuction	−25.9%	1.35	35%	1.51%	46.35
Breast lift	−21.0%	1.27	27%	1.19%	58.76
Varicose vein treatment	−20.9%	1.27	27%	1.18%	58.97
Eyelid surgery	−19.6%	1.24	24%	1.10%	63.47
Thigh lift	−16.2%	1.19	19%	0.89%	78.36
Tummy tuck	−15.5%	1.18	18%	0.85%	82.23
Lower body lift	−15.5%	1.18	18%	0.84%	82.41
Buttock lift	−14.4%	1.17	17%	0.78%	89.18
Nose surgery	−12.7%	1.15	15%	0.68%	102.13
Male breast reduction	−11.6%	1.13	13%	0.62%	112.14
Face-lift	−11.1%	1.13	13%	0.59%	117.56
Upper arm lift	−0.4%	1.00	0%	N/A	N/A
Chin augmentation	+9.6%	0.91	−9%	−0.46%	N/A

Source: Authors' calculations.
Note: N/A = Doubling period cannot be calculated for commodities that have become less rather than more abundant between two points in time.

for laser hair removal every 12.14 years (see Figure 5.25). For more, see Appendix 20.

U.S. cosmetic procedures: the U.S. upskilling worker perspective (1998–2018)

Between 1998 and 2018, the average hourly compensation rates of U.S. upskilling workers rose from $7.75 to $32.06. As such, U.S. upskilling workers saw the average TP of 19 cosmetic procedures fall by 70.5 percent. The TPs of laser hair removal fell the most (−87.3 percent) and chin augmentation the least (−53.3 percent). The average pRA rose by 239 percent, the pRA of laser hair removal increased 686 percent, and the pRA of chin augmentation increased 114 percent.

The average pRAM rose to 3.39. It rose to 7.86 for laser hair removal and 2.14 for chin augmentation. The average CAGR-pRA rose 6.29 percent a

Figure 5.25. U.S. cosmetic procedures: U.S. unskilled worker perspective (1998–2018)

	Change in resource time price	Personal resource abundance multiplier	Change in personal resource abundance	Compound annual growth rate in personal resource abundance	Years to double personal resource abundance
Laser hair removal	−68.1%	3.13	213%	5.87%	12.14
Botox injection	−55.5%	2.25	125%	4.13%	17.11
Chemical peel	−48.8%	1.95	95%	3.41%	20.70
Laser skin resurfacing	−30.7%	1.44	44%	1.85%	37.80
Breast reduction	−28.0%	1.39	39%	1.65%	42.28
AVERAGE	−26.0%	1.35	35%	1.52%	46.04
Breast augmentation	−24.5%	1.32	32%	1.42%	49.27
Liposuction	−20.7%	1.26	26%	1.17%	59.75
Breast lift	−15.5%	1.18	18%	0.85%	82.11
Varicose vein treatment	−15.5%	1.18	18%	0.84%	82.53
Eyelid surgery	−14.0%	1.16	16%	0.76%	91.62
Thigh lift	−10.4%	1.12	12%	0.55%	126.24
Tummy tuck	−9.7%	1.11	11%	0.51%	136.61
Lower body lift	−9.6%	1.11	11%	0.51%	137.08
Buttock lift	−8.5%	1.09	9%	0.44%	156.91
Nose surgery	−6.6%	1.07	7%	0.34%	201.98
Male breast reduction	−5.5%	1.06	6%	0.28%	245.25
Face-lift	−5.0%	1.05	5%	0.25%	272.76
Upper arm lift	+6.5%	0.94	−6%	−0.31%	N/A
Chin augmentation	+17.2%	0.85	−15%	−0.79%	N/A

Source: Authors' calculations.
Note: N/A = Doubling period cannot be calculated for commodities that have become less rather than more abundant between two points in time.

year. It rose at 10.86 percent a year for laser hair removal and 3.88 percent for chin augmentation. Those numbers imply a doubling of the average pRA every 11.36 years, of laser hair removal every 6.73 years, and of chin augmentation every 18.22 years (see Figure 5.26). For more, see Appendix 21.

U.S. cosmetic procedures: summary (1998–2018)

Between 1998 and 2018, U.S. blue-collar workers saw the average TP of cosmetic procedures fall by 30.8 percent, indicating a 45 percent increase in the average pRA. U.S. unskilled workers saw the average TP fall by 26 percent, indicating a 35 percent increase in the average pRA. U.S. upskilling workers saw the average TP fall by 70.5 percent, indicating a 239 percent increase in the average pRA. The average pRAM rose to 1.45, 1.35, and 3.39, respectively. The average CAGR-pRA rose by 1.86 percent

Figure 5.26. U.S. cosmetic procedures: U.S. upskilling worker perspective (1998–2018)

	Change in resource time price	Personal resource abundance multiplier	Change in personal resource abundance	Compound annual growth rate in personal resource abundance	Years to double personal resource abundance
Laser hair removal	−87.3%	7.86	686%	10.86%	6.73
Botox injection	−82.3%	5.64	464%	9.03%	8.01
Chemical peel	−79.6%	4.90	390%	8.27%	8.72
Laser skin resurfacing	−72.4%	3.62	262%	6.64%	10.78
Breast reduction	−71.3%	3.48	248%	6.44%	11.11
AVERAGE	−70.5%	3.39	239%	6.29%	11.36
Breast augmentation	−69.9%	3.32	232%	6.19%	11.54
Liposuction	−68.4%	3.16	216%	5.93%	12.04
Breast lift	−66.3%	2.97	197%	5.59%	12.74
Varicose vein treatment	−66.3%	2.97	197%	5.59%	12.75
Eyelid surgery	−65.7%	2.92	192%	5.50%	12.94
Thigh lift	−64.3%	2.80	180%	5.28%	13.47
Tummy tuck	−64.0%	2.78	178%	5.24%	13.58
Lower body lift	−64.0%	2.78	178%	5.24%	13.58
Buttock lift	−63.5%	2.74	174%	5.17%	13.75
Nose surgery	−62.8%	2.69	169%	5.07%	14.03
Male breast reduction	−62.3%	2.65	165%	5.00%	14.20
Face-lift	−62.1%	2.64	164%	4.97%	14.28
Upper arm lift	−57.6%	2.36	136%	4.38%	16.17
Chin augmentation	−53.3%	2.14	114%	3.88%	18.22

Source: Authors' calculations.

Table 5.5. U.S. cosmetic procedures: summary of the U.S. blue-collar worker perspective, the U.S. unskilled worker perspective, and U.S. upskilling worker perspective (1998–2018)

Cosmetic procedures 1998–2018	Percentage change in resource time price	Personal resource abundance multiplier	Percentage change in personal resource abundance	Compound annual percentage growth rate in personal resource abundance	Years to double personal resource abundance
Blue-collar	−30.8	1.45	45	1.86	37.65
Unskilled	−26.0	1.35	35	1.52	46.04
Upskilling	−70.5	3.39	239	6.29	11.36

Source: Authors' calculations.

a year for U.S. blue-collar workers, 1.52 percent a year for U.S. unskilled workers, and 6.29 percent a year for U.S. upskilling workers. Those figures indicate a doubling of the average pRA every 37.65 years, 46.04 years, and 11.36 years, respectively (see Table 5.5).

The Simon-Ehrlich wager reconsidered (1980–1990, 1980–2018, and 1900–2018)

The original Simon-Ehrlich wager took place between 1980 and 1990. This was a bet on the inflation-adjusted prices of five metals (chromium, copper, nickel, tin, and tungsten) that were selected by Ehrlich and his two partners, John Harte and John P. Holdren.

The wager placed $200 on each of the five commodities for a total of $1,000.[13] Over the next 10 years, inflation increased by 58 percent, and consequently, $1,000 in 1980 became $1,580 in 1990. What happened to the price of the five metals? The nominal price of the five metals hardly moved, increasing from $1,000 to only $1,003.93. The difference between $1,580 and $1,003.93 came to $576.07, or a decline of around 36 percent. That was the amount that Ehrlich mailed to Simon in the form of a personal check on October 11, 1990 (see Chapter 3).

In this section, we will subject the original bet between the two scholars to our time price analysis. We will then extend our time price analysis of the bet to 2018. Finally, we will take it back in time all the way to 1900. Doing so should allow us to see if Simon's win was just a fluke, or if Simon identified a broader trend in the relationship between population growth and the abundance of resources.

The Simon-Ehrlich wager: time pricing the original bet (1980–1990)

As we have argued in previous chapters, however, abundance is not best measured in terms of dollars and cents, as Simon and Ehrlich did, but in terms of time. To persuade his intellectual opponents to accept his bet, Simon generously agreed to use inflation-adjusted prices, which do not fully account for the increase in hourly incomes. The other problem with the bet was that the maximum loss faced by Ehrlich and his partners was only $1,000. Simon, on the other hand, could have lost thousands. That's because prices can only drop by 100 percent, whereas theoretically they can increase ad infinitum. Finally, the Ehrlich team was supremely confident that the prices of the five

Table 5.6. The Simon-Ehrlich five-metal basket: percentage change analysis (September 29, 1980–September 29, 1990)

Five-metal basket	Sept. 29, 1980	Sept. 29, 1990	Percentage change
Nominal price	$1,000.00	$1,003.93	0.4
CPI adjustment factor	1.0000	1.5738	57.4
If nominal was equal to inflation	$1,000.00	$1,580.00	58.0
Difference Ehrlich to Simon		$576.07	
Real price	$1,000.00	$637.90	−36.2
GDP per total hours	$3.24	$5.41	67.0
Time price	308.64	185.57	−39.9

Source: Authors' calculations.

Note: CPI = Consumer Price Index; GDP = gross domestic product.

metals were going to increase. Confidence is typically priced into a bet with odds. If the odds of an event occurring are 95 percent, for example, the wagerer bets $0.95 and gets $1 if the event actually occurs. If the odds are only 5 percent, by contrast, a $0.05 bet yields $1 if the event actually occurs. Simon could have included a probability factor in the bet, but instead, he charitably gave the Ehrlich team even odds.

What would happen, though, if the bet was made using TPs instead of inflation-adjusted dollars? The nominal prices of the five-metal basket, as we have noted, barely moved from $1,000 in 1980 to $1,003.93 in 1990. Over those 10 years, the CPI increased by 57.4 percent. However, the average global nominal GDP per hour worked, which we discussed in the previous chapter, increased by 67 percent from $3.24 in 1980 to $5.41 in 1990. To calculate the TP of the five-metal basket, we divide the nominal prices of the basket by the average nominal GDP per hour worked. We find that the average TP of the five-metal basket fell by almost 40 percent (see Table 5.6). Had Simon and Ehrlich used TPs, Ehrlich would have owed Simon $627.95, or 9.01 percent more than he actually paid.[14]

Remember that the bet between Simon and Ehrlich took into account the prices of the five metals on September 29, 1980, and September 29, 1990. If, on the other hand, we look at the average annual nominal prices of the five metals as reported by the United States Geological Survey (USGS), the

Figure 5.27. The Simon-Ehrlich five-metal basket (1980–1990)

	Change in resource time price	Personal resource abundance multiplier	Change in personal resource abundance	Compound annual growth rate in personal resource abundance	Years to double personal resource abundance
Tin	−72.7%	3.67	267%	13.88%	5.33
Tungsten	−72.6%	3.65	265%	13.81%	5.36
AVERAGE	−54.8%	2.21	121%	8.27%	8.73
Copper	−27.4%	1.38	38%	3.25%	21.67
Chromium	−16.4%	1.20	20%	1.80%	38.81
Nickel	−14.9%	1.18	18%	1.63%	42.91

Source: Authors' calculations.

average TP of the five-metal basket declined by 54.8 percent between 1980 and 1990, indicating a 121 percent increase in the average pRA. The average CAGR-pRA came to 8.27 percent, thus indicating a doubling of the average pRA every 8.7 years (see Figure 5.27). While prices fluctuated between 1980 and 1990, at no point did the five-metal basket become less abundant than it was in 1980 (see Figure 5.28). For more, see Appendix 22.

The Simon-Ehrlich wager: time pricing the bet to the present (1980–2018)

Did Simon get lucky by picking a propitious decade for his bet with Ehrlich, as some scholars argued he did?[15] Let's examine the 1980–2018 data using our methodology.[16] The average TP of the five-metal basket decreased by 57.3 percent, indicating a 134 percent increase in the average pRA. The average CAGR-pRA came to 2.27 percent, thus indicating a doubling of the average pRA every 31 years (see Figure 5.29). Once again, while prices fluctuated between 1980 and 2018, the five-metal basket still became no less abundant at any point than it was in 1980 (see Figure 5.30). For more, see Appendix 23.

The Simon-Ehrlich wager: time pricing the bet back in time (1900–2018)

Finally, we have decided to extend our analysis of the Simon-Ehrlich wager all the way to 1900, which is the earliest year for which we have reliable data for all five Simon-Ehrlich metals. Simon's claim that resource prices decline

Figure 5.28. The Simon-Ehrlich five-metal basket: change in personal resource abundance, percent (1980–1990)

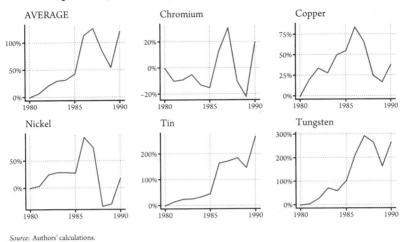

Source: Authors' calculations.

in the face of population growth was, after all, based on his meticulous and scientific evaluation of historical data.

For this analysis, we have once again used average annual nominal price data from the USGS. Between 1900 and 2018, nominal prices of the five-metal basket increased by an average of 3,660 percent.

We were not able to identify a source for good estimates of average global nominal GDP per hour worked for a representative sample of countries and territories prior to 1960, but we do have excellent data on the U.S. blue-collar hourly compensation rate and the U.S. unskilled hourly wage rate going back to the 18th century.[17] We will, therefore, use the last two as our denominators.

The Simon-Ehrlich wager: the U.S. blue-collar worker perspective (1900–2018)

The average nominal U.S. blue-collar worker hourly compensation rate increased by 22,800 percent from $0.14 per hour in 1900 to $32.06 per hour in 2018. To calculate the average TP of the five-metal basket, we will divide the nominal prices of the five metals by the average nominal U.S. blue-collar worker hourly compensation rates.

Figure 5.29. The Simon-Ehrlich five-metal basket (1980–2018)

	Change in resource time price	Personal resource abundance multiplier	Change in personal resource abundance	Compound annual growth rate in personal resource abundance	Years to double personal resource abundance
Tin	−77.5%	4.45	345%	4.01%	17.65
AVERAGE	−57.3%	2.34	134%	2.27%	30.92
Nickel	−57.1%	2.33	133%	2.25%	31.11
Tungsten	−54.7%	2.21	121%	2.11%	33.23
Copper	−39.9%	1.66	66%	1.35%	51.67
Chromium	−6.3%	1.07	7%	0.17%	401.80

Source: Authors' calculations.

We find that the average TP of the five-metal basket fell by 89.2 percent over the analyzed period. The average pRA increased by 828 percent. The average CAGR-pRA rate amounted to 1.91 percent, thus indicating a doubling of the average pRA every 36.7 years (see Figure 5.31). While prices fluctuated between 1900 and 2018, at no point did the five-metal basket become less abundant than it was in 1980 (see Figure 5.32). For more, see Appendix 24.

The Simon-Ehrlich wager: the U.S. unskilled worker perspective (1900–2018)

The average nominal U.S. unskilled worker hourly wage rate increased by 14,100 percent from $0.09 per hour in 1900 to $12.78 per hour in 2018. As such, we find that the average TP of the five-metal basket fell by 82.6 percent over the analyzed period. The average pRA increased by 475 percent. The average CAGR-pRA amounted to 1.49 percent, indicating a doubling of the average pRA every 46.7 years (see Figure 5.33). While prices fluctuated between 1900 and 2018, at no point did the five-metal basket become less abundant than it was in 1980 (see Figure 5.34). For more, see Appendix 25.

The Simon-Ehrlich wager: summary (1980–1990, 1980–2018, and 1900–2018)

In this section, we looked at the Simon-Ehrlich bet from several different perspectives. First, we analyzed the original bet, which started September 29, 1980, and ended September 29, 1990. We found that the average TP

Figure 5.30. The Simon-Ehrlich five-metal basket: change in personal resource abundance, percent (1980–2018)

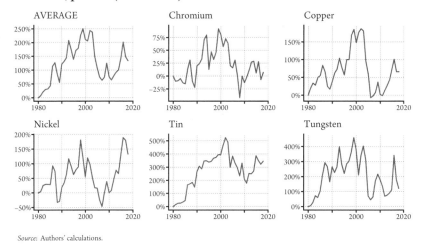

Source: Authors' calculations.

Figure 5.31. The Simon-Ehrlich five-metal basket: U.S. blue-collar worker perspective (1900–2018)

	Change in resource time price	Personal resource abundance multiplier	Change in personal resource abundance	Compound annual growth rate in personal resource abundance	Years to double personal resource abundance
Nickel	−94.8%	19.21	1,821%	2.54%	27.68
Copper	−91.9%	12.41	1,141%	2.16%	32.47
AVERAGE	−89.2%	9.28	828%	1.91%	36.71
Tin	−86.3%	7.31	631%	1.70%	41.11
Chromium	−77.1%	4.37	337%	1.26%	55.44
Tungsten	−67.7%	3.10	210%	0.96%	72.35

Source: Authors' calculations.

fell by 39.9 percent, which is more than the 36.2 percent fall in inflation-adjusted prices that Ehrlich and Simon agreed on. If TPs were in play during the course of the original wager, Ehrlich would have owed Simon another $51.50 because hourly income rose faster than CPI.

Looking at the average annual prices of the five metals, we found that the average TP of the five-metal basket fell by 54.8 percent. That drop would have increased Ehrlich's liability to $865.84, or 50 percent more than he actually paid Simon. The average pRAM rose to 2.21, the average pRA rose to 121.2 percent, the average CAGR-pRA amounted to 8.26 percent, and the implied doubling of the average pRA came to 8.73 years.

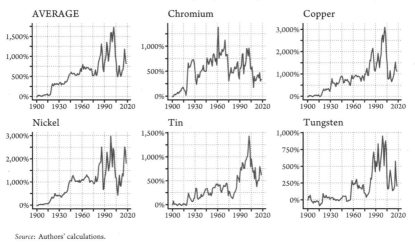

Figure 5.32. The Simon-Ehrlich five-metal basket: change in personal resource abundance, U.S. blue-collar worker perspective, percent (1900–2018)

Source: Authors' calculations.

Next, we brought the bet forward to 2018. We found that the average TP of the five-metal basket fell by 57.3 percent. The average pRAM rose to 2.34, the average pRA rose to 134.2 percent, the average CAGR-pRA amounted to 2.26 percent, and the implied doubling of the average pRA came to 31 years.

We then took the bet backward to 1900 and analyzed TPs from both the U.S. blue-collar worker perspective and the U.S. unskilled worker perspective. With regard to the former, the average TP fell by 89.2 percent. The average pRAM rose to 9.26, the average pRA rose to 826 percent, the average CAGR-pRA amounted to 1.9 percent, and the implied doubling of the

Figure 5.33. The Simon-Ehrlich five-metal basket: U.S. unskilled worker perspective (1900–2018)

	Change in resource time price	Personal resource abundance multiplier	Change in personal resource abundance	Compound annual growth rate in personal resource abundance	Years to double personal resource abundance
Nickel	−91.6%	11.91	1,091%	2.12%	33.01
Copper	−87.0%	7.70	670%	1.74%	40.08
AVERAGE	−82.6%	5.75	475%	1.49%	46.74
Tin	−77.9%	4.53	353%	1.29%	54.11
Chromium	−63.1%	2.71	171%	0.85%	82.00
Tungsten	−47.9%	1.92	92%	0.55%	125.33

Source: Authors' calculations.

Figure 5.34. The Simon-Ehrlich five-metal basket: change in personal resource abundance, U.S. unskilled worker perspective, percent (1900–2018)

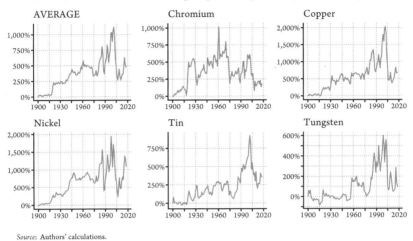

Source: Authors' calculations.

average pRA came to 36.75 years. With regard to the latter, the average TP fell by 82.6 percent. The average pRAM rose to 5.75, the average pRA rose to 474.7 percent, the average CAGR-pRA amounted to 1.49 percent, and the implied doubling of the average pRA came to 46.8 years (see Table 5.7).

Growth rates: personal resource abundance perspective

University of Chicago economist Robert E. Lucas noted that "once one starts to think about . . . [economic growth] it is hard to think about anything else."[18] That is because, as University of Oxford professor Paul Collier wrote, "Growth is not a cure-all, but lack of growth is a kill-all."[19] Put differently, growth does not solve all human problems, but without growth there can be no plenitude of food, sophisticated health care, excellent sanitation, modern transportation, and a plethora of other conveniences that make modern life so much better and more enjoyable than life in the past. Indeed, some of the world's best economic historians have devoted their careers to estimating historical growth rates and figuring out why growth accelerated only over the last two centuries or so. The University of California-Davis economic historian Gregory Clark, for example, noted that

Table 5.7. Summary of the reevaluation of the Simon-Ehrlich wager

Date range	Hourly compensation rate	Years	Percentage change in resource prices	Personal resource abundance multiplier	Percentage change in personal resource abundance	Compound annual percentage growth rate in personal resource abundance	Years to double personal resource abundance
Sept. 29, 1980 to Sept. 29, 1990	Inflation-adjusted	10	−36.2	1.57	56.7	4.60	15.42
Sept. 29, 1980 to Sept. 29, 1990	GDP per hour	10	−39.9	1.66	66.4	5.22	13.61
1980–1990 USGS average prices	GDP per hour	10	−54.8	2.21	121.2	8.26	8.73
1980–2018 USGS average prices	GDP per hour	38	−57.3	2.34	134.2	2.26	30.95
1900–2018	Blue-collar	118	−89.2	9.26	825.9	1.90	36.75
1900–2018	Unskilled	118	−82.6	5.75	474.7	1.49	46.77

Source: Authors' calculations.

Note: GDP = gross domestic product; USGS = United States Geological Survey.

Prior to 1760 the average rate of efficiency advance through technological change in the world economy through millennia was very close to 0. At a world level for example, efficiency growth rates 1000–1500 were 0.02 percent per year, and 1500–1750 still only .045 percent per year. Efficiency growth rates in England 1760–1860 were still modest by modern measures—only about 0.5 percent per year—but such growth rates over 100 years were still a unique break in world economic history.[20]

The Bank of England estimated that global GDP per person grew on average by 0.01 percent a year between 1,000 BCE and 1750 CE. Between 1750 (the start of the Industrial Revolution) and 2000, it averaged 1.5 percent. To put that number in context, prior to 1750, it took 6,000 years for global per capita GDP to double in size. Since 1750, it has taken about 50 years.[21] University of Illinois at Chicago economist and historian Deirdre McCloskey argued that "serious growth happened only after 1800" and puts the figure at "2 percent per capita in PPP [purchasing power parity] conventionally adjusted for inflation."[22] While it is true that different scholars and institutions have come up with slightly different estimates of economic growth in the past, what matters is the comparative enormity of modern economic growth, and on that subject there is little disagreement.

To quote McCloskey again: "The exactitude . . . [of measurement] is inessential." What matters is the "magnitude" of the Great Enrichment, which amounted to "a rise from $2 or $3 a day to over $100, a factor of 30." In that passage, McCloskey was referring to early modernizers such as Japan and Finland. "The worldwide factor since 1800," she estimated, amounted to "10 only, about $2 or $3 to $30 a day."[23] In our calculations (see Chapter 8), global GDP per person per day rose from $2.80 in 1800 to $40 in 2016 (in 2011 dollars). That's an increase of 1,329 percent, or a factor of 14.29.

GDP is a useful but imperfect measure of abundance. It does not, for example, distinguish between GDP increases due to "good" factors, such as expansion of the labor force resulting from a greater acceptance of female workers, and "bad" factors, such as the need to rebuild a city after an earthquake. It does not take into account leisure time, thus treating countries with the same GDP as equally rich but not considering differing total hours of work that went into producing that GDP. It ignores black markets and home production. It does not address the unequal distribution of goods and services, which is especially troubling in countries where income inequality is a product of corruption and political oppression.[24] It is bad at measuring quality differences (between Soviet and American cars, for example) and quality improvements (between an American car in 1980 and an American car in 2020).

Perhaps the most salient shortcoming of GDP "is its inability to fully capture the benefits of technology. Think of a free app on your phone that you rely upon for traffic updates, directions, the weather, instantaneous information, and so on. Because it's free, there's no way to use prices—our willingness to pay for the good—as a measure of how much we value it."[25] Can that shortcoming be overcome? In 1994, Yale University economist and Nobel laureate William D. Nordhaus tried to do just that by time pricing light. He started by measuring the length of time needed to buy artificial light generated by campfires. He then considered various types of lamps and candles, gas and kerosene, and finally the improvements in electric light bulbs. He found that

> The overall improvements in lighting efficiency are nothing short of astounding. The first recorded device, the Paleolithic oil lamp, was perhaps a tenfold improvement in efficiency over the open fire of Peking man, which represents a 0.0004 percent per year improvement. Progression from the Paleolithic lamps to the Babylonian lamps represents an improvement rate of 0.01 percent per year; from Babylonian lamps to candles of the early nineteenth century is an improvement at a more rapid rate of 0.04 percent per year. The Age of Invention showed a dramatic improvement in lighting efficiency, with an increase by a factor of 900, representing a rate of 3.5 percent per year between 1800 and 1992.[26]

In this chapter, we used our methodology to quantify the impact of innovation on the lives of ordinary people. We found that between 1980 and 2018, a basket of 50 commodities essential for human flourishing became 3.37 percent more abundant each year. Between 1960 and 2018, a basket

Table 5.8. Summary of the CAGR-pRA: all data sets

Data set	Range	Years	Items in the data set	Compound annual percentage growth rate in personal resource abundance	Years to double personal resource abundance	Personal resource abundance factor in 100 years
Basic 50	1980–2018	38	50	3.37	20.91	27.51
World Bank 37	1960–2018	58	37	3.10	22.70	21.18
Jacks's 40 blue-collar	1900–2018	118	40	2.78	25.28	15.52
Jacks's 40 unskilled	1900–2018	118	40	2.36	29.72	10.30
Jacks's 26 blue-collar	1850–2018	168	26	2.45	28.64	11.25
Jacks's 26 unskilled	1850–2018	168	26	2.00	35.00	7.24
U.S. food prices blue-collar	1919–2019	100	42	2.49	28.18	11.70
U.S. food prices unskilled	1919–2019	100	42	2.10	33.35	7.99
U.S. finished goods blue-collar	1979–2019	40	35	3.34	21.10	26.72
U.S. finished goods unskilled	1979–2019	40	35	3.06	23.00	20.37
U.S. finished goods upskilling	1979–2019	40	35	5.47	13.02	205.54
U.S. cosmetic procedures blue-collar	1998–2018	20	19	1.86	37.61	6.31
U.S cosmetic procedures unskilled	1998–2018	20	19	1.52	45.95	4.52
U.S. cosmetic procedures upskilling	1998–2018	20	19	6.29	11.36	445.90
Simon-Ehrlich 1980–1990	1980–1990	10	5	8.26	8.73	2,797.71
Simon-Ehrlich 1980–2018	1980–2018	38	5	2.26	31.02	9.34
Simon-Ehrlich 1900–2018 blue-collar	1900–2018	118	5	1.90	36.83	6.57
Simon-Ehrlich 1900–2018 unskilled	1900–2018	118	5	1.49	46.87	4.39
Average				3.12	22.58	21.52

Source: Authors' calculations.

of 37 commodities became 3.10 percent more abundant each year. Those were our estimates for the rise of the average pRA at a global level. Turning to the average pRA in the United States, we found that between 1900 and 2018, a basket of 40 commodities became 2.57 percent more abundant each year. Between 1850 and 2018, a basket of 26 commodities became 2.23 percent more abundant each year. Between 1919 and 2019, U.S. food became 2.3 percent more abundant each year. Thirty-five selected everyday items became 3.96 percent more abundant each year between 1979 and 2019. Even cosmetic procedures became 3.22 percent more abundant each year between 1998 and 2018. These are the averages for all U.S. workers (blue collar, unskilled, and, when applicable, upskilling). Finally, we found that the average pRA increased at a greater speed in more recent decades (see Table 5.8).

It may be difficult to notice improvements amounting to between 3 and 4 percent a year, but that kind of growth means that our abundance doubles every 18 to 24 years. Nordhaus's lighting efficiency increased 3.5 percent a year, which implies a doubling of the abundance of light every 20 years between 1800 and 1992. The CAGR-pRA of 3.12 percent, which was the average of all the data sets that we measured in this chapter, implies a doubling of the pRA every 23 years between 1850 and 2019. Should the CAGR-pRA continue to grow at a 3.12 percent rate, the pRA will increase 21.52 times over the next 100 years.[27]

CHAPTER 6

Population resource abundance: methodology, evidence, and analysis

The world is a closed system in the way that a piano is a closed system. The instrument has only 88 notes, but those notes can be played in a nearly infinite variety of ways. The same applies to our planet. The Earth's atoms may be fixed, but the possible combinations of those atoms are infinite. What matters, then, is not the physical limits of our planet, but human freedom to experiment and reimagine the use of resources that we have.

**Gale L. Pooley and Marian L. Tupy, "The Simon
Abundance Index: A New Way to Measure
Availability of Resources"[1]**

Chapter summary

So far, we have looked at the abundance of resources from the perspective of an individual human being. What about the population as a whole? After all, Thomas Malthus, Paul Ehrlich, and Julian Simon all agreed that there is a discernible relationship between human population growth and the abundance of resources.

Malthus and Ehrlich argued that as the population increased, resources would become less abundant. Simon argued the opposite, that a growing population would increase the abundance of resources because with every hungry mouth comes a brain capable of reason and creativity.

In Chapter 6, therefore, we will use population resource abundance analysis (not to be confused with personal resource abundance analysis) and elasticity of population to quantify the relationship between the abundance of resources and population growth. Those will help us determine whether Simon's or Ehrlich's arguments were correct.

The chapter will conclude by charting the growth in the abundance of resources along a Simon-Ehrlich continuum from superabundance at the one extreme to collapsing abundance at the other extreme. Our analysis of 18 distinct data sets will show that the abundance of resources is increasing at a faster pace than the population is growing. We call that relationship *superabundance*.

What are the components of the population resource abundance analysis?

In Chapter 4, we introduced personal resource abundance analysis. In Chapter 5, we used personal resource abundance analysis to estimate abundance across a wide range of countries and territories, resources, and periods. It is crucial to remember that the two chapters looked at the abundance of resources from the perspective of an individual human being. In this chapter, we will use our population resource abundance analysis to quantify the relationship between the abundance of resources and population growth.[2]

We will begin by estimating the population resource abundance multiplier (PRAM), which will tell us how much more of a resource or resources humanity can get for the same amount of labor between two points in time. Once we have calculated the PRAM, we will then be able to measure the percentage change in population resource abundance (PRA). The PRA will tell us how much better off humanity has become between two points in time. The compound annual growth rate in PRA (CAGR-PRA) will tell us the rate of that improvement. The years to double PRA (YD-PRA) will tell us the length of time required for a resource or resources to become twice as abundant.[3]

We will then measure the sensitivity of changes in abundance to changes in population using three different ways of gauging population elasticity. The time price elasticity of population (TP-EP) will measure the sensitivity of TPs to population growth. The personal resource abundance elasticity of population (pRA-EP) will measure the sensitivity of personal abundance of resources to population growth. Finally, the population resource abundance elasticity of population (PRA-EP) will measure the sensitivity of population resource abundance to population growth.

The chapter will conclude by charting our results within the Simon-Ehrlich Box. The box, which is a visual tool that we have developed, depicts the resource abundance continuum. At one end of the continuum is superabundance, a state of affairs in which personal resource abundance is increasing at a faster rate than the population is growing. At the other end of the continuum is collapsing abundance, a state of affairs in which personal resource abundance decreases at a faster rate than population increases. As you'll see, all of the data sets that we have analyzed in this book fall within the zone of superabundance, hence the title of this book.

Population resource abundance multiplier (PRAM) tells us how much more of a resource a population can get for the same amount of labor between two points in time

The population resource abundance multiplier (PRAM) captures both the size of the population and the personal resource abundance multiplier (pRAM) in one value. Put differently, the PRAM measures changes in

Table 6.1. The population resource abundance multiplier (PRAM), 18 data sets

Data set	Range	Years	Items in the data set	Percentage change in resource time prices	Personal resource abundance multiplier	Percentage change in personal resource abundance	Percentage change in population	Population multiplier	Population resource abundance multiplier start-year	Population resource abundance multiplier end-year
Basic 50	1980–2018	38	50	−71.6	3.52	252.0	71.2	1.71	1.00	6.03
World Bank 37	1960–2018	58	37	−83.0	5.89	489.0	151.8	2.52	1.00	14.83
Jacks's 40 blue-collar	1900–2018	118	40	−96.1	25.37	2,437.0	330.3	4.30	1.00	109.16
Jacks's 40 unskilled	1900–2018	118	40	−93.6	15.73	1,473.0	330.3	4.30	1.00	67.68
Jacks's 26 blue-collar	1850–2018	168	26	−98.3	58.62	5,762.0	1,321.7	14.22	1.00	833.42
Jacks's 26 unskilled	1850–2018	168	26	−96.4	27.82	2,682.0	1,321.7	14.22	1.00	395.53
U.S. food prices blue-collar	1919–2019	100	42	−91.2	11.32	1,032.0	212.4	3.12	1.00	35.36
U.S. food prices unskilled	1919–2019	100	42	−87.8	8.22	722.0	212.4	3.12	1.00	25.68
U.S. finished goods blue-collar	1979–2019	40	35	−72.3	3.61	261.0	44.5	1.44	1.00	5.22

U.S. finished goods unskilled	1979–2019	40	35	−70.9	3.44	244.0	44.5	1.44	1.00	4.97
U.S. finished goods upskilling	1979–2019	40	35	−87.7	8.16	716.0	44.5	1.44	1.00	11.79
U.S. cosmetic procedures blue-collar	1998–2018	20	19	−31.0	1.45	45.0	18.9	1.19	1.00	1.72
U.S. cosmetic procedures unskilled	1998–2018	20	19	−25.9	1.35	35.0	18.9	1.19	1.00	1.61
U.S. cosmetic procedures upskilling	1998–2018	20	19	−70.5	3.39	239.0	18.9	1.19	1.00	4.03
Simon-Ehrlich 1980–1990	1980–1990	10	5	−54.8	2.21	121.2	19.6	1.20	1.00	2.64
Simon-Ehrlich 1980–2018	1980–2018	38	5	−57.3	2.34	134.2	71.2	1.71	1.00	4.01
Simon-Ehrlich 1900–2018 Blue-collar	1900–2018	118	5	−89.2	9.26	825.9	330.3	4.30	1.00	39.84
Simon-Ehrlich 1900–2018 unskilled	1900–2018	118	5	−82.6	5.75	474.7	330.3	4.30	1.00	24.73

Source: Authors' calculations.

Note: Since population size is indexed to 1 in the start-year of the analysis and pRAM is also equal to 1 in the start-year of the analysis, PRAM in the start-year of the analysis will always equal 1.

abundance of resources for entire populations. The relevant equation here is as follows:

$$PRAM_n = Population_n \times pRAM_n$$

We have indexed the size of the population to 1 in the start-year of all of our data sets. Similarly, pRAM is always equal to 1 in the start-year of all of our data sets. Consequently, the PRAM in the start-year of any of our data sets will always equal 1.

Let's look at a concrete example. We index the world's population in 1980 to 1 and the pRAM of the Basic 50 commodities also to 1. By 2018, the world's population rose by 71.2 percent, which can be indexed to 1.71. In the meantime, pRAM increased from 1 to 3.52. As such, we can say that the PRAM of the Basic 50 commodities rose from 1 in 1980 to 6.03 in 2018. The relevant equation here is as follows:

$$PRAM_{2018} = 1.71_{2018} \times 3.52_{2018}$$
$$PRAM_{2018} = 6.03$$

Table 6.1 provides the PRAM values for all 18 Chapter 5 data sets. The PRAM of Jacks's 26 commodities rose the most (833.42) for U.S. blue-collar workers between 1850 and 2018. The PRAM of cosmetic procedures rose the least (1.61) for U.S. unskilled workers between 1998 and 2018.[4]

Percentage change in population resource abundance (PRA) tells us how much better off humanity has become between two points in time

To measure the percentage change in the population resource abundance (PRA), we use the following equation:

$$Percentage\ Change\ in\ PRA =$$
$$((PRAM_{end\text{-}year} - PRAM_{start\text{-}year}) \div PRAM_{start\text{-}year}) \times 100$$

Since the $PRAM_{\text{start-year}}$ is always equal to 1, the equation can be reduced to

$$\text{Percentage Change in PRA} = (PRAM_{\text{end-year}} - 1) \times 100$$

Let us once again use the Basic 50 data set as an example. As can be seen from the following calculation, the PRA of the 50 Basic commodities rose by 502.9 percent between 1980 and 2018.

$$\text{Percentage Change in PRA} = (6.03 - 1) \times 100$$

$$\text{Percentage Change in PRA} = 502.9$$

Table 6.2 provides the percentage change in the PRA values for all 18 Chapter 5 data sets. The PRA of Jacks's 26 commodities rose the most (83,242 percent) for U.S. blue-collar workers between 1850 and 2018. The PRA of cosmetic procedures rose the least (61 percent) for U.S. unskilled workers between 1998 and 2018.[5]

Compound annual growth rate in population resource abundance (CAGR-PRA) tells us the rate of improvement in PRA between two points in time

To calculate the compound annual growth rate in population resource abundance (CAGR-PRA), we use the following equation:

$$\text{CAGR} - \text{PRA} = PRAM_{\text{end-year}}{}^{1/\text{Years}} - 1$$

Let's turn, once again, to our Basic 50 data set. As noted, the PRAM of the Basic 50 grew from 1.0 in 1980 to 6.029 in 2018. That means that the PRA of the Basic 50 basket of commodities grew at a compound annual rate of 4.84 percent. The relevant equation here is as follows:

$$\text{CAGR} - \text{PRA} = 6.029^{1/38} - 1$$

$$\text{CAGR} - \text{PRA} = 4.84$$

Table 6.3 provides the CAGR-PRA values for all 18 Chapter 5 data sets. The CAGR-PRA of the Simon-Ehrlich five-metal basket between 1980 and

Table 6.2. Percentage change in population resource abundance, 18 data sets

Data set	Range	Years	Items in the data set	Population resource abundance multiplier end-year	Percentage change in population resource abundance
Basic 50	1980–2018	38	50	6.03	503
World bank 37	1960–2018	58	37	14.83	1,383
Jacks's 40 blue-collar	1900–2018	118	40	109.16	10,816
Jacks's 40 unskilled	1900–2018	118	40	67.68	6,668
Jacks's 26 blue-collar	1850–2018	168	26	833.42	83,242
Jacks's 26 unskilled	1850–2018	168	26	395.53	39,453
U.S. food prices blue-collar	1919–2019	100	42	35.36	3,436
U.S. food prices unskilled	1919–2019	100	42	25.68	2,468
U.S. finished goods blue-collar	1979–2019	40	35	5.22	422
U.S. finished goods unskilled	1979–2019	40	35	4.97	397
U.S. finished goods upskilling	1979–2019	40	35	11.79	1,079
U.S. cosmetic procedures blue-collar	1998–2018	20	19	1.72	72
U.S. cosmetic procedures unskilled	1998–2018	20	19	1.61	61
U.S. cosmetic procedures upskilling	1998–2018	20	19	4.03	303
Simon-Ehrlich 1980–1990	1980–1990	10	5	2.64	164
Simon-Ehrlich 1980–2018	1980–2018	38	5	4.01	301
Simon-Ehrlich 1900–2018 blue-collar	1900–2018	118	5	39.84	3,884
Simon-Ehrlich 1900–2018 unskilled	1900–2018	118	5	24.73	2,373

Source: Authors' calculations.

Table 6.3. Compound annual growth rate in population resource abundance, 18 data sets

Data set	Range	Years	Items in the data set	Population resource abundance multiplier end-year	Percentage change in population resource abundance	Compound annual percentage growth rate in population resource abundance
Basic 50	1980–2018	38	50	6.03	503	4.84
World Bank 37	1960–2018	58	37	14.83	1,383	4.76
Jacks's 40 blue-collar	1900–2018	118	40	109.16	10,816	4.06
Jacks's 40 unskilled	1900–2018	118	40	67.68	6,668	3.64
Jacks's 26 blue-collar	1850–2018	168	26	833.42	83,242	4.08
Jacks's 26 unskilled	1850–2018	168	26	395.53	39,453	3.62
U.S. food prices blue-collar	1919–2019	100	42	35.36	3,436	3.63
U.S. food prices unskilled	1919–2019	100	42	25.68	2,468	3.30
U.S. finished goods blue-collar	1979–2019	40	35	5.22	422	4.22
U.S. finished goods unskilled	1979–2019	40	35	4.97	397	4.09
U.S. finished goods upskilling	1979–2019	40	35	11.79	1,079	6.36
U.S. cosmetic procedures blue-collar	1998–2018	20	19	1.72	72	2.76
U.S. cosmetic procedures unskilled	1998–2018	20	19	1.61	61	2.39
U.S. cosmetic procedures upskilling	1998–2018	20	19	4.03	303	7.22
Simon-Ehrlich 1980–1990	1980–1990	10	5	2.64	164	10.21
Simon-Ehrlich 1980–2018	1980–2018	38	5	4.01	301	3.72
Simon-Ehrlich 1900–2018 blue-collar	1900–2018	118	5	39.84	3,884	3.17
Simon-Ehrlich 1900–2018 unskilled	1900–2018	118	5	24.73	2,373	2.76
Average						4.38

Source: Authors' calculations.

1990 was the highest (10.21 percent). The CAGR-PRA of cosmetic procedures for U.S. unskilled workers between 1998 and 2018 was the lowest (2.39 percent).[6] Notably, none of these values were negative. Populations grew, and as they did, resources became more abundant.

Years to double population resource abundance (YD-PRA) tells us the length of time required for a resource to become twice as abundant

To calculate the number of years needed for population resource abundance (YD-PRA) to double, we will use the CAGR-PRA values and the NPER function in Excel. This value can also be calculated using the following equation:

$$YD\text{-}PRA = \log(2) \div \log(1 + CAGR\text{-}PRA)$$

Let's start by calculating the PRA doubling period for our Basic 50 commodities. The relevant calculation here is as follows:

$$YD\text{-}PRA = \log(2) \div \log(1 + 0.0484)$$

$$YD\text{-}PRA = 0.693 \div 0.0472$$

$$YD\text{-}PRA = 14.66$$

Table 6.4 provides the YD-PRA values for all 18 Chapter 5 data sets. The YD-PRA of the Simon-Ehrlich five-metal basket between 1980 and 1990 was the lowest (7.13 years). The YD-PRA of cosmetic procedures for U.S. unskilled workers between 1998 and 2018 was the highest (29.29 years).[7]

Elasticities of population measure the sensitivity of changes in abundance to changes in population

In economics, elasticity measures one variable's sensitivity to a change in another variable. If variable x changes by 10 percent while the change in x produces a 5 percent change in the variable y, then the elasticity coefficient

Table 6.4. Years to double population resource abundance, 18 data sets

Data set	Range	Years	Items in the data set	Population resource abundance multiplier end-year	Percentage change in population resource abundance	Compound annual rate of growth in population resource abundance	Years to double population resource abundance
Basic 50	1980–2018	38	50	6.03	503	4.84	14.66
World Bank 37	1960–2018	58	37	14.83	1,383	4.76	14.91
Jacks's 40 blue-collar	1900–2018	118	40	109.16	10,816	4.06	17.43
Jacks's 40 unskilled	1900–2018	118	40	67.68	6,668	3.64	19.41
Jacks's 26 blue-collar	1850–2018	168	26	833.42	83,242	4.08	17.31
Jacks's 26 unskilled	1850–2018	168	26	395.53	39,453	3.62	19.47
U.S. food prices blue-collar	1919–2019	100	42	35.36	3,436	3.63	19.44
U.S. food prices unskilled	1919–2019	100	42	25.68	2,468	3.30	21.36
U.S. finished goods blue-collar	1979–2019	40	35	5.22	422	4.22	16.79
U.S. finished goods unskilled	1979–2019	40	35	4.97	397	4.09	17.29
U.S. finished goods upskilling	1979–2019	40	35	11.79	1,079	6.36	11.24
U.S. cosmetic procedures blue-collar	1998–2018	20	19	1.72	72	2.76	25.45
U.S. cosmetic procedures unskilled	1998–2018	20	19	1.61	61	2.39	29.29
U.S. cosmetic procedures upskilling	1998–2018	20	19	4.03	303	7.22	9.94
Simon-Ehrlich 1980–1990	1980–1990	10	5	2.64	164	10.21	7.13
Simon-Ehrlich 1980–2018	1980–2018	38	5	4.01	301	3.72	18.97
Simon-Ehrlich 1900–2018 blue-collar	1900–2018	118	5	39.84	3,884	3.17	22.20
Simon-Ehrlich 1900–2018 unskilled	1900–2018	118	5	24.73	2,373	2.76	25.50
Average						**4.38**	**16.17**

Source: Authors' calculations.

of x relative to y is 2.0 (that is, $10 \div 5$). A coefficient of 2.0 can be interpreted as a 2 percent change in x corresponding to a 1 percent change in y. In this section, we will use the concept of elasticity to estimate the sensitivity of abundance to changes in population. We will do so from three different perspectives: the time price elasticity of population (TP-EP), the personal resource abundance elasticity of population (pRA-EP), and the population resource abundance elasticity of population (PRA-EP).

Time price elasticity of population (TP-EP) measures the sensitivity of time prices to population growth

To calculate the TP-EP, which measures the sensitivity of TPs to population growth, we use the following equation:

$$\text{TP-EP} = \text{Percentage change in TP} \div \text{Percentage Change in Population}$$

Once more, we turn to our Basic 50 basket of commodities data set. Between 1980 and 2018, the world's population increased by 71.2 percent.[8] Over the same period, the average TP of the Basic 50 commodities that we looked at in Chapter 5 declined by 71.6 percent. Therefore,

$$\text{TP-EP} = -71.6 \div 71.2$$

$$\text{TP-EP} = -1.005$$

As such, we can say that every 1 percent increase in population corresponds to a slightly more than 1 percent decrease in the average TP of the Basic 50 commodities.

Table 6.5 provides the TP-EP values for all 18 Chapter 5 data sets. As can be seen, the TP-EP was the highest (-3.728 percent) for the data set on U.S. cosmetic procedures and upskilling workers, while the TP-EP was the lowest (-0.073) for the Jacks's 26 unskilled worker data set.

Table 6.5. Time price elasticity of population, 18 data sets

Data set	Range	Years	Items in the data set	Percentage change in population	Percentage change in time prices	Time price elasticity of population
Basic 50	1980–2018	38	50	71.2	−71.6	−1.005
World Bank 37	1960–2018	58	37	151.8	−83.0	−0.547
Jacks's 40 blue-collar	1900–2018	118	40	330.3	−96.1	−0.291
Jacks's 40 unskilled	1900–2018	118	40	330.3	−93.6	−0.284
Jacks's 26 blue-collar	1850–2018	168	26	1,321.7	−98.3	−0.074
Jacks's 26 unskilled	1850–2018	168	26	1,321.7	−96.4	−0.073
U.S. food prices blue-collar	1919–2019	100	42	212.4	−91.2	−0.429
U.S. food prices unskilled	1919–2019	100	42	212.4	−87.8	−0.414
U.S. finished goods blue-collar	1979–2019	40	35	44.5	−72.3	−1.625
U.S. finished goods unskilled	1979–2019	40	35	44.5	−70.9	−1.594
U.S. finished goods upskilling	1979–2019	40	35	44.5	−87.7	−1.972
U.S. cosmetic procedures blue-collar	1998–2018	20	19	18.9	−31.0	−1.641
U.S. cosmetic procedures unskilled	1998–2018	20	19	18.9	−25.9	−1.371
U.S. cosmetic procedures upskilling	1998–2018	20	19	18.9	−70.5	−3.728
Simon-Ehrlich 1980–1990	1980–1990	10	5	19.6	−54.8	−2.801
Simon-Ehrlich 1980–2018	1980–2018	38	5	71.2	−57.3	−0.805
Simon-Ehrlich 1900–2018 blue-collar	1900–2018	118	5	330.3	−89.2	−0.270
Simon-Ehrlich 1900–2018 unskilled	1900–2018	118	5	330.3	−82.6	−0.250
Average						**−1.065**

Source: Authors' calculations.

Personal resource abundance elasticity of population (pRA-EP) measures the sensitivity of personal abundance of resources to population growth

To calculate the pRA-EP, which measures the sensitivity of personal abundance of resources to population growth, we use the following equation:

$$pRA\text{-}EP = \text{Percentage Change in pRA} \div \text{Percentage Change in Population}$$

Once more, we turn to our Basic 50 basket of commodities. Between 1980 and 2018, the world's population increased by 71.2 percent. Over the same period, the pRA of the Basic 50 commodities rose by 252 percent (see Chapter 5). Therefore:

$$pRA\text{-}EP = 252 \div 71.2$$

$$pRA\text{-}EP = 3.54$$

As such, we can say that every 1 percent increase in population corresponds to a 3.54 percent increase in the pRA of the Basic 50 commodities.

Table 6.6 provides the pRA-EP values for all 18 Chapter 5 data sets. The pRA-EP was the highest for our U.S. upskilling workers finished goods data set (16.09). It was the lowest for our Simon-Ehrlich unskilled worker data set (1.44).

Population resource abundance elasticity of population (PRA-EP) measures the sensitivity of population abundance of resources to population growth

To calculate the PRA-EP, which measures the sensitivity of population abundance of resources to population growth, we use the following equation:

$$PRA\text{-}EP = \text{Percentage Change in PRA} \div \text{Percentage Change in Population}$$

Table 6.6. Personal resource abundance elasticity of population, 18 data sets

Data set	Range	Years	Items in the data set	Percentage change in personal resource abundance	Percentage change in population	Personal resource abundance elasticity of population
Basic 50	1980–2018	38	50	252.0	71.2	3.54
World Bank 37	1960–2018	58	37	489.0	151.8	3.22
Jacks's 40 blue-collar	1900–2018	118	40	2,437.0	330.3	7.38
Jacks's 40 unskilled	1900–2018	118	40	1,473.0	330.3	4.46
Jacks's 26 blue-collar	1850–2018	168	26	5,762.0	1,321.7	4.36
Jacks's 26 unskilled	1850–2018	168	26	2,682.0	1,321.7	2.03
U.S. food prices blue-collar	1919–2019	100	42	1,032.0	212.4	4.86
U.S. food prices unskilled	1919–2019	100	42	722.0	212.4	3.40
U.S. finished goods blue-collar	1979–2019	40	35	261.0	44.5	5.87
U.S. finished goods unskilled	1979–2019	40	35	244.0	44.5	5.48
U.S. finished goods upskilling	1979–2019	40	35	716.0	44.5	16.09
U.S. cosmetic procedures blue-collar	1998–2018	20	19	45.0	18.9	2.38
U.S. cosmetic procedures unskilled	1998–2018	20	19	35.0	18.9	1.85
U.S. cosmetic procedures upskilling	1998–2018	20	19	239.0	18.9	12.64
Simon-Ehrlich 1980–1990	1980–1990	10	5	121.2	19.6	6.20
Simon-Ehrlich 1980–2018	1980–2018	38	5	134.2	71.2	1.88
Simon-Ehrlich 1900–2018 blue-collar	1900–2018	118	5	825.9	330.3	2.50
Simon-Ehrlich 1900–2018 unskilled	1900–2018	118	5	474.7	330.3	1.44
Average						**4.98**

Source: Authors' calculations.

Let's estimate the PRA-EP for our Basic 50 data set. As noted, the world's population increased by 71.2 percent between 1980 and 2018. Over the same period, the PRA increased by 503 percent. Therefore:

$$PRA\text{-}EP = 503 \div 71.2$$

$$PRA\text{-}EP = 7.06$$

As such, we can say that every 1 percent increase in population corresponds to a 7.06 percent increase in the PRA of the Basic 50 commodities.

Table 6.7 provides the PRA-EP values for all 18 Chapter 5 data sets. The PRA-EP was the highest for our Jacks's 26 blue-collar workers data set (62.98). It was the lowest for our cosmetic procedures for the U.S. unskilled workers data set (3.20).[9]

Population resource abundance analysis: summary

Population resource abundance analysis quantifies the relationship between the abundance of resources and population growth. It helps us evaluate Ehrlich's claim that population growth must result in resource scarcity and Simon's counterclaim that population growth will increase the abundance of resources. The analysis shows that Ehrlich was wrong. As Simon predicted, population growth was accompanied by increasing abundance of resources. In Part Three of this book, we will go further and explain why we believe that population growth not only allows for the increase in the abundance of resources but also is partly responsible for it. For now, let us summarize our findings.

- The population resource abundance multiplier (PRAM) rose in all 18 data sets that we analyzed in Chapter 5. The PRAM of the Jacks's 26 commodities rose the most (833.42) for U.S. blue-collar workers between 1850 and 2018. The PRAM of cosmetic procedures rose the least (1.61) for U.S. unskilled workers between 1998 and 2018 (see column 5 in Table 6.8).
- The percentage change in population resource abundance (PRA) rose in all 18 data sets that we analyzed in Chapter 5. The PRA of

Table 6.7. Population resource abundance elasticity of population, 18 data sets

Data set	Range	Years	Items in the data set	Percentage change in population resource abundance	Percentage change in population	Population resource abundance elasticity of population
Basic 50	1980–2018	38	50	503	71.2	7.06
World Bank 37	1960–2018	58	37	1,383	151.8	9.11
Jacks's 40 blue-collar	1900–2018	118	40	10,816	330.3	32.75
Jacks's 40 unskilled	1900–2018	118	40	6,668	330.3	20.19
Jacks's 26 blue-collar	1850–2018	168	26	83,242	1,321.7	62.98
Jacks's 26 unskilled	1850–2018	168	26	39,453	1,321.7	29.85
U.S. food prices blue-collar	1919–2019	100	42	3,436	212.4	16.18
U.S. food prices unskilled	1919–2019	100	42	2,468	212.4	11.62
U.S. finished goods blue-collar	1979–2019	40	35	422	44.5	9.48
U.S. finished goods unskilled	1979–2019	40	35	397	44.5	8.92
U.S. finished goods upskilling	1979–2019	40	35	1,079	44.5	24.25
U.S. cosmetic procedures blue-collar	1998–2018	20	19	72	18.9	3.83
U.S. cosmetic procedures unskilled	1998–2018	20	19	61	18.9	3.20
U.S. cosmetic procedures upskilling	1998–2018	20	19	303	18.9	16.03
Simon-Ehrlich 1980–1990	1980–1990	10	5	164	19.6	8.41
Simon-Ehrlich 1980–2018	1980–2018	38	5	301	71.2	4.23
Simon-Ehrlich 1900–2018 blue-collar	1900–2018	118	5	3,884	330.3	11.76
Simon-Ehrlich 1900–2018 unskilled	1900–2018	118	5	2,373	330.3	7.18
Average						**15.95**

Source: Authors' calculations.

Table 6.8. Population resource abundance analysis, summary of all 18 Chapter 5 data sets

Data set	Range	Years	Items in the data set	Population resource abundance multiplier end-year	Percentage change in population resource abundance	Compound annual percentage growth rate in population resource abundance	Years to double population resource abundance	Time price elasticity of population	Personal resource abundance elasticity of population	Population resource abundance elasticity of population
Basic 50	1980–2018	38	50	6.03	503	4.84	14.66	−1.01	3.54	7.06
World Bank 37	1960–2018	58	37	14.83	1,383	4.76	14.91	−0.55	3.22	9.11
Jacks's 40 blue-collar	1900–2018	118	40	109.16	10,816	4.06	17.43	−0.29	7.38	32.75
Jacks's 40 unskilled	1900–2018	118	40	67.68	6,668	3.64	19.41	−0.28	4.46	20.19
Jacks's 26 blue-collar	1850–2018	168	26	833.42	83,242	4.08	17.31	−0.07	4.36	62.98
Jacks's 26 unskilled	1850–2018	168	26	395.53	39,453	3.62	19.47	−0.07	2.03	29.85
U.S. food prices blue-collar	1919–2019	100	42	35.36	3,436	3.63	19.44	−0.43	4.86	16.18
U.S. food prices unskilled	1919–2019	100	42	25.68	2,468	3.30	21.36	−0.41	3.40	11.62
U.S. finished goods blue-collar	1979–2019	40	35	5.22	422	4.22	16.79	−1.62	5.87	9.48

U.S. finished goods unskilled	1979–2019	40	35	4.97	397	4.09	17.29	−1.59	5.48	8.92
U.S. finished goods upskilling	1979–2019	40	35	11.79	1,079	6.36	11.24	−1.97	16.09	24.25
U.S. cosmetic procedures blue-collar	1998–2018	20	19	1.72	72	2.76	25.45	−1.64	2.38	3.83
U.S. cosmetic procedures unskilled	1998–2018	20	19	1.61	61	2.39	29.29	−1.37	1.85	3.20
U.S. cosmetic procedures upskilling	1998–2018	20	19	4.03	303	7.22	9.94	−3.73	12.64	16.03
Simon-Ehrlich 1980–1990	1980–1990	10	5	2.64	164	10.21	7.13	−2.80	6.20	8.41
Simon-Ehrlich 1980–2018	1980–2018	38	5	4.01	301	3.72	18.97	−0.80	1.88	4.23
Simon-Ehrlich 1900–2018 blue-collar	1900–2018	118	5	39.84	3,884	3.17	22.20	−0.27	2.50	11.76
Simon-Ehrlich 1900–2018 unskilled	1900–2018	118	5	24.73	2,373	2.76	25.50	−0.25	1.44	7.18
Average						**4.38**	**16.17**	**−1.07**	**4.98**	**15.95**

Source: Authors' calculations.

Jacks's 26 commodities for U.S. blue-collar workers between 1850 and 2018 rose the most: 83,242 percent. The PRA of cosmetic procedures for U.S. unskilled workers between 1998 and 2018 rose the least: 61 percent (see column 6 in Table 6.8).

- The compound annual growth rate in population resource abundance (CAGR-PRA) was calculated for all 18 data sets that we analyzed in Chapter 5. The CAGR-PRA of the Simon-Ehrlich five-metal basket between 1980 and 1990 was the highest (10.21 percent). The CAGR-PRA of cosmetic procedures for U.S. unskilled workers between 1998 and 2018 was the lowest (2.39 percent). For more, see column 7 in Table 6.8.

- The years to double population resource abundance (YD-PRA) was calculated for all 18 data sets that we analyzed in Chapter 5. The YD-PRA of the Simon-Ehrlich five-metal basket between 1980 and 1990 was the lowest (7.13 years). The YD-PRA of cosmetic procedures for U.S. unskilled workers between 1998 and 2018 was the highest (29.29 years). For more, see column 8 in Table 6.8.

- The time price elasticity of population (TP-EP) was calculated for all 18 data sets that we analyzed in Chapter 5. We found that a 1 percent increase in population corresponded to the greatest TP decline with respect to U.S. cosmetic procedures (upskilling worker perspective, −3.73 percent). A 1 percent increase in population corresponded to the smallest TP decline with respect to the Jacks's 26 (blue-collar and unskilled worker perspectives, −0.07 percent).[10] For more, see column 9 in Table 6.8.

- The personal resource abundance elasticity of population (pRA-EP) was calculated for all 18 data sets that we analyzed in Chapter 5. The pRA-EP was the highest for our U.S. upskilling workers finished goods data set (16.09). It was the lowest for our Simon-Ehrlich unskilled worker data set (1.44). For more, see column 10 in Table 6.8.

- The population resource abundance elasticity of population (PRA-EP) was calculated for all 18 data sets that we analyzed in Chapter 5. The PRA-EP was the highest for our Jacks's 26 blue-collar workers data set (62.98). It was the lowest for our cosmetic procedures for U.S. unskilled workers data set (3.20). For more, see column 11 in Table 6.8.

■ **Box 6.1. Compounding miracle (1850–2018)**

Imagine waking up one day to find that abundance had doubled overnight. We would have a great celebration. What if that doubling occurred once every 17.31 years? Our analysis of Jacks's 26 commodities suggests that the population resource abundance multiplier (PRAM) for U.S. blue-collar workers rose at a compound annual rate of 4.08 percent between 1850 and 2018. That means that PRA doubled every 6,318 days (or 17.31 years). That improvement in the standard of living happened gradually—0.0112 percent each day. People don't notice such small changes. Thanks to the miracle of compounding, however, the overall effect of long-term growth can be quite dramatic. What would happen, then, if that trend continued between 2020 and 2100? The PRAM would increase by a factor of 24.5 and the PRA would increase by 2,350 percent. Finally, what would happen if the PRAM rose at 4.38 percent, which is the average of all the PRAM compound annual growth rates that we calculated in this book (see Table 6.8)? Between 2020 and 2100, the PRAM would increase by a factor of 30.85, and the PRA would increase by 2,985 percent. ■

Visualizing population resource abundance

In this section, we will illustrate the growth in population resource abundance (PRA) for each of the 18 data sets that we first encountered in Chapter 5. The goal is to help readers "see" the magnitude of the difference in PRA between the start-year of the analysis and the end-year of the analysis. We will use a red box to indicate PRA in the start-year of the analysis and a green box to indicate PRA in the end-year of the analysis. The horizontal axis denotes population growth, and the vertical axis denotes personal resource abundance (pRA) growth. The start-years and end-years of the respective analyses are depicted in the boxes themselves.

As was already explained, the personal resource abundance multiplier (pRAM) in the start-year of the analysis is always equal to 1. The same is true of population, which is always indexed to 1 in the start-year of the analysis. Consequently, the red box depicting the start-year of the analysis will always

Figure 6.1. Population resource abundance over time: example 1

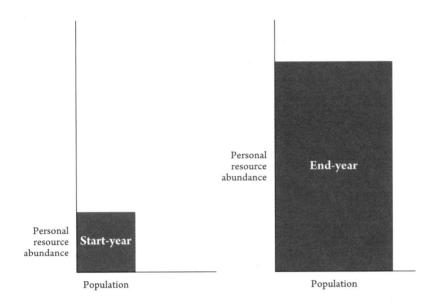

be a square measuring 1 × 1. That way, we can use the same scale to compare relative changes in population and pRA. The green box depicts PRA in the end-year of the analysis. The green box will increase along the horizontal dimension based on the percentage increase in population and along the vertical dimension based on the increase in personal resource abundance, or pRA (see Figure 6.1).

Our next step consists of overlapping the two boxes and noting how much population and pRA have increased along their respective axes. Finally, we add information pertinent to each of the data sets (name of the data set, hourly income rate source, CAGR-PRA, YD-PRA, pRA-EP, and PRA-EP) below each of the visualizations (see Figure 6.2).[11]

Now that we have described the basic structure of the visualization, let us turn to a concrete example. Once again, we will focus on the first data set from Chapter 5, which is the abundance of the 50 Basic commodities tracked by the World Bank between 1980 and 2018. As can be seen in Figure 6.3, the world's population increased from 1.0 to 1.712 or 71.2 percent (see the horizontal axis). Personal resource abundance (pRA) increased from 1.0 to 3.52, or 252 percent (see the vertical axis). The population resource abundance

Figure 6.2. Population resource abundance over time: example 2

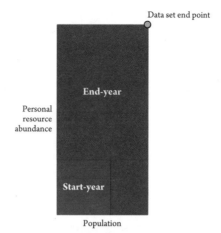

Data set end point

End-year

Personal
resource
abundance

Start-year

Population

Data set name
Hourly income rate source

Compound annual growth rate in population resource abundance

Years to double population resource abundance

Personal resource abundance elasticity of population

Population resource abundance elasticity of population

multiplier (PRAM), therefore, amounts to 3.52×1.71, or 6.03. That means that PRA, which is $(\text{PRAM}_{\text{end-year}} - 1) \times 100$, rose by 503 percent between 1980 and 2018. These three numbers (increases in population, pRA, and PRA) are denoted in the visualization itself.

Below the visualization, there are four additional numbers. The first is the compound annual growth rate in population resource abundance (CAGR-PRA), which came to 4.84 percent and denotes the speed at which PRA increased each year between 1980 and 2018. The second is the number of years required for PRA to double (YD-PRA), which came to 14.66. The third is personal resource abundance elasticity of population (pRA-EP), which shows that, ceteris paribus, a 1 percent increase in population contributed to increasing pRA by 3.54 percent. The fourth is the population resource abundance elasticity of population (PRA-EP), which shows that, ceteris paribus, a 1 percent increase in population contributed to increasing PRA by 7.06 percent.

In the rest of this section, we will visualize the other 17 data sets from Chapter 5 without further explanation (see Figures 6.4 through 6.11).

Figure 6.3. Population resource abundance over time: the Basic 50 commodities (1980–2018)

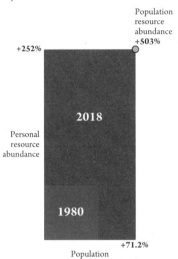

Basic 50
GDP per total hours worked

Compound annual growth rate in population resource abundance:	**4.84%**
Years to double population resource abundance:	**14.66**
Personal resource abundance elasticity of population:	**3.54**
Population resource abundance elasticity of population:	**7.06**

Source: Authors' calculations.

Figure 6.4. Population resource abundance over time: the World Bank 37 commodities (1960–2018)

Population resource abundance +1,383%

+489%

Personal resource abundance

2018

1960

+151.8%
Population

World Bank 37
GDP per total hours worked

Compound annual growth rate in population resource abundance: **4.76%**

Years to double population resource abundance: **14.91**

Personal resource abundance elasticity of population: **3.22**

Population resource abundance elasticity of population: **9.11**

Source: Authors' calculations.

Figure 6.5. Population resource abundance over time: Jacks's 40 commodities, U.S. unskilled and blue-collar worker perspectives (1900–2018)

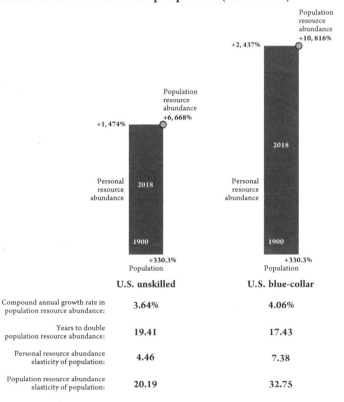

	U.S. unskilled	U.S. blue-collar
Compound annual growth rate in population resource abundance:	3.64%	4.06%
Years to double population resource abundance:	19.41	17.43
Personal resource abundance elasticity of population:	4.46	7.38
Population resource abundance elasticity of population:	20.19	32.75

Source: Authors' calculations.

Figure 6.6. Population resource abundance over time: Jacks's 26 commodities, U.S. unskilled and blue-collar worker perspectives (1850–2018)

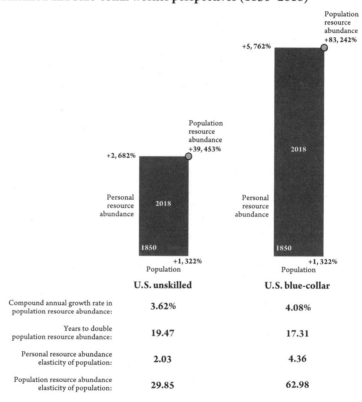

	U.S. unskilled	U.S. blue-collar
Compound annual growth rate in population resource abundance:	3.62%	4.08%
Years to double population resource abundance:	19.47	17.31
Personal resource abundance elasticity of population:	2.03	4.36
Population resource abundance elasticity of population:	29.85	62.98

Source: Authors' calculations.

Figure 6.7. Population resource abundance over time: U.S. food prices, U.S. unskilled and blue-collar worker perspectives (1919–2019)

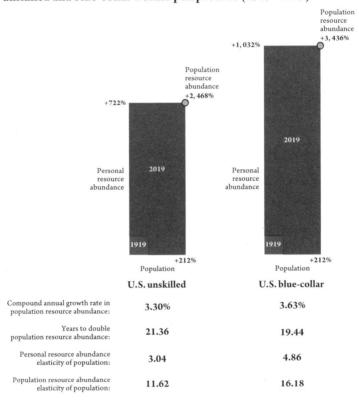

	U.S. unskilled	U.S. blue-collar
Compound annual growth rate in population resource abundance:	3.30%	3.63%
Years to double population resource abundance:	21.36	19.44
Personal resource abundance elasticity of population:	3.04	4.86
Population resource abundance elasticity of population:	11.62	16.18

Source: Authors' calculations.

Figure 6.8. Population resource abundance over time: U.S. finished goods, U.S. unskilled, blue-collar, and upskilling worker perspectives (1979–2019)

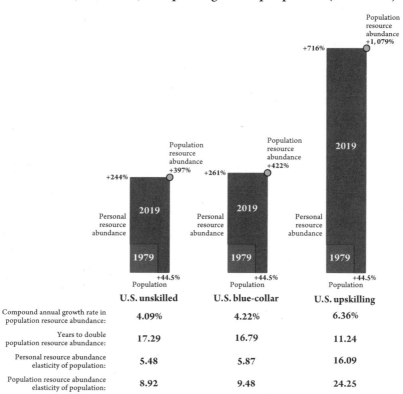

	U.S. unskilled	U.S. blue-collar	U.S. upskilling
Compound annual growth rate in population resource abundance:	4.09%	4.22%	6.36%
Years to double population resource abundance:	17.29	16.79	11.24
Personal resource abundance elasticity of population:	5.48	5.87	16.09
Population resource abundance elasticity of population:	8.92	9.48	24.25

Source: Authors' calculations.

Figure 6.9. Population resource abundance over time: U.S. cosmetic procedures, U.S. unskilled, blue-collar, and upskilling worker perspectives (1998–2019)

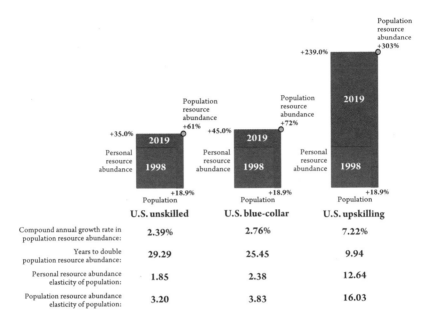

	U.S. unskilled	U.S. blue-collar	U.S. upskilling
Compound annual growth rate in population resource abundance:	2.39%	2.76%	7.22%
Years to double population resource abundance:	29.29	25.45	9.94
Personal resource abundance elasticity of population:	1.85	2.38	12.64
Population resource abundance elasticity of population:	3.20	3.83	16.03

Source: Authors' calculations.

Figure 6.10. Population resource abundance over time: the Simon-Ehrlich five-metal basket (1980–1990 and 1980–2018)

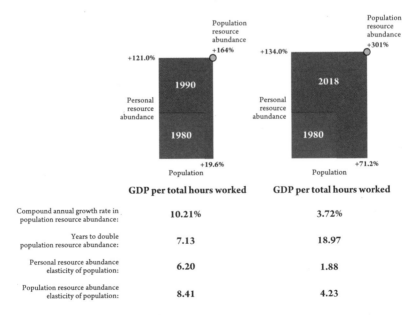

	GDP per total hours worked	GDP per total hours worked
Compound annual growth rate in population resource abundance:	10.21%	3.72%
Years to double population resource abundance:	7.13	18.97
Personal resource abundance elasticity of population:	6.20	1.88
Population resource abundance elasticity of population:	8.41	4.23

Source: Authors' calculations.

Figure 6.11. Population resource abundance over time: the Simon-Ehrlich five-metal basket, U.S. unskilled and blue-collar worker perspectives (1900–2018)

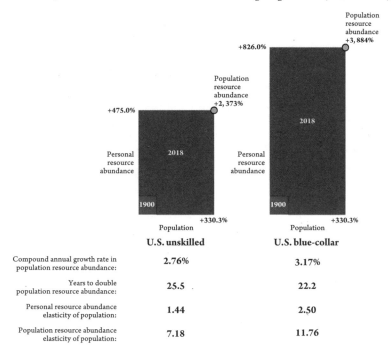

	U.S. unskilled	U.S. blue-collar
Compound annual growth rate in population resource abundance:	2.76%	3.17%
Years to double population resource abundance:	25.5	22.2
Personal resource abundance elasticity of population:	1.44	2.50
Population resource abundance elasticity of population:	7.18	11.76

Source: Authors' calculations.

The Simon-Ehrlich Box: charting population and personal resource abundance

In the previous section, we visualized the growth in abundance of resources relative to the growth in population. In this section, we will chart both variables in the Simon-Ehrlich Box, which is a graphic illustration of the main point of contention between Simon and Ehrlich. Simon argued that each additional human being would make resources more plentiful for the rest of us. Ehrlich argued that each additional human being would make resources more scarce for the rest of us. The Simon-Ehrlich Box therefore depicts an abundance continuum from superabundance at one end where the abundance of resources grows at a faster rate than population growth to collapsing abundance at the other end where the abundance of resources falls at a faster rate than population growth.

In the Simon-Ehrlich Box, the percentage change in population is plotted on the horizontal axis, and the percentage change in pRA is plotted on the vertical axis. Change in population growth ranges from 0 percent to plus 100 percent. We do not deal with declining population scenarios even though negative population growth can occur at both the national and international level. That's because the Simon-Ehrlich debate is solely concerned with the effect of increasing population on the availability of resources.[12] Conversely, change in pRA ranges from minus 100 percent to plus 100 percent because population growth can result in making resources less abundant as well as more abundant. That's especially true of the short run. As Simon put it,

> There is no physical or economic reason why human resourcefulness and enterprise cannot forever continue to respond to impending shortages and existing problems with new expedients that after an adjustment period leave us better off than before the problem arose. . . . Adding more people will cause [short-run] problems, but at the same time there will be more people to solve these problems and leave us with the bonus of lower costs and less scarcity in the long run. . . . The ultimate resource is people—skilled, spirited, and hopeful people who will exert their wills and imaginations for their own benefit, and so inevitably for the benefit of us all.[13]

The zone of decreasing pRA (gray) and the zone of increasing pRA (blue) are divided by the Simon Frontier, a line denoting zero change in pRA regardless of the extent of population growth.

Put differently, if population increases and pRA declines (if, that is, the size of the pizza slice per person becomes smaller when more people come to dinner), we will find ourselves in the gray zone of decreasing pRA. If population increases and so does pRA (i.e., the size of the pizza slice per person becomes larger when more people come to dinner), we will find ourselves in the increasing blue pRA zone. If pRA remains the same while population

Figure 6.12. The Simon-Ehrlich Box with increasing pRA and decreasing pRA zones

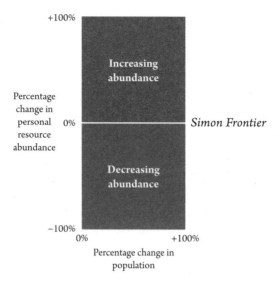

increases (i.e., the size of the slice of pizza per person remains the same when more people come to dinner), we will be moving horizontally along the Simon Frontier (see Figure 6.12).

Ehrlich argued that planetary resources are fixed or declining. They cannot be meaningfully expanded via the application of human reason and ingenuity. Consequently, population growth had to reduce the amount of available resources not only in the short run, but also in the long run. He wrote,

> Since natural resources are finite, increasing consumption obviously must "inevitably lead to depletion and scarcity." Currently there are very large supplies of many mineral resources, including iron and coal. But when they become "depleted" or "scarce" will depend not simply on how much is in the ground but also on the rate at which they can be produced and the amount societies can afford to pay, in standard economic or environmental terms, for their extraction and use. For most resources, economic and environmental constraints will limit consumption while substantial quantities remain. . . . For others, however, global "depletion"—that is,

Figure 6.13. The Simon-Ehrlich Box with increasing pRA, decreasing pRA, and collapsing pRA zones

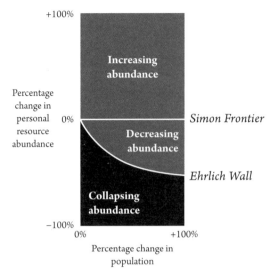

decline to a point where worldwide demand can no longer be met economically—is already on the horizon. Petroleum is a textbook example of such a resource.[14]

The Ehrlich Wall, therefore, denotes a scenario in which pRA decreases in proportion to population increases. If the population increases by 10 percent, in other words, the size of the slice of pizza will shrink by 9.09 percent, and if the population doubles, the size of the slice of pizza will shrink by 50 percent. The relevant equation here is as follows:

$$\text{Percentage Change in pRA at the Ehrlich Wall} = (1 \div (1 + \% \text{ Change in Population})) - 1$$

The Ehrlich Wall separates the decreasing gray pRA zone into two sub-zones. Above the Ehrlich Wall, pRA decreases at a slower rate than population increases, or the size of the slice of pizza per person gets 5 percent smaller for every 10 percent increase in the number of people who come to dinner. Below the Ehrlich Wall is the collapsing pRA subzone where pRA

Figure 6.14. The Simon-Ehrlich Box with superabundance, increasing pRA, decreasing pRA, and collapsing pRA zones

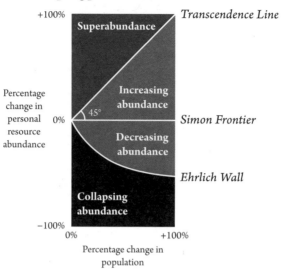

decreases at a faster rate than population increases. The size of the slice of pizza per person gets 10 percent smaller for every 5 percent increase in the number of people who come to dinner. See Figure 6.13.

Note that the Ehrlich Wall is curved, not straight. That's because pRA can only decrease 100 percent, that is, completely.[15] In stark contrast, there is no limit to how much pRA can increase. As time prices approach zero, pRA approaches infinity (see Figure 4.2). The Transcendence Line depicts a situation where the rate of change in pRA increases at the same rate as population grows, or the slice of pizza per person will increase by 10 percent for every 10 percent increase in the number of people who come to dinner.

The Transcendence Line divides the blue zone of increasing pRA into two subzones. Below the line, pRA grows at a rate that is slower than population increase (e.g., the slice of pizza per person increases by 5 percent for every 10 percent more people who come to dinner). Above the line, pRA grows at a rate that is faster than population increase (e.g., the slice of pizza increases by 10 percent for every 5 percent increase in the number of people who come to dinner). We call that last state of affairs superabundance (see Figure 6.14).

Table 6.9. Summary of the structure of the Simon-Ehrlich Box

Zone or line	Relative to population growth, personal resource abundance is:
Superabundance zone	Increasing at a faster rate
Transcendence Line	Increasing at the same rate
Increasing abundance zone	Increasing at a slower rate
Simon Frontier	Not changing
Decreasing abundance zone	Decreasing at a slower rate
Ehrlich Wall	Decreasing at a proportional rate
Collapsing abundance	Decreasing at a faster rate

We have now established the basic structure of the Simon-Ehrlich Box, with the zone of collapsing pRA at the bottom and the superabundance zone at the top. Table 6.9 provides a summary of that structure.

The next step of our analysis will establish which of our 18 data sets belong in which of the four zones: the collapsing pRA zone, the decreasing pRA zone, the increasing pRA zone, and the superabundance zone. To do that, we will be using percentage change in pRA values that were denoted by green bars in the figures in Chapter 5 and percentage change in population values obtained from the United Nations and the United States Census Bureau.

As Table 6.10 shows, all of our Chapter 5 data sets fall into the superabundance zone. In all 18 cases, pRA (column 6) increased at a faster pace than the population grew (column 7). Put differently, the slice of pizza per person increased at a greater rate than the rate at which more and more people arrived for dinner.

Note that the values in columns 6 and 7 correspond to the highlighted area in Figure 6.15. The red and green box on the left represents the visualizations from the previous section, and the orange highlight depicts percentage change in population and the percentage change in pRA.

Table 6.10. Summary of percentage changes in pRA from Chapter 5 and percentage changes in population

Data set	Range	Years	Items in the data set	Percentage change in resource time prices	Percentage change in personal resource abundance	Percentage change in population
Basic 50	1980–2018	38	50	−71.6	252.0	71.2
World Bank 37	1960–2018	58	37	−83.0	489.0	151.8
Jacks's 40 blue-collar	1900–2018	118	40	−96.1	2,437.0	330.3
Jacks's 40 unskilled	1900–2018	118	40	−93.6	1,473.0	330.3
Jacks's 26 blue-collar	1850–2018	168	26	−98.3	5,762.0	1,321.7
Jacks's 26 unskilled	1850–2018	168	26	−96.4	2,682.0	1,321.7
U.S. food prices blue-collar	1919–2019	100	42	−91.2	1,032.0	212.4
U.S. food prices unskilled	1919–2019	100	42	−87.8	722.0	212.4
U.S. finished goods blue-collar	1979–2019	40	35	−72.3	261.0	44.5
U.S. finished goods unskilled	1979–2019	40	35	−70.9	244.0	44.5
U.S. finished goods upskilling	1979–2019	40	35	−87.7	716.0	44.5
U.S. cosmetic procedures blue-collar	1998–2018	20	19	−31.0	45.0	18.9
U.S. cosmetic procedures unskilled	1998–2018	20	19	−25.9	35.0	18.9
U.S. cosmetic procedures upskilling	1998–2018	20	19	−70.5	239.0	18.9
Simon-Ehrlich 1980–1990	1980–1990	10	5	−54.8	121.2	19.6
Simon-Ehrlich 1980–2018	1980–2018	38	5	−57.3	134.2	71.2
Simon-Ehrlich 1900–2018 blue-collar	1900–2018	118	5	−89.2	825.9	330.3
Simon-Ehrlich 1900–2018 unskilled	1900–2018	118	5	−82.6	474.7	330.3

Source: Authors' calculations.

Figure 6.15. Charting population and personal resource abundance: example

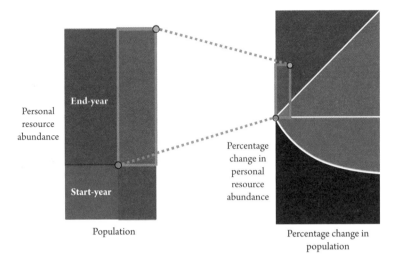

Finally, similar areas from our red and green boxes can be plotted in the Simon-Ehrlich Box (see Figure 6.16). Once again, we see that all of our 18 data sets fall within the superabundance zone (for a detailed view of the Simon-Ehrlich Box with all 18 data sets plotted therein, see Appendixes 31 and 32).

Figure 6.16. Charting population and personal resource abundance: 18 data sets plotted in the Simon-Ehrlich Box

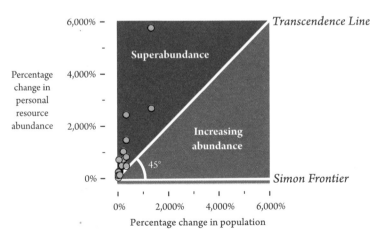

Source: Authors' calculations.
Note: For detailed views of the 18 data sets' placement in the superabundance zone, see Appendixes 31 and 32.

Part Two: Summary

In the second part of this book, we introduced the reader to the Simon Abundance Framework (SAF). The SAF uses bespoke methodology to measure the change in abundance relative to the change in wages. The SAF includes two levels of analysis: personal level and population level. To use a pizza analogy, personal resource abundance measures the size of a slice of pizza per person. Population resource abundance measures the size of the entire pizza pie. Looking at hundreds of commodities, goods, and services over many decades, we found that abundance almost invariably grew, often substantially. In general, we estimate that personal resource abundance grows by over 3 percent per year, thereby doubling every two decades or so. Our population resource abundance analysis showed that resources have been growing more abundant by over 4 percent per year, thereby doubling every 16 years or so. Moreover, it showed that humanity is experiencing superabundance, a condition where abundance is increasing at a faster rate than the population is growing. Data suggest that additional human beings tend to benefit rather than impoverish the rest of humanity. That vindicates Julian Simon's observation with which we started Chapter 3: "Our supplies of natural resources are not finite in any economic sense. Nor does past experience give reason to expect natural resources to become more scarce. Rather, if history is any guide, natural resources will progressively become less costly, hence less scarce, and will constitute a smaller proportion of our expenses in future years."[16]

PART THREE

Human flourishing and its enemies

CHAPTER 7

Humanity's 7-million-year journey from the African rainforest to the Industrial Revolution

The cavemen had the same natural resources at their disposal as
we have today, and the difference between their standard of living
and ours is a difference between the knowledge they could bring
to bear on those resources and the knowledge used today.

Thomas Sowell, *Knowledge and Decisions*[1]

Chapter summary

It is our contention that resources grow more abundant, and not in spite of population growth but (in large part) because of it. Unlike other animals, humans are intelligent beings capable of innovating their way out of shortages through greater efficiency, increased supply, and the development of substitutes. Over time, we have developed sophisticated ways of dealing with adversity, enhancing our chances of survival, and increasing our well-being. How did that happen?

This chapter will take you on a 7-million-year journey during which our ancestors began to climb down from the treetops in African forests, start walking on two legs as bipeds, cooperate with one another and become social beings, develop the theory of mind and division of labor, harness fire, and then sit around the fire telling one another stories, a wonderful mechanism for disseminating accumulated knowledge.

It will explain how our first steps toward civilization—the discovery of agriculture and permanent settlements—led to the emergence of new institutions such as private property, hierarchy, and inequality. These institutions improved our lives by making our food supply more stable and predictable, while at the same time stifling economic and political innovation, at least for a time.

Finally, this chapter will explain the process by which 18th-century Western Europeans became the first people to largely free themselves from the shackles of suffocating political and economic institutions, irrationality, and counterproductive ethics and set the stage for the Era of Innovation and the Great Enrichment.

An apelike creature becomes fully human . . .

Between 6 and 7 million years ago, our ape ancestors took a drastic step that was to have far-reaching consequences. Shifting tectonic plates in Africa had lifted a large swath of low-lying rainforest into a plateau, slowly drying out the forest and transforming it into savannah. This new landscape was problematic for the forest dwellers. The trees had provided safety, shelter, and a reliable source of food, while the savannah was hot, periodically parched, and full of predators. One of the unhappy species forced to leave the protection of the forest was a group of chimp-like apes, the early ancestors of humans. In response to their new environment, these creatures evolved a few significant characteristics.

. . . by learning how to walk and cooperate . . .

The first was bipedalism, or the ability to walk on two legs. Living in the savannah required moving long distances in search of food and water, and walking on two legs is much more energy-efficient than walking on all four. Another benefit of bipedalism is the free use of the hands while traveling. Creatures capable of carrying tools and food with them rather than just leaving everything behind when moving from one place to another would have had a tremendous evolutionary advantage. Unfortunately, we don't have any evidence to suggest that our early ancestors were capable of planning for the future. That's a problem because beings incapable of planning for the future will not see the need to carry useful objects around with them.

In his 2018 book, *The Social Leap*, University of Queensland psychologist William von Hippel provides a likely answer to that conundrum. Most animals don't carry food and water with them because they don't expect to be hungry in the future. While hunger comes in waves, fear would have been omnipresent on the savannah. For a creature that had evolved to hide in the treetops, the sparsely forested grassland full of lions and wild dogs was not a friendly environment. Living in constant fear of predators meant that prehistoric chimps would have desired protection at all times, bypassing the planning limitations. Von Hippel theorizes, therefore, that our ancestors became bipedal partly to carry weapons, such as crude spears.[2]

Even more far-reaching than the invention of weapons was the invention of human cooperation. While a spear-wielding ape is slightly better off than an unarmed one, our ancestors would still be easy pickings for a pride of hungry lions. For added protection, then, the displaced apes formed groups. In a large group, there are more eyes to spot threats and more muscle to dispatch predators. Individuals in more cooperative bands survived to adulthood and bred more often, resulting in a more cooperative species. Furthermore, since living alone was tantamount to a death sentence, selfish apes who didn't care about being ostracized for not pulling their weight died off, resulting in a psychological desire for communal cooperation and a deep-rooted fear of rejection by the group.

Much of the evidence for these theories can be observed in the behavior of modern apes and monkeys. When traveling on the savannah, chimpanzees assemble in larger groups and share more often than they normally do in the forest. Interestingly, they can also be seen carrying long, sharpened sticks. These sticks, though, are used mainly for hunting and foraging, not for self-defense. When attacked by predators, chimpanzees drop their weapons and flee, scrambling desperately for the nearest tree. Baboons also group up and even fight off small predators. Their large, doglike jaws and terrifying canines allow them to tear apart enemies without much cooperation beyond a unified charge. Based on our diminutive jaws and tiny teeth, it's clear that our ancestors had a different defensive strategy.

Teamwork and sticks are better than nothing, but they are not enough to let us drive off a saber-toothed tiger without suffering serious casualties. Eventually, our ancestors developed a vastly more effective method of self-defense, one that relied on both bipedalism and cooperation: throwing stones. Standing allows us to hold objects and aim better, and importantly, it allows the muscles to produce elastic force, increasing the speed and deadliness of the projectile. The benefits of cooperation are just as clear. While throwing a few stones might scare off a coyote, a simultaneous barrage of stones will drive away almost any predator.

Besides protection, von Hippel contends, stone-throwing was used to hunt more efficiently and to steal kills from other predators. Since stone-throwing was so effective, our ancestors gradually became more social and more bipedal over time. Another side effect of bipedalism and cooperation was that capable but uncooperative individuals could now be stoned to death by the group with minimal risk. That meant that communal cooperation or sociality was a more potent evolutionary mechanism than individual brains and brawn.[3]

... embracing sociality and understanding of others ...

The creatures we have described thus far are known to us as *Australopithecus afarensis*. It is to this species that the famous "Lucy" fossil, which lived between 3 and 4 million years ago in East Africa, belongs. These early hominids, while increasingly social and bipedal, had brains more similar to those of chimps than to those of modern humans. That is because the evolutionary pressures that created Lucy—predation and food scarcity—could be overcome without tremendous intelligence. These pressures were part of the physical landscape, a challenging but static environment that didn't require a lot of cognitive ability to navigate. The pressure that resulted in modern humans was the social system itself.

The social landscape is much more dynamic than the physical one. Once banded together in groups sophisticated enough to coordinate ranged bombardment, our ancestors were forced to forge relationships with and avoid being exploited by individuals with divergent and constantly shifting interests. Those who couldn't keep up with the increasingly complex social game either died or were unable to mate. This new pressure created a positive evolutionary cycle. Banding together created more complex social systems, which required bigger brains. Bigger brains needed to be fed, and the best way to get more food was through more cooperation and a more sophisticated social system.

The main cognitive development that arose from this evolutionary cycle is known as the theory of mind. In short, the theory of mind is the ability to understand that other minds can have different reasoning, knowledge, and desires from your own. While that seems basic, a complete theory of mind (apes only have a partial theory of mind) distinguishes us from all other life on Earth. It allows us to determine whether an affront, for example, was intentional, accidental, or forced. It allows us to feel emotions like empathy, pride, and guilt, abilities that are key to a functioning society.

One of the most salutary effects of the theory of mind is the ability to teach and learn. While other animals can teach, it usually takes them an enormous amount of time to learn simple tasks. It takes between three and seven years for infant chimpanzees in the wild, for example, to learn how to crack a nut.[4] That's because other creatures cannot understand what knowledge their student does and doesn't possess. The mothers of chimps, for example, can correct obvious mistakes committed by their offspring, but it is impossible for the former to identify the latter's lack of knowledge that resulted in the mistake in the first place. Humans avoid starting every lesson or teaching moment from scratch by predicting what the student already knows and, therefore, what the student still needs to learn to complete the task.

The development of at least a partial theory of mind began to show its real power among *Homo erectus*, the first human species to colonize the world beyond Africa. They survived the longest out of all of our ancestors, appearing in the fossil records around 2 million years ago and lasting until about 140,000 BCE. That wasn't their only achievement, though. For one, their stone tools are dramatically more sophisticated and have distinct designs that are more advanced than the generic sharpened rock. These implements were specialized for different tasks and were also carried long distances from the production site, thus proving that *Homo erectus* developed the capacity to recognize not only momentary needs but also future ones.

. . . and dividing labor and harnessing fire

This ability to imagine and plan for hypothetical futures opened the gates to an even greater step in human evolution. The stone tool production sites reveal that *Homo erectus* was capable of dividing labor. Rocks were bashed into flakes in one station, and then the flakes were fashioned into more complex tools in another. This constitutes evidence that stronger individuals handled tasks requiring brute force, while more skilled and coordinated workers dealt with more detailed work. Division of labor increased efficiency without any extra workload, allowing even larger and more organized groups of our ancestors to flourish.

Sometime between 1.7 million and 200,000 years ago, the superior brain power of *Homo erectus*, itself a result of increased sociality, enabled our ancestors to control fire. As Matt Ridley explains,

> Fire was not unknown of course. Indeed, at certain seasons it must
> have been a common occurrence to see lightning-ignited grass

fires. Chimpanzees take this natural phenomenon in their stride. Did *Homo erectus* perhaps get into the habit of hanging around such fires and catching small animals that rushed to escape the flames; or to looking for the charred bodies of creatures that got caught in the fire, having found that they tasted good and made a satisfying meal: lizards, rodents, birds' eggs, nuts? Other predators do this kind of fire foraging, notably hawks. Perhaps spreading grass fires on purpose by carrying embers to a new spot became a habit, to encourage new growth of grass to attract herds of game. Or perhaps they borrowed burning sticks to keep warm at night and only then began cooking things.[5]

Fire enabled us to cook, unlocking much-needed calories. Brain tissue requires 22 times the energy of skeletal muscle, and tough, fibrous fruits and tubers would not have been able to provide enough calories for *Homo erectus* to survive. Without fire,

> *Homo erectus* . . . would have to eat roughly 12 pounds of raw plant food a day, or 6 pounds of raw plants plus raw meat. . . . Adding high-energy raw meat does not help much, either—[British paleontologist Richard] Wrangham found data showing that even at chimps' chewing rate, which can deliver them 400 food calories per hour, *Homo erectus* would have needed to chew raw meat for 5.7 to 6.2 hours a day to fulfill its daily energy needs. When it was not gathering food, it would literally be chewing that food for the rest of the day.[6]

Thankfully, fire enabled our ancestors to get around that problem. A nice side effect of softer, cooked food meant we could spend less time chewing and more time socializing during mealtimes. Fire also extended our bedtimes. Before firelight, our ancestors were forced to head home at sunset in fear of vicious nocturnal predators. With fire, however, they could relax around the campfire without fear, enjoying the company of others.

The extra leisure time led not only to increased sociality but also to the development of culture and knowledge. Social interactions morphed into

■ Box 7.1. Breakfast bounty (1919–2019)

Between 1919 and 2019, the time price of breakfast fell by 89.5 percent. For the same length of time required to earn enough money to buy one breakfast in 1919, you could get 9.54 breakfasts in 2019—an 854 percent increase in breakfast abundance. If you are interested in how we got those numbers, read on.

We started by comparing the nominal prices of 12 breakfast items in 1919 with the nominal prices of the same items in 2019. The items included bacon, bread, butter, coffee, cornflakes, Cream of Wheat, eggs, ham, milk, oranges, rolled oats, and sugar. We got the 1919 prices from the U.S. Bureau of Labor Statistics and the 2019 prices from Walmart (see Chapter 5).

We then divided the nominal prices of 12 breakfast items by the nominal hourly compensation rate earned by the average U.S. blue-collar worker. The ratio of a money price divided by the hourly compensation rate is called the time price, or the time required to earn enough money to buy an item.

We found that shoppers in 1919 spent $4.18 (in 1919 dollars) to buy all 12 items. At a compensation rate of $0.43 an hour, blue-collar workers had to work 9.72 hours to stock their breakfast pantry. By 2019, the breakfast bill increased to $32.96, but the hourly compensation rate had increased to $32.36. That means that it took just over 1 hour of work to earn the money needed to buy the same 12 breakfast items.

Compared with blue-collar workers in 1919, blue-collar workers in 2019 spent 90 percent less time earning enough money to buy breakfast. As such, they could enjoy more leisure, learn a new skill, earn money to buy something else, or take a nap. In that sense, innovation, which made all 12 breakfast items more affordable, gave all of us more freedom and more choices.

As Table B7.1.1 shows, all 12 breakfast items became more abundant, with the average time price decreasing by 89.5 percent. The time price of oranges fell the least (73.5 percent), while the time price of eggs fell the most (97.2 percent). Remember that the relationship between percentage change in time price and abundance is geometric, not linear. If an item becomes 50 percent cheaper, you get two items instead of one. A 97.2 percent decline in the time price of eggs means that instead of one egg, you get 36.

Another way of looking at breakfast abundance is to consider how many breakfasts blue-collar workers could get in 2019 for the same length of work needed to buy one breakfast in 1919. This "personal resource abundance" can

Table B7.1.1. Time price analysis of breakfast (1919–2019)

Commodity	1919 BLS nominal price ($)	2019 Walmart nominal price ($)	Percentage change in nominal price 1919–2019	Blue-collar 1919 time price at $0.43 per hour	Blue-collar 2019 time price at $32.36 per hour	Percentage change in time price 1919–2019	1919–2019 personal resource abundance multiplier 1919=1	Percentage change in personal resource abundance 1919–2019
Bacon, sliced, lb.	0.53	3.68	598.3	1.23	0.11	–90.7	10.78	978
Bread, lb., baked weight	0.10	1.28	1,154.9	0.24	0.04	–83.3	6.00	500
Butter, lb.	0.67	3.04	352.4	1.56	0.09	–94.0	16.64	1,564
Coffee, lb.	0.43	4.00	828.1	1.00	0.12	–87.7	8.11	711
Cornflakes, 8 oz. pkg.	0.14	0.40	185.7	0.33	0.01	–96.2	26.34	2,534
Cream of Wheat, 28 oz. pkg.	0.25	3.48	1,286.5	0.58	0.11	–81.6	5.43	443
Eggs, dozen	0.61	1.28	108.8	1.43	0.04	–97.2	36.04	3,504
Ham, sliced, lb.	0.57	3.00	429.1	1.32	0.09	–93.0	14.22	1,322
Milk, fresh, quart	0.15	0.96	523.4	0.36	0.03	–91.7	12.07	1,107
Oranges, dozen	0.53	10.56	1,896.2	1.23	0.33	–73.5	3.77	277
Rolled Oats, lb.	0.08	0.96	1,115.2	0.18	0.03	–83.9	6.19	519
Sugar, granulated, lb.	0.11	0.32	183.2	0.26	0.01	–96.2	26.57	2,557
Summary	4.18	32.96	721.8	9.72	1.02	–89.5	9.54	854

Source: Authors' calculations.
Note: BLS = Bureau of Labor Statistics.

be measured by comparing time prices at two different points in time. We do that by dividing the 1919 time price (9.72 hours) by the 2019 time price (1.02 hours). Given that 9.72 hours ÷ 1.02 hours = 9.54, we can say that for the same length of work required to buy one breakfast in 1919, a blue-collar worker could get 9.54 breakfasts in 2019. That's an 854 percent increase in personal resource abundance.

This 854 percent increase in personal breakfast abundance occurred while the U.S. population rose from 104.5 million to 328.2 million (by 214 percent). Every 1 percent increase in the U.S. population, then, corresponded to a 4.0 percent increase in personal breakfast abundance.

The above data allows us to estimate resource abundance at a group level. We do that by multiplying personal resource abundance by the size of the group. We call that value "population resource abundance." The changes in population resource abundance over time tell us whether resources are becoming more or less abundant for a group, country, or the entire planet.

Considering that personal breakfast abundance rose by 854 percent and the U.S. population grew by 214 percent, we can say that the total U.S. breakfast abundance increased by 2,896 percent $[(9.54 \times 3.14) -1]$. Every 1 percent increase in the U.S. population corresponded to a 13.53 percent increase in the overall size of the U.S. "breakfast pie."

Breakfasts became superabundant—that is, their abundance increased at a faster rate than population growth. When you enjoy your breakfast tomorrow, take a moment to thank all those who have worked to make our breakfasts so plentiful. ∎

storytelling. Stories can be passed down between generations and even between different groups, thereby contributing to the accumulation and dissemination of time-tested wisdom. Each generation can then build upon that knowledge (let's call it "knowledge stacking"), constantly improving the human ability to thrive in any environment. Once fire met the theory of mind, von Hippel avers, society itself became the greatest teacher.[7]

Today, it's clear that what separates humans from all other species is innovation. While other animals might use a rock to crush a shell or a stick to find insects, our inventions have come to dominate Earth, bending the latter better to conform to our desires. The vast scope of humanity's accumulated knowledge is unquestionable, but why did it take so long to produce superabundance?

The agricultural revolution and its consequences . . .

For most of our history, humans were quite egalitarian. As McCloskey wrote,

> "The scientific consensus is that a core characteristic of documented nomadic foragers is their political egalitarianism. Nomadic foragers have no hierarchical social stratification. . . . Leaders (if they exist) have little authority over group members; rotation of roles and functions occur regularly; people come and go as they please; and no person can command or subject group members to act according to one's political aspirations."[8]

Equality, alas, did not mean prosperity. When food was not found, death followed. Some 12,000 years ago or so, humans discovered that a good way of mitigating the risk of starvation was to plant seeds in advance of the next season. As Matt Ridley notes,

> True, a life of farming proved often to be one of drudgery and malnutrition for the poorest, but this was because the poorest were not dead: in hunter-gathering societies those at the margins of society, or unfit because of injury or disease, simply died. Farming kept people alive long enough to raise offspring even if they were poor.[9]

Eventually, this technique, known as agriculture, became our primary means of subsistence. This transition meant we had to settle down. Sedentary farming, a hallmark of the Neolithic Age, allowed us to grow unprecedented amounts of food on a relatively small area of land and store it for emergencies.

. . . including a greater prevalence of disease . . .

Agriculture was a huge step forward in the history of our species, but it came with costs. To start with, nomads had no need for bathrooms. When they despoiled the area that they temporarily occupied with their feces, they moved on. When people started to plant crops, they could no longer move on. Over time, their feces began to infect the water supply, causing diseases such as giardia, typhoid, and cholera. Moreover, the diet of our ancestors deteriorated. Hunter-gatherers enjoyed a healthy diet by eating all the various fruits, roots, and nuts they could find, picking up camp when they plucked the bushes clean. Farmers, on the other hand, had to subsist on grains and other starches. Bacteria that thrive on a starchy diet happen to be quite nasty, whereas good bacteria die out in a starch-heavy environment. The loss of bacterial balance meant that, compared to hunter-gatherers, early farmers were short, sickly, and toothless. While that was a horrible way to live for the individual, farming communities were far more successful than hunter-gathering groups. Farming simply creates more food more reliably than hunting and gathering do. Agriculturalists, in other words, could support much larger populations. And so, over the millennia, farming gradually displaced hunting and gathering, leaving the former as the dominant human lifestyle in many parts of the world.

. . . greater acceptance of private property . . .

As McCloskey noted, foraging societies were relatively equal. No matter how skillful an individual hunter was, hunting was always a bit of a gamble. On some days, the hunter caught nothing. Moreover, the foragers had limited means of preventing food spoliation. As a result, some food (especially game) got shared widely. By contrast, farmers didn't share quite as well. In a foraging group, it is easy to tell who is and who is not working: just keep an eye on the one who never brings back a carcass or berries. The farmer's harvest, on the other hand, is a culmination of months of labor, which makes it difficult to measure how much work everyone put in. People are tempted to slack off, knowing that the hard work of others will ensure a good harvest. This free-rider problem was amplified by the larger size of farming communities. Foragers lived in small bands consisting of their own family and closest friends, a much more trusting and cooperative group than a large farming community full of mere acquaintances. As such, agriculture resulted in a cultural shift from collective ownership to private property. Farmers who owned their land, tools, and harvest could work knowing that they would reap the full benefit of their labor.

. . . and more inequality . . .

In a world of private ownership, differences in ability, effort, and opportunity inevitably lead to income gaps, wealth gaps, and status gaps. Such inequalities are evident even in the transitional stages of agriculture. Among pure hunter-gatherers, there is almost never a designated leader, but among groups that hunt, gather, and tend small gardens, there are hereditary chieftains. Of course, inequality is not exclusively human. Other species exhibit inequality through territoriality. The biggest and most dominant lions have the largest hunting grounds featuring the plumpest buffalo. Interestingly, what determines whether an animal is territorial is the density of the resource it feeds on. Grazing animals are less likely to be territorial since grass is distributed pretty equally, while predators are very territorial since their prey consists of high-calorie bundles. Similarly, foragers who do observe private property norms are those who harvest high-density food. Salmon-fishing Native Americans in the Pacific Northwest, for example, could harvest a whole year's worth of food supply during the salmon runs by drying their catch. As a result, the best fishing spots were claimed by individual families and fiercely defended.

. . . necessitated the justification of hierarchy . . .

After accepting private property and inequality, humans ran into a psychological conflict. How does one justify being (relatively) rich while those around you remain in poverty? We evolved to be social and cooperative animals who are hardwired to help the needy. At the same time, the economics of agriculture dictated that sharing was a bad survival strategy. And so, wrote von Hippel,

> new patterns of thinking were required to mitigate the dissonance that this [wealth] disparity aroused. First and foremost in these psychological changes was the idea that some humans are better

and/or more deserving than others. . . . Once you accept that "fact of nature," why stop at rich and poor? Why not king and peasant, or master and slaves? Of course, that's exactly what happened. Worldwide, egalitarianism was kicked to the curb, and newfound beliefs in innate superiority led to all sorts of human suffering.[10]

To justify their newly discovered hierarchical beliefs, people began to argue that certain bloodlines were better than others, so one lazy son was just seen as an aberration in a line of worthy kings. The logic of hierarchy has been used to justify conquest and oppression throughout history. One great example is imperialism, which was often defended as a way of bestowing the gifts of civilization on so-called savages. Interestingly, when colonialists enforced unequal systems on indigenous people as the Spanish conquistadors did in Latin America, they were fiercely resisted by hunter-gatherers but relatively accepted by native agriculturalists. Farming communities were already taxed and oppressed by the local lords, and ordinary people didn't care too much if the tyrant was a Spaniard or an Inca.

. . . that led to the emergence of new ruling elites

Prior to modernity, the vast majority of governments that had existed consisted of elites exploiting the rest of the population while defending the latter from predation by other elites. Today, government predation is sometimes accompanied by anarchy and lawlessness, as in Nicolás Maduro's Venezuela, but social structures that emerged in the agricultural era were highly hierarchical and relied on brutal enforcement of (often) unjust laws. Different sets of laws imposed different sets of rights and obligations on different people depending on their status within the hierarchy. That's still the case in places like Cuba and North Korea. What distinguishes the modern world from the past, therefore, is not the rule of law but equality before the law. The best way to ensure an equal set of rules is to pit one elite against another. When the elite are homogeneous, as was the case with the plantation owners in the antebellum American South, they will create rules that benefit the plantation owners. When the elite are diverse and include, for example, farmers, industrialists, and bankers, they will create a political and economic system that is more fair. In a heterogeneous society, other groups always outnumber one's own, so equality under the law is in everyone's best interest. It is to that transformation that we shall now turn.

The struggle to constrain the new ruling elite . . .

Private property, inequality, and hierarchy, as we have seen, have emerged alongside early civilizations, which can be defined as societies marked by the presence of cities and writing. In this context, civilization should be understood in contradistinction to the hunting and gathering societies that dominated the globe until about 12,000 years ago. Our use of the word "civilization" should not be read as a term of approval. After all, until very recently, few human populations or cultures that have ever existed could be described as civilized, at least from our contemporary vantage point, and not all "civilized" people are wise, just, or humane.

Human beings nonetheless gradually abandoned their foraging lifestyles because the domestication of crops and animals gave our ancestors a massive advantage in terms of survival. The relative security and predictability of the food supply—the most basic prerequisite for human survival—came at a price, however. Once in place, the new institutions of private property, inequality, and hierarchy helped perpetuate the interests of the governing elite (the aristocracy, the clergy, and soldiers). The elite accounted for a sliver of society (less than 10 percent), while the vast majority of the populace were peasants, compelled to exchange their labor for a modicum of greater security in this life and a promise of a better life after death. In a word, the political and economic institutions of the agrarian era were extractive.

Over time, political and economic institutions became more inclusive, or to put it differently, more reflective of the needs, wants, and desires of ever larger parts of the populace.[11] This process of institutional change differed across the globe and spanned different lengths of time, but most scholars agree on a general long-term trend toward greater inclusivity. The change started in the Western Europe and North America, and it contributed (along with other changes to which we shall turn shortly) to the Great Enrichment during the Age of

Innovation (see Chapter 8). It then spread to other parts of the world and continues to this day. As political and economic institutions have changed, our understanding of private property, inequality, and hierarchy have changed also.

In the agrarian era, property rights were widespread but unequal. They were also often arbitrarily violated by the powerful, be they Egyptian pharaohs, Roman and Chinese emperors, or Russian czars. Today, all people in advanced countries enjoy substantially the same property rights. Moreover, they can usually expect to have their property rights protected with equal vigor. Expropriation and taxation still take place, of course, but they tend not to be arbitrary and have to follow due process. It is, in part, the security of private property that distinguishes today's rich countries, where people have an incentive to save, invest, and innovate, from today's poor countries, where people's private property rights continue to be insecure.

Inequality meant unequal rights and freedoms enjoyed by different groups of people. Think of the differing rights and freedoms of the nobility and the peasants during the ancien régime in France, whites and blacks in the American South, Europeans and Africans in apartheid South Africa, members and nonmembers of the Communist Party in the Soviet Union, and Germans and Jews under national socialism. Today, unequal treatment before the law, be it sexist legislation in Saudi Arabia or anti-Muslim discrimination in China, still persists in some places, but it is universally condemned. That said, not all types of inequality are detrimental to human well-being. Think, for example, of the mathematical genius of Albert Einstein or the business acumen of Jeff Bezos. Such people demonstrate that inequality of ability can benefit all of us.

Finally, hierarchy used to mean an inherent right to rule, be it by individuals such as the Aztec emperor Montezuma, French king Louis XIV, or nations, which would manifest in ways such as the "right" of the Europeans to rule non-Europeans or Aryans to rule non-Aryans. Today, such notions are rightfully scorned. Other forms of hierarchy are unavoidable and, on the whole, beneficial. The hierarchy of competence, for example, often elevates smart people such as U.S. president Thomas Jefferson (1743–1826), visionary entrepreneurs such as the Apple Corporation cofounder Steve Jobs (1955–2011), and remarkable practitioners such as the pioneering South African heart surgeon Christiaan Barnard (1922–2001) to positions of power, prestige, and influence.

... required a transition from extractive to inclusive institutions

In their 2012 book, *Why Nations Fail: The Origins of Power, Prosperity, and Poverty,* Daron Acemoglu from the Massachusetts Institute of Technology and James A. Robinson, formerly of Harvard University and now at the University of Chicago, explored the distinction and the interaction between inclusive political and economic institutions, on the one hand, and extractive political and economic institutions, on the other hand. Their thesis provides one useful prism through which to view differences in economic outcomes between countries as these are manifested in the world today.

Consider North and South Korea. North Korea's extractive economic institutions restrict the autonomy of the individual by setting stringent rules on how people may earn and spend their money. The government uses state education as a propaganda tool, requires everyone to enlist in the military for 10 years, and sets limits on property and business ownership. To the extent that wealth is still created by the citizenry, it is diverted to members of the elite, such as members of the governing party and the top echelons of the military.

By contrast, South Korea's economic institutions are inclusive. People are largely free to earn and spend their money any way they like. The citizenry has access to an open educational system, information, and technology. The property rights of ordinary citizens are protected, and entrepreneurial activity is encouraged. South Korea's market is open and consequently innovative. It produces wealth. That goes a long way toward explaining why South Koreans are at least 22 times richer than their cousins in the North. Ethnicity, culture, history, geography, and climate—which the two largely share—cannot explain that gap, but the existence of different types of institutions in the two countries can and do.

The problem is that, as things stand, economic inclusion is determined by the actions of the state. Market activity requires, among other things, the legal enforcement of contracts, infrastructure for exchange, and protection against fraud. Since government and economic activity are interwoven, economic institutions tend to conform to the objectives of the ruling group of individuals.

Inclusive economic institutions rely on the existence of political institutions characterized by power-sharing and the wide distribution of decision making among the elites, businesses, civil society, and, ultimately, individuals. The elite are, in a word, constrained. Unconstrained decision making, by contrast, centralizes power in the hands of a small elite, or in extreme cases, in one individual. The former fosters competition, coalition building, and accountability. The latter fosters elite predation.

Finally, economic and political institutions tend to reinforce each other. Here, the feedback loop between the governing elite and the rest of the citizenry becomes salient. In extractive political systems, there is a lack of appropriate feedback from the citizens. As such, the elite can use their power to further entrench an extractive economic system that benefits them at the expense of the population as a whole. In an inclusive political system, by contrast, the elite are constantly exposed to citizen feedback, be it in the form of opinion polls or elections. As such, the elite have incentives to improve the functioning of the state, and that includes the creation of more inclusive economic institutions.

■ Box 7.2. If extractive institutions are so bad, why is China booming?

An intelligent reader will have spotted an apparent problem with the argument that inclusive institutions lead to economic growth. The fly in the ointment is economic growth that takes place in countries such as China that have extractive political institutions.[a] For the past few decades, the Chinese governing elite have promoted the development of relatively inclusive economic institutions. Those institutions are much more free than they had been under the totalitarian dictatorship of Mao Zedong (1893–1976). As a rule, governing elites can choose a development model that combines extractive political and relatively inclusive economic institutions so long as they feel in total control of the state.

The Chinese elite were able to free the economy without losing political control through greater centralization of power in the hands of the government. That includes such Orwellian measures as the almost universal surveillance of the population and a "social credit" system that rewards and punishes ordinary citizens in accordance with their loyalty to the ruling regime. In other words, the Chinese elite are secure enough not to fear the people. In return, the elite provide the citizenry with a measure of economic freedom.

The problem is that centralized and extractive political institutions cannot sustain rapid growth in the long term. The Chinese state does not allow for innovation that might threaten the authority of the Communist Party. Concomitantly, "creative destruction," which will be discussed in the next section, is hindered. Such economies do eventually tend to stagnate or even regress. Additionally, extractive political institutions can easily collapse due to infighting between the members of the elite, which can lead to civil war and anarchy. The political elite, in other words, may be tempted to preserve their hold on power by shifting from inclusive economic institutions to extractive ones.[b] Thus, Acemoglu and Robinson conclude, sustained high rates of economic growth can survive only by combining inclusive political and economic institutions. ∎

If prosperity is so good, why doesn't everyone embrace institutions that promote wealth creation?

Ceteris paribus, successful nations combine inclusive political and economic systems, whereas failing nations combine political and economic extractionism. The question is why all nations don't choose inclusive institutions that foster growth and make the society as a whole better off. The Austrian economist Joseph Schumpeter (1883–1950) noted that vibrant and innovative societies create wealth through the process of "creative destruction," or "the incessant product and process innovation mechanism by which new production units replace outdated ones."[12] That process creates losers and resentment. Those threatened with losses, therefore, try to prevent innovation from happening.

During the Industrial Revolution in Britain, which will be discussed in greater detail in the next chapter, new business entities such as textile factories replaced individual clothing producers. The latter attempted to thwart the spread of industrialization by mounting "Luddite" rebellions and smashing stocking frames (machines used to knit fabrics). In addition to economic

changes, the Industrial Revolution produced a dramatic shift in power relations. As peasants left the British countryside to work in factories, the
power of the landed gentry declined. In places where the aristocracy had
more power to start with—Austria-Hungary and Russia, for instance—the
elite initially blocked industrialization rather than lose control. Such actions
can delay the emergence of widespread prosperity by decades, and in some
cases, centuries.

To summarize, powerful groups often resist economic change because
they wish to protect existing power dynamics. Because economic growth
gives rise to winners and losers, the decisions made by the elite can have
grave consequences for its own survival. In some cases, such as that of czar-
ist Russia, the elite chose to maintain political institutions that curbed economic growth. In other cases, extractive political institutions shifted toward
pluralist governments and power sharing. When, where, and why that happened will be discussed in the next section.

Our long struggle to gain the freedom to innovate succeeded . . .

Political and economic changes tend to be heavily influenced by the attitudes
of the elite, whom we define as a relatively small group of people who hold
a disproportionate amount of wealth and power in a society. The elite have
the power to resist and block changes, and they will wish to do so as long as
they perceive those changes as being contrary to their long-term interests.
As we have seen throughout this chapter, political and economic institutions
that dominated human affairs following the discovery of agriculture some
12,000 years ago tended to be extractive ones. Then, a few centuries ago,
politics and economics in Western Europe started to change. In a 2012 essay,
Gregory Clark asked,

> Why was the transition to this modern regime delayed at least
> 10,000 years from the development of settled agriculture? Why
> did it occur in a small country on the fringe of Europe, and not
> in the great center of world population in China? England had a

population in 1760 of 6 million compared to 270 million in Quing China, 31 million in Japan, and at least 100 million in India. Why did it not occur 2,000 years earlier, in the classical civilizations of Europe in Greece or Italy, or in the already developed economy of China?[13]

The goal of this section is to explore some of the possible reasons for the emergence of the Age of Innovation in Western Europe. We will rely on insights of a trio of economic historians: Stephen Davies from the Institute of Economic Affairs in London, who argued that the Age of Innovation arose due to a lucky combination of geopolitical competition and trade with the New World; Joel Mokyr from Northwestern University, who noted the crucial role played by critical rationalism; and Deirdre McCloskey, who argued that the Age of Innovation and the subsequent Great Enrichment happened because of changes in the Western European attitudes to commerce and innovation. Let us explore these theses in greater detail.

. . . because of geopolitical competition . . .

In his 2019 book, *The Wealth Explosion: The Nature and Origins of Modernity*, Davies noted the emergence of the two social classes—the elite and the rest—that we have already discussed. For a long time, he observed, the elite were satisfied with political and economic arrangements that they had imposed. Beginning in the 14th century, however, the incentives that Western European elites faced began to change.

Around 1300, the world cooled. During the Little Ice Age, a 500-year-long period of long, cold winters and short summers, agricultural yields declined and harvest failures increased by 20 percent. The cooling of the climate had an obvious effect: famine. The first was the Great Famine of 1315, when three years of rain decimated European food production and caused starvation and widespread violence. Peasants were forced to eat seed grain and slaughter their livestock, crippling European agriculture.

At the same time, a new threat arose in the East. In central Asia, the bubonic plague appeared among the Mongol armies and quickly spread across their empire. It hit China in 1323, wiping out 40 percent of its population in the first outbreak alone. It then traveled along the newly reopened Silk Road, arriving in Europe in 1347. The plague killed two out of every five people. It is noteworthy that the plague did not affect all areas equally. Urban areas suffered much more than rural ones, sending cities into decline and undermining trade.

Population decline and falling tax revenue and trade increased financial pressure on the ruling elites across the world. Desperate rulers sought to increase revenue in two ways. First, they taxed more widely and heavily. Second, they waged war in order to control a larger portion of the declining tax base. Increased taxation broke the back of the producers who were already struggling with disease and malnutrition, causing uprisings in Europe, China, and India. Across the world, dynasties fell and empires crumbled. Out of the ashes of the old system, a balkanized and highly competitive political order arose.[14]

Starting in the 1400s, political competition caused warfare to go through a number of changes. Historically, with a few exceptions such as the ancient Greeks and Romans, cavalry tended to be the backbone of the army. That is why nomadic herders like the Huns and the Mongols had such a decisive advantage over settled populations. In this period, though, infantry slowly grew in prominence, especially in Europe. Another major change came with the invention of gunpowder. Heavy artillery was originally only used in prolonged sieges, but improvements in metal casting eventually led to the development of lighter and more mobile guns that could be used on the battlefield.

The adoption of personal firearms in the late 16th century further increased infantry dominance in military affairs. Firearms were easier to use than swords, and so armies became larger, if less skilled. Larger armies needed a more structured, hierarchical chain of command, resulting in a more permanent and elaborate military establishment. The ruling elite had to provide the now full-time soldiers with food and shelter, which meant that it needed to build additional infrastructure and secure more funding. Armies became a constant expenditure paid for with current revenue, not just with accumulated treasure. Put differently, a large and expensive military needed a large and efficient tax administration.

This military revolution resulted in a huge geopolitical shift. Since innovation was generally slow, powers that adopted some of these military changes early had a big first-mover advantage. This was especially true for artillery, which is why access to iron ore was key to a state's success. Since the old order had been splintered, states in advantageous locations or with skilled leadership were able to reform their militaries, dominate their regions, and form vast land empires. These "gunpowder empires," such as China, Russia, Mughal India, the Ottoman Empire, and Safavid Iran, became more and more powerful with each conquest and only stopped expanding when confronted with other empires of equal strength.

These new empires controlled the vast majority of Eurasia and a significant portion of the world's productive base. They were also very large. Internal stability was therefore the ruling elite's primary concern. The gunpowder empires reduced predation and exploitation within their borders, leading to some economic growth, but ideas and innovations that threatened the traditional order were suppressed in the name of stability, hindering long-term growth.

There was, as you may have guessed, one major exception to the rule: Europe. Instead of having one regional hegemon, Europe was divided between several constantly competing naval powers. The gunpowder empires were so large that conflict among them would consistently end in a stalemate. As such, the primary danger to sovereignty was internal instability rather than external conquest. In Europe, however, states were smaller, and there was an omnipresent danger of being conquered by a neighbor. This interstate competition meant that Europe was the only continent where the military revolution continued into the 17th century.

To be sure, innovation threatened traditional authority in Europe as much as it did in the rest of Eurasia. The external threat to the ruling elite, however, was so great in Europe that suppression of innovation risked defeat in war and loss of sovereignty. When faced with that unappetizing choice, many European elites decided to allow greater innovation to take place.

Here, the contingent nature of the European political arrangement needs to be emphasized. One family, the House of Habsburg, came very close to uniting Europe under a single banner, in fact. By a series of fortuitous events, Charles V (1500–1558) inherited the duchy of Burgundy, Habsburg lands in Germany, and the kingdoms of Aragon and Castile, which included all of Spain as well as Naples, Sicily, Milan, and the emerging empire in the New World. In 1526, he inherited Hungary and Bohemia and was also crowned the Holy Roman Emperor. During his reign, Charles had the greatest army in Europe. He possessed the Low Countries, which contained the best gunsmiths, and Northern Italy, which controlled the most sophisticated financial system in Europe.

The main obstacle to Charles's European hegemony was the French House of Valois. The Valois fought the Habsburgs with gusto, and while Charles V was often victorious, he was unable to completely subdue the French. The Valois were aided by two factors. First, the Protestant Reformation and the ensuing rebellions by the German Protestant princes threatened Charles's position in the Holy Roman Empire. Second, the Ottoman Empire successfully conquered territory as far west as Vienna, and although they were eventually driven back, the Ottomans remained a constant threat to the Habsburgs's southeastern border.

Following Charles's reign, the Habsburgs continued pursuing hegemony, a struggle that culminated in the outbreak of the Thirty Years War in 1618, which ended with the Peace of Westphalia signed in 1648. This groundbreaking treaty legally divided Europe into sovereign states and set the foundation for the modern international order. The Habsburg quest for pan-European domination came to a definitive end.

Without a single hegemon, Europe remained in a state of constant war and competition. The military revolution thus continued, and European armies became the most advanced in the world by the 1750s. The expanding military needed to be paid for, and economic and scientific innovations were allowed to take place along with military reforms. As mentioned earlier, these changes were hugely destabilizing. That said, European rulers simply could not afford to limit innovation at the risk of falling behind their neighbors. In fact, there was a tremendous incentive for European rulers to initiate programs like the Royal Society in England (1660) and the Académie des Sciences in France (1666), both of which embraced and promoted innovation.

. . . trade with the New World . . .

Along with these geopolitical changes, the global economy went through a major shift beginning in the late 15th century in the form of the Columbian exchange, a series of enormous consequences resulting from European contact with the Americas. Produce from the New World, including tobacco, potatoes, chili peppers, tomatoes, and maize, entered the world trade system. The potato, in particular, was consequential, for it allowed more people to be supported on a smaller area of land, leading to population growth.

Another far-reaching consequence of European trade with the Americas was access to greater quantities of silver. Starting with Vasco da Gama in 1497, European explorers established a sustained maritime connection with Asian markets. Asia was then the center of the world economy and produced highly sought-after goods like porcelain and spices. The problem was that Asian states had little interest in European goods. However, after discovering two massive silver lodes at Potosi and Zacatecas, the Spanish finally had a good that was universally desired.

In subsequent centuries, so much silver entered India and China that the two were able to introduce a uniform silver currency throughout their massive empires. The adoption of silver as currency meant that for the first time in history, there was a universal means of exchange. That removed the need to barter in long-distance trade, making trade much easier and more profitable.

These economic changes meant that as the population recovered from famines, plagues, and wars, long-distance trade returned and even exceeded its previous peak in the 13th century. Urban trade hubs rebounded, and more types of goods were traded, allowing for greater specialization among regions.

. . . revolution in thought . . .

Another transformation in Europe was a revolution in thought. In his 2004 book, *The Gifts of Athena*, Joel Mokyr separated human knowledge into two categories.[15] "Propositional" knowledge refers to what humans believe to be true about the world. Today, propositional knowledge consists of our understanding of concepts like gravity and evolution. These ideas have no direct effect on the day-to-day lives of most people, but they do frame our perception of the world around us. "Prescriptional" knowledge, by contrast, refers to instructions on how to do things like grow crops, cast metal, and navigate the seas.

In the premodern world, the two types of knowledge barely intersected. As such, people had little or no theoretical understanding of why prescriptive knowledge worked. Moreover, they had little or no idea of how to generate new prescriptive knowledge. The English physician Edward Jenner (1749–1823), for example, started to vaccinate his patients against smallpox in 1796. No one knew why Jenner's vaccine worked, though, so vaccinations against other diseases had to wait until the germ theory of disease became widely accepted a century later. Medical, scientific, and technological progress happened as a consequence of random experimentation (which is laborious, slow, and expensive) or accident.

Likewise, advances in prescriptive knowledge had little or no impact on propositional knowledge, and that included false propositional knowledge. Since Greek antiquity, medical practitioners, for example, had subscribed to the humoral theory of medicine, which held that the human body is composed of four basic humors (black bile, yellow bile, phlegm, and blood) that had to be in balance for a patient to be healthy. To the extent that prescriptive knowledge, such as medical treatments, was ever influenced by propositional knowledge, false propositions retarded the advance of human understanding, thus contributing to unnecessary human suffering.

Another key aspect of premodern knowledge was its holistic nature or "comprehension of the parts . . . as intimately interconnected and explicable only by reference to the whole."[16] It relied totally on the belief in a creator deity. As such, human anatomy was seen as a microcosm of astronomy, meaning that any statement about the human body implied something about the cosmic order. That meant that ideas about the natural world had moral implications. If a new discovery undermined one part of the system, it threatened the entire order. Since rulers typically justified their reign with theology, innovation directly threatened their authority. Therefore, scientific innovation was not only difficult but also dangerous. To avoid the destabilizing effects of progress, the rulers often used traditional sources of knowledge as grounds to reject scientific discoveries.

Occasionally, there were periods during which reason prevailed over tradition. In these epochs, which scholars refer to as "efflorescences," philosophical inquirers were permitted to freely question and debate established knowledge. These "ages of reason" usually coincided with a loss of central authority, such as during the Warring States Period in China or the Hellenic period in Europe. Once central authority was restored, however, these efflorescences would always be stamped out by the ruling elite and replaced by orthodoxy and tradition.

One of these ages of reason occurred during the Renaissance, an era when Europeans rediscovered ancient thinkers and began to revere—and eventually question—an idealized vision of the past. There was also an increase in intellectual pluralism, as people were exposed to ideas from other cultures that Europeans encountered during the Age of Discovery. Finally, it was also at this time that the individual in Western Europe was becoming a distinct notion. Identity became a more and more complete and self-contained concept, meaning that people were increasingly seen as more than just the sum of their relationships with others. This cultural shift led to the desire for a more personal and direct relationship with God, one that wasn't filtered through the church.

This underlying desire, along with Catholic abuses, such as church corruption and the selling of indulgences, culminated in the Protestant Reformation that began in 1517 when Martin Luther (1483–1546) nailed his famous Ninety-Five Theses to the door of a church in Wittenberg, Germany (importantly, the arrival of the printing press, which will be discussed at greater length in Chapter 9, made the spread of Luther's ideas impossible to suppress by the Catholic authorities). Since Luther called for a transfer of authority from the Catholic Church to the state, Protestants were supported by many ruling aristocrats across Europe. This schism between the Catholics and Protestants eventually led to religious wars across Europe, including the aforementioned Thirty Years War.

The wars of religion were extremely destructive, killing millions and causing widespread famine and plague. That led to a rise in skepticism, as the different religious schools competed to undermine each other, and the widespread chaos and destruction led many to question whether religion was really worth all the violence it seemed to inspire. Furthermore, people had become exposed to religions in other parts of the world and began to wonder if any religion was truly more legitimate than any other.

As noted, such intellectual turbulence would normally be replaced by a more traditional system. In Europe, however, political and religious divisions remained, in large part due to the Peace of Westphalia. That meant that there was no central intellectual authority and thus no one system to appeal to. Plurality of thought, in other words, persisted at the national level.

Since intellectuals in Europe didn't revert back to trust in traditional authority, they were faced with a philosophical dilemma. Either nothing can be proven to be true, as the skeptics argued, or there was a way to discover truth independent from revelation and authority. A solution was eventually developed in which some types of propositions could be revised if they were shown to be false or insufficient. This way of thinking became known as critical rationalism and is best illustrated by the ideas of two major thinkers whom we encountered in Chapter 1: Francis Bacon (1561–1626) and René Descartes (1596–1650).

Furthermore, since knowledge was now discovered from discrete observations and not an assumption about the whole system, individual discoveries were totally independent of one another. Connections became coincidental, not explanatory. Most consequentially, there was no longer anything morally wrong about questioning established knowledge. Thought and debate could now be free, and knowledge could approach ever closer to truth.

As a consequence, prescriptive and propositional knowledge became connected. Prescriptive knowledge was now used to challenge and refine propositional knowledge, and since propositional knowledge was now rooted in reality, it could serve as an intellectual foundation for prescriptive innovation. Experimentation was no longer reliant on random mistakes but could be consciously pursued using scientific inquiry. Science and technology, in other words, began to help one another.

That is not to say that religion and magic suddenly lost all influence. These were and still are a powerful cultural force, but they had lost their monopoly on intellectual thought. Traditional systems of knowledge persisted, but now, reasoned arguments were not thrown out just because they contradicted a holy text, at least in the European context. For the first time in history, reason was not stamped out by the elite. In highly competitive Europe, the practical military and economic benefits of free thought were essential: the survival of the ruling elite depended on them.

. . . and change in ethics

Concomitant with geopolitical competition, population growth enabled by the Columbian exchange, and the revolution in thought was a change in ethics that governed people's attitudes toward innovation and commerce. Innovation and commerce are intimately connected, for as the American economic historian Deirdre McCloskey noted, innovation "isn't enough [for technological and material progress]. It has got to be tested, whether it is profitable to work."[17] The testing mechanism for the efficacy of innovation, as we shall see in Chapter 9, is trade or commerce. Let us, therefore, look at how European attitudes to innovation and commerce changed over time.

The ancient Greeks and Romans did not have a specific word for innovation. That said, newness or deviation from the norm tended to have political and negative connotations. The Greek historian Herodotus (484–425 BCE), for example, described the reaction of the Persian emperor Darius the Great to the news that the Greeks had sacked the Persian city of Sardis. Darius summoned the governor of the area surrounding Sardis and said to him, "I am informed . . . that your lieutenant [who was in charge of Sardis] has attempted *neotera* (i.e., new things) against me."[18] Similarly, Sallust explained that he had decided to write about the Catiline conspiracy, in which a bankrupt aristocrat tried to overthrow Rome's government in 63 BCE because of "the *novitas* (i.e., newness) of the crime and of the danger arising from it."[19]

When it came to nonpolitical innovation, the ancients were equally suspicious. Three Roman writers—Pliny the Elder (23–79 CE), Petronius (27–66 CE), and Dio Cassius (155–235 CE)—recorded similar anecdotes about a man who invented an unbreakable glass bowl and brought it to Emperor Tiberius (42 BCE–37 CE) in the hope of receiving a reward. Tiberius asked the inventor whether he had told anyone else about his invention. When the inventor said he had not, the emperor had him put to death, lest the unbreakable glass make precious metals (from which cups and bowls were made) valueless. Conversely, Emperor Vespasian (9–79 CE) rewarded a man who had invented a machine capable of carrying heavy columns, but he feared that the machine would worsen Roman unemployment, so he declined to make use of it.[20] The historical record is replete with similar stories.[21]

That does not mean that innovations did not take place. Just think of the printing press, gunnery, and the maritime compass that we encountered in Chapter 1. It also does not mean that individual Europeans failed to appreciate innovations that improved their own lives. As early as 1306, for example, Giordano da Rivalto, a Dominican friar from Pisa, delivered a sermon in which he noted, "It is not twenty years since there was discovered the art of making spectacles which help one to see well, an art which is one of the best and most necessary in the world."[22]

The general or societal attitude toward innovation was nonetheless one of hostility. In the words of American economist Donald J. Boudreaux, this negative attitude to innovation served as a "dishonor tax." "Like all taxes," he wrote, the dishonor tax discouraged the activities on which it fell, while making alternative "untaxed activities relatively more attractive. . . . Innovation that destroyed jobs was indeed held in contempt prior to the modern age."[23]

Let us now turn to commerce. Until relatively recently, most types of commerce and profit-making were universally derided. In Homer's *Odyssey*, for example, the Greek hero Odysseus is insulted for resembling a merchant ship captain "whose one concern is the greedy profit he makes when he sells his goods."[24] Similarly, when the Spartans warned Cyrus the Great not to harm any of the Greek cities, the Persian emperor responded,

> I have never yet been afraid of any men, who have a set place in the middle of their city, where they come together to cheat each other and forswear themselves. Cyrus intended these words as a reproach against all the Greeks, because of their having market-places where they buy and sell.[25]

Plato envisaged an ideal society ruled by "guardians" who had no private property so as not to "tear the city in pieces by differing about 'mine' and 'not mine.'" He observed that "all the classes engaged in retail and wholesale trade . . . are disparaged and subjected to contempt and insults." In the ideal state, Plato averred, only noncitizens should engage in commerce. Conversely, a citizen who becomes a merchant should be punished with imprisonment for "shaming his family."[26]

These were not purely elite sentiments. The primary consumers of Old Attic Comedy, which is exemplified by the works of Aristophanes (446–386 BCE), were the common people. "Again and again," noted the German classicist Victor Ehrenberg, "the comic writers allude to the insidious machinations of the flour-dealers, the innkeepers, the bird-sellers, the wool-merchants, or the fish-mongers."[27] In the classical period (5th and 4th centuries BCE), most of the leading politicians were former manufacturers. When vilified and mocked by the comedians, however, the politicians were "deliberately characterized as tradesmen, as sellers of something." The emphasis was "laid not on them being producers, but on their activities in buying and selling."[28] Even sons of merchants were, by virtue of their birth, objects of ridicule.[29]

In ancient Rome, wrote University of Leeds classicist Donald C. Earl, "All trade was stigmatized as undignified. . . . The word *mercator* [merchant] appears as almost a term of abuse."[30] In the first century BCE, the Roman politician Cicero noted that retail trade is *sordidus* (vile) because retailers "would get no profits without a great deal of downright lying."[31] The Roman masses shared Cicero's attitude. In his comedies, which were aimed at a mass audience, Plautus (254–184 BCE) made "frequent reference to the commercial classes, who are invariably treated with hostility and contempt."[32]

The Roman state was cognizant of the popular sentiments toward merchants. Consider the Edict on Maximum Prices that was promulgated by Emperor Diocletian (244–311 CE) in 301 CE. The edict set the maximum prices of more than 1,200 products, including raw materials, labor, services, animals, and slaves. In the preamble, which sought to justify his actions, Diocletian declared:

> Some people always are eager to turn a profit even on blessings from the gods: they seize the abundance of general prosperity and strangle it. Or again they make much of a year's bad harvest and traffic by the operations of hucksters. Although they each wallow in the greatest riches, with which nations could have been satisfied, they chase after personal allowances and hunt down their chiseling percentages. On their greed, provincial citizens, the logic of our shared humanity urges us to set a limit.[33]

Roman Catholic theologians continued the old imperial hostility toward commerce and profit-making. Consider the *Decretum Gratiani*, which became the recognized standard compilation of canon law from the time of its publication by Italian jurist Gratian (1070–1140) until 1917. Accordingly, "whoever buys something . . . so that it may be a material for making something else, he is no merchant. But the man who buys it in order to sell it unchanged . . . is cast out from God's temple."[34] Protestant theologians agreed. According to the English economic historian R. H. Tawney (1880–1962), Martin Luther "hated commerce and capitalism."[35] In Luther's view, Tawney wrote,

> Christians should earn their living by the sweat of their brow. . . .
> [T]he most admirable life was that of the peasant. . . . The labor of
> the craftsman is [also] honorable, for he serves the community . . .
> [but the Catholic] mendicant orders . . . cover the land with a
> horde of beggars. Pilgrimages, saints' days, and monasteries are
> an excuse for idleness and must be suppressed. Vagrants must be
> either banished or compelled to labor. . . . [T]rade, banking and
> credit, capitalist industry . . . seem[ed] to him to belong to the very
> essence of the kingdom of darkness.[36]

In his 1867 work, *Das Kapital*, Karl Marx approvingly quotes Luther as saying that "great wrong and unchristian thievery and robbery are committed all over the world by merchants."[37] And John Calvin (1509–1564) also noted that the life of the merchant closely resembles that of a prostitute, for it is "full of tricks and traps and deceits."[38]

As Deirdre McCloskey documented in a trilogy of books on the bourgeois era, though, European attitudes toward the merchant class (now called the "bourgeoisie") and its activities started to change around the beginning of the 18th century.[39] She wrote,

> Three centuries ago in places like Holland and England, the talk
> and thought about the middle class began to alter. Ordinary con-
> versations about innovation and markets became more approving.
> The high theorists were emboldened to rethink their prejudice
> against the bourgeoisie, a prejudice by then millenia old. . . . In

northwestern Europe around 1700 the general opinion shifted in favor of the bourgeoisie, and especially in favor of its marketing and innovating. . . . People stopped sneering at market innovativeness and other bourgeois virtues exercised far from the traditional places of honor in the Basilica of St. Peter or the Palace of Versailles or the gory grounds of the First Battle of Breitenfeld.[40]

As we saw in Chapter 1, enlightened thinkers embraced commercial society and credited the latter with all sorts of beneficial consequences, including prosperity, amity, and peace. The former's attitudes toward innovation also changed. Consequently, the English philosopher Jeremy Bentham (1748–1832) noted that "to say all new things are bad, is as much as to say all things are bad, or at any event, at their commencement; for of all the old things ever seen or heard of, there is not one that was not once new."[41] "The result," as McCloskey observed, "was modern economic growth."[42] What accounts for those changes?

■ Box 7.3. Revulsion toward commerce was not restricted to the Western world

Revulsion toward commerce was not restricted to the Western world. As Marcel Maus noted in his 1967 *Manuel d'Ethnographie*, "The Brahman [highest ranking of the four varnas, or social classes, in Hindu India] has invincible pride. He refuses to have anything to do with markets."[c] Likewise, as Robert Klitgaard found in his 1986 work, *Elitism and Meritocracy in Developing Countries: Selection Policies for Higher Education*, the system of competitive examinations for recruiting Chinese state officials between 960 and 1905 were open to all, except for brothel-keepers, entertainers, and merchants.[d] Finally, in the Islamic world,

> The merchant's profits were regarded as a sort of profiteering, the result of speculation, an illegitimate gain; whereas what had been produced by the work of the hand and sweat of the brow—this only was legitimate. . . . The neutral terms like *bazirgan* and *matrabaz*, which are used for merchants in official documents, gained in popular speech such pejorative implications as "profiteer" and "trickster."[e] ■

Prior to the Enlightenment, European states served the financial and dynastic interests of the elite, while the rest of the population was expected to find solace in the afterlife. Ritchie Robertson from Oxford University observed in his 2021 book, *The Enlightenment: The Pursuit of Happiness, 1680–1790*, that the thinkers of the Enlightenment saw the ultimate goal of a society very differently. In their view, society should facilitate the maximization of human welfare (i.e., happiness).[43] As such, luxury, pleasure, and material wealth in general became morally positive and most readily attainable through market-tested innovation.

The Enlightenment, then, helped to undermine traditional feudal institutions and led to a profound change in what was considered the philosophical purpose of government. Remarkably, the ruling elite allowed those changes to happen and even embraced them. That resulted in the emergence of rulers dubbed "enlightened despots" such as Holy Roman Emperor Joseph II (1741–1790), Russian czarina Catherine the Great (1729–1796), the Prussian king Frederick the Great (1712–1786), and the French emperor Napoleon Bonaparte (1769–1821) who coined the phrase, "Everything should be done for the people, nothing by the people."[44]

The change in attitudes toward commerce and innovation parallels the split between premodern and modern society. When "innovator" and "merchant" were hurled as curses, the main goal of the elite was the preservation of the feudal status quo. To preserve their independence in a geopolitically competitive environment, the elite was forced to use innovation and trade to further their existential ends. This shift birthed the modern world in which ordinary men and women were, at last, free to "have a go" at heretofore unknown freedom, dignity, and prosperity.[45]

■ Box 7.4. Western European innovations before the Age of Innovation (1550–1750)

Long before the Age of Innovation, Western Europeans understood that they lived on a technologically and scientifically dynamic continent. Take, for example, the experiences of the Italian Jesuit Matthew (Mateo) Ricci (1552–1610), who lived in China between 1583 and 1610. Shortly after his arrival, "the presence

---

of the wonderful things brought from Europe attracted many." The Chinese are "delighted and amazed when you show them books containing descriptive maps. . . . They simply marvel that whole countries can be viewed in one book. . . . They realize that fundamentally our sciences are more solid than their own and that the Chinese . . . have had a wrong idea of foreigners up to the present, placing them all in the same category and calling them all barbarians."[f]

In Nanking, the chief magistrate "took great pleasure in studying" a map of the world, "wondering that he could see the great expanse of the world depicted on such a small surface." The governor of Nanking, "was so pleased with" one of Ricci's maps that "he had it copied on marble together with a beautifully carved inscription, in praise of the drawing."[g] The maps caused such excitement, because the "Chinese had never seen a geographical exposition of the entire surface of the earth, either in the form of a globe or as presented on the plane surface of a map, nor had they seen the earth's surface divided by meridians, parallels, or degrees; and they knew nothing of an equator, of tropics, of either pole, or of a division of the earth into five zones."[h] The Chinese, Ricci continued,

> are grossly ignorant of what the world in general is like. . . . [T]heir universe was limited to their own fifteen provinces, and in the sea painted around it they had placed a few little islands to which they had given the names of different kingdoms they had heard of. All of these islands put together would not be as large as the smallest of the Chinese provinces. . . . We must mention here another discovery which helped to win the good will of the Chinese. To them . . . the earth is flat and square. . . . They could not comprehend . . . that the earth is a globe . . . and that a globe by its very nature has neither beginning nor end.[i]

Finally, Ricci observed, the Chinese "did not know that the whole surface of the earth is inhabited or that men can live on the opposite side without falling off."[j]

The excitement that Ricci observed did not seem to have had a lasting effect on the Chinese attitude toward innovation. Writing a century or so after Ricci, French Jesuit missionary Louis Le Comte (1655–1728) observed that the Chinese are "fond of the most defective piece of antiquity . . . differing much in this from us [Europeans], who are in love with nothing but the new."[k] Some hundred years later, Sir George Staunton (1781–1859) was so disheartened by the Chinese indifference to his embassy's recommendations for the improvement of Chinese canals that he commented, "In this country they think that everything is excellent and that proposals for improvement would be superfluous if not blameworthy."[l]

The Chinese attitude to innovations is not unique. In 1609, the interim captain-general of Manila, Rodrigo Vivero (1564–1636) got shipwrecked off the coast of Japan. "One day," noted Fernand Braudel, Vivero "was chatting idly with the Shogun's secretary at Yedo.[m] The secretary criticized the Spaniards for their pride, their reserve. He then proceeded to discuss their way of dressing, 'the variety of their costumes, a realm in which they are so inconsistent that they are dressed in a different way every two years.' . . . [The secretary proposed to] show 'by the evidence of traditions and of old papers that his nation had not changed its costume for over a thousand years.'"[n]

Similarly, the French traveler Jean-Baptiste Chardin (1643–1713), who lived in Persia for a decade, observed in 1686, "I have seen Tamberlaine's [Tamerlane's] costume, which is kept in the treasury of Ispahan, and it is cut exactly like the clothes worn here today, without any difference. . . . [The Persians] are not anxious for new discoveries and innovations," for "they believe [that] they possess all that is required in the way of necessities and conveniences for living, and are content to remain so."[o]

This observable technological and scientific dynamism in Western Europe after 1500 should not be confused with the age of sustained innovation that started in the mid-18th century. As Gregory Clark observed,

> There is general agreement, but not unanimity, that modern economic growth occurred long after the major scientific breakthroughs of the sixteenth and seventeenth century. The dogmas of the ancient Greeks which had informed medieval science were discarded in a broad Scientific Revolution, often dated to 1543, that involved advances in physics, astronomy, biology, chemistry, [and] human anatomy. At the same time general levels of literacy rose all across northern Europe, and there was a vast expansion of the amount of printed material. Yet even in economies like England there is little sign of productivity

advance in the interval 1540–1760. In other areas of Europe, such as Italy, there was economic stagnation or decline.[p]

It is, therefore, worth exploring why technological and scientific progress did not translate into massive gains in the European standards of living before the 18th and, especially, the 19th centuries. To that end, Mokyr observed this:

> Inventions in the pre-1700 era . . . were normally the result of serendipitous strokes of luck, flashes of brilliant intuition, learning by doing, and the slow accumulation of incremental improvements of techniques in use. It was "a world of engineering without mechanics, iron-making without metallurgy, farming without soil science, mining without geology, water-power without hydraulics, dye-making without organic chemistry, and medical practice without microbiology and immunology."[q] Technical progress in the eighteenth century came to rely slowly on insights from natural philosophy, on more useful practical mathematics, and on more careful experimental methods borrowed from scientific practice. Once technological progress began to rely on formal and systematic knowledge, the European advantage rapidly became overwhelming.[r]

Mokyr goes on to say, "It was no longer enough to establish that a technique worked; people were curious to know how and why it did, and once they made progress on that front, techniques could be improved further."[s] To the growth of "formal and systematic knowledge," we may add greater liberality (or inclusiveness) of political and economic institutions that allowed for greater freedom of thought, expression and experimentation, as well as the freedom to benefit from inventions and innovations in ways that were relatively secure from predation by the ruling elite. ∎

The stage for modernity is finally set

Geopolitical competition and the survival instincts of the European elite helped to create a fortuitous landscape where new political, economic, scientific, and ethical ideas flourished. Europe, in other words, became more free.

What the continent needed now was people—more human beings willing and able to take advantage of the new liberal atmosphere of greater inclusion and openness.

Fortuitously, the Little Ice Age came to an end and the earth finally began to warm. This more temperate climate, along with the more efficient New World crops such as the potato (in Europe), the sweet potato (in China), and corn (in Africa), led to a significant increase in population. Between 1750 and 1850, the global population rose from about 800 million people to about 1.3 billion.[46] Europe's population more than doubled, from 128 million in 1750 to almost 300 million in 1900.[47]

Rising populations allowed for more specialization and trade resulting in a growth in labor productivity. However, this particular growth spurt didn't last, and Malthusian checks began to restrain long-term population growth. Rising hunger put pressure on the productive system and caused political instability. In India, the Mughal state collapsed. In China, a number of anti-Manchu rebellions took place. There was unrest in the Ottoman Empire and major upheavals in Southern Africa.

Europe also saw a good share of new conflicts, including the Seven Years' War (1756–1763) and the War of American Independence (1775–1783). Yet European states did not collapse, even as some of them assuredly transformed their institutions. Instead, they generally thrived. Why? Because Europe's peculiar geopolitical system, along with revolutions in thought and ethics, enabled the Europeans of the 18th century to become the first people to respond to Malthusian pressures with sustained innovation.

Common-access pastures were enclosed, agricultural production became more specialized, and fertilizer became more widely used. Efficiency was further increased through the use of devices like the seed drill and the threshing machine and the adoption of practices such as selective breeding. These innovations increased productivity so much that fewer people were needed to grow food and labor began to migrate from agriculture to manufacturing.

In previous generations, it had been common for farming households to pursue small-scale industrial activity in their homes. However, as agriculture became more efficient, more and more people became full-time manufacturers. Industry also began to move out of the household and into workshops and factories. Labor, therefore, became less family-oriented and more individualistic and fluid.[48] One salutary consequence of this reorganization of labor was the decline of state-backed production institutions like guilds, thereby creating space for individual entrepreneurship.

There was also tremendous technological innovation. Devices like the Newcomen steam engine (1712) and its subsequent refinement by James Watt (1776) transformed the ways in which energy was harnessed. Innovation also occurred in the European financial sector, with the invention of bills of exchange, capital markets, and tradeable government debt. Capital markets began to pool previously dispersed and illiquid assets, driving the price of capital down. This encouraged investment, which in turn created more plentiful, cheaper capital.

In the political sphere, the state became a distinct entity that was increasingly independent of the hereditary ruling elite. Moreover, the government was increasingly expected to improve the general welfare of the people, rather than perpetuate the goals of a tiny elite. The rational pursuit of science also accelerated, with chemistry replacing alchemy and geology obliterating previous estimates about the age of Earth.

By 1850, the traditional, holistic framework of knowledge and the predatory relationship between the elite and the rest had been completely destroyed. In short, Europe had reached modernity, and there was no longer any way for the ruling elite to stop it. Modern states were so superior to feudalism that the modern way of life spread across the globe, from Britain and the Low Countries to France and Germany, and then to North America and the world beyond.

CHAPTER 8

The Age of Innovation and the Great Enrichment

Nor during the Age of Innovation have the poor gotten poorer, as people are always saying. On the contrary, the poor have been the chief beneficiaries of modern capitalism. It is an irrefutable historical finding, obscured by the logical truth that the profits from innovation go in the first act mostly to the bourgeois rich.

Deirdre McCloskey, *Bourgeois Dignity: Why Economics Can't Explain the Modern World*[1]

Chapter summary

Homo sapiens may well be 300,000 years old.[2] For the first 96 percent of our time on Earth, we were foragers, subsisting on what little we could find or kill. Even after *Homo sapiens* embraced agriculture some 12,000 years ago, progress was painfully slow. People lacked basic medicines and died relatively young. They had no painkillers, and people with ailments spent much of their lives in agonizing pain. Entire families lived in bug-infested dwellings that offered neither comfort nor privacy. They worked in the fields from sunrise to sunset, yet hunger and famines were commonplace. Transportation was primitive, and most people never traveled beyond their native villages or nearest towns. Ignorance and illiteracy were ubiquitous.

In a remarkable and sudden transition, though, standards of living skyrocketed over the last two centuries, first in Western Europe and North America, and then in other parts of the world. The consequences of that increase in economic growth were monumental. For the first time in human history, our species overcame Malthusian limits on production and consumption. The Age of Innovation ushered in unprecedented and even unimaginable improvements in wealth, life expectancy, nutrition, health, clothing, working conditions, and education. Extreme poverty, infant and maternal mortalities, and child labor declined. Eventually, environmental quality started to improve, violence became more rare, and humanity became more moral, as witnessed by such monumental accomplishments as the abolition of the once universal institution of slavery. In Chapter 8, we will look at some of the most beneficial changes that took place over the past 200 years or so.

The Industrial Revolution

The living standards of the masses began to undergo
sustained growth for the first time in history

The Age of Innovation, which started in mid-18th-century Western Europe, before spreading to North America and beyond, brought widespread changes. In those years, no change was more important than the Industrial Revolution. The Industrial Revolution introduced new fuels such as coal and petroleum; new locomotive power such as the steam engine and the internal-combustion engine; new machines such as the spinning jenny and the power loom; and the factory system, which reorganized work and required much greater division of labor and specialization of function. Those increased the use of natural resources and enabled the mass production of manufactured goods.[3]

Improvements in agricultural productivity, which resulted from mechanization and the use of synthetic fertilizer, fed a larger population.[4] That, along with new opportunities for factory work, increased urbanization and contributed to the development of political awareness among the "lower orders." At the same time, wealth became more widely distributed, as landed interests gave way to the interests of the nouveau-riche bourgeoisie. All in all, old patterns of authority were eroded, and society began to become more democratic.

Far-reaching developments, such as the liberalization of trade, allowed the benefits of industrialization to spread globally. Trade volumes rose, costs fell, and, as reflected in the process of price convergence, markets became global. The gold standard and the invention of the telegraph made capital transfers easier. Attracted by higher profits, investment flowed from more developed to less developed countries.

The Industrial Revolution marked a definite break with our Malthusian past. As Robert E. Lucas noted, "For the first time in history, the living standards of the masses of ordinary people have begun to undergo sustained growth. . . . Nothing remotely like this economic behavior is mentioned by the classical economists, even as a theoretical possibility."[5]

■ Box 8.1. Bringing humanity out of darkness (1800–2020)

The University of Illinois at Chicago economist and historian Deirdre Mc-Closkey calls the period beginning in 1800 the Great Enrichment.[a] She notes that inflation-adjusted per capita incomes have risen by 3,000 percent since then. In some ways that's a conservative estimate. U.S. blue-collar workers, for example, saw personal resource abundance of 26 basic commodities increase by 5,762 percent between 1850 and 2018.

Measured in time prices (i.e., the time it takes to earn enough money to buy something), many commodities became 99 percent cheaper. Remember that a 99 percent decrease in time price means that the time it took to earn enough money to buy 1 item at the start of the analysis gets the buyer 100 (i.e., 9,900 percent more) items at the end of the analysis.

Between 1850 and 2018, for example, the U.S. blue-collar worker's personal resource abundance (pRA) of rye, tea, and rice increased 9,840 percent, 10,552 percent, and 11,049 percent, respectively. The pRA of nickel increased by 18,046 percent, and the pRA of sugar increased by 22,583 percent.

The pRA of light has increased even faster. The Nobel Prize–winning economist William Nordhaus estimated that buying one hour of light in 1800 required about 5.37 hours of labor.[b] With advanced LED technology, one hour of light today costs less than 0.16 seconds of labor. That represents a 12,082,400 percent increase in the personal abundance of light.

What about the relationship between population growth and the abundance of light? Remember that we calculate the size of the population resource pie by multiplying personal resource abundance (how much of a resource one hour of labor will buy for one person) by the population size. Comparing the size of the population resource pie at different points in time reveals changes in the population resource abundance (PRA).

Between 1800 and 2020, the pRA of light increased from 1 to 120,825. Over this same period, the world's population increased from 1 billion to 7.8 billion, or 680 percent. The population resource abundance of light in 2020 can thus be calculated as $120,825 \times 7.8$, which amounts to 942,435. Put differently, the PRA of light has increased by 94,243,400 percent since 1800. The PRA of light has been increasing at a compounded annual growth rate of about 6.5 percent, thus doubling every 10.8 years.

Finally, elasticity measures one variable's sensitivity to a change in another variable. Between 1800 and 2020, the PRA of light increased by 94,243,400 percent. Over the same period, the world's population increased by 680 percent. Dividing 94,243,400 by 680 equals 138,593. So, every 1 percent increase in the world's population corresponds to a 138,593 percent increase in the PRA of light. We have experienced an exponential efflorescence of illumination.

The next time you turn on a light switch, please take a moment to appreciate the freedom and creativity of people who toiled to bring humanity out of the darkness. Compared with the illumination of our world today, all of our ancestors really did live in the "dark ages."

Table B8.1.1. Time price analysis of light (1800–2020)

	1800	2020	Percentage change
Personal light abundance indexed to 1800 = 1	1	120,825	12,082,400
Population in billions	1	7.8	680
Population light abundance	1	942,435	94,243,400
Personal light abundance elasticity of population: 17,768%			
Population light abundance elasticity of population: 138,593%			
CAGR of personal light abundance: 5.5%			
CAGR of population light abundance: 6.5%			

Source: Authors' calculations. ∎

The Great Enrichment

Global and American living standards rose 12-fold
and 24-fold, respectively, over the past two centuries

Standards of living are closely tied to economic growth. It is growth that makes all kinds of desiderata (adequate nutrition, better schools, better hospitals) more easily achievable. As Deirdre McCloskey noted, growth "has looked like an ice-hockey stick lying on the ground. It had a long, long horizontal handle . . . extending through the two-hundred-thousand-year history of *Homo sapiens* to 1800 . . . then a wholly unexpected blade, leaping up in the last two out of the two thousand centuries."[6]

Measured in 2011 U.S. dollars, Angus Maddison and a team of economists at the University of Groningen found that the global income per person per day in the reign of Caesar Augustus averaged $2. That's also where it stood when William the Conqueror set sail in 1066 to claim the crown of England. This income stagnation does not imply that no economic growth happened over the intervening millennium. Growth did occur, but it was minuscule, localized, and episodic. In the end, the gains always petered out. The "basic fact, known to every economic historian," wrote Joel Mokyr, was

> that before the Industrial Revolution economic growth was slow, intermittent, and reversible. Years of growth were normally offset by years of decline. Even after the Great Enrichment, episodes of economic decline did happen, but the "good years" began to outweigh the bad ones. Economies became more resilient to outside shocks, whether natural or manmade. Asking "why" economic growth was so weak before the Industrial Revolution may seem otiose, since it was the normal, natural state of affairs. Yet the answers point to the many ways in which "modern" economies differ from traditional ones, and thus underline that the Industrial Revolution was in many ways what the physicists call a "phase transition," a major transformation not only of the level and rate of growth of the system, but rang in an entirely new economic dynamic.[7]

In 1800, the average daily income was $2.80. Put differently, in the 18 centuries that separated Augustus's emperorship and the presidency of Thomas Jefferson, per person daily income rose by less than 40 percent. Again, there were regional differences, but those were not great. At the start of the 19th century, average Americans and Britons were twice as prosperous as the global average, roughly speaking.

Then, suddenly, everything changed. Between 1800 and 1900, the global GDP per person per day doubled. Income grew more than twice as much in one century as it had over the preceding 18 combined. By 2016, the number had risen to $40. In the United States, it stood at $145, and in Africa, the world's poorest continent, at $13. In other words, global and American standards of living rose 14-fold and 24-fold, respectively, over the course of the last two centuries.[8] Global income per person per day rose at a compounded rate of about 1.8 percent per year over the last 100 years. It will reach $166 per person per day in 2100 if the trend continues. In the United States, it will reach $605 per person per day.

Extreme poverty

The share of humanity living on the edge of survival fell from 90 percent in 1820 to less than 10 percent today

Before the modern era, European society was bifurcated between a small minority of the very rich and the vast majority of the very poor. Sébastien Le Prestre de Vauban (1633–1707), a military engineer during the reign of Louis XIV, which lasted from 1643 until 1715, estimated that the French population consisted of 10 percent rich, 50 percent very poor (*fort malaise*), 30 percent who were nearly beggars, and 10 percent who were actually beggars. Likewise, Francesco Guicciardini (1483–1540), an Italian historian and friend of Niccolò Machiavelli, wrote that "except for a few Grandees of the Kingdom [of Spain] who live with great sumptuousness, one gathers that others live in great poverty."[9]

"The majority of the beggars" in late 18th-century Naples, wrote Francesco Pignatelli Principe di Strongoli (1775–1853), "do not have houses; they find nocturnal asylum in a few caves, stables or ruined houses, or (not very different from the last) in houses run by one of their number, with a lantern and a little straw as their sole equipment, entry being obtained in exchange for a grano [a small Neapolitan coin] or slightly more per night . . . they are to be seen there lying like filthy animals, with no distinction of age or sex: all the ugliness and all the offspring which result from this can be imagined. . . . They proliferate, without families, having no relationship with the state except through the gallows and living in such chaos that only God could get his bearings among them."[10]

And what of the children of these poor wretches? Let one gruesome example, which the historian Fernand Braudel cited from the French writer Louis-Sébastien Mercier's 18th-century book, *Tableau de Paris*, suffice.

> Paris had 7,000 to 8,000 abandoned children out of some 30,000 births around 1780. Depositing these children at the poor-house was an occupation in itself. The man carried them on his back "in a padded box which can hold three. They are propped upright in their swaddling clothes, breathing through the top. . . . When [the

carrier] opens his box, he often finds one of them dead; he completes his journey with the other two, impatient to be rid of the load. . . . He immediately sets off once more to start the same task, which is his livelihood, over again."[11]

What was true of Europe was also true of the rest of the world. According to the former chief economist of the World Bank and the former director of the Paris School of Economics, François Bourguignon, and University of Paris economist and former head of the OECD, Christian Morrisson, nearly 90 percent of the world's population lived in extreme poverty as late as 1820, extreme poverty being defined as less than $1.90 per person per day (in 2015 dollars). Put differently, 965 million out of the world's 1.08 billion people lived in extreme poverty, and only 117 million were better off (some by a big margin and some by a tiny margin).[12] By 2015, that had changed: only 734 million people of the world's 7.35 billion people lived in extreme poverty, and 6.62 billion people lived better than that. As such, the share of humanity living in extreme poverty fell to less than 10 percent.

The latest World Bank assessment estimates that the share of the world's inhabitants living in extreme poverty fell below 8 percent in 2020.[13] If we are correct, extreme poverty fell not in spite of population growth but largely because of it. Human ingenuity, not magic, reduced extreme poverty across the globe from 90 percent to less than 9 percent.

To summarize, extreme poverty completely disappeared from Western Europe and North America, and it is now in retreat elsewhere. Today it can be said that absolute poverty is, for the first time in human history, no longer a global problem. Regrettably, it remains an African problem, for it is sub-Saharan Africa where the vast majority of extremely poor people today reside. Thankfully, since the start of the new millenium, sub-Saharan Africa has enjoyed relatively high growth rates, and there is no a priori reason why the region should not see further reductions in extreme poverty in the future.[14]

Life expectancy

Globally, people live more than 22 years
longer than the richest people did in 1900

Human life expectancy at birth averaged approximately 30 years for most of human history. That was in large part because of the sky-high child mortality rate among the rich and poor alike. For example, Queen Anne of Great Britain and Ireland (1665–1714) lost 17 children; several were stillborn, while the child who lived the longest, William, died in 1700 at the age of 11.[15] As Olivia Colman, who portrayed the queen in the 2018 movie *The Favourite* put it, "Some were born as blood, some without breath, and some were with me a very brief time."[16] As late as 1800, 43 percent of children globally died before the age of 5. By 2015, only 4.5 percent of children died so young.[17]

In 1800, life expectancy in Europe and North America started to increase at a sustained rate of about three months per year.[18] Within a century, people living in the richest parts of the world could expect to live to the age of 50. The main reasons for increasing life spans included better nutrition and public health measures, such as water filtration and expansion of sewer networks. Both were coterminous with and enabled by the gradual enrichment of the society as a whole.

In 2017, global life expectancy reached 72.4 years, according to the World Bank.[19] Put differently, an average inhabitant of the planet at birth—say someone living in the Dominican Republic today—can expect to live 22 years longer than an average Briton or American would have expected to live just 120 years ago. Life expectancy in the Western world rose to about 80 in the meantime, and in some countries like Japan, it rose to 88 years.[20]

Finally, what happens if the current trend in life expectancy continues? Ronald Bailey crunched the numbers and found that "life expectancy rising by 3 months annually implies a global average lifespan of 92 years by 2100. However, the 2017 United Nations medium fertility scenario more conservatively projects that average life expectancy will rise from 72 years today to 83 years by the end of this [the 21st] century."[21] We hope that Bailey is correct.

Maternal mortality

The rate will have fallen from 1,000 per 100,000 live births in the first half of the 18th century to 70 by 2030

Lady Sybil Branson, a wealthy British aristocrat in the popular television show *Downton Abbey*, died during childbirth in 1920 in spite of being able to afford the best medical care of the day. The fictional character suffered from a very serious malady. Affecting 6 percent of all pregnancies, pre-eclampsia raises a pregnant woman's blood pressure to dangerously high levels and, if left untreated, often results in violent seizures (eclampsia) that can lead to the death of the mother, the child, or both.[22] Historically, no amount of wealth or privilege was sufficient to save a woman from this horrific condition.

The World Health Organization defines maternal mortality as "the death of a woman while pregnant or within 42 days of termination of pregnancy."[23] Such deaths can occur for a variety of reasons, including bleeding and infection after childbirth, high blood pressure during pregnancy, complications during delivery, and an unsafe abortion. Early statistics are difficult to come by, but British parish records indicate a maternal mortality rate of 1,000 per 100,000 live births in the first half of the 18th century. Since women were pregnant more often than is the case today, the actual risk of dying due to complications from pregnancy was much higher.[24]

In the mid-19th century, a Hungarian physician named Ignaz Semmel-weis (1818–1865) noticed that women who gave birth at home died at a lower rate than women who were assisted by doctors. He hypothesized that doctors, who did not then wash their hands, passed diseases from other patients to pregnant women. Unfortunately, Semmelweis's insight was ignored or dismissed until the French biologist Louis Pasteur (1822–1895) established a definitive link between germs and disease in the 1860s. After doctors started to disinfect their hands, maternal mortality began to fall, a trend that was much enhanced when the Scottish physician and microbiologist Alexander Fleming (1881–1955) discovered the world's first effective antibiotic, which he named penicillin.

As the knowledge of best medical practices spread and pharmaceutical drugs became more affordable, maternal mortality rates plummeted throughout the world. The global maternal death rate fell from 385 per 100,000 live births in 1990 to 216 in 2015, a reduction of 44 percent. In sub-Saharan Africa, the world's poorest region, the rate of maternal deaths fell from 987 to 547 over the same period, a reduction of 45 percent. Globally, maternal mortality rates remain higher among women in far-flung rural areas that are difficult to reach by professional medical staff, cultures in which adolescent pregnancy remains relatively common, and very poor countries without proper medical facilities. That said, the United Nations expects the maternal mortality rate to continue declining and to fall to 70 per 100,000 live births by 2030.[25]

As for preeclampsia, humanity has made much progress. Today, evidence suggests that low-dose aspirin or calcium supplementation can reduce the risk of developing the condition. Moreover, blood pressure monitoring is a routine part of all prenatal medical visits. But the most effective treatment for preeclampsia is early delivery. Advancements in the ability of doctors to induce labor and care for preterm infants—thanks be to the German physician Martin Arthur Couney (1870–1950) for inventing the baby incubator—have thus dramatically improved the odds of survival for preeclamptic women and their children.

Nutrition

In 15th-century England, 80 percent of private expenditure was on food, with 20 percent spent on bread alone

Until relatively recently, people were constantly hungry, and starvation was only ever a few bad harvests away. In 1800, the average food supply in France, which was then and is now one of the world's richest countries, was only 1,846 calories per person per day.[26] To put these figures in perspective, the U.S. Department of Agriculture's Dietary Guidelines estimate that calorie needs per person per day range from 1,600 to 2,000 for women and 1,900 to 2,500 for men. That amounts to an average of 2,000 calories per person per day across sexes and over the entire human lifespan, hence the crude "2,000-calorie diet" that every American knows about.[27]

"We do know that the mass [of the European and global population] lived in a state of undernourishment," wrote University of California, Berkeley, economic historian Carlo M. Cipolla in his 1994 book, *Before the Industrial Revolution: European Society and Economy 1000–1700*. "This gave rise, among other things, to serious forms of avitaminosis. Widespread filth was also the cause of troublesome and painful skin diseases. To this must be added in certain areas the endemic presence of malaria, or deleterious effects of a restricted matrimonial selection, which gave rise to cretinism."[28]

An account of rural life in 16th-century Lombardy found that "the peasants live on wheat . . . and it seems to us that we can disregard their other expenses because it is the shortage of wheat that induces the labourers to raise their claims; their expenses for clothing and other needs are practically non-existent."[29] In 15th-century England, 80 percent of private expenditure was on food. Of that amount, 20 percent was spent on bread alone.[30] By 2020, in comparison, only 8.6 percent of the U.S. personal disposable income was spent on food, a figure which is itself inflated by the large amounts that Americans spend in restaurants.[31] For health reasons, many Americans today avoid eating bread altogether.

By 2017, the French enjoyed a circadian feast of 3,558 calories, with Americans consuming 3,766 calories per person per day, the British 3,428 calories, the Chinese 3,197 calories, and the Indians 2,517 calories. The average global population-weighted food supply per person per day stood at 2,961 calories. In sub-Saharan Africa, the world's poorest region, it stood at 2,449 calories.[32] Famines still occur, but they are becoming more rare and now are always the result of bad economic policies or war.

Back in the 1800s, millions of people starved to death every decade. Famines peaked in the 1870s with more than 20 million deaths. In the 1880s, the least hungry decade in the 19th century, close to 3 million people starved to death worldwide. A smaller number of people died in the troubled 2000s, the hungriest decade in recent memory. The difference is even more stark after accounting for population growth in the past two centuries. The average annual rate of famine deaths per 100,000 people dropped from 19.5 in the 1880s to 4.3 in the 2000s. Between 2010 and 2016, it was only 0.5,[33] which amounts to a 40-fold decline from the 1880s.

■ Box 8.2. Thanksgiving dinner became much cheaper (1986–2020)

Since 1986, the American Farm Bureau Federation has conducted an annual price survey of food items found in a typical Thanksgiving dinner. The items on this shopping list are designed to serve a group of 10 people, with leftovers remaining. The list includes a 16-pound turkey, a 30-ounce pumpkin pie mix, one gallon of milk, a one-pound vegetable tray, 12 bread rolls, two pie shells, one pound of green peas, 12 ounces of fresh cranberries, half a pint of whipping cream, 14 ounces of cubed stuffing, three pounds of sweet potatoes, and several miscellaneous ingredients.[c] What happened to the price of dinner over time?

In nominal terms, the cost of a Thanksgiving dinner price rose from $28.74 in 1986 to $46.90 in 2020, or 63.2 percent. Over the same period, inflation rose by 135 percent.[d] To keep up with inflation, the dinner should have cost about $67.69 in 2020, rather than $46.90. So, adjusted for inflation, the Thanksgiving dinner became $20.79 or 30.7 percent cheaper. What happens, though, if we analyze the cost of Thanksgiving dinner using time prices (TPs)?

Let's look at the data using our three U.S. hourly wage denominators, as described in Chapter 4. To get the time price (TP) of a Thanksgiving dinner, we divide the nominal money price of the meal by the hourly wage rate. That will give us the number of hours required to earn enough money to feed our 10 guests. We can then analyze the change in TPs over time. Note that as long as hourly income is increasing faster than nominal prices, TPs will decrease.

As Table B8.2.1 shows, the nominal price of Thanksgiving dinner increased 63.2 percent between 1986 and 2020, but the unskilled wage rate increased 173.2 percent. That means that the TP of the meal for the U.S. unskilled worker declined from 5.48 hours in 1986 to 3.27 hours in 2020 or 40.3 percent. As such, the U.S. unskilled worker could buy 1.67 Thanksgiving dinners in 2020 for the same length of time of work it took to buy one meal in 1986.

The TP of the Thanksgiving dinner for the U.S. blue-collar worker declined from 2.23 hours in 1986 to 1.38 hours in 2020 or 38 percent. As such, the U.S. blue-collar worker could buy 1.61 Thanksgiving dinners in 2020 for the same length of time of work it took to buy one meal in 1986.

The U.S. unskilled workers who upgraded their skills to become blue-collar workers between 1986 and 2020, saw the TP of a Thanksgiving dinner fall by

Table B8.2.1. Time prices of a Thanksgiving dinner: the U.S. unskilled worker perspective, the U.S. blue-collar worker perspective, and the U.S. upskilling worker perspective (1986–2020)

Thanksgiving Day dinner for 10 people	1986	2020	Percentage change	Dinner multiplier
Nominal money price of dinner	$28.74	$46.90	63.2	
Hourly income rates				
Unskilled	$5.25	$14.34	173.2	
Blue-collar	$12.90	$33.98	163.4	
Upskilling	$5.25	$33.98	547.4	
Time prices in hours				
Unskilled	5.48	3.27	−40.3	1.67
Blue-collar	2.23	1.38	−38.0	1.61
Upskilling	5.48	1.38	−74.8	3.97

Source: Authors' calculations.

Table B8.2.2. Personal resource abundance analysis of Thanksgiving dinner: summary of the U.S. blue-collar worker perspective, the U.S. unskilled worker perspective, and the U.S. upskilling worker perspective (1986–2020)

Thanksgiving dinner 1986–2020	Percentage change in resource time price	Personal resource abundance multiplier	Percentage change in personal resource abundance	Compound annual percentage growth rate in personal resource abundance	Years to double personal resource abundance
Blue-collar	−38.0	1.61	61.4	1.42	49.2
Unskilled	−40.3	1.67	67.4	1.53	45.7
Upskilling	−74.8	3.97	296.7	4.14	17.1

Source: Authors' calculations.

Table B8.2.3. Thanksgiving dinner: the U.S. population analysis (1986–2020)

Thanksgiving Day dinner for 10 people	1986	2020	Percentage change
U.S. population in millions	240	331	37.9
Time prices in hours			
Unskilled	5.48	3.27	−40.3
Blue-collar	2.23	1.38	−38.0
Upskilling	5.48	1.38	−74.8
Working time in millions of hours			
Unskilled	131.4	108.3	−17.6
Blue-collar	53.5	45.7	−14.6
Upskilling	131.4	45.7	−65.2

Source: Authors' calculations.

74.8 percent. These upskilling workers were thus able to buy 3.97 Thanksgiving dinners for the same length of time of work it took them to buy one meal in 1986 (see Table B8.2.2).

Note that the U.S. population rose from 240 million in 1986 to 331 million in 2020, or 37.9 percent. What happened to the total Thanksgiving dinner bill over that 34-year period? If the whole United States consisted of unskilled laborers in 1986, the total Thanksgiving dinner bill would have fallen by 17.6 percent in 2020. If everyone in the United States had been a blue-collar worker in 1986, the total bill would have fallen by 14.6 percent by 2020. If everyone in the United States upskilled from unskilled work to blue-collar work, the total Thanksgiving dinner bill would have fallen by an astonishing 65.2 percent (see Table B8.2.3). ∎

Hygiene and sanitation

Elizabeth I bathed once a month, "whether she needed it or not," but her successor, James I, only washed his fingers

The need to keep human and animal waste away from human contact seems obvious today, but for millennia, that was not the case. Before the emergence of the germ theory of disease and the subsequent public health campaigns, together with the construction of adequate sanitation infrastructure in most of the world, people and waste commingled, with catastrophic results. Countless millions of people got sick or died from diseases such as diarrhea, ascariasis (a type of intestinal worm infection), cholera, hepatitis, trachoma (an infectious disease caused by the bacterium *Chlamydia trachomatis*), polio, schistosomiasis (also known as snail fever and bilharzia), and so on.

In deference to our ancestors, it has to be noted that some cultures, such as ancient Rome, paid due attention to cleanliness. The Romans built numerous public baths, which were accessible even to the very poor for a nominal fee, and a sophisticated system of sewers that enabled Rome to grow and reach a population of over 1 million people around the start of the first millennium. But that feat would not be replicated in Europe until London and Paris achieved it in the 19th century.

In general, however, standards of hygiene were very poor. Most people—even medical "professionals"—tended not to wash their hands, even after going to the bathroom. As a consequence, there was "the prevalence of intestinal worms," which is "a slow, disgusting, and debilitating disease that caused a vast amount of human misery and ill health."[34] Jewish people, who sometimes died at lower rates than the rest of the populace, possibly thanks to the frequent washing of hands that is prescribed by Judaism, were often accused of witchcraft, persecuted, and even killed.[35]

The reluctance to wash was partly a result of the Black Death, which killed between 30 and 60 percent of the European population in the 14th century. According to the medical advice of the day, "once heat and water created openings (pores) through the skin, the plague could easily invade the entire body."[36] As such, even the rich and powerful tended to avoid bathing. Elizabeth I took a bath once a month, "whether she needed it or not," but her successor, James I, only washed his fingers.[37] The *Journal de la Santé*, first published in 1862, was maintained for Louis XIV (1638–1715) by his doctors from infancy until a few years before he died. It described the king's daily life in microscopic detail but mentioned bathing only once.[38]

Sanitation was similarly appalling. English historian Lawrence Stone (1919–1999) observed in his 1977 book, *The Family, Sex and Marriage in England 1500–1800*, that "in towns in the eighteenth century, the city ditches, now often filled with stagnant water, were commonly used as latrines; butchers killed animals in their shops and threw the offal of the carcases into the streets; dead animals were left to decay and fester where they lay; latrine pits were dug close to wells, thus contaminating the water supply. Decomposing bodies of the rich in burial vaults beneath the church often stank out parson and congregation."[39]

A "special problem" in London, Stone wrote, was the "poor holes" or "large, deep, open pits in which were laid the bodies of the poor, side by side, row by row. Only when the pit was filled with bodies was it finally covered with earth."[40] Stone quotes one contemporary writer who observed, "How noisome the stench is that arises from these holes."[41] Furthermore, "great quantities of human excrement were cast into the streets."[42] As Johan Norberg wrote, "When pedestrians heard the shout of 'Gardyloo!' they ran for cover. This phrase, taken from the French for 'Look out for the water,' was your only warning that someone was about to throw their waste out of the window."[43]

Not surprisingly, sanitation was no better on the European mainland. In the middle of the 17th century, Queen Anne of Austria, who was the mother of Louis XIV, noted that "Paris is a horrible place and ill smelling. The streets are so mephitic that one cannot linger there because of the stench of rotting meat and fish and because of a crowd of people who urinate in the streets."[44]

Louis's magnificent palace of Versailles had no proper waste facilities, and people relieved themselves where they stood: in the hallways, behind the curtains, and in the gardens. One 18th-century observer noted that Versailles was "the receptacle of all of humanity's horrors—the passageways, corridors, and courtyards are filled with urine and faecal matter."[45] All that filth was an excellent breeding ground for vermin and disease that periodically decimated the rich and poor alike.

The situation does not appear to have been much better in the non-Western world. In Cairo, wrote one traveler in 1660, "the streets of the town are . . . full here and there of the holes these wretches [i.e., inhabitants] dig to piss in, according to the law, so that the urine should not make them unclean by spurting up at them."[46] In 1694, another traveler observed that the filthiness of unpaved and dusty streets in Isfahan (and, for that matter, all of Persia) "is still further increased by the custom of throwing dead animals, together with the blood of those killed by butchers, on the squares, and of publicly relieving oneself wherever one happens to be."[47]

Today, hygiene is much better throughout the world, and people everywhere wash with greater regularity, helped along by the mass production and distribution of affordable soap, as we shall see in the next section. Moreover, poor sanitation is mostly limited to very poor countries. In sub-Saharan Africa, for example, a mere 30 percent of the population had access to improved sanitation facilities in 2015. That was an improvement from 1990, when only 24 percent did. In other parts of the world, progress has been much faster. In South Asia, which includes very populous countries like India and Bangladesh, the share of the population with access to improved sanitation rose from 20 to 45 percent over the same period. Globally, it increased from 53 to 68 percent.[48]

The United Nations aim to end open defecation by 2030 seems quite optimistic for regions like sub-Saharan Africa and South Asia, but there is no apparent reason why East Asia, Latin America, and the Middle East should not be able to reach the European level of 93 percent or even the North American level of 100 percent by 2030.

Clothing

The purchase of a garment used to be a luxury the common people could only afford a few times in their lives

There is perhaps no greater symbol of the Age of Innovation and the break with Western Europe's agricultural past than the cotton mills. The main products of these mills (buildings housing spinning or weaving machinery for the production of yarn or cloth from cotton) were easily washable cotton clothes and underclothes. That was revolutionary. As Carlo M. Cipolla noted,

> In pre-industrial Europe, the purchase of a garment or cloth for a garment remained a luxury the common people could only afford a few times in their lives. One of the main preoccupations of hospital administration was to ensure that the clothes of the deceased should not be usurped but should be given to lawful inheritors. During epidemics of plague, the town authorities had to struggle to confiscate the clothes of the dead and to burn them: people waited for others to die so as to take over their clothes—which generally had the effect of spreading the epidemic.[49]

Up to the 19th century, poor people wore woolen clothes and underclothes, which itch and are not easy to wash. That practice exacerbated the across-the-board problem of poor hygiene. Lest we forget, most people lived and slept with their domestic animals, including chickens, cows, and pigs, to guard the latter against thieves and predators and to provide the former with additional heat during the long winter months. Eggs, milk, and occasional meat enriched the usually bland diet of bread, and animal waste was needed to fertilize crops. The dangers inherent in using waste as fertilizer were compounded by the fact that people seldom washed their hands or clothes. This led to epidemics and contributed to sky-high mortality rates among our ancestors.

As late as the Battle of Waterloo, in 1815, during which 55,000 men were either killed or wounded, dead soldiers were stripped before being buried. Why would anyone bother stripping the dead, when every hour increased the danger of putrefaction and the spread of disease? The most likely reason for the practice was that clothing was still very expensive and the uniforms were washed, patched, and reused. Just 31 years later, the age-old problem of inadequate clothing was clearly in retreat throughout Western Europe. As the French historian Jules Michelet (1798–1874) wrote in his 1846 book, *Le Peuple,*

> This [i.e., industrialization] was a revolution in France, little noted, but a great revolution nonetheless. It was a revolution in

cleanliness and embellishment of the homes of the poor; underwear, bedding, table linen, and window curtains were now used by
whole classes who had not used them since the beginning of the
world. . . . Machine production . . . brings within the reach of the
poor a world of useful objects, even luxurious and artistic objects,
which they could never reach before. . . . Every [nonrich] woman
used to wear a blue or black dress that she kept for ten years without washing, for fear it might tear to pieces. But now her husband,
a poor worker, covers her in a robe of flowers [i.e., flowery designs]
for the price of a day's labour.[50]

American economic historian David S. Landes (1924–2013) similarly
observed in his 1998 book, *The Wealth and Poverty of Nations: Why Some Are
So Rich and Some So Poor*, that

the principal product of the new technology that we know as the
Industrial Revolution was cheap, washable cotton; and along with
it mass-produced soap made of vegetable oils. For the first time,
the common man could afford underwear, once known as body
linen because that was the washable fabric that the well-to-do
wore next to their skin. He (or she) could wash with soap and even
bathe, although too much bathing was seen as a sign of dirtiness.
Why would clean people have to wash so often? No matter. Personal hygiene changed drastically, so that commoners of the late
nineteenth and early twentieth century often lived cleaner than the
kings and queens of a century earlier.[51]

Today, cheap clothing is readily available throughout the world. As Georgetown University professor of finance and international business Pietra Rivoli
wrote in her 2005 book, *The Travels of a T-Shirt in the Global Economy: An
Economist Examines the Markets, Power, and Politics of World Trade*,

Rich Americans—or even middle-class Americans—excel at throwing things away, and the richer we become, the bigger the mounds
of cast-off clothing swell. The Salvation Army at one time tried

to sell all of the clothing in its stores or to give it away, but the supply now so far outstrips domestic demand that only a fraction of the clothing collected by the Salvation Army stays in the United States. There are nowhere near enough poor people in America to absorb the mountains of castoffs, even if they were given away.[52]

Even in Africa, the world's poorest continent, people are generally adequately clothed. To start with, sub-Saharan Africa imports free second-hand clothing from richer parts of the world. Rivoli notes that sub-Saharan Africans today are so relatively prosperous that they are becoming quite picky about which secondhand clothing they accept from the developed world. "The Africans are every bit as fashion-conscious as the Americans, and know whether lapels are wide or pants have cuffs this year, and make their demands accordingly," she writes.[53] The region also produces vast quantities of clothing, including a number of highly regarded luxury brands.[54]

Child labor

*Prior to mechanized agriculture, there were no food surpluses
to sustain idle hands, not even those of children*

Child labor was once ubiquitous. Take, for example, ancient Rome. As University of Cambridge classicist Mary Beard noted in her 2015 book, *SPQR: A History of Ancient Rome*, "Child labour was the norm. It is not a problem, or even a category, that most Romans would have understood. The invention of 'childhood' and the regulation of what work 'children' could do only came fifteen hundred years later and is still a peculiarly Western preoccupation."[55]

Prior to the mechanization of agriculture, which increased farm productivity, there were no food surpluses to sustain idle hands, not even those of children. "The survival of the family demanded that everybody contributed," wrote Johan Norberg. As such, "it was common for working-class children to start working from seven years of age. . . . In old tapestries and paintings from at least the medieval period, children are portrayed as an integral part of the household economy... [with many working] hard in small workshops and in the home-based industry."[56]

Their working conditions varied, but one 16th-century ordinance in Lombardy found that supervisors of work in rice fields "bring together a large number of children and adolescents, against whom they practice barbarous cruelties.... [They] do not provide these poor creatures with the necessary food, and make them labour as slaves by beating them and treating them more harshly than galley slaves, so that many of the children... die miserably in the farms and neighbouring fields."[57]

As agricultural productivity increased, people no longer had to stay on the farm and grow their own food. They moved to the cities in search of a better life. At first, living conditions were dire, and many children worked in mines and factories. By the middle of the 19th century, however, working conditions started to improve. Economic expansion led to increased competition for labor, and wages grew. That, in turn, enabled more parents to forego their children's labor and send them to school instead.

Between 1851 and 1911, the share of British working boys and girls between the ages of 10 and 14 dropped from 37 and 20 percent, respectively, to 18 and 10 percent. In the United States, the share of working children aged 10 to 13 fell from 12 percent in 1890 to 2.5 percent in 1930. In Italy, 81.3 percent of boys and 46.5 percent of girls between the ages of 10 and 14 had to work in 1881. By 1961, those numbers fell to 4.1 percent and 3.1 percent, respectively.[58]

Legislation eventually enshrined what was already happening in practice by banning child labor. It is nonetheless vital to remember that it was only after a critical mass of children were pulled out of the labor force by their parents that people realized that life without child labor was possible. Similar processes are taking place in the rest of the world today.

According to the International Labor Organization's 2017 report *Global Estimates of Child Labor: Results and Trends 2012–2016*, child laborers as a proportion of all children aged 5 to 17 dropped from 16 percent in 2000 to 9.6 percent in 2016. That year, 19.6 percent of children worked in Africa, 2.9 percent in the Arab states, 4.1 percent in Europe and Central Asia, 5.3 percent in the Americas, and 7.4 percent in Asia and the Pacific.[59]

Work and safety

Between 1856 and 1981, the share of disposable lifetime hours
spent working fell from 50 to 20 percent in Britain

The number of hours worked per day has fluctuated throughout human history. On the basis of their observations of extant hunter-gatherer societies, scholars estimate that our foraging ancestors worked anywhere between 2.8 hours and 7.6 hours per day.[60] Once the foragers secured their food for the day, however, they stopped. The foragers' workday was comparatively short, but their standard of living was consequently lower. Our preagricultural ancestors' wealth—that is, the wealth of most of our ancestors—was limited to the weight of the possessions they could carry on their backs from one location to the next.

The total number of hours worked rose as a result of the agricultural revolution because people were willing to sacrifice free time in exchange for a more stable food supply. Since artificial lighting was prohibitively expensive, daylight regulated the amount of work that could be done on any given day. In the summer, most people worked between 6 and 10 hours in the fields and an additional 3 hours at home. In the winter, shorter days limited the total number of work hours to 8. For religious reasons, Sunday was a day off, and a plethora of feasts broke the monotony of agricultural life.

Our expectations as to what constitutes a good work-life balance are obviously very different from those of hunter-gatherers and early agriculturalists. It makes sense, therefore, to compare today's workload to that at the beginning of the modern era.

Throughout the nineteenth century, the standard workday was longer in the United States than in Britain. In the U.S., the 12-hour day was common during the 1830s and 1840s, and in some sectors (such as steel) [this trend] continued into the 1920s. The standard surveys place the average work day at 11.5 hours between 1830 and 1850, declining to 10 somewhere between 1880 and 1890. In Britain, maximum hours were set at 10 in 1847, while the standard had fallen to 9 by the 1870s, and to 8 in most industries (including steel) by the 1890s.[61]

The overall number of hours worked has declined in tandem with increasing prosperity. Plainly put, the richer the country, the fewer hours people work. Data for developing countries is difficult to come by, but the average number of hours worked per worker in some high-income countries is available. Rockefeller University scholar Jesse H. Ausubel and International Institute for Applied Systems Analysis in Austria researcher Arnulf Grubler estimate, for example, that "although the average career length [in the United Kingdom] has remained around 40 years, the total life hours worked shrank for an average British worker from 124,000 hours in 1856 to 69,000 in 1981. The fraction of disposable lifetime hours spent working declined from 50 percent to 20 percent."[62] In a similar vein, economist Jaap De Koning at Erasmus University in Rotterdam found that in the Netherlands, "men born in 1840 worked on average 118 thousand hours, while it is only 67 thousand hours for the 1950 cohort. As a percent of total number of hours available to a man, the decline is from 23 percent for the 1840 birth cohort to 9 percent for the 1950 birth cohort."[63] Finally, here is Matt Ridley's take on the decline of working hours in America:

> In 1900, when the average lifespan in the United States was forty-seven, when people started work at fourteen, worked sixty-hour weeks and had no possibility of retirement, the percentage of his lifetime that an average man would spend at work was about 25 percent; the rest was spent sleeping, at home, or as a child. Today that figure is about 10 percent, because the average person lives to about eighty, spends about half his or her life in education and retirement, spends only a third of each day (8/24) and five-sevenths of each week at work. A half times a third times five-sevenths is just under 12 per cent. Take off a few weeks' vacation, a little sick leave and the usual holidays like Christmas and you are left with 10 percent. And that's counting the lunch hour as work.[64]

Between 1950 and 2017, Conference Board data suggests that the average number of hours worked per worker per year declined by 28 percent in the Netherlands, 11 percent in the United States, and 17 percent in the United Kingdom. The population-weighted decline in the number of working hours per worker per year declined by 18 percent in high-income countries.[65] Over the same 67-year span, GDP per person, adjusted for purchasing power parity, rose by 337 percent in the Netherlands, 290 percent in the United States, 248 percent in the United Kingdom, and 95 percent in high-income countries as a whole (the figures are in 2016 U.S. dollars).[66] So, people earn more money in exchange for less work.

Over time work has also become easier and safer. As late as the 18th century, an Austrian physician wrote that "in many villages [of the Austrian Empire] the dung has to be carried on human backs up high mountains and the soil has to be scraped in a crouching position; this is the reason why most of the young people [men and women] are deformed and misshapen."[67] Even after the dawn of the Age of Innovation, working conditions remained very poor. As the U.S. president Benjamin Harrison put it in 1892, "American workmen are subjected to peril of life and limb as great as a soldier in time of war."[68]

Steven Pinker estimates that 61 workers per 100,000 employees died in work-related accidents as late as 1913. By 2015 that number had fallen to 3.2, a 95 percent reduction over a little more than a century. A similarly encouraging trend can be observed globally. According to the Workplace Safety and Health Institute in Singapore, 16.4 workers per 100,000 employees died worldwide in 1998. By 2014 that number fell to 11.3, a 31 percent reduction over just 16 years. Considered in a slightly different way, workplace fatalities around the world seem to be falling by almost 2 percentage points every year.[69]

■ Box 8.3. Air travel safety soars (1968–2017)

Professor Arnold I. Barnett from the Massachusetts Institute of Technology analyzed global air travel fatality rates going back to 1968, using data from the Flight Safety Foundation's Aviation Safety Network Accident Database, the World Bank, and other credible sources. He grouped the data by decade to reduce annual spikes in fatalities. Barnett found that between 1968 and 1977, there was 1 death per 350,000 boardings. Between 2008 and 2017, the rate fell to 1 death per 7.9 million boardings (see Figure B8.3.1).[e] Put differently, airline fatality risk fell by 95.6 percent between 1968 and 2017.

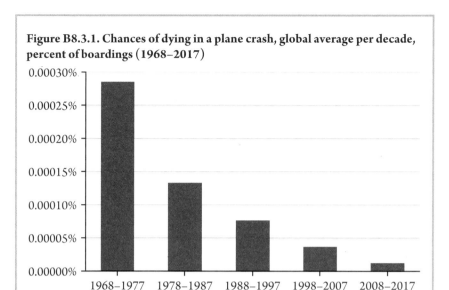

Figure B8.3.1. Chances of dying in a plane crash, global average per decade, percent of boardings (1968–2017)

Source: Authors' calculations.

In developed countries, a passenger's chance of dying in a plane crash between 2008 and 2017 was 1 in 28.8 million. In developing countries, the risk was closer to 1 in 1.3 million, about 30 years behind the global average. Global air safety has been increasing at a compound annual growth rate of about 8.1 percent. At that rate, safety doubles every 8.6 years or so. All the while, the number of air passengers increased by 1,320 percent between 1970 and 2019, from 310 million to 4.4 billion.[f] That implies a compound annual rate of about 5.3 percent. So, flight safety is increasing about 50 percent faster than air traffic. ∎

Education

In 1870, the total length of schooling for people between the ages of 25 and 64 was only about 0.5 years

Informal learning is as old as humanity. Before the advent of writing, however, all of the information that people needed to act in the world was passed down through the generations orally. It was only 5,500 years ago that the first forms of writing emerged. There is much debate about access to education, the length of schooling, and literacy rates in ancient times. A story from the biblical book of Judges, which was probably written in the sixth century BCE, suggests that any random person in ancient Israel could write:

> Gideon son of Joash then returned from the battle by the Pass of Heres. He caught a young man of Sukkoth and questioned him, and the young man wrote down for him the names of the seventy-seven officials of Sukkoth, the elders of the town.[70]

That interpretation of the Hebrew Bible is, alas, contested.[71] More likely, Israelite literacy rates were similar to those in the rest of the ancient world. In his 1989 book, *Ancient Literacy*, Columbia University classicist William V. Harris estimated that no more than 10 percent of the Athenian population was literate in the 5th and 4th centuries BCE. The literate contingent in Athenian society consisted of well-to-do males but excluded poorer men and almost all women and slaves.[72] Parts of ancient societies may have had exceptionally high literacy rates for particular reasons. Literacy in the Roman army, for example, appears to have been quite high. Hence, Polybius could write the following passage in his description of the Roman army's night watch duties:

> The four men chosen by the *optiones* [executive officers or seconds in command of a tactical unit of a Roman legion known as *centuria* or century] from the first squadron, after drawing lots for their respective watches, go to the tribune and get written orders from him stating what stations they are to visit and at what time.[73]

In fact, many Roman soldiers had literary interests. Martial, who was one of the leading Roman poets of the first century CE, boasted that "my book is read to pieces by tough centurions [officers who had begun their careers as common soldiers] serving in the frosty Balkans."[74] That said, Harris concluded that the "classical world, even at its most advanced, was so lacking in the characteristics which produce extensive literacy that we must suppose the majority of the people were always illiterate."[75]

After the fall of Rome, Europe entered what some scholars refer to as the Dark Ages. Schooling, education, and literacy declined, even among the wealthy and powerful. As such, a thousand years after Martial's death, many European potentates could not sign their own names. Illiterate monarchs included the English kings William the Conqueror (1028–1087) and his successor William Rufus (1056–1100); Holy Roman Emperor Conrad II (989–1039) and Frankish king Pepin the Short (714–768). Pepin's son and successor, Charlemagne (748–814), spoke Latin but never learned to write.[76]

Finally, Harris suggests reasons for the relative scarcity of education in the premodern era. First and foremost, high literacy rates require the existence of an extensive school system, which no ancient society possessed. Second, schools that existed catered to the urban elite, but most people were agriculturalists and "rural patterns of living are inimical to the spread of literacy."[77] Third, widespread literacy requires "economic complexity," which was "only attained when the Industrial Revolution took hold," and "semiliterate masses were thought to be indispensable to the state's economic well-being."[78]

By 1820, 85 percent of Danish children had enrolled in a primary school. Other countries with high primary school enrollment rates were Sweden (81 percent), the Netherlands (65 percent), Switzerland (64 percent), Canada (57 percent), New Zealand (56 percent), Bohemia (51 percent), Norway (49 percent), the United States (41 percent), Belgium (36 percent), Australia (35 percent), Austria (35 percent), Germany (21 percent), Bulgaria (19 percent), Poland (18 percent), France (17 percent), Italy (15 percent), the United Kingdom (13 percent), Hungary (13 percent), Iceland (12 percent), and Spain (11 percent). The rest of the world was in the single digits, with most of today's developing countries, such as Bangladesh and Ghana, hovering around zero.[79]

By 1900, 100 percent of age-appropriate children attended school in France, the United States, Denmark, Australia, and Sweden. The United Kingdom caught up with the rest of the advanced countries (98 percent), followed by Norway, Canada, and New Zealand (96 percent), Switzerland (89 percent), Japan (86 percent), Netherlands (84 percent), and Bohemia (82 percent).

Remarkably, Jamaica reached an 80 percent primary school enrollment rate, Barbados reached 72 percent, Trinidad and Tobago 69 percent, and Guyana 62 percent. In no country surveyed was the primary school enrollment rate lower in 1900 than it was in 1820.[80]

Today in all the advanced countries, 100 percent of the age-appropriate children attend primary school. The smallest share of the age-appropriate children attending primary school is in Sudan (60 percent). Other countries at the bottom of the primary school enrollment rate ladder include Niger (62 percent); Ivory Coast (65 percent); Mali (78 percent); Senegal (79 percent); Afghanistan, The Gambia, and Guyana (83 percent); Yemen (86 percent); Lesotho (88 percent); and the Democratic Republic of Congo (89 percent).[81]

As school attendance has increased, the length of schooling has increased along with it. As late as 1870, the global average length of schooling for people between the ages of 25 and 64 is estimated to have been only about 0.5 years. Of that number, primary education accounted for 0.47 years and secondary education for 0.03 years. In a handful of outliers such as Switzerland and the United States, the length of schooling was as high as four years. In France and the United Kingdom, it averaged less than one year. In the world's underdeveloped regions such as sub-Saharan Africa and much of Asia, schooling was negligible and would remain so for decades to come.[82]

By 2010, Korea University economist Jong-Wha Lee and Harvard University economist Robert Barro estimate that the global average length of schooling at all levels of education stood at 8.56 years. That year, primary, secondary, and tertiary schooling amounted to 4.85 years, 3.23 years, and 0.48 years, respectively. It is estimated that by 2040, the four measures of schooling will have increased to 10.52 years in total: 5.03, 4.69, and 0.8 years of primary, secondary, and tertiary education, respectively.[83]

Finally, consider the education gap between the sexes. In ancient Greece, wealthy boys were educated, but wealthy girls were not. In ancient Rome, by contrast, children of both sexes received education, but still, as a general rule, boys' education was almost always prioritized over that of education for girls. That age-old educational gap between boys and girls has closed in the developed world and is in the process of being closed in the developing world. In 1870, girls were schooled an average of 25 percent fewer years than boys in advanced economies. By 2010, girls were schooled for just as long as boys. The improvement is even greater in sub-Saharan Africa. In the world's least developed region, girls enjoyed less than 10 percent of the schooling enjoyed by boys in 1870. In 2010, girls were schooled for 80 percent as long as boys.[84]

■ Box 8.4. Calculating calculation cost (1969–2020)

When U.S. astronaut Buzz Aldrin went to the Moon aboard the *Apollo 11* spacecraft in July 1969, he carried his trusty Pickett N600-ES slide rule. Back then, the calculating device could be purchased for $10.95. In 1969, U.S. blue-collar workers earned about $3.72 per hour and unskilled workers earned $1.72 per hour. It took blue-collar workers 2.94 hours and unskilled workers 6.37 hours to earn enough money to buy a tool that could do about one calculation per second.

In 2020, Apple Corporation introduced the iPhone 12, with a starting price of $699. The iPhone 12's A14 chip can perform 11 trillion operations per second. In 2020, the U.S. blue-collar worker's compensation rate was $33.98 per hour, and the U.S. unskilled worker's hourly wage rate was $14.34 per hour. The new iPhone cost the blue-collar worker 20.57 hours of labor and the unskilled worker 48.74 hours of labor.

So for the same amount of work it took to earn enough money to buy one calculation in 1969, blue-collar workers could buy 1.574 trillion calculations in 2020, and unskilled workers could buy 1.437 trillion calculations (see Table B8.4.1).

That indicates a compound annual growth rate of 51.20 percent for unskilled workers and 51.47 percent for blue-collar workers between 1969 and 2020. Moore's Law suggests a doubling of computing power every two years. The slide rule to iPhone rate indicates a doubling calculation rate of every 20 months.

Table B8.4.1. Time prices of a calculation: comparison of U.S. unskilled workers and U.S. blue-collar workers (1969–2020)

	1969 pickett N600-ES	2020 iPhone 12	Personal resource abundance multiplier
Price	$10.95	$699.00	
Blue-collar hourly wage	$3.72	$33.98	
Blue-collar time price in hours	2.94	20.57	
Operations per second	1	11,000,000,000,000	
Blue-collar time price per calculation	2.94	0.0000000000019	1,574,019,336,379
Unskilled hourly wage	$1.72	$14.34	
Unskilled time price in hours	6.37	48.74	
Unskilled time price per calculation	6.37	0.0000000000044	1,436,647,869,049

Source: Authors' calculations. ■

Liberal democracy

For most of humanity's recorded history, people have lived under some form of autocracy

Modern democracy (the word comes from the Greek words δῆμος [demos, "people"] and κράτος [kratos, "rule"]) is a relatively new phenomenon. For most of recorded human history, people have lived under some form of autocracy. Power was concentrated in the hands of one person such as an absolute monarch or a small group of people such as oligarchs. Even ancient "democracies" such as Athens and Thebes denied the vote to women and slaves.

Crucially, as the Swiss-French writer Henri-Benjamin Constant de Rebecque (1767–1830) pointed out in his 1819 essay, "The Liberty of Ancients Compared with That of Moderns," the ancient Greeks thought that direct democracy was compatible with the complete subjection of the individual citizen to the will of the majority of the assembly. "As a citizen," Constant wrote, "he [i.e., the voter] decides on peace and war; as particular, he is circumscribed, observed, repressed in all his movements."[85]

The moderns, by which Constant meant his 19th-century contemporaries, did not think that the will of the majority as expressed through the elected officials should impede on the private sphere. "The aim of the moderns is to be secure in their private benefits; and 'liberty' is their name for the guarantees accorded by institutions to these benefits."[86] So, liberal democracy, which can be defined as "a system of government in which people consent to their rulers, and rulers, in turn, are constitutionally constrained to respect individual rights" arose in parts of Western Europe and North America in the 18th century.[87] It is essential to keep in mind that the process of democratization was gradual and sometimes nonlinear. Let's look at some data.

The V-Dem Institute is an independent research institute based at the Department of Political Science, University of Gothenburg, Sweden. One of the V-Dem Institute's projects is to measure the extent of liberal democracy around the world going back to the end of the 18th century. Liberal democracy "emphasizes the importance of protecting individual and minority rights against the tyranny of the state and the tyranny of the majority. The liberal model takes a 'negative' view of political power in so far as it judges the quality of democracy by the limits placed on government. This is achieved by constitutionally protected civil liberties, strong rule of law, an independent judiciary, and effective checks and balances that together limit the exercise of executive power."[88]

In 1789, only four countries scored 0.2 or higher on a 0 to 1 scale of liberal democracy. They were the United States (0.26), the United Kingdom (0.23), France (0.21), and Sweden (0.2). By 1900, 23 countries had achieved this level of democracy: New Zealand (0.68), Australia (0.54), Switzerland (0.52), France (0.47), Belgium (0.45), the United Kingdom (0.43), the Netherlands and Norway (0.42), Canada (0.4), the United States (0.38), Denmark (0.37), Iceland (0.33), Sweden (0.32), Uruguay (0.29), Greece (0.27), Chile and Italy (0.24), Austria, Germany and Hungary (0.22), Sri Lanka (0.21), and Argentina and Ecuador (0.2). The 19th century, in other words, saw a historically unprecedented expansion of liberal democracy, a process that accelerated in the post–World War II era. In 1950, the average global score of liberal democracy amounted to 0.2

(the position that Sweden had attained in 1789). By 2019, that figure rose to 0.41. Attesting to the nonlinear nature of the expansion of liberal democracy, the average global score reached its peak in 2012 (0.43). Since then, liberal democracy has retreated slightly. That said, 127 of the 176 countries surveyed in 2019 had a liberal democracy score of at least 0.2, with 38 countries scoring 0.7 and higher.

Environmental quality

Tablecloths were laid just before eating because dust
settled from the fire and they became dingy in hours

One factor driving the massive increase in wealth worldwide is an energy transformation that began in the 19th century. Back in 1800, 98.28 percent of humanity's energy came from the burning of biofuels such as wood and peat and from the muscles of humans and their animals. All are horribly inefficient at generating energy. In 2017, humans used traditional biofuels for only 7.09 percent of the world's energy needs. Over 87 percent of our energy supply came from fossil fuels. While the use of fossil fuels is not without negative side effects, it is superior to burning down Earth's forests to power our economy and keep us warm.[89]

Today, many people are wedded to the romantic view of the premodern era, where people are supposed to have lived in harmony with the bucolic natural environment. In fact, our ancestors had to endure horrific environmental conditions. Let's start with air quality. In 17th century London, English writer and journalist Claire Tomalin observed in her 2002 book, *Samuel Pepys: The Unequalled Self*, "Every household burnt coal. . . . The smoke from their chimneys made the air dark, covering every surface with sooty grime. There were days when a cloud of smoke half a mile high and twenty miles wide could be seen over the city. . . . Londoners spat black."[90]

In a similar vein, Carlo M. Cipolla quoted from the diary of British writer John Evelyn (1620–1706), who wrote in 1661 that "in London, we see people walk and converse pursued and haunted by that infernal smoke. The inhabitants breathe nothing but an impure and thick mist, accompanied by a fuliginous and filthy vapour . . . corrupting the lungs and disordering the entire habit of their bodies."[91]

In the 19th century, indoor air pollution remained a visible problem. In her 2005 book, *Inside the Victorian Home: A Portrait of Domestic Life in Victorian England*, the Canadian historian Judith Flanders noted Ralph Waldo Emerson's observation that "no one . . . [in England] wore white because it was impossible to keep it clean."[92] According to Flanders, hairbrushes looked "black after once using," and tablecloths were laid just before eating, "as otherwise dust settled from the fire and they became dingy in a matter of hours."[93]

The streets were also dirty. John Harrington (1561–1612) invented the toilet in 1596, but bathrooms still remained rare luxuries 200 years later. Chamber pots continued to be emptied into the streets, turning the latter into sewers. To make matters worse, even inhabitants of large towns continued to engage in animal husbandry well into the 18th century. As Braudel noted, "Pigs were reared in freedom in the streets. And the streets were so dirty and muddy that they had to be crossed on stilts, unless wooden bridges were thrown across from one side to the other. . . . As late as 1746, in Venice, it was apparently necessary to forbid the keeping of pigs 'in the city and in the monasteries.'"[94] Much of that filth eventually ended up in rivers, upon which most cities were built.

In 1858, the stench from the River Thames was so bad that "the curtains on the river side of the building were soaked in lime chloride to overcome the smell."[95] The effort was unsuccessful, and this once moved Prime Minister Benjamin Disraeli to flee a committee room "with a mass of papers in one hand, and with his pocket handkerchief applied to his nose," because the stench was so bad. He called the river "a Stygian pool, reeking with ineffable and intolerable horrors."[96]

Keep in mind that even after the Industrial Revolution had begun, much of the pollution was still nonindustrial. English social researcher and journalist Henry Mayhew found that the Thames contained "ingredients from breweries, gasworks, and chemical and mineral manufactories; dead dogs, cats, and kittens, fats, offal from slaughterhouses; street-pavement dirt of every variety; vegetable refuse; stable-dung; the refuse of pig-styes; night-soil; ashes; tin kettles and pans . . . broken stoneware, jars, pitchers, flower-pots, etc.; pieces of wood; rotten mortar and rubbish of different kinds."[97]

Fast-forward to 2015, when the BBC reported that "more than 2,000 seals have been spotted in the Thames over the past decade . . . along with hundreds of porpoises and dolphins and even the odd stray whale. . . . There are now 125 species of fish in the Thames, up from almost none in the 1950s."[98] Similarly, average concentrations of suspended particulate matter in London's air rose from 390 micrograms per cubic meter in 1800 to a peak of 623 in 1891, before falling to 16 in 2016.[99] Today, the air in the capital of the United Kingdom ranks as one of the cleanest among the world's major cities, and environmental quality has much improved in other rich countries as well.

There can be no doubt that industrialization did great damage to the environment during the second half of the 19th century. On the other hand, it also created wealth that allowed advanced societies to build better sanitation facilities and spurred the creation of an enlightened populace with a historically unprecedented concern over the environment and a willingness to pay for its stewardship through somewhat higher taxation. As Don Boudreaux wrote,

> To live harmoniously with nature is to understand and accept natural forces. The greater this understanding and acceptance, the greater the harmony. Because we know so much more today than we did before about physics, chemistry, meteorology, biology, physiology, metallurgy, and on and on with our ologies and urgies, we live so much more harmoniously with nature. . . . It is we today, with our knowledge of how to irrigate fields using science and engineering, and how to make and administer antibiotics, who live harmoniously with nature. . . . Only people who understand these [natural] forces and how to counteract or reinforce or sustain or alter them with other natural forces can be truly said to live harmoniously with nature. It is science—rational thought, skepticism, critical inquiry—that furthers greater harmony with nature.[100]

Morality

Once-common practices such as slavery and human
sacrifice are now extremely rare or nonexistent

Not only are we richer; we are also more moral. The ever-widening circle of empathy, as the Australian philosopher Peter Singer identified in his 2011 book, *The Expanding Circle: Ethics, Evolution, and Moral Progress*, started with our family, then the foraging group that roamed the ancient savannah, then the city, and later the nation-state. The process got a massive shot in the arm during the Enlightenment, which insisted that humanistic values were universal, which is to say applicable to everyone. As Thomas Jefferson (1743–1826), a major Enlightenment figure, put it in the American Declaration of Independence, "We hold these Truths to be self-evident, that all Men are created equal, that they are endowed by their Creator with certain unalienable Rights, that among these are Life, Liberty, and the Pursuit of Happiness."[101]

This does not mean that our political and economic institutions became inclusive overnight. The process, as we already noted, was gradual. Take slavery, for example. The practice can be traced to Sumer, a Mesopotamian civilization that flourished between 4,500 and 1,900 BCE. The early laws of the Babylonians, who overran Sumer in the 18th century BCE, appear to have taken ownership of one person by another for granted. The Code of Hammurabi states, "If a slave says to his master, 'You are not my master,' if they convict him his master shall cut off his ear."[102] Over the succeeding 4,000 years, chattel slavery would be practiced, at one point or another, by every major civilization.

Prior to the Age of Innovation, humanity depended on energy produced primarily by people and animals. An extra pair of field hands was always welcome, and conquered people, if they escaped execution, were frequently put to work as slaves. Slavery existed in ancient Egypt, India, Greece, China, Rome, and pre-Columbian America. The Arab slave trade took off during the Muslim conquests of the Middle Ages. The word "slave" may originally have been a linguistically corrupted reference to the Slavic peoples of Central and Eastern Europe who were enslaved by the Holy Roman Emperor Otto the Great (912–973).[103] Millions of Africans were brought to the New World to be used as slaves in the Caribbean and the southeastern United States, though by far the largest number of African slaves ended up in Brazil. Slavery was also common among African peoples, especially in West Africa, and it persisted until very recently. In fact, Mauritania became the last country to outlaw slavery in 1981.

Slavery gradually disappeared from Europe during the course of the second millennium, though various forms of lesser bondage such as feudal dues and serfdom remained throughout much of the continent until the mid-1800s. The abolitionist movement, which aimed to eliminate chattel slavery in Europe's imperial possessions, began in the late 18th century. It was led, in large part, by Quakers, who were heavily influenced by the ideals of the Enlightenment. Gustav Jönsson noted in a widely praised 2018 article in *Areo Magazine* that

> when Samuel Johnson published his *Dictionary of the English Language* in 1755, there was no entry for abolition. Abolitionism was a novelty that the Enlightenment introduced, not an inheritance from earlier centuries. The examples of Anthony Benezet and the Quakers illustrate this. Benezet was a man of singular vigor and moral clarity. . . . Benezet wrote several screeds against slavery, culminating in the 1771 publication of *Some Historical Account of Guinea, Its Situation, Produce, and the General Disposition of Its Inhabitants: An Inquiry into the Rise and Progress of the Slave Trade, Its Nature, and Lamentable Effects.* [The British philosopher] A. C. Grayling writes that this tract "lit the touchpaper that was Enlightenment sensibility."[104]

In fact, revolutionary France abolished slavery throughout the French Empire in 1794. That decision was reversed by the French Emperor Napoleon Bonaparte in 1802. France again abolished slavery in her overseas possessions in 1848. Meanwhile, the British Parliament made it illegal for British traders to import slaves into territories belonging to foreign powers, a measure intended to punish Napoleonic France. A year later, the Slave Trade Act banned the slave trade as a whole, though many slaves continued to be held in bondage. In 1833, the Slavery Abolition Act banned slavery throughout Britain's colonies.

Today it is *de rigueur* to criticize the Europeans and the Americans for partaking in the slave trade in the first place and for taking too long to abolish the practice. It is worth repeating, then, that slavery was one of the oldest human institutions, present on all continents and among all races. While some people, such as the Stoics, condemned slavery, a broader movement against the practice had to wait until society became rich enough not to need slave labor and humane (or enlightened) enough to see all humans as equal in dignity. That society was the rapidly modernizing Western European and North American society of the early to mid-19th century.

Some people, like the British philosopher John Gray, deny the possibility of moral progress. As he wrote, "I define progress . . . as any kind of advance that's cumulative, so that what's achieved at one period is the basis for later achievement that then, over time, becomes more and more irreversible. In science and technology, progress isn't a myth. However, the myth is that the progress achieved in science and technology can occur in ethics, politics, or more simply, civilisation."[105]

Gray's pessimism, though, is difficult to reconcile with the near disappearance of once common practices such as cannibalism, executions for witchcraft or heresy, dueling, bear baiting, cockfighting (and other animal combat sports), legally sanctioned wife-beating, and the exposure of unwanted infants. Human sacrifice has been looked down on since the Roman times. Today, no rational being believes that sacrificing virgins can bring about better harvests. Better fertilization and pest control are much safer bets for farmers.

A civilizational collapse could resurrect some abhorrent practices, but some of the knowledge and internalized ethical precepts that humanity has so painstakingly accumulated will surely remain, thus moderating peoples' behavior even in the darkest of times. In the meantime, we have to reconcile ourselves to the fact that progress is "self-cloaking." The better things get, the more we will be on the lookout for things to worry about.

Violence

Conflict was the default position in international relations
as late as the early 19th century, but today it is peace

The Enlightenment, which underpinned the modern era, had a profound impact on the decline of violence over the past 250 years or so. In his 1795 essay *Perpetual Peace*, for example, Immanuel Kant discouraged national leaders from instigating war, advocated greater transparency in decision-making, criticized wars of conquest, and favored the free flow of goods and people. Kant and other philosophers of that era argued that conflict can and should be resolved through the application of reasoned arguments and negotiated settlements. The call for a peaceful conflict resolution went hand in hand with another Enlightenment ideal: humanism. This view, which we discussed in the previous section, holds that humans can feel sympathy not only for the people in their immediate surroundings, such as their families, but for humanity as a whole. The combined emphasis on reason and humanism led Enlightenment thinkers to condemn slavery, religious conflict, monarchical despotism, and the various forms of sadistic corporal punishments still common at the time.

Another goal of the Enlightenment was the widespread adoption of representative forms of government. As we saw in Chapter 7, governments that are more inclusive answer to a wider array of interests. Despotic governments, by contrast, answer to one person or to a small ruling elite. Inclusive governments tend to be more circumspect before engaging in conflict because the cost of war falls on a much wider group of citizens, including those who make the decision to go to war. Conversely, despotic governments are more effective at insulating themselves from the cost of war. Under despotic regimes, the cost of war tends to be borne by the voiceless and the powerless.

Moreover, democratic countries, to give inclusive governments of today their proper name, do not go to war against one another. They instead engage in trade, creating a mutual economic interdependence that further lowers the chance of military conflict breaking out. In a 2006 paper, "Trade, Peace and Democracy: An Analysis of Dyadic Dispute," Solomon W. Polachek from the State University of New York at Binghamton and Carlos Seiglie from Rutgers University estimate that "a doubling of trade leads to a 20 percent diminution of belligerence."[106] Trade also increases the wealth of ordinary citizens who live under inclusive political systems. They have more to lose and are thus less likely to support policies that may undermine their standards of living.

Perhaps most remarkably, the spread of Enlightenment ideas, such as those expressed by Kant, have helped change how we think about war itself. In his posthumously published 1832 book, *On War*, the Prussian General Carl von Clausewitz (1780–1831) famously noted that "war is a mere continuation of policy by other means."[107] Conflict, in other words, was the default position in international relations as late as the early 19th century. Today, it is peace. As Steven Pinker wrote, "The world's nations have committed themselves to not waging war except in self-defense or with the approval of the United Nations Security Council. . . . Any country that indulges in a war of conquest can expect opprobrium, not acquiescence, from the rest."[108] Even countries that do engage in nefarious activities abroad such as Russia in Ukraine and Iran in Syria tend to eschew outright declarations of war and seek to justify their actions as acts of "self-defense."

Before proceeding, let's recognize the obvious. We live in a world that is still disfigured by violence. As we discussed in Chapter 1, though, progress is not about comparing the world we live in with utopia. It is about comparing today with the past, and the past was much more violent than the present. As late as the mid-17th century, for example, major powers were almost constantly at war. Contrast that state of human affairs with today. There has not been a war between two or more major powers since the United States and China fought over the Korean peninsula in the early 1950s. International conflicts (i.e., conflicts between different nation-states) are relatively uncommon, the Russian invasion of Ukraine notwithstanding. The world has plenty of civil wars to worry about, but those too have been in decline, at least since the end of the Cold War in 1991.[109] Fewer wars have meant fewer deaths. The rate of battle deaths per 100,000 people reached a post–World War II peak of 23 in 1953. By 2016, it had fallen by about 95 percent.[110]

A similar trend can be observed with regard to genocides. According to Frank Chalk and Kurt Jonassohn of Concordia University, mass killings of unarmed civilians have "been practiced in all regions of the world and during all periods in history."[111] In the first half of the 20th century, well-known acts of mass murder included the Turkish genocide against the Armenians and the German extermination of 6 million Jews. Partly as a result of the Holocaust, the global death rate among civilians reached 350 per 100,000 during World War II. Since that time, genocides have claimed fewer lives. The mass murder of unarmed civilians in the second half of the 20th century peaked during the Bangladesh War of Independence in 1971 when the global death rate temporarily rose to 49 people per 100,000. Since the start of the third millennium, it has been very low. It peaked at 2 per 100,000 in 2004 and has stood at statistical zero since 2005.[112] That does not mean that mass murder has disappeared, though. According to the Uppsala Conflict Data Program, "intentional attacks on civilians by governments and formally organized armed groups" accounted for 7,088 lost lives in 2017.[113]

The level of interpersonal violence has also decreased. According to Cambridge University criminologist Manuel Eisner, the annual homicide rate in 14th-century Florence amounted to 150 murders per 100,000 people. In 15th-century England, it hovered around 24 per 100,000. In the Netherlands, it ranged between 30 and 60 per 100,000. In 16th-century Rome, it ranged from 30 to 80 per 100,000. Between the mid-15th and the mid-17th centuries, Sweden experienced homicide rates of up to 60 per 100,000. In the Middle Ages, most people resolved their disputes through physical violence. For better and for worse, central governments gradually gained a monopoly on violence and clamped down on interpersonal violence. In the 19th century, criminal justice systems finally became professionalized and municipal police forces began to appear. In 2003, the intentional homicide rate in the abovementioned countries stood at around 1 per 100,000.[114] Some countries, like Honduras and South Africa, continue to experience medieval homicide rates, but those countries are exceptional. "As the rule of law, fairer judicial systems, and better policing have spread to more countries around the world," wrote Ronald Bailey, "the global homicide rate according to the Institute of Health Metrics and Evaluation has dropped from 6.4 per 100,000 in 1990 to 5.3 per 100,000 in 2017."[115]

CHAPTER 9

Where do innovations come from? The crucial roles played by population growth and freedom

The main ingredient in the secret sauce that leads to innovation is freedom. Freedom to exchange, experiment, imagine, invest, and fail; freedom from expropriation or restriction by chiefs, priests, and thieves; freedom on the part of consumers to reward the innovations they like and reject the ones they do not.

Matt Ridley, *How Innovation Works:*
And Why It Flourishes in Freedom[1]

Chapter summary

Committees don't have ideas. Algorithms don't have ideas. Machines don't have ideas—at least not yet. So far, ideas have always been a product of human intelligence. Those ideas lead to inventions, and in turn, inventions tested by the market lead to innovations that drive economic growth and rises in the standards of living. That is why all human beings deserve dignity, respect, and liberty: to think up, experiment with, and market their ideas.

Culture provides the incentives that either encourage or discourage individuals to manifest their ideas in reality. Individuals, who lack equal legal rights, and face onerous regulatory burdens, confiscatory taxation, or insecure property rights, will be disincentivized from turning their ideas into inventions and innovations. Conversely, people who function under conditions of legal equality, sensible regulation, moderate taxation, and secure property rights will apply their talents to their benefit and, ultimately, to that of society.

Although we live in a world of a limited number of atoms, there are virtually infinite ways to arrange those atoms. The possibilities for creating new value are thus immense. For value to be created, however, humans need a relatively free market. Knowledge is dispersed in the minds of millions of individuals. That knowledge reveals itself in prices. The price system is a learning system because it creates public information that allows people to exchange things they value for things they value even more. In this chapter, we will build and explain our own human innovation model (see Figure 9.1).

Our human innovation framework . . .

Human innovation is the chief means by which people create wealth and escape poverty. As Matt Ridley noted in his 2020 book, *How Innovation Works: And Why It Flourishes in Freedom,*

> Innovation is the most important fact about the modern world, but
> one of the least well understood. It is the reason most people today
> live lives of prosperity and wisdom compared with their ances-
> tors, the overwhelming cause of the great enrichment of the past

few centuries, the simple explanation of why the incidence of extreme poverty is in global freefall for the first time in history: from 50 percent of the world population to 9 percent in my lifetime.[2]

One might imagine that wealth consists of money or other liquid assets, but as economists see it, wealth is anything that we value. Likewise, capital is anything that we can use to create value.[3] We discover and create value by continuously using our various forms of capital—human, physical, intellectual, and financial—innovatively. Human innovation organizes and reorganizes existing forms of capital to make them more productive and, hence, more valuable. It also creates new capital. Wealth creation, then, is really capital innovation.

The process of innovation and wealth creation both generates and depends on the use of lots of dynamic, temporary, local, and personal information. Most information belongs to the last category, which makes it most valuable to a well-functioning economy. People respond to the incentives that information creates in the form of costs, prices, and values, and that brings us to the most fundamental component of the enriching process: cultural capital. Cultural capital includes the freedom to imagine, create, act, cooperate, and discover. Freedom allows for the creation and dissemination of correct information, which incentivizes human beings to drive the process of enrichment ever forward.

Human innovation is a complex process. Modeling simplifies complexity. This chapter is our effort to articulate a model of human innovation. We recognize that many thinkers have made contributions to the effort to understand the process of innovation, and our model incorporates much of their thinking. Adam Smith, for example, argued that economic growth was driven by the division of labor, specialization, trade, and savings. The American economist Douglass North (1920–2015), along with Robinson and Acemoglu, argued that inclusive social and economic institutions were at the root of the Great Enrichment. Joel Mokyr and Deirdre McCloskey focus on culture and ideas. American writer William Rosen (1955–2016) thought that the key to economic growth was the patent system, while Julian Simon argued that innovation was driven by the size and density of the population and by freedom. Paul Romer, in the meantime, said it was

Figure 9.1. The Human Innovation Framework

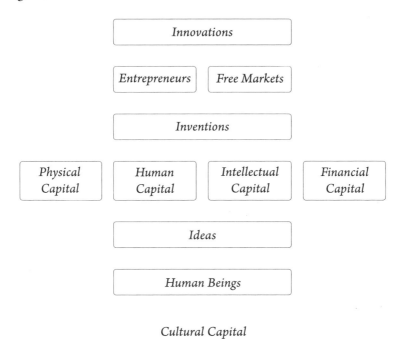

| Innovations |

| Entrepreneurs | Free Markets |

| Inventions |

| Physical Capital | Human Capital | Intellectual Capital | Financial Capital |

| Ideas |

| Human Beings |

Cultural Capital

Source: Authors.

the nonrivalrous nature of ideas.[4] We shall return to these thinkers later in this chapter.

. . . starts with a tolerant, cooperative, and trusting cultural capital . . .

Our innovation framework begins with cultural capital. Everyone lives in some place on the planet, and different places have different cultures. Cultural capital is the foundation of our model. Cultural capital works to create and connect or "synergize" all the other types of capital with one another. As we shall see, cultural capital includes many things. Fundamentally, however, cultural capital is concerned with people's treatment of one another. Vernon Smith, the Nobel Prize–winning economist from Chapman University in California, noted that "the human capacity for fellow feeling, in particular for mutual fellow feeling, is the primary mechanism through which we are socialized creatures."[5] He, with coauthor Bart Wilson, calls this feeling "humanomics" and credits Adam Smith's 1759 book *The Theory of Moral Sentiments* for that insight. The very first sentence in *The Theory of Moral Sentiments*, in fact, reads, "How selfish soever man may be supposed, there are evidently some principles in his nature, which interest him in the fortune of others, and render their happiness necessary to him, though they derive nothing from it, except the pleasure of seeing it."[6] We have discussed the development of human sociality at length in Chapter 7.

The feeling of sociality, which is either underdeveloped or altogether lacking among nonhuman animals, changed over time and is manifested in different ways today. Deirdre McCloskey's great contribution to the discussion of economic growth was to identify specific forms of sociality that have enabled humanity to flourish in recent centuries. She noted that the increased spread and appreciation of human dignity, respect, and liberty were the foundations of the Great Enrichment. In numerous works—including *The Bourgeois Virtues: Ethics for an Age of Commerce* (2006), *Bourgeois Dignity: Why Economics Can't Explain the Modern World* (2010), and *Bourgeois Equality: How Ideas, Not Capital or Institutions, Enriched the World* (2016)—she advanced the idea that people need to be free to "have a go." All humans, she argued, have the capacity to create value because they can make others happy. That freedom to "have a go" may seem obvious to those of us who live in politically and economically free societies today, but people in the past did not think in this way. Even today, there are parts of the world where people who belong to the "wrong" class, ethnicity, race, sex, or sexual orientation are not free to "have a go." That holds us all back. How many Mozarts and Einsteins is humanity not benefiting from because hundreds of millions of people throughout the world are still not free to "have a go"?

To humanomics, we can also add other aspects of cultural capital, including the rule of law, property rights, and the enforcement of contracts. Stable money, nonpunitive and nonarbitrary taxation, and a reasonable and predictable regulatory environment also contribute to the cultural foundations of innovation because they build trust. A culture in which people trust one another will perform better than a culture in which people don't trust one another.

One of the chief reasons for the success of the Jews in medieval Europe and that of the Chinese diaspora in more recent times was the relatively high level of trust in those closely knit communities. Even today, as research by Harvard University political scientist Robert Putnam shows, homogeneous societies are more trustful than heterogeneous ones are.[7] That should not be altogether surprising, since over the millenia, we have evolved in small groups of people who have shared common interests, survival strategies, and (very often) familial connections. Thankfully, trust among more diverse people can be enhanced through the evolution of "trusted" institutions. Countries with a reputation for an impartial legal system and speedy, cost-efficient dispute resolution mechanisms, for example, tend to register a higher level of trust than societies that lack either. Consider the ease with which an ordinary person of any class, ethnicity, race, sex, and sexual orientation can open a bank account and obtain credit in the United States today. Using a credit card, diverse people can purchase anything they want online or in a shop from complete strangers. Similarly, consider the ease with which people can buy and sell property. Land surveying, titles recording, transaction services, and transparent public records make this process relatively smooth and comparatively effortless in advanced countries. Not so in the developing world.[8] In developing economies, financial interactions tend to be cash-based and often happen only among people who already know one another. Such limits on the range of transactions limit value creation, and less trusting societies tend to be less prosperous.

History shows that not all cultures are equally conducive to innovation and growth. Different cultures have developed different values, expectations, and norms, which then impact the scope and speed of progress. These cultural differences often depend on a differing worldview or cognitive orientation of an individual or society. The worldview of a person and a society will determine what they believe to be true, good, and beautiful. Worldviews influence the political structure, the political structure determines the legal system, and the legal system looms large in determining the economic system. Cultures that help people cooperate and trust one another and that place a high value on human freedom and dignity tend to thrive. Cultures that protect the status quo and discourage creative destruction with heavy regulation and social stigma tend to flounder.

Let's look at one specific example. Millions of words have been spoken and written about the cofounder of the Apple Corporation, Steve Jobs. He was born in San Francisco, California, in 1955 and was adopted at birth by Paul and Clara Jobs. His birth father was born and raised in Syria. Jobs grew up in Mountain View and Los Altos, neighborhoods densely populated with engineers and innovators who shared California's culture of freedom and entrepreneurship. By the time he died of cancer in 2011, Jobs had turned Apple into one of the most valuable companies on the planet. Apple was not a computer company or a cell-phone company. It was, above all, an innovation company.

Jobs was able to create trillions of dollars in value for humanity, because he enjoyed a culture that awarded risk, creativity, and discipline. What would the world look like today if Jobs had been born and raised in Syria instead of Silicon Valley? How many Steve Jobses live in Syria or similar places today? It is a great tragedy for human flourishing and prosperity that billions of people live in cultures that discourage or prevent innovation. Thousands, perhaps tens of thousands, of potentially world-changing entrepreneurs remain inactive because they are forced to live in places with little cultural capital. Put differently, culture is the soil and the entrepreneur is the seed.[9]

Keep in mind, however, that cultures can and do change. China during the Song Dynasty (960–1279) led the world in technological progress, generating such inventions as movable print, gunpowder, and the magnetic compass. When the Venetian merchant Marco Polo (1254–1324) visited the kingdom shortly after the Song dynasty was replaced by the Mongolian Yuan Dynasty in the late 13th century, he was amazed by China's riches and power. In particular, he noted the size and density of Chinese cities (he called Hangzhou "beyond dispute the finest and the noblest in the world"),[10] the heavy traffic of its waterways, the riches of its markets, the extent of the public works, and the efficiency of its postal service.[11] By the time of the Italian Jesuit Matteo Ricci's trip to China in the late 16th century, the country was already in the midst of technological stagnation, in which it would remain for the next 400 years.

Likewise, the Islamic Golden Age between the 8th and 13th centuries was characterized by great cultural, economic, and scientific flourishing. Conversely, Europe fell into the "Dark Ages" after the fall of Rome, and the Renaissance was, in part, propelled forward by hand-copied Arabic translations of ancient Greek and Roman texts that Europe had already lost and had to rediscover via the Muslim world. Once again, cultures changed. The German goldsmith Johannes Gutenberg (c. 1400–1468), to give one example, perfected the printing press in the mid-15th century, thereby accelerating the Renaissance, the Age of Discovery, the Scientific Revolution, and the Reformation. Conversely, a narrow-minded outlook in the Islamic world, which prioritized protection of the employment of scribes over the mass production of printed books, prevented the adoption of the printing press until 1727, when a Hungarian emigrant known by his adopted name of Ibrahim Mutafarraqa (1670–1745) was permitted to open a printing press in Constantinople, only to have it shut down again in 1742. Put differently, a culture of openness (freedom, inclusivity, and risk-taking) is, to a great extent, a choice made by actual human beings. The same is true of its opposite.

. . . that allows for an unprecedented number of people . . .

The importance of population growth, which forms another element in our framework, has been recognized by scholars past and present. Julian Simon famously noted that the human population had to reach a critical mass, urban density, and a certain degree of freedom before humanity could enter the Age of Innovation and escape absolute poverty.[12] He agreed with Adam Smith that larger populations create larger markets that can absorb the high fixed costs associated with many innovations. Larger populations, Smith observed, also allow for more specialization and production of niche products.[13] Let us look at the importance of population growth in greater detail.

In *The Rational Optimist*, Ridley explains the process of innovation in terms of sex. Imagine how slow evolution would be if animals were to reproduce asexually. There would be random mutations in each generation, but those mutations would be restricted to one lineage only. Sex brings the genes of two separate individuals (including their mutations) together, thereby drastically increasing the speed of evolution. Ideas obey the same principles. More people can generate more ideas. Even if only a small fraction of humans can generate a good idea, the number of good ideas will grow in proportion to population growth.

Furthermore, freedom multiplies the production of ideas, thereby accelerating the speed of human progress. People who are free to interact with one another are more likely to combine two or more ideas into a new idea. China and India, for example, were the world's most populous countries long before they liberalized their economies in 1978 and 1991, respectively. Both were dirt-poor, giving rise to the joke that the Chinese (and the Indians) were successful everywhere except for China (and India). Since liberalization, both countries' economies grew massively, with China becoming the second-largest economy and India the fifth-largest economy in the world in 2020 (at current U.S. dollar exchange rates).[14]

Between 1820 and 2015, the world population rose from 1.09 billion to 7.38 billion, an increase of 6.8 times.[15] Over the same period, the world economy grew from $1.2 trillion to $108 trillion, or 90 times (the figures are in 2011 U.S. dollars).[16] The population, then, grew at a compounded rate of slightly less than 1 percent per year, while GDP grew at a compounded rate of 2.33 percent per year. That may not seem like much of a difference, but the effect of compounding over 200 years ensured that the economy would grow 13 times faster than the population, thereby producing a 14-factor increase in the average global income we noted in Chapter 5.[17]

The division of labor, or specialization, helps in the production of new ideas as well. By assigning specific tasks to the individuals who are most skilled in those tasks, humans are able to radically increase the efficiency of the economy. When the best hunters hunt and the best toolmakers craft tools, society saves a lot of time and resources. Moreover, hunters can now devote all their energy to hunting, and craftsmen can concentrate on crafting. Both become more skilled in the performance of their tasks and better aware of the shortcomings in the production processes that can be addressed through further improvements. The chances of new inventions and innovations thus increase. Crucially, the benefits of the division of labor rise with population growth, since bigger groups of people can specialize more than small groups of people can.

Consider one example. Some 35,000 years ago, humans populated Australia, including its southeastern corner, which would eventually become Tasmania. These people lived a hunter-gatherer lifestyle but had developed some basic technologies like bone tools, cold-weather clothing, fishhooks, and traps. Around 10,000 years ago, melting ice filled the low-lying plains that separated Tasmania and Australia, creating an impassable strait and isolating the Tasmanians. At the time of the European arrival in the 17th century, there were only about 5,000 Tasmanians on the island. They were virtually naked and hadn't made a bone tool in thousands of years. By contrast, Australian aboriginals had not only retained their existing technology but also invented new things such as the returning boomerang.

So what went wrong in Tasmania? Ridley argues that the island's technological backslide occurred because Tasmania could not support enough people to maintain their level of technology, let alone to invent new technologies. Consider the process of human learning. In general, people learn new skills by copying experts in the field. The best fishermen teach the next generation to fish, and the best toolmakers teach the new generation to make tools. Larger, more specialized populations have plenty of experts, while small populations have very few. That simple fact means that small populations are significantly more vulnerable to technological regression.

What if, for example, the most knowledgeable expert refuses to teach anyone at all or is killed by a venomous snake before he gets the chance to take on a student? What if a storm wipes out all of the fishermen at once on a fishing trip? Through a pure accident, generations of accumulated knowledge are destroyed. The destruction of knowledge can also happen through ecological change. Imagine that fish suddenly become relatively scarce in Tasmania. Since fishing is now a waste of time, nobody bothers to learn how to fish. In one generation, all the old fishermen are dead, and their skill set is lost. In a small, isolated population, accidents and ecological change slowly eat away at technology.

Small populations are also less likely to innovate. During its 10,000 years of separation, Tasmania only produced two unique innovations of note. One was a rather pitiful boat made of reeds that would sink after just a few hours in the water. The other was a technique of deep-sea diving to collect lobsters and clams that was practiced by women, a somewhat disappointing result of 10 millennia of evolution, especially when contrasted with Tasmania's astounding technological losses over the same period. To repeat, bigger populations are capable of more specialization and require more specialized goods. As a consequence, a bigger population has more experts in every field.

More specialization, in turn, results in a greater probability of new ideas, inventions, and innovations.

The only sure way for smaller populations to thrive is to trade. On Tierra del Fuego, an island with about the same landmass and population as Tasmania, the people possessed traps, nets, hooks, harpoons, clothing, and canoes. That happened because, unlike the Tasmanians, the inhabitants of Tierra del Fuego traded with mainland South America. Despite their small population, the Fuegians were able to access the larger continental market, allowing them to prevent technological regression and benefit from the specialization developed on the South American mainland. If all their fishermen were eaten by sharks, they could ask their neighbors across the channel how to cast a line. If the last man who knew how to make a hook had a heart attack, they could relearn the skill from continental toolmakers or just trade pearls for some fishhooks every few months. University of Toulouse physicist Cesar Hidalgo and Harvard University economic development specialist Ricardo Hausmann put it like this:

> Because individuals are limited in what they know, the only way societies can expand their knowledge base is by facilitating the interaction of individuals with different knowledge sets in increasingly complex webs of organizations and markets.[18]

So, innovation relies on population growth and the freedom to exchange goods and ideas. The larger the population, the larger the market. The larger the market, the more specialized a population can become. The more specialized a population becomes, the more prosperous it grows. Furthermore, a higher degree of specialization makes innovation more likely and technological regression less likely.

. . . to turn their ideas into inventions and innovations

The next element in our framework is human ideas. Innovation requires inventions, and inventions begin with ideas. Though artificial intelligence may supplement or complement human ideas at some point in the future, only humans are capable of producing new ideas at present. The American economist Don Boudreaux noted, "The human mind is the ultimate resource because it, and only it, creates all of the other economically valuable inputs that we call 'resources.'"[19] That said, ideas leading to new inventions and innovations are a bit of a mystery. We don't know who will have them or when they will appear.

In fact, most people don't invent or innovate anything. In their 2018 paper "Did Humans Evolve to Innovate with a Social Rather Than Technical Orientation?," University of Queensland psychologists William von Hippel and Thomas Suddendorf noted a British study showing that only 6 percent of people reported modifying or innovating a product in the past three years. The share of innovators was even lower in other countries (e.g., 5.4 percent in Finland, 5.2 percent in the United States, and 3.7 percent in Japan).[20]

Those low numbers may seem strange, given that human achievement is largely measured by technological advancement. But, as we explained in Chapter 7, human evolution is defined by social, rather than technical, innovation. Figuring out how to throw a stone is a technical problem, but using stones to ward off predators requires a social solution (i.e., coordinated bombardment). *Homo erectus* invented tools that were superior to those produced by its ancestors, but the division of labor, which improved the manufacture of those tools and enabled our ancestors to hunt large animals, was entirely social. Finally, fire increased our capacity to extract calories from food, but without using the former for social gatherings, we would never have developed the rich and diverse cultures that made it possible to accumulate knowledge. Technology makes our lives easier, but the success of our species is contingent on our ability to cooperate and organize as a society.

Moreover, since the evolutionary fitness of individual humans is based primarily on their ability to cooperate, most people choose a social solution over a technical one when confronted with a problem. If you need to put sunscreen on your back, it's easier to ask your friend to rub it in for you than to MacGyver your own lotion-rubbing apparatus. The only reason not to ask for help would be that you didn't have any friends around or—and this is crucial—that you had a unique personality characteristic that made asking for help unappealing.

Less social individuals appear to be more likely to invent a technical solution rather than a social one, which makes intuitive sense. People who would prefer to solve a problem by themselves would be more likely to invent something. Besides intuition, lots of data suggest a negative correlation between sociality and technical innovation. "Engineers and physical scientists show higher levels of autistic traits (one of which is diminished social orientation) than people in the humanities and social sciences," von Hippel and Suddendorf noted. "Unsurprisingly, engineers and physical scientists are also more likely than people in the humanities and social sciences to hold patents and are also more likely to innovate products for their own use. As a notable example, Silicon Valley is a hotbed of technical innovation and also features an unusual concentration of people on the autism spectrum."[21]

This pattern, the two psychologists observe, extends also to sex differences. Why? On average, women are more social than men. In terms of work preferences, for example, the former are more interested in working with other people, while the latter are more interested in working with things, such as tools and computers. Moreover, men are 4 to 10 times as likely to be on the autism spectrum as women are. Perhaps unsurprisingly, a study by the UK Intellectual Property Office found that women "account for just under 13 percent of patent applications globally."[22] This discrepancy cannot fully be explained by past sex discrimination. Europe, for example, has made great strides toward equality between the sexes, yet as a 2007 study found, the share of patents held by female engineers was four times lower than the share of female engineers in the labor force.[23] In other words, technical innovation seems to be disproportionately—though by no means exclusively—a domain of somewhat autistic males.[24]

Autism, notes the American psychologist Robert Plomin in his 2018 book, *Blueprint: How DNA Makes Us Who We Are*, is not a distinct illness or disease. Rather, it is a long spectrum of traits related to social, emotional, and communication skills.[25] Autistic individuals may, for example,

> not point at objects to show interest, not look at objects when another person points at them, have trouble relating to others or not have an interest in other people at all, avoid eye contact and want to be alone, have trouble understanding other people's feelings or

talking about their own feelings . . . appear to be unaware when people talk to them (but respond to other sounds), be very interested in people (but not know how to talk, play, or relate to them), repeat or echo words or phrases said to them (or repeat words or phrases in place of normal language), have trouble expressing their needs using typical words or motions . . . repeat actions over and over again, have trouble adapting when routine changes, have unusual reactions to the way things smell, taste, look, feel, or sound, and lose skills they once had (for example, stop saying words they were using).[26]

Furthermore, autistic individuals tend to exhibit a particular combination of the Big Five Personality Traits.[27] Namely, they tend to be "more neurotic and less extroverted, agreeable, conscientious, and open to experience."[28] In a word, they tend to be, as Melissa A. Schilling from New York University's Stern School of Business noted, "quirky" or eccentric.[29] Liberal societies—which is to say free, open, or inclusive ones—are relatively good at accommodating eccentricities. But will that continue? Remember that in the long run, social evolution (and natural selection) favors conformism and social innovation. Inventors and innovators, by contrast, tend to exhibit eccentric traits and favor technical innovations. If social pressure (norms, mores, speech codes) prevents eccentric people from flourishing, society will tend toward technological stagnation. Conversely, a society that tolerates eccentricity will enhance its potential for technological innovation.

As we write, dark clouds are forming over the horizon. They include a decline in viewpoint diversity,[30] an ever-growing emphasis on equity (i.e., equality of outcome between sexes, races, sexual orientations, etc.)[31] and punishment for unorthodox thinking.[32] Political correctness and increasingly complex speech codes are particularly challenging for neurodiverse or neurodivergent individuals, as the University of New Mexico psychologist Geoffrey Miller noted, including people with attention deficit hyperactivity disorder (ADHD), Tourette syndrome, social communication disorder, posttraumatic stress disorder (PTSD), bipolar disorder, schizophrenia, and a variety of other paranoid, schizoid, schizotypal, histrionic, narcissistic, borderline, and antisocial personality disorders.[33]

Simply put, liberal societies appear to be growing less tolerant of eccentricity, and that could have profound consequences for the future of invention and innovation. For what it's worth, we believe that it would be a great mistake to purge academia and the private sector of individuals with quirky behavioral patterns or peculiar views on hot-button social issues. Humanity should not have to forgo a cure for cancer or a new source of plentiful and reliable energy because the researchers involved are "objectionable" in some way.[34] Put differently, we should not sacrifice technological, scientific, and medical progress on the altar of "niceness." To maximize invention and innovation, society should celebrate inventors and innovators in general, and quirky individuals in particular.

The process of turning inventions into innovations . . .

Human beings have been inventing and innovating for millions of years, but economic progress has been painfully slow. It has only been over the past two centuries or so that economic growth has skyrocketed. A major reason for that explosive growth, we argue, is population growth combined with greater freedom to think, speak, and experiment. This beneficial combination—people plus freedom—allowed inventing and innovation to be sustainable over a long period for the first time in human history. We call that period the Age of Innovation. What's the difference between invention and innovation?

Inventions begin with ideas that emerge from the human mind. Individual human intelligence and consciousness (or alertness to new opportunities) are keys to the process of innovation. Human intelligence includes the power to reason, create, and communicate. Reasoning is the ability to identify patterns, weigh evidence, project future scenarios, and make decisions. Creativity manifests itself in new ideas. Oral and written language enable human beings to communicate complex ideas with one another across space and time, allowing knowledge to grow and be shared. Individuals then demonstrate their ideas with inventions. Finally, people test their inventions in the marketplace. An innovation, therefore, is a market-successful (or, to use Deirdre McCloskey's term, "trade-tested") invention.

This distinction between invention and innovation is imperative. People invent a lot of things, many of which are useless or even harmful. *Time* magazine has compiled a list of the worst inventions of all time, including New Coke, Clippy, CueCat, hydrogenated oils, Honeygar, hydrogen blimps, hair in a can, red dye no. 2, the Ford Pinto, the parachute jacket, Betamax, the baby cage, the hula chair, the Pontiac Aztek, the Snuggie for dogs, the Mizar flying car, and olestra.[35] As such, people need market forces to discover whether their inventions are really valuable. The market is the metaphorical place in which inventors learn the value of their inventions (or, to be more precise, a process of discovery through which they learn that). Without the freedom to buy and sell, we cannot ascertain useful information about the value of an invention. Once the market gives its stamp of approval to an invention, the invention becomes an innovation. An innovation, in turn, creates positive net value for humanity.

That said, only a small fraction of the trillions of ideas that come into being become inventions, and of those inventions, only a small fraction become innovations. Consider the data. On June 19, 2018, the U.S. Patent and Trademark Office issued its 10-millionth utility patent using the current numbering system that started in 1836. The idea of patents for intellectual property was recognized by the American founders in the U.S. Constitution that came into force in 1789. In article 1, section 8, clause 8, the U.S. Constitution states that the U.S. Congress has the power "to promote the Progress of Science and useful Arts, by securing for limited Times to Authors and Inventors the exclusive Right to their respective Writings and Discoveries." George Washington, the first president of the United States, actually signed the first patent, which was issued in 1790 to Samuel Hopkins for improvements in "the making of potash and pearl ash."[36] While many valuable inventions are not patented, only around 5 percent of the 2.1 million patents that are currently active (most patents expire after 20 years) are commercially profitable. That statistic suggests that only 105,000 inventions patented in the United States in the last 20 years meet the test of market success. Of course, we all benefit from expired patents, as the knowledge that they contain becomes free to use.

Finally, keep in mind that there are a variety of innovations. Professor Clayton Christensen (1952–2020) of the Harvard Business School, for example, wrote about disruptive innovations (a new product or service that starts operating from the low end of the market, slowly moves up the value chain, and finally replaces the incumbent product or service), sustaining innovations (an innovation that aims to improve the quality and feature of the current product offering), and efficiency innovations (innovations that try to do more with less in the manufacture of a product). Others have defined incremental innovation, architectural innovation, and radical innovation. That said, all innovations fall into two broad categories: consumption innovations and capital innovations. Consumption innovations create products and services that are consumed by "end users" or customers. (An end user is the person who ultimately uses a particular product. A customer is a person who performs the purchasing transaction. If a single person purchases and ends up using the product, that person is both an end user and a customer.) Capital innovations are products and services that contribute to the development of innovations that are still new. They include "explicit organizational knowledge residing in an organization's intellectual property, business designs, business process techniques, patents, copyrights and trade secrets (among other factors) which enables organizations to build a competitive advantage either through economies of scale and scope or differentiation."[37]

. . . usually requires a rearrangement of existing physical capital . . .

Physical capital, wrote Harvard University economist Gregory Mankiw, "consists of man-made goods (or input into the process of production) that assist in the production process."[38] Real estate, equipment, and inventory are examples of physical capital. All physical capital consists of a finite number of atoms, the basic building blocks of ordinary matter. Combining and recombining those atoms in new ways has long been the stuff of innovation. In a 2015 article, "Economic Growth," the Nobel Prize–winning New York University economist Paul Romer observed that while there may be a fixed number of atoms in the universe, there is virtually an infinite number of ways to arrange and rearrange those atoms. Therefore, the value creation process is also virtually unlimited. Romer writes,

> Every generation has perceived the limits to growth that finite resources and undesirable side effects would pose if no new recipes

or ideas were discovered. And every generation has underestimated the potential for finding new recipes and ideas. We consistently fail to grasp how many ideas remain to be discovered. The difficulty is the same one we have with compounding. Possibilities do not add up. They multiply.... To get some sense of how much scope there is for more such discoveries, we can calculate as follows. The periodic table contains about a hundred different types of atoms. If a recipe is simply an indication of whether an element is included or not, there will be 100×99 recipes like the one for bronze or steel that involve only two elements. For recipes that can have four elements, there are $100 \times 99 \times 98 \times 97$ recipes, which is more [than] 94 million. With up to 5 elements, more than 9 billion. Mathematicians call this increase in the number of combinations "combinatorial explosion." Once you get to 10 elements, there are more recipes than seconds since the big bang created the universe. As you keep going, it becomes obvious that there have been too few people on earth and too little time since we showed up, for us to have tried more than a minuscule fraction of all the possibilities.[39]

Nuclear fission is a perfect example of the new ways in which human beings can literally rearrange atoms—or, in the case of nuclear power, "split" them—to produce a brand-new source of energy, one that does not emit any carbon dioxide into the atmosphere. Nuclear fusion, should it ever become economically viable, will rearrange atoms in the opposite way by crushing them together to produce energy that will be even safer than nuclear fission.

An iron bridge and an asphalt road are likewise exercises in atom rearrangement. Iron is a metal that has been present in Earth's core since the formation of our planet some 4.5 billion years ago. In the past, it was used to make cookware and weaponry. But large-scale bridge building had to wait until the 19th century, when humans figured out that steel, which even the ancients were familiar with, could be mass-produced using the Bessemer process.[40] Similarly, asphalt, which is a sticky, black, and highly viscous liquid form of petroleum, had been known to the "ancient Mesopotamians [who] used it to waterproof temple baths and water tanks."[41] The Phoenicians used it to caulk their ships, and the Romans used it to seal their aqueducts. Only in the 20th century, however, did we start using a specific mix of asphalt, sand, stone, and gravel to pave our roads, streets, and airport runways, thus enhancing our ability to travel and conduct *doux commerce* ("sweet commerce").

Physical capital such as the aforementioned energy, roads, and bridges can assist in the production process, but physical capital need not be a prerequisite for innovation. Rather, it tends to be a consequence of innovation. The United States, for example, became the world's largest economy at the end of the 19th century and a global superpower during the course of World War II, yet only 4 percent of U.S. roads were paved as late as 1900.[42] In fact, the U.S. federal government was not involved in road construction until 1916, and the construction of the American interstate highway system did not begin until 1956. So, ideas usually lead to new physical capital rather than vice versa. To quote Donald J. Boudreaux: "It's true that nature created . . . materials, but nature did not transform them into resources. This all-important transformation was the product exclusively of human creativity, intellect, and effort."[43]

■ Box 9.1. Housing is more abundant (1970–2019)

The American economic and financial writer Bill Bonner noted that "it cost $23,000 in 1970 to put a roof over [one's] head. Today, it's $240,000."[a] What he forgot to mention is that the average house in 1970 was 1,500 square feet. Today it's closer to 2,700 square feet.[b] The nominal rate per square foot in 1970 was about $15.33, compared with $88.89 in 2019.

The nominal price of a square foot of housing in 1970 was $15.33, and the U.S. blue-collar hourly compensation rate was $3.93, indicating a time price (TP) of 3.9 hours per square foot. In 2019, the nominal price of a square foot of housing was $88.89, and the U.S. blue-collar hourly compensation rate was $32.36, indicating a TP of 2.75 hours per square foot. Those figures indicate that the price of housing declined by almost 30 percent between 1970 and 2019.

In 1970, the U.S. unskilled hourly wage rate was $1.85, indicating a TP of 8.28 hours per square foot. In 2019, the U.S. unskilled hourly wage rate was $13.66. As such, the TP of one square foot of housing amounted to 6.50 hours. That indicates that the price of housing declined by almost 21.5 percent between 1970 and 2019. The U.S. upskilling workers saw their hourly compensation rate rise

---

Table B9.1.1. Personal resource abundance analysis of housing in the United States: summary of the U.S. blue-collar worker perspective, the U.S. unskilled worker perspective, and the U.S. upskilling worker perspective (1970–2019)

Housing per sq. ft. 1970–2019	Percentage change in resource time price	Personal resource abundance multiplier	Percentage change in personal resource abundance	Compound annual percentage growth rate in personal resource abundance	Years to double personal resource abundance
Blue-collar	−29.6	1.42	42	0.72	96.8
Unskilled	−21.5	1.27	27	0.49	140.5
Upskilling	−66.9	3.02	202	2.28	30.8

Source: Authors' calculations.

Note: sq. ft. = square foot.

from $1.85 in 1970 to $32.36 in 2019. The TP of one square foot of housing, therefore, declined from 8.28 hours to 2.75 hours, or 66.8 percent (see Table B9.1.1).

Note that household size in 1970 was more than 3 persons. In 2019, it was closer to 2.5, so square footage per person has more than doubled, from about 500 to 1,080. Contemporary homes, of course, are also much more energy efficient. They come with better, bigger, and more numerous bathrooms, closets, and garages; are equipped with better and more numerous home appliances; and almost always include modern features such as central air conditioning and granite countertops.

Where houses have gotten significantly more expensive, they have usually done so due to highly restrictive zoning and regulatory requirements, which have artificially raised the price of land. On average, however, we are getting much more house for much less effort. ∎

. . . which tends to depend on a relatively advanced human capital . . .

Human capital was already recognized by Adam Smith. In *The Wealth of Nations*, Smith pondered "the acquired and useful abilities of all the inhabitants or members of the society."[44] He noted that the acquisition of talents by the maintenance of the acquirer during his education, study, or apprenticeship, always costs a real expense, which is a capital fixed and realized, as it were, in his person. Those talents, as they make a part of his fortune, so do they likewise of that of the society to which he belongs. The improved dexterity of a workman may be considered in the same light as a machine or instrument of trade which facilitates and abridges labor and which, though it costs a certain expense, repays that expense with a profit.[45]

More recently, Nobel Prize–winning University of Chicago economist Gary Becker (1930–2014) wrote that "human capital analysis starts with the assumption that individuals decide on their education, training, medical care, and other additions to knowledge and health by weighing the benefits and costs. Benefits include cultural and other nonmonetary gains along with improvement in earnings and occupations, while costs usually depend mainly on the foregone value of the time spent on these investments."[46] Put differently, we value education because learning provides us with the opportunity to further increase our knowledge and skills. Skills are actionable knowledge.

Other aspects of human capital include integrity and trust. As Warren Buffett has remarked, "I look for three things in a person: intelligence, and a high energy level, and integrity. If they don't have the latter, the first two will kill you."[47] Being worthy of trust is one of the most valuable human capital traits one can possess. That's especially true in the context of a free economy, where individuals and companies tend to interact on the basis of their respective reputations. (In nonfree economies, the state may dictate economic interactions between two parties irrespective of the latter's ability to fulfill their part of the contract.) Connected to integrity and trust is the network that someone has developed. Who you know can be as valuable as what you know, if not more so.

Human capital also includes a person's life expectancy, health, leadership skills, personality, and network. Life expectancy is a proxy for the health of a country. The greater the number of years of life, the greater potential for human capital to create more value. Human capital is an active asset. No matter how much knowledge and skills one might have, these assets remain inactive capital without health. Leadership skills are also important. Whether innate or learned, this element of human capital can be exceptionally valuable in guiding people and companies between different courses of action and accompanying opportunity costs.

Other enhancers of human capital are personality traits that give people the ability to work in teams and be pleasant and inspiring. Note, however, that different economic activities require different personality traits. As we have already discussed, inventors and innovators succeed in generating new ideas precisely because they do not seek the approval of the people around them. Once new ideas are produced, the people responsible for actualizing them and marketing them tend to be precisely the kinds of people who are pleasant and try to get along.

What's truly beautiful about humanity is that our social and technical innovations complement each other. Less social people might invent more often, but they need a predominantly social population in order for their inventions to proliferate and benefit humanity as a whole. Furthermore, as we saw with toolmaking, stones, and fire, society multiplies the positive effects of technical innovation. The internet is a great modern example of that social dynamic. As a technology, it's a groundbreaking platform for instant communication, but human sociality made it useful. Wikipedia is the largest collection of human knowledge in history, and it's entirely based on independent researchers who want to share their findings with the world. As a result, everyone has benefited from it.

To improve such human capital as knowledge, skills, and relationships with others, people must believe that they live in a society that will reward those improvements in the future. In the past, people believed in the strict stratification of human society into slaves, peasants, nobility, and priests. That order, they thought, was preordained and made vertical mobility impossible. A son born to a blacksmith would take over his father's business and pass on that enterprise down to his son. That this sort of stasis could go on for many generations is attested by the rise of "professional" last names, such as Smith, Potter, Cooper, Mason, Tyler, and so on. Thus John, the son of Peter the Smith, became John Smith, and so on.

Similarly, people who still live in societies that are socially immobile or antagonistic to entrepreneurship are typically disincentivized from investing in their own futures. Why, for example, should a person study (invest in his or her future) if university tenure is awarded on the basis of nepotism rather than on merit? Why should a person build a business if that enterprise can be stolen by a well-connected army general? So, the organization and reorganization of human capital also depend on an idea, namely, on the idea of progress or the belief that the future can be better for individuals and their descendants.

. . . that's enhanced by a previously accumulated intellectual capital . . .

The generation of new ideas consists of combining or recombining other (often previously generated) ideas.[48] This intellectual capital includes all of humanity's store of knowledge. Knowledge can be possessed by individuals, organizations, and the general public. It is stored in bits, ideas, methods, patents, recipes, and other ways of doing things.[49] Paul Romer made the distinction between physical capital (i.e., atoms) and intellectual capital (i.e., bits) in his 1993 paper, "Idea Gaps and Object Gaps in Economic Development." He wrote that "even [Adam] Smith recognized that . . . objects are of no inherent value as inputs without knowledge of how to combine them in ways that generate valuable output."[50]

Once again, not all countries possess the same amount of intellectual capital. Advanced economies are increasingly being referred to as "knowledge" or "bit" economies, while some other countries, including the tragically poor Burundi and Central African Republic, are yet to undergo industrialization at all. Mercifully, countries that lack intellectual capital to spur innovation and growth can access "ideas that are available in the rest of the world . . . partly through unimpeded flows of the capital goods that are produced in the industrialized nations of the world. These goods embody many new ideas."[51] Economic development, Romer noted,

> requires a mechanism for ensuring adequate flows of the large quantity of disembodied ideas that are used in production. The government of a poor country can therefore help its residents by creating an economic environment that offers an adequate reward

to multinational corporations when they bring ideas from the rest of the world and put them to use with domestic resources. . . . [Those ideas] include the innumerable insights about packaging, marketing, distribution, inventory control, payments systems, information systems, transactions processing, quality control, and worker motivation that are all used in the creation of economic value in a modern economy.[52]

Dissemination of intellectual capital, then, also depends on ideas. Specifically, it depends on abandoning the discredited idea of economic self-reliance, characterized by protectionism and most famously questioned by Adam Smith and David Ricardo (1772–1823), as well as embracing free trade. That's to say that innovation and economic development depend on an intellectual shift from a mindset that sees foreign investment and the operation of multinational corporations (MNCs) as tools of capitalist exploitation, to a mindset that sees foreign investment and MNCs as sources of valuable and growth-enhancing knowledge.[53]

Romer also notes that ideas are nonrivalrous and nonexcludable goods. A nonrivalrous good such as a telecast or streaming television documentary can be watched or "consumed" by everyone at the same time. A Snickers bar, in contrast, is a rival good, for it can be consumed by only one person (or a very limited number of people). A nonexcludable good such as national defense covers everyone. Once it is provided, people cannot be excluded from enjoying it, even if they want to. Private parking, in contrast, is an excludable good; people who don't pay for a parking spot don't get to enjoy it. Romer worries that the generation or production of new ideas may be retarded by their nonrivalrous and nonexcludable characteristics. The solution to that problem, he believes, includes the expansion of public funding on research and development (R&D).

Since government revenue is finite, someone will have to decide who gets the taxpayer support and who does not. Should politicians and bureaucrats make those kinds of decisions? And what is the likelihood that public investments in R&D will be more effective and efficient than private ones? The answers to those questions are beyond the scope of this book. But the British scientist Terence Kealey and British economist Martin Ricketts contend that researchers tend to thrive on sharing their knowledge with one another as part of reciprocal social relationship networks. Thus, they argue that lack of government funding of R&D may be less of a problem in retarding future innovation than is often assumed.[54]

. . . is powered by liquid and sophisticated financial capital . . .

Financial capital includes institutions and innovations that deal with money and risk, and how those two are measured and managed. Regardless of the presence of all of the other capitals, the innovation process doesn't really function unless inventors and entrepreneurs can rely on a moderately stable currency, incorporate businesses, borrow money, buy or sell shares, purchase insurance, and have a common language to understand financial performance.

To innovate, people need to have faith in the future. A stable currency is a vital component of a stable society. Between 1700 and 1914, to give one example, Great Britain generated an immense amount of economic progress. George Gilder pointed out that along with transforming physics and co-developing calculus, the English polymath Sir Isaac Newton (1643–1727) also served as the master of the mint. During his tenure, Great Britain moved to the gold standard, which ensured the stability of the pound sterling and provided the monetary structure of the British Empire during one of the greatest periods of economic growth ever experienced by the human race.[55]

The limited liability company (LLC), which is a legal business entity authorized to operate by the state, is another salutary component of financial capital. The Dutch East India Company (Vereenigde Oostindische Compagnie, or VOC) was established in 1602 and is commonly considered to be the first modern corporation. The VOC limited the liability of the stockholders in the event of business failure to the amount that they invested in the company. (Before the invention of the LLC, stockholders could lose everything, including their private possessions and even their freedom.) Today, corporations can raise millions of dollars from thousands of investors who enjoy limited risk. That allows societies to take on large and complex projects that non-LLCs could never attempt.

Banks serve as financial intermediaries, providing people with the ability to create value for one another by lending and borrowing. Bank deposits are lent to borrowers while earning interest for lenders (that is, for depositors). Prior to the rise of modern banking—a crucial component of financial capital—lending and borrowing tended to happen mostly among people who knew each other (and, therefore, were aware of the contracting parties' respective reputations). Modern banks still rely on the reputations of borrowers through, for instance, credit scores, but the sheer volume of transactions and the size of each bank's lending network lower the risk to individual lenders, thus allowing for more and riskier lending.[56] That can lead to problems, such as the 2008 banking crisis, but most scholars agree that modern banking is a source of much greater liquidity than would otherwise be the case. Greater liquidity, in turn, stimulates faster growth.

Another key aspect of financial capital is a stock exchange or a bourse. These are organized markets for buying and selling financial instruments such as government bonds, promissory notes, securities, commodities, corporate shares, and other investments. The term "bourse" is common in Europe and is based on the Bruges residence of textile merchant Robbrecht van der Buerse (c. 1265–c. 1319), where Hanseatic and Italian merchants and financiers began gathering and trading in the 1300s.[57] Stock markets first emerged in Amsterdam, London, New York, and Paris. Most countries have since developed their own stock markets, including new exchanges in Vietnam and Saudi Arabia. The ability to easily buy and sell financial instruments on exchanges increases financial liquidity and allows risk to be spread across large numbers of individual investors that have different valuations and risk tolerances.[58]

Insurance is a vital part of financial capital that allows contracting parties to diversify and share risks. By knowing the maximum financial downside of their investment (i.e., of losing the insurance premium and specified deductibles), insured entities, be they individuals or corporations, can take greater risks with the potential for higher returns. Different approaches to managing these kinds of risks were practiced by the Chinese and the Babylonians in the 3rd and 2nd millennia BCE, respectively. The latter enshrined their insurance system in the aforementioned Code of Hammurabi, though the first known insurance contract dates to Genoa in 1347.[59] Today, insurance is a major component of the U.S. economy, amounting to $1.22 trillion in 2018.[60]

Double-entry accounting or bookkeeping is another aspect of financial capital, which was practiced all the way back in ancient Rome. In 70 CE, for example, Pliny the Elder described the structure of double-entry accounting as "on one page all the disbursements are entered, on the other page all the receipts; both pages constitute a whole for each operation of every man."[61] As the Australian author Jane Gleeson-White noted in her book, *Double Entry: How the Merchants of Venice Created Modern Finance*, "You could itemize the profits in each account, so you knew which products you were doing well in and which you weren't. Then you could start to think about how you would change your business activities. It was just a whole revolution in the way of thinking about business and trade."[62] The longevity of double-entry bookkeeping attests to its usefulness to commerce and economic development.

. . . and enabled by relatively free markets

In Chapter 4, we described the functioning of free markets and offered reasons for their necessity. To summarize, the market is the place and the process for discovering what's valuable. It is where inventions are tested for their value-creating power. It is where learning occurs. As Cesar Hidalgo and Ricardo Hausmann noted, "A modern society can amass large amounts of productive knowledge because it distributes bits and pieces of knowledge among its many members. But to make use of it, this knowledge has to be put back together through organizations and markets."[63]

To maximize the learning that can occur in markets, buyers and sellers must be free to come and go, and prices must be free to rise and fall. University of Nebraska-Omaha economics professor Arthur M. Diamond observed that an invention is much more worthy of attention, praise, and reward if it is designed and constructed so that it can succeed in the market. The question that markets answer is this: "Is it [the product] made well enough, cheaply enough, with the right set of features, and with key complementary goods in place, so that it could be sold for a profit?"[64]

Free markets serve one other beneficial role in human society: they build trust and cooperation. Competition, as everyone knows, is an essential part of a capitalist economy. It drives businesses to innovate and to provide consumers with less costly and better products. If businesses fail to innovate, they go under. The marketplace can be a brutal place (just think of the way in which Netflix dispatched Blockbuster). "Capitalism without failure is like religion without sin," as the American economist Allan H. Meltzer (1928–2017) once put it. "It doesn't work."[65] Capitalism is also one of the most cooperative of human endeavors, though. Goods and services are traded among strangers and across vast distances, guided to a great degree by the price mechanism and by the reputation of the trading parties. Repeated transactions among trading parties encourage trustworthiness, a moral side-product of capitalism that we do not spend enough time talking about, let alone celebrating.

In the short run, competition produces winners and losers (although over the long run it is very difficult to find anyone in a market society who does not daily enjoy substantial gains or "wins" from market competition). As Amazon expanded, for example, neighborhood bookstores shuttered across the United States. Some people thought that was a great tragedy, for bookstores provided a pleasant way to browse through publications and, sometimes, to meet interesting people. Ultimately, however, the convenience of the internet, along with superior choices and lower prices, proved to be more valuable to the average customer. Amazon and its clientele won, while your local bookseller lost. The losers who emerge from capitalist competition appear to confirm a zero-sum bias in the human brain. It is for that reason that many people tend to focus on the closed local bookstores, rather than revel in the falling prices and increased choice made possible by Amazon.[66] Where did that bias come from?

For hundreds of thousands of years that we spent wandering the planet as hunter-gatherers, the success of one group of people, often related by family bonds, came at the expense of another group. When the resources in an area occupied by group A ran out, group A moved onto a territory occupied by group B, provoking conflict. Conflict still continues to define the interaction among animals. Humans, by contrast, evolved additional ways of interacting with one another. Permanent settlements were a key part of that process. Strangers who settled next to one another had to learn how to cooperate. In that process, they either acquired a reputation for trustworthiness, or they became social outcasts excluded from a larger economy.

As a result of cooperation, humanity advanced so much that by the time of the Roman Republic, the Latin term *civis* became a root word for both the city and civilization. Over time, the city-state gave way to the nation-state, and the nation-state became a part of a global economy. As human cooperation expanded, so did our economic horizons. That was both an unambiguously moral phenomenon and an economic one. People who might have otherwise hated each other were brought together in the pursuit of profit. So trade allows everyone to participate in the dignity of this value-creating process of mutual interdependencies. Our wealth grows as we specialize and become more and more dependent on and cooperative with each other. F. A. Hayek suggests that markets perform a "catallactic" function. He wrote that "the term 'catallactics' is derived from the Greek verb *katallattein* (or *katallassein*), which meant, significantly, not only 'to exchange' but also 'to admit into the community' and '*to change from enemy into friend*' [emphasis added]."[67]

■ Box 9.2. U.S. domestic airfares fell in price (1995–2019)

In 1995, the average U.S. domestic airfare was about $288.[c] In 2019, it was closer to $345.[d] That amounts to a 19.8 percent increase in nominal price. However, over the intervening 24 years, the U.S. blue-collar worker hourly compensation rate increased from $16.66 to $32.36, or 94.2 percent. As such, the time price (TP) of an average U.S. domestic airfare dropped from 17.2 hours to 10.7 hours, or 38.1 percent. That means that for the same length of work that bought one U.S. domestic airfare in 1995, a U.S. blue-collar worker could get 1.62 airfares in 2019 (see Table B9.2.1).

Between 1995 and 2019, the U.S. unskilled worker's hourly wage rate rose from $7.00 to $13.66, or 95.1 percent. As such, the TP of an average U.S. domestic airfare dropped from 41 hours to 25.3 hours, or 38.4 percent. That means that for the same length of work that bought one U.S. domestic airfare in 1995, a U.S. unskilled worker could get 1.62 airfares in 2019.

Table B9.2.1. Personal resource abundance analysis of U.S. domestic airfares (1995–2019)

Airfares	1995	2019	Percentage change 1995–2019	Personal resource abundance multiplier 1995 = 1	Percentage change in personal resource abundance 1995–2019	Compound annual percentage growth rate in personal resource abundance	Years to double personal resource abundance
Nominal price	$287	$345	20.2				
Blue-collar	$16.66	$32.36	94.2				
Time price	17.2	10.7	−38.1	1.62	61.6	2.0	34.7
Unskilled	$7.00	$13.66	95.1				
Time price	41.0	25.3	−38.4	1.62	62.3	2.0	34.3
Upskilling	$7.00	$32.36	362.3				
Time Price	41.0	10.7	−74.0	3.85	284.6	5.8	12.4

Source: Authors' calculations.

Table B9.2.2. Personal resource analysis of U.S. domestic airfares: summary of the U.S. blue-collar worker perspective, the U.S. unskilled worker perspective, and the U.S. upskilling worker perspective (1995–2019)

Airfares 1995–2019	Percentage change in resource time price	Personal resource abundance multiplier	Percentage change in personal resource abundance	Compound annual percentage growth rate in personal resource abundance	Years to double personal resource abundance
Blue-collar	−38.1	1.62	62	2.02	34.7
Unskilled	−38.4	1.62	62	2.04	34.3
Upskilling	−74.0	3.85	285	5.77	12.4

Source: Authors' calculations.

Over the same period, the U.S. upskilling worker's hourly compensation rose from $7.00 to $32.36, or 362.3 percent. As such, the TP of an average U.S. domestic airfare dropped from 41 hours to 10.7 hours, or 74 percent. That means that for the same length of work that bought one U.S. domestic airfare in 1995, a U.S. upskilling worker could get 3.85 airfares in 2019. So, depending on their efforts to upgrade their human capital, the U.S. domestic airfares have been getting between 16 and 76 minutes cheaper for American workers every year (see Table B9.2.2). ∎

The oft-forgotten heroes of progress are the entrepreneurs . . .

Much has been written about the role of the entrepreneur in the innovation process. George Gilder, for example, noted that "the key role of entrepreneurs, like the most crucial role of scientists, is not to fill in the gaps in an existing market or theory, but to generate entirely new markets or theories. They stand before a canvas as empty as any painter's; a page as blank as any poet's."[68] While there are many types of entrepreneurship, we focus on entrepreneurs as risk-takers in our human innovation model.[69] It is these risk-takers who try to convert inventions into innovations by using different

forms of capital. In the remainder of this chapter, we will look at the entrepreneurial endeavors of two men: Johannes Gutenberg and James Watt.

. . . like the perfecter of the printing press, Johannes Gutenberg . . .

The printing press is one of the most consequential innovations in history.
The value of creating, storing, transmitting, and learning knowledge in the
form of mass-produced, affordable books cannot be overestimated. That was
especially true during the Protestant Reformation (1517–1648) that led,
among other things, to higher school enrollment and literacy rates, narrower
gender gaps in school enrollment and literacy rates, higher public spending on
schooling, higher numeracy, the Protestant work ethic, the spread of market-
friendly attitudes and faster economic development, the growth of Protestant cities, greater entrepreneurship among religious minorities in Protestant
states, the development of the post-Westphalian state system and interjuris-
dictional competition, poor relief and a nascent welfare system, and eventually
the modern conception of separation of church and state.[70]

Johannes Gutenberg, who greatly improved the movable printing press
in the mid-15th century in the German city of Mainz, had to combine and
refine a number of key existing technologies. As such, the Gutenberg printing press is a prime example of combinatorial innovation that we first encountered when discussing Paul Romer's ideas. The Chinese, for example,
had invented movable-type printing in the 11th century. Gutenberg improved the Chinese technology by developing hand-molded matrices made
out of more durable lead and other metal alloys. The Chinese had also developed papermaking around 100 BCE. Europeans mechanized papermaking
with water-powered paper mills, reducing the price of paper to one-sixth of
the cost of parchment that the Chinese had used. One of Gutenberg's first
partners, in fact, was Andreas Heilman, a paper mill owner. Gutenberg was
also able to use newer, oil-based inks that were far superior to their water-
based alternatives. Also beneficial was the fact that the Latin alphabet had
only two dozen letters, as opposed to the 40,000 ideographs in the Chinese
language. We also note the importance of eyeglasses, which were developed
in Northern Italy in the 13th century, a discovery that created additional

demand for books. In the meantime, winemakers in Germany were developing screw presses to extract juices from grapes. Gutenberg refined these presses so they could provide for a more even pressing experience. He also added a movable under-table system that allowed paper sheets to be changed quickly.

Essential to Gutenberg's success was the existence of a relatively unconstrained market. As Jeremiah Dittmar of the London School of Economics and Skipper Seabold from Civis Analytics note, "Regulation was light . . . [because] printing fell outside guild regulation and was one of the first industries in European history in which firms organized production."[71] Free from burdensome restrictions, Gutenberg was able to develop and market his ideas. He was also able to access human capital when he partnered with other businessmen and hired craftsmen with the knowledge and skills he needed to realize his vision. Moreover, he was able to utilize financial capital when he borrowed significant sums from his brother-in-law, Andreas Dritzehn, and 1,600 guilders ($167,000 in 2020 U.S. dollars) from a German banker named Johann Fust (1400–1466).

In summary, Gutenberg proved his ideas in the marketplace by using physical, human, intellectual, and financial forms of capital. In doing so, his discovery helped to unleash great social, political, and economic changes that continue to reverberate today. Fortunately, Gutenberg lived in a place and time that allowed him to apply his talents. In the much more repressive China, the printing press was an invention. In less repressive Europe, it became an innovation. Gutenberg's career confirms Mark Twain's observation that "substantially all ideas are second-hand, consciously and unconsciously drawn from a million outside sources."[72]

. . . and the refiner of the steam engine, James Watt

James Watt was born in Scotland in 1736. He was trained as an instrument maker and became interested in steam engine technology. The steam engine had been around for many centuries, even showing up in the toys of Egyptian children in Alexandria in the first century CE. Watt's contribution to technological progress was to invent new instruments that dramatically improved the efficiency of steam engines that powered the Industrial Revolution.

Chief among these instruments was a separate condenser. As *Encyclopedia Britannica* explains,

> While repairing a model Newcomen steam engine in 1764 [Newcomen developed a less efficient steam engine in 1712], Watt was impressed by its waste of steam. In May 1765, after wrestling with the problem of improving it, he suddenly came upon a solution—the separate condenser, his first and greatest invention. Watt had realized that the loss of latent heat (the heat involved in changing the state of a substance—e.g., solid or liquid) was the worst defect of the Newcomen engine and that therefore condensation must be effected in a chamber distinct from the cylinder but connected to it.[73]

As a young man, Watt worked at the University of Glasgow, where he became friends with Adam Smith. It is fitting, then, that Watt's improved steam engine entered the market on March 8, 1776, one day before the publication of Adam Smith's *The Wealth of Nations*. Another professor whom Watt befriended was a physicist and chemist named Joseph Black. Black helped Watt learn chemistry and also financially supported Watt's experimentation and invention. In 1767, Watt formed a partnership with John Roebuck, who provided the former with financial and human capital. Watt needed skilled ironworkers and precision machinists to perfect his designs. He borrowed the technology of John Wilkinson's cannon-boring techniques to develop the necessary piston and cylinder components. By that time, Great Britain had developed a patent system, an intellectual innovation aimed at incentivizing invention.[74]

In 1769, Watt and Roebuck took out their famous patent, "A New Invented Method of Lessening the Consumption of Steam and Fuel in Fire Engines."[75] Roebuck eventually went bankrupt and sold his patent rights to Matthew Boulton in 1775. After this, Boulton & Watt became one of the most important engineering and manufacturing firms of the Industrial Revolution.

In conclusion, Watt acted within our innovation framework, combining his ideas with physical, human, intellectual, and financial capital. He also enjoyed access to great cultural capital and a relatively free market. It was through the market that Watt the inventor became Watt the innovator and entrepreneur.

■ Box 9.3. DNA sequencing for everyone (2003–2020)

The Human Genome Project was an international effort to map the entire human genome with its 3 billion base pairs. The project was launched in 1990 and concluded its work in 2003, 50 years after Nobel Prize–winning molecular biologists James Watson and Francis Crick discovered the double-helix structure of DNA.

The U.S. government contributed $3.8 billion toward the project, though the cost of the actual sequencing was lower.[e] Dr. Eric Green, director of the National Human Genome Research Institute, recalled that "the first genome cost us about a billion dollars. . . . Now [in 2020] when we sequence a person's genome, it's less than $1000, so that's a million-fold reduction."[f]

Note that blue-collar worker hourly compensation (wages and benefits) rates increased from $21.54 to $32.54 (51 percent) between 2003 and 2020. Consequently, it would have cost that worker 46,425,255 hours of work to earn enough money to buy his or her DNA sequence in 2003 but only 30.73 hours of work to do so in 2020.

The time price of DNA sequencing, in other words, dropped by 99.99993 percent. For the same hours of work required to earn the money to buy one DNA sequence in 2003, a blue-collar worker can get more than 1.5 million sequences today. That amounts to over a 150 million percent increase in DNA sequencing abundance.

Now a group of Chinese entrepreneurs at the Beijing Genomics Institute (BGI) hope to get the price down to $100 using a robotic arm and a roomful of chemical baths and imaging machines.[g] Rade Drmanac, chief scientific officer of Complete Genomics, a division of BGI, noted that at $100, genetic sequencing could soon be common for every child at birth.[h]

A decrease in the cost of DNA sequencing from $1 billion to $100 over 20 years would imply a compound rate of decline of 6.5 percent a month. (Adjusting for the time price puts the compound rate of decline at 7.13 percent per month.) Moore's Law indicates that prices of computing decline at 2.85 percent a month. The cost of DNA sequencing per genome, then, may yet amount to the fastest price decline in history. ■

CHAPTER 10

The enemies of progress from the Romantics to the extreme environmentalists

Left-wing and right-wing political ideologies have themselves become secular religions, providing people with a community of like-minded brethren, a catechism of sacred beliefs, a well-populated demonology, and a beatific confidence in the righteousness of their cause.

Steven Pinker, *Enlightenment Now: The Case for Reason, Science, Humanism, and Progress*[1]

Chapter summary

The arrival of modernity was also accompanied by fundamental social changes. The end of old certainties, including rigid hierarchies that limited social mobility and religious beliefs that could not withstand the onslaught of scientific discoveries, proved profoundly disorienting to the public in general and intellectuals in particular. The rise of the bourgeoisie, and the concomitant diminution in the power and prestige of the nobility and the clergy, led to a great deal of envy and resentment. The weakening and the eventual retreat of traditional religion led to the rise of pseudoreligious fads like spiritualism and mesmerism, as well as alternative explanations of history and of "man's role in the universe." The void left behind by the collapse of the ancien régime would eventually be filled by a plethora of new theories, including racism, national socialism, communism, and, most recently, an increasingly militant strand of environmentalism.

We will discuss the rise of environmentalism in 19th-century Europe in general and Germany in particular, and its eventual importation into the United States. As we will show, environmentalism contained within itself anti-bourgeois and anti-capitalist sentiments from its beginning, eventually culminating in a comprehensive condemnation of modernity and liberal civilization. We will then turn to the rising strand of anti-humanism in the modern environmentalism movement that, in its mildest form, advocates in favor of anti-natalism and, in its most destructive form, flirts with genocide. Next, we will discuss the rise of eco-anxiety that is causing depression and disillusionment. Finally, we will contend that environmentalism has acquired many aspects of traditional religion and is increasingly fulfilling the role of the latter in societies in which traditional beliefs have receded.

The failed ideas of the Counter-Enlightenment, such as racism, fascism, and Marxism . . .

In addition to the broader trends that we discussed in Chapter 8, the modern era ushered in many inventions that nearly every denizen of modernity interacts with routinely, so routinely, in fact, that these interactions are taken for granted. Many life-saving and life-enhancing inventions and innovations were unknown to our ancestors living in the middle of the 18th century, including electricity and the lightbulb, trains, motorcars, reinforced concrete, airplanes, microwave ovens, air conditioning, landline phones and mobile phones, transistors and the radio, cameras and video recorders, televisions, solar cells, optic fiber cables, microchips, lasers, calculators, batteries and fuel cells, the World Wide Web and the computer, aspirin and antibiotics, cortisone, pacemakers, artificial hearts, MRI scans and gene therapies, vaccines, and many other life-saving and life-enhancing inventions and innovations. Life, in other words, has become better, not worse, for an increasing number of people who inhabit our planet.

As Arthur Herman notes in *The Idea of Decline on Western History*, though, modernity has not always been universally welcomed. The backlash started after the French Revolution went off the rails and ushered in the Reign of Terror, Napoleonic despotism, and Europe-wide conflict. People yearned for the stability of the prerevolutionary years. Denounced as barbaric relics of the past during the Enlightenment, the Catholic Church, the monarchy, and the landed aristocracy were now seen as medieval Europe's honorable legacy. Gothic architecture surged in popularity, and books about knights, maidens, and chivalry became immensely popular. The French poet Charles Baudelaire (1821–1867), for example, claimed that "there are but three groups worthy of respect: the priest, the warrior, and the poet. To know, to kill, and to create."[2] All three were vanishing from society, leaving only ennui, the fatal boredom that settles in after decadence sucks the creative energy from human beings.

The chief source of European decadence, the critics felt, was the bourgeoisie. They saw the rising middle class as spiritually dead, pursuing material pleasures over higher goals. Born shortly after the Napoleonic Wars, French writer Joseph Arthur de Gobineau (1816–1882) expanded this critique of modernity in a more radical direction. Gobineau was the son of a disgraced aristocrat and spent his formative years watching the death of his ancestors' way of life. He was a conservative, shared the Romantic distaste for modern society, and blamed his failed literary career on capitalism. The bloody 1848 revolutions in Europe seemed to justify Gobineau's pessimism. In 1853, he wrote his *Essay on the Inequality of the Human Races*, which claimed that biological decline was the driving force behind history. In his time, his book was the latest iteration of the myth of an ancient, perfect race that we encountered in Chapter 1.

In 1788, English philologist William Jones (1746–1794) noticed that Latin, Greek, and the Germanic languages were grammatically similar, suggesting a shared ancestral language. Later, German philologist Friedrich Schlegel (1772–1829) argued that this language was Sanskrit and that it had been spoken by the Aryans. Gobineau argued that the priests, warriors, and poets of every great empire were the descendants of that ancient race and he believed that Aryan blood was the source of vital energy and creative power. Each time the Aryans conquered a lesser race, however, the former interbred with the latter. That corrupted the Aryan blood, Gobineau claimed, and sent civilization into decline. In Europe, the Aryans were said to be Gobineau's ancestors, the Germanic aristocrats who spawned the mixed-race bourgeoise. The 1848 revolutions, he thought, were an attack of the mongrel hordes on the last remnants of Aryan purity. Gobineau's race theory was not well received in France, for it argued that the French were culturally and racially degenerate, but it did find better reception in Germany, where the Enlightenment was already under attack. From the 18th century onward, Germans constantly contrasted *Helden* (heroes) with their polar opposites, *Händler* (merchants or salespeople), who were especially Jews, Britons, and Americans.[3] Germanophiles such as the British philosopher Houston Chamberlain (1855–1927) adapted Gobineau's ideas to German conditions. Chamberlain argued that modern Germans, the last Aryans of Europe, were being tainted by Latins, French, Greeks, and, most of all, Jews. To Chamberlain, race was more than genetics. It included thought, art, and religion. To save themselves from decline, Germans supposedly needed to reject the lesser races in the bedroom, remove them from the academy, and expel them from Germany.

Swiss historian Jacob Burckhardt (1818–1897) founded a parallel theory of decline. In his theory, however, human society was unstable regardless of race. Stability, he averred, was to be found in a balance between three pillars of society: religion, government, and culture. If one of the three grew too much or decayed too much, balance was lost and crisis ensued. The first European crisis, Burckhardt thought, was the collapse of Rome, which was precipitated by the overexpansion of the empire and overextension of its government. The second, the Protestant Reformation, was the result of the growth of an oppressive religion. Democracy, he thought, created the third great crisis. The working class, which suffered from capitalist exploitation, now had the power to tear the economic system down. In order to survive, then, the state had to obey the will of the masses. At the same time, popular participation became a justification for increased state power. Burckhardt predicted that mass politics, the death of religion and tradition, and the power of modern military technology, would turn the nation into a tyrannical war machine. The crisis, Burckhardt thought, was essentially cultural. Capitalism and individualism undermined high culture, exploited workers, and reduced life to the simple pursuit of wealth. Worst of all, individualism had abolished traditional morality, leaving only the worship of power.

The German philosopher Friedrich Nietzsche (1844–1900) shared Burkhardt's distaste for capitalism. Nietzsche in fact hated all forms of modernity, including socialism. He saw modernity as rationalistic and egocentric and therefore spiritually empty. However, unlike Burckhardt, Nietzsche didn't think the ancien régime was any better. The latter was particularly contemptuous of Western religious tradition. In Nietzsche's view, Christianity was a failed religion that continued to infect modernity with "kindness" and "self-control," thus sapping Western creativity. The way out of societal degeneration wasn't to be found in a return to the old way of life but in pushing forward toward something new. Nietzsche hoped to see the emergence of a new elite consisting of giants ("Roman Caesars with the soul of Christ") who would impose their physical and psychological vitality on others. The desire to dominate, which Nietzsche termed the "will to power," would give humanity its creative energy, despite its destructive character.[4] The return of creative energy, however, required the rejection of the entire foundation of western morality. Nietzsche concluded that the giants he sought were outcasts—immoralists, who fully rejected both good and evil.

While some theories of biological or social decline were based on the interpretation of history, another equally insidious theory arose that purportedly accorded with the principles of science. Charles Darwin's theory of natural selection demonstrated how living things evolve over time. Food scarcity, predation, and reproductive fitness culled the weakest members of the species, allowing only the fittest individuals to reproduce. Some 19th-century thinkers came to believe that modern society created perverse incentives that could retard social evolution. The French sociologist Émile Durkheim (1858–1917), for example, thought that overspecialization and the stress of industrial society made people excessively delicate, thus leading to anxiety, depression, and suicide.[5] To protect humanity from degeneration, Durkheim argued, society had to be changed. Institutions such as the family, labor unions, and the state had to provide the sense of unity that kept people calm and healthy.

Instead of changing society to better fit humanity, as Durkheim desired, eugenicists wished to change humanity to advance broader social goals. Francis Galton, whom we met in Chapter 1, theorized that the complexity of industrial society meant that only 1 person in 4,000 had the physical and mental talent to advance civilization. He worried that, over time, the unfit masses would overwhelm the talented minority and doom society to mediocracy. Galton's solution was state-enforced natural selection. In Galton's own words, "what nature does blindly, slowly, and ruthlessly, man may do providentially, quickly, and kindly."[6] While in Western Europe and North America, the worst of the eugenics movement was limited to sterilization, in Germany it contributed to genocide. Gobineau's deterministic vision of racial decline melded easily with the seemingly scientific method of eugenics. In the 1930s, the rise of national socialism gave the German state the power to turn theory into practice.

The United States was not immune to the European doom and gloom. From the very beginning, one of the founding fathers and the second U.S. president, John Adams (1735–1826), predicted that liberty and democracy would allow the American masses to be controlled by demagogues who would corrupt and destroy the nation. His great-grandson, Henry Adams (1838–1919), abhorred the new millionaire industrialist class that had replaced the old Puritan elite, and he also hated the giant cities of immigrants that sprung up across the nation. The new elites, he observed, held political power over these emerging metropoles. Money bought votes, votes gave power, and power brought more money. Henry concluded that the American public could not be trusted with democracy. What America needed was a natural aristocracy, an educated Protestant class to guide them.

With some justification, Henry argued that the culture of liberty in America had sprung from the hardworking Anglo-Saxon Protestants who founded the United States (his ancestors, that is), and worried that material progress was undermining both. While Henry's Anglo-Saxon thesis was cultural, other scholars, such as the American historian Herbert Baxter Adams (no relation of Henry's) espoused a Teutonic "germ theory," which traced the practice of democracy from the decision making among ancient Germanic tribes to the parliamentary practices in Great Britain and ultimately to the representative form of government in the United States, where it flourished in its fullest and most mature form. It wasn't much of an intellectual jump to claim that immigrants were tainting the freedom-loving blood of Anglo-Saxon Americans. This idea was taken up most dramatically by the Ku Klux Klan, which envisioned themselves as the saviors of white America, denouncing and attacking blacks, Catholics, Eastern and Southern Europeans, and Jews.

Henry's brother, Brooks Adams (1848–1927), argued that industry created monopolies with so much power that they would destroy liberty and society. The state, he believed, had to intervene to reverse the trend toward monopoly. In his book *The Law of Civilization and Decay*, Brooks turned this theory into a historical law, arguing that Rome was destroyed by big agriculture that consumed independent freeholders. The U.S. president Theodore Roosevelt (1858–1919) was much taken by Brooks and sought to extend the government's control over U.S. businesses. Brooks, in turn, welcomed Roosevelt's imperialism, because it increased the power of the state. His prescription for a well-functioning society was a powerful, militaristic government run by a technocratic elite that would neuter the capitalists and save the nation from decline.

In Germany, meanwhile, Nietzsche's sister and caretaker Elisabeth Förster-Nietzsche (1846–1935) took control of her ailing brother's writings. After modifying them to fit her own anti-Semitic and nationalist beliefs, Nietzsche's ideas exploded in popularity. War, Nietzsche maintained, is a great source of vital energy. "I am glad about the military development of Europe; also of the internal states of anarchy: the time of repose and Chinese ossification, which Galiani predicted for this century, is over," he wrote. "Personal manly *virtu* of the body, is regaining value, estimation becomes more physical, nutrition meatier. Beautiful men are again becoming possible. Pallid hypocrisy (with mandarins at the top, as Comte dreamed) is over. The barbarian in each of us is affirmed; also the wild beast," Nietzsche continued.[7]

One of Nietzsche's young followers was Oswald Spengler (1880–1936), the child of a middle-class family who rebelled against the stifling morality of his parents' generation. Spengler found refuge in Munich, where a subclass of radical writers and artists were influencing the newly literate masses. The Munich scene was full of cultural pessimists and nationalists. They saw Germans as the only people in Western Europe who were relatively unspoiled by industrial civilization and who were engaged in a constant struggle against modernity. So as tensions rose in Europe during the first decade of the 20th century and war seemed ever closer, the Munich intellectuals cheered on the looming troubles.

In his 1918 book, *The Decline of the West*, Spengler argued that all major cultures and civilizations follow a cyclical pattern of growth and decline. The "spring" and "summer" stages are marked by vitality that leads to the flourishing of art, literature, religion, and philosophy. The "fall" and "winter" stages, by contrast, see a decline in creative endeavors and a focus on money, industry, politics, and expansionism. Not all is lost, however, for when one civilization declines, another rises to take its place. Spengler thought that Western civilization had entered a final stage and would self-destruct in a desperate struggle for power. The one hope, Spengler claimed, was that Germany could fight through the chaos and wrench a new culture from the ashes of war.[8]

After the Great War, Spengler's book became immensely popular. His hope for German reconstruction lay in the war veterans who, vitalized by battle, would lead the country into the future. Like Brooks Adams, Spengler envisioned a militarized, socialist command economy, but one that was characterized by the Prussian tradition of obedience. Classical "individual" liberty was replaced by an inner freedom that was found by serving the goals of a nation. The state, the people, and industry, Spengler prophesied, would fuse into a single entity, the ultimate expression of Nietzsche's will to power. The National Socialists shared Spengler's vision and repeatedly tried to recruit the philosopher to their ranks, but Spengler was in no rush to join a party that was based on mass politics and racism, rather than on his preferred Prussian militaristic tradition. He died in 1936, prophesying that the Third Reich had no more than 10 years to live.

While Spengler and Hitler pursued revolutions in Munich, another school of philosophy was developing at the Institute of Social Research in Frankfurt. The Frankfurt School, whose members included philosophers Max Horkheimer (1895–1973) and Theodor Adorno (1903–1969), pioneered a new and more pessimistic version of Marxism than the one we encountered in Chapter 1. Like other theories of decline, the new theory was rooted in the idea of degeneration. Everything that was once blamed on physical degeneration such as crime, mental illness, and atavism was now pinned on bourgeois capitalism. Horkheimer, who took over leadership of the institute in 1929, thought that the destructiveness of capitalism went beyond economics, affecting the habits and thoughts of the people. This cultural criticism was based on Marx's early writings, which argued that as the capitalist division of labor separates the workers from the product of their labor, it reduces them to a status of mere machines. Having lost their humanity, the proletariat becomes soulless and idiotic, a trend that Adorno believed he detected in their love for jazz.

After Hitler's rise to power, the Frankfurt School fled to Columbia University in New York City. Stunned by the support that the National Socialists obtained from the working class, the Frankfurt School philosophers theorized that fascism was actually the inevitable and final stage of modern civilization. Adorno and Horkheimer traced this trend all the way back to the Enlightenment, arguing that relentless pursuit of power through reason created a cycle of alienation and domination that climaxed in totalitarianism. This expansive critique covered Josef Stalin's Soviet Union as well, for it claimed that any industrial society was doomed to the same fate, regardless of its ideology. In fact, ideology was the tool that allowed these totalitarian societies to function. The Frankfurt School's mission, like that of Nietzsche's nihilists, was to tear off these cultural blindfolds and expose the reality of power relations within modern societies.

In France, philosophes combined the Frankfurt School's assertion that rationality destroyed freedom with the Nietzschean critique of bourgeois society. The result of this marriage of ideas was existentialism. French philosopher Jean-Paul Sartre (1905–1980) thus argued that true freedom was found by choosing one's own values, just like Nietzsche's prototypical post-nihilist was supposed to have done. The bourgeois vision of the world, he believed, was more than just cultural tyranny. It restricted freedom by imposing its false values onto the people. Early in his life, Sartre held that engaging with society destroyed freedom by turning humans from individuals into products of civilization. Sartre later pivoted, arguing that freedom could be found by complete immersion in the present (that is, in politics). To Sartre, engagement with communism, a cause that sought to change the status quo, was the way to reclaim his individualism. He reached this conclusion with the help of the French philosopher Maurice Merleau-Ponty (1908–1961).

Merleau-Ponty argued that even though the future is incomprehensible, humanity has to decide at certain times between radically different paths. He saw the Cold War as one of these moments, a coin toss between two visions of the future. Merleau-Ponty chose communism. To be sure, he saw both sides in the Cold War as violent, but preferred Stalin's Soviet Union, because "a regime which acknowledged its violence might have in it more genuine humanity."[9] Sartre adopted Merleau-Ponty's perspective but was driven much more by his fear of the United States than by his love of the Soviet Union. Sartre did not see communism as a path to class liberation but believed that combating the bourgeois ideology was more pressing than other considerations.

Sartre had two key intellectual heirs. One was Frantz Fanon (1925–1961), a Marxist theorist from Martinique who became obsessed with Sartre's conception of the liberating effects of violence. To Sartre, peacefulness was simply modern morality imposed upon the rest of the world. As such, violent acts were a form of resistance to bourgeois ideology. Fanon fused violence with decolonization, arguing that violent acts were key to revealing the true nature of Africans, a nature that European culture had previously suppressed. In his own words, "to shoot down a European is to kill two birds with one stone, to destroy an oppressor and the man he [the European] oppresses [i.e., the colonized mind of an African] at the same time."[10]

Sartre's other heir was the French philosopher Michel Foucault (1926–1984), who expanded Sartre's critique of bourgeois ideology even further. To Foucault, civilization was the systematic categorization and segregation of everything deemed irrational, imprisoning the human mind in a cage of reason—the same way that modern society confined social deviants in prisons. Every single aspect of modern culture—its patriarchal family, its penal system, and even its furniture—was based on domination. In spite of all that was apparently wrong with it, though, bourgeois capitalism was neither dead nor dying. Instead, it was being reinvigorated under the leadership of Margaret Thatcher (1925–2013) in the United Kingdom and the presidency of Ronald Reagan (1911–2004) in the United States. As such, Foucault broke with Sartre and concluded that engagement in politics (i.e., using reasoned arguments to convince the electorate to elect politicians willing and able to implement desired social and economic changes) was akin to finding comfort in the cage. With the collapse of communism, the critics of modernity retreated to European and American universities, where their ideas became institutionalized. Today, the likes of the American linguist Noam Chomsky and the American writer Jonathan Kozol continue to argue that modern society in general, and the United States in particular, are already totalitarian. Instead of murdering the citizenry outright, though, the bourgeoisie uses capitalism, government, and mass culture to pacify it.

While fascism and Marxism fell out of favor over the course of the 20th century, broadly socialist ideas continue to enjoy substantial though not majority support by the public, especially on the left of the political spectrum and among the younger generation. According to a 2019 Gallup poll, "39 percent of Americans said they . . . [had] a positive opinion of socialism, while 57 percent view[ed] it negatively."[11] A year later, Gallup found that "65 percent of Democrats . . . [said] they have a favorable view [of socialism, which is] contrasted sharply with 9 percent of Republicans and 41 percent of independents."[12] The same poll also found "that 49 percent of millennials and Gen Zers have a positive view of socialism, contrasted with 39 percent of Gen Xers and a still lower 32 percent of baby boomers and traditionalists (those aged 55 and older)."[13] In a similar vein, a 2016 YouGov poll found that 45 percent of Germans had a favorable view of socialism and 26 percent of Germans had a favorable view of capitalism. Conversely, 26 percent of Germans had an unfavorable view of socialism and 47 percent of Germans had an unfavorable view of capitalism. In Great Britain, 36 percent of respondents had a favorable view of socialism and 33 percent had a favorable view of capitalism. Conversely, 32 percent of Britons had an unfavorable view of socialism, while 39 percent of Britons had an unfavorable view of capitalism.[14]

■ Box 10.1. Television prices: something to look at (1997–2019)

In 1997, the Sharp and Sony corporations introduced their first 42-inch flat-screen televisions, which cost about $15,000 each.[a] That year, the U.S. blue-collar hourly compensation rate was about $18.12 per hour, indicating a time price (TP) of a large flat-screen TV of 828 hours. In 2019, a 43-inch liquid-crystal-display television (LCD-TV) set could be purchased at Walmart for $148.[b] With the U.S. blue-collar hourly compensation rate rising to about $32.36, the TP of an LCD-TV fell to 4.6 hours. The TP, in other words, fell by 99.45 percent, indicating a personal resource abundance multiplier of 181 at a compound annual growth rate of personal resource abundance of 26.7 percent. From the perspective of the U.S. blue-collar worker, in other words, the abundance of 42-inch LCD-TVs doubled every 2.9 years between 1997 and 2019 (see Table B10.1.1).

The hourly wage of U.S. unskilled workers increased from $7.49 to $13.66. As such, the TP of a 42-inch LCD-TV fell by 99.46 percent, indicating a 185 personal resource abundance multiplier, 26.8 percent compound annual growth rate in personal resource abundance, and a doubling of the abundance of LCD-TVs every 2.9 years. U.S. workers who moved from unskilled jobs to blue-collar employment saw their hourly compensation rate increase from $7.49 to $32.36. For U.S. upskilling workers, the TP of large flat-screen TVs fell by 99.8 percent, indicating a personal resource abundance multiplier of 438, suggesting a compound annual growth rate of 31.8 percent and a doubling of personal resource abundance every 2.5 years (see Table B10.1.2).

What about time equality? Between 1997 and 2019, the U.S. blue-collar worker saved 823 hours of work on the purchase of a 42-inch LCD-TV, while the U.S. unskilled worker saved 1,992 hours of work to buy that product. Instead of costing roughly one year of work for an unskilled worker, a 42-inch LCD-TV now costs just a little bit more than one day of work. For every 1 hour of work saved by blue-collar workers, unskilled workers saved 2.42 hours. Innovation, in other words, increased time equality (see Figure B10.1.1). Instead of measuring income inequality, we should measure time inequality. That will give us a better sense of the improvements in the standards of living.

Table B10.1.1. Personal resource abundance analysis of 42-inch LCD-TVs in the United States (1997–2019)

Flat-screen TV	1997	2019	Percentage change 1997–2019	Personal resource abundance multiplier 1997 = 1	Percentage change in personal resource abundance 1997–2019	Compound annual percentage growth rate in personal resource abundance	Years to double personal resource abundance
Nominal price	$15,000	$148	−99.0				
Blue-collar	$18.12	$32.36	78.6				
Time price	828	4.6	−99.45	181.00	18,000	26.7	2.9
Unskilled	$7.49	$13.66	82.4				
Time price	2,003	10.8	−99.46	184.84	18,384	26.8	2.9
Upskilling	$7.49	$32.36	332.0				
Time price	2,003	4.6	−99.8	437.88	43,688	31.8	2.5

Source: Authors' calculations.

Note: LCD-TV = liquid-crystal-display television.

Table B10.1.2. Personal resource abundance analysis of 42-inch LCD-TVs in the United States: summary of the U.S. unskilled worker perspective, the U.S. blue-collar worker perspective, and the U.S. upskilling worker perspective (1997–2019)

Large flat-screen TVs 1997–2019	Percentage change in resource time price	Personal resource abundance multiplier	Percentage change in personal resource abundance	Compound annual percentage growth rate in personal resource abundance	Years to double personal resource abundance
Blue-collar	−99.4	181.00	18,000	26.65	2.9
Unskilled	−99.5	184.84	18,384	26.78	2.9
Upskilling	−99.8	437.88	43,688	31.84	2.5

Source: Authors' calculations.

Figure B10.1.1. Time prices of 42-inch LCD TVs in the United States: unskilled worker perspective and blue-collar worker perspective (1997–2019)

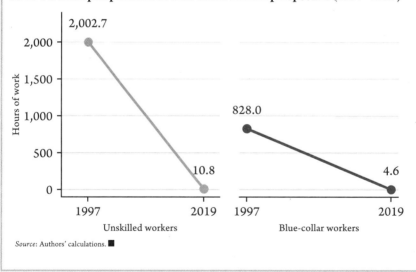

Source: Authors' calculations. ∎

. . . were soon joined by another, related idea, that of radical environmentalism . . .

Environmentalism, the most recent theory of decline, has substantially replaced the discredited notions of racism, national socialism, and communism, but is also rooted in Romanticism. The scholars of the Enlightenment thought that reason could coexist in harmony with nature. As the Romantics saw it, the human tendency to use reason to dominate the natural world would bring about humanity's downfall. The machine embodied the division between the two schools of thought. To many of the 18th and 19th century thinkers whom we met in Chapter 1, the machine was a harbinger of progress. To the Romantics, it meant the coming of an apocalypse.

The English poet William Blake (1757–1827), for example, lamented how the pastoral landscapes of Britain were now pockmarked with "dark, Satanic mills."[15] He described London, the peak of modern development, as full of "marks of weariness" and "marks of woe."[16] Worse, the hard-working bourgeoisie that pushed society forward was becoming spiritless, empty, and philistine in its pursuit of profit. The overly specialized industrial economy created so much easy wealth and luxury that materialism became inescapable. In the future, the spirit would wither, and society would fall into the trap of stagnation that characterized, in the European view, the Eastern civilizations at the turn of the 19th century.

The writings of H. G. Wells (1866–1946) show the Englishman's concern over both machines and spiritual degradation. In his 1895 science-fiction novella, *The Time Machine*, Wells described how almost 1 million years in the future, industrial society had split humanity into two degenerate races: brute cave-dwelling Morlocks (i.e., the workers) and banal and weak Eloi (i.e., the upper classes). In another one of his novels, *The War of the Worlds* (1898), he described Martians taking over Earth with advanced machines only to be struck down by natural pathogens. To Wells, technology was not only at war with nature: it was, above all, a war that technology could not win.

The word "ecology" was actually coined by a German biologist, Ernst Haeckel (1834–1919), "who applied the term *Ökologie* to the 'relation of the animal both to its organic as well as its inorganic environment.'"[17] Haeckel's *Ökologie* was central to his philosophy of monism, which dictated that the universe was one united, dynamic, and purposeless process. Haeckel wanted monism to replace Christianity in Germany. He thought that his philosophy would help to spread communitarian values and end the biological hierarchy that is present in Abrahamic religions and that gives humanity a privileged status over other creatures.

While Haeckel never accomplished his goal of replacing Christianity, his monism was very popular in fin de siècle Germany, a country that was obsessed with the Romantic view of nature and deeply ambivalent about commerce, urbanization, and industrialization. The German Youth Movement, for example, started in 1896. It consisted of a number of organizations devoted to outdoor activities. The movement grew immensely popular, with some 8 million German children affiliated with it in one form or another by 1938. It was for the German Youth Movement that the German philosopher Ludwig Klages (1872–1956) wrote his 1913 essay "Man and Earth." He wrote,

> Today we see ever-increasing hordes huddled together in our big cities, where they grow accustomed to the soot belching from the chimneys and the thunderous turmoil of the streets, where the nights are as bright as the days. These urban masses believe that they have had an adequate introduction to the world of nature as soon as they've caught a glimpse of a potato-field, or seen a single starling perched upon a branch of an emaciated roadside tree. But, to anyone who recalls the sounds and scents of the German landscape of seventy years ago, from out of the words and images in which these memories are embodied[,] a wind would arise to pronounce a warning reproach to the lost souls of today as soon they begin to regurgitate their weather-proof platitudes about "economic development," "necessities," and "culture." ... An unparalleled orgy of destruction has seized mankind, and it is "civilization" that has unleashed this lust for murder, so that the earth withers before its noxious breath. These are indeed the fruits of "progress"![18]

German Romanticism aligned with *völkisch* nationalism and was eventually co-opted by the National Socialists. The German philosopher and National Socialist Martin Heidegger (1889–1976) distilled the ideas of

German Romanticism into a comprehensive critique of Western life. To that end, he identified two nature-destroying forces. First came technology, which gave humanity the ability to dominate nature. Second came capitalism, which destroyed any connection between nature and the product of work (or economic output).

According to some advocates of the National Socialist worldview, the Aryan, with his connection to blood and soil, was the perfect man to re-unite humanity with nature. Organic farming was encouraged by members of the Nazi state machinery such as Minister of Agriculture Richard W. Darré (1895–1953), for it harmonized the relationship between humans and the land.[19] Even the Reichsführer of the Schutzstaffel Heinrich Himmler (1900–1945) taught his SS recruits to respect animal life and banned vivisections under the Nazi regime. (Himmler was much less squeamish about the value of human life and the inhumane medical experiments on prisoners of the regime he served and its genocidal goals.)

In the United States, environmentalism took longer to emerge. According to the *Journal of the U.S. Environmental Protection Agency*, "many environmental ideas [in America] first crystallized in 1962. That year saw the publication of Rachel Carson's *Silent Spring*, first in serial form in the *New Yorker* and then as a Houghton Mifflin best seller." In her book, Carson (1907–1964) attacked the "indiscriminate use of pesticides . . . causing a revolution in public opinion."[20] Within a year, the U.S. Congress passed the 1963 Clean Air Act, giving the U.S. federal government more power to regulate the environment.[21]

Five years later, as we explained at length in Chapter 3, Paul Ehrlich's book *The Population Bomb* caused a sensation of similar proportions. The book, which sold millions of copies and was translated into many languages, warned of the coming depletion of natural resources and put Malthusianism firmly back on the intellectual agenda.

The speed and extent of environmentalist triumphs in the United States are noteworthy. The year 1970 kicked off with the celebration of the first Earth Day, on April 22. As Ronald Bailey remembers,

> About 20 million Americans turned out for the first Earth Day on April 22, 1970. Lectures and rallies took place at more than 2,000

college campuses, 10,000 elementary and high schools, and thousands of other places across the country. Forty-two states adopted resolutions endorsing Earth Day, and Congress recessed so that legislators could participate in the activities in their districts. It is sometimes described as, up to that time, the largest public demonstration in history.[22]

In September of that same year, the U.S. Congress beefed up the 1963 Clean Air Act. By December, President Richard M. Nixon helped create the Environmental Protection Agency. Private environmental organizations also flourished, along with more militant groups like Greenpeace (which was established in 1971). Over 2,000 communes sprung up across the nation, striving to create real, ecologically balanced microsocieties. To get a sense of the intellectual atmosphere at that time, consider a small sample of pronouncements "from authority" carried by the press.

- In a speech at the University of Rhode Island on November 16, 1970, Harvard University biology professor and Nobel laureate George Wald predicted, "Civilization will end within 15 or 30 years unless immediate action is taken against problems facing mankind."[23]
- In a June 1970 issue of *Field & Stream* magazine, Washington University biologist Barry Commoner wrote, "We are in an environmental crisis which threatens the survival of this nation and of the world as a suitable place of human habitation."[24]
- On April 23, 1970, a *New York Times* editorial titled "The Good Earth" noted that "man must stop pollution and conserve his resources, not merely to enhance existence but to save the race from intolerable deterioration and possible extinction."[25]
- In an April 1970 interview with *Mademoiselle* magazine, Paul Ehrlich claimed, "Population will inevitably and completely outstrip whatever small increases in food supplies we make. The death rate will increase until at least 100–200 million people per year will be starving to death during the next ten years."[26]
- In a 1969 essay titled "Eco-Catastrophe!," Ehrlich asserted, "Most of the people who are going to die in the greatest cataclysm in the

history of man have already been born. . . . [By 1975,] some experts feel that food shortages will have escalated the present level of world hunger and starvation into famines of unbelievable proportions. Other experts, more optimistic, think the ultimate food-population collision will not occur until the decade of the 1980s."[27]

- In the Spring 1970 issue of *The Living Wilderness*, environmental advocate Denis Hayes mourned, "It is already too late to avoid mass starvation."[28]

- In the same issue, Peter Gunter, a professor at North Texas State University, declared, "Demographers agree almost unanimously on the following grim timetable: by 1975 widespread famines will begin in India; these will spread by 1990 to include all of India, Pakistan, China and the Near East, Africa. By the year 2000, or conceivably sooner, South and Central America will exist under famine conditions. . . . By the year 2000, thirty years from now, the entire world, with the exception of Western Europe, North America, and Australia, will be in famine."[29]

- In a January 1970 issue of *Life* magazine, an article titled "Ecology: A Cause Becomes a New Mass Movement" proclaimed, "In a decade, urban dwellers will have to wear gas masks to survive air pollution. . . . By 1985 air pollution will have reduced the amount of sunlight reaching earth by one half."[30]

- In the February 1970 issue of *Time* magazine, ecologist Kenneth Watt lamented, "At the present rate of nitrogen buildup, it's only a matter of time before light will be filtered out of the atmosphere and none of our land will be usable."[31]

- In the same issue, Watt forecasted, "By the year 2000, if present trends continue, we will be using up crude oil at such a rate . . . that there won't be any more crude oil. You'll drive up to the pump and say, 'Fill 'er up, buddy,' and he'll say, 'I am very sorry, there isn't any.'"[32]

- A *Newsweek* article published on January 26, 1970, speculated, "[One] theory assumes that the earth's cloud cover will continue to thicken as more dust, fumes, and water vapor are belched into the atmosphere by industrial smokestacks and jet planes. Screened from the sun's heat, the planet will cool, the water vapor will fall and freeze, and a new Ice Age will be born."[33]

- In a speech at Swarthmore College on April 19, 1970, Watt concluded, "The world has been chilling sharply for about twenty years. If present trends continue, the world will be about four degrees colder for the global mean temperature in 1990, but eleven degrees colder in the year 2000. This is about twice what it would take to put us into an ice age."[34]

As the 1970s rolled on, American environmentalism became increasingly anti-capitalist. Arthur Herman avers that it was the American writer Charles A. Reich (1928–2019) who brought the German ideas to America with his book *The Greening of America* (1970) and notes that "modern ecology [in the United States] . . . replayed the same enthusiasms that had animated every modern cultural regeneration movement since the German Romantics."[35] Reich's book was a bestseller both in 1970 and 1971, topping the *New York Times* bestseller list on December 27, 1970. According to Reich,

> Work and living have become more and more pointless and empty. There is no lack of meaningful projects that cry out to be done, but our working days are used up in work that lacks meaning: making useless or harmful products, or servicing the bureaucratic structures. For most Americans, work is mindless, exhausting, boring, servile and hateful, something to be endured while "life" is confined to "time off." At the same time our culture has been reduced to the grossly commercial; all cultural values are for sale, and those that fail to make a profit are not preserved. Our life activities have become artificial, vicarious and false to our genuine needs, activities fabricated by others and forced upon us.[36]

That is exactly the Marxist critique of capitalism as "alienation" of labor. Instead of acknowledging that fact, however, Reich veers straight into environmentalism. Yet, like a typical Marxist, he even predicts revolutionary turmoil. "There is a revolution coming," Reich prophesied, and its "ultimate creation will be a new and enduring wholeness and beauty—a renewed relationship of man to himself, to other men, to society, to nature, and to the land."[37]

Other voices critical of capitalism's effect on the environment soon emerged. They included the American biologist Barry Commoner (1917–2012), who argued that modern society was unsustainable. Unlike Ehrlich, who focused on overpopulation, Commoner focused on capitalist production techniques (pollution-causing detergents and synthetic textiles, for instance) and advocated in favor of "eco-socialism." In 1972, the British economist Barbara Ward (1914–1981) and the French American microbiologist René Dubos (1901–1982) warned that the exponential economic growth of industrial society threatened the survival of the entire planet. For these environmentalists, wealth generation was no longer capitalism's saving grace. It was a problem that needed to be tackled.

By the 1980s, environmental demands had become more radical. The Norwegian philosopher Arne Naess (1912–2009), for example, thought that reforming industrial society was not enough. Instead, he called for a change of the culture that allowed any amount of ecological destruction to exist at all. Like Haeckel's monism, Naess's philosophy of "deep ecology" concluded that the problem with modernity was that it placed humans above other lifeforms, creating an inflated ego that enables our species to destroy nature.

In 1986, the American social theorist Murray Bookchin (1921–2007) published *The Modern Crisis*, in which he called for the replacement of environmentally destructive capitalism. Embracing deep ecology, Bookchin's utopia was radically egalitarian, with men, women, plants, and animals living on equal terms, and promoting each other's well-being. As he saw it, such utopia had existed for thousands of years in the form of primitive societies. Bookchin's ideas amounted to a total inversion of human progress. Civilization, he averred, was just domination over nature, wrenching away the last remnants of a paradise that still existed among the aborigines of Africa and South America.

In his 1991 book *In the Absence of the Sacred*, American activist and author Jerry Mander likewise claimed that primitive societies are based on a rejection of modernity, not ignorance of it. In Mander's view, the subsistence lifestyle is a conscious cultural choice to avoid civilization. To this day, deep ecologists view primitive societies as not only ecologically harmonious but free of the cultural desire to exploit nature.

In 1992, U.S. vice president Al Gore published his book *Earth in the Balance*. Gore's critique of modern society is a fusion of old ideas: modern society is ecologically destructive, materialist, shallow, and shields us from authentic experiences. The culprit, however, is new. This time, the fault is with human nature itself. In Gore's vision, culture at its most basic level represents control over nature. Stone tools and cave paintings are just rudimentary attempts to impose artificial order on the organic world. The West, capitalism, technology, and even sexism and racism, are extensions of the innate human desire to dominate.

Some ecologists began to salivate at the thought of the end of the world. Writers like American author Edward Abbey (1927–1989), and even U.S. domestic terrorists like the "Unabomber" Ted Kaczynski, dreamed of dams bursting and cities crumbling, forcing the last remnants of humanity to return to a primitive lifestyle. The French explorer Jacques-Yves Cousteau (1910–1997) called the idea of getting rid of suffering and disease "not altogether a beneficial one" and urged that "we must eliminate 350,000 people per day."[38]

American environmentalist Christopher Manes called HIV/AIDS "the necessary solution" to environmental degradation.[39] Paraphrasing Voltaire, he said that "if the AIDS epidemic didn't exist, radical environmentalists would have to invent one."[40] Finally, Richard Preston from the *New York Times* wondered in his 1994 bestseller, *The Hot Zone: A Terrifying True Story*, whether extremely deadly viruses such as Ebola and Marburg may be the biosphere's reaction against "the human parasite" and the "cancerous rotouts" of advanced industrial societies.[41]

. . . which is increasingly influenced by anti-humanism . . .

As we write these words, it is clear that anti-humanism has become firmly established within some parts of the environmentalist movement. In May 2019, for example, a CNN report on the newly released report of the

United Nations' Intergovernmental Science Policy Platform on Biodiversity and Ecosystem Services asserted that "we must act now; consuming less; polluting less; having fewer children"[42] to prevent an environmental catastrophe. To emphasize the supposed link between population growth and a coming planetary disaster, CNN interviewed none other than Paul Ehrlich, who noted that

> for a species that names itself *Homo sapiens*, the wise man, we are being incredibly stupid. The other organisms on our planet are our life support systems. You don't have to worry about them if you don't care about eating, if you don't care about breathing, if you don't care about having freshwater and so on, then you can just forget about it and die. I am very, very optimistic about what we could do in theory. I am very pessimistic about what we will do [in practice].[43]

In a February 2019 question-and-answer session that was livestreamed on Instagram, Congresswoman Alexandria Ocasio-Cortez, a rising star of the U.S. Democratic Party, told her viewers that unless humanity takes urgent action on carbon dioxide (CO_2) emissions, there is no hope for the future. "It is basically a scientific consensus that the lives of our children are going to be very difficult, and it does lead young people to have a legitimate question: is it OK to still have children?"[44]

Likewise, Bill Maher opined in April 2019 that

> the great under-discussed factor in the climate crisis is there are just too many of us and we use too much shit. Climate deniers like to say, "There's no population problem, just look out the window of an airplane. So much open space down there." But it's not about space, it's about resources. Humans are already using 1.7 times the resources the planet can support. . . . We don't need smaller carbon footprints [sic], we need less [sic] feet. . . . It's no wonder millennials are freaking out about having kids. They and Generation-Z are waking up en masse to the idea that way too early in their lifetimes the planet is going to be a shit show. . . . Everyone talks about falling

birth rates like it means something is desperately wrong with the country. They're depressed! They're not f*&#@ng enough! Whatever problems are caused by falling birth rates aren't nearly as dire as those brought on by overpopulation. In 1900, there were less than two billion people on Earth, now it's approaching eight. We can't just keep on like this. The world is just too crowded. When was the last time you sat comfortably on an airplane? Wouldn't it be nicer to just have fewer people around? The best thing you can do for the earth is to not have kids, die, and stay dead.[45]

The logical continuation of the Malthusian concern with population growth, as Chelsea Follett noted, is the Voluntary Human Extinction Movement (Vhemt).[46] According to its American founder Les Knight, Vhemt (pronounced "vehement") is gaining traction among the young. "In the last year," Knight told the British newspaper the *Daily Mail* in January 2019, "I've seen more and more articles about people choosing to remain child-free or to not add more to their existing family than ever. I've been collecting these stories and last year was just a groundswell of articles, and, in addition, there have been articles about human extinction."[47]

He is right. Recent articles embracing the benefits of human extinction include the *New Yorker*'s "The Case for Not Being Born," NBC News's "Science Proves Kids Are Bad for Earth. Morality Suggests We Stop Having Them," and the *New York Times* polemic "Would Human Extinction Be a Tragedy?" The last piece muses that "our species possesses inherent value, but we are devastating the earth and causing unimaginable animal suffering.... It may well be, then, that the extinction of humanity would make the world better off."[48] In a similar vein, the American business magazine *FastCompany* released a disturbing video titled "Why Having Kids Is the Worst Thing You Can Do for the Planet" in April 2019.[49]

In November 2019, the British daily newspaper *The Guardian* ran an article titled "I Wish I'd Never Been Born: The Rise of the Anti-Natalists." In the article, the author, Rebecca Tuhus-Dubrow, introduced anti-natalism with a story about an Indian man who, as a symbolic gesture, decided to sue his parents on the grounds that they should not have begotten him without his consent. The lawsuit's intent was to set an ethical precedent, according to which the net effect of bringing life into the world is, by definition, negative, thus rendering all procreation objectively immoral.

As the author explained, "[the] basic tenet of anti-natalism is . . . that life, even under the best of circumstances . . . [is] a harm and an imposition." Anti-natalism hinges on the idea that every human life involves some amount of suffering, that suffering cannot be offset by happiness, and that reducing suffering regardless of happiness is the key moral imperative of society. It logically follows that the goal of eliminating suffering altogether requires the complete extinction of human beings.

Tuhus-Dubrow credits South African philosopher David Benatar with introducing the term "anti-natalism" and taking leadership of the modern anti-natalist movement. Benatar has attracted followers such as Dallas-based YouTuber Dana Wells, who also goes by the title "The Friendly Antinatalist" online. Wells felt "annoyed" when questioned about why she didn't have children and discovered anti-natalism while seeking like-minded people who could empathize with her. Wells now uses her platform to spread the anti-natalist message, encourage the philosophy's adherents, and "address tensions among true anti-natalists."

As with any philosophy, the definition of "true" anti-natalism is a contentious subject. One group of anti-natalists are "the childfree." These people don't want children themselves, but they do not consider all procreation to be unethical. Another group consists of "denatalists." These people disapprove of procreation only under certain conditions. Wells does not consider the two aforementioned groups to be "true" anti-natalists. "Real anti-natalism," Wells avers, "means opposing all births, under all circumstances."

True anti-natalists, though united by the common overarching goal of human extinction, are split into two camps: those who prioritize human extinction and those who advocate the extinction of all sentient life. Wells and Benatar fall into the latter category, which, understandably, is largely composed of vegans.

Tuhus-Dubrow then explores the relationship between anti-natalists and climate activists, finding that the two groups' adherents often have similar concerns, practical lifestyles, and perspectives on the state of the world.

These similarities are most intriguing when they coincide with the often-radical differences between each group's ultimate goals. Climate activists may fear having children for two main reasons. First, some activists are pessimistic enough to believe that the ecological state of the world today—and especially of tomorrow—is so bad that "inflicting" it on a child would be unjust. Second, many climate activists believe that each new life brought into the world will consume an unjust amount of scarce resources, generate emissions, and ultimately endanger the planet and fellow humans.

While climate activists and true anti-natalists may both consider procreation immoral, they often have remarkably different reasons for thinking so. "Ultimately," as Tuhus-Dubrow explains, "the goals of the two camps diverge sharply." No matter how strongly climate activists oppose procreation, most of them do so because they fear human extinction and believe that suffering is a mere obstacle to happiness. By contrast, for "true" anti-natalists, "extinction is the dream."

While Tuhus-Dubrow acknowledges that there is increasing opposition to procreation globally, she notes that this opposition is "mostly in the context of the climate crisis." It is interesting to note that anti-natalism owes part of its recent growth to its proximity to this supposed crisis, but in David Benatar's own words, "It's not clear . . . that the world is getting worse."

True anti-natalists, Tuhus-Dubrow concludes, may offer a useful perspective on the "general pessimism" that has allowed both movements to rise. True anti-natalists are more likely to acknowledge the improving state of the world because their core belief is that the world can never improve enough to morally justify procreation anyway. True anti-natalists, then, "can help us appreciate that uncertainty and pain are an inherent part of a sentient existence—even if we disagree with them about whether the bargain is worth it."[50]

Most anti-natalists are content with voluntary reduction of birth rates. Others hope to achieve that goal through government enforcement. Prominent environmentalists, including Johns Hopkins University bioethicist Travis Rieder and science popularizer Bill Nye, have advocated in favor of special taxes or other state-imposed penalties on those with "too many children."[51]

Bowdoin College philosopher Sarah Conly's 2015 book, *One Child: Do We Have a Right to More?*, noted that "we live in a world where a burgeoning global population has started to have a major and destructive environmental impact. The results, including climate change and the struggle for limited resources, appear to be inevitable aspects of a difficult future." She acknowledged that "many view procreation as an essential component of the right to personal happiness and autonomy" and noted "the dominant view . . . that the government does not have the right to impose these restrictions on its own citizens, for the sake of future people who have yet to exist."

Conly ultimately decided that "not only is it wrong to have more than one child in the face of such [environmental] concerns, we do not even retain the right to do so." Personal "autonomy and personal rights are not unlimited, especially if one's body may cause harm to anyone, and that the government has a moral obligation to protect both current and future citizens," she concluded.[52]

In Chapter 1, we noted Wojcik's observation that "there is an inherent romance to the apocalypse, which gives the disillusioned something to look forward to—even if they do expect to die." Follett found that, true to form, many "anti-natalists believe that a world without humans, or with significantly fewer of them, would eventually revert to a pollution-free paradise with abundant natural resources. As one human extinction proponent put it in January 2020 in a letter to his local paper, 'In approximately 20,000 years after human extinction, this magnificent resistant biosphere will return to its perfection.'"[53]

As COVID-19 spread around the world in early 2020, some environmental extremists rejoiced at the growing death toll. Stanford University environmental science graduate student Sierra Garcia has compiled some horrifying instances of such rejoicing. One archetypal example is a tweet with about 300,000 likes proclaiming, "Wow. . . . Earth is recovering. . . . Coronavirus is Earth's vaccine. We're the virus."[54]

Unfortunately, such attitudes can be found also among prominent individuals. A Quebec politician and radio talk-show host, Luc Ferrandez, praised the virus for reducing Wuhan's carbon footprint.[55] The *New York Times* has noted that an upside of social distancing efforts is that they may help fight climate change, and CNN ran the headline, "There's an Unlikely Beneficiary of Coronavirus: The Planet."[56]

The BBC's environmental correspondent has gleefully reported that air pollution and CO_2 emissions have been falling rapidly as the virus has spread.[57] Some environmentalists, pleased that the COVID-19 pandemic and the concomitant economic crisis slashed the CO_2 emissions, worried that once things get better, post-recession economies will see a surge in harmful emissions.[58]

The most extreme adherents of anti-humanism are people who do not rely on persuasion or government action, but instead take matters into their own hands and start to cull the members of the human race at least in part for the sake of the planet's environment.

Just minutes before shooting 22 people in an El Paso Walmart on August 3, 2019, the shooter, Patrick Crusius, released a manifesto titled "The Inconvenient Truth," a reference to the former U.S. vice president Al Gore's 2006 climate change documentary.

"Our lifestyle is destroying the environment of our country," he wrote. "But god damn most of y'all are just too stubborn to change your lifestyle. So the next logical step is to decrease the number of people in America using resources. If we can get rid of enough people, then our way of life can become more sustainable."[59]

The people in the United States that Crusius wanted to kill were Hispanics, a group that Crusius believed would give the U.S. Democratic Party a permanent electoral advantage. In return for the Hispanic support, Crusius reasoned, the Democrats will keep the borders open, thus leading to further immigration. Crusius was clearly a white supremacist, but he partly justified his murderousness with Malthusian ideas.

He was not the first shooter to do so. In the opening statement of his manifesto, Crusius declared that he was inspired by Brenton Tarrant, an Australian man who killed 51 people at two mosques in New Zealand on March 15, 2019.

Tarrant's manifesto, titled "The Great Replacement," is similar to Crusius's, although the former targeted Muslims in New Zealand rather than Hispanics in the United States. In one section of his manifesto, Tarrant blamed climate change on higher birth rates in predominantly nonwhite countries, stating that "the invaders are the ones overpopulating the world. Kill the invaders, kill the overpopulation, and by doing so save the environment."[60]

Later, he wrote that "there is no Green future with never ending population growth, the ideal green world cannot exist in a world of 100 billion, 50 billion, or even 10 billion people. Continued immigration into Europe is environmental warfare and ultimately destructive to nature itself."[61]

Tarrant himself seems to have been inspired by Anders Behring Breivik, a right-wing extremist who killed 77 people in a bombing and shooting spree on the Norwegian island of Utøya on July 22, 2011. Breivik too had a manifesto, a rambling 1,500-page compendium that at one point called for a global population cap of 2.5 billion people to avoid environmental destruction.[62]

Crusius, Tarrant, and Breivik represent a global mass killer phenomenon inspired by a new ideology dubbed eco-fascism. Broadly speaking, eco-fascists combine white nationalism with environmentalist extremism, thus giving a new meaning to the concept of "blood and soil."

Malthusian killers, though, are not limited to the far right. Beginning in the late 1970s, militant Luddite Ted Kaczynski, popularly known as the "Unabomber," sent bombs to prominent figures in academia and industry with the objective of toppling industrial society itself and returning humanity to a foraging existence.

Kaczynski's manifesto focused on the effects of modern life on human culture and psychology, rather than the environment. He acknowledged that focus in his introduction, stating that "for practical reasons we have to confine our discussion to areas that have received insufficient public attention. . . . Since there are well-developed environmental and wilderness movements, we have written very little about environmental degradation or the destruction of wild nature, even though we consider these to be highly important."[63]

Still, when he did mention the environment, he lamented the loss of Malthusian checks on population growth. "One of the effects of the intrusion of industrial society has been that . . . controls on population have been thrown out of balance. Hence the population explosion, with all that that implies," he wrote. "No one knows what will happen as a result of ozone depletion, the greenhouse effect and other environmental problems that cannot yet be foreseen."[64]

The motives of Connor Betts, who police say shot and killed 10 people in Dayton, Ohio, on August 4, 2019, are more enigmatic. Betts was shot dead by police at the scene of the massacre, and no manifesto has yet been discovered. He did leave tweets and scattered anecdotes that somewhat illuminate his thinking. Betts's Twitter account was staunchly leftist.

After the Parkland school shooting on February 14, 2018, Betts condemned gun violence, writing on Republican U.S. senator Rob Portman's

Twitter feed, "How much did they pay you to look the other way? 17 kids are dead. If not now, when?"[65] He also endorsed militant socialism and anti-fascism with tweets like "I want socialism, and I'll not wait for the idiots to finally come round understanding," and "Kill every fascist."[66]

Betts was also clearly pro-immigration, using Alexandria Ocasio-Cortez's rhetoric (she compared U.S. immigrant holding facilities to World War II concentration camps) and tweeting out, "Cut the fences down. Slice ICE tires. Throw bolt cutters over the fences."[67]

Yet Betts appears to have shared some environmental concerns. He retweeted a statement from a Twitter user called "@fingerblaster," who argued that "if we don't have a right to a life-sustaining climate, we could probably argue that murder is also legal."[68] He also shared a tweet from "@AliceAvizandum," who advocated "behead[ing] all oil executives with katanas" as a solution to climate change. Another retweet was from "@fazolisfacts," who depicted Smokey Bear wearing a red bandana emblazoned with the hammer and sickle and holding a sign reading "Remember! The planet isn't dying, it's being killed."[69]

These are worrying trends, but it would be wrong to conclude this section by implying that all environmentally conscious individuals are comfortable with the anti-humanist and anti-natalist extremists who dominate the head-lines. After all, the authors of this book consider themselves environmentally conscious individuals. In our book, in fact, we are happy to draw on the wisdom of such "eco-modernists" and "eco-pragmatists" as Michael Schellen-berger, whom we shall meet later in this chapter, and Jesse Ausubel, whom we met in Chapter 1. Whether these scholars' emphases on a compromise between the well-being of the human race and good stewardship of the environment gain the traction that they deserve is, alas, an open question.

. . . and marked by the rise of eco-anxiety

While eco-anxiety is not listed in the U.S. Diagnostic and Statistical Manual of Mental Disorders, "mental health professionals do use the term eco-anxiety within the field of eco-psychology, a branch that deals with people's psychological relationships with the rest of nature and how this impacts their identity, well-being, and health."[70] In fact, the American Psychiatric Association described eco-anxiety as "a chronic fear of environmental doom" in

2017 and noted that climate change's effect on mental health can manifest as "trauma and shock, post-traumatic stress disorder, anxiety, depression, substance abuse, aggression, reduced feelings of autonomy and control, feelings of helplessness, fatalism, and fear."[71]

A growing body of evidence suggests that environmental concerns are contributing to increased levels of anxiety around the world. In 2021, for example, researchers at the University of Bath polled 10,000 young people between the ages of 16 and 25 in Australia, Brazil, Finland, France, Great Britain, India, Nigeria, the Philippines, Portugal, and the United States. This study is the latest and most comprehensive survey of young people's perception of the environmental state of the planet. The researchers found that, on average, 83 percent of respondents thought that "people have failed to care for the planet." Seventy-five percent thought that the "future is frightening." Fifty-six percent thought that "humanity is doomed." Fifty-five percent thought that they will have "less opportunity than [their] parents." Finally, 39 percent stated that they were "hesitant to have children."[72]

Some of the results were strikingly similar. For example, 78 percent of Americans and 76 percent of Nigerians felt that "people have failed to care for the planet." Seventy-eight percent of Americans and 70 percent of Nigerians felt that the "future is frightening." Forty-six percent of Americans and 42 percent of Nigerians felt that "humanity is doomed." Forty-four percent of Americans and 49 percent of Nigerians felt that they will have "less opportunity than [their] parents." Finally, 36 percent of American respondents and 23 percent of Nigerian respondents (but 41 percent of Indian respondents) stated that they were "hesitant to have children."

On the one hand, the universality of doom and gloom about the state of the planet may seem somewhat surprising, given that people living in richer countries tend to enjoy a much better quality of the environment than people living in poorer countries. To give just one example, the Environmental Performance Index, which was developed by Yale University and Columbia University and which quantifies the environmental performance of national policies, is regularly topped by the richest nations on Earth. In 2018, the top 10 countries were (in descending order) Switzerland, France, Denmark, Malta, Sweden, the United Kingdom, Luxembourg, Austria, Ireland, and Finland. The bottom 10 were (in descending order) the Central African

Republic, Niger, Lesotho, Haiti, Madagascar, Nepal, India, the Democratic Republic of the Congo, Bangladesh, and Burundi.[73]

On the other hand, all humans suffer from a number of negativity biases, which we discussed in Chapter 1. These biases tend to make us underestimate or filter out that which is good, while focusing a disproportionate amount of our attention on that which is bad. The universality of these psychological traits may help to explain why respondents who enjoy a much better quality of the environment perceive the state of the planet in ways that are fairly similar to respondents suffering from a much worse quality of the environment. Unfortunately, our negativity biases also make us underappreciate or ignore the real progress that humans have made in tackling environmental problems in the past. Furthermore, they militate against an attitude of rational optimism about our ability to solve environmental problems in the future. It is in this context that the role of improving standards of living cannot be overemphasized.

Economists have long suspected that there is a link between increasing prosperity and heightened concerns for the environment. According to the environmental Kuznets curve (EKC), a hypothesis with a large following in the field of economics, the environment worsens in tandem with economic growth until a certain income per person is reached. At that point, resources start flowing toward environmental protection, and the ecosystem is restored.[74]

As such, a 2006 paper found that "among 50 nations with extensive forests reported in the Food and Agriculture Organization's comprehensive Global Forest Resources Assessment 2005, no nation where annual per person gross domestic product exceeded $4,600 had a negative rate of growing stock change."[75] Put differently, societies with per capita incomes above $6,200 (in 2019 dollars) either stopped deforestation or experienced afforestation (a development of new forests). Similar EKC effects have been observed with regard to water and air pollution, as well as emissions of sulfur dioxide, nitrogen oxide, lead, chlorofluorocarbons, sewage, and other environmental hazards.

Conversely, a dramatic drop in the standards of living can have serious repercussions for the environment. Following the collapse of the Zimbabwean economy in the early 2000s, for example, people started killing the previously protected wildlife to feed their families.[76] Similarly, following the collapse of the Venezuelan economy in the mid-2010s, desperate Venezuelans killed and ate animals from the zoo in the nation's capital of Caracas.[77]

Part of the answer to tackling the problem of global eco-anxiety, therefore, must surely rest in the one thing that many extreme environmentalists are adamantly opposed to: rapid and sustained economic development in poor countries.

Is environmentalism becoming a secular religion?

Michael Shellenberger is an American environmentalist who won *Time* magazine's Hero of the Environment award in 2008 and founded a California-based think tank called Environmental Progress. "At 17," Shellenberger wrote, "I lived in Nicaragua to show solidarity with the Sandinista socialist revolution. At 23 I raised money for Guatemalan women's cooperatives. In my early 20s I lived in the semi-Amazon doing research with small farmers fighting land invasions. At 26 I helped expose poor conditions at Nike factories in Asia. I became an environmentalist at 16 when I threw a fundraiser for Rainforest Action Network. At 27 I helped save the last unprotected ancient redwoods in California. In my 30s I advocated renewables and successfully helped persuade the Obama administration to invest $90 billion into them."[78]

For many years, Shellenberger observed environmentalist rhetoric grow increasingly apocalyptic. "But then last year [2019], things spiraled out of control," he wrote in a 2020 article. "Alexandria Ocasio-Cortez said 'The world is going to end in 12 years if we don't address climate change.' Britain's most high-profile environmental group claimed 'Climate Change Kills Children.' The world's most influential green journalist, Bill McKibben, called climate change the 'greatest challenge humans have ever faced' and said it would 'wipe out civilizations.'"[79] And so, Shellenberger decided to write a book, analyzing the environmentalist obsession with the apocalypse.

In *Apocalypse Never: Why Environmental Alarmism Hurts Us All*, Shellenberger noted that nature is imbued with mysticism that can produce intense artistic and spiritual inspirations, but it can also make nature difficult to consider rationally. Shellenberger brings up the appeal-to-nature fallacy as an example. A person who appeals to nature argues that natural things, say compost, are better than artificial things, say synthetic fertilizer, just because they are natural. Of course, artificial things are as much a part of nature as anything else, and most people would consider "natural" things like cancer and earthquakes to be pretty bad. The appeal-to-nature is obviously irrational, but it still pervades discourse around the environment. Genetically modified crops have the potential to return acres of farmland to wild animals, for example, but they are often criticized as being unnatural and therefore unhealthy for humans and the environment.[80]

Another common myth about nature is that it is a self-regulating, harmonious whole with a natural equilibrium that humans are destroying. When Earth's history is considered, though, it is clear that there is no ideal balance for humans to upset. Nature is in fact constantly changing, and the Carboniferous period was no "better" or "worse" than the Jurassic one. While it is true that some threats to the planet, such as an asteroid impact, would certainly cause ecological collapse, Shellenberger noticed that environmental activists could not provide clear evidence that environmental changes, such as melting ice, deforestation, and (potentially) shifting ocean currents, will "add up to an apocalyptic sum greater than their parts."[81] If Earth is not a harmonious whole, where does the idea of nature as an ideally balanced and interconnected system come from?

Shellenberger points to religion.[82] In Judaism and Christianity, the natural world is said to be the product of intelligent design, with every creature playing a part of God's grand design. We have encountered the notion of holisticity or grand design in Chapter 7. Likewise, many environmentalists see each species as an essential part of the larger ecosystem or biosphere. Thus, when humans extinguish one species, the theory goes, they set off a chain reaction of extinctions that will eventually result in the extinction of humanity itself, an original sin leading to the apocalypse described in the Book of Revelations, so to speak.

Environmentalists are not usually devout Christians,[83] but the myths and morals of Judaism and Christianity are deeply rooted in Western culture. It is reasonable, then, that these religious traditions may be subconsciously shaping the foundational beliefs of environmentalism, thereby creating a new, secular religion. Shellenberger explains how "in the Judeo-Christian tradition, human problems stem from our failure to adjust ourselves to God," while "in the apocalyptic environmental tradition, human problems stem from our failure to adjust ourselves to nature."[84] In this secular religion, God is replaced by nature and the priesthood is replaced by scientists who are tasked with interpreting the natural order of things.

To Shellenberger's observations, we can add Michael Crichton's analysis of the parallels between traditional religion and apocalyptic environmentalism. As the American author (1942–2008) noted in 2003,

> If you look carefully, you see that environmentalism is in fact a perfect 21st-century remapping of traditional Judeo-Christian beliefs and myths. There's an initial Eden, a paradise, a state of grace, and unity with nature, there's a fall from grace into a state of pollution as a result of eating from the tree of knowledge, and as a result of our actions there is a judgment day coming for us all. We are all energy sinners, doomed to die, unless we seek salvation, which is now called sustainability. Sustainability is salvation in the church of the environment. Just as organic food is its communion, that pesticide-free wafer that the right people with the right beliefs, imbibe.[85]

In addition to being similar in structure, environmentalism fulfills the same psychological needs as religion does. Saving Earth is portrayed as a grand struggle for existence, turning environmentalists into righteous heroes and providing additional sources of meaning to the lives of many. These religious qualities are not necessarily bad. To be happy, humans need to find meaning somehow, but as Shellenberger notes, "It has become increasingly apocalyptic, destructive, and self-defeating," leading "its adherents to demonize their opponents . . . restrict power and prosperity" and spread "anxiety and depression."[86] How did that happen?

The apocalyptic side of environmentalism, Shellenberger argues, rises from anxieties about the nature of human progress. After religion was separated from science during the Enlightenment, knowledge was no longer derived from the holy scriptures. Our understanding of the world became more accurate, but certainty and stability, which humans derived from religion, was by and large lost. Over time, scientific advances became the norm and seemed unstoppable. The positive effects of scientific progress, such as rising standards of living, became routine, and the explicit link between innovation and human betterment faded into the background. Instead, new technologies become feared, with some people worrying that continued technological progress could lead to the end of civilization.

Rather than striving for a green utopia, as the environmentalists of yesteryear did, the contemporary green movement has become obsessed with fear, predicting the end of the world by technology-induced climate change. Shellenberger recounted his experience at the Extinction Rebellion protest in Trafalgar Square in London. He noted that while the protestors were demographically similar to the members of an older Earth First! group (i.e., white, wealthy, and educated), the members of Extinction Rebellion were uniquely obsessed with death. He wrote that he saw "large banners with the word DEATH on them," "women wearing black mourning veils," and "dead-silent activists" with "blood-red gowns" and "ghost-white" face paint.[87]

To explain this apocalyptic trend, Shellenberger borrows from *The Denial of Death*, a 1973 book by American anthropologist Ernest Becker (1924–1974). Fear of death, Becker wrote, is a core part of our subconscious. We realize our own mortality early in our lives and spend the later part dealing with it, often subconsciously. One way we deal with death, Becker observed, is to create an "immortality project," a way of ensuring that we leave some sort of legacy after we are dead.[88] This could mean having children, starting a business, or creating art. The key part of someone's immortality project is that they are the hero of the story, the selfless parent, the bold entrepreneur, or the eccentric painter.

Environmentalism functions as an immortality project by offering a psychological escape from mortality. Shellenberger mentions research showing that "children who engage with climate activism have better mental health than kids who know about climate change but don't do anything about it."[89] He notes how the rise in climate alarmism has coincided with increased levels of anxiety, depression, and suicide in the United States and Europe, with "seventy percent of American teenagers call[ing] anxiety and depression a major problem."[90]

Like any immortality project, environmentalism requires a narrative to function properly. One such narrative concerns heroic environmental activists and scientists combating the villains of industry. But any story that contains villains also creates anger, and that can be dangerous. Carbon emissions, for example, are not born from evil intentions, but "are a by-product of energy consumption," which is a necessary part of eliminating global poverty.[91] Were environmentalists successful in reducing the use of fossil fuels in developing countries, the world's poorest and most vulnerable people would suffer. Constructive anger, Shellenberger wrote, can change the system, but nihilistic anger threatens a great deal of destruction.

Besides anger, apocalyptic environmentalism creates a lot of sadness. It is a pessimistic worldview that holds that the pursuit of prosperity will drive our species extinct. Shellenberger recalled from experience that "the more apocalyptic environmentalist books and articles I read, the sadder and more anxious I felt."[92] He noted that while environmentalists can escape depression through their movement, the narrative that they push inflames anxieties that are already rising in modern society.

Ours is a secular book, not a religious tract. Our values are humanistic. We value life because we value our own lives and those of our friends and families. We neither welcome nor condemn the decline in organized religion as a source of meaning. We acknowledge it as a fact of modern life. In a similar vein, we recognize that, to cope with dying, human beings have evolved a strong desire for the transcendent. Finally, we observe that in the absence of traditional religion, the need for the transcendent is being filled by something else, including, as Williams College scholar Jason Josephson Storm found in his 2017 book, *The Myth of Disenchantment: Magic, Modernity, and the Birth of the Human Sciences*, new-age spirituality, paranormal beliefs, pagan nature worship, and the like.

The decline of religion in rich countries (and among the educated and increasingly prosperous global elite) has created a void that is increasingly filled by environmentalism. As the University of Illinois at Chicago economist, historian, and Christian Deirdre McCloskey put it in her 2010 book, *Bourgeois Dignity: Why Economics Can't Explain the Modern World*,

> [Environmentalism] is taught now as a civic religion in the American schools (and with an even more fevered rhetoric in Germany and the Netherlands and especially in Sweden).... [In Sweden the] worship starts at home and in the kindergartens, with stories

of the beneficent troll Mulle [a popular children's character], and is carried on in the rest of the school, taking up substantial parts of the curriculum in the manner of religious instruction. By adulthood every Swede is a passionate nature worshiper, and spends her Sundays picking berries in the woods. Humans need such contact with the transcendent (though the theologians observe that worshiping anything short of God has the problem of idolatry for things that will pass). Sweden nowadays is no more a secular country than it was in the time of Norse gods, or of Lutheranism. The Swedes disdain Allah, yet worship passionately the transcendence of Mulle. . . . The environmental left has now worshipfully adopted Malthus, not on fresh scientific evidence but on the mathematical "logic" that "resources must" be limited. (Such evidence-free logic, requiring no wearisome study of the social sciences or of social facts, might explain why a mechanical environmentalism appeals to so many physical and especially biological scientists.) Forget about Marx, says the new left of 2010. Hurrah for Malthus.[93]

Reason, we contend, is needed to reveal the quasi-religious role that the belief in the coming of an environmental apocalypse plays in the lives of many well-meaning but increasingly unreasonable individuals. Evidence, we insist, provides rational grounds for cautious optimism about the state of the planet.

Part Three: Summary

In the third part of this book, we looked at some of the main reasons for the growth in abundance. We noted that, unlike nonhuman animals, people flourished by developing sophisticated ways of cooperating and gaining knowledge. Not only do we trade more intensively and extensively than other species do; more importantly, we constantly innovate. It is innovation that distinguishes relatively slow Smithian growth (i.e., a process of adding more people, land, and capital to the production processes) from the relatively fast Schumpeterian growth (i.e., a process of economic expansion powered by technological change).[94] The process of innovation, however, can be disruptive and thus threatening to the status quo. As a result of that "problem," innovation has tended to be discouraged or even snuffed out by the powerful. Over time, however, geopolitical competition has compelled institutions in some Western European countries to become more economically and politically inclusive. There were also coterminous revolutions in Western European thought and ethics, especially ordinary people's attitudes to innovation and commerce. It was chiefly these fortuitous developments that allowed human ingenuity to shine, thereby freeing an ever-growing share of the world's population from relative stagnation and the Malthusian trap.

Unfortunately, the reasons for human flourishing—liberalism (in its original European sense, not its current American sense), openness, and inclusivity—are neither widely known nor appreciated. Parts of humanity had hardly begun to experience historically unprecedented improvements in longevity, nutrition, education, and so on, before competing conceptions of human flourishing emerged. Throughout the 19th century and well into the 20th, extreme nationalism (including a variety of racist, imperialist, and fascistic doctrines) and socialism (including communism, Maoism, and national socialism) competed with liberalism for world supremacy. One by one, challenges to liberalism were defeated or discredited. The anti-liberal vacuum, we argue, was gradually and increasingly filled by an extreme form of environmentalism. No doubt, some will object that the harm done by environmental extremism cannot be compared to the destructiveness of prior anti-liberal ideologies, yet it is impossible to deny that monomaniacal commitment to extreme forms of environmentalism could lead to gross human rights abuses, as happened in China and India. The ideology of extreme environmentalism and its proponents are anti-natalist, anti-humanist, anti-growth, and anti-progress. Most worryingly, extreme environmentalism and its proponents are growing more radical, as befits a new and increasingly popular form of a secular religion.

Can superabundance endure?

The world's problem is not too many people, but lack of
political and economic freedom.

Julian Simon, *The Ultimate Resource 2* [1]

In 2018, we started to collaborate on an update of the famous Simon-Ehrlich
wager. Instead of focusing on real or inflation-adjusted prices of commodities as Simon and Ehrlich did, we set out to estimate the change in the abundance of resources relative to changes in incomes. We also extended the
period of analysis from 10 years (1980–1990) to 37 years (1980–2017). Finally, we extended the number of the analyzed commodities from 5 to 50.
Our original study, "The Simon Abundance Index: A New Way to Measure
Availability of Resources," came out in December 2018. Between 1980 and
2017, we found, the average time price of commodities fell by 64.7 percent.
Over the same period, the world population increased by 69.3 percent. That
meant that the average time price of commodities declined by 0.934 percent
for every 1 percent increase in population. We also found that the abundance
of resources grew at a compounded annual growth rate of 4.32 percent, thus
implying that population-level resources were 379.6 percent more abundant

in 2017 than they were in 1980.[2] Those findings whetted our appetites. Over the next three years, we refined our methodology and expanded the scope of our inquiry. The result of those efforts, dear reader, is this book.

From the vantage point of people living in advanced societies today, most past humans faced almost unimaginable hardships. Violence, disease, and starvation, which still bedevil the lives of the unfortunates living in some of the world's poorest countries, were compounded by deep and universal ignorance. To our ancestors, some of the most basic facts about the universe and the individual's place in it were unknown. To cope with suffering and to infuse life with higher meaning, humans developed religion. The early religions, as well as all the great religions today, reflected the tragic world of yesteryear. To be more precise, they reflected a human psychology that was trying to make sense of a life that had, in Thomas Hobbes's famous words, "no arts; no letters; no society; and which is worst of all, continual fear, and danger of violent death; and the life of man, solitary, poor, nasty, brutish, and short."[3] Much of the world has changed, especially in the past two centuries or so, but human psychological traits (and our genes) evolve at a slower pace. Surrounded by historically unprecedented plenty and tranquility, our "stone-age minds" consequently keep on perceiving reality through the prism of a set of negative biases that make us think that the world is in much worse shape than it really is. The reasons for pessimism change, but the ancestral brain that directs our lives today craves its daily fix of fear and anxiety.

In this book, we focused on one ancient source of despair that, judging by some recent movies as well as part of the public debate, continues to resonate with people today: the fear of overpopulation and the concomitant exhaustion of natural resources. That fear was, of course, real for thousands of years, and Thomas Malthus, its most prominent proponent, deserves credit for being a decent historian. Paradoxically, Malthus penned his influential thesis—human population grows geometrically, while food production can only grow arithmetically—just as the world was starting to undergo fundamental change. In the late 18th century, some Western European nations and their colonial offshoots started to break out of the Malthusian trap. Their mortality rates started to fall, incomes began to rise, and nutrition improved.

By many measures, life became better. With time, much of the rest of the world followed in Western Europe's footsteps by adopting, however partially and imperfectly, liberal institutions, liberal ethics, and liberal commitments to open inquiry, science, and technology. In this post-Malthusian world, our species flourished and multiplied. In 1800, there were 1 billion of us. By 1950, there were 2.5 billion people in the world, a number that would rise to 7.8 billion in 2020.

The fear of "unsustainable" population growth led to the intellectual battle between the Malthusian Paul Ehrlich and the cornucopian Julian Simon, the hero of this book. The wager between the two men inspired thousands of books and articles. This book offers a new perspective on the relationship between population and resources. We believe that the most meaningful way to estimate the abundance of resources is through the prism of hourly wages. As Simon himself recognized, "A more personal—but often relevant—test of scarcity is whether you and I and others feel that we can afford to buy the material. That is, the relationship between price and income may matter. If the price of food stays the same but income falls sharply, then we feel that food is more scarce. By a similar test, if our wages rise while the price of oil remains constant, our fuller pockets lead us to feel that oil is getting less scarce."[4] To that end, we estimated the abundance of resources at the personal level and at the population level. We looked at many different resources and wage rates in different countries and over different periods, the longest being 168 years. On average, we estimate that personal resource abundance grew by more than 3 percent per year, thereby doubling every two decades or so. We also estimate that population resource abundance grew by more than 4 percent per year on average, thereby doubling every 16 years or so. Moreover, we found that in all the data sets we analyzed, abundance grew at a faster rate than population did during the same period. We call that state of affairs *superabundance*. Based on those findings, we concluded that additional human beings tend to benefit, rather than impoverish, the rest of humanity.[5]

Can superabundance continue? Superabundance, we believe, depends on two main components: people and freedom. People who are free to think, speak, read, publish, and interact with others generate ideas, and market-tested ideas lead to progress. The more people the planet has and the more freedom they enjoy, the greater the likelihood that new good ideas will be generated to tackle the problems that still remain and those that will arise in the future. Consider just one such problem. Fossil fuels have freed humanity from reliance on human and animal muscle and ushered in the modern era dominated first by the steam engine and later by the combustion engine. But they have also contributed to the warming of the planet that we are currently experiencing. Nuclear fission is a very safe and reliable source of energy that emits no CO_2 into the atmosphere, but most countries refuse to build new nuclear reactors partly because of highly publicized accidents at places like Chernobyl and Fukushima.[6] Nuclear fusion could be safer still.[7] During the nuclear fusion process, smaller atoms fuse into larger ones, releasing huge amounts of energy. Alas, nuclear fusion is difficult, and to make it viable, humanity needs to go on innovating.

By analogy, during the innovation process, elements of capital are fused into new creations, generating potentially enormous amounts of value. Since ideas are not made of matter, the laws of thermodynamics do not apply. Innovations can thus create exponential new value. But will we continue to innovate? We can see at least three potential threats on the horizon. The first is an environmental panic–induced decline of the global population. The second is a potentially serious decline in the freedom of expression. The third is the omnipresent danger of further restrictions of the freedom of the market. Let us look at them in turn.

To start with, we take no position on the optimal size of the world's population, except to note that population growth has dramatically enhanced, rather than retarded, economic growth and standards of living since the dawn of the Age of Innovation. As was already explained and extensively documented, coercive policies and other incentives that aim to reduce family size are neither helpful nor moral. Quite the opposite is true. They harm economic growth and, much more importantly, cause great suffering and even death.[8] But we are also opposed to government measures that would coerce or otherwise incentivize people to have more children. The human population should reflect the free choices of individual men and women. While that freedom could reduce population growth and, consequently, retard economic growth, we believe that human freedom is more important than economic growth.[9] Government policies, including various incentive structures such as taxation and regulation, should be tailored in ways that will have no impact on population growth. If such an impact cannot be avoided, government policies should err on the side of population growth and not on the side of population decline. That being said, even in free societies that do not coerce or incentivize parental decisions in one way or another, parental choices are not made in an intellectual vacuum.

Ceteris paribus, the nostrums of extreme environmentalism can reduce population growth when they are thoughtlessly repeated by policymakers, academics, social media influencers, religious leaders, celebrities, and, above all, the news media. The impact of persistent fearmongering is readily discernible. Since we started writing this book, the British daily newspaper *The Guardian*, for example, ran an article that quoted a 27-year-old woman saying, "I feel like I can't in good conscience bring a child into this world and force them to try and survive what may be apocalyptic conditions."[10] The BBC wrote about a couple who decided not to have children. "We've come to this decision on a personal basis," says Morgan, 30, who shares [her partner] Bickner's views on birth. "I wanted to mitigate my own carbon footprint and my own impact as much as I could."[11] The *New York Times* told a story of Lori Day, a woman suffering from "terrifying anxiety" and "recurring nightmares about her daughter's safety . . . triggered by the prospect of catastrophic climate change."[12] The *New York Post*, in the meantime, opined, "Life is already exhausting enough. And the world is broken and burning. Who would want to bring new, innocent life into a criminally unequal society situated on a planet with catastrophically rising sea levels?"[13]

These are not mere anecdotes. Recent surveys show that parents who feel that having more children harms the planet or, worse, puts the future of the entire species at risk, are less inclined to have more children, or to have any children at all. A 2020 study in the journal *Climatic Change*, for example, "found that "59.8 percent of [American] respondents [between the ages of 27 and 45] reported being 'very' or 'extremely concerned' about the carbon footprint of procreation, [and] 96.5 percent of respondents were 'very' or 'extremely concerned' about the well-being of their existing, expected, or hypothetical children in a climate-changed world. This was largely due to an overwhelmingly negative expectation of the future with climate change."[14] A year later, a global study that we mentioned in Chapter 10 found that

39 percent of respondents globally and 36 percent of respondents in the United States were "hesitant to have children" because of environmental considerations.[15] Finally, the analysts at Morgan Stanley, a U.S. investment banking company, found that the "movement to not have children owing to fears over climate change is growing and impacting fertility rates quicker than any preceding trend in the field of fertility decline."[16]

The population replacement level is 2.1 children per woman. Out of the world's 200 countries and territories, 89 had a total fertility rate of 2 or less in 2018. The list of countries and territories with lower-than-replacement total fertility rates is disproportionately populated (forgive the pun) by advanced jurisdictions that are most concerned with environmental issues, including France (1.9); Sweden (1.8); Denmark, the United Kingdom, and the United States (1.7); Germany, the Netherlands, and Norway (1.6); Austria, Canada, and Switzerland (1.5); Finland, Japan, and Portugal (1.4); Italy and Spain (1.3); and South Korea (1).[17] The list of countries and territories with below-replacement total fertility rate and the list of countries and territories most concerned about the environment do not map onto one another perfectly. Furthermore, the total fertility rate declines with income, education, and opportunities for women to earn a living outside the home. We take no issue with those developments and processes, and nothing we write should be read as an attack on parents' autonomy to have as many children as they please. But we insist that in many advanced jurisdictions with low total fertility rates, parents are being unduly influenced by a pervasive anti-natalist sentiment, which we described in Chapter 10. What we are calling for, therefore, is a more balanced and factual debate about population growth that includes a discussion of the benefits of population growth and the dangers inherent in population decline. This leads to the second threat to superabundance: restrictions on the freedom of expression.

Governments have generally curtailed freedom of expression much more often than not, and speech continues to be restricted in many countries today. Certain subjects such as the existence of a particular deity or the movement of the heavenly bodies have been taboo, and in some places, they remain so today. People proclaiming these taboos such as the priests and the shamans spoke from "authority," but without logic or evidence. They enforced these taboos with ostracism, exile, imprisonment, torture, and even death. The great contribution of the Enlightenment to human progress was to insist that the right to free speech was absolute, that no subject was off-limits to the discussion, that no expression of any opinion could be punished, and that logic and evidence were required before a claim could be accepted as truthful. It was that set of enlightened values that helped Western Europe gradually break free of deep ignorance and widespread superstition and embark on a journey toward global scientific and technological preeminence and a historically unprecedented degree of prosperity.

Unfortunately, the light of the Enlightenment had not been lit in all parts of the globe. Just consider Afghanistan under the Taliban or North Korea under the Kim dynasty. Worryingly, it is burning somewhat less brightly in some advanced countries as well. Speakers deemed "controversial" and "problematic" are being banned from speaking on university campuses—the very places that are supposed to be devoted to the pursuit of free inquiry—by a minority of noisy and sometimes violent protesters.[18] Inconvenient questions about "sensitive" issues such as the extent of climate change, and the long-term threats posed by global warming are being silenced in the media, and their proponents are being condemned as "denialists."[19] Instead of relying on evidence, such as that contained in "big data" and long-term trends, we are asked to prioritize and generalize from individual people's "lived experience."[20] Instead of seeing logic and math as quintessentially objective, we are being asked to see the two as at best subjective and at worst racist.[21] Instead of searching for the objective truth, we are asked to believe "his truth" and "her truth."[22]

In other words, many of the values of the Enlightenment appear to be in a bit of a retreat. As a consequence of that trend, a growing share of the population in some advanced countries is increasingly self-censoring what they say.[23] Orwellian "doublethink," by which individual men and women say one thing publicly while reserving their real feelings for the privacy of their homes, is emerging even in countries where people used to feel free to publicly say exactly what they thought privately.[24] Some argue that limits on free expression of some people are tolerable if they prevent hurting other people's feelings.[25] To be sure, politeness and consideration are welcome traits, but self-censorship in matters of civic importance can have far-reaching consequences. Lest we forget, many facts commonly accepted today, such as heliocentrism and natural selection, started as intellectual heresies that offended, discomfited, and hurt the feelings of many people when they were first proposed. Moreover, self-censorship is particularly difficult for people on whom we disproportionately rely to advance technological and scientific progress. Steve Jobs, for example, was a famously difficult boss, while James Watson, the codiscoverer of the structure of DNA, is a provocateur with a penchant for shocking and offending people.[26] As noted in Chapter 9, some of the most brilliant minds belong to neurodivergent individuals. A question: Should humanity forgo additional discoveries simply because future inventors and innovators fail the test of "niceness" or decide to censor themselves? We believe that the answer should be a resounding "no."

Let's now turn to the free market. Further restrictions on the free functioning of the market, we believe, are the third main threat to superabundance. As we already noted, inventors must test their ideas in the marketplace. It is in the marketplace that inventors discover if their ideas can create additional value or not. To reveal the value of an idea, markets must be free. Buyers and sellers, in other words, must come and go as they please, and prices must be allowed to freely increase and decrease. Market-generated profits and losses tell us a great deal about value creation because rising and falling prices capture the personal preferences of billions of buyers and sellers. Conversely, restrictions on the functioning of the market, such as limits on profits and the socialization of losses, prevent the emergence of valuable knowledge. George Gilder argues that wealth is knowledge, and growth is learning. Communist and socialist economies have failed to generate wealth because they have not had markets to help them distinguish between what's valuable (or relatively valuable, such as different uses for the same commodity, which is a key question when it comes to the efficient allocation of capital) and what's not valuable. In other words, they have failed to learn.

As far as we can tell, there has never been a completely free economy anywhere in the world. In every country, governments have always interfered with market freedom to some extent.[27] That said, many countries and territories have enjoyed a high degree of economic freedom in the past, and many continue to do so today. The *Economic Freedom of the World* report copublished by the Fraser Institute in Canada and the Cato Institute in the United States, for example, estimates that Hong Kong and Singapore were the world's freest economies in 2018. On a scale from 0 to 10, the two scored 8.94 and 8.65 respectively.[28] The rest of the 163 nations and territories surveyed were less free, with Venezuela being the worst performer (3.34 out of 10).[29] In recent decades, economic freedom grew, and the global average rose from 6.63 in 2000 to 6.98 in 2018. Economic freedom has declined in some of the world's centers of innovation, though, and this includes the United States, where it fell from 8.67 in 2000 to 8.22 in 2018, and the United Kingdom, where it fell from 8.52 to 8.08 over the same period.

The free market, or to use a more loaded term, capitalism, produces more wealth and higher standards of living than any other economic system that humanity has conceived and implemented. The differences in economic performance between North and South Korea, East and West Germany, Chile and Venezuela, Botswana and Zimbabwe, not to mention the United States and the Soviet Union, speak for themselves. In spite of that generally recognized fact, capitalism has never enjoyed anything close to universal long-term support. In fact, quite the opposite is true. As one commentator put it, "There have been innumerable political parties called socialist. In the history of the world, there has never been a single political party called capitalist. There is not even a name for a supporter of capitalism. A socialist champions socialism; a democrat champions democracy. But a capitalist is someone who owns and manipulates capital."[30] That's because capitalism rubs against some very deeply ingrained parts of human nature, and human nature is important. As Leda Cosmides, John Tooby, and their coauthor Jerome H. Barkow from Dalhousie University put it in their 1992 book, *The Adapted Mind: Evolutionary Psychology and the Generation of Culture*:

> What we think of as all of human history—from, say, the rise of the Shang, Minoan, Egyptian, Indian, and Sumerian civilizations—and everything we take for granted as normal parts of life—agriculture, pastoralism, governments, police, sanitation, medical care, education, armies, transportation, and so on—are all novel products of the last few thousand years. In contrast to this, our ancestors spent the last two million years as Pleistocene hunter-gatherers, and, of

course, several hundred million years before that as one kind of forager or another. These relative spans are important because they establish which set of environments and conditions defined the adaptive problems the mind was shaped to cope with: Pleistocene conditions, rather than modern conditions.[31]

Among the relevant psychological characteristics that humans developed in the Pleistocene were our propensities toward tribalism, egalitarianism, and zero-sum thinking. We evolved in small bands composed of between 25 and 200 individuals. We all knew each other and were often related to one another. Everyone knew who contributed to the band's survival and who shirked his or her responsibilities. Cheaters and free riders were targets of anger and, sometimes, punishment. Just as consequentially, cheaters and free riders lost valuable cooperative partners. The latter would work with more reliable or generous individuals instead.

In such bands, sharing food was common. Storing food for future consumption was not practical for semi nomadic people. So when hunter-gatherers acquired more food than their families could consume, they "stored" it in the form of social obligations, that is, they shared it with other members of the band in the expectation that the favor would be returned in the future. How widely the foragers shared food was sensitive to whether the variation in the foraging success was primarily due to luck or effort. Luck played a large role in hunting success. Hunters who worked hard often came home with nothing. So meat was shared widely within the band (it was a way of pooling risk or a buffer against hunger). When effort played a larger role in foraging success as it did with regard to the gathering of many plant foods, sharing was more targeted. Gathered foods were shared primarily within the family and with specific reciprocation partners.

Moreover, the volume of personal possessions was limited by what our ancestors could carry on their backs as they moved from one location to another, so the accumulation of property and wealth inequality could not have been major concerns. Also, like other animals, we have evolved to form hierarchies of dominance. An individual's survival and ability to pass on his genes were enhanced if he could rise within a group and control access to greater resources. On the other hand, humans also evolved to form co-alitions, in which less dominant individuals cooperated to take down the stronger, more successful group members. Finally, sharing and cooperation among hunter-gatherers ended at the band's edge, so to speak. In a world without specialization and trade, disproportionate gains by one band often came at the expense of another band. By forming aggressive coalitions, men could expand their band's foraging territories or gain more wives by cooper-ating to kill men from other bands.

The hunter-gatherer psychology helps to explain our contemporary at-titudes to the extent and freedom of the market.[32] Consider, for example, the provision of health care. When a hunter got sick or injured, he could not go on hunting for food. His sickness or injury was a double blow to the band. Not only did the stricken hunter cease to contribute to the band's survival, but he also needed to be fed and cared for. Furthermore, no one could guarantee that a stricken hunter would ever be able to hunt again, so it made sense for humans to evolve the feelings of compassion and to surround themselves by caring individuals. The feelings of compassion and the acts of caring contrast with calculated and profit-seeking exchanges in the marketplace. Employers, for example, tend to pay wages and provide benefits to their employees to make money (that is, the employer calculates that the productivity of the employee outweighs the cost of the employee's compensation), not because they care about the employees' welfare.

Put differently, our brains interpret market exchanges as signs of social distance, whereas illness or injury activates our hunter-gatherer intuitions about helping others. The notion of socialized medicine as a universal fix to the problem of bad luck, which is usually the cause of sickness or injury, satisfies those intuitions. Conversely, the notion of market-based health care is completely counterintuitive and would remain so even when it could be conclusively shown that people get better results from a market-based health care system. Note that people are much less sympathetic to the government paying for the health care of patients whose illness is not caused by bad luck, such as smokers with lung cancer. When people want to argue for helping patients with lung cancer, they usually turn to arguments about addiction: he or she could not help smoking, the evil tobacco company knowingly sold an addictive product to him or her as a teenager, and so on. In other words, many arguments about the various aspects of the welfare state and the extent of market exchanges follow directly from the different sharing rules that evolved to deal with the variance of fortunes due to luck versus effort.

To summarize, the psychology that evolved when our ancestors lived in small hunter-gatherer groups prepared us to cope with a world of personal cooperation and exchange in small communities. It did not prepare us to cope with a world of impersonal cooperation and exchange among millions of people (a typical advanced economy) or billions of people (the global economy). In a way, the complexity of the modern economy outran the ability of our stone-age minds to understand it. Yet it is that transition from personal simplicity to impersonal complexity that makes capitalism so effective at producing great wealth. To complicate matters further, the extended marketplace of millions or billions of people enables enterprising individuals with value-creating ideas to amass greater wealth than they would be able to amass while catering to small communities. That wealth inequality rubs against our egalitarian predispositions and zero-sum thinking. Finally, our tribalism helps explain why we continue to resent other nations and suspect them of thriving at our expense even when we do consent to trade with them.

To understand capitalism—let alone to appreciate its benefits—requires all of us to distinguish between the personal and the impersonal, between the simple and the complex, and between the limited and the extended. The ever-insightful F. A. Hayek put it this way:

> Part of our present difficulty is that we must constantly adjust our lives, our thoughts and our emotions, in order to live simultaneously within different kinds of orders according to different rules. If we were to apply the unmodified, uncurbed, rules of the micro-cosmos (i.e., of the small band or troop, or of, say, our families) to the macro-cosmos (our wider civilization), as our instincts and sentimental yearnings often make us wish to do, we would destroy it. Yet if we were always to apply the rules of the extended order to our more intimate groupings, we would crush them. So we must learn to live in two sorts of world at once.[33]

Striking the balance between the implementation of those two sets of rules is a difficult task, and we often fail to do so. When we do fail—as we did most recently in Venezuela—the results can be catastrophic. The collapse of Venezuela's "21st-century socialism" should provide a warning to future generations, but the same was expected (largely to no avail) from dozens of socialist failures in the 20th century. As such, we suspect that the defense of free markets will remain a never-ending struggle because of the predispositions of the stone-age mind.

We hope that those readers who made it to the end of this book will appreciate how far humanity has come and the sheer improbability of what it has accomplished. Struggling against conflict, hunger, and disease, we have managed to gradually gain the upper hand. In a world trending toward entropy, we have succeeded in creating a complex and superabundant civilization. We have done so because humans are a unique kind of animal, one that has developed a cooperative culture that allows for the accumulation and sharing of knowledge. That knowledge, in turn, helps to make our society gentler and more prosperous. Population growth and freedom are crucial parts of that positive feedback loop. It is free people, not machines or deities, who generate new ideas, and it is free people who test those new ideas against other people's ideas in the marketplace. The process of knowledge and value creation is at the heart of humanity's moral and material progress. It is what enables our civilization to bend toward goodness and superabundance. Let us try to keep it that way.

ACKNOWLEDGMENTS

We wish to thank the Searle Freedom Trust for its support in researching this book. Our thanks also go to Connor Hansen and Larissa Lee, and to the Cato Institute interns, including Robert Arnold, Sarah Barron, John Burzawa, Adam Fink, Kathryn Paravano, and Michael Peterson. Malcolm Cochran and Bradley Dowell were especially helpful with article summaries and the checking of references. David Simon provided us with extensive notes pertaining to the life, career, and thoughts of his father, Julian. We are deeply grateful to Don Boudreaux, Pierre Desrochers, and Jason Kuznicki for reviewing the full manuscript and for suggesting pertinent changes to the text. Specific chapters were reviewed by David Boaz, Matt Clancy, Leda Cosmides, Stephen Davies, Arthur Diamond, Chelsea Follett, Stephen Hicks, Terence Kealey, Michael McCullough, Jeffrey Miron, Steven Pinker, Clay Routledge, Michael Shellenberger, Matthew Slaboch, Aaron Steelman, Ian Vásquez, and William von Hippel. We are grateful for their insights. Finally, our thanks go to Luis Ahumada Abrigo, Guillermina Sutter Schneider, Eleanor O'Connor, Onur Yoruk, Emma Evans, Marcy Gessel, Kate Hall, Barbara Hart, Karen Ingebretsen, Kevin Morrow, and Linda Stringer, who helped to design and edit this book. The errors that remain are our own.

APPENDIXES

Appendix 1. Concepts, abbreviations, and equations

Concept	Abbreviation	Equation
Time price	TP	Nominal money price ÷ Nominal hourly income
Percentage change in time price	PCTP	$(\text{Time price}_{end} \div \text{Time price}_{start}) - 1$
Percentage change in population	PCP	$(\text{Population}_{end} \div \text{Population}_{start}) - 1$
Time price elasticity of population	TP-EP	Percentage change in time price ÷ percentage change in population
Personal resource level of analysis		
Personal resource abundance multiplier	pRAM	$(\text{Time price}_{start} \div \text{Time price}_{end})$
Percentage change in personal resource abundance	pRA	Personal resource abundance multiplier − 1
Compound annual growth rate of personal resource abundance	CAGR-pRA	Personal resource abundance multiplier $^{1/Years} - 1$
Years to double personal resource abundance	YD-pRA	$(\text{Log}(2) - \text{Log}(1)) \div \text{Log}(1+\text{CARG-pRA})$, or $0.30103 \div \text{Log}(1+\text{CARG-pRA})$, or $\approx 70 \div \text{CARG-pRA}$
Personal resource abundance elasticity of population	pRA-EP	Percentage change in personal resource abundance ÷ percentage change in population
Population resource level of analysis		
Population resource abundance multiplier	PRAM	$\text{Population}_{end} \times$ Personal resource abundance multiplier
Percentage change in population resource abundance	PRA	Population resource abundance multiplier − 1
Compound annual growth rate of population resource abundance	CAGR-PRA	Population resource abundance multiplier $^{1/Years} - 1$
Years to double population resource abundance	YD-PRA	$(\text{Log}(2) - \text{Log}(1)) \div \text{Log}(1+\text{CARG-PRA})$, or $0.30103 \div \text{Log}(1+\text{CARG-PRA})$, or $\approx 70 \div \text{CARG-PRA}$
Population resource abundance elasticity of population	PRA-EP	Percentage change in population resource abundance ÷ percentage change in population

Notes: Personal resource abundance multiplier is indexed to 1 in the base year; population resource abundance multiplier is indexed to 1 in the base year.

Appendix 2. Average global nominal GDP per hour worked in 28 countries and territories (1960–2018)

Year	Nominal GDP per total hours worked ($)	Year	Nominal GDP per total hours worked ($)
1960	0.77	1990	7.07
1961	0.82	1991	7.42
1962	0.89	1992	7.77
1963	0.94	1993	7.81
1964	1.02	1994	8.31
1965	1.09	1995	9.06
1966	1.17	1996	9.12
1967	1.22	1997	8.98
1968	1.28	1998	8.92
1969	1.36	1999	9.17
1970	1.46	2000	9.34
1971	1.54	2001	9.14
1972	1.74	2002	9.35
1973	2.03	2003	10.24
1974	2.24	2004	11.23
1975	2.48	2005	11.86
1976	2.64	2006	12.46
1977	2.91	2007	13.58
1978	3.37	2008	14.51
1979	3.80	2009	14.01
1980	4.17	2010	14.97
1981	4.22	2011	17.54
1982	4.08	2012	18.53
1983	4.11	2013	19.61
1984	4.25	2014	20.75
1985	4.40	2015	20.45
1986	5.11	2016	21.27
1987	5.72	2017	22.30
1988	6.32	2018	23.65
1989	6.50		

Sources: World Bank, Conference Board, and www.measuringworth.com.

Note: GDP = gross domestic product.

Appendix 3. Average global nominal GDP per hour worked in 42 countries and territories (1980–2018)

Year	GDP per capita ($)	Annual hours worked	GDP per capita per hour worked ($)
1980	2,507	2,166	1.16
1981	2,550	2,161	1.18
1982	2,482	2,155	1.15
1983	2,487	2,150	1.16
1984	2,535	2,145	1.18
1985	2,616	2,140	1.22
1986	3,036	2,134	1.42
1987	3,391	2,129	1.59
1988	3,726	2,124	1.75
1989	3,836	2,118	1.81
1990	4,241	2,113	2.01
1991	4,420	2,108	2.10
1992	4,622	2,103	2.20
1993	4,626	2,097	2.21
1994	4,897	2,092	2.34
1995	5,367	2,087	2.57
1996	5,412	2,081	2.60
1997	5,322	2,076	2.56
1998	5,239	2,071	2.53
1999	5,364	2,066	2.60
2000	5,468	2,060	2.65
2001	5,367	2,055	2.61
2002	5,504	2,050	2.69
2003	6,100	2,044	2.98
2004	6,786	2,039	3.33

(Continued)

Appendix 3 *(continued)*

Year	GDP per capita ($)	Annual hours worked	GDP per capita per hour worked ($)
2005	7,259	2,034	3.57
2006	7,767	2,028	3.83
2007	8,641	2,023	4.27
2008	9,363	2,018	4.64
2009	8,768	2,013	4.36
2010	9,480	2,007	4.72
2011	10,410	2,002	5.20
2012	10,521	1,997	5.27
2013	10,688	1,991	5.37
2014	10,850	1,986	5.46
2015	10,147	1,981	5.12
2016	10,182	1,976	5.15
2017	10,693	1,970	5.43
2018	11,464	1,965	5.83

Sources: World Bank, Conference Board, and www.measuringworth.com.
Note: GDP = gross domestic product.

Appendix 4. Average nominal U.S. hourly income (1850–2018)

Year	U.S. unskilled wage ($)	U.S. blue-collar compensation ($)	U.S. upskilling compensation ($)
1850	0.05	0.06	N/A
1851	0.05	0.06	N/A
1852	0.05	0.07	N/A
1853	0.05	0.07	N/A
1854	0.06	0.07	N/A
1855	0.06	0.07	N/A
1856	0.06	0.07	N/A
1857	0.06	0.07	N/A
1858	0.06	0.08	N/A
1859	0.06	0.08	N/A
1860	0.06	0.08	N/A
1861	0.06	0.08	N/A
1862	0.06	0.09	N/A
1863	0.07	0.10	N/A
1864	0.08	0.11	N/A
1865	0.09	0.11	N/A
1866	0.09	0.11	N/A
1867	0.09	0.11	N/A
1868	0.09	0.11	N/A
1869	0.09	0.11	N/A
1870	0.09	0.11	N/A
1871	0.09	0.12	N/A
1872	0.09	0.12	N/A
1873	0.08	0.12	N/A
1874	0.08	0.12	N/A
1875	0.08	0.12	N/A

(Continued)

Appendix 4 (*continued*)

Year	U.S. unskilled wage ($)	U.S. blue-collar compensation ($)	U.S. upskilling compensation ($)
1876	0.07	0.11	N/A
1877	0.07	0.11	N/A
1878	0.07	0.11	N/A
1879	0.07	0.11	N/A
1880	0.07	0.11	N/A
1881	0.07	0.11	N/A
1882	0.08	0.11	N/A
1883	0.08	0.11	N/A
1884	0.08	0.12	N/A
1885	0.08	0.12	N/A
1886	0.08	0.12	N/A
1887	0.08	0.13	N/A
1888	0.08	0.13	N/A
1889	0.08	0.13	N/A
1890	0.08	0.13	N/A
1891	0.08	0.13	N/A
1892	0.08	0.13	N/A
1893	0.08	0.14	N/A
1894	0.08	0.13	N/A
1895	0.08	0.13	N/A
1896	0.08	0.13	N/A
1897	0.08	0.13	N/A
1898	0.08	0.13	N/A
1899	0.08	0.13	N/A
1900	0.09	0.14	N/A
1901	0.09	0.14	N/A
1902	0.09	0.15	N/A

Year	U.S. unskilled wage ($)	U.S. blue-collar compensation ($)	U.S. upskilling compensation ($)
1903	0.09	0.15	N/A
1904	0.09	0.15	N/A
1905	0.10	0.16	N/A
1906	0.10	0.16	N/A
1907	0.11	0.17	N/A
1908	0.10	0.16	N/A
1909	0.10	0.17	N/A
1910	0.11	0.18	N/A
1911	0.10	0.18	N/A
1912	0.10	0.19	N/A
1913	0.11	0.20	N/A
1914	0.11	0.20	N/A
1915	0.11	0.20	N/A
1916	0.14	0.24	N/A
1917	0.17	0.29	N/A
1918	0.21	0.36	N/A
1919	0.25	0.43	N/A
1920	0.29	0.54	N/A
1921	0.24	0.48	N/A
1922	0.22	0.44	N/A
1923	0.24	0.48	N/A
1924	0.25	0.51	N/A
1925	0.25	0.50	N/A
1926	0.25	0.51	N/A
1927	0.26	0.52	N/A
1928	0.26	0.52	N/A

(Continued)

Appendix 4 *(continued)*

Year	U.S. unskilled wage ($)	U.S. blue-collar compensation ($)	U.S. upskilling compensation ($)
1929	0.26	0.52	N/A
1930	0.26	0.53	N/A
1931	0.25	0.51	N/A
1932	0.22	0.45	N/A
1933	0.22	0.44	N/A
1934	0.26	0.53	N/A
1935	0.27	0.54	N/A
1936	0.27	0.55	N/A
1937	0.31	0.63	N/A
1938	0.32	0.64	N/A
1939	0.32	0.64	N/A
1940	0.33	0.67	N/A
1941	0.37	0.74	N/A
1942	0.42	0.86	N/A
1943	0.46	0.98	N/A
1944	0.48	1.05	N/A
1945	0.50	1.06	N/A
1946	0.55	1.13	N/A
1947	0.62	1.30	N/A
1948	0.66	1.41	N/A
1949	0.69	1.46	N/A
1950	0.72	1.55	N/A
1951	0.78	1.72	N/A
1952	0.83	1.83	N/A
1953	0.89	1.94	N/A
1954	0.93	1.97	N/A
1955	0.97	2.05	N/A

Year	U.S. unskilled wage ($)	U.S. blue-collar compensation ($)	U.S. upskilling compensation ($)
1956	1.02	2.16	N/A
1957	1.07	2.24	N/A
1958	1.12	2.39	N/A
1959	1.16	2.45	N/A
1960	1.21	2.54	N/A
1961	1.25	2.60	N/A
1962	1.29	2.71	N/A
1963	1.33	2.83	N/A
1964	1.37	2.89	N/A
1965	1.41	3.00	N/A
1966	1.47	3.14	N/A
1967	1.54	3.29	N/A
1968	1.62	3.52	N/A
1969	1.72	3.72	N/A
1970	1.85	3.93	N/A
1971	1.99	4.26	N/A
1972	2.14	4.59	N/A
1973	2.28	4.95	N/A
1974	2.45	5.44	N/A
1975	2.66	6.02	N/A
1976	2.91	6.53	N/A
1977	3.15	7.15	N/A
1978	3.40	7.77	N/A
1979	3.69	8.34	N/A
1980	4.06	9.12	4.06
1981	4.40	10.00	4.55

(Continued)

Appendix 4 *(continued)*

Year	U.S. unskilled wage ($)	U.S. blue-collar compensation ($)	U.S. upskilling compensation ($)
1982	4.63	10.80	4.96
1983	4.83	11.22	5.34
1984	5.01	11.78	5.72
1985	5.18	12.50	6.14
1986	5.28	12.90	6.48
1987	5.40	13.05	6.81
1988	5.60	13.58	7.28
1989	5.79	14.00	7.74
1990	6.03	14.41	8.24
1991	6.26	14.93	8.77
1992	6.43	15.63	9.34
1993	6.60	16.12	9.86
1994	6.78	16.56	10.38
1995	6.99	16.66	10.81
1996	7.23	16.84	11.28
1997	7.49	18.12	12.24
1998	7.75	18.18	12.69
1999	8.00	18.75	13.37
2000	8.30	19.36	14.12
2001	8.81	19.36	14.64
2002	8.95	21.02	15.94
2003	9.25	21.54	16.69
2004	9.25	23.07	17.98
2005	9.44	23.92	18.96
2006	9.67	24.37	19.73
2007	9.87	25.07	20.67
2008	10.45	25.87	21.81

Year	U.S. unskilled wage ($)	U.S. blue-collar compensation ($)	U.S. upskilling compensation ($)
2009	10.47	26.15	22.44
2010	10.24	26.44	23.03
2011	10.40	26.88	23.84
2012	10.87	27.15	24.58
2013	10.89	27.92	25.68
2014	11.26	29.40	27.49
2015	11.35	30.55	29.03
2016	11.63	31.95	30.88
2017	12.00	32.39	31.85
2018	12.78	32.06	32.06

Sources: World Bank, Conference Board, and MeasuringWorth, www.measuringworth.com.
Note: N/A = not applicable.

Appendix 5. The Basic 50 and the World Bank 37 nominal price data adjustment

We eliminated three crude oil data sets (Brent, Dubai, and West Texas Intermediate) because the data contained therein were already reflected in "Crude oil, average." There were three categories for coal. Only Australian coal was tracked back to 1980, so we did not include the other two. There were four types of natural gas: the United States, Europe, Japan, and an average. We dropped the average and included the three individual markets. We did so because the three markets are largely independent, and international prices of natural gas can vary considerably. We created a single average for the prices of coffee (combining Arabica and Robusta). We retained just one measure of the price of tea, which is the average of the prices in Colombo, Kolkata, and Mombasa. We also combined coconut oil and copra (from which coconut oil is derived). We combined ground nuts and groundnut oil. We included palm oil, but not palm kernel oil, which was not tracked until 1996. We combined soybeans, soybean oil, and soybean meal into one category. "Rice, Thai 5 percent" and "Wheat, U.S. HRW" had the most complete price histories, and so we included them. We eliminated "Banana, Europe" because it didn't start until 1997. There were three sugar indexes: U.S., Europe, and World. We combined those into one average category. We combined Cameroon and Malaysian logs into an average category. We combined Cameroon and Malaysian sawnwood into an average as well. There were two rubber categories, but we eliminated "Rubber, TSR20," because it has been tracked only since 1999. We combined diammonium phosphate, phosphate rock, triple superphosphate, urea, and potassium chloride into one price measure called "Fertilizer." The two wool grades were combined into an average.

Appendix 6. The Basic 50: commodity perspective (1980–2018)

Commodity	Units	1980 nominal price ($)	2018 nominal price ($)	Percentage change in nominal price 1980–2018	GDP per hour worked 1980 time price at $3.24 per hour	GDP per hour worked 2018 time price at $15.88 per hour	Percentage change in time price 1980–2018	1980–2018 personal resource abundance multiplier 1980 = 1	Percentage change in personal resource abundance 1980–2018	Compound annual percentage growth rate in personal resource abundance	Years to double personal resource abundance
Aluminum	$/mt	1,774.91	2,108.48	18.8	548.49	132.74	−75.8	4.13	313.2	3.80	18.56
Bananas	$/lb	0.34	0.57	67.9	0.11	0.04	−65.8	2.92	192.4	2.86	24.55
Barley	$/mt	78.23	125.89	60.9	24.17	7.93	−67.2	3.05	205.0	2.98	23.62
Beef	$/kg	2.76	4.20	52.2	0.85	0.26	−69.0	3.23	222.6	3.13	22.49
Chicken	$/kg	0.76	2.24	194.7	0.23	0.14	−40.0	1.67	66.5	1.35	51.64
Coal	$/mt	40.14	107.02	166.6	12.40	6.74	−45.7	1.84	84.1	1.62	43.16
Cocoa	$/kg	2.60	2.29	−11.9	0.80	0.14	−82.1	5.57	457.3	4.62	15.33
Coconut oil	$/mt	673.83	996.87	47.9	208.23	62.76	−69.9	3.32	231.8	3.21	21.96
Coffee	$/kg	3.35	2.40	−28.5	1.04	0.15	−85.4	6.86	586.1	5.20	13.68
Copper	$/mt	2,182.09	6,529.80	199.2	674.31	411.08	−39.0	1.64	64.0	1.31	53.22
Corn	$/mt	125.26	164.41	31.3	38.71	10.35	−73.3	3.74	274.0	3.53	19.97
Cotton	$/kg	2.06	2.01	−2.4	0.64	0.13	−80.1	5.03	403.1	4.34	16.30

Commodity	Unit										
Crude oil	$/bbl	36.87	68.35	85.4	11.39	4.30	−62.2	2.65	164.8	2.60	27.05
Fertilizer	$/mt	150.84	258.59	71.4	46.61	16.28	−65.1	2.86	186.3	2.81	25.04
Fish meal	$/mt	504.43	1,525.10	202.3	155.88	96.01	−38.4	1.62	62.4	1.28	54.35
Gold	$/tz	607.86	1,269.23	108.8	187.84	79.90	−57.5	2.35	135.1	2.27	30.81
Groundnuts etc.	$/mt	2,095.33	2,766.08	32.0	647.50	174.14	−73.1	3.72	271.8	3.52	20.06
Hides	¢/lb	0.46	0.58	26.3	0.14	0.04	−74.3	3.89	288.6	3.64	19.40
Iron ore	$/dmtu	28.09	69.75	148.3	8.68	4.39	−49.4	1.98	97.7	1.81	38.65
Lamb	$/kg	2.88	5.87	103.8	0.89	0.37	−58.5	2.41	140.8	2.34	29.97
Lead	$/mt	905.75	2,240.44	147.4	279.90	141.05	−49.6	1.98	98.4	1.82	38.43
LNG, Japan	$/mmbtu	5.70	10.65	86.9	1.76	0.67	−61.9	2.63	162.7	2.57	27.28
Logs	$/cm	223.60	341.63	52.8	69.10	21.51	−68.9	3.21	221.3	3.12	22.57
Natural gas, Eur.	$/mmbtu	4.22	7.68	82.0	1.30	0.48	−62.9	2.70	169.7	2.65	26.55
Natural gas, U.S.	$/mmbtu	1.59	3.16	98.7	0.49	0.20	−59.5	2.47	147.0	2.41	29.13
Nickel	$/mt	6,518.68	13,114.06	101.2	2,014.42	825.59	−59.0	2.44	144.0	2.38	29.53
Oranges	$/kg	0.40	0.79	97.5	0.12	0.05	−59.8	2.49	148.5	2.42	28.93

(Continued)

Commodity	Units	1980 nominal price ($)	2018 nominal price ($)	Percentage change in nominal price 1980–2018	GDP per hour worked			1980–2018 personal resource abundance multiplier 1980 = 1	Percentage change in personal resource abundance 1980–2018	Compound annual percentage growth rate in personal resource abundance	Years to double personal resource abundance
					1980 time price at $3.24 per hour	2018 time price at $15.88 per hour	Percentage change in time price 1980–2018				
Palm oil	$/mt	583.69	638.66	9.4	180.37	40.21	−77.7	4.49	348.6	4.03	17.55
Platinum	$/tz	679.10	879.55	29.5	209.86	55.37	−73.6	3.79	279.0	3.57	19.77
Plywood	¢/sheet	273.78	494.70	80.7	84.60	31.14	−63.2	2.72	171.7	2.66	26.36
Pork	$/lb	0.82	0.62	−24.4	0.25	0.04	−84.6	6.50	549.7	5.05	14.08
Pulpwood	$/mt	536.54	875.00	63.1	165.80	55.09	−66.8	3.01	201.0	2.94	23.90
Rapeseed	$/mt	572.37	829.63	44.9	176.87	52.23	−70.5	3.39	238.7	3.26	21.59
Rice	$/mt	410.74	420.67	2.4	126.93	26.48	−79.1	4.79	379.3	4.21	16.81
Rubber	$/kg	1.42	1.57	10.6	0.44	0.10	−77.5	4.44	344.0	4.00	17.67
Salmon	$/kg	7.98	7.52	−5.8	2.47	0.47	−80.8	5.21	421.0	4.44	15.96
Sawnwood	$/cm	396.10	683.97	72.7	122.40	43.06	−64.8	2.84	184.3	2.79	25.21
Shrimp	$/kg	10.14	12.24	20.7	3.13	0.77	−75.4	4.07	306.6	3.76	18.78

Silver	$/tz	20.80	15.71	−24.5	6.43	0.99	−84.6	6.50	549.9	5.05	14.07
Sorghum	$/mt	128.86	168.59	30.8	39.82	10.61	−73.3	3.75	275.2	3.54	19.92
Soybeans etc.	$/mt	385.42	529.62	37.4	119.10	33.34	−72.0	3.57	257.2	3.41	20.69
Sugar	$/kg	0.59	0.41	−30.9	0.18	0.03	−85.9	7.11	610.6	5.30	13.43
Sunflower oil	$/mt	556.01	900.81	62.0	171.82	56.71	−67.0	3.03	203.0	2.96	23.76
Tea	$/kg	1.66	2.85	71.6	0.51	0.18	−65.0	2.86	186.0	2.80	25.06
Tin	$/mt	16,774.88	20,145.21	20.1	5,183.81	1,268.24	−75.5	4.09	308.7	3.77	18.71
Tobacco	$/mt	2,275.86	4,862.91	113.7	703.29	306.14	−56.5	2.30	129.7	2.21	31.67
Uranium	$/lb	31.79	20.30	−36.1	9.82	1.28	−87.0	7.69	668.7	5.51	12.91
Wheat	$/mt	172.73	203.89	18.0	53.38	12.84	−76.0	4.16	315.8	3.82	18.48
Wool	¢/kg	628.78	1,591.69	153.1	194.31	100.20	−48.4	1.94	93.9	1.76	39.77
Zinc	$/mt	761.22	2,922.38	283.9	235.23	183.98	−21.8	1.28	27.9	0.65	107.17
Average				64.9			−71.6	3.52	251.8	3.37	20.94

Source: Authors' calculations.

Note: bbl = barrel; cm = cubic meters; dmtu = dry metric tonne unit; Eur. = Europe; GDP = gross domestic product; lb = pound; kg = kilogram; LNG = liquefied natural gas; mmbtu = metric million British thermal unit; mt = metric ton; tz = troy ounce.

Appendix 7. The Basic 50: country and territory perspective (1980–2018)

	1980 GDP per hour worked ($)	2018 GDP per hour worked ($)	1980–2018 percentage change in hourly rate	Percentage change time price Basic 50 index	Basic 50 commodities personal resource abundance multiplier	Percentage change in personal resource abundance 1980–2018	Compound annual percentage growth rate in personal resource abundance	Years to double personal resource abundance
China[a]	0.16	9.18	5,522.9	−97.5	40.30	3,930	10.22	7.1
South Korea	1.66	29.32	1,667.8	−92.1	12.67	1,167	6.91	10.4
Sri Lanka	0.48	5.76	1,101.5	−88.4	8.61	761	5.83	12.2
Ireland	8.47	99.51	1,074.2	−88.1	8.42	742	5.77	12.4
Thailand	0.55	6.12	1,019.0	−87.5	8.02	702	5.63	12.7
Singapore	4.97	43.91	784.2	−84.2	6.34	534	4.98	14.3
Hong Kong	5.21	43.30	730.5	−83.2	5.95	495	4.81	14.8
India	0.32	2.46	674.3	−82.0	5.55	455	4.61	15.4
Portugal	4.11	26.27	538.5	−78.1	4.58	358	4.08	17.3
Bangladesh	0.31	1.88	515.1	−77.3	4.41	341	3.98	17.8
Indonesia	0.70	4.26	506.3	−77.0	4.35	335	3.94	17.9
Turkey	2.50	14.39	474.8	−75.7	4.12	312	3.80	18.6
New Zealand	8.06	45.09	459.7	−75.1	4.01	301	3.72	19.0
Australia	12.41	66.15	433.1	−73.8	3.82	282	3.59	19.7

Finland	12.33	65.45	430.8	−73.7	3.80	280	3.58	19.7
Norway	20.93	108.94	420.5	−73.2	3.73	273	3.53	20.0
Pakistan	0.46	2.39	414.9	−72.9	3.69	269	3.50	20.2
Iceland	17.02	87.08	411.7	−72.7	3.67	267	3.48	20.3
Austria	12.52	62.97	403.0	−72.3	3.60	260	3.43	20.5
Malaysia	2.25	10.76	378.9	−70.9	3.43	243	3.30	21.4
United States	15.51	73.64	374.9	−70.6	3.40	240	3.28	21.5
Denmark	17.93	84.91	373.6	−70.5	3.39	239	3.27	21.6
Germany	13.95	66.04	373.2	−70.5	3.39	239	3.27	21.6
Japan	9.04	42.26	367.5	−70.2	3.35	235	3.23	21.8
Chile	3.94	18.04	357.9	−69.5	3.28	228	3.18	22.2
Luxembourg	23.24	103.68	346.1	−68.7	3.20	220	3.11	22.7
Spain	9.58	42.69	345.9	−68.7	3.20	220	3.10	22.7
Switzerland	20.02	88.30	341.2	−68.4	3.16	216	3.08	22.9
Peru	1.56	6.90	340.8	−68.3	3.16	216	3.07	22.9
Brazil	2.37	10.35	336.3	−68.0	3.13	213	3.05	23.1
United Kingdom	12.61	52.50	316.2	−66.5	2.98	198	2.92	24.1

(Continued)

Appendix 7 (*continued*)

	1980 GDP per hour worked ($)	2018 GDP per hour worked ($)	1980–2018 percentage change in hourly rate	Percentage change time price Basic 50 index	Basic 50 commodities personal resource abundance multiplier	Percentage change in personal resource abundance 1980–2018	Compound annual percentage growth rate in personal resource abundance	Years to double personal resource abundance
Philippines	0.91	3.69	307.6	−65.8	2.92	192	2.86	24.6
Argentina	3.75	15.25	307.2	−65.7	2.92	192	2.86	24.6
Italy	11.95	47.42	296.8	−64.8	2.84	184	2.79	25.2
Canada	13.43	52.97	294.4	−64.6	2.83	183	2.77	25.3
Colombia	1.90	7.28	283.6	−63.6	2.75	175	2.70	26.0
France	17.39	65.12	274.4	−62.7	2.68	168	2.63	26.7
Belgium	19.81	72.32	265.0	−61.8	2.62	162	2.56	27.4
Greece	7.41	25.41	242.7	−59.3	2.46	146	2.39	29.3
Netherlands	20.42	68.67	236.4	−58.5	2.41	141	2.34	29.9
Sweden	21.60	67.37	211.8	−55.3	2.23	123	2.14	32.8
Mexico	4.36	10.27	135.5	−40.8	1.69	69	1.39	50.3
Average	**3.24**	**15.88**	**390.9**	**−71.6**	**3.52**	**252**	**3.37**	**20.9**

Source: Authors' calculations.

Note: GDP = gross domestic product; Hong Kong = Hong Kong SAR, China.

a. The Conference Board presents the Chinese data in two series, China (Alternative) and China (Official). The former is based on alternative growth estimates, while the latter is based on official data. We use the China (Alternative) series. For more information on the Conference Board's alternative growth measures for China, please refer to https://www.conference-board.org/pdf_free/FAQ-for-China-GDP-vs4_10nov15.pdf.

Appendix 8. The World Bank 37: commodity perspective (1960–2018)

Commodity	Units	1960 nominal price ($)	2018 nominal price ($)	Percentage change in nominal prices 1960–2018	GDP per hour worked 1960 time price at $0.77 per hour	GDP per hour worked 2018 time price at $23.65 per hour	Percentage change in time prices 1960–2018	1960–2018 personal resource abundance multiplier 1960 = 1	Percentage change in personal resource abundance 1960–2018	Compound annual percentage growth rate in personal resource abundance	Years to double personal resource abundance
Aluminum	$/mt	511.47	2,108.48	312.2	661.67	89.15	−86.5	7.42	642	3.52	20.06
Bananas	$/lb	0.14	1.10	669.9	0.18	0.05	−74.8	3.97	297	2.41	29.14
Barley	$/mt	20.15	125.89	524.6	26.07	5.32	−79.6	4.90	390	2.78	25.30
Beef	$/kg	0.74	4.20	469.6	0.95	0.18	−81.4	5.37	437	2.94	23.91
Chicken	$/kg	0.30	2.24	647.4	0.39	0.09	−75.6	4.09	309	2.46	28.52
Cocoa	$/kg	0.59	2.29	289.4	0.76	0.10	−87.3	7.86	686	3.62	19.50
Coconut oil	$/mt	312.33	996.87	219.2	404.05	42.15	−89.6	9.59	859	3.97	17.79
Coffee	$/kg	0.81	2.40	196.1	1.05	0.10	−90.3	10.33	933	4.11	17.21
Copper	$/mt	678.76	6,529.80	862.0	878.08	276.08	−68.6	3.18	218	2.01	34.75
Corn	$/mt	44.50	164.41	269.5	57.57	6.95	−87.9	8.28	728	3.71	19.02
Cotton	$/kg	0.65	2.01	207.8	0.85	0.09	−89.9	9.94	894	4.04	17.50

(Continued)

Commodity	Units	1960 nominal price ($)	2018 nominal price ($)	Percentage change in nominal prices 1960–2018	GDP per hour worked		Percentage change in time prices 1960–2018	1960–2018 personal resource abundance multiplier 1960 = 1	Percentage change in personal resource abundance 1960–2018	Compound annual percentage growth rate in personal resource abundance	Years to double personal resource abundance
					1960 time price at $0.77 per hour	2018 time price at $23.65 per hour					
Crude oil	$/bbl	1.63	68.35	4,093.1	2.11	2.89	37.0	0.73	−27	−0.54	−127.58
Fertilizer	$/mt	34.19	258.59	656.4	44.23	10.93	−75.3	4.05	305	2.44	28.77
Gold	$/tz	35.27	1,269.23	3,498.6	45.63	53.66	17.6	0.85	−15	−0.28	−247.83
Groundnut oil	$/mt	327.00	1,446.21	342.3	423.03	61.15	−85.5	6.92	592	3.39	20.79
Iron ore	$/dmtu	11.42	69.75	510.8	14.77	2.95	−80.0	5.01	401	2.82	24.95
Lead	$/mt	198.85	2,240.44	1,026.7	257.24	94.73	−63.2	2.72	172	1.74	40.24
Logs	$/cm	31.94	269.70	744.4	41.32	11.40	−72.4	3.62	262	2.24	31.23
Natural gas, Eur.	$/mmbtu	0.40	7.68	1,797.8	0.52	0.32	−38.0	1.61	61	0.83	84.17
Natural gas, U.S.	$/mmbtu	0.14	3.16	2,153.6	0.18	0.13	−26.3	1.36	36	0.53	131.48
Nickel	$/mt	1,631.00	13,114.06	704.1	2109.95	554.46	−73.7	3.81	281	2.33	30.08
Oranges	$/kg	0.13	0.79	507.7	0.17	0.03	−80.1	5.04	404	2.83	24.87
Palm oil	$/mt	224.42	638.70	184.6	290.32	27.00	−90.7	10.75	975	4.18	16.93

Platinum	$/tz	83.50	879.55	953.3	108.02	37.19	−65.6	2.90	190	1.86	37.70
Rice, Thai	$/mt	107.35	420.67	291.9	138.87	17.79	−87.2	7.81	681	3.61	19.56
Rubber	$/kg	0.78	1.57	100.6	1.01	0.07	−93.4	15.25	1,425	4.81	14.76
Sawnwood	$/cm	149.17	727.94	388.0	192.98	30.78	−84.1	6.27	527	3.22	21.90
Shrimp	$/kg	1.61	12.24	662.1	2.08	0.52	−75.1	4.01	301	2.43	28.92
Silver	$/tz	0.91	15.71	1,619.8	1.18	0.66	−43.8	1.78	78	1.00	69.78
Sorghum	$/mt	36.58	168.59	360.9	47.32	7.13	−84.9	6.64	564	3.32	21.24
Soybeans etc.	$/mt	132.25	529.62	300.5	171.09	22.39	−86.9	7.64	664	3.57	19.77
Sugar	$/kg	0.10	0.41	288.3	0.14	0.02	−87.3	7.88	688	3.62	19.47
Tea	$/kg	1.03	2.85	176.6	1.33	0.12	−91.0	11.06	1,006	4.23	16.73
Tin	$/mt	2,196.73	20,145.21	817.1	2841.82	851.74	−70.0	3.34	234	2.10	33.37
Tobacco	$/mt	1,736.87	4,862.91	180.0	2246.91	205.60	−90.8	10.93	993	4.21	16.81
Wheat	$/mt	57.99	209.93	262.0	75.02	8.88	−88.2	8.45	745	3.75	18.83
Zinc	$/mt	246.19	2,922.38	1,087.0	318.49	123.56	−61.2	2.58	158	1.65	42.46
Average				**766.9**			**−83.0**	**5.89**	**489**	**3.10**	**22.67**

Source: Authors' calculations.

Note: bbl = barrel; cm = cubic meters; dmtu = dry metric tonne unit; Eur = Europe; GDP = gross domestic product; lb = pound; kg = kilogram; LNG = liquefied natural gas; mmbtu = metric million British thermal unit; mt = metric ton; tz = troy ounce.

Appendix 9. The World Bank 37: country and territory perspective (1960–2018)

	1960 GDP per hour worked ($)	2018 GDP per hour worked ($)	Percentage change 1960–2018 GDP per hour worked	Percentage change time price World Bank 37 index	World Bank 37 commodities personal resource abundance multiplier	Percentage change in personal resource abundance 1960–2018	Compound annual percentage growth rate in personal resource abundance	Years to double personal resource abundance
Australia	2.28	66.15	2,806	−82.1	5.60	460	3.01	23.3
Austria	0.93	62.97	6,639	−92.3	12.97	1,197	4.52	15.7
Belgium	1.67	72.32	4,243	−88.0	8.36	736	3.73	18.9
Brazil	0.27	10.35	3,690	−86.3	7.30	630	3.49	20.2
Canada	2.91	52.97	1,718	−71.4	3.50	250	2.18	32.1
Chile	0.72	18.04	2,392	−79.2	4.80	380	2.74	25.6
China[a]	0.08	9.18	10,797	−95.2	20.98	1,998	5.39	13.2
Colombia	0.41	7.28	1,688	−71.0	3.44	244	2.15	32.5
Denmark	1.55	84.91	5,368	−90.5	10.53	953	4.14	17.1
Finland	1.15	65.45	5,568	−90.8	10.91	991	4.21	16.8
France	1.47	65.12	4,326	−88.3	8.52	752	3.76	18.8
Greece	0.54	25.41	4,562	−88.9	8.98	798	3.86	18.3
Hong Kong	0.45	43.30	9,507	−94.6	18.49	1,749	5.16	13.8
Ireland	0.76	99.51	12,960	−96.0	25.14	2,414	5.72	12.5

Italy	0.89	47.42	5,256	−90.3	10.31	931	4.10	17.2
Japan	0.43	42.26	9,774	−94.7	19.01	1,801	5.21	13.7
Mexico	0.60	10.27	1,623	−69.8	3.32	232	2.09	33.5
Netherlands	1.40	68.67	4,796	−89.4	9.43	843	3.94	17.9
Norway	1.67	108.94	6,433	−92.0	12.58	1,158	4.46	15.9
Peru	0.35	6.90	1,858	−73.5	3.77	277	2.31	30.3
Portugal	0.43	26.27	6,002	−91.5	11.75	1,075	4.34	16.3
Singapore	0.63	43.91	6,884	−92.6	13.44	1,244	4.58	15.5
South Korea	0.24	29.32	12,290	−95.8	23.85	2,285	5.62	12.7
Spain	0.46	42.69	9,194	−94.4	17.89	1,689	5.10	13.9
Sweden	2.17	67.37	3,009	−83.3	5.98	498	3.13	22.5
Switzerland	1.74	88.30	4,984	−89.8	9.79	879	4.01	17.6
United Kingdom	1.42	52.50	3,588	−85.9	7.10	610	3.44	20.5
United States	4.04	73.64	1,721	−71.5	3.51	251	2.19	32.1
Average	**0.77**	**23.65**	**2,960**	**−79.6**	**5.89**	**489**	**3.10**	**22.7**

Source: Authors' calculations.

Note: Eur. = Europe; GDP = gross domestic product; Hong Kong = Hong Kong SAR, China.

a. The Conference Board presents the Chinese data in two series, China (Alternative) and China (Official). The former is based on alternative growth estimates, while the latter is based on official data. We use the China (Alternative) series. For more information on The Conference Board's alternative growth measures for China, please refer to https://www.conference-board.org/pdf_free/FAQ_for-China-GDP-vs4_10nov15.pdf.

Appendix 10. Jacks's 40 commodities: the U.S. blue-collar worker perspective (1900–2018)

| Commodity | 1900 nominal price indexed to 1900 = 100 | 2018 nominal price indexed to 1900 = 100 | Percentage change in nominal price 1900–2018 | Blue-collar worker rate | | Percentage change in time price 1900–2018 | 1900–2018 personal resource abundance multiplier 1900 = 1 | Percentage change in personal resource abundance 1900–2018 | Compound annual percentage growth rate in personal resource abundance | Years to double personal resource abundance |
				1900 time price at $0.14 per hour	2018 time price at $32.06 per hour					
Aluminum	100.0	252.13	152.1	714.3	7.9	−98.9	90.83	8,983	3.86	18.29
Barley	100.0	1,289.19	1,189.2	714.3	40.2	−94.4	17.76	1,676	2.45	28.67
Bauxite	100.0	763.46	663.5	714.3	23.8	−96.7	30.00	2,900	2.90	24.25
Beef	100.0	5,612.24	5,512.2	714.3	175.1	−75.5	4.08	308	1.19	58.66
Chromium	100.0	5,735.88	5,635.9	714.3	178.9	−75.0	3.99	299	1.17	59.58
Coal	100.0	7,440.88	7,340.9	714.3	232.1	−67.5	3.08	208	0.95	73.38
Cocoa	100.0	658.34	558.3	714.3	20.5	−97.1	34.78	3,378	3.03	23.24
Coffee	100.0	1,415.72	1,315.7	714.3	44.2	−93.8	16.18	1,518	2.37	29.63
Copper	100.0	1,889.66	1,789.7	714.3	58.9	−91.7	12.12	1,112	2.12	33.06
Corn	100.0	895.07	795.1	714.3	27.9	−96.1	25.58	2,458	2.76	25.44
Cotton	100.0	971.39	871.4	714.3	30.3	−95.8	23.57	2,257	2.69	26.10
Cottonseed	100.0	939.90	839.9	714.3	29.3	−95.9	24.36	2,336	2.72	25.83

Gold	100.0	6,137.05	6,037.0	714.3	191.4	−73.2	3.73	273	1.11	62.64
Hides	100.0	724.65	624.7	714.3	22.6	−96.8	31.60	3,060	2.94	23.89
Iron ore	100.0	2,052.64	1,952.6	714.3	64.0	−91.0	11.16	1,016	2.05	34.20
Lamb	100.0	4,893.85	4,793.8	714.3	152.6	−78.6	4.68	368	1.31	53.45
Lead	100.0	2,402.70	2,302.7	714.3	74.9	−89.5	9.53	853	1.91	36.59
Manganese	100.0	4,179.04	4,079.0	714.3	130.4	−81.8	5.48	448	1.44	48.49
Natural gas	100.0	4,419.32	4,319.3	714.3	137.8	−80.7	5.18	418	1.39	50.14
Nickel	100.0	1,139.43	1,039.4	714.3	35.5	−95.0	20.10	1,910	2.55	27.49
Palm oil	100.0	708.99	609.0	714.3	22.1	−96.9	32.30	3,130	2.96	23.74
Peanuts	100.0	864.24	764.2	714.3	27.0	−96.2	26.50	2,550	2.79	25.17
Petroleum	100.0	11,692.62	11,592.6	714.3	364.7	−48.9	1.96	96	0.57	122.71
Phosphate	100.0	1,263.82	1,163.8	714.3	39.4	−94.5	18.12	1,712	2.46	28.47
Platinum	100.0	4,701.54	4,601.5	714.3	146.6	−79.5	4.87	387	1.34	52.10
Pork	100.0	365.70	265.7	714.3	11.4	−98.4	62.62	6,162	3.54	19.94
Potash	100.0	422.39	322.4	714.3	13.2	−98.2	54.22	5,322	3.41	20.66
Rice	100.0	556.96	457.0	714.3	17.4	−97.6	41.12	4,012	3.17	22.19

(Continued)

| Commodity | 1900 nominal price indexed to 1900 = 100 | 2018 nominal price indexed to 1900 = 100 | Percentage change in nominal price 1900–2018 | Blue-collar worker rate | | | 1900–2018 personal resource abundance multiplier 1900 = 1 | Percentage change in personal resource abundance 1900–2018 | Compound annual percentage growth rate in personal resource abundance | Years to double personal resource abundance |
				1900 time price at $0.14 per hour	2018 time price at $32.06 per hour	Percentage change in time price 1900–2018				
Rubber	100.0	132.16	32.2	714.3	4.1	−99.4	173.27	17,227	4.43	16.00
Rye	100.0	948.13	848.1	714.3	29.6	−95.9	24.15	2,315	2.71	25.90
Silver	100.0	2,424.45	2,324.5	714.3	75.6	−89.4	9.45	845	1.90	36.73
Steel	100.0	3,046.47	2,946.5	714.3	95.0	−86.7	7.52	652	1.71	40.89
Sugar	100.0	461.89	361.9	714.3	14.4	−98.0	49.58	4,858	3.33	21.13
Sulfur	100.0	719.86	619.9	714.3	22.5	−96.9	31.81	3,081	2.95	23.84
Tea	100.0	891.61	791.6	714.3	27.8	−96.1	25.68	2,468	2.77	25.41
Tin	100.0	3,397.76	3,297.8	714.3	106.0	−85.2	6.74	574	1.62	43.23
Tobacco	100.0	2,432.70	2,332.7	714.3	75.9	−89.4	9.41	841	1.90	36.79
Wheat	100.0	751.18	651.2	714.3	23.4	−96.7	30.49	2,949	2.91	24.14
Wool	100.0	1,143.83	1,043.8	714.3	35.7	−95.0	20.02	1,902	2.55	27.52
Zinc	100.0	3,271.75	3,171.8	714.3	102.1	−85.7	7.00	600	1.65	42.39
Average			2,250.3			−96.1	25.37	2,437	2.75	25.51

Source: Authors' calculations.

Appendix 11. Jacks's 40 commodities: the U.S. unskilled worker perspective (1900–2018)

Commodity	1900 nominal price indexed to 1900 = 100	2018 nominal price indexed to 1900 = 100	Percentage change in nominal price 1900–2018	Unskilled worker rate		Percentage change in time price 1900–2018	1900–2018 personal resource abundance multiplier 1900 = 1	Percentage change in personal resource abundance 1900–2018	Compound annual percentage growth rate in personal resource abundance	Years to double personal resource abundance
				1900 time price at $0.09 per hour	2018 time price at $12.78 per hour					
Aluminum	100.0	252.13	152.1	1,111.1	19.7	−98.2	56.32	5,532	3.48	20.29
Barley	100.0	1,289.19	1,189.2	1,111.1	100.9	−90.9	11.01	1,001	2.05	34.09
Bauxite	100.0	763.46	663.5	1,111.1	59.7	−94.6	18.60	1,760	2.51	27.98
Beef	100.0	5,612.24	5,512.2	1,111.1	439.1	−60.5	2.53	153	0.79	88.11
Chromium	100.0	5,735.88	5,635.9	1,111.1	448.8	−59.6	2.48	148	0.77	90.23
Coal	100.0	7,440.88	7,340.9	1,111.1	582.2	−47.6	1.91	91	0.55	126.56
Cocoa	100.0	658.34	558.3	1,111.1	51.5	−95.4	21.57	2,057	2.64	26.63
Coffee	100.0	1,415.72	1,315.7	1,111.1	110.8	−90.0	10.03	903	1.97	35.48
Copper	100.0	1,889.66	1,789.7	1,111.1	147.9	−86.7	7.51	651	1.72	40.55
Corn	100.0	895.07	795.1	1,111.1	70.0	−93.7	15.86	1,486	2.37	29.59
Cotton	100.0	971.39	871.4	1,111.1	76.0	−93.2	14.62	1,362	2.30	30.49
Cottonseed	100.0	939.90	839.9	1,111.1	73.5	−93.4	15.11	1,411	2.33	30.12

(Continued)

Appendix 11 (*continued*)

| Commodity | 1900 nominal price indexed to 1900 = 100 | 2018 nominal price indexed to 1900 = 100 | Percentage change in nominal price 1900–2018 | Unskilled worker rate | | Percentage change in time price 1900–2018 | 1900–2018 personal resource abundance multiplier 1900 = 1 | Percentage change in personal resource abundance 1900–2018 | Compound annual percentage growth rate in personal resource abundance | Years to double personal resource abundance |
				1900 time price at $0.09 per hour	2018 time price at $12.78 per hour					
Gold	100.0	6,137.05	6,037.0	1,111.1	480.2	−56.8	2.31	131	0.71	97.50
Hides	100.0	724.65	624.7	1,111.1	56.7	−94.9	19.60	1,860	2.55	27.49
Iron ore	100.0	2,052.64	1,952.6	1,111.1	160.6	−85.5	6.92	592	1.65	42.29
Lamb	100.0	4,893.85	4,793.8	1,111.1	382.9	−65.5	2.90	190	0.91	76.78
Lead	100.0	2,402.70	2,302.7	1,111.1	188.0	−83.1	5.91	491	1.52	46.04
Manganese	100.0	4,179.04	4,079.0	1,111.1	327.0	−70.6	3.40	240	1.04	66.87
Natural gas	100.0	4,419.32	4,319.3	1,111.1	345.8	−68.9	3.21	221	0.99	70.07
Nickel	100.0	1,139.43	1,039.4	1,111.1	89.2	−92.0	12.46	1,146	2.16	32.42
Palm oil	100.0	708.99	609.0	1,111.1	55.5	−95.0	20.03	1,903	2.57	27.29
Peanuts	100.0	864.24	764.2	1,111.1	67.6	−93.9	16.43	1,543	2.40	29.22
Petroleum	100.0	11,692.62	11,592.6	1,111.1	914.9	−17.7	1.21	21	0.16	420.99
Phosphate	100.0	1,263.82	1,163.8	1,111.1	98.9	−91.1	11.24	1,024	2.07	33.81
Platinum	100.0	4,701.54	4,601.5	1,111.1	367.9	−66.9	3.02	202	0.94	74.00

Pork	100.0	365.70	265.7	1,111.1	28.6	−97.4	38.83	3,783	3.15	22.35
Potash	100.0	422.39	322.4	1,111.1	33.1	−97.0	33.62	3,262	3.02	23.27
Rice	100.0	556.96	457.0	1,111.1	43.6	−96.1	25.50	2,450	2.78	25.26
Rubber	100.0	132.16	32.2	1,111.1	10.3	−99.1	107.44	10,644	4.04	17.49
Rye	100.0	948.13	848.1	1,111.1	74.2	−93.3	14.98	1,398	2.32	30.22
Silver	100.0	2,424.45	2,324.5	1,111.1	189.7	−82.9	5.86	486	1.51	46.27
Steel	100.0	3,046.47	2,946.5	1,111.1	238.4	−78.5	4.66	366	1.31	53.14
Sugar	100.0	461.89	361.9	1,111.1	36.1	−96.7	30.74	2,974	2.95	23.88
Sulfur	100.0	719.86	619.9	1,111.1	56.3	−94.9	19.73	1,873	2.56	27.43
Tea	100.0	891.61	791.6	1,111.1	69.8	−93.7	15.93	1,493	2.37	29.55
Tin	100.0	3,397.76	3,297.8	1,111.1	265.9	−76.1	4.18	318	1.22	57.19
Tobacco	100.0	2,432.70	2,332.7	1,111.1	190.4	−82.9	5.84	484	1.51	46.36
Wheat	100.0	751.18	651.2	1,111.1	58.8	−94.7	18.90	1,790	2.52	27.83
Wool	100.0	1,143.83	1,043.8	1,111.1	89.5	−91.9	12.41	1,141	2.16	32.47
Zinc	100.0	3,271.75	3,171.8	1,111.1	256.0	−77.0	4.34	334	1.25	55.72
Average			**2,250.3**			**−93.6**	**15.73**	**1,473**	**2.36**	**29.68**

Source: Authors' calculations.

Appendix 12. Jacks's 26 commodities: the U.S. blue-collar worker perspective (1850–2018)

Commodity	1850 nominal price indexed to 1900 = 100	2018 nominal price indexed to 1900 = 100	Percentage change in nominal price 1850–2018	Blue-collar worker rate — 1850 time price at $0.06 per hour	Blue-collar worker rate — 2018 time price at $32.06 per hour	Percentage change in time price 1850–2018	1850–2018 personal resource abundance multiplier 1850 = 1	Percentage change in personal resource abundance 1850–2018	Compound annual percentage growth rate in personal resource abundance	Years to double personal resource abundance
Barley	108.66	1,289.19	1,086.5	1,810.9	40.2	−97.8	45.04	4,404	2.29	30.58
Beef	71.43	5,612.24	7,757.1	1,190.5	175.1	−85.3	6.80	580	1.15	60.74
Coal	88.32	7,440.88	8,325.1	1,472.0	232.1	−84.2	6.34	534	1.11	63.04
Cocoa	74.32	658.34	785.9	1,238.6	20.5	−98.3	60.32	5,932	2.47	28.40
Coffee	129.26	1,415.72	995.3	2,154.3	44.2	−98.0	48.79	4,779	2.34	29.96
Copper	107.70	1,889.66	1,654.6	1,795.0	58.9	−96.7	30.45	2,945	2.05	34.09
Corn	91.88	895.07	874.1	1,531.4	27.9	−98.2	54.85	5,385	2.41	29.08
Cotton	125.37	971.39	674.8	2,089.6	30.3	−98.5	68.96	6,796	2.55	27.51
Gold	100.00	6,137.05	6,037.0	1,666.7	191.4	−88.5	8.71	771	1.30	53.81
Hides	60.00	724.65	1,107.8	1,000.0	22.6	−97.7	44.24	4,324	2.28	30.73
Lamb	72.88	4,893.85	6,614.8	1,214.7	152.6	−87.4	7.96	696	1.24	56.14
Lead	128.97	2,402.70	1,763.0	2,149.5	74.9	−96.5	28.68	2,768	2.02	34.70

Nickel	386.95	1,139.43	194.5	6,449.1	35.5	−99.4	181.46	18,046	3.14	22.39
Palm oil	109.09	708.99	549.9	1,818.2	22.1	−98.8	82.22	8,122	2.66	26.41
Pork	51.27	365.70	613.3	854.5	11.4	−98.7	74.91	7,391	2.60	26.98
Rice	116.22	556.96	379.2	1,936.9	17.4	−99.1	111.49	11,049	2.85	24.70
Rye	176.38	948.13	437.6	2,939.6	29.6	−99.0	99.40	9,840	2.78	25.32
Silver	199.38	2,424.45	1,116.0	3,323.0	75.6	−97.7	43.94	4,294	2.28	30.78
Steel	54.22	3,046.47	5,518.3	903.7	95.0	−89.5	9.51	851	1.35	51.70
Sugar	196.08	461.89	135.6	3,268.0	14.4	−99.6	226.83	22,583	3.28	21.47
Tea	177.74	891.61	401.6	2,962.3	27.8	−99.1	106.52	10,552	2.82	24.94
Tin	57.43	3,397.76	5,816.4	957.2	106.0	−88.9	9.03	803	1.32	52.91
Tobacco	168.58	2,432.70	1,343.1	2,809.6	75.9	−97.3	37.03	3,603	2.17	32.24
Wheat	91.18	751.18	723.8	1,519.7	23.4	−98.5	64.86	6,386	2.51	27.91
Wool	112.70	1,143.83	914.9	1,878.3	35.7	−98.1	52.65	5,165	2.39	29.38
Zinc	80.24	3,271.75	3,977.2	1,337.4	102.1	−92.4	13.11	1,211	1.54	45.26
Average			**2,299.9**			**−98.3**	**58.62**	**5,762**	**2.45**	**28.60**

Source: Authors' calculations.

Appendix 13. Jacks's 26 commodities: the U.S. unskilled worker perspective (1850–2018)

Commodity	1850 nominal price indexed to 1900=100	2018 nominal price indexed to 1900=100	Percentage change in nominal price 1850–2018	Unskilled worker rate			1850–2018 personal resource abundance multiplier 1850=1	Percentage change in personal resource abundance 1850–2018	Compound annual percentage growth rate in personal resource abundance	Years to double personal resource abundance
				1850 time price at $0.05 per hour	2018 time price at $12.78 per hour	Percentage change in time price 1850–2018				
Barley	108.66	1,289.19	1,086.5	2,156.4	100.9	−95.3	21.38	2,038	1.84	38.03
Beef	71.43	5,612.24	7,757.1	1,417.6	439.1	−69.0	3.23	223	0.70	99.37
Coal	88.32	7,440.88	8,325.1	1,752.8	582.2	−66.8	3.01	201	0.66	105.66
Cocoa	74.32	658.34	785.9	1,474.9	51.5	−96.5	28.63	2,763	2.02	34.71
Coffee	129.26	1,415.72	995.3	2,565.2	110.8	−95.7	23.16	2,216	1.89	37.06
Copper	107.70	1,889.66	1,654.6	2,137.4	147.9	−93.1	14.46	1,346	1.60	43.60
Corn	91.88	895.07	874.1	1,823.5	70.0	−96.2	26.04	2,504	1.96	35.73
Cotton	125.37	971.39	674.8	2,488.2	76.0	−96.9	32.74	3,174	2.10	33.38
Gold	100.00	6,137.05	6,037.0	1,984.6	480.2	−75.8	4.13	313	0.85	82.07
Hides	60.00	724.65	1,107.8	1,190.8	56.7	−95.2	21.00	2,000	1.83	38.25
Lamb	72.88	4,893.85	6,614.8	1,446.4	382.9	−73.5	3.78	278	0.79	87.62
Lead	128.97	2,402.70	1,763.0	2,559.6	188.0	−92.7	13.61	1,261	1.57	44.60

Nickel	386.95	1,139.43	194.5	7,679.4	89.2	−98.8	86.13	8,513	2.69	26.13
Palm oil	109.09	708.99	549.9	2,165.0	55.5	−97.4	39.03	3,803	2.21	31.78
Pork	51.27	365.70	613.3	1,017.5	28.6	−97.2	35.56	3,456	2.15	32.61
Rice	116.22	556.96	379.2	2,306.4	43.6	−98.1	52.92	5,192	2.39	29.34
Rye	176.38	948.13	437.6	3,500.4	74.2	−97.9	47.18	4,618	2.32	30.21
Silver	199.38	2,424.45	1,116.0	3,956.9	189.7	−95.2	20.86	1,986	1.82	38.33
Steel	54.22	3,046.47	5,518.3	1,076.1	238.4	−77.8	4.51	351	0.90	77.26
Sugar	196.08	461.89	135.6	3,891.4	36.1	−99.1	107.67	10,667	2.82	24.89
Tea	177.74	891.61	401.6	3,527.4	69.8	−98.0	50.56	4,956	2.36	29.68
Tin	57.43	3,397.76	5,816.4	1,139.7	265.9	−76.7	4.29	329	0.87	80.00
Tobacco	168.58	2,432.70	1,343.1	3,345.6	190.4	−94.3	17.58	1,658	1.72	40.62
Wheat	91.18	751.18	723.8	1,809.6	58.8	−96.8	30.79	2,979	2.06	33.98
Wool	112.70	1,143.83	914.9	2,236.6	89.5	−96.0	24.99	2,399	1.93	36.18
Zinc	80.24	3,271.75	3,977.2	1,592.5	256.0	−83.9	6.22	522	1.09	63.71
Average			2,299.9			−96.4	27.82	2,682	2.00	35.01

Source: Authors' calculations.

Appendix 14. U.S. food prices: the U.S. blue-collar worker perspective (1919–2019)

Commodity	1919 BLS nominal price ($)	2019 Walmart nominal price ($)	Percentage change in nominal price 1919–2019	Blue-collar worker rate — 1919 time price at $0.43 per hour	Blue-collar worker rate — 2019 time price at $32.36 per hour	Percentage change in time price 1919–2019	1919–2019 personal resource abundance multiplier 1919 = 1	Percentage change in personal resource abundance 1919–2019	Compound annual percentage growth rate in personal resource abundance	Years to double personal resource abundance
Bacon, sliced, lb.	0.53	3.68	598.3	1.23	0.11	−90.7	10.78	978	2.41	29.16
Bananas, dozen	0.32	2.16	579.2	0.74	0.07	−91.0	11.08	1,008	2.43	28.82
Beans, baked, no. 2 can	0.17	1.40	748.5	0.38	0.04	−88.7	8.87	787	2.21	31.76
Beans, navy, lb.	0.12	1.42	1,113.7	0.27	0.04	−83.9	6.20	520	1.84	37.99
Bread, lb., baked weight	0.10	1.28	1,154.9	0.24	0.04	−83.3	6.00	500	1.81	38.70
Butter, lb.	0.67	3.04	352.4	1.56	0.09	−94.0	16.64	1,564	2.85	24.65
Cabbage, lb.	0.06	1.26	1,932.3	0.14	0.04	−73.0	3.70	270	1.32	52.95
Cheese, lb.	0.42	3.20	665.6	0.97	0.10	−89.8	9.83	883	2.31	30.33
Chuck roast, lb.	0.25	4.47	1,680.9	0.58	0.14	−76.3	4.23	323	1.45	48.10
Coffee, lb.	0.43	4.00	828.1	1.00	0.12	−87.7	8.11	711	2.12	33.12
Cornflakes, 8 oz. pkg.	0.14	0.40	185.7	0.33	0.01	−96.2	26.34	2,534	3.33	21.19
Cornmeal, lb.	0.07	0.46	590.9	0.15	0.01	−90.8	10.89	989	2.42	29.03
Corn, canned, no. 2 can	0.20	0.60	204.6	0.46	0.02	−96.0	24.71	2,371	3.26	21.61

Cream of Wheat, 28 oz. pkg.	0.25	3.48	1,286.5	0.58	0.11	−81.6	5.43	443	1.71	40.98
Crisco, lb.	0.36	2.84	700.0	0.83	0.09	−89.4	9.41	841	2.27	30.92
Eggs, dozen	0.61	1.28	108.8	1.43	0.04	−97.2	36.04	3,504	3.65	19.34
Flour, wheat, lb.	0.07	0.67	846.5	0.17	0.02	−87.4	7.95	695	2.09	33.43
Ham, sliced, lb.	0.57	3.00	429.1	1.32	0.09	−93.0	14.22	1,322	2.69	26.11
Hens, lb.	0.41	1.16	186.4	0.94	0.04	−96.2	26.27	2,527	3.32	21.21
Lamb, lb.	0.37	6.94	1,775.7	0.86	0.21	−75.1	4.01	301	1.40	49.89
Lard, lb.	0.37	1.75	371.7	0.86	0.05	−93.7	15.95	1,495	2.81	25.03
Macaroni, lb.	0.19	0.80	321.1	0.44	0.02	−94.4	17.87	1,687	2.93	24.04
Milk, evaporated, 15–16 oz. can	0.16	0.90	473.2	0.37	0.03	−92.4	13.13	1,213	2.61	26.92
Milk, fresh, quart	0.15	0.96	523.4	0.36	0.03	−91.7	12.07	1,107	2.52	27.83
Nut margarine, lb.	0.35	5.13	1,382.7	0.80	0.16	−80.3	5.08	408	1.64	42.67
Onions, lb.	0.08	0.98	1,206.7	0.17	0.03	−82.6	5.76	476	1.77	39.59
Oranges, dozen	0.53	10.56	1,896.2	1.23	0.33	−73.5	3.77	277	1.34	52.23
Peas, canned, no. 2 can	0.19	0.60	224.3	0.43	0.02	−95.7	23.20	2,220	3.19	22.04
Plate beef, lb.	0.19	2.96	1,466.1	0.44	0.09	−79.2	4.81	381	1.58	44.16
Pork chops, lb.	0.42	2.46	489.9	0.97	0.08	−92.2	12.76	1,176	2.58	27.22

(Continued)

Appendix 14 (*continued*)

Commodity	1919 BLS nominal price ($)	2019 Walmart nominal price ($)	Percentage change in nominal price 1919–2019	Blue-collar worker rate 1919 time price at $0.43 per hour	Blue-collar worker rate 2019 time price at $32.36 per hour	Percentage change in time price 1919–2019	1919–2019 personal resource abundance multiplier 1919 = 1	Percentage change in personal resource abundance 1919–2019	Compound annual percentage growth rate in personal resource abundance	Years to double personal resource abundance
Potatoes, lb.	0.04	0.60	1,614.3	0.08	0.02	−77.2	4.39	339	1.49	46.86
Prunes, lb.	0.26	3.52	1,253.8	0.60	0.11	−82.0	5.56	456	1.73	40.41
Raisins, seeded, lb.	0.18	2.45	1,231.5	0.43	0.08	−82.3	5.65	465	1.75	40.02
Rib roast, lb.	0.31	8.97	2,793.5	0.72	0.28	−61.6	2.60	160	0.96	72.52
Rice, lb.	0.15	0.44	189.5	0.35	0.01	−96.2	26.00	2,500	3.31	21.28
Rolled oats, lb.	0.08	0.96	1,115.2	0.18	0.03	−83.9	6.19	519	1.84	38.01
Round steak, lb.	0.35	7.74	2,111.4	0.81	0.24	−70.6	3.40	240	1.23	56.60
Salmon, canned, lb.	0.33	3.36	921.3	0.77	0.10	−86.4	7.37	637	2.02	34.70
Sirloin steak, lb.	0.39	6.82	1,635.4	0.91	0.21	−76.9	4.34	334	1.48	47.25
Sugar, granulated, lb.	0.11	0.32	183.2	0.26	0.01	−96.2	26.57	2,557	3.33	21.13
Tea, lb.	0.64	22.24	3,396.9	1.48	0.69	−53.5	2.15	115	0.77	90.44
Tomatoes, canned, no. 2 can	0.17	0.80	370.6	0.40	0.02	−93.7	15.99	1,499	2.81	25.00
Average			979.5			−91.2	11.32	1,032	2.46	28.57

Source: Authors' calculations.

Note: BLS = Bureau of Labor Statistics; lb. = pound; oz. = ounce; pkg. = package.

Appendix 15. U.S. food prices: the U.S. unskilled worker perspective (1919–2019)

| Commodity | 1919 BLS nominal price ($) | 2019 Walmart nominal price ($) | Percentage change in nominal price 1919–2019 | Unskilled worker rate | | Percentage change in time price 1919–2019 | 1919–2019 personal resource abundance multiplier 1919=1 | Percentage change in personal resource abundance 1919–2019 | Compound annual percentage growth rate in personal resource abundance | Years to double personal resource abundance |
				1919 time price at $0.25 per hour	2019 time price at $13.66 per hour					
Bacon, sliced, lb.	0.53	3.68	598.3	2.11	0.27	-87.2	7.83	683	2.08	33.68
Bananas, dozen	0.32	2.16	579.2	1.27	0.16	-87.6	8.05	705	2.11	33.23
Beans, baked, no. 2 can	0.17	1.40	748.5	0.66	0.10	-84.5	6.44	544	1.88	37.20
Beans, navy, lb.	0.12	1.42	1,113.7	0.47	0.10	-77.8	4.51	351	1.52	46.05
Bread, lb, baked weight	0.10	1.28	1,154.9	0.41	0.09	-77.1	4.36	336	1.48	47.09
Butter, lb.	0.67	3.04	352.4	2.69	0.22	-91.7	12.09	1,109	2.52	27.81
Cabbage, lb.	0.06	1.26	1,932.3	0.25	0.09	-62.8	2.69	169	0.99	70.03
Cheese, lb.	0.42	3.20	665.6	1.67	0.23	-86.0	7.14	614	1.99	35.25
Chuck roast, lb.	0.25	4.47	1,680.9	1.00	0.33	-67.4	3.07	207	1.13	61.79
Coffee, lb.	0.43	4.00	828.1	1.73	0.29	-83.0	5.89	489	1.79	39.08
Cornflakes, 8 oz. pkg.	0.14	0.40	185.7	0.56	0.03	-94.8	19.14	1,814	3.00	23.48
Cornmeal, lb.	0.07	0.46	590.9	0.26	0.03	-87.4	7.91	691	2.09	33.51

(Continued)

Appendix 15 (continued)

Commodity	1919 BLS nominal price ($)	2019 Walmart nominal price ($)	Percentage change in nominal price 1919–2019	Unskilled worker rate		Percentage change in time price 1919–2019	1919–2019 personal resource abundance multiplier 1919 = 1	Percentage change in personal resource abundance 1919–2019	Compound annual percentage growth rate in personal resource abundance	Years to double personal resource abundance
				1919 time price at $0.25 per hour	2019 time price at $13.66 per hour					
Corn, canned, no. 2 can	0.20	0.60	204.6	0.79	0.04	−94.4	17.95	1,695	2.93	24.00
Cream of Wheat, 28 oz. pkg.	0.25	3.48	1,286.5	1.00	0.25	−74.6	3.94	294	1.38	50.51
Crisco, lb.	0.36	2.84	700.0	1.42	0.21	−85.4	6.84	584	1.94	36.06
Eggs, dozen	0.61	1.28	108.8	2.45	0.09	−96.2	26.19	2,519	3.32	21.23
Flour, wheat, lb.	0.07	0.67	846.5	0.28	0.05	−82.7	5.78	478	1.77	39.52
Ham, sliced, lb.	0.57	3.00	429.1	2.27	0.22	−90.3	10.34	934	2.36	29.68
Hens, lb.	0.41	1.16	186.4	1.62	0.08	−94.8	19.09	1,809	2.99	23.50
Lamb, lb.	0.37	6.94	1,775.7	1.48	0.51	−65.7	2.92	192	1.08	64.78
Lard, lb.	0.37	1.75	371.7	1.49	0.13	−91.4	11.59	1,059	2.48	28.29
Macaroni, lb.	0.19	0.80	321.1	0.76	0.06	−92.3	12.99	1,199	2.60	27.03
Milk, evaporated, 15–16 oz. can	0.16	0.90	473.2	0.63	0.07	−89.5	9.54	854	2.28	30.73
Milk, fresh, quart	0.15	0.96	523.4	0.62	0.07	−88.6	8.77	777	2.20	31.92
Nut margarine, lb.	0.35	5.13	1,382.7	1.39	0.38	−72.9	3.69	269	1.31	53.11
Onions, lb.	0.08	0.98	1,206.7	0.30	0.07	−76.1	4.18	318	1.44	48.42

Item										
Oranges, dozen	0.53	10.56	1,896.2	2.12	0.77	−63.5	2.74	174	1.01	68.78
Peas, canned, no. 2 can	0.19	0.60	224.3	0.74	0.04	−94.1	16.86	1,586	2.87	24.54
Plate beef, lb.	0.19	2.96	1,466.1	0.76	0.22	−71.4	3.49	249	1.26	55.44
Pork chops, lb.	0.42	2.46	489.9	1.67	0.18	−89.2	9.27	827	2.25	31.13
Potatoes, lb.	0.04	0.60	1,614.3	0.14	0.04	−68.7	3.19	219	1.17	59.76
Prunes, lb.	0.26	3.52	1,253.8	1.04	0.26	−75.2	4.04	304	1.41	49.65
Raisins, seeded, lb.	0.18	2.45	1,231.5	0.74	0.18	−75.7	4.11	311	1.42	49.07
Rib roast, lb.	0.31	8.97	2,793.5	1.24	0.66	−47.1	1.89	89	0.64	108.90
Rice, lb.	0.15	0.44	189.5	0.61	0.03	−94.7	18.89	1,789	2.98	23.59
Rolled oats, lb.	0.08	0.96	1,115.2	0.32	0.07	−77.8	4.50	350	1.52	46.08
Round steak, lb.	0.35	7.74	2,111.4	1.40	0.57	−59.6	2.47	147	0.91	76.56
Salmon, canned, lb.	0.33	3.36	921.3	1.32	0.25	−81.3	5.35	435	1.69	41.31
Sirloin steak, lb.	0.39	6.82	1,635.4	1.57	0.50	−68.3	3.15	215	1.15	60.39
Sugar, granulated, lb.	0.11	0.32	183.2	0.45	0.02	−94.8	19.31	1,831	3.00	23.41
Tea, lb.	0.64	22.24	3,396.9	2.55	1.63	−36.1	1.56	56	0.45	155.03
Tomatoes, canned, no. 2 can	0.17	0.80	370.6	0.68	0.06	−91.4	11.62	1,062	2.48	28.26
Average			**979.5**			**−87.8**	**8.22**	**722**	**2.13**	**32.90**

Source: Authors' calculations.

Note: BLS = Bureau of Labor Statistics; lb. = pound; oz. = ounce; pkg. = package.

Appendix 16. U.S. finished goods: the U.S. blue-collar worker perspective (1979–2019)

	1979 nominal price ($)	2019 nominal price ($)	Percentage change in nominal prices 1979–2019	Blue-collar worker rate 1979 time price at $8.34 per hour	Blue-collar worker rate 2019 time price at $32.36 per hour	Percentage change in time prices 1979–2019	1979–2019 personal resource abundance multiplier 1979=1	Percentage change in personal resource abundance 1979–2019	Compound annual percentage growth rate in personal resource abundance	Years to double personal resource abundance
APPLIANCES						−74.8	3.97	297	3.51	20.10
Slow cooker	27.99	39.99	42.9	3.36	1.24	−63.2	2.72	172	2.53	27.75
Dutch oven	34.99	49.99	42.9	4.20	1.54	−63.2	2.72	172	2.53	27.75
Skillet	24.99	24.99	0.0	3.00	0.77	−74.2	3.88	288	3.45	20.45
Coffeemaker	14.79	19.99	35.2	1.77	0.62	−65.2	2.87	187	2.67	26.29
Toaster	9.79	8.88	−9.3	1.17	0.27	−76.6	4.28	328	3.70	19.08
Blender	49.49	39.99	−19.2	5.93	1.24	−79.2	4.80	380	4.00	17.67
Can opener	11.99	8.88	−25.9	1.44	0.27	−80.9	5.24	424	4.23	16.74
Food processor	38.99	20.99	−46.2	4.68	0.65	−86.1	7.21	621	5.06	14.04
Vacuum	334.95	219.99	−34.3	40.16	6.80	−83.1	5.91	491	4.54	15.61
Dishwasher	389.95	582.00	49.2	46.76	17.99	−61.5	2.60	160	2.42	29.02
Washer	298.00	409.19	37.3	35.73	12.64	−64.6	2.83	183	2.63	26.69
Dryer	228.00	337.49	48.0	27.34	10.43	−61.9	2.62	162	2.44	28.77

MEN'S						−72.0	3.57	257	3.23	21.78
Watch	19.99	44.95	124.9	2.40	1.39	−42.0	1.73	73	1.37	50.82
Shaver	32.88	33.69	2.5	3.94	1.04	−73.6	3.79	279	3.38	20.82
Wallet	12.00	9.99	−16.8	1.44	0.31	−78.5	4.66	366	3.92	18.01
Suit	69.99	79.99	14.3	8.39	2.47	−70.5	3.40	240	3.10	22.68
Pants	15.99	25.00	56.3	1.92	0.77	−59.7	2.48	148	2.30	30.50
Cardigan	17.99	12.99	−27.8	2.16	0.40	−81.4	5.37	437	4.29	16.49
CHILDREN'S						−69.8	3.31	231	3.04	23.16
Crib	130.97	115.99	−11.4	15.70	3.58	−77.2	4.38	338	3.76	18.77
Pants	16.99	23.90	40.7	2.04	0.74	−63.7	2.76	176	2.57	27.33
Pajamas	8.99	23.99	166.9	1.08	0.74	−31.2	1.45	45	0.94	74.07
Panties	5.99	5.00	−16.5	0.72	0.15	−78.5	4.65	365	3.92	18.04
WOMEN'S						−69.8	3.31	231	3.04	23.15
Camisole	9.00	4.00	−55.6	1.08	0.12	−88.5	8.73	773	5.57	12.80
Blazer	25.00	29.99	20.0	3.00	0.93	−69.1	3.23	223	2.98	23.62
Belt	6.00	8.00	33.3	0.72	0.25	−65.6	2.91	191	2.71	25.96
Pants	14.00	29.99	114.2	1.68	0.93	−44.8	1.81	81	1.50	46.67

(Continued)

Appendix 16 (*continued*)

	1979 nominal price ($)	2019 nominal price ($)	Percentage change in nominal prices 1979–2019	Blue-collar worker rate		Percentage change in time prices 1979–2019	1979–2019 personal resource abundance multiplier 1979 = 1	Percentage change in personal resource abundance 1979–2019	Compound annual percentage growth rate in personal resource abundance	Years to double personal resource abundance
				1979 time price at $8.34 per hour	2019 time price at $32.36 per hour					
Sweater	8.99	17.50	94.7	1.08	0.54	−49.8	1.99	99	1.74	40.20
Gold necklace	10.00	39.99	299.9	1.20	1.24	3.1	0.97	−3	−0.08	
Blow dryer	14.99	18.99	26.7	1.80	0.59	−67.4	3.06	206	2.84	24.77
Gloves	17.00	17.70	4.1	2.04	0.55	−73.2	3.73	273	3.34	21.08
Sheer hose	2.75	3.17	15.3	0.33	0.10	−70.3	3.37	237	3.08	22.84
MISCELLANEOUS						−72.4	3.62	262	3.27	21.55
Butcher block	99.95	69.99	−30.0	11.98	2.16	−82.0	5.54	454	4.37	16.19
Bicycle	128.99	129.00	0.0	15.47	3.99	−74.2	3.88	288	3.45	20.45
Utensil set	9.99	18.84	88.6	1.20	0.58	−51.4	2.06	106	1.82	38.43
Jogging shoes	15.49	19.99	29.1	1.86	0.62	−66.7	3.01	201	2.79	25.19
Average						**−72.3**	**3.61**	**261**	**3.26**	**21.60**

Source: Authors' calculations.

Appendix 17. U.S. finished goods: the U.S. unskilled worker perspective (1979-2019)

	1979 nominal price ($)	2019 nominal price ($)	Percentage change in nominal prices 1979-2019	Unskilled worker rate — 1979 time price at $3.69 per hour	Unskilled worker rate — 2019 time price at $13.66 per hour	Percentage change in time prices 1979-2019	1979-2019 personal resource abundance multiplier 1979=1	Percentage change in personal resource abundance 1979-2019	Compound annual percentage growth rate in personal resource abundance	Years to double personal resource abundance
APPLIANCES						-73.6	3.79	279	3.39	20.81
Slow cooker	27.99	39.99	42.9	7.59	2.93	-61.4	2.59	159	2.41	29.12
Dutch oven	34.99	49.99	42.9	9.48	3.66	-61.4	2.59	159	2.41	29.12
Skillet	24.99	24.99	0.0	6.77	1.83	-73.0	3.70	270	3.33	21.18
Coffeemaker	14.79	19.99	35.2	4.01	1.46	-63.5	2.74	174	2.55	27.52
Toaster	9.79	8.88	-9.3	2.65	0.65	-75.5	4.08	308	3.58	19.71
Blender	49.49	39.99	-19.2	13.41	2.93	-78.2	4.58	358	3.88	18.22
Can opener	11.99	8.88	-25.9	3.25	0.65	-80.0	5.00	400	4.10	17.23
Food processor	38.99	20.99	-46.2	10.57	1.54	-85.5	6.88	588	4.94	14.38
Vacuum	334.95	219.99	-34.3	90.77	16.10	-82.3	5.64	464	4.42	16.03
Dishwasher	389.95	582.00	49.2	105.68	42.61	-59.7	2.48	148	2.30	30.52
Washer	298.00	409.19	37.3	80.76	29.96	-62.9	2.70	170	2.51	27.96
Dryer	228.00	337.49	48.0	61.79	24.71	-60.0	2.50	150	2.32	30.25

(Continued)

	1979 nominal price ($)	2019 nominal price ($)	Percentage change in nominal prices 1979–2019	Unskilled worker rate — 1979 time price at $3.69 per hour	Unskilled worker rate — 2019 time price at $13.66 per hour	Percentage change in time prices 1979–2019	1979–2019 personal resource abundance multiplier 1979 = 1	Percentage change in personal resource abundance 1979–2019	Compound annual percentage growth rate in personal resource abundance	Years to double personal resource abundance
MEN'S						−70.6	3.41	241	3.11	22.62
Watch	19.99	44.95	124.9	5.42	3.29	−39.3	1.65	65	1.25	55.62
Shaver	32.88	33.69	2.5	8.91	2.47	−72.3	3.61	261	3.26	21.58
Wallet	12.00	9.99	−16.8	3.25	0.73	−77.5	4.45	345	3.80	18.58
Suit	69.99	79.99	14.3	18.97	5.86	−69.1	3.24	224	2.98	23.59
Pants	15.99	25.00	56.3	4.33	1.83	−57.8	2.37	137	2.18	32.17
Cardigan	17.99	12.99	−27.8	4.88	0.95	−80.5	5.13	413	4.17	16.96
CHILDREN'S						−68.3	3.16	216	2.92	24.11
Crib	130.97	115.99	−11.4	35.49	8.49	−76.1	4.18	318	3.64	19.38
Pants	16.99	23.90	40.7	4.60	1.75	−62.0	2.63	163	2.45	28.65
Pajamas	8.99	23.99	166.9	2.44	1.76	−27.9	1.39	39	0.82	84.71
Panties	5.99	5.00	−16.5	1.62	0.37	−77.5	4.43	343	3.79	18.61

WOMEN'S						−68.4	3.16	216	2.92	24.10
Camisole	9.00	4.00	−55.6	2.44	0.29	−88.0	8.33	733	5.44	13.08
Blazer	25.00	29.99	20.0	6.78	2.20	−67.6	3.09	209	2.86	24.60
Belt	6.00	8.00	33.3	1.63	0.59	−64.0	2.78	178	2.59	27.15
Pants	14.00	29.99	114.2	3.79	2.20	−42.1	1.73	73	1.38	50.68
Sweater	8.99	17.50	94.7	2.44	1.28	−47.4	1.90	90	1.62	43.14
Gold necklace	10.00	39.99	299.9	2.71	2.93	8.0	0.93	−7	−0.19	
Blow dryer	14.99	18.99	26.7	4.06	1.39	−65.8	2.92	192	2.72	25.86
Gloves	17.00	17.70	4.1	4.61	1.30	−71.9	3.56	256	3.22	21.86
Sheer hose	2.75	3.17	15.3	0.75	0.23	−68.9	3.21	221	2.96	23.76
MISCELLANEOUS						−71.1	3.45	245	3.15	22.36
Butcher block	99.95	69.99	−30.0	27.09	5.12	−81.1	5.29	429	4.25	16.65
Bicycle	128.99	129.00	.0	34.96	9.44	−73.0	3.70	270	3.33	21.18
Utensil set	9.99	18.84	88.6	2.71	1.38	−49.1	1.96	96	1.70	41.11
Jogging shoes	15.49	19.99	29.1	4.20	1.46	−65.1	2.87	187	2.67	26.31
Average						**−71.0**	**3.44**	**244**	**3.14**	**22.42**

Source: Authors' calculations.

Appendix 18. U.S. finished goods: the U.S. upskilling worker perspective (1979–2019)

| | 1979 nominal price ($) | 2019 nominal price ($) | Percentage change in nominal prices 1979–2019 | Upskilling worker rate | | | Percentage change in time prices 1979–2019 | 1979–2019 personal resource abundance multiplier 1979 = 1 | Percentage change in personal resource abundance 1979–2019 | Compound annual percentage growth rate in personal resource abundance | Years to double personal resource abundance |
				1979 time price at $3.69 per hour	2019 time price at $32.36 per hour						
APPLIANCES							−88.9	8.98	798	5.64	12.63
Slow cooker	27.99	39.99	42.9	7.59	1.24		−83.7	6.14	514	4.64	15.28
Dutch oven	34.99	49.99	42.9	9.48	1.54		−83.7	6.14	514	4.64	15.28
Skillet	24.99	24.99	0.0	6.77	0.77		−88.6	8.77	777	5.58	12.77
Coffeemaker	14.79	19.99	35.2	4.01	0.62		−84.6	6.49	549	4.79	14.83
Toaster	9.79	8.88	−9.3	2.65	0.27		−89.7	9.67	867	5.84	12.22
Blender	49.49	39.99	−19.2	13.41	1.24		−90.8	10.85	985	6.14	11.63
Can opener	11.99	8.88	−25.9	3.25	0.27		−91.6	11.84	1,084	6.37	11.22
Food processor	38.99	20.99	−46.2	10.57	0.65		−93.9	16.29	1,529	7.23	9.94
Vacuum	334.95	219.99	−34.3	90.77	6.80		−92.5	13.35	1,235	6.69	10.70
Dishwasher	389.95	582.00	49.2	105.68	17.99		−83.0	5.88	488	4.53	15.66

Washer	298.00	409.19	37.3	80.76	12.64	-84.3	6.39	539	4.74	14.95
Dryer	228.00	337.49	48.0	61.79	10.43	-83.1	5.92	492	4.55	15.58
MEN'S						-87.6	8.07	707	5.36	13.28
Watch	19.99	44.95	124.9	5.42	1.39	-74.4	3.90	290	3.46	20.37
Shaver	32.88	33.69	2.5	8.91	1.04	-88.3	8.56	756	5.51	12.91
Wallet	12.00	9.99	-16.8	3.25	0.31	-90.5	10.53	953	6.06	11.78
Suit	69.99	79.99	14.3	18.97	2.47	-87.0	7.67	667	5.23	13.61
Pants	15.99	25.00	56.3	4.33	0.77	-82.2	5.61	461	4.41	16.08
Cardigan	17.99	12.99	-27.8	4.88	0.40	-91.8	12.15	1,115	6.44	11.10
CHILDREN'S						-86.6	7.48	648	5.16	13.78
Crib	130.97	115.99	-11.4	35.49	3.58	-89.9	9.90	890	5.90	12.09
Pants	16.99	23.90	40.7	4.60	0.74	-84.0	6.23	523	4.68	15.15
Pajamas	8.99	23.99	166.9	2.44	0.74	-69.6	3.29	229	3.02	23.30
Panties	5.99	5.00	-16.5	1.62	0.15	-90.5	10.51	951	6.06	11.79

(Continued)

Appendix 18 (*continued*)

| | 1979 nominal price ($) | 2019 nominal price ($) | Percentage change in nominal prices 1979–2019 | Upskilling worker rate | | Percentage change in time prices 1979–2019 | 1979–2019 personal resource abundance multiplier 1979 = 1 | Percentage change in personal resource abundance 1979–2019 | Compound annual percentage growth rate in personal resource abundance | Years to double personal resource abundance |
				1979 time price at $3.69 per hour	2019 time price at $32.36 per hour					
WOMEN'S						−86.6	7.48	648	5.16	13.77
Camisole	9.00	4.00	−55.6	2.44	0.12	−94.9	19.73	1,873	7.74	9.30
Blazer	25.00	29.99	20.0	6.78	0.93	−86.3	7.31	631	5.10	13.94
Belt	6.00	8.00	33.3	1.63	0.25	−84.8	6.58	558	4.82	14.72
Pants	14.00	29.99	114.2	3.79	0.93	−75.6	4.09	309	3.59	19.67
Sweater	8.99	17.50	94.7	2.44	0.54	−77.8	4.51	351	3.83	18.42
Gold necklace	10.00	39.99	299.9	2.71	1.24	−54.4	2.19	119	1.98	35.31
Blow dryer	14.99	18.99	26.7	4.06	0.59	−85.6	6.92	592	4.96	14.33
Gloves	17.00	17.70	4.1	4.61	0.55	−88.1	8.42	742	5.47	13.01
Sheer hose	2.75	3.17	15.3	0.75	0.10	−86.9	7.61	661	5.20	13.66

MISCELLANEOUS						−87.8	8.18	718	5.40	13.19
Butcher block	99.95	69.99	−30.0	27.09	2.16	−92.0	12.52	1,152	6.52	10.97
Bicycle	128.99	129.00	0.0	34.96	3.99	−88.6	8.77	777	5.58	12.77
Utensil set	9.99	18.84	88.6	2.71	0.58	−78.5	4.65	365	3.92	18.04
Jogging shoes	15.49	19.99	29.1	4.20	0.62	−85.3	6.80	580	4.91	14.47
Average						**−87.7**	**8.16**	**716**	**5.39**	**13.21**

Source: Authors' calculations.

Appendix 19. U.S. cosmetic procedures: the U.S. blue-collar worker perspective (1998–2018)

| | 1998 nominal price ($) | 2018 nominal price ($) | Percentage change in nominal prices 1998–2018 | Blue-collar worker rate | | | 1998–2018 personal resource abundance multiplier 1998=1 | Percentage change in personal resource abundance 1998–2018 | Compound annual percentage growth rate in personal resource abundance | Years to double personal resource abundance |
				1998 time price at $18.18 per hour	2018 time price at $32.06 per hour	Percentage change in time prices 1998–2018				
Botox injection	424	311	-26.7	23.32	9.70	-58.4	2.40	140	4.48	15.80
Breast augmentation	3,001	3,735	24.5	165.07	116.50	-29.4	1.42	42	1.76	39.78
Liposuction	2,562	3,350	30.8	140.92	104.49	-25.9	1.35	35	1.51	46.35
Breast lift	3,439	4,790	39.3	189.16	149.41	-21.0	1.27	27	1.19	58.76
Tummy tuck	4,058	6,046	49.0	223.21	188.58	-15.5	1.18	18	0.85	82.23
Chemical peel	821	693	-15.6	45.16	21.62	-52.1	2.09	109	3.75	18.82
Laser hair removal	452	238	-47.3	24.86	7.42	-70.1	3.35	235	6.23	11.47
Eyelid surgery	2,187	3,100	41.7	120.30	96.69	-19.6	1.24	24	1.10	63.47
Breast reduction	4,936	5,864	18.8	271.51	182.91	-32.6	1.48	48	1.99	35.10

Facelift	4,895	7,672	56.7	269.25	239.30	−11.1	1.13	13	0.59	117.56
Nose surgery	3,304	5,087	54.0	181.74	158.67	−12.7	1.15	15	0.68	102.13
Laser skin resurfacing	2,276	2,601	14.3	125.19	81.13	−35.2	1.54	54	2.19	31.96
Male breast reduction	2,534	3,949	55.8	139.38	123.18	−11.6	1.13	13	0.62	112.14
Upper arm lift	2,643	4,640	75.6	145.38	144.73	−0.4	1.00	0	0.00	
Sclerotherapy (varicose veins)	269	375	39.4	14.80	11.70	−20.9	1.27	27	1.18	58.97
Thigh lift	3,516	5,195	47.8	193.40	162.04	−16.2	1.19	19	0.89	78.36
Chin augmentation	1,482	2,865	93.3	81.52	89.36	9.6	0.91	−9	−0.46	
Lower body lift	5,377	8,014	49.0	295.76	249.97	−15.5	1.18	18	0.84	82.41
Buttock lift	3,648	5,507	51.0	200.66	171.77	−14.4	1.17	17	0.78	89.18
Average						**−30.8**	**1.45**	**45**	**1.86**	**37.65**

Source: Authors' calculations.

Appendix 20. U.S. cosmetic procedures: the U.S. unskilled worker perspective (1998–2018)

| | 1998 nominal price ($) | 2018 nominal price ($) | Percentage change in nominal prices 1998–2018 | Unskilled worker rate | | | 1998–2018 personal resource abundance multiplier 1998 = 1 | Percentage change in personal resource abundance 1998–2018 | Compound annual percentage growth rate in personal resource abundance | Years to double personal resource abundance |
				1998 time price at $7.75 per hour	2018 time price at $12.78 per hour	Percentage change in time prices 1998–2018				
Botox injection	424	311	−26.7	54.71	24.33	−55.5	2.25	125	4.13	17.11
Breast augmentation	3,001	3,735	24.5	387.23	292.25	−24.5	1.32	32	1.42	49.27
Liposuction	2,562	3,350	30.8	330.58	262.13	−20.7	1.26	26	1.17	59.75
Breast lift	3,439	4,790	39.3	443.74	374.80	−15.5	1.18	18	0.85	82.11
Tummy tuck	4,058	6,046	49.0	523.61	473.08	−9.7	1.11	11	0.51	136.61
Chemical peel	821	693	−15.6	105.94	54.23	−48.8	1.95	95	3.41	20.70
Laser hair removal	452	238	−47.3	58.32	18.62	−68.1	3.13	213	5.87	12.14
Eyelid surgery	2,187	3,100	41.7	282.19	242.57	−14.0	1.16	16	0.76	91.62
Breast reduction	4,936	5,864	18.8	636.90	458.84	−28.0	1.39	39	1.65	42.28

Facelift	4,895	7,672	56.7	631.61	600.31	−5.0	1.05	5	0.25	272.76
Nose surgery	3,304	5,087	54.0	426.32	398.04	−6.6	1.07	7	0.34	201.98
Laser skin resurfacing	2,276	2,601	14.3	293.68	203.52	−30.7	1.44	44	1.85	37.80
Male breast reduction	2,534	3,949	55.8	326.97	309.00	−5.5	1.06	6	0.28	245.25
Upper arm lift	2,643	4,640	75.6	341.03	363.07	6.5	0.94	−6	−0.31	
Sclerotherapy (varicose veins)	269	375	39.4	34.71	29.34	−15.5	1.18	18	0.84	82.53
Thigh lift	3,516	5,195	47.8	453.68	406.49	−10.4	1.12	12	0.55	126.24
Chin augmentation	1,482	2,865	93.3	191.23	224.18	17.2	0.85	−15	−0.79	
Lower body lift	5,377	8,014	49.0	693.81	627.07	−9.6	1.11	11	0.51	137.08
Buttock lift	3,648	5,507	51.0	470.71	430.91	−8.5	1.09	9	0.44	156.91
Average						**−26.0**	**1.35**	**35**	**1.52**	**46.04**

Source: Authors' calculations.

Appendix 21. U.S. cosmetic procedures: the U.S. upskilling worker perspective (1998–2018)

| | 1998 nominal price ($) | 2018 nominal price ($) | Percentage change in nominal prices 1998–2018 | Upskilling worker rate | | | 1998–2018 personal resource abundance multiplier 1998 = 1 | Percentage change in personal resource abundance 1998–2018 | Compound annual percentage growth rate in personal resource abundance | Years to double personal resource abundance |
				1998 time price at $7.75 per hour	2018 time price at $32.06 per hour	Percentage change in time prices 1998–2018				
Botox injection	424	311	−26.7	54.71	9.70	−82.3	5.64	464	9.03	8.01
Breast augmentation	3,001	3,735	24.5	387.23	116.50	−69.9	3.32	232	6.19	11.54
Liposuction	2,562	3,350	30.8	330.58	104.49	−68.4	3.16	216	5.93	12.04
Breast lift	3,439	4,790	39.3	443.74	149.41	−66.3	2.97	197	5.59	12.74
Tummy tuck	4,058	6,046	49.0	523.61	188.58	−64.0	2.78	178	5.24	13.58
Chemical peel	821	693	−15.6	105.94	21.62	−79.6	4.90	390	8.27	8.72
Laser hair removal	452	238	−47.3	58.32	7.42	−87.3	7.86	686	10.86	6.73
Eyelid surgery	2,187	3,100	41.7	282.19	96.69	−65.7	2.92	192	5.50	12.94
Breast reduction	4,936	5,864	18.8	636.90	182.91	−71.3	3.48	248	6.44	11.11

Facelift	4,895	7,672	56.7	631.61	239.30	−62.1	2.64	164	4.97	14.28
Nose surgery	3,304	5,087	54.0	426.32	158.67	−62.8	2.69	169	5.07	14.03
Laser skin resurfacing	2,276	2,601	14.3	293.68	81.13	−72.4	3.62	262	6.64	10.78
Male breast reduction	2,534	3,949	55.8	326.97	123.18	−62.3	2.65	165	5.00	14.20
Upper arm lift	2,643	4,640	75.6	341.03	144.73	−57.6	2.36	136	4.38	16.17
Sclerotherapy (varicose veins)	269	375	39.4	34.71	11.70	−66.3	2.97	197	5.59	12.75
Thigh lift	3,516	5,195	47.8	453.68	162.04	−64.3	2.80	180	5.28	13.47
Chin augmentation	1,482	2,865	93.3	191.23	89.36	−53.3	2.14	114	3.88	18.22
Lower body lift	5,377	8,014	49.0	693.81	249.97	−64.0	2.78	178	5.24	13.58
Buttock lift	3,648	5,507	51.0	470.71	171.77	−63.5	2.74	174	5.17	13.75
Average						**−70.5**	**3.39**	**239**	**6.29**	**11.36**

Source: Authors' calculations.

Appendix 22. The Simon-Ehrlich five-metal basket (1980–1990)

| | 1980 nominal price ($) | 1990 nominal price ($) | Percentage change in nominal prices 1980–1990 | GDP per hours worked | | | 1980–1990 personal resource abundance multiplier 1980 = 1 | Percentage change in personal resource abundance 1980–1990 | Compound annual percentage growth rate in personal resource abundance | Years to double personal resource abundance |
				1980 time price at $3.24 per hour	1990 time price at $5.41 per hour	Percentage change in time prices 1980–1990				
Chromium	638	892	39.8	197.16	164.91	−16.4	1.20	20	1.80	38.81
Copper	2,234	2,712	21.4	690.35	501.39	−27.4	1.38	38	3.25	21.67
Nickel	6,230	8,860	42.2	1,925.21	1,638.04	−14.9	1.18	18	1.63	42.91
Tin	18,700	8,520	−54.4	5,778.71	1,575.18	−72.7	3.67	267	13.88	5.33
Tungsten	18,500	8,480	−54.2	5,716.91	1,567.78	−72.6	3.65	265	13.81	5.36
Average			**−1.0**			**−54.8**	**2.21**	**121**	**8.27**	**8.73**

Source: Authors' calculations.

Note: GDP = gross domestic product.

Appendix 23. The Simon-Ehrlich five-metal basket (1980–2018)

| | 1980 nominal price ($) | 2018 nominal price ($) | Percentage change in nominal prices 1980–2018 | GDP per hours worked | | Percentage change in time prices 1980–2018 | 1980–2018 personal resource abundance multiplier 1980 = 1 | Percentage change in personal resource abundance 1980–2018 | Compound annual percentage growth rate in personal resource abundance | Years to double personal resource abundance |
				1980 time price at $3.24 per hour	2018 time Price at $15.88 per hour					
Chromium	638	2,933	359.7	197.16	184.65	−6.3	1.07	7	0.17	401.80
Copper	2,234	6,586	194.8	690.35	414.64	−39.9	1.66	66	1.35	51.67
Nickel	6,230	13,114	110.5	1,925.21	825.59	−57.1	2.33	133	2.25	31.11
Tin	18,700	20,639	10.4	5,778.71	1,299.31	−77.5	4.45	345	4.01	17.65
Tungsten	18,500	41,109	122.2	5,716.91	2,587.98	−54.7	2.21	121	2.11	33.23
Average			159.5			−57.3	2.34	134	2.27	30.92

Source: Authors' calculations.

Note: GDP = gross domestic product.

Appendix 24. The Simon-Ehrlich five-metal basket: the U.S. blue-collar worker perspective (1900–2018)

| | 1900 nominal price ($) | 2018 nominal price ($) | Percentage change in nominal prices 1900–2018 | Blue-collar worker rate | | Percentage change in time prices 1900–2018 | 1900–2018 personal resource abundance multiplier 1900 = 1 | Percentage change in personal resource abundance 1900–2018 | Compound annual percentage growth rate in personal resource abundance | Years to double personal resource abundance |
				1900 time price at $0.14 per hour	2018 time price at $32.06 per hour					
Chromium	56	2,933	5,137.5	400.00	91.48	−77.1	4.37	337	1.26	55.44
Copper	357	6,586	1,744.9	2,550.00	205.44	−91.9	12.41	1,141	2.16	32.47
Nickel	1,100	13,114	1,092.2	7,857.14	409.05	−94.8	19.21	1,821	2.54	27.68
Tin	659	20,639	3,031.8	4,707.14	643.76	−86.3	7.31	631	1.70	41.11
Tungsten	556	41,109	7,293.6	3,971.43	1,282.24	−67.7	3.10	210	0.96	72.35
Average			3,660.0			−89.2	9.28	828	1.91	36.71

Source: Authors' calculations.

Appendix 25. The Simon-Ehrlich five-metal basket: the U.S. unskilled worker perspective (1900–2018)

	1900 nominal price ($)	2018 nominal price ($)	Percentage change in nominal prices 1900–2018	Unskilled worker rate		Percentage change in time prices 1900–2018	1900–2018 personal resource abundance multiplier 1900 = 1	Percentage change in personal resource abundance 1900–2018	Compound annual percentage growth rate in personal resource abundance	Years to double personal resource abundance
				1900 time price at $0.09 per hour	2018 time price at $12.78 per hour					
Chromium	56	2,933	5,137.5	622.22	229.50	−63.1	2.71	171	0.85	82.00
Copper	357	6,586	1,744.9	3,966.67	515.36	−87.0	7.70	670	1.74	40.08
Nickel	1,100	13,114	1,092.2	12,222.22	1,026.13	−91.6	11.91	1,091	2.12	33.01
Tin	659	20,639	3,031.8	7,322.22	1,614.93	−77.9	4.53	353	1.29	54.11
Tungsten	556	41,109	7,293.6	6,177.78	3,216.64	−47.9	1.92	92	0.55	125.33
Average			3,660.0			−82.6	5.75	475	1.49	46.74

Source: Authors' calculations.

Appendix 26. Population resource cost, 18 data sets

Data set	Range	Years	Items in the data set	Percentage change in time prices	Time prices in end-year with start year indexed to 1.0	Population in end-year with start-year indexed to 1.0	Total costs start-year	Total costs end-year
Basic 50	1980–2018	38	50	−71.6	0.284	1.71	1.00	0.486
World Bank 37	1960–2018	58	37	−83.0	0.170	2.52	1.00	0.428
Jacks's 40 blue-collar	1900–2018	118	40	−96.1	0.039	4.30	1.00	0.170
Jacks's 40 unskilled	1900–2018	118	40	−93.6	0.064	4.30	1.00	0.274
Jacks's 26 blue-collar	1850–2018	168	26	−98.3	0.017	14.22	1.00	0.243
Jacks's 26 unskilled	1850–2018	168	26	−96.4	0.036	14.22	1.00	0.511
U.S. food prices blue-collar	1919–2019	100	42	−91.2	0.088	3.12	1.00	0.276
U.S. food prices unskilled	1919–2019	100	42	−87.8	0.122	3.12	1.00	0.380
U.S. finished goods blue-collar	1979–2019	40	35	−72.3	0.277	1.44	1.00	0.400

U.S. finished goods unskilled	1979–2019	40	35	−70.9	0.291	1.44	1.00	0.420
U.S. finished goods upskilling	1979–2019	40	35	−87.7	0.123	1.44	1.00	0.177
U.S. cosmetic procedures blue-collar	1998–2018	20	19	−31.0	0.690	1.19	1.00	0.820
U.S. cosmetic procedures unskilled	1998–2018	20	19	−25.9	0.741	1.19	1.00	0.881
U.S. cosmetic procedures upskilling	1998–2018	20	19	−70.5	0.295	1.19	1.00	0.351
Simon-Ehrlich 1980–1990	1980–1990	10	5	−54.8	0.452	1.20	1.00	0.541
Simon-Ehrlich 1980–2018	1980–2018	38	5	−57.3	0.427	1.71	1.00	0.731
Simon-Ehrlich 1900–2018 blue-collar	1900–2018	118	5	−89.2	0.108	4.30	1.00	0.465
Simon-Ehrlich 1900–2018 unskilled	1900–2018	118	5	−82.6	0.174	4.30	1.00	0.749

Source: Authors' calculations.

Appendix 27. Percentage change in population resource cost, 18 data sets

Data set	Range	Years	Items in the data set	Total costs start-year	Total costs end-year	Percentage change in total cost
Basic 50	1980–2018	38	50	1.00	0.486	−51.4
World Bank 37	1960–2018	58	37	1.00	0.428	−57.2
Jacks's 40 blue-collar	1900–2018	118	40	1.00	0.170	−83.0
Jacks's 40 unskilled	1900–2018	118	40	1.00	0.274	−72.6
Jacks's 26 blue-collar	1850–2018	168	26	1.00	0.243	−75.7
Jacks's 26 unskilled	1850–2018	168	26	1.00	0.511	−48.9
U.S. food prices blue-collar	1919–2019	100	42	1.00	0.276	−72.4
U.S. food prices unskilled	1919–2019	100	42	1.00	0.380	−62.0
U.S. finished goods blue-collar	1979–2019	40	35	1.00	0.400	−60.0
U.S. finished goods unskilled	1979–2019	40	35	1.00	0.420	−58.0
U.S. finished goods upskilling	1979–2019	40	35	1.00	0.177	−82.3
U.S. cosmetic procedures blue-collar	1998–2018	20	19	1.00	0.820	−18.0
U.S. cosmetic procedures unskilled	1998–2018	20	19	1.00	0.881	−11.9
U.S. cosmetic procedures upskilling	1998–2018	20	19	1.00	0.351	−64.9
Simon-Ehrlich 1980–1990	1980–1990	10	5	1.00	0.541	−45.9
Simon-Ehrlich 1980–2018	1980–2018	38	5	1.00	0.731	−26.9
Simon-Ehrlich 1900–2018 blue-collar	1900–2018	118	5	1.00	0.465	−53.5
Simon-Ehrlich 1900–2018 unskilled	1900–2018	118	5	1.00	0.749	−25.1

Source: Authors' calculations.

Appendix 28. Compound annual growth rate in population resource cost, 18 data sets

Data set	Range	Years	Items in the data set	Total costs start-year	Total costs end-year	Percentage change in total cost	Compound annual percentage rate of growth in total cost
Basic 50	1980–2018	38	50	1.00	0.486	−51.4	−1.88
World Bank 37	1960–2018	58	37	1.00	0.428	−57.2	−1.45
Jacks's 40 blue-collar	1900–2018	118	40	1.00	0.170	−83.0	−1.49
Jacks's 40 unskilled	1900–2018	118	40	1.00	0.274	−72.6	−1.09
Jacks's 26 blue-collar	1850–2018	168	26	1.00	0.243	−75.7	−0.84
Jacks's 26 unskilled	1850–2018	168	26	1.00	0.511	−48.9	−0.40
U.S. food prices blue-collar	1919–2019	100	42	1.00	0.276	−72.4	−1.28
U.S. food prices unskilled	1919–2019	100	42	1.00	0.380	−62.0	−0.96
U.S. finished goods blue-collar	1979–2019	40	35	1.00	0.400	−60.0	−2.26
U.S. finished goods unskilled	1979–2019	40	35	1.00	0.420	−58.0	−2.15

(Continued)

Appendix 28 (continued)

Data set	Range	Years	Items in the data set	Total costs start-year	Total costs end-year	Percentage change in total cost	Compound annual percentage rate of growth in total cost
U.S. finished goods upskilling	1979–2019	40	35	1.00	0.177	–82.3	–4.24
U.S. cosmetic procedures blue-collar	1998–2018	20	19	1.00	0.820	–18.0	–0.99
U.S. cosmetic procedures unskilled	1998–2018	20	19	1.00	0.881	–11.9	–0.63
U.S. cosmetic procedures upskilling	1998–2018	20	19	1.00	0.351	–64.9	–5.10
Simon-Ehrlich 1980–1990	1980–1990	10	5	1.00	0.541	–45.9	–5.97
Simon-Ehrlich 1980–2018	1980–2018	38	5	1.00	0.731	–26.9	–0.82
Simon-Ehrlich 1900–2018 blue-collar	1900–2018	118	5	1.00	0.465	–53.5	–0.65
Simon-Ehrlich 1900–2018 unskilled	1900–2018	118	5	1.00	0.749	–25.1	–0.24

Source: Authors' calculations.

Appendix 29. Years to half population resource cost, 18 data sets

Data set	Range	Years	Items in the data set	Total cost start year	Total cost end year	Percentage change in total costs	Compound annual percentage growth rate in personal resource abundance	Years to half total cost
Basic 50	1980–2018	38	50	1.00	0.486	−51.4	−1.88	36.5
World Bank 37	1960–2018	58	37	1.00	0.428	−57.2	−1.45	47.3
Jacks's 40 blue-collar	1900–2018	118	40	1.00	0.170	−83.0	−1.49	46.1
Jacks's 40 unskilled	1900–2018	118	40	1.00	0.274	−72.6	−1.09	63.1
Jacks's 26 blue-collar	1850–2018	168	26	1.00	0.243	−75.7	−0.84	82.2
Jacks's 26 unskilled	1850–2018	168	26	1.00	0.511	−48.9	−0.40	173.5
U.S. food prices blue-collar	1919–2019	100	42	1.00	0.276	−72.4	−1.28	53.8
U.S. food prices unskilled	1919–2019	100	42	1.00	0.380	−62.0	−0.96	71.6
U.S. finished goods blue-collar	1979–2019	40	35	1.00	0.400	−60.0	−2.26	30.3
U.S. finished goods unskilled	1979–2019	40	35	1.00	0.420	−58.0	−2.15	32.0

(Continued)

Appendix 29 (*continued*)

Data set	Range	Years	Items in the data set	Total cost start year	Total cost end year	Percentage change in total costs	Compound annual percentage growth rate in personal resource abundance	Years to half total cost
U.S. finished goods upskilling	1979–2019	40	35	1.00	0.177	−82.3	−4.24	16.0
U.S. cosmetic procedures blue-collar	1998–2018	20	19	1.00	0.820	−18.0	−0.99	69.9
U.S. cosmetic procedures unskilled	1998–2018	20	19	1.00	0.881	−11.9	−0.63	109.2
U.S. cosmetic procedures upskilling	1998–2018	20	19	1.00	0.351	−64.9	−5.10	13.2
Simon-Ehrlich 1980–1990	1980–1990	10	5	1.00	0.541	−45.9	−5.97	11.3
Simon-Ehrlich 1980–2018	1980–2018	38	5	1.00	0.731	−26.9	−0.82	84.1
Simon-Ehrlich 1900–2018 blue-collar	1900–2018	118	5	1.00	0.465	−53.5	−0.65	106.7
Simon-Ehrlich 1900–2018 unskilled	1900–2018	118	5	1.00	0.749	−25.1	−0.24	282.6
Average							**−1.80**	**73.86**

Appendix 30. Population resource cost elasticity of population, 18 data sets

Data set	Range	Years	Items in the data set	Percentage change in population	Percentage change in total cost	Total cost elasticity of population
Basic 50	1980–2018	38	50	71.2	−51.4	−0.72
World Bank 37	1960–2018	58	37	151.8	−57.2	−0.38
Jacks's 40 blue-collar	1900–2018	118	40	330.3	−83.0	−0.25
Jacks's 40 unskilled	1900–2018	118	40	330.3	−72.6	−0.22
Jacks's 26 blue-collar	1850–2018	168	26	1,321.7	−75.7	−0.06
Jacks's 26 unskilled	1850–2018	168	26	1,321.7	−48.9	−0.04
U.S. food prices blue-collar	1919–2019	100	42	212.4	−72.4	−0.34
U.S. food prices unskilled	1919–2019	100	42	212.4	−62.0	−0.29
U.S. finished goods blue-collar	1979–2019	40	35	44.5	−60.0	−1.35
U.S. finished goods unskilled	1979–2019	40	35	44.5	−58.0	−1.30
U.S. finished goods upskilling	1979–2019	40	35	44.5	−82.3	−1.85
U.S. cosmetic procedures blue-collar	1998–2018	20	19	18.9	−18.0	−0.95
U.S. cosmetic procedures unskilled	1998–2018	20	19	18.9	−11.9	−0.63
U.S. cosmetic procedures upskilling	1998–2018	20	19	18.9	−64.9	−3.43
Simon-Ehrlich 1980–1990	1980–1990	10	5	19.6	−45.9	−2.35
Simon-Ehrlich 1980–2018	1980–2018	38	5	71.2	−26.9	−0.38
Simon-Ehrlich 1900–2018 blue-collar	1900–2018	118	5	330.3	−53.5	−0.16
Simon-Ehrlich 1900–2018 unskilled	1900–2018	118	5	330.3	−25.1	−0.08

Source: Authors' calculations.

Appendix 31. Detailed view of the Simon-Ehrlich Box, up to 100 percentage change in population and 800 percentage change in personal resource abundance

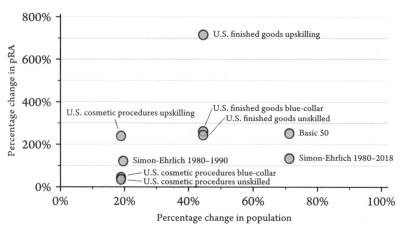

Appendix 32. Detailed view of the Simon-Ehrlich Box, up to 1,500 percentage change in population and 6,000 percentage change in personal resource abundance

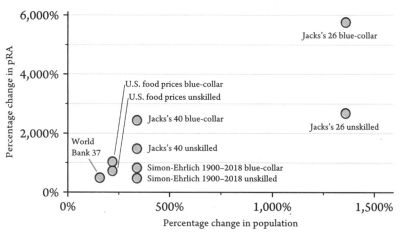

Appendix 33. Quizzes

Quiz 1. Time prices and personal resource abundance

Learning Objectives

- Calculate the time price (TP).
- Calculate the percentage change in time prices (PCTP).
- Calculate the personal resource abundance multiplier (pRAM).
- Calculate the percentage change in personal resource abundance (pRA).
- Calculate the compound annual growth rate in personal resource abundance (CAGR-pRA).
- Calculate the years to double personal resource abundance (YD-pRA).

Assume the following:

	Nominal price ($)	Hourly income ($)
1980	75	15
2020	60	30

1. What are the TPs for each year?
2. What is the PCTP?
3. What is the pRAM?
4. How much has the pRA increased?
5. What is the CAGR-pRA?
6. What is the YD-pRA?

Answers

1. 5, 2
2. −60%
3. 2.50
4. 150%
5. 2.32%
6. 20.26

Quiz 2. Population and resources (population resource abundance)

Learning Objectives

- Calculate the population resource abundance multiplier (PRAM).
- Calculate the percentage change in population resource abundance (PRA).
- Calculate the compound annual growth rate in population resource abundance (CAGR-PRA).

- Calculate the years to double population resource abundance (YD-PRA).
- Calculate the personal resource abundance elasticity of population (pRA-EP).
- Calculate the population resource abundance elasticity of population (PRA-EP).
- Calculate the time price elasticity of population (TP-EP).

Assume the following:

	Resource abundance multiplier	Population
1980	1.00	1.00
2020	2.50	1.70

1. What are the population resource abundance multipliers for each year?
2. What is the percentage change in population resource abundance?
3. What is the compound annual growth rate in population resource abundance?
4. How many years will it take to double population resource abundance?
5. What is the personal resource abundance elasticity of population?
6. What is the population resource abundance elasticity of population?
7. What is the time price elasticity of population?

Answers

1. 1.00, 4.25
2. 325%
3. 3.68%
4. 19.16
5. 2.14
6. 4.64
7. −0.86

NOTES

Citations and notes for the text appear as numbered endnotes. The lettered endnotes used in some chapters pertain to the boxed text.

Epigraph

Fernand Braudel, *Civilization and Capitalism, 15th–18th Century*, vol. 1, *The Structures of Everyday Life* (Berkeley: University of California Press, 1992), p. 31.

Introduction

[1] "Supply and Demand of Natural Resources: An Unequal Balance," *BBC/Bitesize* (online study support resource), accessed February 26, 2021.

[2] In absolute terms, the world's population rose from 4.5 billion people to 7.6 billion people between 1980 and 2018 (United Nations Population Division: World Population Prospects 2019).

[3] That 252 percent increase in abundance of commodities translates to a compounded growth rate of 3.4 percent per year and a doubling of abundance every 21 years.

[4] We are not the first writers to note the falling prices of resources. Since the 1960s, the time when the supposed "scarcity" of resources became a major concern, a number of eminent economists and demographers noted that prices of resources tended to decline over the long run. They included Carnegie Mellon University economist Neil Potter (1915–2008), Resources for the Future economist Francis T. Christy (1926–2009), Washington University economist Harold J. Barnett (1917–1987), Cornell University economist Chandler Morse (1906–1988), Harvard University economist Dale Jorgensen, Harvard University economist Zvi Griliches (1930–1999), University of Southern California economist Richard Easterlin, Yale University economist William Nordhaus, Duke University economist Allen Kelley (1937–2017), Harvard University economist Simon Kuznets (1901–1985), and Danish economist Ester Boserup (1910–1999). For a more detailed discussion of previous literature on the falling prices of resources, see Pierre Desrochers and Vincent Geloso, *Snatching the Wrong Conclusions from the Jaws of Defeat: A Resourceship Perspective on Paul Sabin's The Bet: Paul Ehrlich, Julian Simon, and Our Gamble over Earth's Future*, (New Haven, CT: Yale University Press, 2013), appearing in *New Perspectives on Political Economy: A Bilingual Interdisciplinary Journal* 12, no. 1–2 (2016): 32–33.

[5] Adam Smith, *An Inquiry into the Nature and Causes of the Wealth of Nations* (London: Methuen Publishing, 1904), Book I, Chapter II.

[6] Smith, *Wealth of Nations*.

[7] Ridley continues, "I am not talking about swapping favors—any old primate can do that. There is plenty of 'reciprocity' in monkeys and apes: you scratch my back and

I scratch yours. . . . Such reciprocity is an important human social glue, a source of cooperation and a habit inherited from the animal past that undoubtedly prepared human beings for exchange. But it is not the same thing as exchange. Reciprocity means giving each other the same thing (usually) at different times. Exchange—call it barter or trade if you like—means giving each other different things (usually) at the same time: simultaneously swapping two different objects." Matt Ridley, *The Rational Optimist* (New York: HarperCollins, 2010), pp. 56–57.

8 Fernand Braudel, *Civilization and Capitalism, 15th–18th Century*, vol. 1, *The Structures of Everyday Life* (Berkeley: University of California Press, 1992), p. 334.

9 "Food: All Cereal Brands," Walmart (website), accessed April 12, 2020.

10 For a complete list of our concepts, abbreviations, and equations, see Appendix 1.

11 The Consumer Price Index (CPI), for example, has four serious limitations. First, "the substitution bias causes certain increases in price to be overstated because it ignores the presence of substitutes." Second, the "representation of novelty results in a temporary distortion of the actual cost of living after the introduction of new products." Third, the "effects of quality changes cannot always be represented accurately because the quality is extremely hard to measure." Fourth, "the CPI may not accurately report the level of inflation experienced by an individual, because it measures the price level and inflation based on a typical consumer." Raphael Zeder, "Limitations of the Consumer Price Index (CPI)," *Quickonomics* (blog), accessed August 6, 2020.

12 See John Tierney, "Betting on the Planet," *New York Times Magazine*, Dec. 2, 1990.

13 John P. Holdren and Paul R. Ehrlich, *Global Ecology: Readings Toward a Rational Strategy for Man* (New York: Harcourt Brace Jovanovich, 1971), p. 7.

14 Paul R. Ehrlich et al., "No Middle Way on the Environment," *Atlantic Monthly* 280, no. 6 (December 1997): pp. 98–104.

15 Simon recognized the importance of time prices. He wrote, "A more personal, but often relevant, test of scarcity is whether you and I and others feel that we can afford to buy the material. That is, the relationship between price and income may matter. If the price of food stays the same but income falls sharply, then we feel that food is more scarce. By a similar test, if our wages rise while the price of oil remains constant, our fuller pockets lead us to feel that oil is getting less scarce." Ultimately, however, Simon decided to challenge Ehrlich using real or inflation-adjusted prices, probably assuming that the latter would be more likely to accept the wager. See Julian L. Simon, *The Ultimate Resource 2* (Princeton, NJ: Princeton University Press, 1996), pp. 25–26.

16 True, once upon a time they did, but that has not been the case since about 1800.

Chapter 1

1 *Avengers: Infinity War*, directed by Anthony Russo and Joe Russo (2018; Burbank, CA: Marvel Studios, 2018), DVD.

2 P. J. O'Rourke, *All the Trouble in the World: The Lighter Side of Overpopulation, Famine, Ecological Disaster, Ethnic Hatred, Plague, and Poverty* (New York: The Atlantic Monthly Press, 1994), p. 2.

3 For more on this subject, see J. B. Bury, *The Idea of Progress: An Inquiry into Its Origin and Growth* (New York: Dover Publications, 1932).

4 For more on this subject, see Martin J. Wiener, *English Culture and the Decline of the Industrial Spirit, 1850–1980*, 2nd edition (Cambridge: Cambridge University Press, 1981).

5 John Bowden, "Ocasio-Cortez: 'World Will End in 12 Years' If Climate Change Not Addressed," *The Hill*, January 22, 2019.

6 Statistics for *Avengers: Infinity War* appear on Box Office Mojo, accessed September 11, 2019.

7 Pamela McClintock, "Average Price of a Movie Ticket Rises to $9.11 in 2018," *Hollywood Reporter*, January 23, 2019.

8 Thanos's slaughter is eventually reversed. In *Avengers: Endgame*, the superheroes go back in time and defeat Thanos in an epic battle that claims the life of Iron Man.

9 Mary K. Bloodsworth-Lugo and Carmen R. Lugo-Lugo, *Projecting 9/11: Race, Gender, and Citizenship in Recent Hollywood Films* (Lanham: Rowman and Littlefield, 2015), p. 159, quoted in Wynn Gerald Hamonic, "Global Catastrophe in Motion Pictures as Meaning and Message: The Functions of Apocalyptic Cinema in American Film," *Journal of Religion & Film* 21, no. 1 (April 1, 2017).

10 Hamonic, "Global Catastrophe in Motion Pictures," p. 1.

11 *Kingsman: The Secret Service*, directed by Matthew Vaughn (Twentieth Century Fox, Los Angeles, CA, 2014), DVD.

12 *Inferno*, directed by Ron Howard (Columbia Pictures, Culver City, CA, 2016), DVD.

13 *Real Time with Bill Maher*, season 17, episode 19, "Episode #17.19," written by Samantha Matti, featuring Bill Maher, George F. Will, Charlie Sykes, aired June 14, 2019, on HBO.

14 The biblical book of Genesis says, "And out of the ground made the Lord God to grow every tree that is pleasant to the sight, and good for food; the tree of life also in the midst of the garden, and the tree of the knowledge of good and evil" (Gen. 2:9).

15 *Encyclopaedia Britannica Online*, s.v. "Mappō Buddhism," accessed October 23, 2021.

16 Zhuangzi, *The Complete Works of Zhuangzi*, trans. Burton Watson (New York: Columbia University Press, 2013), pp. 122–23.

17 Alan Levinovitz, *Natural: How Faith in Nature's Goodness Leads to Harmful Fads, Unjust Laws, and Flawed Science* (Boston: Beacon Press, 2020), p. 67.

18 Hesiod, *Works and Days* (Cambridge, MA: William Heinemann Ltd., 1914), lines 110–20.

19 Hesiod, *Works and Days*, lines 175–80.

20 See Aeschylus, *Prometheus Bound*, lines 128–284; Sophocles, *Antigone*, lines 332–75; and Euripides, *The Suppliant Women*, lines 195–200.

21 Bury, *The Idea of Progress*, p. 8.

22 Sallust, *The War with Catiline*, Section 2.

23 Tacitus, *Annals*, Book 3, Chapter 26.

24 "But after the earth was infected with heinous crime, and each one banished justice from their grasping mind, and brothers steeped their hands in fraternal blood, the son ceased grieving over departed parents, the sire craved for the funeral rites of his first-born that freely he might take of the flower of unwedded step-mother, the

unholy mother, lying under her unknowing son, did not fear to sully her household gods with dishonor: everything licit and lawless commingled with mad infamy turned away from us the just-seeing mind of the gods." See Catullus, *Poem 64* (London: Smithers, 1894).

25 Livy, *History of Rome*, Preface.
26 Seneca, *Natural Questions*, Book VII.
27 Bury, *The Idea of Progress*, p. 15.
28 Lucretius, *De Rerum Natura*, Book V, lines 1436–65.
29 Bury, *The Idea of Progress*, p. 17.
30 Sushil Mittal, Gene Thursby, eds., *Hindu World* (Routledge: London, 2012), p. 284.
31 "The Buddhist Universe," *BBC* (study resource), last updated November 23, 2009.
32 Plato, *Statesman* (Cambridge, MA: William Heinemann Ltd., 1921), http://www.perseus.tufts.edu/hopper/text?doc=Perseus%3Atext%3A1999.01.0172%3Atext%3DStat.%3Asection%3D272a. See also Corinne Gartner and Claudia Yau, "The Myth of Cronus in Plato's Statesman: Cosmic Rotation and Earthly Correspondence," *Apeiron* 53, no. 4 (2017): 437–62, https://doi.org/10.1515/apeiron-2017-0047.
33 Marcus Aurelius, *Meditations*, Book XI, Section 1.
34 In Book VIII of his *Republic*, Plato discusses five types of regimes: aristocracy, timocracy, oligarchy, democracy, and tyranny. See http://www.perseus.tufts.edu/hopper/text?doc=Perseus%3Atext%3A1999.01.0168%3Abook%3D8. In Book II of his *Politics*, Aristotle distinguished between political innovations (i.e., departure from the ideal norm), which he thought were bad, and scientific innovations, which he thought could lead to improvement. See http://www.perseus.tufts.edu/hopper/text?doc=Perseus:abo:tlg,0086,035:2.
35 "What Is Anacyclosis?" Our Philosophy page, Anacyclosis Institute, accessed October 23, 2021.
36 Arthur Herman, *Idea of Decline in Western History* (New York: Simon and Schuster, 2007), pp. 16–17.
37 *Encyclopaedia Britannica Online*, s.v. "Vohu Manah (Zoroastrianism)," accessed September 11, 2019.
38 "Key Beliefs in Judaism," *BBC/Bitesize* (online study support resource), accessed October 23, 2021.
39 "Key Beliefs in Islam," *BBC/Bitesize* (online study support resource), accessed October 23, 2021.
40 Bury, *The Idea of Progress*, p. 21.
41 Bury, *The Idea of Progress*, p. 24.
42 Bury, *The Idea of Progress*, p. 24.
43 Clay Routledge, Andrew A. Abeyta, and Christina Roylance, "Death and End Times: The Effects of Religious Fundamentalism and Mortality Salience on Apocalyptic Beliefs," *Religion, Brain & Behavior* 8, no. 1 (June 2016): 21–30, https://doi.org/10.1080/2153599X.2016.1238840.
44 Daniel N. Wojcik, *The End of the World as We Know It: Faith, Fatalism, and Apocalypse in America* (New York: NYU Press, 1997). More recent works on apocalyptic

thinking include Alison McQueen's *Political Realism in Apocalyptic Times* (Cambridge: Cambridge University Press, 2017) and Mark Lilla's *The Shipwrecked Mind: On Political Reaction* (New York: New York Review Books, 2016).

45 "Total Economy Database," Conference Board (online data set: "*TED 1*"), accessed March 27, 2020.

46 "Total Economy Database," Conference Board (online data set: "*TED 1*"), accessed March 27, 2020.

47 "Life Expectancy at Birth, Total (Years)," World Bank (online data set), accessed March 27, 2020.

48 "Mortality Rate, Infant (Per 1,000 Live Births)," World Bank (online data set), accessed March 27, 2020.

49 "Food Supply, per Person, per Day, Calories," Human Progress (online data set), accessed September 12, 2019.

50 "Health Facts," U.S. Department of Health and Human Services (online data set), accessed September 12, 2019 (site discontinued).

51 "Food Supply, Per Person, Per Day, Calories," Human Progress (online data set), accessed September 12, 2019.

52 Dickson Abanimi Amugsi et al., "Prevalence and Time Trends in Overweight and Obesity Among Urban Women: An Analysis of Demographic and Health Surveys Data from 24 African Countries," *BMJ Open* 7, no. 10 (October 2017): https://doi.org/10.1136/bmjopen-2017-017344.

53 Ronald Bailey and Marian L. Tupy, *Ten Global Trends Every Smart Person Should Know: And Many Others You Will Find Interesting* (Washington: Cato Institute, 2020), p. 81.

54 Ronald Bailey, "Impending Defeat for the Four Horsemen of the Apocalypse," *Reason*, August 3, 2019.

55 Max Roser, "War and Peace," Our World in Data, accessed September 12, 2019.

56 Steven Pinker, *Enlightenment Now: The Case for Reason, Science, Humanism, and Progress* (New York: Viking Press, 2018), p. 161.

57 "School Enrollment, Primary (% Net)," World Bank (online data set), accessed March 27, 2020.

58 "School Enrollment, Secondary (% Gross)," World Bank (online data set), accessed March 30, 2020.

59 "School Enrollment, Tertiary (% Gross)," World Bank (online data set), accessed March 30, 2020.

60 "Literacy Rate, Adult Male (% of Males Ages 15 and Above)," World Bank (online data set), accessed March 30, 2020.

61 "Literacy Rate, Adult Female (% of Females Ages 15 and Above)," World Bank (online data set), accessed March 30, 2020.

62 "Literacy Rate, Youth Female (% of Females Ages 15–24)," World Bank (online data set), accessed March 30, 2020.

63 "Literacy Rate, Youth Male (% of Males Ages 15–24)," World Bank (online data set), accessed March 30, 2020.

[64] "Poverty Headcount Ratio at $1.90 a Day (2011 PPP) (% of Population)," World Bank (online data set), accessed March 30, 2020.

[65] "Poverty Headcount Ratio at $1.90 a Day (2011 PPP) (% of Population)," World Bank (online data set), accessed March 30, 2020.

[66] John D. Sutter, "Slavery's Last Stronghold," *CNN Interactive*, March 2012, accessed September 12, 2019.

[67] Drew Desilver, "Despite Global Concerns about Democracy, More than Half of Countries Are Democratic," Pew Research Center, May 14, 2019.

[68] Bailey and Tupy, *Ten Global Trends.*

[69] Xiao-Peng Song et al., "Global Land Change from 1982 to 2016," *Nature* 560, no. 1 (August 2018): 639.

[70] Ronald Bailey, "Global Tree Cover Has Expanded More than 7 Percent Since 1982," *Reason*, September 4, 2018.

[71] Bailey and Tupy, *Ten Global Trends*, p. 25.

[72] Jesse H. Ausubel, "Peak Farmland and Potatoes" (plenary address, 2014 Potato Business Summit of the United Potato Growers of America, San Antonio, January 8, 2014).

[73] UNEP-WCMW and IUCN, "Protected Planet Report 2016: How Protected Areas Contribute to Achieving Global Targets for Biodiversity," working paper, Cambridge, United Kingdom, 2016.

[74] Bailey and Tupy, *Ten Global Trends*, p. 133.

[75] Jan Luiten van Zanden, *How Was Life? Global Well-Being Since 1820* (Paris: OECD Publishing, 2014); "Global SO_2 Emissions," Our World in Data, accessed October 23, 2021; Z. Klimont, S. J. Smith, and J. Cofala, "The Last Decade of Global Anthropogenic Sulfur Dioxide: 2000–2011 Emissions," *Environmental Research Letters* 8, no. 1 (January 9, 2013), https://doi.org/10.1088/1748-9326/8/1/014003.

[76] "Volume of Sulfur Dioxide Emissions in the U.S. from 1970 to 2019," Statista (online data set), April 2020.

[77] "CO_2 Emissions Kg per 2010 US$ of GDP," World Bank (online data set), accessed March 30, 2020.

[78] "Environmental Impacts of Natural Gas," Union of Concerned Scientists, June 19, 2014.

[79] Hannah Ritchie and Max Roser, "CO_2 and Greenhouse Gas Emissions," Our World in Data, accessed March 30, 2020.

[80] Hannah Ritchie and Max Roser, "CO_2 Emissions," Our World in Data, accessed February 3, 2021.

[81] "Water Productivity, Total (Constant 2010 US$ GDP per Cubic Meter of Total Freshwater Withdrawal)," World Bank (online data set), accessed September 12, 2019.

[82] Andrew McAfee, *More from Less: The Surprising Story of How We Learned to Prosper Using Fewer Resources—and What Happens Next* (New York: Charles Scribner's Sons, 2019), p. 101.

[83] "In sustainability parlance," wrote Pierre Desrochers in a recent paper, "relative decoupling refers to environmental impacts growing at a slower rate than population

or consumption. This is achieved through productivity gains from increased agricultural yields to lower energy inputs per unit of output. Absolute decoupling describes declining overall impacts independent of population and consumption trends. It is most commonly achieved through resource substitution such as the reduction in the number of work horses and mules brought about by the advent of the truck, tractor, and the automobile; the reduction in greenhouse gas emissions that resulted from the substitution of coal by natural gas in electricity generation; or the replacement of paper by electronic devices." See Pierre Desrochers, "The Paradoxical Malthusian. A Promethean Perspective on Vaclav Smil's *Growth: From Microorganisms to Megacities* (MIT Press, 2019) and *Energy and Civilization: A History* (MIT Press, 2017)," *Energies* 13, no. 20: 5306, https://doi.org/10.3390/en13205306.

[84] The term "progress" is not to be confused with "progressivism," a political movement that, at least in the American context, advocates for a greater role of the government in fostering social and economic change.

[85] Bury, *The Idea of Progress*, pp. 38–39.

[86] Bury, *The Idea of Progress*, p. 40. All three inventions were known to the ancient Chinese, although the extent of the European borrowing, as opposed to independent discoveries of the compass and the printing press, continues to be subject to much scholarly debate.

[87] Bury, *The Idea of Progress*, p. 65.

[88] Bury, *The Idea of Progress*, p. 65.

[89] Bury, *The Idea of Progress*, p. 78.

[90] As the American author George Gilder succinctly put it, "Wealth is essentially knowledge." George Gilder, "Wealth Is Essentially Knowledge," *Wall Street Journal*, December 20, 2013.

[91] "Peace is the natural effect of trade. Two nations who traffic with each other become reciprocally dependent, for if one has an interest in buying, the other has an interest in selling, and thus their union is founded on their mutual necessities," Charles-Louis de Secondat, Baron de La Brède et de Montesquieu, *The Spirit of the Laws* (London: T. Evans, 1777), Book XX.

[92] Francis Hutcheson, *A System of Moral Philosophy*, vol. 1 (London: Andrew Millar, 1755), p. 281.

[93] The word "civilization" originally meant being ruled by the Romans, but after the fall of Rome, it came to mean being ruled "well." Eventually, it came to refer to a "civilizing process" by which a society began to detest "murder, incest, and cannibalism" and adopted institutions like contracts, friendship, marriage, and the family instead. See Herman, *Idea of Decline*, p. 21.

[94] William Robertson, *The History of the Reign of the Emperor Charles V,* vol. 1 (London: W. Strahan, 1769), Section 1, p. 81.

[95] Charles de Secondat, Baron de Montesquieu, *The Spirit of the Laws*, trans. Anne M. Cohler, Basia Carolyn Miller, and Harold Samuel Stone (Cambridge: Cambridge University Press, 1989), p. 338.

[96] James Boswell, *The Life of Samuel Johnson* (London: I. Pitman & Sons, 1907), p. 502.

[97] Voltaire, *Letters on England*, trans. Leonard Tancock (New York: Penguin, 1980), letter 6, p. 41.

[98] These trends were clear to contemporary observers such as the English philosopher Herbert Spencer (1820–1903), who thought that increased "industrialism," which was Spencer's term for the gradual departure from agricultural feudalism in Europe, decreases political inequalities in "two ways: firstly, by creating a class having power derived otherwise than from territorial possessions or official positions and secondly, by generating ideas and sentiments at variance with the ancient assumptions of class superiority." Herbert Spencer, *The Principles of Sociology*, vol. 2, (New York: D. Appleton, 1882), p. 306.

[99] Marie-Jean-Antoine-Nicolas Caritat, Marquis de Condorcet, *Outlines of a Historical View of the Progress of the Human Mind: Being a Posthumous Work of the Late M. de Condorcet* (Chicago: G. Langer, 2009), pp. 364–65.

[100] Herman, *Idea of Decline*, p. 26.

[101] Edward Gibbon, *The History of the Decline and Fall of the Roman Empire*, vol. 3, Chapter 38, (London: Penguin Classics, 1996).

[102] James Anthony Froude, "Calvinism," in *Short Studies on Great Subjects,* vol. 2 (London: Longmans, Green and Co., 1871), p. 25.

[103] Jean-Jacques Rousseau, *A Discourse on Inequality* (London: Penguin, 1984), p. 38.

[104] Jean-Jacques Rousseau, *The Basic Political Writings,* trans. Donald A. Cress (Indianapolis, IN: Hackett, 2012), p. 79.

[105] Geneviève Rousselière, "Rousseau on Freedom in Commercial Society," *American Journal of Political Science* 60, no. 2 (April 2016): 352–363.

[106] G. W. F. Hegel, *Elements of the Philosophy of Right* (Cambridge: Cambridge University Press, 1991), Section 331; G. W. F. Hegel, "Philosophy of History" in *Selections*, ed. Jacob Loewenberg (New York: C. Scribner's Sons, 1929), pp. 388–89.

[107] For one instance, see Karl Marx and Friedrich Engels, *The Communist Manifesto and Its Relevance for Today* (Chippendale, Australia: Resistance Books, 1998), pp. 21–25.

[108] Herman, *Idea of Decline*, p. 36.

[109] Translation: "The higher goal of colonization is civilization."

[110] Stéphane Courtois et al., *Black Book of Communism* (Cambridge, MA: Harvard University Press, 1999), p. 15.

[111] Mussolini was a member of the National Directorate of the Italian Socialist Party and editor of that party's official newspaper, *Avanti!*

[112] See Benito Mussolini, speech delivered before the Chamber of Deputies, December 9, 1928, Palazzo Venezia, Rome; G. W. F. Hegel, "Philosophy of Law" in *Selections*, ed. Jacob Loewenberg (New York: C. Scribner's Sons, 1929), pp. 443–44, 447.

[113] See also, "I am not only the conqueror, but also the executor of Marxism . . . I had only to develop logically what social democracy repeatedly failed in because of its attempt to realize its evolution within the framework of democracy. National Socialism is what Marxism might have been if it could have broken its absurd and artificial ties with democratic order." Both quotes appear in Hermann Rauschning, *The Voice of Destruction* (New York: Putnam, 1940), pp. 185–86.

114 Oxford English Dictionary Online, s.v. "Progress," in Oxford English Dictionary Online, accessed September 11, 2019.

115 Pinker, *Enlightenment Now*, p. 51.

116 Pinker, *Enlightenment Now* p. 51.

117 Bury, *The Idea of Progress*, p. 236.

118 Immanuel Kant, *Idea for a General History with a Cosmopolitan Aim* (1784), quoted in Paul Guyer, "The Crooked Timber of Mankind," in *Kant's Idea for a Universal History with a Cosmopolitan Aim*, eds. Amélie Rorty and James Schmidt (Cambridge: Cambridge University Press, 2009), p. 129.

119 The phrase "Our modern skulls house a Stone-Age mind" was first used by the science journalist William Allman in his 1995 book *Stone Age Present: How Evolution Has Shaped Modern Life—from Sex, Violence, and Language to Emotions, Morals, and Communities*. For more, see Leda Cosmides and John Tooby, "Evolutionary Psychology: A Primer," UCSB Center for Evolutionary Psychology, accessed September 11, 2019.

120 "Homo sapiens," Smithsonian Museum of Natural History, Human Evolution Evidence (online study support resource), accessed September 11, 2019.

121 Daniel Kahneman, *Thinking, Fast and Slow* (New York: Farrar, Strauss, and Giroux, 2013), p. 282.

122 Peter H. Diamandis and Steven Kotler, *Abundance: The Future Is Better Than You Think* (New York: Free Press, 2012), p. 32.

123 Mark Trussler and Stuart Soroka, "Consumer Demand for Cynical and Negative News," *International Journal of Press/Politics* 19, no. 3 (2014): 360–379, https://doi.org/10.1177/1940161214524832.

124 Pinker, *Enlightenment Now*, p. 41.

125 Pinker, *Enlightenment Now*, p. 50.

126 Matt Ridley, *The Rational Optimist* (New York: HarperCollins, 2010), p. 280.

127 Robert Heilbroner, ed., *The Essential Adam Smith* (New York: W. W. Norton & Company), 106.

128 John Mueller and Mark G. Stewart, "How Safe Are We? Asking the Right Questions about Terrorism," *Foreign Affairs*, August 15, 2016.

129 Roy F. Baumeister, Ellen Bratslavsky, Catrin Finkenauer, and Kathleen D. Vohs, "Bad Is Stronger than Good," *Review of General Psychology* 5, no. 4 (December 1, 2001): 323–370, https://doi.org/10.1037/1089-2680.5.4.323.

130 Adam Smith, *The Theory of Moral Sentiments* (Los Angeles: Logos Books, 2018), 46.

131 Johan Galtung and Mari Holmboe Ruge, "The Structure of Foreign News," *Journal of Peace Research* 2, no. 1 (1965): 64–91.

132 David E. Levari et al., "Prevalence-Induced Concept Change in Human Judgement," *Science* 360, no. 6396 (June 29, 2018): 1465–67, https://doi.org/10.1126/science.aap8731.

133 "The Problem with Solving Problems," *Science Daily*, June 28, 2018.

134 Morgan Housel, "The Seduction of Pessimism," Collaborative Fund, June 13, 2017.

135 Deborah Solomon, "The Science of Second-Guessing," *New York Times Magazine*, December 12, 2004.

136 Vernon L. Smith, "The Economy Will Survive the Coronavirus," *Wall Street Journal*, April 5, 2020.

137 Housel, "The Seduction of Pessimism."

138 Thomas Babington Macaulay, *Essays, Critical and Miscellaneous* (Boston: Philips, Sampson and Company, 1859), p. 115.

Chapter 2

1 Thomas Robert Malthus, *An Essay on the Principle of Population, as It Affects the Future Improvement of Society, with Remarks on the Speculations of Mr. Godwin, M. Condorcet, and Other Writers* (London: J. Johnson, 1798), p. 61.

2 The exact range for the world's population in 1800 was between 813 million and 1.13 billion. "Historical Estimates of World Population," United States Census Bureau, accessed September 13, 2019.

3 Aristotle, *The Poetics of Aristotle* (Project Gutenberg, 2008), part XIII.

4 Aleksandr Solzhenitsyn, *The Gulag Archipelago* (New York: Harper and Row, 1979), p. 173.

5 *Avengers: Infinity War*, directed by Anthony Russo and Joe Russo.

6 Translation: "To understand all is to forgive all."

7 United Nations, *The Determinants and Consequences of Population Trends: New Summary of Findings of Interaction of Demographic, Economic and Social Factors* (New York: United Nations, 1973–1978), p. 33.

8 United Nations, *Determinants and Consequences*, p. 34.

9 United Nations, *Determinants and Consequences*, p. 34.

10 United Nations, *Determinants and Consequences*, p. 34.

11 United Nations, *Determinants and Consequences*, p. 34.

12 United Nations, *Determinants and Consequences*, pp. 34–35.

13 United Nations, *Determinants and Consequences*, p. 35.

14 United Nations, *Determinants and Consequences*, pp. 35–36.

15 United Nations, *Determinants and Consequences*, pp. 36–37.

16 "Historical Estimates of World Population," United States Census Bureau (online data set), accessed September 13, 2019.

17 Pierre Desrochers and Joanna Szurmak, "The Terrors of Dr. Suzuki," *C2C Journal*, February 6, 2019.

18 United Nations, *Determinants and Consequences*, p. 37.

19 United Nations, *Determinants and Consequences*, p. 37.

20 David Hume, *Essays Moral, Political, and Literary*, 3rd edition (London: Longmans, Green, and Co., 1882), p. 384.

21 Joseph de Maistre, *Against Rousseau: On the State of Nature and On the Sovereignty of the People*, trans. and ed. Richard A. Lebrun (Montreal: McGill-Queen's Press, MQUP, 1996), p. 157.

22 Malthus may have learned about the difference between geometric and arithmetic growth rates while studying mathematics at the University of Cambridge. He then applied that knowledge to this thinking about population growth.

23 Malthus, *Principle of Population*, Chapter 1. Paul Ehrlich would echo those sentiments in 1970. "Population will inevitably and completely outstrip whatever small increases in food supplies we make," Ehrlich predicted in *Mademoiselle* magazine. "The death rate will increase until at least 100–200 million people per year will be starving to death during the next ten years" (quoted in Ronald Bailey, "Earth Day Turns 50," *Reason*, May 2020).

24 Malthus, *Principle of Population*, Chapter 7.

25 Note that Malthus revised his 1798 essay on five more occasions. In addition to the six editions of his essay, he also published *A Summary View on the Principle of Population* in 1830. It is from that last work that the "preventive checks" quote comes from. See Thomas Malthus, *An Essay on the Principle of Population and a Summary View of the Principle of Population* (London: Penguin Books, 1985), p. 250.

26 Edward Anthony Wrigley and Roger Schofield, *The Population History of England, 1541–1871: A Reconstruction* (Cambridge, MA: Harvard University Press, 1981), Table 7.8, pp. 208–9.

27 Ryland Thomas and Samuel H. Williamson, "What Was the U.K. GDP Then?" Measuring Worth, accessed August 6, 2020.

28 Gregory Clark, "The Long March of History: Farm Wages Population and Economic Growth, England 1209–1869," *Economic History Review* 60, no. 1 (July 10, 2006), https://doi.org/10.1111/j.1468-0289.2006.00358.x.

29 "Ratio," Lexico Online Dictionary, accessed August 6, 2020.

30 The relevant equation is $[1 \div (1 - 0.303)] = 1.43$.

31 Gregory Clark, *A Farewell to Alms: A Brief Economic History of the World* (Princeton, NJ: Princeton University Press, 2007), p. 81.

32 Pierre Desrochers and Joanna Szurmak, *Population Bombed: Exploding the Link between Overpopulation and Climate Change* (London: Global Warming Policy Foundation, 2018), pp. 19–30.

33 John P. Holdren partnered with Paul Ehrlich and John Harte in their famous bet against Julian Simon, a topic that will be discussed at length in Chapter 3.

34 Milton Friedman and Rose Friedman, *Free to Choose: A Personal Statement* (Boston: Houghton Mifflin Harcourt, 1980), p. 13.

35 Desrochers and Szurmak, *Population Bombed*, p. 25.

36 John Dryzek, *The Politics of the Earth: Environmental Discourses* (Oxford: Oxford University Press, 2005), p. 52.

37 Desrochers and Szurmak, *Population Bombed*, pp. 37–47.

38 As will be explained in Chapters 7 and 9, population growth is a necessary but insufficient precondition for sustaining innovation and growth. People also need the freedom to speak and associate (i.e., to exchange ideas), property rights to incentivize them to discover new things, markets to test their ideas, the rule of law to ensure that they benefit from their discoveries, etc. These institutions are a cause and an effect of innovation (i.e., a virtuous cycle). China, in spite of a massive population, was a very poor place, until greater freedom and better institutions allowed the country to flourish.

[39] Desrochers and Szurmak, *Population Bombed*, p. 44.

[40] Paul Pojman and Louis P. Pojman, *Food Ethics* (Towson, MD: Cengage Learning, 2011), p. 75.

[41] Desrochers and Szurmak, *Population Bombed*, p. 47.

[42] Quoted in Julian L. Simon, *The Ultimate Resource 2* (Princeton, NJ: Princeton University Press, 1996), p. 30.

[43] The Club of Rome, which was established in 1968, "is an organization of individuals who share a common concern for the future of humanity and strive to make a difference. . . . [Its] mission is to promote an understanding of the global challenges facing humanity and to propose solutions through scientific analysis, communication and advocacy." See "About Us" section, Club of Rome, accessed September 16, 2019.

[44] Donella H. Meadows, Dennis L. Meadows, Jørgen Randers, and William W. Behrens III, *The Limits to Growth: A Report for the Club of Rome's Project on the Predicament of Mankind* (Washington: Potomac Associates, 1972).

[45] The *Ecologist* was a British environmental journal (later magazine) published between 1970 and 2009.

[46] "A Blueprint for Survival," editorial, *New York Times*, accessed September 16, 2019.

[47] Edward Goldsmith and Robert Allen, "A Blueprint For Survival," *The Ecologist* 2, no. 1 (January 1972): 1.

[48] Chelsea Follett, "Neo-Malthusianism and Coercive Population Control in China and India: Overpopulation Concerns Often Result in Coercion," Cato Institute Policy Analysis no. 897, July 21, 2020.

[49] Lena Edlund et al., "More Men, More Crime: Evidence from China's One-Child Policy," IZA discussion paper no. 3214, December 2007, quoted in Follett, "Neo-Malthusianism."

[50] Mei Fong, "One Child: The Story of China's Most Radical Experiment" (London: OneWorld Publications, 2016), p. 77, quoted in Follett, "Neo-Malthusianism."

[51] Susan Greenhalgh, "Controlling Births and Bodies in Village China," *American Ethnologist* 21, no. 1 (1994): 23, quoted in Follett, "Neo-Malthusianism."

[52] Verna Yu, "'I could hear the baby cry. They Killed My Baby . . . Yet I Couldn't Do A Thing': The Countless Tragedies of China's One Child Policy," *South China Morning Post*, November 15, 2015, quoted in Follett, "Neo-Malthusianism."

[53] "The Brutal Truth," *The Economist*, June 23, 2012, quoted in Follett, "Neo-Malthusianism."

[54] "Forced Late-Term Abortions Must Not Be Tolerated," *Global Times*, June 13, 2012, quoted in Follett, "Neo-Malthusianism."

[55] "When and What Happened: Timeline of Emergency, the Darkest Phase of Democracy in India," *India TV News Desk*, June 25, 2019.

[56] Emma Tarlo, *Unsettling Memories: Narratives of the Emergency in Delhi* (Berkeley: University of California Press, 2003), pp. 27–28.

[57] Follett, "Neo-Malthusianism," pp. 12–13.

[58] Follett, "Neo-Malthusianism," p. 13.

[59] Henry Kamm, "India State Is Leader in Forced Sterilization," *New York Times*, August 13, 1976, quoted in Follett, "Neo-Malthusianism."

[60] Tarlo, p. 165, quoted in Follett, "Neo-Malthusianism."

[61] Tarlo, p. 148, quoted in Follett, "Neo-Malthusianism."

[62] Follett, "Neo-Malthusianism," p. 15.

Box 2.1

[a] "Biological Extinction | Paul R. Ehrlich," YouTube, uploaded by Casina Pio IV, Paul R. Ehrlich, "Biological Extinction" (lecture, PAS-PASS Workshop, Casina Pio IV, Vatican City, February 27–March 1, 2017).

[b] Charles C. Mann, "The Book That Incited a Worldwide Fear of Overpopulation," *Smithsonian*, January 2018.

[c] Helen Raleigh, "China's 'One-Child Policy' Inflicted Billions with Unspeakable Suffering," *The Federalist*, September 29, 2020.

[d] Justin Parkinson, "Five Numbers That Sum Up China's One-Child Policy," *BBC News*, October 29, 2015.

[e] "Too Many Men," *Washington Post*, April 18, 2018.

[f] Paul Ehrlich (@PaulREhrlich), "China to End One-Child Policy, Allowing Families Two Children, http://nyti.ms/1kVju7L, GIBBERING INSANITY—THE GROWTH-FOREVER GANG," Twitter, October 29, 2015, 9:31a.m., accessed September 10, 2021.

[g] $[[(1 + 3.03) \times (1 + 0.758)] - 1]$.

[h] $[(6.59 \times 1.848) - 1]$.

Chapter 3

[1] Julian L. Simon, *The Ultimate Resource 2* (Princeton: Princeton University Press, 1996), p. 6.

[2] From Latin *cornu copiae*, which means the "horn of plenty" or a mythological hollow horn filled with the inexhaustible gifts of celebratory fruits. See also John Tierney, "Betting on the Planet," *New York Times Magazine*, Dec. 2, 1990.

[3] The scholars who most influenced his thinking included the Austrian economist F. A. Hayek (1899–1992), American economist Milton Friedman (1912–2006), and Belarussian (later American) economist Simon Kuznets (1901–1985). Simon became a senior fellow at the Cato Institute in Washington, DC.

[4] Simon, *Ultimate Resource 2*, p. 12.

[5] Simon, *Ultimate Resource 2*, p. 367.

[6] Simon, *Ultimate Resource 2*, p. xxxi.

[7] Simon, *Ultimate Resource 2*, p. xxxi.

[8] Simon, *Ultimate Resource 2*, p. xxxi.

[9] Letter quoted in personal communication from David Simon, July 12, 2019.

[10] Simon, *Ultimate Resource 2*, p. 605.

[11] Paul Sabin, *The Bet: Paul Ehrlich, Julian Simon, and Our Gamble over Earth's Future* (New Haven, CT: Yale University Press, 2013), p. 207.

[12] Quoted in personal communication from David Simon, July 12, 2019.

[13] Quoted in personal communication from David Simon, July 12, 2019.

14 Quoted in personal communication from David Simon, July 12, 2019.

15 Pierre Desrochers and Joanna Szurmak, "From Blue Collar Icon to Green Radical," *New Geography*, May 29, 2020.

16 Jan Dennis, "Airline Overbooking Policy Well Known, and So Too Should Be Its Creator," *Illinois News Bureau*, August 3, 2009.

17 Dennis, "Airline Overbooking Policy."

18 The full quote is this: "Most biologists and ecologists look at population growth in terms of the carrying capacity of natural systems. Julian [Simon] was not handicapped by being either. As an economist, he could see population growth in a much more optimistic light." See Kenneth N. Gilpin, "Julian Simon, 65, Optimistic Economist, Dies," *New York Times*, February 12, 1998.

19 Paul Ehrlich, *The Population Bomb* (New York: Ballantine Books, 1968), p. 1.

20 Ehrlich, *Population Bomb*, p. 11.

21 Tierney, "Betting on the Planet."

22 *The Carson Podcast*, April 12, 2018, https://carsonpodcast.com/dr-paul-ehrlich/.

23 Quoted in Tierney, "Betting on the Planet."

24 Tierney, "Betting on the Planet."

25 Tierney, "Betting on the Planet."

26 Tierney, "Betting on the Planet."

27 Simon, *Ultimate Resource 2*, p. 35.

28 Bernard Dixon, *What Is Science For?* (New York: Harper, 1973), p. 198.

29 Paul R. Ehrlich, "An Economist in Wonderland," *Social Science Quarterly* 62, no. 1 (March 1981): 46.

30 Paul R. Ehrlich, "That's Right—You Should Check It for Yourself," *Social Science Quarterly* 63, no. 2 (June 1982): 386.

31 Paul R. Ehrlich and Anne H. Ehrlich, *Healing the Planet* (Reading, MA: Addison-Wesley, 1991), p. 229.

32 Tierney, "Betting on the Planet."

33 Tierney, "Betting on the Planet."

34 Paul R. Ehrlich and Anne H. Ehrlich, "Can a Collapse of Global Civilization Be Avoided?" *Proceedings of the Royal Society B* 280, no. 1754 (January 9, 2013), https://doi.org/10.1098/rspb.2012.2845.

35 "Biological Extinction | Paul R. Ehrlich," YouTube, uploaded by Casina Pio IV, Paul R. Ehrlich, "Biological Extinction" (lecture, PAS-PASS Workshop, Casina Pio IV, Vatican City, February 27–March 1, 2017).

36 Regis, "The Doomslayer."

37 Julian L. Simon, *The State of Humanity* (Cambridge, MA: Blackwell, 1995), p. 654.

38 Kenneth Ewart Boulding, "Fun and Games with the Gross National Product: The Role of Misleading Indicators in Social Policy," quoted in H. W. Helfrich, *The Environmental Crisis: Man's Struggle to Live With Himself* (New Haven: Yale University Press, 1970), pp. 157–70.

39 Paul R. Ehrlich, "An Economist in Wonderland," *Social Science Quarterly* 62, no. 1 (March 1981): 46.

[40] Mark Sagoff, "The Rise and Fall of Ecological Economics: A Cautionary Tale," *The Breakthrough*, January 13, 2012.

[41] Michael Shellenberger, *Apocalypse Never: Why Environmental Alarmism Hurts Us All* (New York: Harper Collins, 2020), pp. 243–44.

[42] Bill McKibben, "A Special Moment in History," *Atlantic Monthly* 281, no. 5 (May 1998): 55–78.

[43] Michael E. Mann (@MichaelEMann), "Climate change is simply one axis in a multi-dimensional problem that is environmental sustainability. They all stem from the same problem—too many people using too many natural resources. We probably already exceed the planet's carrying capacity by a factor of eight," Twitter post, January 29, 2019, 7:34 p.m., https://twitter.com/michaelemann/status /1090407949770674176.

[44] Adam Wernick, "Biodiversity Loss Has an Enormous Impact on Humans, According to a UN Report," *The World*, April 21, 2018.

[45] Gabrielle Walker, "Newsmaker of the Year: Rajendra Pachauri," *Nature* 450, no. 20 (December 27, 2007): 1150–55, https://doi.org/10.1038/4501150a.

[46] James Kanter, "Scientist: Warming Could Cut Population to 1 Billion," *New York Times*, March 13, 2009.

[47] Pierre Desrochers and Joanna Szurmak, *Population Bombed: Exploding the Link between Overpopulation and Climate Change* (London: Global Warming Policy Foundation, 2018), p. 107.

[48] In August 2020, for example, a monthly peer-reviewed scientific journal called *Nature Ecology & Evolution* published a study based on 36 meta analyses of more than 4,600 individual studies covering the last 45 years of research on ecological thresholds. A threshold "corresponds to a level of environmental pressure that creates a discontinuity in the ecosystem response to this pressure. Thresholds and tipping points pervade environmental policy documents as they allow definition of levels of pressure below which ecosystem responses remain within 'safe ecological limits' and above which response magnitudes and their variances increase disproportionately." Nine German, French, Irish, and Finnish ecologists found that "threshold transgressions were rarely detectable, either within or across meta-analyses. Instead, ecological responses were characterized mostly by progressively increasing magnitude and variance when pressure increased. Sensitivity analyses with modelled data revealed that minor variances in the response are sufficient to preclude the detection of thresholds from data, even if they are present. The simulations reinforced our contention that global change biology needs to abandon the general expectation that system properties allow defining thresholds as a way to manage nature under global change. Rather, highly variable responses, even under weak pressures, suggest that 'safe-operating spaces' are unlikely to be quantifiable." See Helmut Hillebrand et al., "Thresholds for Ecological Responses to Global Change Do Not Emerge from Empirical Data," *Nature Ecology & Evolution* 4, no. 1502–1509 (August 17, 2020), https://doi.org/10.1038 /s41559-020-1256-9.

[49] Ted Nordhaus and Sam Haselby, "The Earth's Carrying Capacity for Human Life Is Not Fixed," *Aeon*, July 5, 2018.

[50] Ronald Bailey and Marian L. Tupy, *Ten Global Trends Every Smart Person Should Know: And Many Others You Will Find Interesting* (Washington: Cato Institute, 2020), p. 13.

[51] Desrochers and Szurmak note that "the idea that effective attempts to address climate change must involve population control—and that population control in itself is insufficient if overall mass consumption keeps increasing—has become a new form of what author Greg Easterbrook calls 'collapse anxiety,' which he defined as a 'widespread feeling that the prosperity [of the developed world] cannot really be enjoyed because the Western lifestyle may crash owing to economic breakdown, environmental damage, resource exhaustion . . . or some other imposed calamity.'" Desrochers and Szurmak, *Population Bombed*, p. 2.

[52] Jesse H. Ausubel and Paul E. Waggoner, "Dematerialization: Variety, Caution, and Persistence," *PNAS* 105, no. 35 (September 2, 2008): 12774–79, https://doi.org/10.1073/pnas.0806099105.

[53] "As argued three decades ago by economist and demographer Mikhael Bernstam . . . throughout the second half of the twentieth century market economies became wealthier and cleaner while centrally planned ones stagnated or even regressed while becoming increasingly polluted. Bernstam considered this outcome the 'most important reversal in economic and environmental history since the Industrial Revolution.' A short version of his analysis is that this result can be attributed to the cost minimization paradigm of market economies as opposed to the input maximization of centrally planned ones. His most relevant insight for this essay, however, is that discharges into the environment declined in market economies for reasons ranging from spontaneous energy transitions (e.g., the substitution of coal and fuel oil by natural gas and hydro-electricity) to the development and adoption of better pollution control and disposal technologies made possible by increased wealth (e.g., from sewage treatment and landfilling to waste incineration and [deep] underground injection of hazardous wastes). The elimination or proper handling of waste (i.e., uselessly processed resources and economically useless production—scrap, spills, slag, discards, refuses and other processing losses; destroyed primary resources; losses of intermediary and final output in transportation and storage), rather than greater material use as a result of increased production and consumption, thus ultimately determined the impact of economic growth on the environment." See Pierre Desrochers, "The Paradoxical Malthusian. A Promethean Perspective on Vaclav Smil's *Growth: From Microorganisms to Megacities* (MIT Press, 2019) and *Energy and Civilization: A History* (MIT Press, 2017)," *Energies* 13, no. 20: 5306, https://doi.org/10.3390/en13205306.

[54] Arnulf Grubler et al., "A Low Energy Demand Scenario for Meeting the 1.5 °C Target and Sustainable Development Goals without Negative Emission Technologies," *Nature Energy* 3, no. 1 (June 4, 2018): 515–27, https://doi.org/10.1038/s41560-018-0172-6.

55 Joel Mokyr, "The Past and the Future of Innovation: Some Lessons from Economic History," working paper, National Bureau of Economic Research, May 2017, p. 24.

56 Nordhaus and Haselby, "Earth's Carrying Capacity."

57 Jesse H. Ausubel, Iddo K. Wernick, and Paul E. Waggoner, "Peak Farmland and the Prospect for Land Sparing," *Population and Development Review* 38 (February 2013): 221–242, https://doi.org/10.1111/j.1728-4457.2013.00561.x.

58 Bailey and Tupy, *Ten Global Trends*, p. 111.

59 Emily Atkin, "Really, Michael Moore?" *Heated*, April 27, 2020; Benjamin Tincq, "10 Reasons 'Planet of the Humans' Gets Everything Wrong on Climate and Energy," *Medium*, April 26, 2020; Tom Athanasiou, "Why 'Planet of the Humans' Is Crap," *EcoEquity*, April 23, 2020; Josh Fox, "Meet the New Flack for Oil and Gas: Michael Moore," *The Nation*, April 30, 2020; Leah C. Stokes, "Michael Moore Produced a Film about Climate Change That's a Gift to Big Oil," *Vox*, April 28, 2020.

60 "Big Wind's Dirty Little Secret: Toxic Lakes and Radioactive Waste," Institute for Energy Research, October 23, 2013.

61 Megan Brenan, "Americans' Trust in Mass Media Edges Down to 41%," Gallup, September 26, 2019.

62 Myron Ebell and Steven J. Milloy, "Wrong Again: 50 Years of Failed Eco-Pocalyptic Predictions," Competitive Enterprise Institute, September 18, 2019.

63 George Getze, "Dire Famine Forecast by '75," *Salt Lake Tribune*, November 17, 1967.

64 Robert Reinhold, "Foe of Pollution Sees Lack of Time; Asserts Environmental Ills Outrun Public Concern," *New York Times,* August 10, 1969.

65 James B. Ayres, "Scientists Predict a New Ice Age by the 21st Century," *Boston Globe*, April 16, 1970.

66 Victor Cohn, "U.S. Scientist Sees New Ice Age Coming," *Washington Post,* July 9, 1971.

67 Anthony Tucker, "Space Satellites Show New Ice Age Coming Fast," *The Guardian,* January 29, 1974.

68 "Another Ice Age?" *Time*, June 24, 1974.

69 Walter Sullivan, "International Team of Specialists Finds No End in Sight to 30-Year Cooling Trend in Northern Hemisphere," *New York Times*, January 5, 1978.

70 "More Droughts Likely, Expert Tells Senators," *Miami News*, June 24, 1988.

71 "Prepare for Long, Hot Summers," *Lansing State Journal*, December 12, 1988.

72 "Threat to Islands," Canberra Times, September 26, 1988.

73 "Rising Seas Could Obliterate Nations: U.N. Officials," Associated Press, June 30, 1989.

74 Charles Onians, "Snowfalls Are Now Just a Thing of the Past," *Independent,* March 20, 2000.

75 Suzy Hansen, "Stormy Weather: Floods, Droughts, Hurricanes and Disease Outbreaks; An Expert Explains Why Climate Changes Give Us Yet Another Reason to Find Terror in the Skies," *Salon*, October 23, 2001.

76 George Monbiot, "Why Vegans Were Right All Along—Famine Can Only Be Avoided if the Rich Give Up Meat, Fish, and Dairy," *The Guardian*, December 23, 2002.

77 Mark Townsend and Paul Harris, "Now the Pentagon Tells Bush: Climate Change Will Destroy Us," *The Guardian*, February 21, 2004.

78 Seth Borenstein, "NASA Scientist: 'We're Toast,'" *Argus-Press*, June 24, 2008.

79 Robert Verkaik, "Just 96 Months to Save World, Says Prince Charles," *Independent*, July 9, 2009.

80 "Gordon Brown: We Have Fewer Than Fifty Days to Save Our Planet from Catastrophe," *Independent* (transcript of speech, Major Economies Forum, London, October 20, 2009).

81 Douglas Stanglin, "Gore: Polar Ice Cap May Disappear by Summer 2014," *USA Today*, December 14, 2009.

82 Nafeez Ahmed, "Ice-Free Arctic in Two Years Heralds Methane Catastrophe—Scientist," *The Guardian*, July 24, 2013.

83 Nafeez Ahmed, "U.S. Navy Predicts Summer Ice-Free Arctic by 2016," *The Guardian*, December 9, 2013.

84 Jeryl Bier, "French Foreign Minister: '500 Days to Avoid Climate Chaos,'" *Washington Examiner*, May 14, 2014. On September 29, 2015, the *Washington Examiner* followed up its original story with an article by Jeryl Bier titled "Planet Still Standing 500 Days after French Foreign Minister Warned of 'Climate Chaos.'"

85 Coral Davenport, "Major Climate Report Describes a Strong Risk of Crisis as Early as 2040," *New York Times*, October 7, 2018.

86 Chris Mooney and Brady Dennis, "The World Has Just Over a Decade to Get Climate Change under Control, U.N. Scientists Say," *Washington Post*, October 7, 2018.

Chapter 4

1 Julian L. Simon, *The Ultimate Resource 2* (Princeton, NJ: Princeton University Press, 1996), p. 525.

2 Lionel Robbins, *An Essay on the Nature and Significance of Economic Science* (London: Macmillan, 1932), p. 15.

3 Abundance has a variety of definitions, including a very large quantity of something; the state or condition of having a copious quantity of something; plentifulness, profusion, copiousness, amplitude, affluence, lavishness, bountifulness, infinity, opulence, exuberance, or luxuriance; plentifulness of the good things of life; and prosperity. See *Lexico Online Dictionary*, s.v. "Abundance," accessed August 21, 2020.

4 "Ethics Explainer: Naturalistic Fallacy," The Ethics Center, March 15, 2016.

5 We are grateful to William von Hippel for alerting us to the complexities of status anxiety. Personal correspondence, January 2, 2021.

6 Steven Pressman, "Why Inequality Is the Most Important Economic Challenge Facing the Next President," *The Conversation*, October 16, 2016.

7 Jonathan Kelley and M. D. R. Evans, "Societal Inequality and Individual Subjective Well-Being: Results from 68 Societies and Over 200,000 Individuals, 1981–2008," *Social Science Research* 62 (February 2017): 1–23, https://doi.org/10.1016/j.ssresearch.2016.04.020.

8   William D. Nordhaus, "Schumpeterian Profits in the American Economy: Theory and Measurement," National Bureau of Economic Research, working paper no. 10433, 2004, https://doi.org/10.3386/w10433.

9   "2011 Forbes 400 Net Worth: #39 Steve Jobs," *Forbes*, September 1, 2011.

10 Jobs's $7 billion divided by 2.2 percent comes to $318 billion, so Jobs's customers received $311 billion from the $318 billion that Jobs created in terms of social value.

11 "Apple, Inc.," Yahoo Finance (stock price display), accessed January 3, 2021.

12 "Apple, Inc.," Yahoo Finance (stock price display), accessed January 3, 2021.

13 Richard Layard, *Happiness: Lessons from a New Science* (London: Penguin Books, 2006), p. 47.

14 In his 2018 book, *12 Rules for Life: An Antidote to Chaos*, University of Toronto psychologist Jordan Peterson urges his readers to follow his fourth rule, which states, "Compare yourself to who you were yesterday, not to who someone else is today." Jordan B. Peterson, *12 Rules for Life: An Antidote to Chaos* (Toronto: Random House Canada, 2018), p. 83.

15 Chelsea Follett, "U.S. President's Son Dies of an Infected Blister?" *Human Progress*, March 1, 2016.

16 As Pierre Desrochers recently noted, "Carbon fuels, metals, sand, clay, silicon, potash, and phosphate, among others, have thus allowed through many transactions much developmental work and constantly improved manufacturing processes to drastically reduce overall demand for wild fauna such as whales (whale oil, baleen, perfume base), birds (feathers), elephants, polar bears, alligators, and countless other wild animals (ivory, fur, skin); trees and other plants (lumber, firewood, charcoal, rubber, pulp, dyes, green manure); agricultural products (fats and fibers from livestock and crops, leather, dyes and pesticides from plants); work animals (horses, mules, oxen); and human labor in various forms (lumbering, weeding)." See Pierre Desrochers, "The Paradoxical Malthusian. A Promethean Perspective on Vaclav Smil's *Growth: From Microorganisms to Megacities* (MIT Press, 2019) and *Energy and Civilization: A History* (MIT Press, 2017)," *Energies* 13, no. 20: 5306, https://doi.org /10.3390/en13205306.

17 Adam Smith, *An Inquiry into the Nature and Causes of the Wealth of Nations* (London: W. Strahan and T. Cadell, 1776), Book 1, Chapter 5.

18 George Gilder, *Life After Google: The Fall of Big Data and the Rise of the Blockchain Economy* (New York: Simon and Schuster, 2018), pp. 259–60.

19 Michael Cox and Richard Alm of Southern Methodist University in Dallas, Texas, greatly expanded the idea of time prices in their 1997 article, "Time Well Spent: The Declining Real Cost of Living in America." In it, they compared prices of household items in the 1897 Sears, Roebuck, and Company catalog to 1997 prices and food items from 1919 to 1997. They also looked at the cost of housing, electricity, mattresses, air conditioners, kitchen appliances, clothing, cars, gasoline, haircuts, movie tickets, airline flights, cruises, college education, fast food, televisions, VCRs, and movie cameras, calculators, cell phones, microwaves, and a number of other items. See W. Michael Cox and Richard Alm, "Time Well Spent: The Declining Real Cost

of Living in America," Federal Reserve Bank of Dallas, February 24, 1997. They expanded their analysis in their 1999 book, *Myths of Rich and Poor*, and their article "Onward and Upward" in the O'Neil Center 2015–2016 Annual Report. See William J. O'Neil Center for Global Markets and Freedom, *2015–16 Annual Report: Onward and Upward! Bet on Capitalism: It Works*, accessed February 27, 2021. Professor Don Boudreaux at George Mason University in Fairfax, Virginia, has also done lots of analysis using this "simple but brilliant method of measuring changes" on historical prices found in Sears catalogs. In 2006, he analyzed over 400 goods from the 1975 catalog and found that time prices were significantly lower for most products. See Donald J. Boudreaux, "The Myth of American Middle-Class Stagnation," American Institute of Economic Research, July 29, 2019.

[20] For a complete list of our concepts, abbreviations, and equations, see Appendix 1.

[21] "The Consumer Price Index (CPI) measures changes over time in the general level of prices of goods and services that a reference population acquires, uses, or pays for consumption" ("Consumer Price Index," Organisation for Economic Co-Operation and Development, April 16, 2013).

[22] "Retail Price of Bananas in the United States from 1995 to 2019," Statista (online data set), February 2020.

[23] See Appendix 4.

[24] See "GDP (Current US$)—World," World Bank (online data set), accessed March 19, 2020; "Total Hours Worked," Conference Board (online data set), accessed March 19, 2020.

[25] "Total Hours Worked," Conference Board (online data set), accessed March 19, 2020.

[26] "GDP Per Capita in 2018 US$," Conference Board (online data set), accessed March 19, 2020.

[27] For more details, see Appendix 2.

[28] For more details, see Appendix 3.

[29] Lawrence H. Officer and Samuel H. Williamson, "Annual Wages in the United States Unskilled Labor and Manufacturing Workers, 1774–Present," Measuring Worth (online data set), accessed March 19, 2020.

[30] According to Measuring Worth (see https://www.measuringworth.com), the money wage of unskilled labor "is an index of the average money wage of a 'common' or unskilled laborer. Until the late 19th century, common labor usually meant outdoor work on or off farms, in tasks that required no training. With the growth of manufacturing, those in the factory called 'laborers' or helpers were regarded as unskilled. After WWII, the unskilled were not counted separately, so the index is constructed from the compensation of such jobs as janitors, porters, and cleaners." See Officer and Williamson, "Annual Wages in the United States." Similarly, production workers' compensation "is restricted to production workers, also called blue-collar workers, hourly rated workers, or non-office workers. The series includes both money earnings and benefits. Thus, it is legitimately an average-hourly-compensation series and is expressed as the number of dollars per work-hour. Of

course, there are production workers in other sectors, but this series covers only manufacturing. Workers on salary (white-collar workers, office workers, nonproduction workers), such as clerks and executives, are excluded."

31 Note that prior to World War II, nonwage benefits were negligible. Hence, unskilled wages and blue-collar compensation rates were nearly identical.

32 For more, see Appendix 4.

33 That's because TPs are calculated using nominal prices divided by hourly income. The rate of change in TPs between points in time is what we are ultimately interested in.

34 "The Economic Policy Institute (EPI) is a 501 (c)(3) non-profit American, left-leaning think tank based in Washington, D.C., that carries out economic research and analyzes the economic impact of policies and proposals." See Wikipedia, s.v. "Economic Policy Institute," last edited February 24, 2022. The Bureau of Labor Statistics (BLS) is a U.S. government agency.

35 Gregory Clark, *A Farewell to Alms: A Brief Economic History of the World* (Princeton: Princeton University Press, 2008), pp. 3–4.

36 See, for example, Deirdre McCloskey, *Bourgeois Dignity: Why Economics Can't Explain the Modern World* (Chicago: University of Chicago Press, 2010), p. 70.

37 The Gini measures inequality on a scale from 0 to 1, with 0 denoting perfect equality in income (all people have exactly the same income) and 1 denoting a perfect inequality in income (one person has all the income).

38 "Commodity Markets," World Bank, accessed March 20, 2020; "IMF Primary Commodity Prices," International Monetary Fund, March 10, 2020.

39 Note that prior to our calculations, we had to adjust the original data sets a little. For example, the World Bank provides nominal price data for three types of crude oil (Brent, Dubai, and West Texas Intermediate). We thought that reporting three very similar prices of crude oil in our overall price index was excessive. As such, we averaged the three prices of crude oil to come up with a crude oil average. Our adjustments are described in detail in Appendix 5.

40 David S. Jacks, "From Boom to Bust: A Typology of Real Commodity Prices in the Long Run," National Bureau of Economic Research, working paper no. 18874, 2018, https://doi.org/10.3386/w18874.

41 Jacks put his commodities into two general categories: "to be grown" and "in the ground." This distinction could also be explained as "farmed" or "mined." See Jacks, "From Boom to Bust." He further divided his commodities into seven categories: animal products, energy products, grains, metals, minerals, precious metals, and soft commodities (such as coffee). Jacks created an overall index for his 40 commodities and considered three ways to weight the items: (1) equal shares, (2) weighted by 1975 production values, and (3) weighted by 2011 production values. He determined that the 1975 production values weighting was the least objectionable for his overall index. Jacks was trying to identify overall price trends and commodity price cycles (booms and busts). He concluded that since 1900, real commodity prices had risen modestly. He also found that there are discernible patterns of price commodity cycles (booms and busts). Finally, he noted that demand shocks are typically

followed by supply responses that return prices to their pre-demand shock level or even to a lower level (this fits well with Simon's thinking). Our analysis goes beyond real commodity prices and calculates TPs of commodities over time.

[42] Marian L. Tupy, "Julian Simon Was Right: A Half-Century of Population Growth, Increasing Prosperity, and Falling Commodity Prices," *Cato Institute Economic Development Bulletin*, no. 29 (February 16, 2018): p. 7.

[43] Tupy, "Julian Simon Was Right," p. 7.

Chapter 5

[1] Julian L. Simon, *The Ultimate Resource 2* (Princeton, NJ: Princeton University Press, 1996), p. 9.

[2] As you read our commodities sections, always keep in mind that the number of commodities and the length of the period analyzed are determined by data availability, not cherry-picking by the authors.

[3] We have selected the 40-year period for three reasons. First, many politicians from both the left and the right of the political spectrum in the United States maintain that American standards of living have stagnated since the onset of globalization in the early 1980s, but as we will show, many of the most commonly purchased items in the United States have become much more affordable. Second, technological change makes product comparisons more difficult over time. While a pound of beef is the same in 1919 and 2019, a 1979 record player is incomparably inferior to an iPod. Third, a 40-year period allows us to add a new denominator to our analysis. The "up-skilling" hourly compensation rate reflects the experiences of those U.S. workers who start as unskilled laborers but become blue-collar workers over the course of their working lives.

[4] We chose 1900 because that is the earliest year for which we have the relevant commodity data.

[5] Note that there were five energy items in the Basic 50, but energy indirectly shows up in all of the commodities as part of their discovery, production, and transportation costs.

[6] Those countries are Austria, Belgium, Brazil, Chile, Denmark, France, Germany, Greece, Iceland, Italy, Luxembourg, Mexico, the Netherlands, Peru, Portugal, Spain, and Sweden.

[7] Those countries are Chile, China, Colombia, Peru, and South Korea.

[8] Nut margarine is margarine made principally from coconut and peanut oils churned with soured whole or skimmed milk and salt.

[9] Beef plate (also known as plate beef or the short plate) is a forequarter cut from the belly of the cow, just below the rib cut.

[10] United States Bureau of Labor Statistics, *Retail Prices, 1913 to December 1919*, Bulletin of the United States Bureau of Labor Statistics, no. 270 (February 1921): 176–83, accessed February 27, 2021, https://fraser.stlouisfed.org/title/161/item/5364.

[11] Remember that when the pRAM of an item falls below 1, the item becomes less abundant.

[12] Remember that when the pRAM of an item falls below 1, the item becomes less abundant.

[13] Simon originally proposed a $10,000 bet. He later reduced that amount to $1,000. Ehrlich and his two partners were disappointed and reluctantly accepted the lower wager. Since they lost the bet, Simon reduced their losses by 90 percent and saved them $5,185.

[14] $1,573.81 \times 39.9$ percent $= \$627.95$.

[15] See, for example, Katherine. A. Kiel, Victor Matheson, and Kevin Golembiewski, "Luck or Skill? An Examination of the Ehrlich–Simon Bet," *Ecological Economics* 69, no. 7 (May 15, 2010): 1365–7, https://doi.org/10.1016/j.ecolecon.2010.03.007.

[16] Once again, we rely on the average annual nominal prices of the five metals as reported by the USGS.

[17] As a reminder, we do not provide upskilling analysis for periods longer than 40 years.

[18] Robert E. Lucas, *On the Mechanics of Economic Development* (Amsterdam: North Holland, 1988), p. 5.

[19] Paul Collier, *The Bottom Billion: Why the Poorest Countries Are Failing and What Can Be Done About It* (Oxford: Oxford University Press, 2007), p. 190.

[20] Gregory Clark, "Review Essay: The Enlightened Economy: An Economic History of Britain, 1700–1850 by Joel Mokyr," *Journal of Economic Literature* 50, no. 1 (March 2012): 86.

[21] "How Has Growth Changed Over Time?," Bank of England, October 7, 2020.

[22] Deirdre Nansen McCloskey, "How Growth Happens: Liberalism, Innovism, and the Great Enrichment," DeirdreMcCloskey.com, November 29, 2018.

[23] McCloskey, "How Growth Happens."

[24] Mark Thoma, "Why GDP Fails As a Measure of Well-Being," *CBS News*, January 27, 2016.

[25] Thoma, "Why GDP Fails."

[26] William D. Nordhaus, "Do Real Output and Real Wage Measures Capture Reality? The History of Lighting Suggests Not," in *The Economics of New Goods*, ed. Timothy F. Bresnahan and Robert J. Gordon (Chicago: University of Chicago Press, 1997), p. 38.

[27] If something grows at a 4.71 percent annual rate for 100 years, it will become 100 times larger in a century. This relationship is calculated as 1 plus the CAGR-pRA raised to the power of 100. Between 1960 and 2018, to give one example, the pRA of rubber grew at 4.8 percent per year. So, 1 + .048 raised to the power of 100 would amount to 108.7. In other words, rubber would become 108.7 times more abundant in 100 years.

Boxes 5.1–5.3

[a] Sabir Shah, "The History and Evolution of Sugar, a Luxurious and Valuable Commodity." *News International*, April 13, 2020.

[b] The National Archives of the United Kingdom, "Currency Converter: 1270–2017," November 28, 2018.

c   Juliet Schor, "Preindustrial Workers Had a Shorter Workweek than Today's," in *The Overworked American: The Unexpected Decline of Leisure* (New York: Basic Books, 2008), accessed September 10, 2021.

d   Results for "Sugar," Tesco (website), accessed September 10, 2021.

e   William Hageman, "Pepper's History Spiced with Dark Moments," *Chicago Tribune*, September 7, 2018.

f   William Shakespeare, *Romeo and Juliet*, Complete Works of William Shakespeare, MIT, 4.4.1-6.

g   "The Sweet and Sour History of Sugar Prices" Winton, April 6, 2017.

h   "Data," Simon Fraser University (online data set), accessed September 10, 2021.

i   "Domino Sugar, Pure Cane, Granulated (10 Lb.)," Walmart (website), accessed 10 September 2021.

j   "Sugar Commodity," *Markets Insider*, Business Insider, accessed September 10, 2021.

k   "Mahindra Bolero Maxi Truck Price in New Delhi," Trucks Dekho, accessed December 12, 2020; "Brand-new China JAC 4WD roll bar pickup, pickup truck for sale," Alibaba, accessed December 12, 2020.

l   "1970 Ford F-100 Prices and Values," J. D. Power, accessed December 12, 2020.

m   Lawrence H. Officer and Samuel H. Williamson, "Annual Wages in the United States Unskilled Labor and Manufacturing Workers, 1774–Present," Measuring Worth (online data set), accessed March 19, 2020.

n   W. Michael Cox and Richard Alm, *Time Well Spent: The Declining Real Cost of Living in America*, Federal Reserve Bank of Dallas, February 24, 1997.

o   "6000 BTU-Air Conditioners," Walmart (website), accessed October 12, 2019.

p   "Average Energy Prices for the United States, Regions, Census Divisions, and Selected Metropolitan Areas," U.S. Bureau of Labor Statistics (online data set), accessed December 12, 2020; "CPI for All Urban Consumers (CPI-U)," U.S. Bureau of Labor Statistics (online data set), accessed December 12, 2020.

Chapter 6

1   Gale L. Pooley and Marian L. Tupy, "The Simon Abundance Index: A New Way to Measure Availability of Resources," Cato Institute Policy Analysis no. 857, December 4, 2018.

2   As a reminder, personal resource abundance measures the size of a slice of pizza per person. Population resource abundance measures the size of the entire pizza pie.

3   The YD-PRA will be estimated by the NPER function in Excel. The NPER function, which was already described in a section in Chapter 4 called "Years to double personal resource abundance (YD-pRA) tells you the length of time required for a resource to become twice as abundant," tells you the length of time required for a resource to become twice as abundant.

4   The PRAM can also be measured from the perspective of the population resource cost (PRC). If the PRC of resources declines, the PRAM of resources increases. The following equation is similar to the one we used to measure the PRAM, except that

instead of using the pRAMs, we use the TPs from Chapter 5. The relevant equation here is $PRC_n = Population_n \times TP_n$. To calculate the PRC, we have indexed the size of the population to 1 in the start-year of all of our data sets. Similarly, any TP will always equal 1 in the start-year of all of our data sets. Consequently, the PRC in the start-year of any of our data sets will always equal 1. Let's look at a concrete example. In 1980, the world's population was indexed to 1 and the TP of the Basic 50 commodities also amounted to 1. By 2018, the world's population rose by 71.2 percent, which can be indexed to 1.71. In the meantime, the TP declined by -71.6 percent. The relevant equation here is $PRC_{2018} = 1.71_{2018} \times (1 - 0.716)_{2018}$; $PRC_{2018} = 1.71 \times 0.284$; $PRC_{2018} = 0.486$. As such, we can say that the PRC of the Basic 50 commodities declined from 1 in 1980 to 0.486 in 2018. Appendix 26 shows the PRC values for all 18 Chapter 5 data sets. As can be seen, the PRC of the Jacks's 40 commodities for U.S. blue-collar workers declined the most (from 1 in 1900 to 0.170 in 2018), while the PRC of cosmetic procedures for unskilled U.S. workers declined the least (from 1 in 1998 to 0.881 in 2018).

[5] To measure the percentage change in population resource cost (PRC) between two points in time, we use the following equation: Percentage change in PRC = $((PRC_{end\text{-}year} - PRC_{start\text{-}year}) \div PRC_{start\text{-}year}) \times 100$. Since $PRC_{start\text{-}year}$ is always equal to 1, the equation can be reduced to Percentage change in PRC = $(PRC_{end\text{-}year} - 1) \times 100$. Let us once again use the Basic 50 data set as an example. As can be seen from the following calculation, the PRC of the 50 Basic commodities declined by -51.4 percent between 1980 and 2018: Percentage change in PRC = $(0.486 - 1) \times 100$; Percentage change in PRC = -51.4. Appendix 27 provides percentage change in PRC values for all Chapter 5 data sets. The PRC of Jacks's 40 commodities declined the most (-83 percent) for U.S. blue-collar workers between 1900 and 2018. The PRC of cosmetic procedures declined the least (-11.9 percent) for U.S. unskilled workers between 1998 and 2018.

[6] To calculate the compound annual growth rate in population resource cost (CAGR-PRC), we use the following equation: CAGR-PRC = $(PRC_{end\text{-}year}^{1/Years} - 1) \times 100$. Let's turn once again to our Basic 50 data set. As noted, the PRC of the Basic 50 basket of commodities declined from 1.0 in 1980 to 0.486 in 2018. That means that the PRC of the Basic 50 basket of commodities declined at a compound annual rate of -1.88 percent. The relevant equation here is CAGR-PRC = $(0.486^{1/38} - 1) \times 100$; CAGR-PRC = -0.0188×100; CAGR-PRC = -1.88 percent. Appendix 28 provides CAGR-PRC values for all Chapter 5 data sets. The CAGR-PRC of the Simon-Ehrlich five-metal basket between 1980 and 1990 decreased the fastest (-5.97 percent). The CAGR-PRC of the Simon-Ehrlich five-metal basket fell the slowest (-0.24 percent) for unskilled U.S. workers between 1900 and 2018.

[7] To calculate the number of years needed for a population resource cost (YH-PRC) to halve, we will use CAGR-PRC values and the following equation: YH-PRC = $\log(0.5) \div \log(1 + CAGR\text{-}PRC)$. Let's start by calculating the PRC halving period for our Basic 50 commodities. The relevant calculation here

is YH-PRC $= \log(0.5) \div \log(1 - 0.0188)$; YH-PRC $= -0.301 \div 0.0082$; YH-PRC $= 36.7$. Appendix 29 provides YH-PRC values for all Chapter 5 data sets. The YH-PRC of the Simon-Ehrlich five-metal basket between 1980 and 1990 was the lowest (7.13 years). The YH-PRC of cosmetic procedures for U.S. unskilled workers between 1998 and 2018 was the highest (29.29 years).

[8] "World Population Prospects, 2018," United Nations Department of Economic and Social Affairs (online data set), August 28, 2019.

[9] Population resource cost elasticity of population (PRC-EP) measures the sensitivity of PRC to population growth. PRC-EP allows us to establish how much a 1 percent increase in population changes the PRC between the start-year of the analysis and the end-year of the analysis. The relevant calculation is PRC-EP = Percentage Change in PRC ÷ Percentage Change in Population. Let's estimate PRC-EP for our Basic 50 data set. As noted, the world's population increased by 71.2 percent between 1980 and 2018. Over the same period, PRC decreased from 1.0 to 0.486, or by -51.4 percent. Dividing -51.4 by 71.2 indicates a value of -0.72. The relevant equation here is PRC-EP $= -51.4 \div 71.2$; PRC-EP $= -0.72$. As such, we can say that for every 1 percent increase in population, PRC decreased by 0.72 percent. Appendix 30 provides PRC-EP values for all Chapter 5 data sets. As can be seen, PRC-EP was the highest (-3.43 percent) for U.S. cosmetic procedures and upskilling worker data sets, while PRC-EP was the lowest (-0.04) for the Jacks's 26 unskilled worker data set.

[10] Note that TPs can only decline by 100 percent. In contrast, the population can increase by more than 100 percent. TP-EP is consequently most helpful when populations increase by less than 100 percent. PRA-EP and pRA-EP use the same scale (both population and abundance can grow infinitely), thus providing a higher level of information.

[11] We leave out TP-EP because this visualization does not include negative values.

[12] For more, see Stein Emil Vollset et al., "Fertility, Mortality, Migration, and Population Scenarios for 195 Countries and Territories from 2017 to 2100: A Forecasting Analysis for the Global Burden of Disease Study," *Lancet* 396, no. 10258 (July 14, 2020), https://doi.org/10.1016/S0140-6736(20)30677-2.

[13] Julian L. Simon, *The Ultimate Resource 2* (Princeton, NJ: Princeton University Press, 1996), pp. 345–46, 348.

[14] Paul R. Ehrlich et al., "No Middle Way on the Environment," *Atlantic Monthly* 280, no. 6 (December 1997): 98–104.

[15] Mathematically speaking, there is no "one for one" offset between a 1 percent increase in population and a 1 percent decrease in the size of the slice of pizza per person. As noted, if the population increases by 10 percent, the size of the slice of pizza does not shrink by 10 percent. Instead, it shrinks "only" by 9.09 percent. If the population doubles (i.e., increases by 100 percent), the size of the slice of pizza will fall by 50 percent. In reality, of course, the size of the slice of pizza per person will only decrease up to a point where it is too small to feed anyone. After that, famine ensues and population growth ceases or is reversed.

[16] Simon, *Ultimate Resource 2*, p. 6.

Chapter 7

1. Thomas Sowell, *Knowledge and Decisions* (New York: Basic Books, 1980), p. 47.

2. William von Hippel, *The Social Leap: The New Evolutionary Science of Who We Are, Where We Come From, and What Makes Us Happy* (New York: Harper Collins, 2018), pp. 41–43.

3. Von Hippel, *The Social Leap,* pp. 23–30.

4. See Tetsuro Matsuzawa, "Field Experiments on Use of Stone Tools by Chimpanzees in the Wild," in *Chimpanzee Cultures,* ed. Richard W. Wrangham, W. C. McGrew, Frans B. M. de Waal, and Paul G. Heltne (Cambridge, MA: Harvard University Press, 1996), pp. 351–70.

5. Matt Ridley, *How Innovation Works: And Why It Flourishes in Freedom* (New York: HarperCollins, 2020), pp. 236–37.

6. Rachael Moeller Gorman, "Cooking Up Bigger Brains," *Scientific American,* January 1, 2008.

7. Von Hippel, *The Social Leap,* pp. 44–47.

8. Deirdre Nansen McCloskey, "Fukuyama Was Correct: Liberalism *Is* the Telos of History," *Journal of Contextual Economics—Schmollers Jahrbuch* 139, nos. 2–4 (August 2019): 285–303.

9. Ridley, *How Innovation Works,* p. 221.

10. Von Hippel, *The Social Leap,* p. 75.

11. In England, for example, the high nobility started to assert their rights against the arbitrary power of the kings as early as 1215, but a full-fledged constitutional monarchy emerged only after the Glorious Revolution of 1688. Parliament originally consisted of nobles, bishops, and shire representatives, and the franchise was restricted to a tiny number of propertied men that only gradually and fitfully expanded over time. The Reform Acts of 1832 and 1867 expanded the franchise further. By the time of the Representation of the People Act of 1884, some 60 percent of all men could vote. All men over the age of 21 and "qualified" women over the age of 30 got the vote in 1918, but equal enfranchisement of all women had to wait until 1928.

12. Ricardo J. Caballero, "Creative Destruction," Massachusetts Institute of Technology, accessed September 25, 2019.

13. Gregory Clark, "Review Essay: The Enlightened Economy. An Economic History of Britain, 1700–1850 by Joel Mokyr," *Journal of Economic Literature* 50, no. 1 (March 2012): 86.

14. Stephen Davies, *The Wealth Explosion: The Nature and Origins of Modernity* (Brighton, UK: Edward Everett Root, 2019), pp. 104–9.

15. Joel Mokyr, *The Gifts of Athena: Historical Origins of the Knowledge Economy* (Princeton, NJ: Princeton University Press, 2011).

16. Archie Hobson, ed., *The Oxford Dictionary of Difficult Words* (Oxford: Oxford University Press, 2004), p. 208.

17. Abby W. Schachter, "5 Questions for Deirdre McCloskey," *CAPX,* December 10, 2015.

[18] Herodotus, *The History*, trans. Henry Cary (London: Henry George Bohn, 1856), book 5, chap. 106, sect. 1, p. 349.

[19] Sallust, *The War With Catiline* (London: Loeb Classical Library, 1921).

[20] See Pliny the Elder, *Natural History*, trans. D. E. Eicholz, Harris Rackham, and William Henry Samuel Jones (Cambridge, MA: Harvard University Press, 1962), books XXXVI–XXXVII, p. 195; Petronius, *Satyricon*, trans. Sarah Ruden (Indianapolis: Hackett Publishing Company, 2000), p. 51; Cassius Dio Cocceianus, *Roman History*, trans. Earnest Cary and Herbert Baldwin Foster (London: William Heinemann, 1914), book LVII.

[21] For more, see Bruce Bartlett, "Is Industrial Innovation Destroying Jobs?," Cato Institute, accessed February 27, 2021.

[22] Danièle Cybulskie, "Medieval Eyeglasses: Wearable Technology of the Thirteenth Century," Medievalists.net.

[23] Donald J. Boudreaux, "Deirdre McCloskey and Economists' Ideas about Ideas," *Liberty Matters*, July 1, 2014.

[24] Homer, *The Odyssey*, trans. Stephen Mitchell (New York: Simon and Schuster, 2013), p. 97.

[25] Herodotus, *History of Herodotus*, trans. George Rawlinson (London: John Murray, 1875), vol. 1, p. 276.

[26] Plato, *The Dialogues of Plato, (The Republic, Timaeus, Critias)*, trans. Benjamin Jowett, vol. 3 (Oxford: Oxford University Press, 1892), book 5, sect. 159.

[27] Victor Ehrenberg, *The People of Aristophanes (Routledge Revivals): A Sociology of Old Attic Comedy* (Abingdon-on-Thames, UK: Routledge, 2015), p. 114.

[28] Ehrenberg, *The People of Aristophanes*, pp. 119–22.

[29] Aristophanes, *Acharnians*, lines 457, 478; Aristophanes, *Frogs*, line 840; Aristophanes, *The Knights*, line 19; Aristophanes, *Women at the Thesmophoria*, lines 387, 456.

[30] Donald C. Earl, *The Political Thought of Sallust* (Indianapolis: Hackett, 1966), p. 27.

[31] Marcus Tullius Cicero, *De Officiis*, trans. Walter Miller (New York: The MacMillan Company, 1913), p. 153.

[32] Earl, *Political Thought of Sallust*, p. 27.

[33] Antony Kropff, "New English translation of the Price Edict of Diocletianus," Academia, April 27, 2016.

[34] Gratian, *Decretum*, pt. 1, dist. lxxxviii, cap. Xi, quoted in R. H. Tawney, *Religion and the Rise of Capitalism* (London: Verso, 2015), p. 35.

[35] Tawney, *Rise of Capitalism*, p. 53.

[36] Tawney, *Rise of Capitalism*, pp. 82–4.

[37] Karl Marx, *Capital: The Process of Capitalist Production as a Whole*, trans. Ernest Untermann (Chicago: Charles H. Kerr, 1909), vol. 3, p. 390.

[38] Ronald Wallace, *Calvin, Geneva, and the Reformation: A Study of Calvin as Social Reformer, Churchman, Pastor, and Theologian* (Eugene, OR: Wipf and Stock Publishers, 1998), p. 86.

[39] The Online Etymology Dictionary provides the following definition: "bourgeoisie (n.) 1707, 'body of freemen in a French town,' hence 'the French middle class,' also

extended to that of other countries, from French *bourgeois*, from Old French *burgeis*, *borjois* (12c.) 'town dweller' (as distinct from 'peasant'), from *borc* 'town, village,' from Frankish **burg* 'city.' . . . Communist use for 'the capitalist class generally' attested from 1886." See "bourgeoisie," Online Etymology Dictionary, accessed August 11, 2020.

[40] Deirdre McCloskey, *Bourgeois Dignity: Why Economics Can't Explain the Modern World* (Chicago: University of Chicago Press, 2010), p. 7; see also Deirdre McCloskey, *The Bourgeois Virtues: Ethics for an Age of Commerce* (Chicago: University of Chicago Press, 2006); Deirdre McCloskey, *Bourgeois Equality: How Ideas, Not Capital or Institutions, Enriched the World* (Chicago: University of Chicago Press, 2016).

[41] Jeremy Bentham, *The Book of Fallacies: From Unfinished Papers of Jeremy Bentham* (London: John and H. L. Hunt, 1824), p. 144.

[42] Deirdre McCloskey, "Bourgeois Dignity: A Revolution in Rhetoric," *Cato Unbound*, October 4, 2010.

[43] See Ritchie Robertson, *The Enlightenment: The Pursuit of Happiness, 1680–1790* (New York: HarperCollins, 2021), chap. 1.

[44] Earl John Russell, *The Life and Times of Charles James Fox* (London: Richard Bentley, 1866), vol. 3, p. 400.

[45] McCloskey, *Bourgeois Dignity*, p. 372.

[46] "Historical Estimates of World Population," United States Census Bureau (online data set), accessed September 13, 2019.

[47] David Levine, "The Population of Europe: Early Modern Demographic Patterns," Encyclopedia.com.

[48] "The movement of progressive societies has been uniform in one respect," noted the British jurist and historian Sir Henry Sumner Maine (1822–1888). "Through all its course it has been distinguished by the gradual dissolution of family dependency," Maine continued. In ancient times, people were "regarded and treated not as individuals, but always as members of a particular group. Everybody is first a citizen, and then, as a citizen, he is a member of his order. . . . Next, he is a member of a gens, house of clan. . . . His individuality was swallowed up in his family." Quoted in Alberto Mingardi, *Herbert Spencer* (London: Bloomsbury, 2011), p. 62.

Boxes 7.1–7.4

[a] Something similar could be said about Chile, South Korea, and Taiwan before they transitioned to democracy.

[b] It may in fact be the case that Chinese economic institutions have grown more extractive under the leadership of Xi Jinping, who became the general secretary of the Chinese Communist Party in 2012 and president of the People's Republic of China in 2013. The unexplained disappearance of business leaders such as Jack Ma (founder of the e-commerce giant Alibaba), the growing use of forced labor such as that performed by the hundreds of thousands of Uyghurs imprisoned in the so-called "reeducation camps," and the increased government involvement in the economy have reduced China's economic freedom since 2015, according to the Fraser Institute's *Economic Freedom of the World* report, thus placing China in the least

economically free quartile in the world. For more, see "Economic Freedom," Fraser Institute, accessed February 27, 2020, www.freetheworld.com.

c Quoted in James A. Boon, *Verging on Extra-Vagance: Anthropology, History, Religion, Literature, Arts . . . Showbiz* (Princeton, NJ: Princeton University Press, 1999), p. 158.

d Robert E. Klitgaard, *Elitism and Meritocracy in Developing Countries: Selection Policies for Higher Education* (Baltimore, MD: Johns Hopkins University Press, 1986), p. 12.

e Halil Inalcik, *The Ottoman Empire: Conquest, Organization, and Economy* (Farnham, UK: Variorum Reprints, 1978), p. 105.

f Matthew Ricci and Nicolas Trigault, *China in the Sixteenth Century: The Journals of Matthew Ricci, 1583–1610,* trans. Louis J. Gallagher, S.J. (New York: Random House, 1953), p. 201.

g Ricci and Trigault, *China in the Sixteenth Century,* pp. 301–2.

h Ricci and Trigault, *China in the Sixteenth Century,* p. 326.

i Ricci and Trigault, *China in the Sixteenth Century,* pp. 166–67.

j Ricci and Trigault, *China in the Sixteenth Century,* p. 325.

k Quoted in David S. Landes, *The Wealth and Poverty of Nations: Why Some Are So Rich and Some So Poor* (New York: W. W. Norton, 1998), p. 342.

l Quoted in Landes, *The Wealth and Poverty of Nations,* p. 342.

m Yedo or Edo was the de facto capital of Japan during the Tokugawa shogunate. See Fernand Braudel, *Civilization and Capitalism, 15th–18th Century,* vol. I, *The Structure of Everyday Life* (Berkeley: University of California Press, 1992), p. 323.

n Braudel, *Civilization and Capitalism,* p. 323.

o Tamerlane (1336–1405) was the Turco-Mongol founder of the Timurid Empire. See Braudel, *Civilization and Capitalism,* pp. 323–4.

p Clark, "Review Essay: The Enlightened Economy."

q Joel Mokyr, "Long-Term Economic Growth and the History of Technology," in *Handbook of Economic Growth,* eds. Philippe Aghion and Steven Durlauf, vol. 1 (Amsterdam: Elsevier, 2005), pp. 1113–80.

r Joel Mokyr, "The Past and the Future of Innovation: Some Lessons from Economic History" (working paper, National Bureau of Economic Research, May 2017), p. 8.

s Mokyr, "The Past and the Future of Innovation," p. 12.

Chapter 8

1 Deirdre McCloskey, *Bourgeois Dignity: Why Economics Can't Explain the Modern World* (Chicago: University of Chicago Press, 2010), p. 70.

2 Scholars assumed that we evolved 200 millennia ago, but a recently analyzed skull from a cave called Jebel Irhoud in Morocco suggests that our species is much older. For more, see Ann Gibbons, "World's Oldest *Homo Sapiens* Fossils Found in Morocco," *Science Magazine,* June 7, 2017.

3 As the British economic historian Edward Anthony Wrigley argued, the organic economy "escaped from the problem of the fixed supply of land and of its organic products by using mineral raw materials. Thus, the typical industries of the [Industrial Revolution]

produced iron, pottery, bricks, glass and inorganic chemicals, or secondary products made from such materials, above all an immense profusion of machines, tools and consumer products fashioned out of iron and steel. The expansion of such industries could continue to any scale without causing significant pressure on the land, whereas the major industries of an organic economy, textiles, leather and construction, for example, could grow only if more wool, hides or wood were produced which in turn implied the commitment of larger and larger acreages to such ends, and entailed fiercer and fiercer competition for a factor of production whose supply could not be increased. Meeting all basic human needs for food, clothing, housing, and fuel, inevitably meant mounting pressure on the same scarce resource." See E. A. Wrigley, *Continuity, Chance and Change* (Cambridge: Cambridge University Press, 1988), p. 5.

4   According to the German American agricultural economist Karl Brandt (1899–1975), agricultural productivity accelerated after the Great War, which "brought the internal combustion engine into general use for agriculture, first in America and later elsewhere. The truck, tractor, and combine were some of the machines in which it was applied. Millions of horses were replaced, and millions of feed acres were released for food production. Enormous savings in manpower and in production costs became possible. New varieties of plants made available for crop production many areas that previously could be used only for scanty grazing. Research in animal nutrition and genetics also led to much greater efficiency in converting feed into animal products." See Karl Brandt, "The Marriage of Nutrition and Agriculture" in *Food for the World*, ed. Theodore William Schultz (Chicago: University of Chicago Press, 1945), pp. 134–48.

5   Robert E. Lucas, "The Industrial Revolution: Past and Future" in *Lectures on Economic Growth* (Cambridge, MA: Harvard University Press, 2002), p. 109.

6   McCloskey, *Bourgeois Dignity*, p. 2.

7   Joel Mokyr, "The Past and the Future of Innovation: Some Lessons from Economic History" (working paper, National Bureau of Economic Research, May 2017), 4.

8   Authors' calculations based on data from Maddison Historical Statistics. See Maddison Historical Statistics (online data set), Groningen Growth and Development Centre (online) at the University of Groningen, January 11, 2018.

9   Carlo M. Cipolla, *Before the Industrial Revolution: European Society and Economy 1000–1700* (New York: W. W. Norton & Company, 1994), p. 11.

10   Fernand Braudel, *Civilization and Capitalism, 15th–18th Century*, vol. I, *The Structure of Everyday Life* (Berkeley: University of California Press, 1992), p. 532.

11   Braudel, *Civilization and Capitalism*, p. 491.

12   Esteban Ortiz-Ospina, "Does the Impressive Historical Decline in Poverty Capture Nonmarket Transactions?" *Our World in Data,* January 23, 2017.

13   "World Poverty Clock," World Data Lab (website) created by the World Bank, accessed March 25, 2020.

14   Kristofer Hamel, Baldwin Tong, and Martin Hofer, "Poverty in Africa Is Now Falling—But Not Fast Enough," *Future Development*, Brookings Institution,

March 28, 2019; Landry Signé and Ameenah Gurib-Fakim, "The High-Growth Promise of an Integrated Africa" (op-ed), Brookings Institution, August 2, 2019.

[15] That's how the British Crown transitioned from the House of Stuart to the House of Hanover.

[16] Mark Kermode, "The Favourite Review—Colman, Weisz, and Stone Are Pitch-Perfect," *The Guardian*, December 30, 2018.

[17] Max Roser, Hannah Ritchie, and Bernadeta Dadonaite, "Child and Infant Mortality," *Our World in Data*, November 2019.

[18] Ronald Bailey and Marian L. Tupy, *Ten Global Trends Every Smart Person Should Know: And Many Others You Will Find Interesting* (Washington: Cato Institute, 2020), p. 55.

[19] "Life Expectancy at Birth, Total (Years)," World Bank (online data set), accessed September 27, 2019.

[20] "Life Expectancy at Birth," World Bank.

[21] Bailey and Tupy, *Ten Global Trends*, p. 55.

[22] Chelsea Follett and Marian L. Tupy, "Plummeting Maternal Mortality Rates Are a Sign of Progress," *Human Progress,* October 5, 2018.

[23] "Health Statistics and Information Systems," World Health Organization (online data set), accessed September 27, 2019.

[24] Bailey and Tupy, *Ten Global Trends*, p. 63.

[25] Bailey and Tupy, *Ten Global Trends*, p. 63.

[26] Max Roser and Hannah Ritchie, "Food Supply," *Our World in Data* (online data set), accessed March 20, 2020.

[27] Marian L. Tupy, "The Battle to Feed All of Humanity Is Over. Humanity Has Won," *Quillette*, February 11, 2020.

[28] Cretinism is a medical condition characterized by physical deformity and learning disabilities that is caused by congenital thyroid deficiency. See Cipolla, *Before the Industrial Revolution*, p. 75.

[29] Cipolla, *Before the Industrial Revolution*, p. 18.

[30] Cipolla, *Before the Industrial Revolution*, p. 19.

[31] "Budget Share for Total Food Dropped by 10 Percent in 2020, a New Historical Low," U.S. Department of Agriculture, last updated July 9, 2021.

[32] Personal calculations and data from "New Food Balances," UN Food and Agriculture Organization (online data set), accessed March 20, 2020.

[33] Joe Hasell, "Famine Mortality over the Long Run," *Our World in Data,* March 22, 2018.

[34] Lawrence Stone, *The Family, Sex and Marriage in England 1500–1800* (London: Weidenfeld & Nicolson, 1977), p. 79.

[35] Richard S. Levy, *Antisemitism: A Historical Encyclopedia of Prejudice and Persecution,* (Santa Barbara, CA: ABC-CLIO, 2005), vol. 1, p. 763. "Panic emerged again during the scourge of the Black Death in 1348 when widespread terror prompted a revival of the well poisoning charge. In areas where Jews appeared to die of the plague in fewer numbers than Christians, possibly because of better hygiene and greater isolation, lower mortality rates provided evidence of Jewish guilt."

36 Katherine Ashenburg, *The Dirt on Clean: An Unsanitized History* (New York: Farrar, Straus, and Giroux, 2014), p. 94.

37 Ashenburg, *The Dirt on Clean*, p. 99.

38 "Journal of the Health of Louis XIV Written by Drs. Vallot, L'Aquin, and Fagon, All Three Successively His First Physicians," *New York Times*, July 27, 1862; Marian L. Tupy, "Some Perspective on What We Have to Be Thankful for," *Los Angeles Times*, November 26, 2014.

39 Stone, *Family, Sex and Marriage*, p. 78.

40 Stone, *Family, Sex and Marriage*, p. 78.

41 Stone, *Family, Sex and Marriage*, p. 78.

42 Stone, *Family, Sex and Marriage*, p. 78.

43 Johan Norberg, *Progress: Ten Reasons to Look Forward to the Future* (London: Oneworld Publications, 2017), p. 34.

44 Cipolla, *Before the Industrial Revolution*, p. 87.

45 Norberg, *Ten Reasons to Look Forward*, p. 33.

46 Braudel, *Civilization and Capitalism*, p. 508.

47 Braudel, *Civilization and Capitalism*, p. 508.

48 Bailey and Tupy, *Ten Global Trends*, p. 147.

49 Cipolla, *Before the Industrial Revolution*, p. 20.

50 Jules Michelet, *Le Peuple*, trans. by G. H. Smith (New York: D. Appleton & Company, 1846), p. 49.

51 David S. Landes, *The Wealth and Poverty of Nations: Why Some Are So Rich and Some So Poor* (New York: W. W. Norton, 1998), p. *xviii*.

52 Pietra Rivoli, *The Travels of a T-Shirt in the Global Economy: An Economist Examines the Markets, Power, and Politics of World Trade* (Hoboken, NJ: Wiley, 2014), p. 216.

53 Rivoli, *The Travels of a T-Shirt*, p. 224.

54 Alden Wicker, "African-Made Luxury Fashion Is Making a Comeback," *Vogue Business*, August 5, 2019.

55 Mary Beard, *SPQR: A History of Ancient Rome* (New York: W. W. Norton & Company, 2015), p. 449.

56 Norberg, *Ten Reasons to Look Forward*, p. 86.

57 Cipolla, *Before the Industrial Revolution*, p. 46.

58 Bailey and Tupy, *Ten Global Trends*, p. 101.

59 Bailey and Tupy, *Ten Global Trends*, p. 101.

60 Gregory Clark, *A Farewell to Alms: A Brief Economic History of the World* (Princeton, NJ: Princeton University Press, 2008), p. 64.

61 Laura Cruz and Joel Mokyr, *The Birth of Modern Europe: Culture and Economy, 1400–1800: Essays in Honor of Jan de Vries* (Leiden, Netherlands: Brill Publishers, 2010), p. 233.

62 Jesse H. Ausubel and Arnulf Grubler, "Working Less and Living Longer: Long-Term Trends in Working Time and Time Budgets," *Technological Forecasting and Social Change* 50 (1995): 113–31.

[63] Jaap de Koning, "The Reduction of Life Hours of Work Since 1850: Estimates for Dutch Males," *SEOR Studies in Social History*, working paper (October 2016): http://doi.org/10.13140/RG.2.2.13516.41609.

[64] Matt Ridley, *How Innovation Works: And Why It Flourishes in Freedom* (New York: HarperCollins, 2020), p. 293.

[65] "Total Economy Database," Conference Board (online data set), accessed April 12, 2019.

[66] "Total Economy Database," Conference Board.

[67] Cipolla, *Before the Industrial Revolution*, p. 46.

[68] Marian L. Tupy, "How the Market Helped to Make Workplaces Safer," *Human Progress*, September 15, 2018.

[69] Bailey and Tupy, *Ten Global Trends*, p. 99.

[70] Judges 8:13–14 (NIV translation).

[71] Ian M. Young, "Israelite Literacy: Interpreting the Evidence: Part I." *Vetus Testamentum* 48, no. 2 (1998): 239–53.

[72] William V. Harris, *Ancient Literacy* (Cambridge, MA: 1989), pp. 102–3.

[73] Polybius, *The Histories* (Cambridge MA: Harvard University Press, 2011), book 6, sects. 35–36.

[74] Juvenal, "Satire XV–Compassion, Not Hatred," in *The Satires*, trans. A. S. Kline (London: Loeb Classical Library, 2004).

[75] Harris, *Ancient Literacy*, p. 13.

[76] Jeffrey Sypeck, *Becoming Charlemagne: Europe, Baghdad, and the Empires of 800* (New York: HarperCollins, 2006), pp. 6, 13.

[77] Harris, *Ancient Literacy*, p. 17.

[78] Harris, *Ancient Literacy*, p. 18.

[79] Max Roser and Esteban Ortiz-Ospina, "Global Education," *Our World in Data*, accessed February 27, 2021.

[80] Roser and Ortiz-Ospina, "Global Education."

[81] Roser and Ortiz-Ospina, "Global Education."

[82] Bailey and Tupy, *Ten Global Trends*, p. 47.

[83] Bailey and Tupy, *Ten Global Trends*, p. 47.

[84] Robert J. Barro and Jong-Wha Lee, "Barro-Lee Education Attainment for Population Aged 15–24, 1870–2010," Barro-Lee (online data set), June 4, 2018.

[85] Benjamin Constant, "The Liberty of the Ancients Compared with That of the Moderns," Early Modern Texts (website), accessed February 27, 2021, p. 2.

[86] Constant, "The Liberty of the Ancients," p. 6.

[87] "Liberal Democracy," Encyclopedia.com, February 21, 2021.

[88] "V-Dem Dataset—Version 10," Varieties of Democracy Project (online data set), accessed February 27, 2021, https://doi.org/10.23696/vdemds20.

[89] Hannah Ritchie and Max Roser, "Energy," *Our World in Data*, accessed March 23, 2020.

[90] Claire Tomalin, *Samuel Pepys: The Unequalled Self* (New York: Knopf Doubleday, 2007), p. 5.

91 Cipolla, *Before the Industrial Revolution*, p. 88.

92 Judith Flanders, *Inside the Victorian Home: A Portrait of Domestic Life in Victorian England* (New York: W. W. Norton & Company, 2004), p. 27.

93 Flanders, *Inside the Victorian Home*, p. 108.

94 Braudel, *Civilization and Capitalism*, pp. 482–83.

95 Carlo Manfredi, *Addressing the Climate in Modern Age's Construction History: Between Architecture and Building Services Engineering* (New York: Springer, 2019), p. 5.

96 Marian L. Tupy, "Pollution in Pre-Industrial Europe," *Human Progress*, February 20, 2019.

97 Tupy, "Pollution in Pre-Industrial Europe."

98 Sophie Hardach, "How the Thames River Was Brought Back from the Dead," BBC, November 12, 2015.

99 Hannah Ritchie, "What the History of London's Air Pollution Can Tell Us about the Future of Today's Growing Megacities," *Our World in Data*, June 20, 2017.

100 Don Boudreaux, "Living in Harmony with Nature," *Cafe Hayek*, April 9, 2005.

101 Thomas Jefferson, The Declaration of Independence, retrieved from the National Archives (website), July 4, 1776.

102 Code of Hammurabi, retrieved online from Wright State University, accessed March 23, 2020.

103 Some researchers suggest that the two words are merely homonyms. See Alexey Timofeychev, "Myths of Russian History: Does the Word 'Slav' Derive from 'Slave'?" *Russia Beyond*, July 17, 2017.

104 Gustav Jönsson, "Did the Enlightenment Endorse Slavery?" *Aero Magazine*, November 18, 2018.

105 Marian L. Tupy, "Is Moral Progress Real or Just a Myth?" *Human Progress*, January 18, 2019.

106 Solomon W. Polachek and Carlos Seiglie, "Trade, Peace and Democracy: An Analysis of Dyadic Dispute," Institute for the Study of Labor Discussion working paper no. 2170, July 25, 2006.

107 Carl von Clausewitz, *On War*, trans. Col. J. J. Graham (London: Kegan Paul, Trench, Trubner & Co., 1918), vol. 1, chap. 1, sect. 24.

108 Steven Pinker, *Enlightenment Now: The Case for Reason, Science, Humanism, and Progress* (New York: Viking Press, 2018), p. 163.

109 "Global Conflict Trends: Assessing the Qualities of Systemic Peace," *Global Conflict Trends*, Center for Systemic Peace, accessed March 23, 2020.

110 Bailey and Tupy, *Ten Global Trends*, p. 85.

111 Frank Chalk and Kurt Jonassohn, *The History of Genocide: Analyses and Case Studies* (Montreal: Montreal Institute for Genocide Studies, 1990), p. *xvii*. See also Steven Pinker, *The Better Angels of Our Nature: Why Violence Has Declined* (New York: Penguin Group, 2011), p. 333.

112 Bailey and Tupy, *Ten Global Trends*, p. 87.

113 "Recorded Fatalities in UCDP Organized Violence 1989–2017," Uppsala Conflict Data Program (online data set), Uppsala University, accessed March 24, 2020.

[114] Manuel Eisner, "Long-Term Historical Trends in Violent Crime," *Crime and Justice* 30 (2003): 83–142.

[115] Bailey and Tupy, *Ten Global Trends*, p. 81.

Boxes 8.1–8.4

[a] Deirdre McCloskey and Art Carden, *Leave Me Alone and I'll Make You Rich: How the Bourgeois Deal Enriched the World*, (Chicago: University of Chicago Press, 2020), p. *xi*.

[b] William D. Nordhaus, "Do Real Output and Real Wage Measures Capture Reality? The History of Lighting Suggests Not," in *The Economics of New Goods*, ed. Timothy F. Bresnahan and Robert J. Gordon (Chicago: University of Chicago Press, 1997), p. 38.

[c] "Farm Bureau Survey: Thanksgiving Dinner Cost Down 4%," American Farm Bureau Federation, November 20, 2020.

[d] "CPI Inflation Calculator," U.S. Bureau of Labor Statistics, accessed December 12, 2020.

[e] Andy Pasztor, "The Airline Safety Revolution," *Wall Street Journal*, April 16, 2021.

[f] "Air Transport, Passengers Carried." World Bank (data set), accessed September 10, 2021.

Chapter 9

[1] Matt Ridley, *How Innovation Works: And Why It Flourishes in Freedom* (New York: HarperCollins, 2020), p. 359.

[2] Ridley, *How Innovation Works*, p. 4.

[3] George Gilder argues that wealth is knowledge and growth is learning, so growth is learning how to create knowledge. Our definition of wealth is more expansive than Gilder's. We define wealth as anything that people value. While growth in knowledge does indeed contribute to wealth creation, we believe that wealth includes health, friendships, beauty, and the like. That said, we agree with Gilder that knowledge is a key to the wealth created by innovation.

[4] Unlike a rival good, such as a Snickers bar that can feed only one person, everyone can consume the same knowledge at the same time. There may in fact be more knowledge after we jointly consume the individual knowledge that we share. As such, knowledge is not just additive. It can be, and often is, exponential.

[5] Vernon L. Smith and Bart J. Wilson, *Humanomics: Moral Sentiments and the Wealth of Nations for the Twenty-First Century* (Cambridge: Cambridge University Press, 2019), p. 11.

[6] Adam Smith, The Theory of Moral Sentiments; or, An Essay Towards an Analysis of the Principles by which Men Naturally Judge Concerning the Conduct and Character, First of Their Neighbours, and Afterwards of Themselves, ed. Dugald Stewart (London: Henry George Bohn,1853).

[7] Robert D. Putnam, "*E Pluribus Unum*: Diversity and Community in the Twenty-First Century—The 2006 Johan Skytte Prize Lecture," *Scandinavian Political Studies* 30, no. 2 (June 15, 2007): 137–174, https://doi.org/10.1111/j.1467-9477.2007.00176.x.

[8] For more, see Hernando De Soto, *The Mystery of Capital: Why Capitalism Triumphs in the West and Fails Everywhere Else* (New York: Basic Books, 2007).

9   For the religiously inclined, here is the how the Bible puts it: "Behold, there went out a sower to sow: And it came to pass, as he sowed, some fell by the wayside, and the fowls of the air came and devoured it up. And some fell on stony ground where it had not much earth; and immediately it sprang up, because it had no depth of earth: But when the sun was up, it was scorched; and because it had no root, it withered away. And some fell among thorns, and the thorns grew up, and choked it, and it yielded no fruit. And other fell on good ground, and did yield fruit that sprang up and increased; and brought forth, some thirty, and some sixty, and some an hundred." Mark 4:3–9 (King James Version).

10 *The Book of Ser Marco Polo: The Venetian Concerning Kingdoms and Marvels of the East* (selected excerpts online), trans. Sir Henry Yule (London: John Murray, 1903), p. 185, accessed October 7, 2020.

11 *The Book of Ser Marco Polo*, pp. 167, 179–180, 182, 190–191, and 480.

12 Julian Simon, *The Great Breakthrough and Its Causes* (Ann Arbor: University of Michigan Press, 2000), p. 36.

13 Likewise, Paul Romer agrees with Simon on the correlation between urban populations, freedom, and economic growth. See Paul Romer, "Economic Growth," PaulRomer.Net, October 12, 2015.

14 Caleb Silver, "The Top 25 Economies in the World," Investopedia, December 24, 2020.

15 Max Roser, Hannah Ritchie, and Esteban Ortiz-Ospina, "World Population Growth," *Our World in Data*, May 2019.

16 Max Roser, "Economic Growth," *Our World in Data*, accessed October 7, 2020.

17 In terms of GDP per person, income grew from $1,101 in 1820 to $14,634 in 2015 ($1.2 trillion divided by 1.09 billion and $108 trillion divided by 7.38 billion). "GDP Per Capita, 1820 to 2018," *Our World in Data*, accessed October 23, 2021.

18 Cesar Hidalgo and Ricardo Hausmann, ed., *The Atlas of Economic Complexity: Mapping Paths to Prosperity* (Cambridge, MA: MIT Press, 2014), p. 18.

19 Donald J. Boudreaux, "There Are No Natural Resources," American Institute for Economic Research, November 13, 2018.

20 William von Hippel and Thomas Suddendorf, "Did Humans Evolve to Innovate with a Social Rather than Technical Orientation?," *New Ideas in Psychology* 51 (December 2018): 34, https://doi.org/10.1016/j.newideapsych.2018.06.002.

21 Von Hippel and Suddendorf, "Evolve to Innovate."

22 Von Hippel and Suddendorf, "Evolve to Innovate."

23 Paola Giuri et al., "Inventors and Invention Processes in Europe: Results from the PatVal-EU Survey," *Research Policy* 36, no. 8 (October 2007): 1111, https://doi.org/10.1016/j.respol.2007.07.008.

24 Note that this is a statistical generalization about overlapping bell curves. Many women are more mechanically gifted and innovative than most men.

25 Robert Polmin, *Blueprint: How DNA Makes Us Who We Are* (Cambridge, MA: MIT Press, 2018).

26 "Autism Spectrum Disorder (ASD): Signs and Symptoms," Centers for Disease Control and Prevention, accessed September 30, 2020.

27 The first is consciousness (impulsive, disorganized versus disciplined, careful). The second is agreeableness (suspicious, uncooperative versus trusting, helpful). The third is neuroticism (calm, confident versus anxious, pessimistic). The fourth is openness to routine (prefers routine, practical versus imaginative, spontaneous), and the fifth is extroversion (reserved, thoughtful versus sociable, fun-loving). For more, see Annabelle G. Y. Lim, "The Big Five Personality Traits," *Simply Psychology*, June 15, 2020.

28 Roberta A. Schriber, Richard W. Robins, and Marjorie Solomon, "Personality and Self-Insight in Individuals with Autism Spectrum Disorder," *Journal of Personality and Social Psychology* 106, no. 1 (January 2014): 112–30.

29 See Melissa A. Schilling, *Quirky: The Remarkable Story of the Traits, Foibles, and Genius of Breakthrough Innovators Who Changed the World* (New York: Public Affairs, 2018).

30 Jonathan Haidt, "Viewpoint Diversity in the Academy," accessed October 23, 2021.

31 Percy Deift, Svetlana Jitomirskaya, and Sergiu Klainerman, "As US Schools Prioritize Diversity over Merit, China Is Becoming the World's STEM Leader," *Quillette*, Aug. 19, 2021.

32 Bo Winegard, "I've Been Fired. If You Value Academic Freedom, That Should Worry You," *Quillette*, Mar. 6, 2020.

33 Geoffrey Miller, "The Neurodiversity Case for Free Speech," *Quillette*, July 18, 2017.

34 For more about objectionable traits of inventors and innovators, see Maelle Gavet, *Trampled by Unicorns: Big Tech's Empathy Problem and How to Fix It* (New York: Wiley, 2020).

35 "The 50 Worst Inventions," *Time*, May 27, 2010.

36 "First U.S. Patent Issued Today in 1790," Suiter Swantz, July 31, 2020.

37 H. Y. Sonya Hsu and Peter P. Mykytyn, Jr., "Intellectual Capital," in *Encyclopedia of Knowledge Management* (Hershey, PA: Idea Group Reference, 2006), 274–80.

38 N. Gregory Mankiw and Mark P. Taylor, *Economics*, 3rd ed. (Boston: Cengage Learning, 2014), p. 2.

39 Paul Romer, "Economic Growth," PaulRomer.Net, October 12, 2015.

40 "The Bessemer Process was the first inexpensive industrial process for the mass production of steel from molten pig iron prior to the open-hearth furnace. The key principle is the removal of impurities from the iron by oxidation by blowing air through the molten iron." See "Bessemer Process," The National Iron & Steel Heritage Museum, accessed February 27, 2020.

41 "The History of Asphalt," Virginia Asphalt Association, accessed February 27, 2020.

42 Transportation Research Board and National Research Council, *Assessing and Managing the Ecological Impacts of Paved Roads* (Washington: The National Academies Press, 2005), p. 3.

43 Donald J. Boudreaux, "There Are No Natural Resources."

44 Adam Smith, *An Inquiry into the Nature and Causes of the Wealth of Nations* (London: Methuen Publishing, 1904), Book 2, Chapter 1.

45 Smith, *Wealth of Nations*, Book 2, Chapter 1.

46 Gary S. Becker, *Accounting for Tastes* (Cambridge, MA: Harvard University Press, 1998), p. 145.

47 Marcel Schwantes, "Warren Buffett Looks for Intelligence and Initiative When Hiring People. But without This Third Trait, 'the First Two Will Kill You,'" *Inc.*, December 3, 2018.

48 Mokyr observed that "the political disasters that followed 1914, while devastating in the short run, did not set long-run global growth rates back in any significant fashion in a way comparable to what happened to Germany after the thirty-years war or for that matter to the Roman Empire after 200 A.D. Growth based on the expansion of useful knowledge is not easy to arrest, much less reverse. It is hard and perhaps impossible for a society to 'unlearn' what has been learned, especially if the knowledge is distributed over a large population and made widely accessible through printing, to say nothing of electronic media." See Joel Mokyr, "The Past and the Future of Innovation," https://conference.nber.org/conf_papers/f100966.pdf, p. 14.

49 Patents provide a legal incentive to create new knowledge. The United States followed the British patent model and enshrined the idea of incentivizing new inventions with patents in the U.S. Constitution. Some scholars have argued that patents discourage innovation and should be done away with. That's because patents usually last for 20 years, and anyone wishing to use a product that's under a patent must pay for a license to use that product. Other scholars have argued that the production of new knowledge requires a tradeoff between the incentives that patents provide and the harm they cause by temporarily postponing the generation of new knowledge. These scholars find time-limited patents reasonable. Still others have made the case for changing the length of patents for different products. See Matt Ridley, "A Welcome Turn Away from Patents," *Wall Street Journal*, June 21, 2013; Arthur M. Diamond, Jr., *Openness to Creative Destruction* (Oxford: Oxford University Press, 2019), p. 139.

50 Paul Romer, "Idea Gaps and Object Gaps in Economic Development," *Journal of Monetary Economics* 32, no. 3 (December 1993): 549, https://doi.org/10.1016/0304-3932(93)90029-F.

51 Paul Romer, "Idea Gaps," 548.

52 Paul Romer, "Idea Gaps," 548.

53 Cesar Hidalgo and Ricardo Hausmann make a similar point when they write, "We can distinguish between two kinds of knowledge: explicit and tacit. Explicit knowledge can be transferred easily by reading a text or listening to a conversation. . . . And yet, if all knowledge had this characteristic, the world would be very different. Countries would catch up very quickly to frontier technologies, and the income differences across the world would be much smaller than those we see today. The problem is that crucial parts of knowledge are tacit and therefore hard to embed in people. . . . Because it is hard to transfer, tacit knowledge is what constrains the

process of growth and development. Ultimately, differences in prosperity are related to the amount of tacit knowledge that societies hold and to their ability to combine and share this knowledge." See Cesar Hidalgo and Ricardo Hausmann, ed., *The Atlas of Economic Complexity: Mapping Paths to Prosperity* (Cambridge, MA: MIT Press, 2014), p. 16.

[54] Terence Kealey and Martin Ricketts, "Innovative Economic Growth: Seven Stages of Understanding," Cato Economic Policy Brief 3, April 6, 2020.

[55] George Gilder, *Life after Google: The Fall of Big Data and the Rise of the Blockchain Economy* (Washington: Regnery Publishing, 2018), 12–13.

[56] A credit score is a numerical representation of a person's or a company's creditworthiness. The score is based on analyses of credit reports pertaining to people's or companies' financial behaviors. Private companies such as Dun & Bradstreet, FICO, Experian, and Equifax collect credit information on companies and persons. The aforementioned pass their findings on to banks, mortgage lenders, and credit card companies. That ensures that as an expression of prudent financial behavior, creditworthiness is rewarded with, for example, lower interest rates.

[57] Will Kenton, "Bourse," Investopedia, June 23, 2020.

[58] In 1971, NASDAQ, which was initially an acronym for the National Association of Securities Dealers Automated Quotations, was established as an electronic exchange. On May 1, 1975, brokerages were allowed to charge varying commission rates. For the previous 180 years, trading fees were set at fixed prices. Charles Schwab was the first firm to offer discount brokerage services. Discount brokers are common today. A retail investor now can open an online trading account for as little as $1 and trade for as little as $1 per trade or less than $0.01 per share. Smartphone apps now allow users to research and trade stocks and other financial instruments. Most recently, firms started to provide the ability to trade "fractions" of shares for as little as $1. These innovations will further diversify risk and increase liquidity.

[59] James Franklin, *The Science of Conjecture: Evidence and Probability Before Pascal* (Baltimore, MD: Johns Hopkins University Press, 2001), 274–77.

[60] "Facts + Statistics: Industry Overview," Insurance Information Institute, accessed October 8, 2020.

[61] Quoted in Jane Gleeson-White, *Double Entry: How the Merchants of Venice Created Modern Finance* (New York: W. W. Norton, 2012), p. 294.

[62] Gleeson-White, *Double Entry*, p. 294.

[63] Hidalgo and Hausmann, *The Atlas of Economic Complexity*, pp. 7–8.

[64] Diamond, *Creative Destruction*, p. 5.

[65] Allan H. Meltzer, *Why Capitalism?* (New York: Oxford University Press, 2012), p. 13.

[66] Note that just before the start of the COVID-19 pandemic, the trend in U.S. bookselling was very much toward smarter, friendlier, and often highly specialized brick-and-mortar bookstores, which were once again opening faster than they were closing. The pandemic and the subsequent lockdowns ruined that trend, but the shift away from large online booksellers shows that innovation never stops. It can happen in very old industries or in industries that have lately been revolutionized.

[67] F. A. Hayek, *Law, Legislation, and Liberty* (Chicago: University of Chicago Press, 1978), p. 108.

[68] George Gilder, *The Spirit of Enterprise* (New York: Simon & Schuster, 1984), p. 145.

[69] Different types of entrepreneurship include the small business, the large company, and scalable startup entrepreneurship; social and innovative entrepreneurship; hustler and imitator entrepreneurship; researcher entrepreneurship; and buyer entrepreneurship. For more, see "The 9 Different Types of Entrepreneurship," Indeed, March 20, 2020.

[70] Over time, printing presses became cheaper and more efficient. In the 17th and 18th centuries, newspapers were widely circulated in Western European coffee-houses (coffee drinking came to Europe from America thanks to the Columbian exchange and gradually became very popular), where new political, economic, financial, and scientific ideas were debated. Important texts, which were previously only available in Latin, became available in the vernacular. Once again, the crucial role of Europe's geopolitical competition cannot be underestimated. According to Deirdre McCloskey, "from the Vatican's Index of Forbidden Books in 1559 down to British prosecutions under the Official Secrets Act, censorship was undermined by publication in other jurisdictions in fragmented Europe, first Venice and then Basel and Holland, and by smuggling the resulting product." As such, it became impossible to regulate or censor any of the written works in circulation. That helped to spur the Glorious Revolution of 1688, thus leading to the establishment of a more liberal English polity and the continued spread of liberal ideas to other parts of Western Europe. See Deirdre McCloskey, *Bourgeois Equality: How Ideas, Not Capital or Institutions, Enriched the World* (Chicago: University of Chicago Press, 2016), p. 391.

[71] Jeremiah Dittmar and Skipper Seabold, "Gutenberg's Moving Type Propelled Europe toward the Scientific Revolution," *LSE Business Review*, March 19, 2019.

[72] Mark Twain, "To Helen Keller, in Wrentham, Mass.," in *The Writings of Mark Twain* (New York: Gabriel Wells, 1917), vol. 35, p. 731.

[73] Peter W. Kingsford, s.v. "James Watt," *Encyclopaedia Britannica Online*, accessed April 20, 2020.

[74] The efficacy of patents to spur innovation is disputed to this day. For more, see previous section on intellectual capital.

[75] Alexander Hammond, "James Watt: The 18th-Century Scotsman Who Became a Hero of Human Progress," Foundation of Economic Education, March 12, 2019.

Boxes 9.1–9.3

[a] Bill Bonner, "The Average Man Is Worse Off Today Than He Was in 1970," *Bill Bonner's Diary*, accessed September 27, 2019.

[b] Evan Comen and Michael B. Sauter, "The Size of a Home the Year You Were Born," 24/7 Wall Street, updated January 6, 2020.

[c] "Annual U.S. Domestic Average Itinerary Fare in Current and Constant Dollars," Bureau of Transportation Statistics (online data set), accessed November 2, 2020.

[d] "Annual U.S. Domestic Average Itinerary Fare in Current and Constant Dollars," Bureau of Transportation Statistics.

^e "Human Genome Project Information Archive 1990–2003," Human Genome Project Budget, accessed September 10, 2021.

^f Katie Jennings, "How Human Genome Sequencing Went from $1 Billion a Pop to under $1,000," *Forbes*, October 28, 2020.

^g Antonio Regalado, "China's BGI Says It Can Sequence a Genome for Just $100," *MIT Technology Review*, April 2, 2020.

^h Edd Gent, "$100 Genome Sequencing Will Yield a Treasure Trove of Genetic Data," Singularity Hub, March 8, 2020.

Chapter 10

1 Steven Pinker, *Enlightenment Now: The Case for Reason, Science, Humanism, and Progress* (New York: Viking Press, 2018), p. 32.

2 Charles Baudelaire, *Intimate Journals* (Mineola, NY: Dover Publications, 2006), p. 75.

3 H. D. Schmidt, "Anti-Western and Anti-Jewish Tradition in German Historical Thought," Yearbook of the Leo Baeck Institute 4, no. 1 (January 1, 1959): 37–60, https://doi.org/10.1093/leobaeck/4.1.37.

4 The phrase "Roman Caesar with Christ's soul" appears in Friedrich Nietzsche, The Will to Power: An Attempted Transvaluation of All Values, trans. Anthony M. Ludovici (London: T.N. Foulis, 1913), p. 380, https://www.gutenberg.org/files/52915/52915-h/52915-h.htm.

5 Arthur Herman, *The Idea of Decline in Western History* (New York: Simon and Schuster, 2007), p. 129.

6 Herman, *Idea of Decline*, p. 133.

7 Friedrich Nietzsche, *The Will to Power*, trans. Walter Kaufmann and R.J. Hollingdale (New York: Random House, 1967), entry 127, http://nietzsche.holtof.com/Nietzsche_the_will_to_power/the_will_to_power_book_I.htm.

8 Oswald Spengler, *The Decline of the West* (Oxford: Oxford University Press, 1991).

9 Maurice Merleau-Ponty, *Humanism and Terror: An Essay on the Communist Problem* (Boston: Beacon Press, 1990), p. xv.

10 Frantz Fanon, *The Wretched of the Earth*, trans. Richard Philcox (New York, NY: Grove Press, 2005), 22–24.

11 Jeffrey M. Jones and Lydia Saad, "U.S. Support for More Government Inches Up, but Not for Socialism," Gallup, November 18, 2019.

12 Frank Newport, "Public Opinion Review: Americans' Reactions to the Word 'Socialism,'" Gallup, March 6, 2020.

13 Newport, "Reactions to the Word 'Socialism.'"

14 Will Dahlgreen, "British People Keener on Socialism Than Capitalism," YouGov, February 23, 2016.

15 There is some controversy as to whether the "dark, Satanic mills" referred to flour mills and other industrial structures that became a common part of the landscape during the Industrial Revolution or whether the "dark, Satanic mills" referred to "Blake's personal mythology in which Satan is described as a miller who grinds

down human souls." Jason Whittaker, "Almost Everything You Know about the Hymn 'Jerusalem' Is Wrong," *Prospect Magazine*, December 26, 2019.

16 William Blake, "Milton: A Poem in Two Books," accessed from the William Blake Archive on April 13, 2020, http://www.blakearchive.org/copy/milton.b?descId =milton.b.illbk.02.

17 Stuart L. Pimm and Robert Leo Smith, "Ecology," *Encyclopedia Britannica,* accessed April 20, 2020.

18 Ludwig Klages, "Man and Earth," accessed from the Revilo P. Oliver Archive (website) on April 15, 2020, http://www.revilo-oliver.com/Writers/Klages /Man_and_Earth.html.

19 Peter Staudenmaier, "Organic Farming in Nazi Germany: The Politics of Biodynamic Agriculture, 1933–1945," *Environmental History* 18, no. 2 (April 2013): 383–411, https://epublications.marquette.edu/hist_fac /82/.

20 Jack Lewis, "The Birth of EPA," U.S. Environmental Protection Agency, November 1985, https://archive.epa.gov/epa/aboutepa/birth-epa.html.

21 University of Toronto researcher Pierre Desrochers contends that the official EPA history obfuscates the role played by the U.S. eugenicists, such as Fairfield Osborn and William Vogt, in the birth of the U.S. environmentalist movement. In the post–World War II environment, Desrochers argues, eugenics became toxic and leading eugenicists re-invented themselves as scholars concerned with overpopulation." See Pierre Desrochers and Christine Hoffbauer, "The Postwar Intellectual Roots of the Population Bomb. Fairfield Osborn's 'Our Plundered Planet' and William Vogt's 'Road to Survival' in Retrospect," *Electronic Journal of Sustainable Development* 1, no. 3 (January 1, 2009).

22 Ronald Bailey, "Earth Day Turns 50," *Reason*, May 2020.

23 "The End of Civilization Feared by Biochemist," *New York Times*, November 18, 1970.

24 Barry Commoner, "Super Technology . . . Will It End the Good Life?," *Field & Stream,* June 1970, 59–60.

25 "The Good Earth," *New York Times*, April 23, 1970.

26 Quoted in Thomas Robertson, *The Malthusian Moment: Global Population Growth and the Birth of American Environmentalism, Studies in Modern Science, Technology, and the Environment* (New Brunswick: Rutgers University Press, 2012), p. 189.

27 Paul Ehrlich, "Eco-Catastrophe!," *Ramparts* 6, no. 3 (July 17, 1969): 24–28.

28 Denis Hayes, "Environmental Teach-In," *The Living Wilderness* 34, no. 109 (Spring 1970): 12–13.

29 Peter Gunter, "Mental Inertia and Environmental Decay: The End of an Era," *Living Wilderness* 34, no. 109 (Spring 1970): 3–5.

30 "Ecology: A Cause Becomes a New Mass Movement," *Life,* January 30, 1970.

31 "Fighting to Save the Earth from Man," *Time*, February 2, 1970.

32 "Fighting to Save the Earth from Man," *Time.*

33 "The Ravaged Environment," *Newsweek*, January 26, 1970.

34 Kenneth Watt, "First Earth Day" (speech, Swarthmore College, Swarthmore, PA, April 19, 1970).

35 Arthur Herman, *The Idea of Decline in Western History* (New York: Simon and Schuster, 2007), p. 415.

36 Charles A. Reich, *The Greening of America* (New York: Random House, 1970), p. 15.

37 Reich, *The Greening of America*, p. 11.

38 Bahgat Elnadiand and Adel Rifaat, "Interview of Jacques-Yves Cousteau," *UNESCO Courier*, (November 1991): 8–13.

39 Miss Ann Thropy, "Population and AIDS," Earth First! 7, no. 5 (May 1, 1987): 33, http://www.environmentandsociety.org/sites/default/files/key_docs/rcc00098005 -7-5_2.pdf. (Miss Ann Thropy was the pen name for Christopher Manes.)

40 Miss Ann Thropy, "Population and AIDS."

41 Richard Preston, *The Hot Zone: A Terrifying True Story* (New York: Random House, 1994), p. 287.

42 "Transcripts, May 6, 2019," CNN, May 6, 2019, http://www.cnn.com/TRAN SCRIPTS/1905/06/nday.04.html.

43 Tom Elliott (@tomselliott). 2019. "CNN: If we don't start 'having fewer children,' a million species will die. . . . Note that the 'expert' they interview is Paul Ehlrich, the discredited 'Population Bomb' prof who's been predicting imminent mass starvation since the 1960s." Twitter, May 6, 2019, 8:02 a.m. ET. https://twitter.com /tomselliott/status/1125370345081454594.

44 Matthew Taylor, "Is Alexandria Ocasio Cortez Right to Ask if the Climate Means We Should Have Fewer Children?," *The Guardian,* February 27, 2019.

45 Ian Schwartz, "Maher: 'Falling Birth Rates Are a Good Thing'; World Is 'Too Crowded,'" *Real Clear Politics,* April 13, 2019.

46 Chelsea Follett, "How Anti-Humanism Is Gaining Ground," *Human Progress*, May 8, 2019.

47 Dusica Sue Malesevic, "Live Long and . . . Go Extinct: The Worldwide Crusade by People Who Say Having Children Is So Damaging to the Planet That the Only Answer Is for Humanity to DIE OUT Voluntarily," *Daily Mail,* January 16, 2019.

48 Todd May, "Would Human Extinction Be a Tragedy?" *New York Times,* December 17, 2018.

49 *Fast Company*, "Why Having Kids is the Worst Thing You Can Do for the Planet," April 10, 2019.

50 Rebecca Tuhus-Dubrow, "I Wish I'd Never Been Born: The Rise of the Anti-Natalists," *The Guardian*, November 14, 2019.

51 Follett, "How Anti-Humanism Is Gaining Ground"; Jennifer Ludden, "Should We Be Having Kids in the Age of Climate Change?," NPR, August 18, 2016; Chris Perez, "Bill Nye: Should We Penalize Parents for Having 'Extra Kids'?," *New York Post,* April 26, 2017.

52 Sarah Conly, *One Child: Do We Have a Right to More?* (Oxford: Oxford University Press, 2015), overview of book.

53 Follett, "How Anti-Humanism Is Gaining Ground."

54 Sierra Garcia, "'We're the Virus': The Pandemic Is Bringing Out Environmentalism's Dark Side," *Grist*, March 30, 2020.

55 Barrett Wilson, "Quebec Politician Praises Coronavirus for Reducing Carbon Footprint in Wuhan," *Post Millennial*, January 25, 2020.

56 John Schwartz, "Social Distancing? You Might Be Fighting Climate Change, Too," *New York Times*, March 13, 2020; Rebecca Wright, "There's an Unlikely Beneficiary of Coronavirus: The Planet," CNN, March 17, 2020.

57 Matt McGrath, "Coronavirus: Air Pollution and CO_2 Fall Rapidly as Virus Spreads," *BBC News*, March 19, 2020.

58 Ryan Heath, "Emissions Are Down Thanks to Coronavirus, but That's Bad," *Politico*, March 13, 2020.

59 Jeffrey A. Tucker, "To Fight Hate, Celebrate Capitalism," American Institute for Economic Research, August 6, 2019.

60 Brenton Harrison Tarrant, "The Great Replacement," accessed online at Il Foglio, March 15, 2019, p. 29, https://www.ilfoglio.it/userUpload/The_Great_Replacementconvertito.pdf.

61 Tarrant, "The Great Replacement," p. 48.

62 Anders Behring Breivik, "A European Declaration of Independence," accessed from *Washington Post*, July 22, 2011, pp. 1203–5.

63 "Text of Unabomber Manifesto," accessed from *New York Times*, May 26, 1996.

64 "Text of Unabomber Manifesto," accessed from *New York Times*.

65 Flowers for Atomsk (@iamthespookster). "@robportman hey rob. How much did they pay you to look the other way? 17 kids are dead. If not now, when?" Twitter, February 14, 2018 (account deactivated).

66 Flowers for Atomsk (@iamthespookster), comment in response to Buzzfeed. "Kill every fascist." Twitter, 2018 (account deactivated).

67 Yaron Steinbuch, Amanda Woods, and Aaron Feis, "Inside the Dark Thoughts and Far-Left Leanings of Dayton Shooter Connor Betts," *New York Post*, August 6, 2019.

68 Flowers for Atomsk (@iamthespookster), retweet of @fingerblaster. "If we don't have a right to a life-sustaining climate we could probably argue that murder is also legal," June 2019 (account deactivated).

69 Flowers for Atomsk (@iamthespookster), retweet of @fazolisfacts. "Remember! The planet isn't dying, it's being killed." Twitter, August 1, 2019 (account deactivated).

70 Jennifer Huizen, "What to Know about Eco-Anxiety," Medical News Today, December 19, 2019.

71 Susan Clayton, Christie Manning, Kirra Krygsman, and Meighen Speiser, *Mental Health and Our Changing Climate: Impacts, Implications, and Guidance* (Washington: American Psychological Association and ecoAmerica, 2017).

72 Elizabeth Marks et al, "Young People's Voices on Climate Anxiety, Government Betrayal and Moral Injury: A Global Phenomenon," p. 6. Preprint, posted September 7, 2021.

73 Z. A. Wendling et al., *2018 Environmental Performance Index* (New Haven, CT: Yale Center for Environmental Law & Policy, 2018).

[74] Soumyananda Dinda, "Environmental Kuznets Curve Hypothesis: A Survey," *Ecological Economics* 49, no. 4 (August 1, 2004): 431–55, https://doi.org/10.1016/j.ecolecon.2004.02.011.

[75] Pekka E. Kauppi et al., "Returning Forests Analyzed with the Forest Identity," *Proceedings of the National Academy of Sciences* 103, no. 46 (November 14, 2006): 17574–9, https://doi.org/10.1073/pnas.0608343103.

[76] Julian Rademeyer, "Zimbabwe's Government Is Standing By as Its Wildlife Is Slaughtered," *The Guardian*, August 25, 2016.

[77] Lenin Danieri and Isaac Urrutia, "Police Believe Thieves Steal Venezuela Zoo Animals to Eat Them," Reuters, August 16, 2017.

[78] Michael Shellenberger, "On Behalf of Environmentalists, I Apologize for the Climate Scare," *Quillette*, June 30, 2020.

[79] Shellenberger, "I Apologize for the Climate Scare."

[80] See also Alan Levinovitz, *Natural: How Faith in Nature's Goodness Leads to Harmful Fads, Unjust Laws, and Flawed Science* (Boston, MA: Beacon Press, 2020).

[81] Michael Shellenberger, *Apocalypse Never: Why Environmental Alarmism Hurts Us All* (New York: Harper Collins, 2020), p. 262.

[82] While we rely on Shellenberger's analysis in this section, he was not the first person to point to the quasi-religious fervor of the environmentalists in general and Malthusians in particular. For example, an "anonymous writer of a review essay published in *The Economist* in 1854 argued that Malthusian beliefs were often held with a 'fervour quite religious' by some of the 'leading minds of society.' Natural constraints, these people believed, ultimately mandated 'no remedy [other than] starving out the people, horrible as it is.' Humanity therefore had to turn its back on 'great discoveries and improvements, which render humanity more productive,' for they would only make things worse down the road. Fortunately, *The Economist* contributor wrote, Malthusian notions that the barrier to progress was 'becoming more formidable' and that 'progress is always in a diminishing ratio' were 'flatly and emphatically contradicted by the history of society all over the world.' Indeed, 'as men have been multiplied [so much faster than formerly],' industry had 'become productive in the compound ratio of their numbers and their skill,' and in every civilized society an increasingly smaller portion of the population was then sufficient to feed everyone. As he put it, the Malthusian doctrine was by then so discredited that 'nobody, except a few mere writers, now troubles himself about Malthus on Population,' although these errors may yet 'linger in the Universities, the appropriate depositories of what is obsolete and practically unimportant.'" Pierre Desrochers, "The Paradoxical Malthusian. A Promethean Perspective on Vaclav Smil's *Growth: From Microorganisms to Megacities* (MIT Press, 2019) and *Energy and Civilization: A History* (MIT Press, 2017)," Energies 13, no. 20: 5306, https://doi.org/10.3390/en13205306. "Sadly," Desrochers noted, "many later university professors and social activists . . . proved very apt at promoting the Malthusian perspective and creating a constant stream of new catastrophist scenarios. When their teachings prevailed, human suffering followed, from forced sterilizations to wars of aggression." [Authors' note:

"wars of aggression" refers to Adolf Hitler's justification of German expansionism in the 1930s on Malthusian grounds.] Other authors who noted the link between environmental extremism and religion include the American economist Robert H. Nelson (1944–2018) in his 2010 book, *The New Holy Wars: Economic Religion Versus Environmental Religion in Contemporary America*, and Deirdre McCloskey in her 2010 book, *Bourgeois Dignity: Why Economics Can't Explain the Modern World.*

[83] The American philosopher Eric Hoffer (1902–1983) noted that "Mass movements can rise and spread without belief in a god, but never without a belief in a devil." Eric Hoffer, quote from "The True Believer, Thoughts on the Nature of Mass Movements," accessed on Quotes, GoodReads, https://www.goodreads.com/quotes/359582-hatred-is-the-most-accessible-and-comprehensive-of-all-the.

[84] Shellenberger, *Apocalypse Never*, p. 264.

[85] Michael Crichton, "Remarks to the Commonwealth Club" (speech, San Francisco, CA, September 15, 2003).

[86] Shellenberger, *Apocalypse Never*, p. 265.

[87] Shellenberger, *Apocalypse Never*, p. 267.

[88] Shellenberger, *Apocalypse Never*, p. 268.

[89] Shellenberger, *Apocalypse Never*, p. 268.

[90] Shellenberger, *Apocalypse Never*, p. 269.

[91] Shellenberger, *Apocalypse Never*, p. 272.

[92] Shellenberger, *Apocalypse Never*, p. 273.

[93] McCloskey, *Bourgeois Dignity*, pp. 433–34.

[94] See Joel Mokyr, *A Culture of Growth: The Origins of the Modern Economy* (Princeton, NJ: Princeton University Press, 2017).

Box 10.1

[a] Erick Kristian, "The Biggest CRT Televisions," Techwalla, accessed December 12, 2020.

[b] "Shop TVs by Size," Walmart (website), accessed December 12, 2019.

Conclusion

[1] Julian L. Simon, *The Ultimate Resource 2* (Princeton, NJ: Princeton University Press, 1996), p. 495

[2] Gale L. Pooley and Marian L. Tupy, "The Simon Abundance Index: A New Way to Measure Availability of Resources," Cato Institute Policy Analysis no. 857, December 4, 2018.

[3] Thomas Hobbes, *Leviathan*, part i, chap. xiii, 9 (1651). See https://www.gutenberg.org/files/3207/3207-h/3207-h.htm.

[4] Simon, *Ultimate Resource*, 25–26.

[5] The evidence from 18 data sets suggests that a 1 percent increase in population corresponds to between 3 percent and 63 percent increase in the population resource abundance. Other factors such as the quality of economic and political institutions also play a role. A population increase in countries dominated by extractive economic and political institutions such as Maoist China or "License Raj" India, in other

words, is highly unlikely to produce large abundance gains. Disaggregating the different contributions to abundance growth will be the focus of the authors' future efforts.

6 Hannah Ritchie, "What Are the Safest and Cleanest Sources of Energy?," *Our World in Data*, February 10, 2020.

7 "Fusion vs Fission," EuroFusion, accessed January 20, 2021.

8 Stanford University economist Charles I. Jones discusses the negative impact of population decline on economic growth in his 2020 paper, "The End of Economic Growth? Unintended Consequences of a Declining Population." See https://web.stanford.edu/~chadj/emptyplanet.pdf.

9 As things stand, the world's population is projected to peak at 9.8 billion people at around 2080 and fall to 9.5 billion by 2100. Ronald Bailey and Marian L. Tupy, *Ten Global Trends Every Smart Person Should Know: And Many Others You Will Find Interesting* (Washington: Cato Institute, 2020), p. 13.

10 Damian Carrington, "Climate 'Apocalypse' Stopping People Having Children—Study," *The Guardian*, November 20, 2020.

11 Ted Scheinman, "The Couples Rethinking Kids Because of Climate Change," BBC, October 1, 2019.

12 Dani Blum, "How Climate Anxiety Is Shaping Family Planning," *New York Times*, April 1, 2020.

13 Suzy Weiss, "'Humans Are a Mistake': Why More Young Women Are Getting Sterilized," *New York Post*, October 27, 2021.

14 M. Schneider-Mayerson and K. L. Leong. "Eco-Reproductive Concerns in the Age of Climate Change," *Climatic Change* 163 (2020): 1007–23, https://doi.org/10.1007/s10584-020-02923-y.

15 Elizabeth Marks et al, "Young People's Voices on Climate Anxiety, Government Betrayal and Moral Injury: A Global Phenomenon," p. 6. Preprint, posted September 7, 2021.

16 Sam Shead, "Climate Change Is Making People Think Twice about Having Children," CNBC, August 12, 2021.

17 "Fertility Rate, Total (Births Per Woman)," World Bank (online data set), accessed January 21, 2021.

18 See Peter Beinart, "A Violent Attack on Free Speech at Middlebury," *The Atlantic*, March 6, 2017; Donald Alexander Downs, *Free Speech and Liberal Education: A Plea for Intellectual Diversity and Tolerance* (Washington: Cato Institute, 2020); and Eric Kaufmann, "Academic Freedom in Crisis: Punishment, Political Discrimination, and Self-Censorship," working paper, Center for the Study of Partisanship and Ideologly, March 1, 2021.

19 Liam Deacon, "The Dangerous Rise of Climate Censorship," *Spiked*, March 8, 2021; Alex Berezow, "Meet the Scientific Outcasts and Mavericks," American Council on Science and Health, June 3, 2016.

20 Kwame Anthony Appiah, "Why Are Politicians Suddenly Talking about Their 'Lived Experience'?," *The Guardian*, November 14, 2020.

21 See Tukufu Zuberi and Eduardo Bonilla-Silva, *White Logic, White Methods: Racism and Methodology* (Lanham, MD: Rowman & Littlefield Publishers, 2008); and Elise Takahama, "Is Math Racist? New Course Outlines Prompt Conversations about Identity, Race in Seattle Classrooms," *Chicago Tribune*, October 10, 2019.

22 Conor Friedersdorf, "The Difference Between Speaking 'Your Truth' and 'The Truth,'" *The Atlantic*, January 18, 2018.

23 Emily Ekins, "Poll: 62% of Americans Say They Have Political Views They're Afraid to Share," Cato Institute, July 22, 2020.

24 Natan Sharansky, "The Doublethinkers," *Tablet*, February 11, 2021.

25 Ulrich Baer, "What 'Snowflakes' Get Right about Free Speech," *New York Times*, April 24, 2017.

26 Dylan Love, "16 Examples of Steve Jobs Being a Huge Jerk," *Business Insider*, October 25, 2011; Tom Abate, "Nobel Winner's Theories Raise Uproar in Berkeley, Geneticist's Views Strike Many as Racist, Sexist", *San Francisco Chronicle*, November 13, 2000, retrieved on October 24, 2007; C. Thompson and A. Berger, 2000, "Agent Provocateur Pursues Happiness," *British Medical Journal* 321 (7252): 12, https://doi.org/10.1136/bmj.321.7252.12; "UK Museum Cancels Scientist's Lecture," ABC News, October 17, 2007; David Reich, *Who We Are and How We Got Here* (Oxford: Oxford University Press, 2019), p. 263.

27 See, for example, Robert L. Schuettinger and Eamonn F. Butler's *Forty Centuries of Wage and Price Controls: How Not to Fight Inflation* (Washington: Heritage Foundation, 2014).

28 Cato Institute and Fraser Institute, *Economic Freedom of the World 2020*, accessed January 3, 2021.

29 Because of the lack of data, the *Economic Freedom of the World 2020* data set does not include some of the most repressive countries, such as Cuba and North Korea.

30 Steven Farron, "Ayn Rand's Totalitarian Sense of Life," *Liberty*, December 2, 2020.

31 Jerome H. Barkow, Leda Cosmides, and John Tooby, *The Adapted Mind: Evolutionary Psychology and the Generation of Culture* (New York: Oxford University Press, 1992), p. 5.

32 The hunter-gathering psychology also helps to explain why it was relatively uncontroversial for many governments to pass huge spending bills at the start of the COVID-19 pandemic. It was not the lack of effort that prevented most people from working. Instead, they were prevented from earning money by the government-enforced stay-at-home orders. The authors of this book, for example, continued to scribble away from the comfort of their homes, while restaurant workers and dry cleaners were out of luck. Moreover, it helps explain why the later spending bills such as the $1.9 trillion American Rescue Plan, which was passed by the U.S. Congress after the U.S. economy had already largely reopened, were much more controversial.

33 F. A. Hayek, *The Fatal Conceit: The Errors of Socialism* (Chicago: University of Chicago Press, 1988), p. 18.

INDEX

Note: Information in figures and tables is indicated by *f* or *t*; n designates a numbered note.

in population resource abundance multiplier, 202t

in time price elasticity of population, 211t

in years to double population resource abundance, 209t

Baudeau, Nicolas, 53

Baudelaire, Charles, 361

Bauer, Peter, 59–60

Baumeister, Roy, 43

Beard, Mary, 301

Becker, Ernest, 394

Becker, Gary, 343

Before the Industrial Revolution: European Society and Economy, 1000–1700 (Cipolla), 292

Benatar, David, 383

Benezet, Anthony, 317

Bernstam, Mikhael, 500n53

Bessemer process, 340, 518n40

Better Angels of Our Nature, The: Why Violence Has Declined (Pinker), 29

Betts, Connor, 387–88

Big Five Personality Traits, 336, 522n27

bipedalism, 243

birth control, 51, 63, 89

Black, Joseph, 356

Blake, William, 373, 526n15

Bloodsworth-Lugo, Mary K., 12

Blueprint for Survival, A (Goldsmith and Allen), 61–62

Blueprint: How DNA Makes Us Who We Are (Plomin), 335–36

Bodin, Jean, 29, 52

Boltzmann, Ludwig, xiii

Bongaarts, John, 57

Bonner, Bill, 341

Bookchin, Murray, 379

bookkeeping, 349

bookstores, 350, 524n66

Boserup, Ester, 485n4

Boudreaux, Donald J., 270, 315, 334, 341

Boulding, Kenneth, 56, 82–83

Boulton, Matthew, 356

Bourgeois Dignity: Why Economics Can't Explain the Modern World (McCloskey), 281

bourgeoisie, 31–34, 272, 283, 360–62, 367–69, 373, 512n39

Bourguignon, François, 288

bourse, 348

Brandt, Karl, 59, 515n4

Bratslavsky, Ellen, 43

Braudel, Fernand, 3, 276, 287, 314

breakfast, time price of, 248, 249t, 250

Breivik, Anders Behring, 387

Brown, Harrison, 58

Brown, Lester R., 78

Bryson, Reid, 57

bubonic plague, 261–62

Buddhism, 14, 16

Buffett, Warren, 343

Burckhardt, Jacob, 362–63

Bury, John Bagnell, 15, 30, 38–39

Caesar Augustus, 18, 51, 53

CAGR-pRA. *See* compound annual growth rate of personal resource abundance (CAGR-pRA)

CAGR-PRC. *See* compound annual growth rate in population resource cost

Calvin, John, 272

Cannan, Edwin, 59

capitalism

in Burckhardt, 363

cooperation and, 350

environment and, 379

exploitative, 36

in Horkheimer, 367

innovism *vs.*, 163

Luther and, 272

public opinion of, 369

carbon dioxide, 27, 340, 381

Cardano, Gerolamo, 29–30

Caritat, Nicolas de, 33

Carrier, Willis, 177

carrying capacity, 4, 72, 78–79, 84, 87, 498n18, 499n43

Carson, Rachel, 375

Catullus, 15, 487n24

Chalk, Frank, 320

Chanakya, 51

Chardin, Jean-Baptiste, 276

Charlemagne, 20

Charles V, Holy Roman Emperor, 20, 263–64

child labor, 301–2

Chile, 5013n–a

chimpanzees, 244–46

China, 60–67, 80, 170, 258–59, 265, 274–76, 329, 331, 495n38, 5013n–b

Christchurch mosque shootings, 386

Christensen, Clayton, 338–39

Christy, Francis T., 485n4

Cicero, 271

Cipolla, Carlo M., 292, 299, 313–14

Clark, Colin, 60

Clark, Gregory, 55, 127, 260–61, 276–77

Clausewitz, Carl von, 319–20

Clean Air Act, 375–76

climate change, 81, 83–84, 91–93, 385–86, 389, 403–5, 499n43. *See also* eco-anxiety; environmentalism

clothing, 298–301

Club of Rome, 61, 65, 496n43

Cold War, 320, 368

in population resource abundance, 206t,
216t–17t, 227f, 235t
in population resource abundance elasticity
of population, 215t
in population resource abundance
multiplier, 203t
in time price elasticity of population, 211t
in years to double population
resource abundance, 209t
fire, 246–47
Flanders, Judith, 314
Fleming, Alexander, 106, 290
Follett, Chelsea, 62, 64, 68, 106, 382
Fontenelle, Bernard Le Bovier de, 30
food prices, 162–67, 166f, 168f, 169t, 196t
in compound annual growth rate of population resource abundance, 207t
in personal resource abundance elasticity of
population, 213t
in population resource abundance, 206t,
216t, 226f, 235t
in population resource abundance elasticity
of population, 215t
in population resource abundance multiplier,
202t
in time price elasticity of population, 211t
in years to double population resource
abundance, 209t
food supply, 23, 53, 59, 242, 255, 291–92
Förster-Nietzsche, Elisabeth, 365–66
Foucault, Michel, 368–69
Fourth Eclogue (Virgil), 18
Francis, Pope, 84
Frankfurt School, 367–68
freedom of expression, 402, 404–5
French Revolution, 361
Freudenburg, William, 75
Friedman, Milton, 57, 497n3
Froude, James Anthony, 34
Fust, Johann, 355

Galton, Francis, 35, 364
Galtung, Johan, 43
Gandhi, Indira, 68
Gandhi, Sanjay, 68–69
GDP. *See* gross domestic product (GDP)
Genesis, book of, 487n14
genocide, 24, 37, 320, 360
George, Henry, 59
German Youth Movement, 374
Gibbon, Edward, 33
Gifts of Athena, The (Mokyr), 265
Gilbert, Daniel, 44
Gilder, George, 59, 112, 353, 406, 491n90, 520n3
Gini, Corrado, 127

Gini coefficient, 127–28, 128f–29f
Gleeson-White, Jane, 349
global warming, 91–93. *See also* climate change;
environmentalism
Glorious Revolution of 1688, 511n11, 525n70
Gobineau, Joseph Arthur de, 361–62
Godwin, William, 53
Goodall, Jane, 57
Gore, Al, 380, 386
Gratian, 272
Gray, John, 318
Great Enrichment, 194, 242, 255–56, 283,
285–86, 325, 327
*Great Escape, The: Health, Wealth, and the
Origins of Inequality* (Easterbrook), 28
Great Famine of 1315, 261
Green, Eric, 357
Greening of America, The (Reich), 378
Greenpeace, 376
Griliches, Zvi, 485n4
gross domestic product (GDP), 120–23,
122f–23f, 194–95
growth rates, personal resource abundance and,
192–97, 193t, 196t
Grubler, Arnulf, 86, 303–4, 500n54
Guicciardini, Francesco, 287
Guizot, François, 33
Gunter, Peter, 377
Gutenberg, Johannes, 330, 354–55

Haeckel, Ernst, 373–74
hands, 243
Hansen, James, 91
Happiness: Lessons from a New Science (Layard),
105–6
Harrington, John, 314
Harris, William V., 307–8
Harrison, Benjamin, 304
Harte, John, 4, 80
Hausmann, Ricardo, 333, 349, 523n53
Hawking, Stephen, 44–45
Hayek, Friedrich, 75–76, 351, 410, 497n3
Hayes, Denis, 377
Hegel, Georg Friedrich, 35
Heidegger, Martin, 374–75
Heilbroner, Robert, 57–58
Heins, James, 77
Herman, Arthur, 31, 33, 361
Herodotus, 269
Hesiod, 14, 17, 31
Hidalgo, Cesar, 333, 523n53
Himmler, Heinrich, 375
History of Rome (Livy), 15
Hitler, Adolf, 36, 367, 531n82
HIV/AIDS, 25, 380

Hobbes, Thomas, 30
Hoffer, Eric, 531n83
Holdren, John P., 4, 56, 58, 80
Home, Henry, 31
Homer, 270
Homo erectus, 120, 246–47, 334
Hong Kong, 406–7
Horkheimer, Max, 367
Horpedahl, Jeremy, 126
Hot Zone, The: A Terrifying True Story (Preston), 380
hourly income, time prices and, 119–29, 122f–26f, 128f–29f, 130t
Housel, Morgan, 44–45
housing, 341–42, 342t
How Innovation Works: And Why It Flourishes in Freedom (Ridley), 323–25
Human Genome Project, 357
Hume, David, 30–31, 53
hunter-gatherer lifestyle, 251–53, 303, 350, 407–10, 533n32
Hutcheson, Francis, 30–31
hygiene, 296–98, 300, 516n35

Ibn Khaldun, 51–52
Idea of Decline on Western History, The (Herman), 361
Idea of Progress, The: An Inquiry into Its Origin and Growth (Bury), 15, 487n3
immortality, 394
inclusivity, of institutions, 257–59
income inequality, 25, 104–6, 127–29, 128f–29f, 130t, 195
increasing abundance zone, 234, 234t
India, 68–70, 170, 265, 298, 331
individualism, 363, 368
Industrial Revolution, 86, 105, 127, 194, 259–60, 282–84, 285t, 514n3, 526n15
inequality, 25, 104–6, 127–29, 128f–29f, 130t, 195, 252–53, 255–56
infant mortality, 23, 50
inflation, 3, 110, 112–13, 131, 293, 486n11
innovation
    before Age of Innovation, 274–77
    capital and, 339–42
    competition and, 349–50
    consumption, 339
    creative destruction and, 259
    cultural capital and, 326–30, 326f
    disruptive, 338–39
    entrepreneurship and, 353–57
    financial capital and, 347–49
    framework, 324–37, 326f
    freedom and, 323, 327
    free market and, 349–51

historical attitudes toward, 269–70
human capital and, 342–45
as human characteristic, 250–51
institutional change and, 255–56
intellectual capital and, 345–47
from invention to, 337–53, 342t, 352t–53t
military, 262–63
modernity and, 279
prices and, 5
time prices and, 3
wealth creation and, 325
innovism, 163
Inside the Victorian Home: A Portrait of Domestic Life in Victorian England (Flanders), 314
insurance, 121, 135, 348–49
intelligence, 2–3
In the Absence of the Sacred (Mander), 379–80
intrauterine devices (IUDs), 63
IPAT, 84
It's Better Than It Looks: Reasons for Optimism in an Age of Fear (Easterbrook), 28
IUDs. *See* intrauterine devices (IUDs)

Jacks, David S., 130, 149
Jacks's 26 commodities, 156–61, 157f–61f, 196t, 219
    in compound annual growth rate of population resource abundance, 207t
    in personal resource abundance elasticity of population, 213t
    in population resource abundance, 206t, 216t, 225f, 235t
    in population resource abundance elasticity of population, 215t
    in population resource abundance multiplier, 202t
    in time price elasticity of population, 211t
    in years to double population resource abundance, 209t
Jacks's 40 commodities, 149–55, 151f–55f, 156t, 196t
    in compound annual growth rate of population resource abundance, 207t
    in personal resource abundance elasticity of population, 213t
    in population resource abundance, 206t, 216t, 224f, 235t
    in population resource abundance elasticity of population, 215t
    in population resource abundance multiplier, 202t
    in time price elasticity of population, 211t
    in years to double population resource abundance, 209t
Jacobs, Jane, 59

Jefferson, Thomas, 256, 316
Jenner, Edward, 266
Jevons, William Stanley, 57–58
Jobs, Steve, 104–5, 256, 328–29
Johnson, Samuel, 32
Johnson, Steven, 59
Jonassohn, Kurt, 320
Jones, William, 362
Jönsson, Gustav, 317

Kaczynski, Ted, 380, 387
Kahn, Herman, 60, 73
Kahneman, Daniel, 40–41
Kant, Immanuel, 39, 318–19
Kasun, Jacqueline, 59–60
Kelley, Jonathan, 104
Klages, Ludwig, 374
Klitgaard, Robert, 273
Knight, Les, 382
knowledge
    cooperation and, 30
    explicit, 523n53
    in human evolution, 247–50
    premodern, 266
    prescriptional, 265–66, 268
    propositional, 265
    stacking, 250
    tacit, 523n53
    wealth as, xvi–xvii
Knowledge and Decisions (Sowell), 241
Kotler, Steven, 41
Kropotkin, Pyotr, 60
Ku Klux Klan, 365
Kuran, Timur, 76
Kuznets, Simon, 485n4, 497n3

labor
    child, 301–2
    costs, money prices or, xiv–xv
    division of, 51, 58, 242, 246–47, 325, 331
    personal resource abundance and, 136
    population resource abundance and, 201
    productivity, 278
ladder of information hierarchy, 100
Landes, David S., 300
Landsberg, Hans, 60
land use, 87
Laudato Si (Pope Francis), 84
Law of Civilization and Decay, The (Adams), 365
Layard, Richard, 105–6
Le Comte, Louis, 275–76
Lectures on Justice, Police, Revenue and Arms (Adam Smith), 31
Lee, Jong-Wha, 309, 518n84
Leetaru, Kalev, 41

Le Prestre de Vauban, Sébastien, 287
Leroy-Beaulieu, Pierre Paul, 36
Levari, David, 44
Levinovitz, Alan, 14
liberal democracy, 311–13
life expectancy, 22–23, 289, 343
light, 284, 285t
limited liability company (LLC), 347
Limits to Growth, The (Club of Rome), 61
Litan, Robert E., 77
literacy, 24, 37, 278, 306–8
Livy, 15
LLC. *See* limited liability company (LLC)
Lorenz, Max, 127
Louis XIV, King of France, 20
Louis XVI, King of France, 31
Lucas, Robert E., 192, 283
Lucretius, 16, 488n88
"Lucy" (*Australopithecus* fossil), 245
Luddites, 259
Lugo-Lugo, Carmen R., 12, 487n9
Luther, Martin, 267, 272
Lütken, Otto Diedrich, 56
Lutz, Wolfgang, 85

Ma, Jack, 513n–b
Macaulay, Thomas Babington, 45–46
Machiavelli, Niccolò, 52, 56
Machlup, Fritz, 59
Maddison, Angus, 285
Maduro, Nicolás, 254
Maher, Bill, 13, 381–82
Maine, Henry Sumner, 513n48
Malthus, Thomas, xi, 34, 47, 53–57, 375, 382, 386–88, 396, 400–401 405, 415, 494n22, 495n25, 530n82
Malthusian trap, 52–53, 78
Mander, Jerry, 379–80
Manes, Christopher, 380
Mann, Charles C., 65
Mann, Michael E., 499n43
Mao Zedong, 258
Marcus Aurelius, 17
Marggraf, Andreas Sigismund, 164
market. *See also* trade
    competition and, 349–50
    cooperation and, 349–50
    as information exchange process, 110–11
    innovation and, 274, 338, 349–51
    restrictions, superabundance, and, 406–7
    ruling elites and, 257
    in Voltaire, 32
Marshall, Alfred, xvii, 58
Martial (Roman poet), 307, 308
Marx, Karl, 35–36, 272

Marxism, 36, 360, 367–69, 378
Maslow, Abraham, 38
maternal mortality, 290–91
Matthew, Gospel of, 19
Maus, Marcel, 273
Mayhew, Henry, 314
McAfee, Andrew, 28, 85
McCloskey, Deirdre, 163, 194, 251, 261, 269,
    272–73, 281, 283, 285, 325, 327, 337,
    395–96, 525n70
McKibben, Bill, 83, 391
media scaremongering, 89–93
Meltzer, Allan H., 350
Mercier, Louis-Sébastien, 287–88
Merleau-Ponty, Maurice, 368
Michelet, Jules, 299–300
Milanovic, Branko, 127
military innovation, 262–63
Mill, John Stuart, xvii, 57
Millar, John, 31
Miller, Geoffrey, 336
mind, theory of, 245–46
modernity, 277–79, 360–61
Mokyr, Joel, 86, 261, 265, 277, 286, 325, 523n48
monism, 373–74
Montesquieu, 32, 491n90
Moore, Michael, 88–89
More from Less: The Surprising Story of How We
    Learned to Prosper Using Fewer Resources—
    and What Happens Next (McAfee), 28, 85
Morse, Chandler, 59, 485n4
Mueller, John, 43
Mussolini, Benito, 36, 492n112
Mutafarraqa, Ibrahim, 330
Myth of Disenchantment, The: Magic, Modernity,
    and the Birth of the Human Sciences
    (McCloskey), 395–96

Naess, Arne, 379
nationalism, 37, 365–66, 374–75, 387, 398
Natural: How Faith in Nature's Goodness Leads
    to Harmful Fads, Unjust Laws, and Flawed
    Science (Levinovitz), 14, 487n17, 530n80
naturalistic fallacy, 103
natural selection, 363–64. See also evolution
Nazis, 366, 374–75
Neanderthal, 120
Newton, Isaac, 347
New World, 264–65
Nietzsche, Friedrich, 363
Nixon, Richard, 57, 376
Norberg, Johan, 28, 297, 301
Nordhaus, Ted, 84
Nordhaus, William, xiv, xiv–xv, 105, 195,
    284, 485n4

North, Douglass, 325
North Korea, 254, 257
nuclear fission, 340, 402
nutrition, 3, 23, 291–95, 294t–95t
Nye, Bill, 384

Observations Concerning the Distinction of
    Ranks in Society (Millar), 31
Ocasio-Cortez, Alexandria, 381, 388, 391
Odyssey (Homer), 270
Officer, Lawrence H., 123, 130
oil market, 131
One Child: Do We Have a Right to More? (Conly),
    384–85
one-child policy, 61–67, 80
On the Origin of Species (Darwin), 35
On War (Clausewitz), 319–20
Organization of Petroleum Exporting Countries
    (OPEC), 131
O'Rourke, P. J., 10
Osborn, Henry Fairfield, 58, 527n21

Pachauri, Rajendra K., 84
pandemic, 385–86, 533n32
Pasteur, Louis, 290
patents, 338, 523n49
PCTP. See percentage change in time price
    (PCTP)
Peace of Westphalia, 264
percentage change in personal resource abun-
    dance (pRA), 116t, 117–18
percentage change in time price (PCTP),
    113–15, 116t
Perry, Mark J., 173
personal resource abundance (pRA), 66–67,
    101, 136, 144
    airfares and, 352t–53t
    changes in, 235t, 236f
    commodities and, 136–61, 138f–39f,
        141f–42f, 145f–48f, 151f–55f, 156t,
        157f–61f
    cosmetic procedures and, 173–84, 174f–75f,
        176t, 178t, 180t, 182f–84f, 184t
    Ehrlich Wall and, 232–33, 232f
    finished goods and, 167–73, 168f, 169t,
        171t, 172f
    food prices and, 162–67, 166f, 168f, 169t
    growth rates and, 192–97, 193t, 196t
    housing and, 342t
    increase in, 284
    population resource abundance or,
        508n2
    Simon-Ehrlich Box and, 230–32, 231f–32f
    televisions and, 371t–72t
    Transcendence Line and, 233, 233f

personal resource abundance elasticity of population (pRA-EP), 201, 212, 218

personal resource abundance multiplier (pRAM), 115–17, 116t, 117f–18f, 136, 144, 150, 168f, 182f, 201
  for basic 50 commodities, 138f, 141f
  for cosmetic procedures, 183f–84f
  for finished goods, 172f, 174f–75f
  for food, 166f
  for Jacks's 26 commodities, 157f, 159f
  for Jacks's 40 commodities, 151f, 153f
  population resource cost and, 508n4
  for Simon-Ehrlich five-metal basket, 187f, 189f–91f
  for World Bank 37 commodities, 145f, 147f

Petronius, 269

Petty, William, 59

Peuple, Le (Michelet), 299–300

Philosophical Review of the Successive Advances of the Human Mind (Turgot), 31

physiocratic school, 52

Pignatelli Principe di Strongoli, Francesco, 287

Pinker, Steven, 24, 29, 37, 41, 320, 359

plague, 261–62

plane crashes, 305–6, 306f

Planet of the Humans (film), 88

Plato, 17, 51, 270, 488n34

Plautus, 271

Pliny the Elder, 269

Plomin, Robert, 335–36

Poetics (Aristotle), 48–49

Polachek, Solomon W., 319

Politics (Aristotle), 488n34

Polybius, 17–18, 307

Pope Francis, 84

Population and Development in Poor Countries (Simon), 73

Population Bomb, The (Ehrlich), 78, 81, 375

Population Bombed: Exploding the Link between Overpopulation and Climate Change (Desrochers and Szurmak), 56

Population Matters: People, Resources, Environment, and Immigration (Simon), 73

population resource abundance (PRA), 101, 204–5, 216t
  components of, 200–208, 202t–3t, 206t–7t
  personal resource abundance or, 508n2
  visualization of, 219–21, 220f–29f

population resource abundance elasticity of population (PRA-EP), 201, 212–13.213t, 215t, 221

population resource abundance multiplier (PRAM), 201–4, 202t–3t, 214, 219–21, 508n4

population resource cost (PRC), 508n4, 509n5

population resource cost elasticity of population (PRC-EP), 510n9

Portman, Rob, 387–88

Potter, Neil, 485n4

poverty
  in China, 67
  decrease in, 24, 282, 287–88
  extreme, 287–88
  innovation and, 324

pRA. See personal resource abundance (pRA)

PRA. See population resource abundance (PRA)

pRA-EP. See personal resource abundance elasticity of population (pRA-EP)

PRA-EP. See population resource abundance elasticity of population (PRA-EP)

pRAM. See personal resource abundance multiplier (pRAM)

PRAM. See population resource abundance multiplier (PRAM)

PRC. See population resource cost (PRC)

Preston, Richard, 380

prices. See also time prices (TP)
  in ancient Rome, 271
  competition and, 111
  as measure of abundance, 109–11

printing press, 330, 354–55, 525n70

progressivism, 491n84

Progress: Ten Reasons to Look Forward to the Future (Norberg), 28

Prometheus Bound (Aeschylus), 15

Protestant Reformation, 267, 354, 363

Putnam, Robert, 328

Quakers, 32, 164, 317

racism, 361–62, 365–66, 373, 380

Rational Optimist, The (Ridley), 28, 42, 330

Reagan, Ronald, 369

Rebecque, Henri-Benjamin Constant de, 311–12

Reform Acts, 511n11

Reich, Charles A., 378–79

religion
  apocalyptic thought and, 21
  as defining feature of humanity, 21
  environmentalism as, 391–96
  wars of, 267

Renaissance, 267

Representation of the People Act, 511n11

Republic (Plato), 488n34

resource abundance information hierarchy, 106–19, 116t, 117f–18f

resource quantity, as useless measurement, 107–8

Ricardo, David, 346

Ricci, Mateo, 274–75, 329

Vivero, Rodrigo, 276
Vogt, William, 57–58, 527n21
Voltaire, 32
von Hippel, William, 243–44, 253–54,
    334–35

Wald, George, 376
Ward, Barbara, 379
War of the Worlds, The (H. G. Wells), 373
water, 27–28, 108, 297
Watson, James, 406
Watson, Robert, 84
Watt, James, 279, 355–56
Watt, Kenneth, 377–78
*Wealth and Poverty of Nations, The: Why Some
    Are So Rich and Some So Poor* (Landes),
    300
*Wealth Explosion, The: The Nature and Origins
    of Modernity* (Davies), 261
Wealth of Nations, The (Smith), 2, 342–43
Wells, Dana, 383
Wells, H. G., 373
*Why Nations Fail: The Origins of Power, Pros-
    perity, and Poverty* (Acemoglu), 257
Williamson, Samuel H., 123
Wilson, Bart, 327
wind turbines, 88
Wojcik, Daniel, 21, 385
work hours, 303–5
World Bank 37 commodities, 143–49, 145f–48f,
    196t
    in compound annual growth rate of
        population resource abundance, 207t
    in personal resource abundance elasticity
        of population, 213t
    in population resource abundance, 206t,
        216t, 223f, 235t

in population resource abundance elasticity
    of population, 215t
in population resource abundance multiplier,
    202t
in time price elasticity of population, 211t
in years to double population resource
    abundance, 209t
World War I, 366
World War II, 24, 37, 177, 312, 320, 341
Wrigley, Edward Anthony, 514n3

Xi Jinping, 513n–b

YD-pRA. *See* years to double personal
    resource abundance (YD-pRA)
YD-PRA. *See* years to double population
    resource abundance (YD-PRA)
years to double personal resource abundance
    (YD-pRA), 119, 168f, 182f, 508n3
    for basic 50 commodities, 138f, 141f
    calculation of, 509n7
    for cosmetic procedures, 183f–84f
    for finished goods, 172f, 174f–75f
    for food, 166f
    for Jacks's 26 commodities, 157f, 159f
    for Jacks's 40 commodities, 151f, 153f
    for Simon-Ehrlich five-metal basket, 187f,
        189f–91f
    for World Bank 37 commodities, 145f, 147f
years to double population resource abundance
    (YD-PRA), 201, 208, 209t, 218, 221, 508n3

Zhou Enlai, 61
Zhuang Zhou, 14
Zimbabwe, 390
Zimmermann, Erich, 60
Zoroastrianism, 18

ABOUT THE AUTHORS

Gale L. Pooley is an associate professor of business management at Brigham Young University-Hawaii. He has taught economics and statistics at Alfaisal University in Riyadh, Saudi Arabia; Brigham Young University-Idaho; Boise State University; and the College of Idaho. Pooley has held professional designations from the Appraisal Institute, the Royal Institution of Chartered Surveyors, and the CCIM Institute. He has published articles with *National Review*, HumanProgress.org, *The American Spectator*, the Foundation for Economic Education, the *Utah Bar Journal*, the *Appraisal Journal*, *Quillette*, *Forbes*, and *RealClearMarkets*. Pooley is a senior fellow with the Discovery Institute, a board member of HumanProgress.org, and a scholar with Hawaii's Grassroot Institute. His major research activity has been the Simon Abundance Index, which he coauthored with Marian Tupy.

Marian L. Tupy is the editor of HumanProgress.org, a senior fellow at the Cato Institute's Center for Global Liberty and Prosperity, and coauthor of the Simon Abundance Index. He specializes in globalization and global well-being and the politics and economics of Europe and Southern Africa. He is the coauthor of *Ten Global Trends Every Smart Person Should Know: And Many Others You Will Find Interesting* (Cato Institute, 2020). His articles have been published in the *Financial Times*, the *Washington Post*, the *Los Angeles Times*, the *Wall Street Journal*, *The Atlantic*, *Newsweek*, the *UK Spectator*, *Foreign Policy*, and various other outlets in the United States and overseas. He has appeared on BBC, CNN, CNBC, MSNBC, Fox News, Fox Business, and other channels. Tupy received his BA in international relations and classics from the University of Witwatersrand in Johannesburg, South Africa, and his PhD in international relations from the University of St. Andrews in Great Britain.

ABOUT THE CATO INSTITUTE

Founded in 1977, the Cato Institute is a public policy research foundation dedicated to broadening the parameters of policy debate to allow consideration of more options that are consistent with the principles of limited government, individual liberty, and peace. To that end, the Institute strives to achieve greater involvement of the intelligent, concerned lay public in questions of policy and the proper role of government.

The Institute is named for *Cato's Letters*, libertarian pamphlets that were widely read in the American Colonies in the early 18th century and played a major role in laying the philosophical foundation for the American Revolution.

Despite the achievement of the nation's Founders, today virtually no aspect of life is free from government encroachment. A pervasive intolerance for individual rights is shown by government's arbitrary intrusions into private economic transactions and its disregard for civil liberties. And while freedom around the globe has notably increased in the past several decades, many countries have moved in the opposite direction, and most governments still do not respect or safeguard the wide range of civil and economic liberties.

To address those issues, the Cato Institute undertakes an extensive publications program on the complete spectrum of policy issues. Books, monographs, and shorter studies are commissioned to examine the federal budget, Social Security, regulation, military spending, international trade, and myriad other issues.

In order to maintain its independence, the Cato Institute accepts no government funding. Contributions are received from foundations, corporations, and individuals, and other revenue is generated from the sale of publications. The Institute is a nonprofit, tax-exempt, educational foundation under Section 501(c)3 of the Internal Revenue Code.

CATO INSTITUTE
1000 Massachusetts Ave. NW
Washington, DC 20001
www.cato.org